A TEXTBOOK OF

Practical Botany II

TAXONOMY, ECONOMIC BOTANY, EMBRYOLOGY, ANATOMY, ECOLOGY, PHYSIOLOGY, BIOSTATISTICS, CYTOLOGY AND GENETICS

By

DR. ASHOK M. BENDRE

FORMERLY–HEAD,
DEPARTMENT OF BOTANY

AND

DR. ASHOK KUMAR

FORMERLY, READER IN BOTANY
MEERUT COLLEGE
MEERUT

RASTOGI
PUBLICATIONS

SHIVAJI ROAD, MEERUT-250 002, INDIA

A TEXTBOOK OF

Practical Botany II

TAXONOMY, ECONOMIC BOTANY, EMBRYOLOGY, ANATOMY, ECOLOGY, PHYSIOLOGY, BIOSTATISTICS, CYTOLOGY AND GENETICS

FOR UNDERGRADUATE STUDENTS

SEVENTH EDITION

NEW DELHI OFFICE :
9, RANI JHANSI ROAD
(MOTIA KHAN)
NEW DELHI - 110 055

HINDI EDITION
IS ALSO AVAILABLE

Practical
Botany II

ISBN : 978-81-7133-877-1

TITLE CODE NO. : **B-15**

SECOND REPRINT (SEVENTH EDITION) : 2021–2022

PRICE : ₹ 465.00 ONLY

PUBLISHED BY RAKESH KUMAR RASTOGI FOR RASTOGI PUBLICATIONS, 'GANGOTRI' SHIVAJI ROAD, MEERUT - 250002
website: www.rastogipublications.com email: info@rastogipublications.com
PRINTED AT INDIAN PRESS, MEERUT. INDIA.
PHONES: (0121)2516080, 2515142 (JMD / 08011/INN06015)

Preface to the Present Edition

In the last decade there had been tremendous developments in biological sciences, which resulted in the establishment of several new branches viz. Molecular Biology, Biotechnology, Environmental Biology, Toxicology, Biostatistics, etc. This necessiated the revision of university syllabi to incorporate the study of these advancements. Several new experiments now appear in practical syllabi too. The author felt the need of thoroughly revising the present book of ***A Text Book of Practical Botany Vol II*** to provide latest and uptodate study material to the students. In conformity with the requirement of the revised syllabi, new chapters such as Biostatistics, Environmental Biology, Cell Biology, Illustrated Glossary of Anatomical Terms, etc. have been included in the book. Almost every chapter has been rewritten and modified. The book has taxonomic description of 112 species of plants belonging to 40 families. These are expected to cover almost all common plants available for practical classes throughout the country. The chapter on Anatomy now includes the study of cell inclusions and epidermal studies. The present chapter on Cytology and Genetics now carries additional exercises on Mendelism and the study of plant cell organelles and chromosomes. In the end, Appendix has been added which includes few additional helpful techniques and recipes of reagents, stains, fixing, agents, etc. The index has also been included that deals with the chapterwise lists of botaincal names to facilitate easy location of the plants and the subject matter of the book.

I am sure that the present revised and enlarged edition will prove more useful to the students and teachers. I shall be grateful to receive valuable suggestions and comments for further improvement of the book.

–Ashok Bendre

Preface to the First Edition

Comprehensive practical study is a supplement to the theoretical classroom knowledge. It helps to understand the subject more precisely. It necessitates to follow a few disciplines, inside the laboratory. This book tries to outline, few of such instructions. Laboratory work also indulges in observations and its record. Own observations are significant towards the contribution of learning the subject. The book is, therefore, designed as a reference rather than copy-down instrument. The book is fairly illustrated and many possible details have been incorporated. It is hoped that this book will serve as a faithful guide to the students.

We are highly indebted to Dr. Naresh Chandra, Reader, Rajasthan University, Jaipur, for valuable guidance and help during the preparation of this book and also to Dr. Narendra Pal Sexena, D.N. College, Meerut and Dr. Virendra Singh, Meerut College, Meerut, for the interest they have shown. Suggestions for improvement will be thankfully accepted.

– The Authors

Department of Botany
Meerut College
Meerut

Contents

11. Experiments in Plant Physiology 389 – 443

Appendix 444 – 449

Index 450 – 452

(B-15/00119600)

1

Introduction to Laboratory

Preamble

Science is a systematised study based on facts and observations. It involves curiosity, inquisitiveness and unbiased analysis. Most of the scientific work is done in a laboratory. It provides an opportunity to a person with scientific frame of mind to see and study various aspects of an object under observation. Hence, a biology student too is obliged to attend laboratory work-out with utmost sincerity, honesty and inquisitiveness.

Laboratory Etiquette

The study of living things in laboratory requires that facilities provided are properly used.

One is expected to complete the assigned work within a specified time. This requires proper utilization and planning of time. One should, therefore, keep busy with own work and wherever necessary consult the teacher alone.

Laboratory provisions should be handled with utmost care. At the end of the laboratory period, working space should be left clean and in order.

Laboratory exercise to be performed should be read in advance and one is expected to arrive to the class theoretically prepared.

Work Plan

1. Listen and understand the instructions and information given by teacher-in-charge.
2. Work out or observe the materials carefully.
3. Mount to prepare slides as per requirements.
4. Study the preparations or specimen carefully.
5. Draw suitable diagrams in a proper sequence and label them in your practical record.
6. Write down the observations sequentially and watch carefully if variations occur.
7. Get your work checked by teacher-in-charge and make necessary corrections.

Necessary Instruments

The variety of instruments required depends upon the nature of work. It has, however, been found convenient to prepare a small kit in suitable containers such as a pencil box containing

1. a pair of forceps,
2. two fine, long handle, dissecting needles,
3. glass droppers,
4. good and sharp razor,
5. safety blade,
6. a fine hair brush,
7. a pair of sharpened pencils,
8. pencil eraser,
9. a clean and soft handkerchief and
10. practical record with cover file and spare pages, etc.

Microscope

It is the most indispensable instrument in a biology laboratory, so much so that it comes to be called 'The primary instrument of the biologists'. It helps to increase the resolving power (property to distinguish objects lying very close as separate bodies) of human eye which fails to recognise objects lying closer between 0.01 to 0.25 mm.

Some common types of microscopes are listed below –

1. dissecting microscope,
2. compound microscope,
3. binocular microscope,
4. phase contrast microscope and
5. electron microscope, etc.

Of these, dissecting microscope and compound microscope are very commonly used by the students.

[I] Dissecting microscope

It is used for dissection, specially during taxonomic studies, embryo separation, etc.

Construction. It consists of basal foot, a vertical limb, stage and a lens. The basal foot is a stand. The limb has an attached stage made of glass plate. A folded arm which can be moved

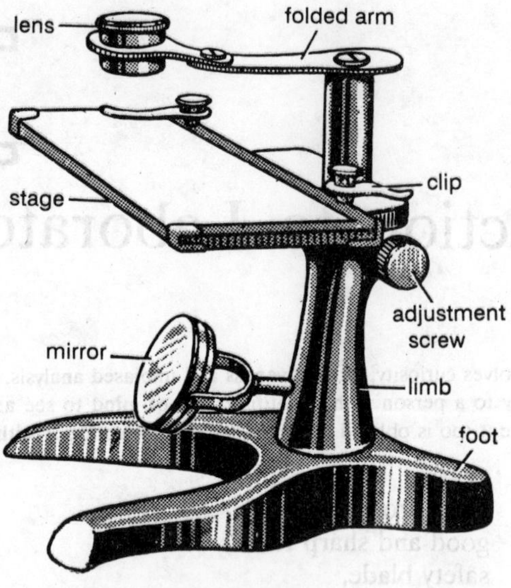

Fig. 1. A dissecting microscope.

vertically holds the lens. A mirror is attached at the base of the limb.

Mechanical operation. 1. Move the lens and adjust it over the object.

2. Illuminate the object suitably by adjusting the mirror.
3. Focus the object by using adjustment screw.

[II] Compound microscope

It is one of the most commonly used and by far the most suitable microscope in the Botany Laboratory. At one time, it employs one ocular (eye piece) and one objective, in working position. As such, it is also known as monocular-mono-objective microscope.

Construction. The microscope is built around a strong basal foot and a vertical limb. The foot supports the vertical limb.

A round, rectangular or square stage is fixed to the limb. It is provided with spring clips to hold the slide in position.

A movable or fixed sub-stage is situated directly below the stage. It is provided with an iris diaphragm and condenser lens. Iris diaphragm is a wheel-shaped metal disc to regulate the aperture, through which light rays reach the condenser and are passed to an object. Condenser is a system of two or more lenses under the stage which receives parallel light rays from mirror and converge them at the level of stage.

A movable concave mirror is fixed at the lowermost part of the limb to focus a converging

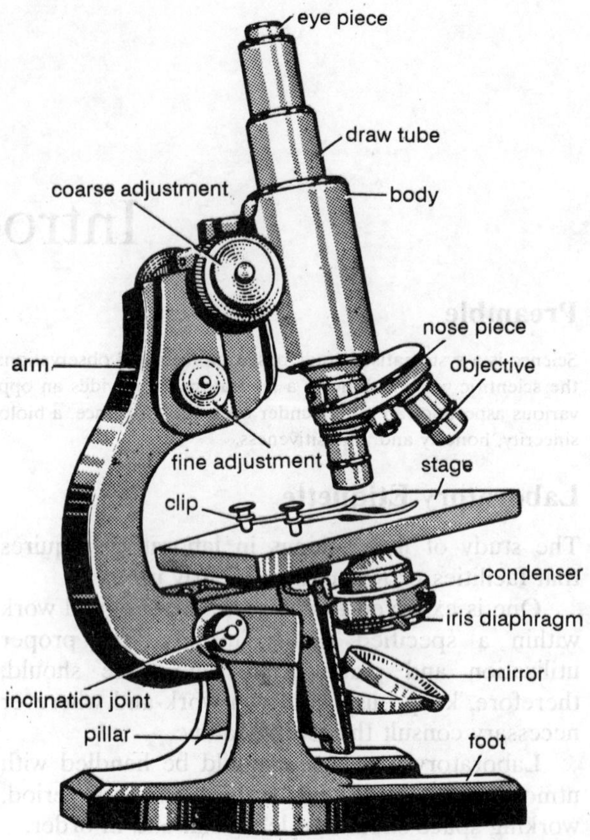

Fig. 2. A compound microscope.

cone of rays at the level of specimen. Whether day or artificial light is used as a source, concave mirror converges the light if there are no condensing lenses.

Body of the microscope is composed of a tube. At the upper end of the tube, is an ocular (eye piece) which can be changed for lower or higher values of magnifications. At the lower end of this tube is a revolving nose-piece with about three objectives viz. low power, high power and oil immersion. These magnifications range from 3.2x to 100x. The conventional low power objective is 10x.

Tube of the microscope is vertically movable with the help of coarse and fine adjustment screws on the limb, operated by a rack and pinion system. Coarse adjustment moves the tube rapidly while fine adjustment screw does it gradually.

Mechanical operation. 1. Microscope is placed in maximum diffuse light. Direct sunlight is harmful for the eyes. The northern light is most suitable. If light source is artificial, filter (preferably blue coloured) is used.

2. Light is adjusted by turning the mirror towards the source of light and also by moving the sub-stage up and down, as well as with the help of iris diaphragm.
3. A prepared slide is placed on the stage. Object is adjusted just over the stage aperture.
4. The object is located and focussed with a low-power objective using coarse adjustment.
5. If higher magnification is desired, nose-piece is turned to next higher power. Fine adjustment can be used freely at this stage, while the use of coarse adjustment by avoided.
6. High power objective and subsequent higher powers are used only when object is properly mounted under coverslip.
7. The object should always be observed with both eyes open.

Care. 1. Before and after the use, all the lenses and metal parts including stage should be cleaned. The lenses are cleaned with tissue paper, muslin cloth or clean and soft handkerchief.

2. Microscope is kept covered when not in use. Proper cases, plastic bags, bell jars or even a clean cloth can be used.
3. Objectives should not be ordinarily removed from the nosepiece.
4. Operating screws, condenser, iris diaphragm, mirror and stage or stage clips should always be handled carefully.

Other Laboratory Provisions

Some other provisions available in the laboratory include staining rack, dropping bottles, slides, cover glasses, watch glasses, petri dishes, beakers, enamel trays, wash bottles, spirit lamp, hone, strop, dusters, etc. Some of these are described below.

1. Staining rack. It is mostly made of wood to hold the dropping bottles. The capacity of number of bottles per rack varies.

2. Dropping bottle. The stains, chemicals, mounting media, etc., are stored in these bottles. This glass bottle has a narrow mouth fitted with a slotted cock. Cock is provided with a beak that permits the liquid to flow out in drops.

3. Slides. The size of slide is mostly 3" × 1" (25 mm × 75 mm). It is about 1 mm thick. These are used to mount the material under study.

4. Cover glasses. The cover glasses are mounted on the object when the preparation is finally ready. These may be either square or round shaped. The standard thickness of the coverslip is 0.17 mm.

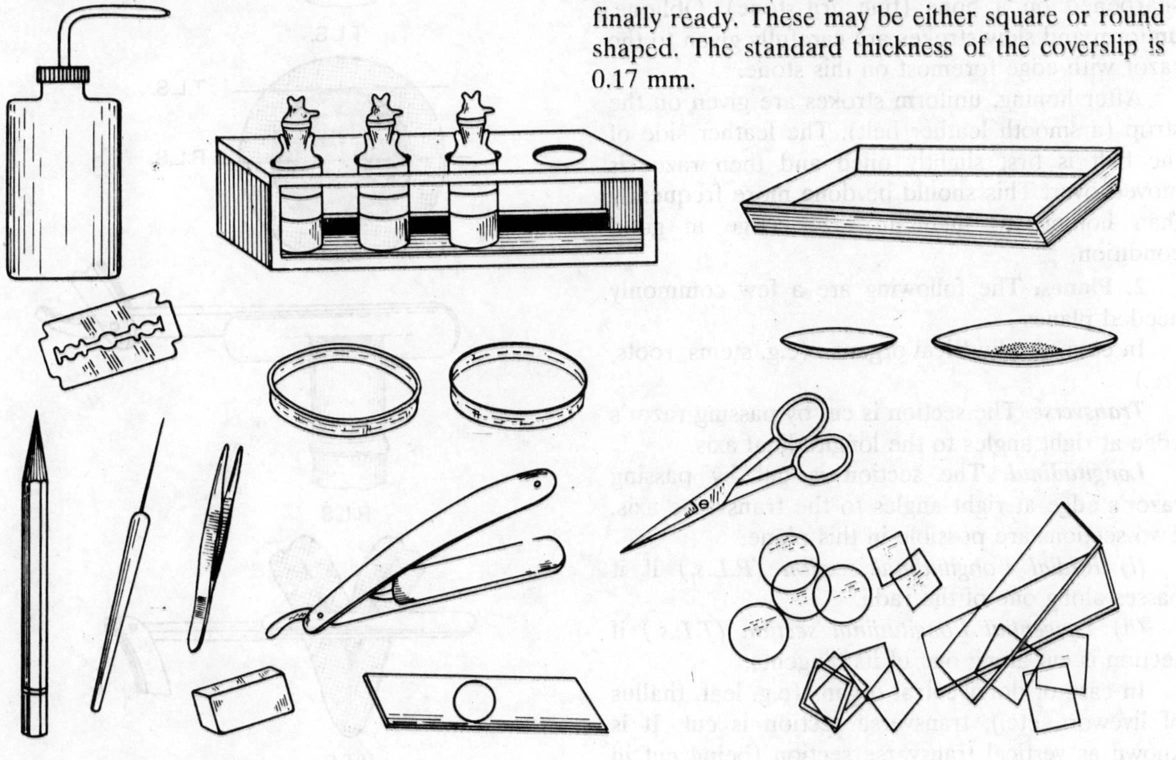

Fig. 3. Some laboratory provisions and necessary instruments.

Fixing Agents and Preservatives

The plants or plant parts, collected fresh need to be immediately killed (fixed) and subsequently preserved for a long time.

For this purpose, a few chemicals are used which do not cause any structural disturbance or distortion of the material. Carnoy's fluid, Formalin-aceto-alcohol, Formalin-propiono-alcohol, Randolph's modified Navashin fluid and Bouin's fluid are some of the common agents used. (See appendix for preparations).

Plants are generally fixed immediately after collection but these can also be fixed after bringing them to laboratory. The collected material must be always kept completely immersed in preservatives.

Laboratory Techniques

[I] Section cutting

Sections of preserved material are cut in suitable planes for histological and ecological studies. Razor is suitable for cutting the sections in laboratory.

1. Honing and stropping. Razor should be sharp and free from nicks. Hence, it should be sharpened on a hone (fine grit-stone). Oblique, uniform and slow strokes are carefully given to the razor with edge foremost on this stone.

After honing, uniform strokes are given on the strop (a smooth leather belt). The leather side of the belt is first slightly oiled and then razor is moved over. This should be done more frequently than honing, to maintain razor edge in good condition.

2. Planes. The following are a few commonly needed planes –

In case of cylindrical organs : (e.g. stems, roots, etc.)

Transverse. The section is cut by passing razor's edge at right angles to the longitudinal axis.

Longitudinal. The section is cut by passing razor's edge at right angles to the transverse axis. Two sections are possible in this plane.

(i) Radial Longitudinal section (R.L.s.) if it passes along one of the radii.

(ii) Tangential Longitudinal section (T.L.s.) if section is cut along one of its tangents.

In case of dorsiventral organs (e.g. leaf, thallus of livewort, etc.), transverse section is cut. It is known as vertical transverse section (being cut in vertical plane).

3. Method. Following steps would be useful for section cutting.

1. **Soft, thin and small materials are placed in pith either by piercing a hole with a needle or by splitting it longitudinally with a blade. The piths used include carrot and radish roots, potato tubers, etc.**
2. **A razor must be held properly to cut the section. The handle and the blade of the razor should be at right angles to one another. The handle should remain free while the index**

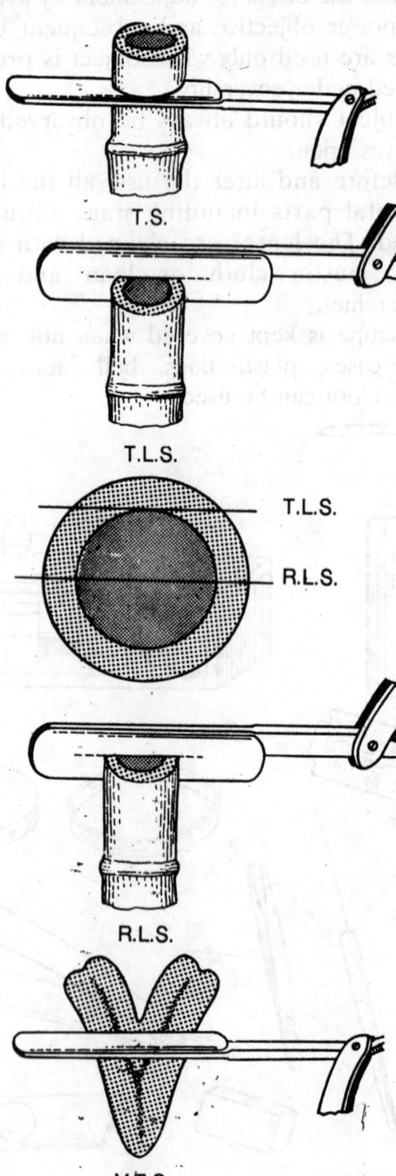

Fig. 4. Planes for section cutting.

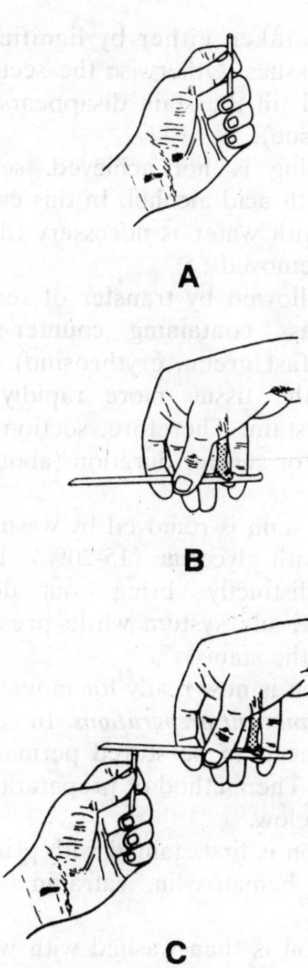

Fig. 5. Method of section cutting. **A.** holding the material, **B.** correct way of holding the razor, **C.** holding the material and stroke of the razor.

finger is placed on the hooked end of the razor; 1st, 2nd and 3rd fingers pressed against the thick back edge of the razor and thumb against the milled surface of the thick shank of blade.

3. The material or the pith with embedded material is held between the thumb and the fingers of the left hand.
4. The material in the left hand and the razor's edge should form right angle.
5. The razor is now moved quickly over the material and the stroke is completed in one action only.
6. More and more uniform strokes are used till desired quality and number of sections are obtained. Care is taken to keep the material and the razor flooded with water.
7. Sections float in water on the razor's edge. These are carefully lifted by a fine camel hair brush and then transferred to a watch glass containing water.
8. After the section cutting is over, the razor is wiped dry and clean without disturbing the edge. It is honed, stropped and encased.
9. The sections which float on water in the watch glass are considered to be thin.
10. These sections are lifted by a hair brush, placed on a slide in a drop of water and observed through microscope. A thin and uniform section is selected for staining.

[II] Stains and staining

The selected sections need to be stained. The stains help to distinguish different tissues, cells or inclusions from one another by developing specific colours. Acetocarmine, Aniline blue, Crystal violet, Erythrosine, Hematoxylins, Fast green, Light green and Safranin are some of the commonly used stains. (See appendix for preparation)

1. Specificity. Most of the stains are specific in reaction and are purposely used so that definite structures or substances are stained. The following are some of the stains used for staining different structures.

Achromatic figure
Aniline blue
Erythrosine
Fast green
Light green

Cellulose cell wall
Aniline blue
Delafield hematoxylin
Fast green
Light green

Lignified cell wall
Crystal violet
Safranin

Suberised cell wall
Safranin

Cytoplasm
Aniline blue
Erythrosine
Fast green
Light green

Cutinised cell wall
Crystal violet
Erythrosine
Safranin

Callose
Aniline blue

Chitin
Safranin

Proteins
Safranin

Mitochondria
Crystal violet

Plastids
Crystal violet
Iron hematoxylin

Nucleus
Crystal violet
Hematoxylin
Safranin

Chromosomes
Hematoxylin
Safranin

2. Single stains. Safranin or fast green is used alone to stain filaments of algae, fungi, sections of bryophytes, spores of pteridophytes, pollen grains of gymnosperms, etc. Aniline blue or safranin is suitable for algae.

Following is the common method of staining.

1. The material is kept in a watch glass. A few drops of stain are added so that the material is immersed in the stain.
2. The material is allowed to remain so for a few minutes and allowed to take stain. The time required varies with materials.
3. After the stain is taken up, the excess of stain is washed off in water. The washing is repeated till stain stops coming out.
4. In some cases, excess stain is removed by acid water or acid alcohol if water alone fails to do so.
5. The stained material is ready for mounting.

Fungi are stained in cotton blue as given below.

(i) A drop of cotton blue (prepared in lacto-phenol) is placed on a slide.
(ii) Fungal hyphae is now placed in this drop.
(iii) The slide is run over the flame of the spirit lamp so that the stain is warmed up.
(iv) The preparation is now ready for mounting.

3. Combinations. Commonly two or more stains are employed wherever tissue differentiation is found. Combination of acidic and basic dyes of contrasting colours is of general use. This permits the distinction of woody tissue from non-woody tissue. The following few combinations are commonly recommended–

1. hematoxylin and safranin,
2. safranin and fast green,
3. safranin and aniline blue,
4. safranin and crystal violet and
5. crystal violet and erythrosine.

4. Staining procedures. There are two types of preparations–semi-permanent and permanent. The procedures differ in both the cases. These are given below.

(a) For semi-permanent and temporary preparations. Certain preparations are made for temporary use. The material is studied and the slide is then discarded. The method for staining them is given below.

1. The selected sections are transferred from watch glass containing water to another watch glass containing principal stain (e.g. hematoxylin, safranin or crystal violet).
2. The sections are allowed to remain in the stain for sometime (for about 4-5 minutes).
3. Excess amount of stain is removed by washing the sections repeatedly with water. (This can be seen under the microscope. The stain should be taken either by lignified or non-lignified tissues. Otherwise the section should be washed till the stain disappears from one type of tissue).
4. If destaining is not achieved, sections are washed with acid alcohol. In this case, further washing with water is necessary till traces of acid are removed.
5. This is followed by transfer of sections to a watch glass containing counter-stain (e.g. safranin, fast green, erythrosine). This stain acts on the tissue more rapidly than the principal stain. Therefore, section is kept in this stain for shorter duration (about a minute or two).
6. Excess of stain is removed by washing stained sections with glycerine (15-20%). The section should distinctly bring out demarcation between tissue system while preserving the colour of the stain.
7. The section is now ready for mounting.

(b) For permanent preparations. In certain cases preparations need to be stored permanently as a future record. The method of preparation followed is described below.

1. The section is first stained with principal stain (aqueous hematoxylin, safranin or crystal violet).
2. The section is then washed with water till no more stain dissolves and water remains colourless.
3. Section is passed through a graded series of alcohol for dehydration. A watch glass is filled with requisite amount of alcohol, (beginning with 30% alcohol) and the section is transferred to it. This watch glass should always be covered with another larger one. In order not to disturb the section, used alcohol is removed by glass dropper. All the 30% alcohol is replaced with 50% alcohol. This procedure is repeated till 70% of alcohol grade is reached.
4. At this stage, counterstain is employed (e.g. safranin, fast green or erythrosine prepared in 80% or 90% alochol).
5. This stain acts quickly and as such section is washed immediately after the requisite time is over.
6. Destaining is done by washing sections with 90% or 100% alcohol.
7. The section is now transferred to absolute alcohol to complete the dehydration.

8. Clearing now begins with 25% of xylol (25 cc of xylol and 75 cc of absolute alcohol). The sections are gradually passed through xylol series of 25%, 50%, 70%, 90% and finally transferred to pure xylol. If dehydration is not complete, pure xylol turns white or turbid. At ths stage section should be passed through reverse series.
9. Pure xylol is the last stage of clearing. Section is now ready for mounting.
10. Mounting is done in Canada balsam.

Specific schemes for staining combinations
(for temporary and semi-permanent preparations)

1. Hematoxylin & safranin	**2. Safranin & fast green or aniline blue**
Select a section ↓ Stain with hematoxylin ↓ Wash with water ↓ Wash with ammonia water till stain turns blue (tap water is suitable if alkaline). ↓ Wash with water ↓ Stain with safranin ↓ Wash with glycerine ↓ Mount in glycerine	Select a section ↓ Stain with safranin (for 4-5 minutes) ↓ Wash with water ↓ Destain with acid alcohol if necessary ↓ Wash repeatedly with water ↓ Stain with fast green or aniline blue (for about a minute) ↓ Wash with glycerine ↓ Mount in glycerine

Specific schemes for staining combinations
(for permanent preparations)

1. Hematoxylin & safranin	**2. Safranin & fast green** **3. Crystal violet & erythrosine**
Select a section (If necessary use mordant) ↓ Stain in hematoxylin (If necessary destain with mordant) ↓ Wash in ammonia water or tap water ↓ Dehydration with 30% alcohol ↓ 50% alcohol ↓ 70% alcohol ↓	Select a section Stain in aqueous safranin/ Crystal violet ↓ Change water, until colourless ↓ Dehydration with 30% alcohol ↓ 50% alcohol ↓ 70% alcohol ↓ 90% alcohol ↓
Stain with safranin ↓ Destain with 70% alcohol ↓ 90% alcohol ↓ Absolute alcohol ↓ Clear with 25% xylol ↓ 50% xylol ↓ 70% xylol ↓ 90% xylol ↓ Pure xylol ↓ Mount in Canada balsam.	Stain with fast green/ erythrosine ↓ Destain with 90% alcohol ↓ Absolute alcohol ↓ Clearing or de-alcoholizing with 25% xylol ↓ 50% xylol ↓ 70% xylol ↓ 90% xylol ↓ Pure xylol ↓ Mount in Canada balsam.

[III] Mounting an object

Mounting is necessary to properly position an object for clear view. Lactophenol, glycerine and glycerine jelly are used for temporary mounting while Canada balsam is used for permanent mounting.

1. Mounting media. Following are some of the common media.

(a) Canada balsam. It is a resin obtained from a conifer—*Abies balsamea*, most suitable for permanent slide preparation. The material to be mounted should come through alcohol (dehydration) and xylol (clearing) series.

(b) Lactophenol. It is a mixture of equal parts of phenol crystals, lactic acid, glycerine (sometimes two parts) and distilled water. Stains may be mixed with this medium (e.g. cotton blue in lactophenol used to stain fungi) or copper acetate is added to preserve green colour of the pigment.

(c) Glycerine. Pure glycerine diluted to 15-25% is widely used. Semi-permanent and temporary preparations are mounted in glycerine.

(d) Glycerine jelly. Jelly is also used for mounting. It is made of gelatin 1 : glycerine 7 water 6.

Warm the gelatin for two hours by adding water. Phenol (1%) is added later. Add crystals of safranin if desired. Allow the solution to cool and settle into jelly.

Many other mounting media like cedar oil, dammar, balsam, venetian turpentines and synthetic resins are also used.

2. Care. Following care should be taken during mounting.

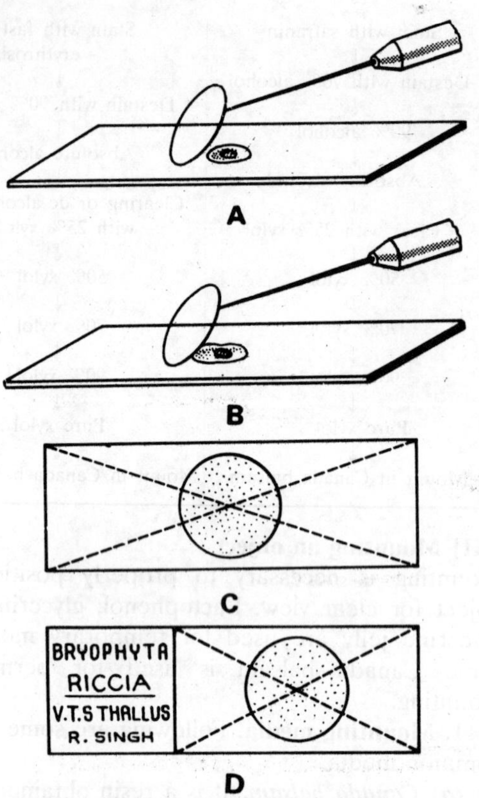

Fig. 6. Method of mounting coverslip.

1. Object should be mounted in the centre of the slide. A simple method may prove suitable for this purpose. Take a piece of thick and white cardboard sheet larger than the size of the slide. Place the slide over it. Draw lines along all the four edges. Join all the four corner points diagonally by two lines. The point, where these two lines meet, gives the centre of the slide. While mounting an object, place the slide over this drawn sheet and an object on the central point.
2. No air bubbles should enter the medium while mounting. This results in drying of medium and preparation is spoiled. To avoid air bubbles, touch one side of the coverslip to the drop of mounting medium on the slide. Support the coverslip by needle and lower it gradually before finally removing it.
3. Use the necessary small quantity of mounting medium so that it does not flow on to the slide. If so, use little lesser quantity for the next preparation. The extra amount can be soaked by touching a piece of blotting paper to the edge of the coverslip.
4. Preparation should be clean, hence the edges of slide and the coverslip alone should be held between the fingers.
5. Labels are pasted uniformly on one side of the prepared slide. It should carry the name of the division or generic and specific names, the part mounted and the section's plane. At the bottom, the name of the student who had prepared the slide be written.

3. Sealing the coverslip. Temporary preparations can be sealed with Canada balsam, gum, dammar, nail polish, etc. Such a preparation is called a semi-permanent preparation.

Sealing is done by simply painting the edges of the coverslip with sealing agent in such a way that the space between the slide and the coverslip gets filled with the agent. It should prevent mounting medium from drying.

Similarly ringing table should be used for sealing the round coverslips. The use of Canada balsam in ringing is more convenient.

Record of Work

After the preparations are ready, these should be carefully observed, salient features noted and drawn on a practical record sheet. The following suggestions would prove useful.

1. Always use a sharp and pointed pencil for thin and uniform lines.
2. Punched holes should be on the left hand side of the drawing sheet.
3. Diagrams of the entire plant or its various aspects are drawn on the same page. The diagrams of other specimens should in no case be drawn on the same page.
4. The sequence of the diagrams should always be—external features, anatomy and then reproduction.
5. For anatomical studies an outline diagram followed by a cellular sketch of its suitable sector are drawn one above the other on the same page.
6. All the parts of the diagram must be labelled. Capital letters are used for labelling. The labels are arranged one below the other in a row.
7. Labelling lines should never cross one another. Beautification and shading is not required until specific effects are to be produced.

8. Every diagram must have caption at its bottom (e.g. T.s. stem).
9. Date is written in the left hand corner of the page.
10. Classification and name of the plant are given in the right hand corner of the sheet.
11. The description is written either on the reverse side of the drawing sheet or on a new facing page.
12. During description only technical terms are used. The points of identification are added in the end.
13. Anatomical studies are described as others. A section should be described starting from epidermis to the central region; give thickness of layer (how many cells deep), shape and size of the cells constituting it. Also give in details the structure of stele and vascular bundle.

Collection

Field work is one of the most essential part in the Botanical study. It permits to come across many types of plants, otherwise not seen and available in the laboratory. It is, therefore, advisable to go round many localities and explore their vegetation. Organised excursions or outings, led by experienced persons, add to the knowledge of common plants in nature.

While on a collection trip, local or outstation, following things are to be carried along.

(1) Containers. For packing the collected material, preferably carry plastic unbreakable containers or polythene bags.

(2) Preservatives. Formalin-Acetic-Alcohol (FAA) or Alcohol 70% or Alcohol 90%, and/or Formalin 6%-10%.

(3) Other requirements. Scalpel knife, blade, forceps, pencil, paper, a hand lens, a bag or vasculum for keeping plants or plant press with many newspapers or blotting papers.

After collecting the plant, it should be immediately killed and preserved or pressed to avoid its rotting and dehydration. Plants are either sprinkled or immersed with a little of the killing agent at the spot. On return to the laboratory collected material should be transferred to new and suitable containers with fresh preservative. The plants should be completely immersed in the preservative.

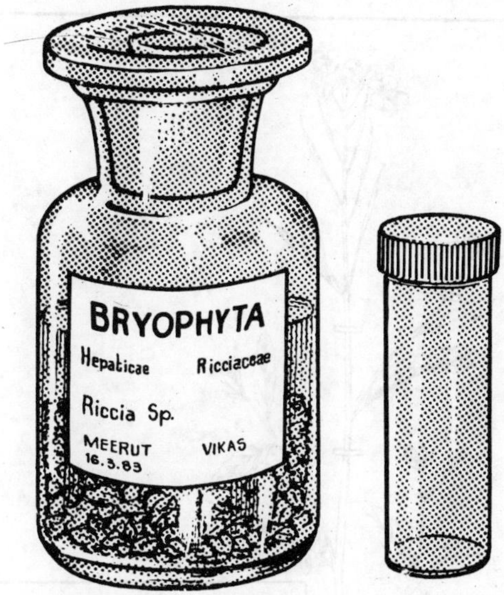

Fig. 7. Collection bottles.

A few plants e.g. filamentous algae, fungi, reproductive parts of bryophytes, fertile parts of pteridophytes and different parts of gymnosperms and angiosperms if collected in large quantities, are preserved in containers. But if materials (except a few algae and fungi) are collected in lesser quantities a herbarium sheet is prepared. Even if large quantity of such plants is available, one plant with fertile parts be preserved in the form of a herbarium sheet, while others should be packed in a container.

Every tube should be labelled. It is desired to write the name of the specimen, place and date of collection. The place of collection and date should also be written on a small piece of white card with a pencil, on the spot and inserted in the container. On return to laboratory, material is identified with the help of standard books. A label bearing name of the division and class to which the material belongs, the name of the material, date and place of collection and also the name of student is pasted on the container. All the containers should be of uniform size as far as possible.

Herbarium

A collection of dried plant specimen, mounted on sheets is known as herbarium. Freshly-picked specimen are dried and pasted on mounting paper of regulation-sized herbarium sheets. The purpose

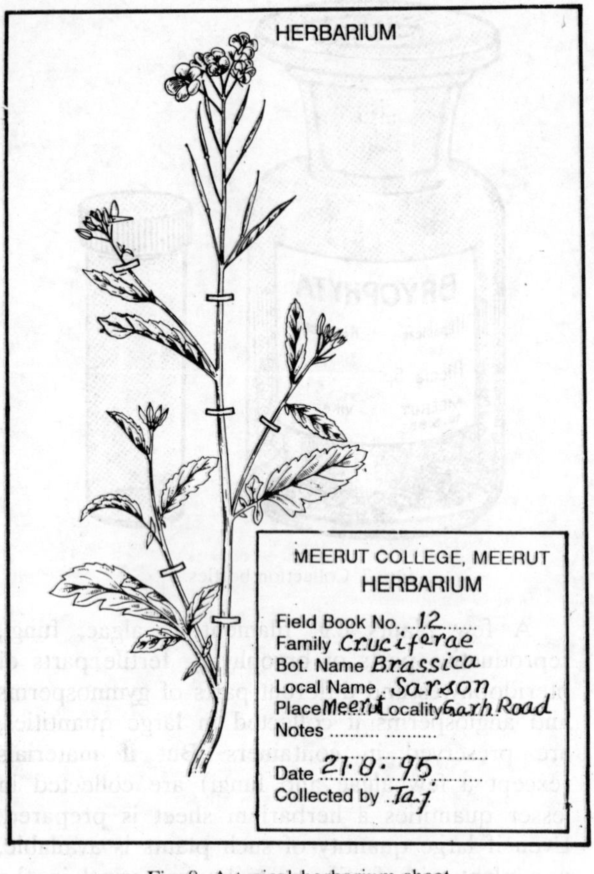

Fig. 8. A typical herbarium sheet.

of such a collection is to study the vegetation of a locality and maintain its record.

[I] Preparation of herbarium sheets

1. Equipment. On excursion, for the collection of plants, several items required to be carried include –

1. Trowel or pick,
2. Collecting can (vasculum) or field plant press,
3. Heavy laboratory plant press,
4. Blotting papers or newspapers,
5. Collecting sheets,
6. Mounting sheets,
7. Gum, gummed tape, labels, notebook, pen and pencil, etc.

Trowel or pick is used to dig out the plant as a whole wherever possible. A light-weight field press is most practical. It is made by taking two pieces of plyboard or heavy binder's board of 12" × 17" size. These are held together by two pieces of heavy cord or straps tied or buckled together and press can be carried over the shoulders. A heavy plant press carries sheets of size at least 11.5 × 17 inches. It is made of iron and tied and tightened by iron chain and screws. This is used for pressing specimen after they are brought to the laboratory. Vasculum may be used in case only a small number of plants are to be brought back.

2. Collection. Collected plants are placed in the collecting sheets. The most practical size is 16.5 × 23 inches; when folded 16.5 × 11.5 inches. Old newspapers serve this purpose to an appreciable extent and a large supply should always be included in the kit.

A specimen collected should represent root, stem, leaves and flowers. The plants are placed between the sheets or newspapers in such a way that relation between different organs is maintained. Herbaceous plants, 2 feet or less higher, may be collected entire. These can be bent to V or N shape whenever necessary. The most desirable is to collect a branch, about one foot high, containing leaves and flowers. In cases, where entire plant or branch cannot be folded to the size of herbarium sheet, only reproductive and fruiting parts and a stem with a few leaves are collected.

Delicate reproductive parts collapse even if pressed fresh. These can be pressed perfectly by applying bits of moist paper to the fresh reproductive structures and spreading them when plants are placed in the press. If parts of the herbaceous plant are thick and difficult to dry, split them before placing on the collecting sheet.

Water plants collapse if dried by usual method. These should be rolled up in wet paper when in the field and brought to the laboratory. On return to the laboratory, these plants are placed in water and floated out on sheets of white paper. The sheets are taken out of water carefully, so that the various parts do not cohere. The white sheets are placed in the blotting paper and then dried as usual.

After specimen has been collected and placed in collecting sheet, it is kept in plant press. This collecting sheet be placed in between blotting papers, one on either side.

While on collection it is important to note date, locality, habitat, height, method of branching, colour of reproductive parts, common name, etc. This should be noted separately in a field-book.

3. Pressing. The collecting sheets should be transferred to a heavy laboratory press. It must be remembered that specimen would acquire the same shape, as on collecting sheet, after pressing. The press is securely tightened. It may also be equally useful if field press is kept under heavy weight. The press should be placed in a warm, well-aired place to dry.

After 24 hours, press is taken out and opened. The old newspapers and blotting sheets are replaced by new unused ones. At least such 3-4 changes are given at an interval of 2-3 days. An average specimen takes about a week for complete drying. Sometimes to hasten the process of drying, plant press may be placed near the source of heat.

4. Mounting. The specimen are ready for mounting once they are completely dry. The standard size of the sheet is 16.5 × 11.5 inches. However, 16 × 10 inches size also has been used. The paper should be of good weight and not thin and flexible. The quality should be so, that it does not turn yellow even with a considerable lapse of time.

To mount, one of the following methods would be found convenient –

1. The gum is spread on a glass plate and specimen is laid on it. As soon as all the parts come in contact with gum, it is lifted and then placed in a position on a mounting sheet.
2. The specimen is inverted and painted with gum by a brush and then transferred to a mounting sheet.
3. The specimen is placed on a herbarium sheet and small strips of gummed tape or cellulose tape are pasted at suitable places, so that most of the part remains loose.

After mounting the specimen, a label is pasted in the right hand lower corner of the sheet. This carries information regarding botanical name of the plant, common name, date, collector's name, place of collection, etc.

5. Arrangement of sheets. The sheets, are finally arranged in accordance with standard classification (preferably Bentham and Hooker's for Angiosperms or the most accepted ones for other groups of plants). The sheets are arranged into groups according to species, genera, families, classes, orders, series and sub - divisions, etc. Each group is placed in a separate envelope, slightly larger than the herbarium sheets (e.g. 17 × 12 or 17 × 11 inches). Each of such envelopes must be labelled and a proper index be written or pasted over it.

6. Care of sheets. Herbarium sheets are often attacked by museum pests, fungi, etc. To guard against them, specimen are fumed with carbon bisulphide, 3-4 times a year. Mounted specimen may also be treated with mercuric bichloride or copper sulphate. To prevent them from attack, powdered naphthalene balls or gamaxene powder be also spread from time to time. This ensures durability and long life of the herbarium sheet.

2

The Method of Studying Angiospermic Plant

There are two major parts of the study of an angiospermic plant. These are
(1) The list of characters of the plant, its classification and identification and
(2) drawing the diagrams of plant, flower and specific parts of flower.

The characters of the plant are written in a serial order on a page of practical record. Floral formula is also written alongwith the description. After the description, classfication based on these characters is drawn and the plant is identified upto its family.

Another page is generally used to draw a complete plant, longitudinal section of a flower, androecium or a stamen, transverse section of ovary and floral diagram.

This chapter is written to inform the students about these essentials. These are given under following headings.

I. Serial list of characters used to describe plants.
II. Alternative terms and illustrated terminology.
III. Floral formula
IV. Classification and identification
V. The diagrams
VI. The floral diagram.

I. Serial List of Characters Used to Describe Plants

Angiospermic plants are described by a special method. Only technical terms are used for their description. There are several alternative terms for every character of an organ. Of these, only one appropriate term is chosen and then written in a place meant for it in a particular series of terms. These terms and their serial are given under **II.** Alternative Terms and Illustrated Terminology. Followings are the terms used to describe plants.

1. Habit

2. Root

3. Stem

[I] Habit ......
[II] Type of stem ......
[III] External shape ......
[IV] Branching ......
[V] Interior ......
[VI] Surface ......
[VII] Colour of stem ......
[VIII] Other characters ......

4. Leaf

[I] Bearing of leaf ......
[II] Phyllotaxy ......
[III] Stipules and thier types ......
[IV] Type of leaf ......
[V] Leaf attachment ......
[VI] Leaf shape ......
[VII] Leaf margin ......
[VIII] Leaf apex ......
[IX] Leaf surface ......
[X] Venation ......
[XI] Texture of leaf ......
[XII] Other special characters (if any) ......

5. Inflorescence

Type ......

6. Flower

[I] Bracts and bracteoles ......
[II] Attachment of flower ......
[III] Presence of floral whorls ......
[IV] Symmetry ......
[V] Presence of reproductive whorls ......
[VI] Number of floral parts ......
[VII] Position of floral organs on thalamus ......
[VIII] Arrangement of floral organs ......
[IX] Colour ......
[X] Other special characters (if any) ......

7. Calyx
[I] Number of sepals ......
[II] Cohesion ......
[III] Aestivation ......
[IV] Duration of calyx ......

8. Corolla
[I] Number of petals ......
[II] Cohesion ......
[III] Aestivation ......
[IV] Shape of corolla ......
[V] Colour of corolla ......
[VI] Appendages of corolla ......

9. Perianth
When calyx and corolla can not be differentiated.
[I] Number of tepals ......
[II] Number of whorls ......
[III] Cohesion ......
[IV] Type ......
[V] Aestivation ......
[VI] Colour of tepals ......

10. Androecium
[I] Number of stamens ......
[II] Fertility ......
[III] Cohesion of stamens ......
[IV] Adhesion of stamens ......
[V] Sequence of staminal whorls ......
[VI] Length of filaments ......
[VII] Position of stamens ......
[VIII] Number of locules ......
[IX] Attachment of filament to anther ......
[X] Type of connectives ......
[XI] Dehiscence ......

11. Gynoecium
[I] Number of carpels ......
[II] Cohesion of carpels ......
[III] Position of ovary ......
[IV] Number of locules ......
[V] Number of ovules in each locule ......
[VI] Placentation ......
[VII] Disc ......
[VIII] Style ......
[IX] Stigma ......

12. Fruits
Type

13. Floral Formula

14. Classification and identification
Class
Sub-class
Series
Order
Family

II. Alternative Terms and Illustrated Terminology

1. HABIT

Habit. Characteristic form or bodily appearance of an organism (Fig. 1).

Alternative Terms

Herb/Shrub/Tree/Any other peculiarity as Climber, Epiphyte, Parasite, Saprophyte, Insectivore, Symbiont, etc.

(The habit of the plant can be understood only if the plant is provided with roots or seen growing in nature.)

Meaning of Alternative Terms

1. Herb. A plant with soft stem-annual, biennial or perennial- whose aerial portion is relatively short lived; *e.g., Ranunculus*.

2. Shrub. Perennial, woody plant of relatively low stature, typically with several stems arising from or near the ground; shrubs do not have a clear stem; *e.g., Capparis*.

3. Tree. A perennial woody plant with a single trunk; *e.g., Melia*.

4. Climber. Plant with thin and long stems, with diffuse branches and special organs of attachment by means of which it clings to the neighbouring objects; *e.g., Clematis, Tecoma*.

5. Epiphyte. A plant that grows upon other plants, but does not absorb food from them as do the parasites *e.g.*, *Vanda, Vanilla* (orchid), Fig. 1.

6. Parasite. A plant that grows upon other living plants or animals and obtains its food material from them. On the basis of their complete or incomplete dependence, the parasite may either be called total parasite *viz. Cuscuta reflexa, Orobanche, Balanophora,* etc. or partial parasite *viz. Viscum album, Loranthus, Santalum,* etc. (Fig. 1).

7. Saprophyte. A plant that grows in places rich in decaying organic subtances, deriving its nutrition from them; *e.g., Monotropa, Neottia* (Fig. 1).

8. Insectivore. Plants which trap the small insects and digest their protein matter; *e.g., Drosera, Utricularia, Nepenthes,* etc. (Fig. 1).

9. Symbiont. Two organisms living together in such a way that they appear to be the parts of the

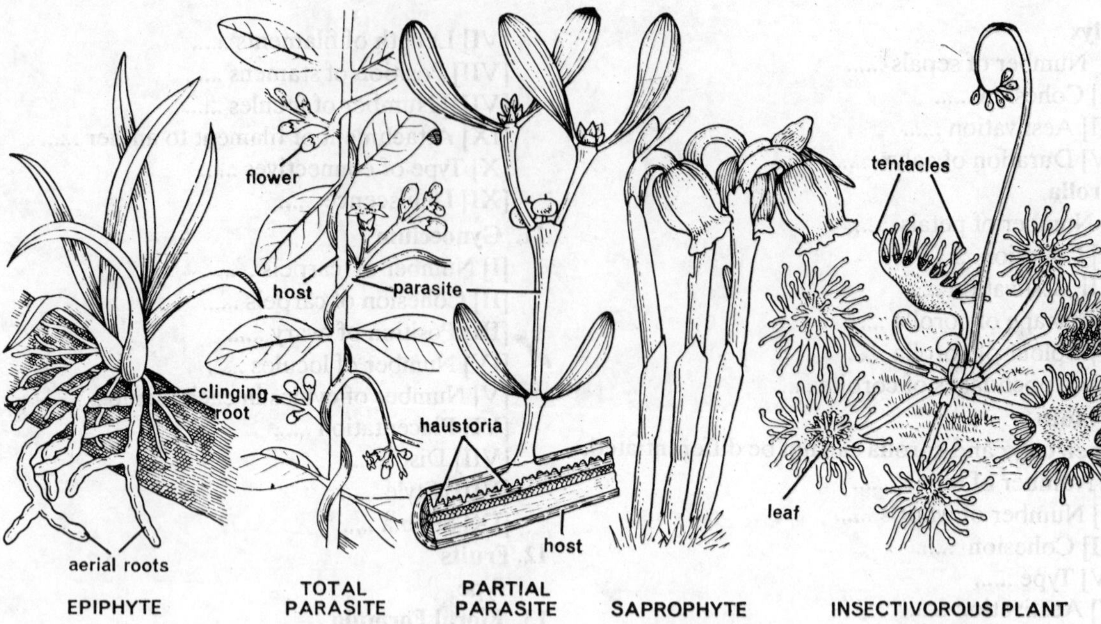

Fig. 1. Some plant habits.

same plant, and are of mutual benefit to each other; *e.g.,* Mycorrhiza, Lichens, *Rhizobium* in root nodules of papilionaceae.

2. ROOT

Root. A part of the plant axis that mostly grows towards the soil and is concerned with absorption of water and minerals.

Alternative Terms

Tap/Adventitious-if adventitious then type of adventitious root.

Meaning of Alternative Terms

1. Tap. A stout, tapering main root arising from the radicle and from which arise smaller lateral branches *e.g., Morus* (Fig. 2A).

2. Adventitious. Roots that grow from any part of the body other than the radicle; *e.g.,* Sugarcane, *Bryophyllum* (Fig. 2B).

3. STEM

Stem. Main axis of the plant; leaf and flower bearing as distinguished from root bearing axis.

[I] Habit

Alternative Terms

Herbaceous/ Woody

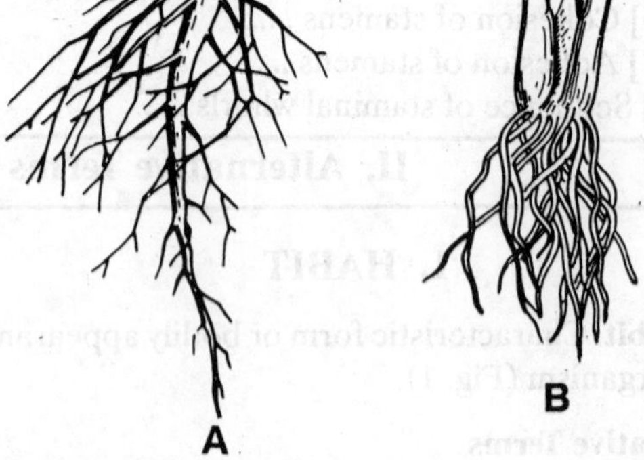

Fig. 2. Types of roots. A. Tap root, B. Adventitious root.

Meaning of Alternative Terms

1. Herbaceous. A term referring to any non-woody plant; *e.g., Fumaria, Ranunculus.*

2. Woody. Trees and shrubs in which increase in diameter of stems and roots continues from year to year; *e.g., Bauhinia, Melia.*

[II] Types of Stem

Alternative Terms

Aerial/Underground/Specialised

1. If **aerial** – erect/weak

(a) if **erect** then – caudex / culm / scape / excurrent / deliquescent

(b) if **weak** then – **(i) trailing** e.g. prostrate/ decumbent / diffuse.

(ii) creeping *e.g.* runner/stolon/ offset/sucker

(iii) climbing *e.g.* rootlet climber/hook climber/ tendril climber/leaf climber/ twiner/ liana.

2. If **underground** – rhizome/tuber/bulb/corm.

3. If **specialised** – phylloclade / cladode.

Meaning of Alternative Terms

1. Aerial. Which remains above ground in air; *e.g., Sesbania, Abutilon, Ipomoea*.

(a) Erect. A rigid and strong stem holding itself in an upright position; *e.g., Sesbania.* These are of following 5 types.

(i) Caudex. An unbranched, stout, cylindrical stem, marked with scars of fallen leaves; *e.g.,* palms.

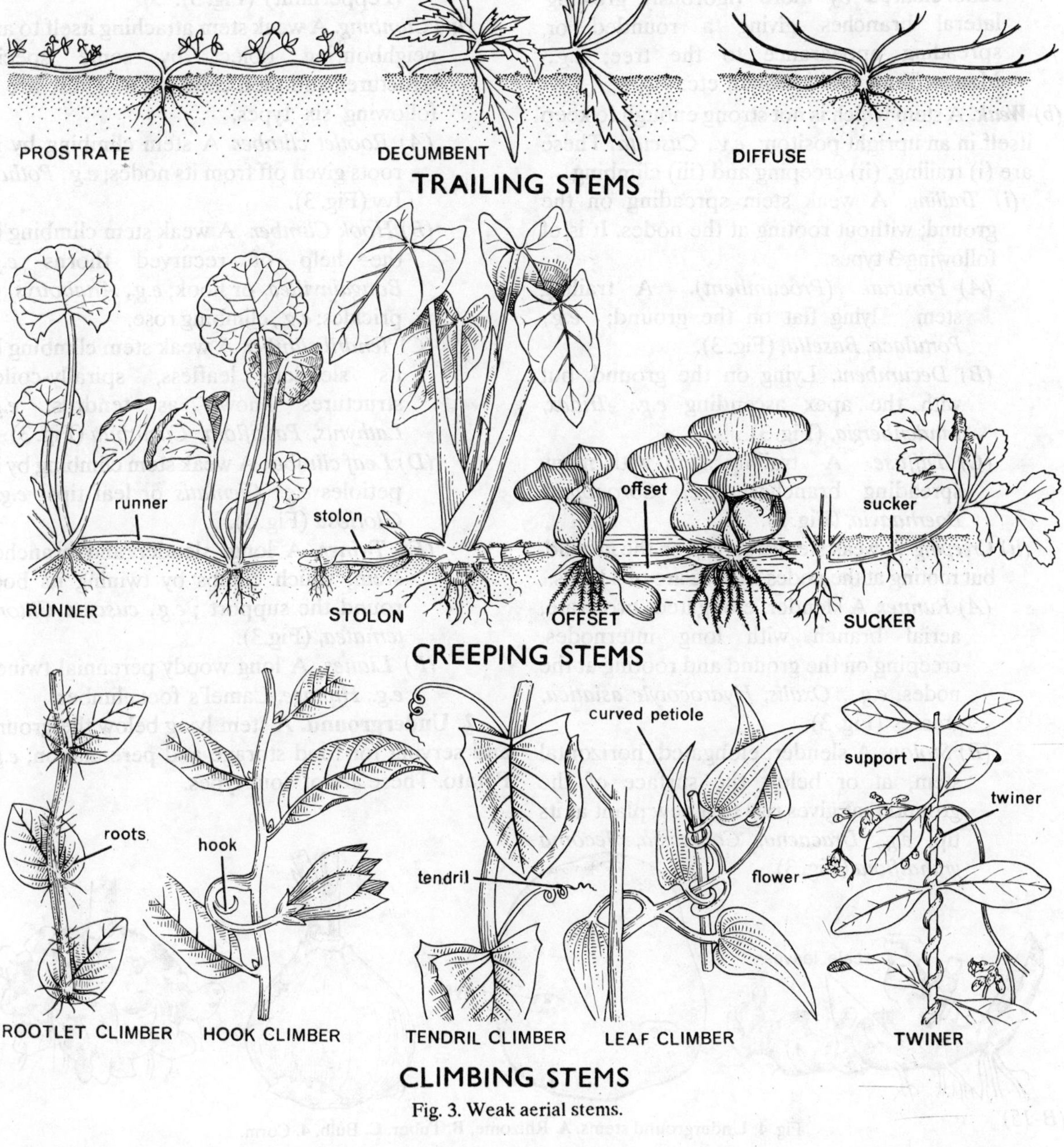

Fig. 3. Weak aerial stems.

(ii) Culm. A jointed stem with solid nodes and hollow internodes; *e.g.,* Bamboo, Wheat.

(iii) Scape. A leafless, usually unbranched flowering shoot produced by an underground stem; *e.g.,* Onion, Canna, Tuberose.

(iv) Excurrent. When the main axis continues growth and the lateral branches develop regularly giving a conical appearance to the tree; *e.g., Polyalthia longifolia, Casuarina*.

(v) Deliquescent. When the main axis in growth is subordinated by more vigorously growing lateral branches giving a rounded or spreading appearance to the tree; *e.g.,* Mango, Teak, Gold Mohur, etc.

(b) Weak. A stem which is not strong enough to keep itself in an upright positon; *e.g., Cuscuta*. These are (i) trailing, (ii) creeping and (iii) climbing.

(i) Trailing. A weak stem spreading on the ground; without rooting at the nodes. It is of following 3 types.

(A) Prostrate (Procumbent). A trailing stem lying flat on the ground; *e.g., Portulaca, Basella*, (Fig. 3).

(B) Decumbent. Lying on the ground, but with the apex ascending *e.g., Tridax, Lindenbergia,* (Fig. 3).

(C) Diffuse. A trailing stem with many spreading branches; *e.g., Coronopus, Boerhaavia,* (Fig. 3).

(ii) Creeping. A weak stem creeping on the ground, but rooting at the nodes. These are of 4 types.

(A) Runner. A slender, elongated, prostrate, aerial branch with long internodes, creeping on the ground and rooting at the nodes, *e.g.* , *Oxalis, Hydrocotyle asiatica,* grasses (Fig. 3).

(B) Stolon. A slender, elongated, horizontal stem, at or below the surface of the ground that gives rise to a new plant at its tip; *e.g., Dracaena, Colocasia, Tecoma grandiflora* (Fig. 3).

(C) Offset. A horizontal, short, more or less thickened, prostrate branch, producing at the apex a tuft of leaves above and a cluster of small roots below; *e.g., Pistia, Salvinia, Eichhornia,* (Fig. 3).

(D) Sucker. A creeping stem developing from the underground part of the stem but growing obliquely upwards and directly giving rise to a leafy shoot or a new plant; *e.g., Chrysanthemum, Mentha piperita* (Peppermint) (Fig. 3).

(iii) Climbing. A weak stem attaching itself to any neighbouring object by some special structures and then climbing it. These are of following six types.

(A) Rootlet climber. A stem climbing by its roots given off from its nodes; *e.g., Pothos,* Ivy (Fig. 3).

(B) Hook Climber. A weak stem climbing by the help of recurved thorns *e.g., Bougainvillea,* or hook; *e.g., Artabotrys* or prickles; *e.g.*, climbing rose.

(C) Tendril climber. A weak stem climbing by its slender, leafless, spirally-coiled structures known as tendrils; *e.g., Lathyrus, Passiflora, Cucurbita* (Fig. 3).

(D) Leaf climber. A weak stem climbing by its petioles *e.g., Clematis* or leaf tips *e.g.* , *Gloriosa* (Fig. 3).

(E) Twiner. A long, slender and branched stem, which climbs by twining its body round the support ; *e.g., cuscuta Clitoria ternatea,* (Fig.3).

(F) Lianes. A long woody perennial twiner; *e.g., Hiptage,* Camel's foot climber.

2. Underground. A stem lying below the ground and serving for food storage and perennation; *e.g.,* Potato. These are of four types.

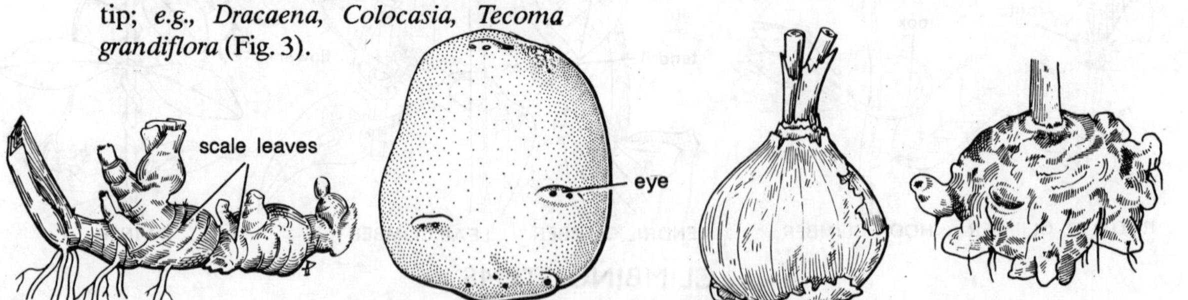

Fig. 4. Underground stems. **A.** Rhizome, **B.** Tuber, **C.** Bulb, **4.** Corm.

(a) ***Rhiozme.*** A horizontal underground stem, distinguished from the root by the presence of nodes and internodes and some times bud and scale-like leaves at the nodes, often thickened and containing accumulated food; *e.g.*, Ginger, Turmeric, Ferns (Fig. 4).

(b) ***Tuber.*** A much enlarged portion of an underground stem provided with buds on the sides and tip; *e.g.*, Potato, *Cyperus* (Fig. 4).

(c) **Bullb.** An underground and reduced stem, composed chiefly of enlarged and fleshy leaf bases; *e.g.,* Onion, Tulip, Garlic (Fig. 4).

(d) ***Corm.*** A short, thickened, underground stem, upright in position in which the food is accumulated; *e.g.*, *Amorphophallus, Crocus (Fig.4).*

3. Specialized stems.

(a) ***Phylloclade.*** A green, flattened or rounded succulent stem having many internodes and with leaves either feebly developed or modified into spines; *e.g., Opuntia, Euphorbia tirucalii* Fig. 5

(b) ***Cladode.*** It is a phylloclade of one internode *(Asparagus)* or two internodes *(Ruscus)* only, (Fig. 5).

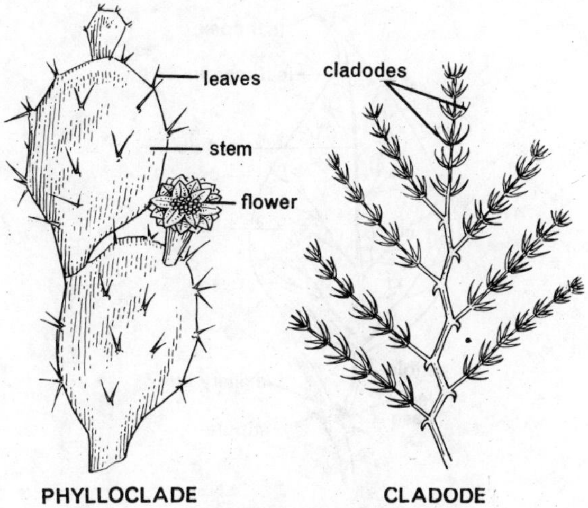

Fig. 5. Specialised stems.

[III] External shape

Alternative Terms

Cylindrical/ Angular- if angular then number of angles.

Meaning of Alternative Terms

1. Cylindrical. A stem which is circular in a transverse section; *e.g.,* Lemon (Fig. 6).

2. Angular. A stem which shows many lateral angles in a transverse section; *e.g., Asparagus, Coriandrum* (Fig. 6).

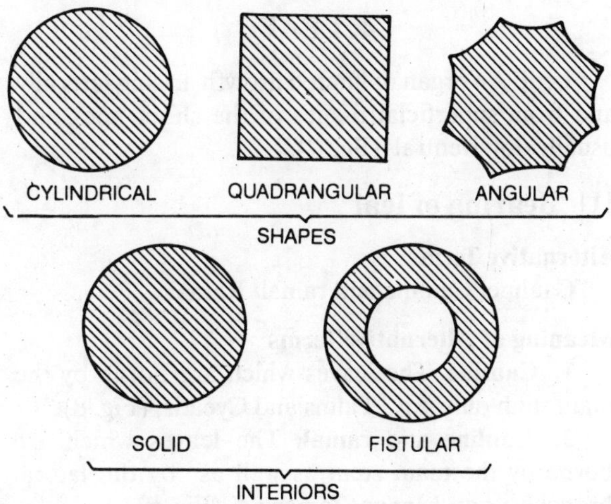

Fig. 6. Stem shapes and interiors.

[IV] Branching

Alternative Terms

Branched/ Unbranched

Meaning of Alternative Terms

1. Branched. A stem with many lateral shoots; *e.g., Ranunculus.*

2. Unbranched. A stem without lateral shoots; *e.g.*, Palms.

[V] Interior

Alternative Terms

Solid/ Fistular

Meaning of Alternative Terms

1. Solid. A stem having a filled interior; *e.g.,* Lemon (Fig. 6).

2. Fistular. A stem having a hollow interior; *e.g.,* Bamboo, Wheat (Fig. 6).

[VI] Surface

Alternative Terms

Glabrous/ Hairy

Meaning of Alternative Terms

1. **Glabrous.** Not hairy, *e.g.,* Lemon,
2. **Hairy.** Covered with hairs; *e.g., Calotropis.*

[VII] Colour of the stem

[VIII] Any other Character

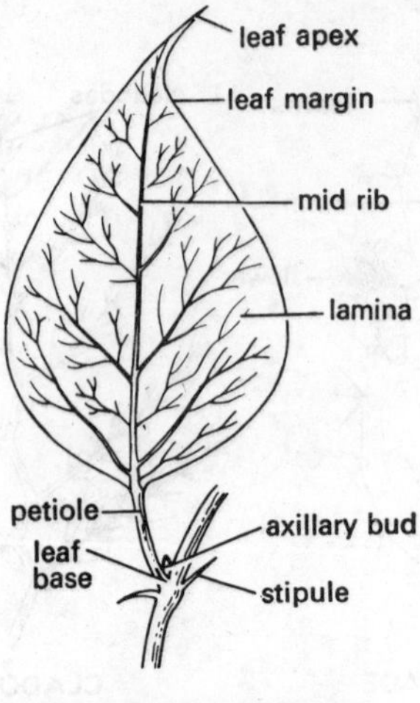

Fig. 7. Leaf and its parts.

4. LEAF

Leaf. An organ of limited growth arising laterally and from superficial tissues of the shoot apex and usually dorsiventral (Fig. 7).

[I] Bearing of leaf

Alternative Terms

Cauline/ Cauline and ramal/ Ramal.

Meaning of Alternative Terms

1. **Cauline.** The leaves which are borne by the main stem only; *e.g.,* Palms and Cycads, (Fig. 8).
2. **Cauline** and **ramal.** The leaves which are borne by the main stem as well as by the lateral branches; *e.g.,* Mango, Tamarind, (Fig. 8).
3. **Radical.** The leaves which arise from a reduced underground stem; *e.g.,* Onion, (Fig. 8).

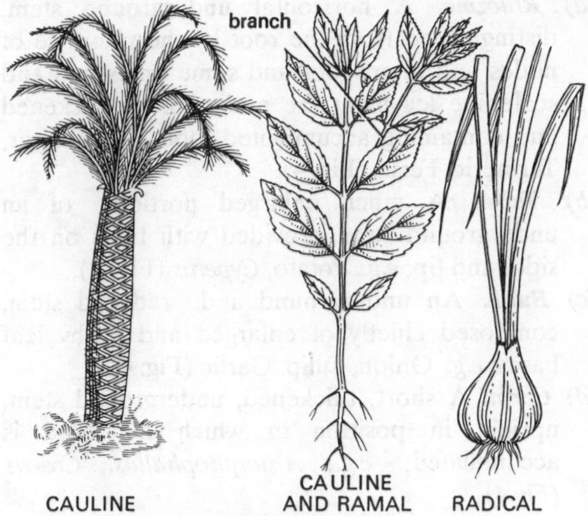

Fig. 8. Bearing of leaves on stem.

[II] Phyllotaxy

Phyllotaxy. Arrangement of leaves on stem.

Alternative Terms

Alternate (spiral)/ Opposite/ Whorled

1. If **alternate** then (a)1/2 or two ranked or distichous, (b) 1/3 or three ranked or tristichous, (c) 2/5 or five ranked or pentastichous, (d) 3/8 or eight ranked or octastichous.
2. If **opposite** whether decussate/ superposed.

Meaning of Alternative Terms

1. **Alternate** or **spiral.** A single leaf arising at each node; *e.g., Ipomoea*. It is of following types.

(a) 1/2 **or** ***two-ranked.*** **Third leaf stands over the first and there is one spiral between the two leaves;** *e.g.,* Gramineae, Ginger, *Ravenala* (Fig. 9).

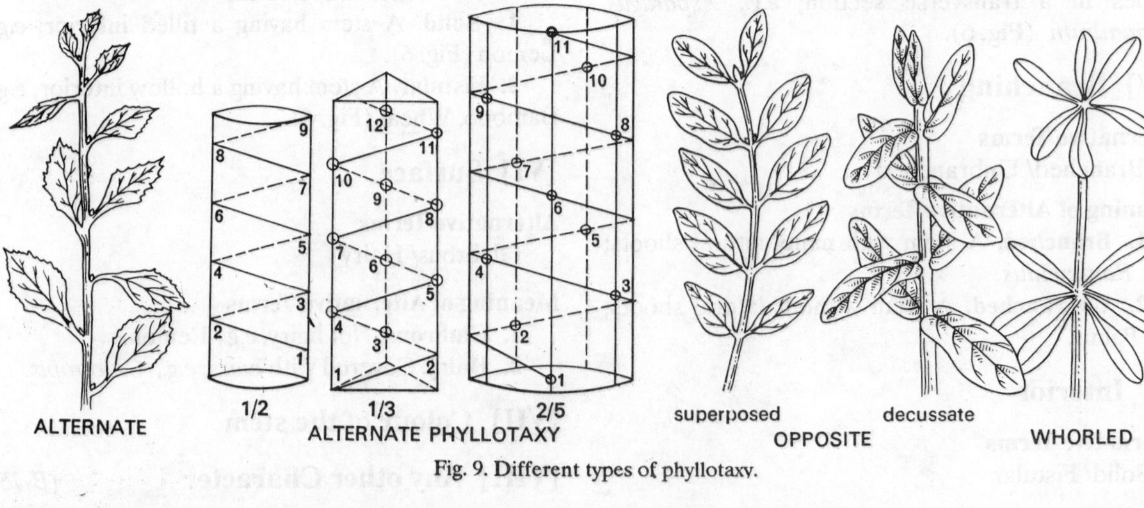

Fig. 9. Different types of phyllotaxy.

(b) 1/3 or ***three-ranked.*** Fourth leaf stands over the first and there is one spiral between the two leaves; *e.g. Cyperus rotundus* (Fig. 9).

(c) 2/5 or ***five-ranked.*** Sixth leaf stands over the first and there are two spirals between the two leaves; *e.g.* China rose. This is the most common type of alternate phyllotaxy (Fig. 9).

(d) 3/8 or ***eight-ranked.*** Ninth leaf stands over the first and there are three spirals between the two leaves; *e.g.,* Papaya.

2. Opposite. Term applied to leaves or buds occurring in pairs at a node; *e.g., Ixora.*

(a) Decussate. A pair of leaves that stands at right angle to the next upper or lower pair; *e.g., Calotropis, Mussaenda, Tabernaemontana* (Fig. 9).

(b) Superposed. A pair of leaves that stands directly over a pair in the same plane; *e.g.,* Guava, *Quisqualis, Carissa* (Fig. 9).

3. Whorled. More than two leaves at each node arranged in a circle or whorl; *e.g., Alstonia* (Fig. 9).

[III] Stipules and their Types

Stipule. An appendage on both the sides of basal part of a leaf.

Stipel. Stipule-like appendage at the base of leaflets of a compound leaf.

Alternative Terms

Exstipulate/Stipulate

If **stipulate** then type of stipules-Free lateral / Scaly /Adnate/Interpetiolar/ Intrapetiolar / Ochreate / Foliaceous / Spinous / Tendrillar / Convolute (ventral)

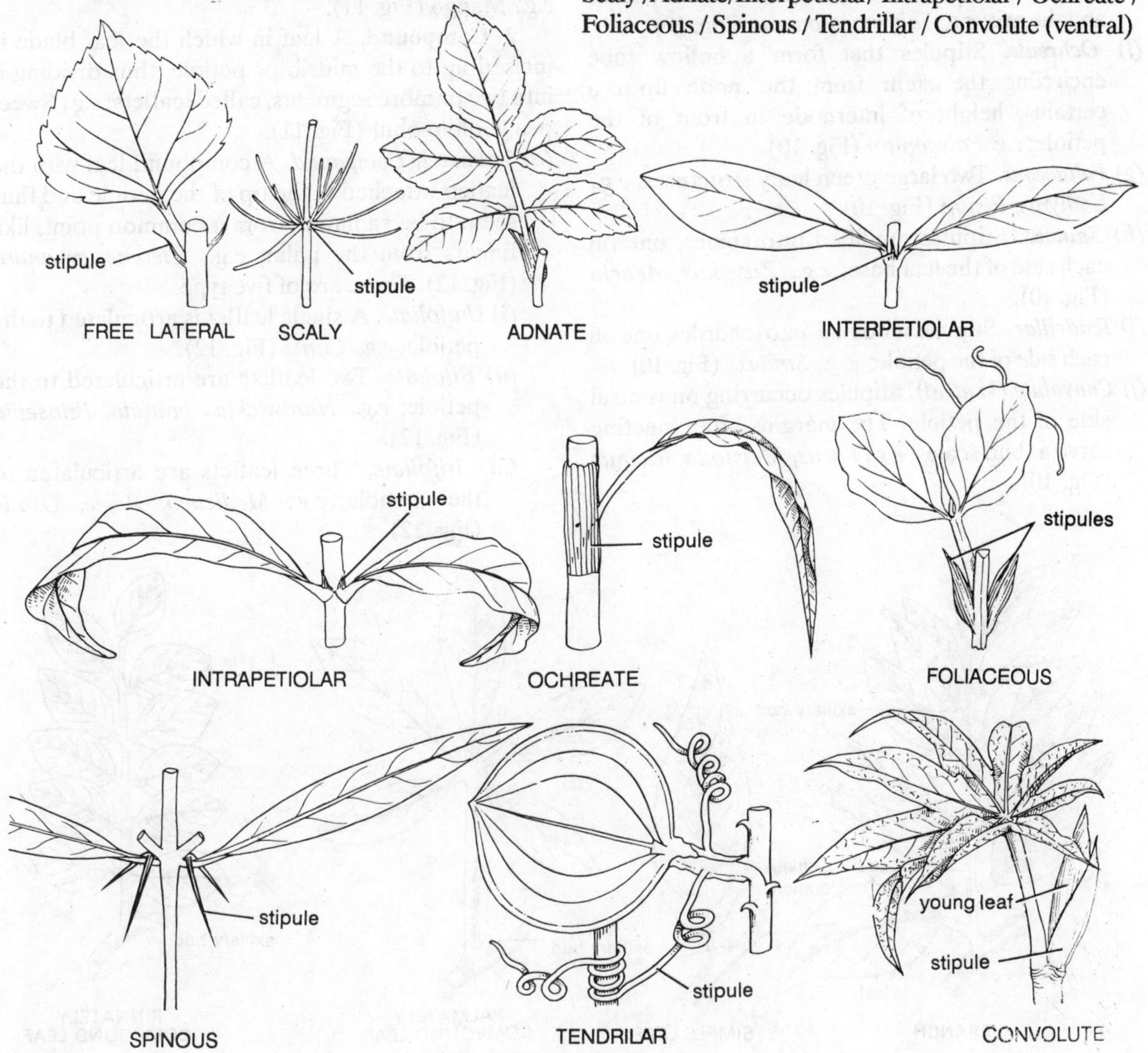

Fig. 10. Different types of stipules.

Meaning of Alternative Terms

1. Extipulate. Stipules absent, *e.g., Ipomoea*.

2. Stipulate. Stipules present, *e.g.*, Rose.

(a) Free-lateral. Two free stipules borne on the two sides of leaf base; *e.g.,* China rose (Fig. 10).

(b) Scaly. Small dry scales, usually two in number, borne on two sides of the leaf base; *e.g., Spergula, Desmodium* (Fig. 10).

(c) Adnate. Two lateral stipules that grow adhering to the petiole up to a certain height thus making it somewhat winged; *e.g.,* Rose (Fig. 10).

(d) Interpetiolar. Two stipules lying between the petioles of opposite or whorled leaves; *e.g., Ixora, Mussaenda* (Fig. 10).

(e) Intrapetiolar. Stipules situated between the petiole and the axis; *e.g., Tabernaemontana* (Fig. 10).

(f) Ochreate. Stipules that form a hollow tube encircling the stem from the node up to a certain height of internode in front of the petiole; *e.g. Polygonum* (Fig. 10).

(g) Foliaceous. Two large green leafy structures; *e.g., Lathyrus, Pisum* (Fig. 10).

(h) Spinous. Stipules modified into spines, one on each side of the leaf base; *e.g., Zizyphus, Acacia* (Fig. 10).

(i) Tendrillar. Stipules modified into tendriles, one on each side of the petiole; *e. g., Smilax,* (Fig. 10).

(j) Convolute (Ventral). Stipules occurring on ventral side of the petiole. The margins after meeting serve as bud scales; *e.g., Fucus, Magnolia, Ricinus* (Fig. 10).

[IV] Types of Leaves

Alternative Terms

Simple/Compound

If **compound** then – palmately compound or pinnately compound

(1) If **palmately compound**- Unifoliate / Bifoliate/ Trifoliate/ Quadrifoliate/ Multifoliate (Digitate).

(2) If **pinnately compound**- Unipinnate (then either paripinnate or imparipinnate) / bipinnate/ tripinnate/ decompound.

Meaning of Alternative Terms

1. Simple. A leaf which may be entire or incised to any depth, but not down to the midrib or petiole; *e.g.,* Mango (Fig. 11).

2. Compound. A leaf in which the leaf blade is incised up to the midrib or petiole, thus dividing it into two or more segments, called leaflets; *e.g.,* Sweet pea, Gold mohur (Fig. 11).

(a) Palmately Compound. A compound leaf with the leaflets attached at the tip of the petiole and thus seem to be radiating from a common point, like fingers from the palm; e.g., *Cleome gynandra* (Fig. 12). These are of five type.

(i) Unifoliate. A single leaflet is articulated to the petiole; *e.g., Citrus* (Fig. 12).

(ii) Bifoliate. Two leaflets are articulated to the petiole; *e.g., Hardwickia binnata, Prinsepia* (Fig. 12).

(iii) Trifoliate. Three leaflets are articulated to the petiole; *e.g., Medicago, Aegle, Oxalis* (Fig. 12).

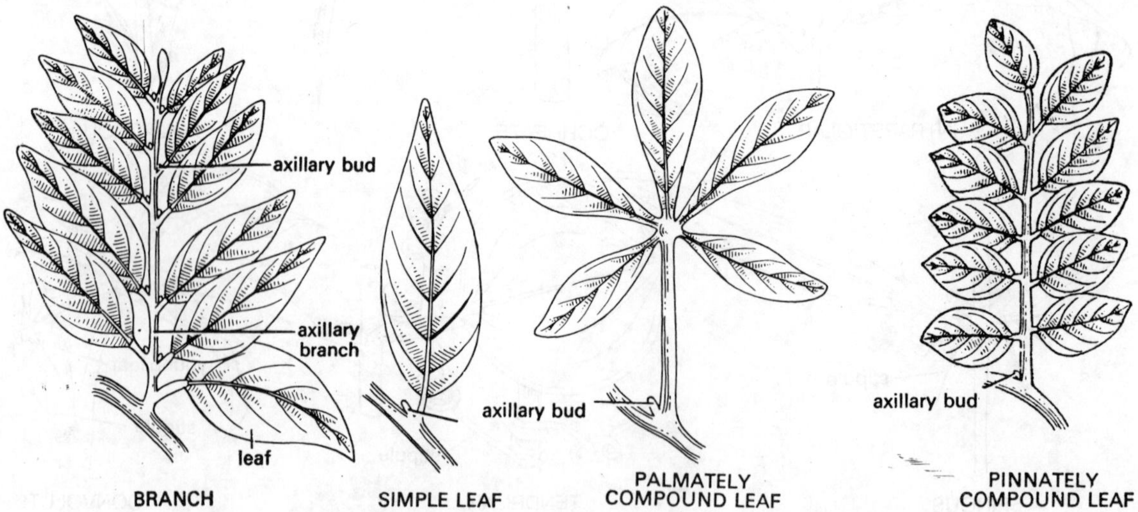

Fig. 11. Branch and types of leaves. (Note the position of axillary bud in each case).

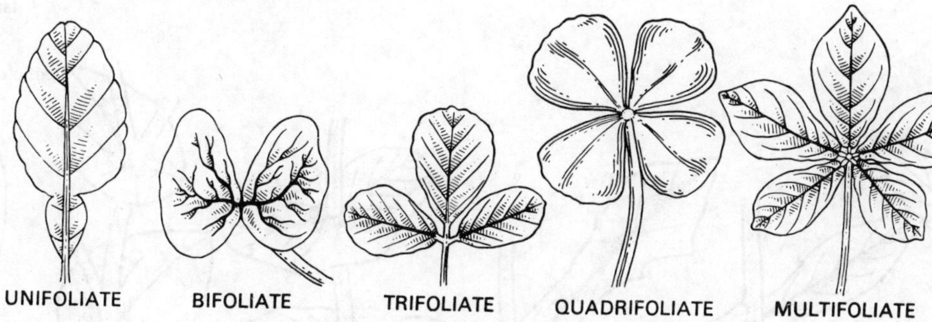

Fig. 12. Palmately compound leaves.

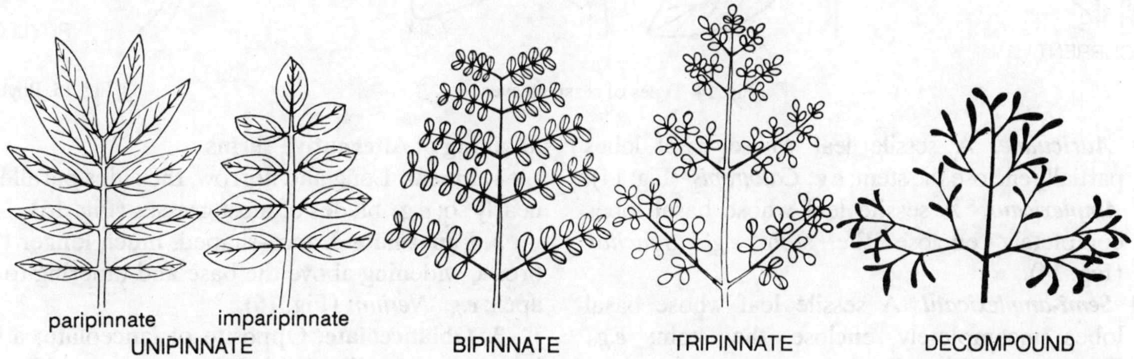

Fig. 13. Pinnately compound leaves.

(iv) Quadrifoliate. Four leaflets are articulated to the petiole; *e.g., Paris quadrifolia, Marsilea* (Fig. 12).

(v) Multifoliate (Digitate). Five or more leaflets are articulated to the petiole and spreading like fingers from the palm; *e.g., Cleome (= Gynandropsis), Bombax* (Fig. 12).

(b) Pinnately Compound. A compound leaf with the leaflets arranged along the sides of common axis, the rachis; *e.g.,* Tamarind (Fig. 11 & 13).

(i) Unipinnate. A pinnately compound leaf bearing the leaflets directly on the rachis; *e.g., Cassia* (Fig. 13).

(A) Paripinnate. A unipinnate leaf with even number of leaflets *e.g.,* Tamarind, *Cassia* sp. (Fig. 13).

(B) Imparipinnate. A unipinnate leaf with odd number of leaflets, *e.g.,* Rose, *Melia* (Fig. 13).

(ii) Bipinnate. A twice pinnate compound leaf i.e. , the midrib produces secondary axes on which the leaflets are borne; *e.g., Acacia, Mimosa pudica* (Fig. 13).

(iii) Tripinnate. A thrice pinnate compound leaf i.e., the secondary axes produce the tertiary axes which bear the leaflets; *e.g., Moringa* (Fig. 13).

(iv) Decompound. A compound leaf which is more than thrice pinnate; *e.g., Coriandrum* (Fig. 13).

[V] Leaf Attachment

Alternative Terms

Sessile/Petiolate

1. If **sessile** then - Decurrent/ Auriculate/ Amplexicaul/Semi- amplexicaul/Connate/Perfoliate.

2. If **petiolate** then the petiole may be Filiform/Terete/Striate/Grooved/ Flattened.

If leaves are cmpound then find out if **petiolulate.**

Meaning of Alternative Terms

1. Sessile. A leaf without stalk, *e.g., Dianthus*.

(a) Decurrent. A sessile leaf with a winged leaf base and the wing extending down the stem so that latter also seems to be winged; *e.g., Laggera pterodonta* (Fig. 14).

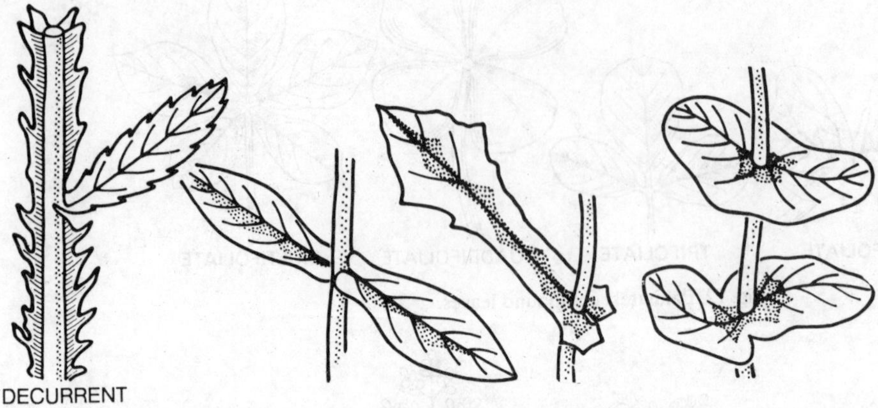

Fig. 14. Types of sessile leaves.

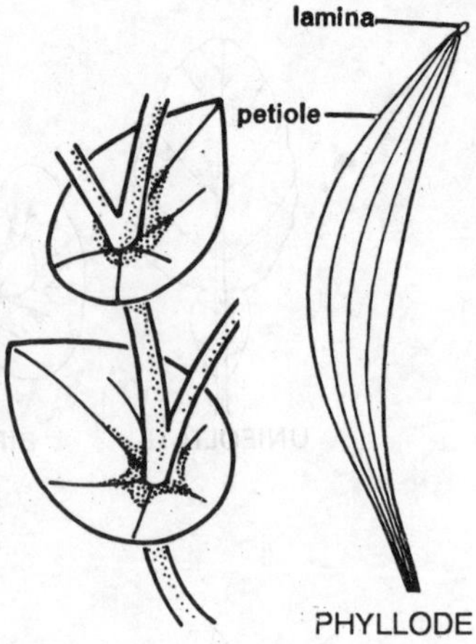

Fig. 15. Phyllode.

(b) ***Auriculate.*** A sessile leaf whose basal lobes partially enclose the stem; *e.g., Calotropis* (Fig. 14).

(c) ***Amplexicaul.*** A sessile leaf whose basal lobes completely enclose the stem; *e.g., Sonchus* (Fig. 14).

(d) ***Semi-amplexicaul.*** A sessile leaf whose basal lobes incompletely enclose the stem; *e.g., Ranunculus* (Fig. 14).

(e) ***Connate.*** Two sessile opposite leaves meeting each other across the stem and fusing together; *e.g., Lonicera flava* (Fig. 14).

(f) ***Perfoliate.*** A sessile leaf whose basal lobes meet across the stem and fuse together so that the latter seems to pass through the leaf blade; *e.g., Aloe perfoliata* (Fig. 14).

2. Petiolate. A stalked leaf; *e.g.,* China rose.

(a) ***Filiform.*** A long and slender petiole; *e.g., Ricinus.*

(b) ***Terete.*** A cylindrical petiole being circular in cross section; *e.g., Ipomoea.*

(c) ***Striate.*** A petiole marked with longitudinal lines; *e.g., Ficus.*

(d) ***Grooved.*** A petiole provided with a long furrow.

(e) ***Phyllode.*** A sickle-shaped petiole flattened like a leaf; *e.g., Acacia auriculiformis.*

[VI] Leaf Shapes

Alternative Terms

Linear/Lanceolate/Oblanceolate/Rotund (orbicular) / Elliptical (oval) / Ovate / Obovate / Spathulate / Oblique / Oblong / Reniform / Cordate/ Sagittate/ Hastate / Lyrate / Acicular / Cuneate / Falcate / Lorate / Runcinate / Deltoid / Rhombate.

Meaning of Alternative Terms

1. Linear. Long and norrow, the sides parallel or nearly so; *e.g.,* blades of most grasses (Fig. 16).

2. Lanceolate. Lance-shaped, much longer than broad, widening above the base and tapering to the apex; *e.g., Nerium* (Fig. 16).

3. Oblanceolate. Opposite of lanceolate; a leaf broader at the distal third than at the middle and tapering toward the base; *e.g., Gnaphalium* (Fig. 16).

4. Rotund. (Orbicular). A leaf blade circular in outline; *e.g.,* Garden nasturtium, water-lily (Fig. 16).

5. Elliptical. Oval in outline narrowed to rounded ends and widest at or about the middle; *e.g.,* Guava (Fig. 16).

6. Ovate. With an outline like that of hen's egg; i.e. broader at the base than at the apex; *e.g.,* China rose (Fig. 16).

7. Obovate. The reverse of ovate, the apical half broader than the basal; *e.g., Cassia obtusifolia* leaflet (Fig. 16).

8. Spathulate. Spoon-shaped i.e., broad and round at the top and narrow towards the base; *e.g., Calendula, Mazus japonicus* (Fig. 16).

9. Oblique. Slanting i.e., the two halves of the leaf are unequal; *e.g.,* Leaflets of Margosa (Fig. 16).

10. Oblong. Longer than broad and with the margin running more or less parallel up to its length; *e.g.,* Banana (Fig. 16).

11. Reniform. Kidney-shaped; *e.g., Centella asiatica* (Fig. 16).

12. Cordate. Heart-shaped; with a sinus and rounded lobes at the base and ovate in general outline; *e.g.,* Betel (Fig. 16).

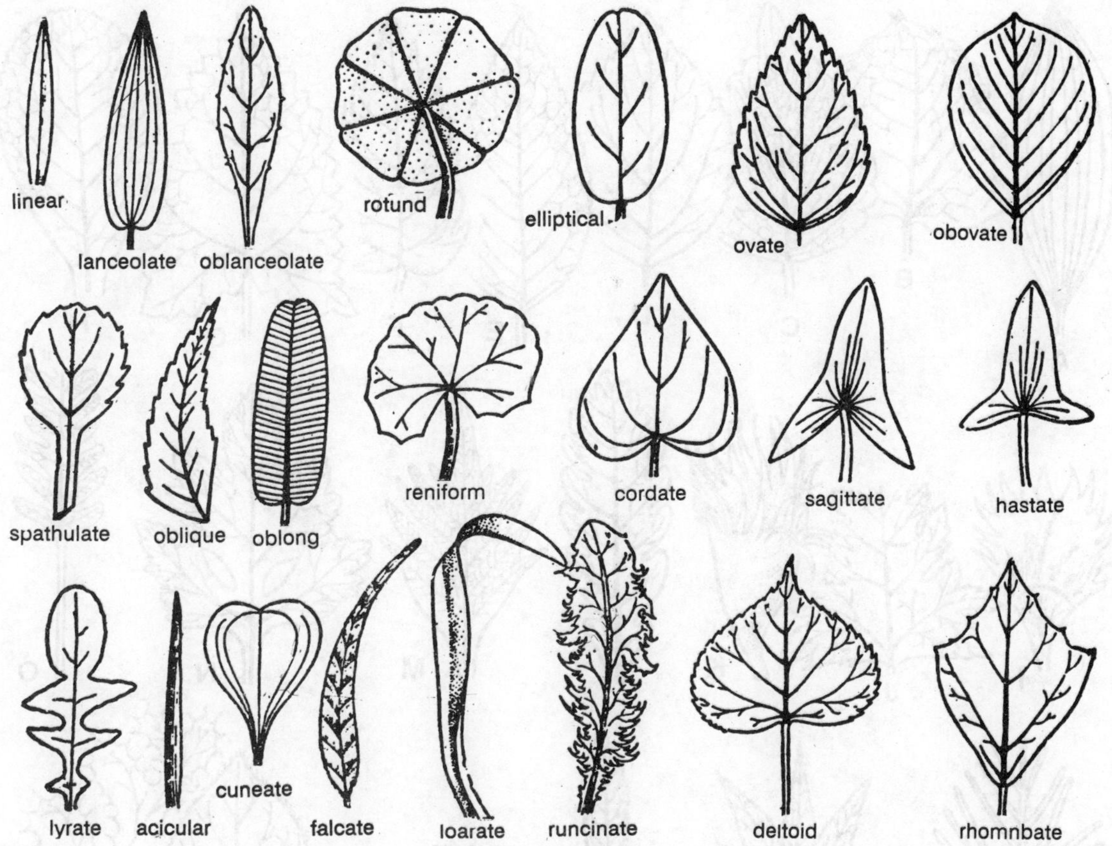

Fig. 16. Leaf shapes.

13. Sagittate. Like an arrowhead i.e. triangular with the basal lobes pointing downward or concavely toward the stalk; *e.g., Sagittaria sagittifolia,* Arum (Fig. 16).

14. Hastate. Like an arrowhead in form; but the basal lobes directed outward; *e.g., Rumex hastatus, Typhonium* (Fig. 16).

15. Lyrate. Like a lyre in form i.e. pinnatifid but with an enlarged terminal lobe and smaller lower lobes; *e.g.,* Mustard (Fig. 16).

16. Acicular. Needle-shaped i.e., long, narrow and cylindrical; *e.g.,* Pine, Onion (Fig. 16).

17. Cuneate. A wedge-shped leaf i.e., triangular with the narrow end at point of attachment; *e.g., Oxalis corymbosa* (Fig. 16).

18. Falcate. Sickle-shaped; *e.g., Eucalyptus* (Fig. 16).

19. Lorate. Strap-shaped; *e.g., Vallisneria* (Fig. 16).

20. Runcinate. Coarsely serrate to sharply incised with the teeth pointing toward the base; *e.g.,* Poppy (Fig. 16).

21. Deltoid. Delta-like; *e.g., Abutilon* (Fig. 16).

22. Rhombate. Shaped like a rhombus (Fig. 16).

[VII] Leaf Margins

Alternative Terms

Entire / Undulate / Crenate / Serrate / Serrulate/ Biserrate / Dentate/Denticulate/ Incised/ Lacerate/ Laciniate / Lobed / Cleft / Parted / Pinatifid / Pectinate/ Palmate/ Palmatifid/ Pedate/ Crispate/ Ciliate/ Spinous.

Meaning of Alternative Terms

1. Entire. An even and smooth leaf margin; *e.g.,* Madar, Mango, etc. (Fig. 17A).

2. Udulate or **Sinuate.** Wavy (up and down and not in and out); *e.g., Polyalthia* (Fig 17 B)

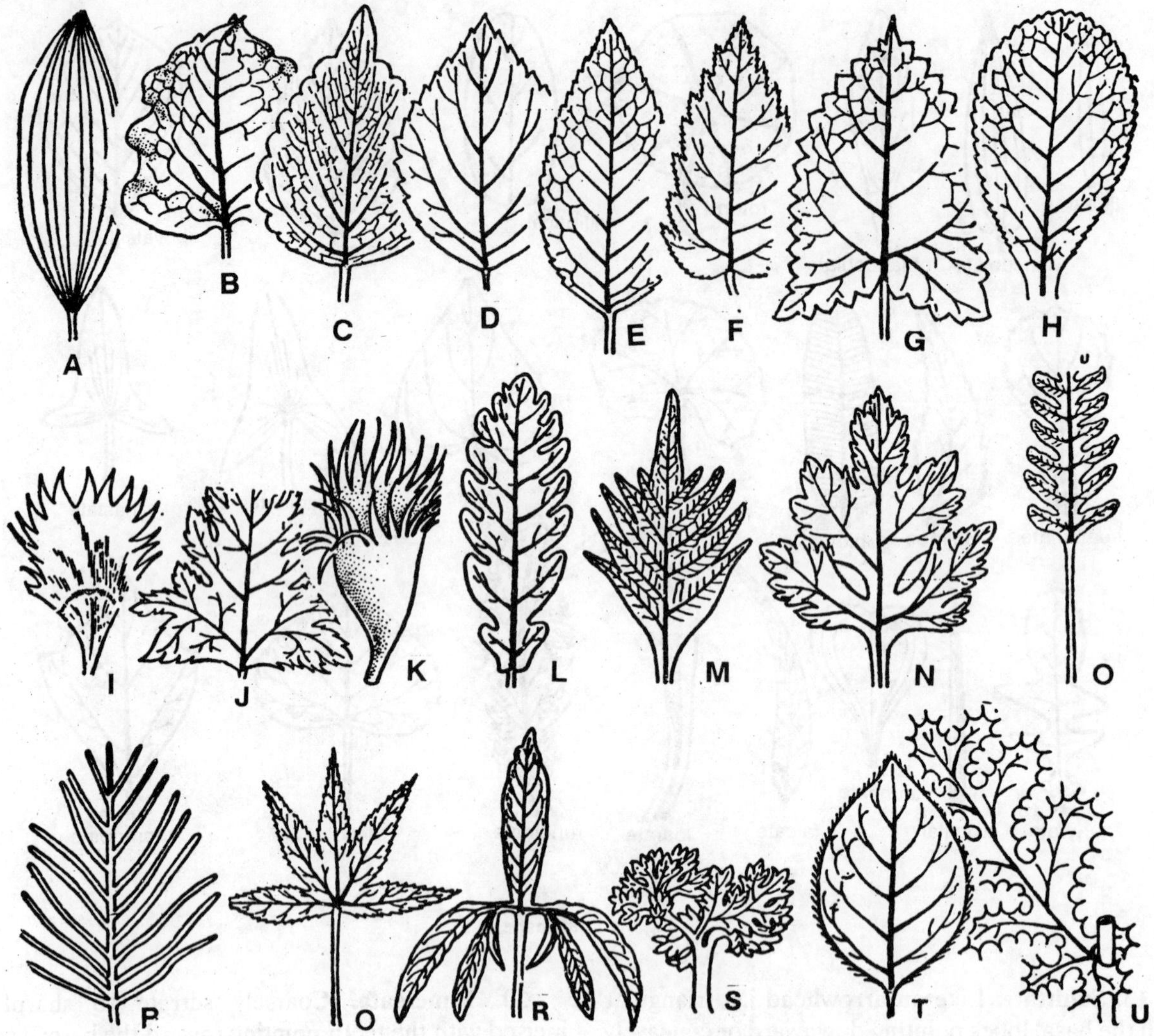

Fig. 17. Leaf margins. A. Entire; B. Undulate; C. Crenate; D. Serrate; E. Serrulate; F. Biserrate; G. Dentate; H. Denticulate; I. Incised; J. Lacerate; K. Laciniate; L. Lobed; M. Cleft; N. Parted; O. Pinnatifid: P. Pectinate; Q. Palmate: R. Pedate; S. Crispate; T. Ciliate; U. Spinous.

3. Crenate. Shallowly round toothed; *e.g., Bryophyllum,Hydrocotyle* (Fig. 17 C).

4. Serrate. Margin cut like the teeth of a saw and the teeth directed upward, *e.g.,* China rose (Fig. 17 D).

5. Serrulate. Minutely serrate; *e.g., Prunus persica* (Fig.17 E).

6. Biserrate. Doubly serrate, each tooth serrated again (Fig. 17 F).

7. Dentate. With sharp spreading, rather coarse indentations or teeth that are perpendicular to the margin; *e.g.,* Melon, (Fig. 17G).

8. Denticulate. Minutely dentate; *e.g., Coccinia cordifolia, Luffa cylindrica,* (Fig. 17H).

9. Incised. Cut irregularly, more or less deeply and sharply; and intermediate condition between tooth and lobes, (Fig. 17I).

10. Lacerate. Torn;irregularly cleft or cut, as in many genera of Ranunculaceae, (Fig. 17J).

11. Laciniate. Cut into narrow pointed lobes, (Fig. 17K).

12. Lobed. Margin divided into many lobes; *e.g., Ranunculus,* (Fig. 17L).

13. Cleft. Divided in or about the middle into divisions, as palmately or pinnately cleft leaf; *e.g.,* many ferns (Fig. 17 M).

14. Parted. Cut not quite to the base (Fig. 17 N).

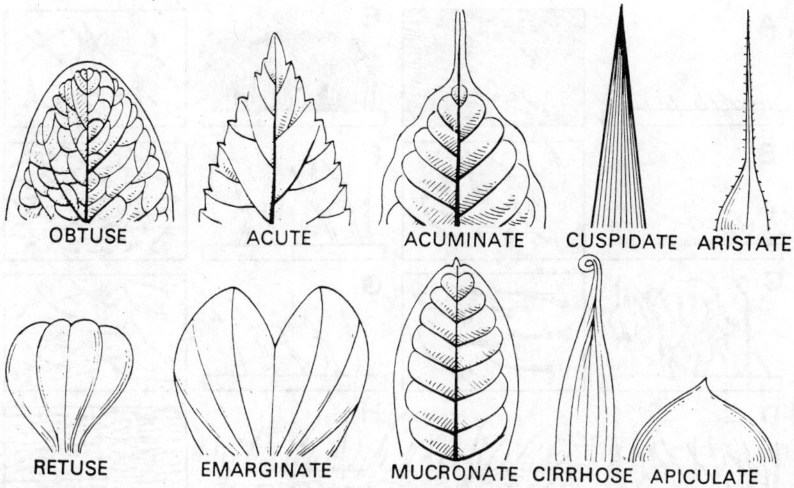

Fig. 18. Leaf apices.

15. Pinnatifid. Cleft or parted in a pinnate way; *e.g., Asplenium alternans* (Fig. 17 O).

16. Pectinate. Comb-like or pinnated with very close narrow divisions (Fig. 17 P).

17. Palmate. Lobed or divided into a palm-like fashion; *e.g.,* Castor (Fig. 17 Q).

18. Palmatifid. Cut about half-way down in a palmate form; *e.g,* Castor.

19. Pedate. A palmately lobed or divided leaf of which the two side lobes are again divided or cleft (Fig. 17 R).

20. Crispate. Curled, extremely undulate; *e.g., Tagetis* (Fig. 17 S).

21. Ciliate. Bearing hairs on the margin; *e.g., Cleome viscosa, Peristrophe* (Fig.17 T).

22. Spinous. Provided with spines; *e.g., Argemone* (Fig. 17 U).

[VIII] Leaf Apices

Alternative Terms

Obtuse/ Acute/ Acuminate/ Caudate/ Cuspidate/ Truncate / Aristate / Retuse / Emarginate / Mucronate/ Cirrhose/ Apiculate.

Meaning of Alternative Terms

1. Obtuse. Blunt or rounded; *e.g.,* Banyan (Fig. 18).

2. Acute. Sharp, ending in a point forming an acute angle; *e.g.,* China rose (Fig. 18).

3. Acuminate (Caudate). An apex drawn out into a long slender tail, *e.g., Ficus religiosa* (Fig. 18).

4. Cuspidate. A leaf ending in a long, rigid, spiny point, *e.g.,* Pineapple and Date palm (Fig. 18).

5. Truncate. Appearing as if cut off at the end; *e.g., Caryota urens.*

6. Aristate. Bearing a stiff bristle-like awn, tapered to a very narrow, much elongated apex (Fig.18).

7. Retuse. An opbtuse or truncate apex furnished with a shallow notch; *e.g., Oxalis corymbosa* (Fig. 18).

8. Emarginate. An apex provided with a deep notch; *e.g., Bauhinia* (Fig. 18).

9. Mucronate. A rounded apex terminated abruplty in a short point; *e.g.,* Leaflet of *Cassia obtusifolia* (Fig. 18).

10. Cirrhose. Tendrillar and coiled; *e.g., Gloriosa* (Fig. 18).

11. Apiculate. Terminated by a short, sharp flexible point; *e.g., Dalbergia* (Fig. 18).

[IX] Leaf Surfaces

Alternative Terms

Glabrous/ Rough/ Glutinous/ Glaucous/ Spiny/ Hairy-if hairy whether Pubescent/ Puberulous Tomentose/ Villous/ Velutinous/ Wooly/ Pilose/ Scabrous/ Hispid/ Stellate/ Hirsute/ Strigose/ Sericeous.

Meaning of Alternative Terms

1. Glabrous. A smooth surface free from hairs or outgrowths of any kind *e.g.,* China rose.

2. Rough. A surface which is somewhat harsh to touch; *e.g., Petrea.*

3. Glutinous. A surface covered with a sticky exudation; *e.g.,* Tobacco.

4.. Glaucous. Green and shining; *e.g., Citrus.*

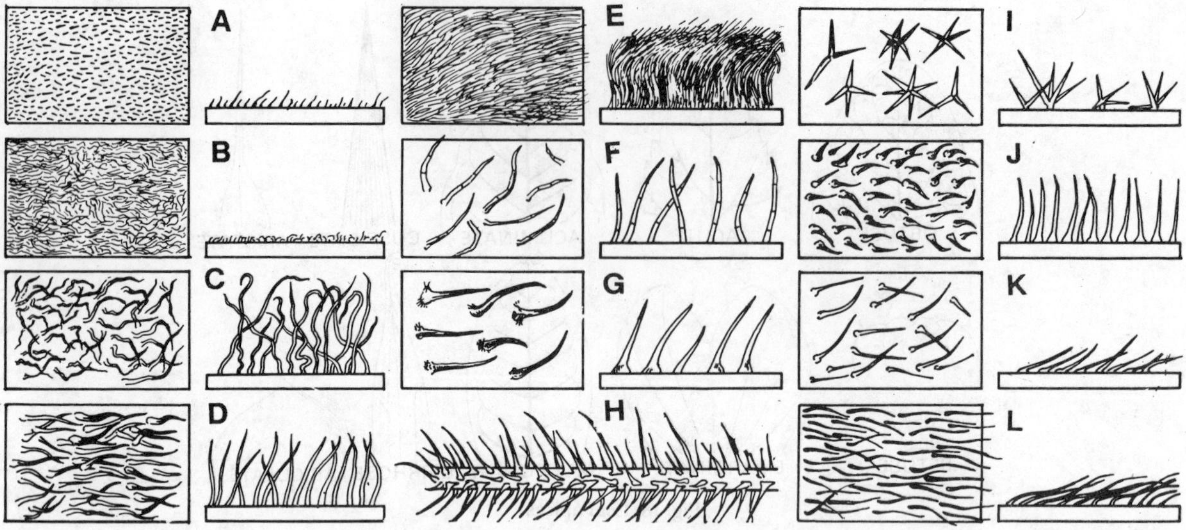

Fig. 19. Kinds of hairs (surface view at left, sectional view at rigtht). A. Puberulous; B. Tomentose; C. Villous; D. Velutinous; E. Wooly; F. Pilose; G. Scabrous; H. Hispid; I. Stellate; J. Hirsute; K. Strigose; L. Sericeous.

5. Spiny. Covered with spines; *e.g., Argemone.*

6. Hairy. A surface covered with hairs.

(a) ***Pubescent.*** Covered with soft, short, straight hairs.

(b) ***Puberulous.*** Minutely pubescent (Fig. 19A).

(c) ***Tomentose.*** Densely covered with long, soft, wool-like hairs (Fig. 19B).

(d) ***Villous.*** Thickly covered with long, soft hairs (Fig.19C).

(e) ***Velutinous.*** Clothed with a velvety covering composed of erect, straight, moderately firm hairs. (Fig. 19 D).

(f) ***Wooly.*** Denesly covered with soft, long, curled hairs looking like wool (Fig. 19 E).

(g) ***Pilose.*** Thinly covered with long, soft hairs (Fig. 19 F).

(h) ***Scabrous.*** Feeling roughish or gritty to touch. (Fig. 19 G).

(i) ***Hispid.*** Beset with rigid or bristly hairs (Fig. 19H).

(j) ***Stellate.*** Star-like hairs having radiating branches; hairs once or twice forked are often treated as stellate (Fig. 19 I).

(k) ***Hiruste.*** Provided with rather rough or coarse hairs (Fig. 19 J).

(l) ***Strigose.*** With sharp, appressed straight hairs, stiff and often basally swollen (Fig. 19 K).

(m) ***Sericeous.*** Provided with silky hairs (Fig. 19L).

[X] Venation

Venation. The arrangement of vascular bundles or veins in a leaf.

Alternative Terms

Reticulate/ Parallel.

Then see whether unicostate or multicostate.

If multicostate whether convergent or Divergent.

Meaning of Alternative Terms

1. Reticulate. The pattern of venation in which the veinlets are irregularly distributed, forming a network (Fig. 20).

(a) ***Unicostate.*** Having only one principal vein, that gives off many lateral veins which proceed toward margin or apex of the leaf; *e.g.,* Mango, Banyan (Fig. 20).

(b) ***Multicostate.*** Having many principal veins arising from tip of petiole and proceeding upwards or outwards (Fig. 20).

(i) Convergent. Many principal veins arising from the tip of petiole, run in a curved manner and converge toward the apex of leaf blade; *e.g., Cinnamomum* (Fig. 20).

(ii) Divergent. Many principal veins arising from the tip of petiole diverge from one another towards the margins of leaf blade; *e.g.,* Castor, Cucumber (Fig. 20).

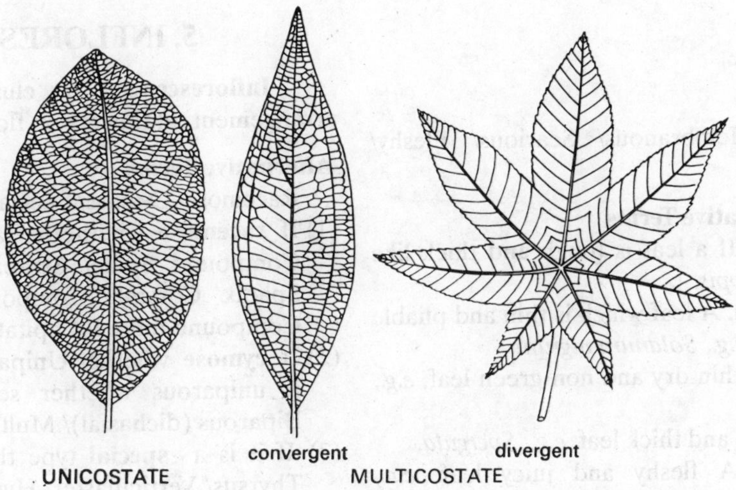

Fig. 20. Reticulate venation.

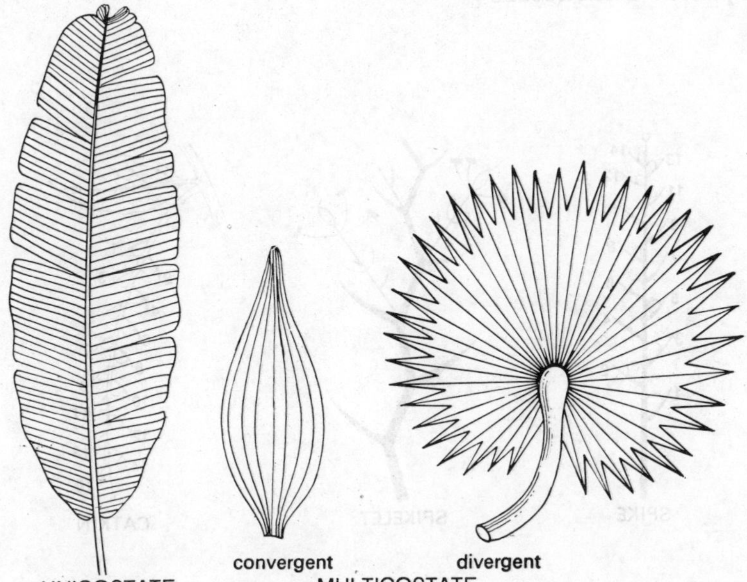

Fig. 21. Parallel venation.

2. Parallel. The pattern of venation in which the veins run parallel to each other. In this type there are no veinlets and no network is formed (Fig. 21).

(a) Unicostate. Having only one principal vein that gives off many lateral veins which proceed toward the margin or apex of leaf blade in a more or less parallel manner; *e.g.,* Canna, Banana (Fig. 21).

(b) Multicostate. Having many principal veins arising from the tip of the petiole and proceeding upwards or outwards (Fig. 21).

(i) Convergent. Many principal veins arising from the base of the leafblade converage towards its apex or less parallel manner; e.g., Grasses such as Wheat, Bamboo (Fig.21).

(ii) Divergent. Many principal veins arising from the tip of the petiole, diverge towards the margin of leaf blade in a more or less parallel manner; *e.g.,* Fan palms (Fig. 21).

[XI] Texture

overall structure.

Alternative Terms

Coriaceous/ Membranous/ Scarious/ Fleshy/ Succulent.

Meaning of Alternative Terms

1. Coriaceous. If a leaf is tough and thick like leather; *e.g., Calotropis.*

2. Membranous. A leaf which is thin and pliable like a membrane; *e.g., Solanum nigrum.*

3. Scarious. A thin dry and non-green leaf; *e.g., Asparagus.*

4. Fleshy. A soft and thick leaf; *e.g., Spergula.*

5. Succulent. A fleshy and juicy leaf; *e.g., Bryophyllum.*

[XII] Other Special Characters

5. INFLORESCENCE

Inflorescence. A cluster of flowers or arrangement of flowers on floral axis.

Alternative Terms

Racemose/ Cymose/ Special type/ Solitary flowers.

(1) If **racemose** whether a Raceme/ Panicle/ Spike/ Compound Spike/ Strobile/ Spikelet/ Catkin/ Spadix/ Corymb/ Compound corymb/ Umbel/ Compound umbel/ Capitate/ Capitulum.

(2) If **cymose** whether Uniparous (monochasial) – if uniparous whether scorpioid or helicoid/ Biparous (dichasial)/ Multiparous (Polychasial).

(3) If it is a **special** type then is it a Cyathium/ Thyrsus/ Verticillaster/ Hypanthodium.

(4) If flower is **solitary** see whether it is terminal or axillary.

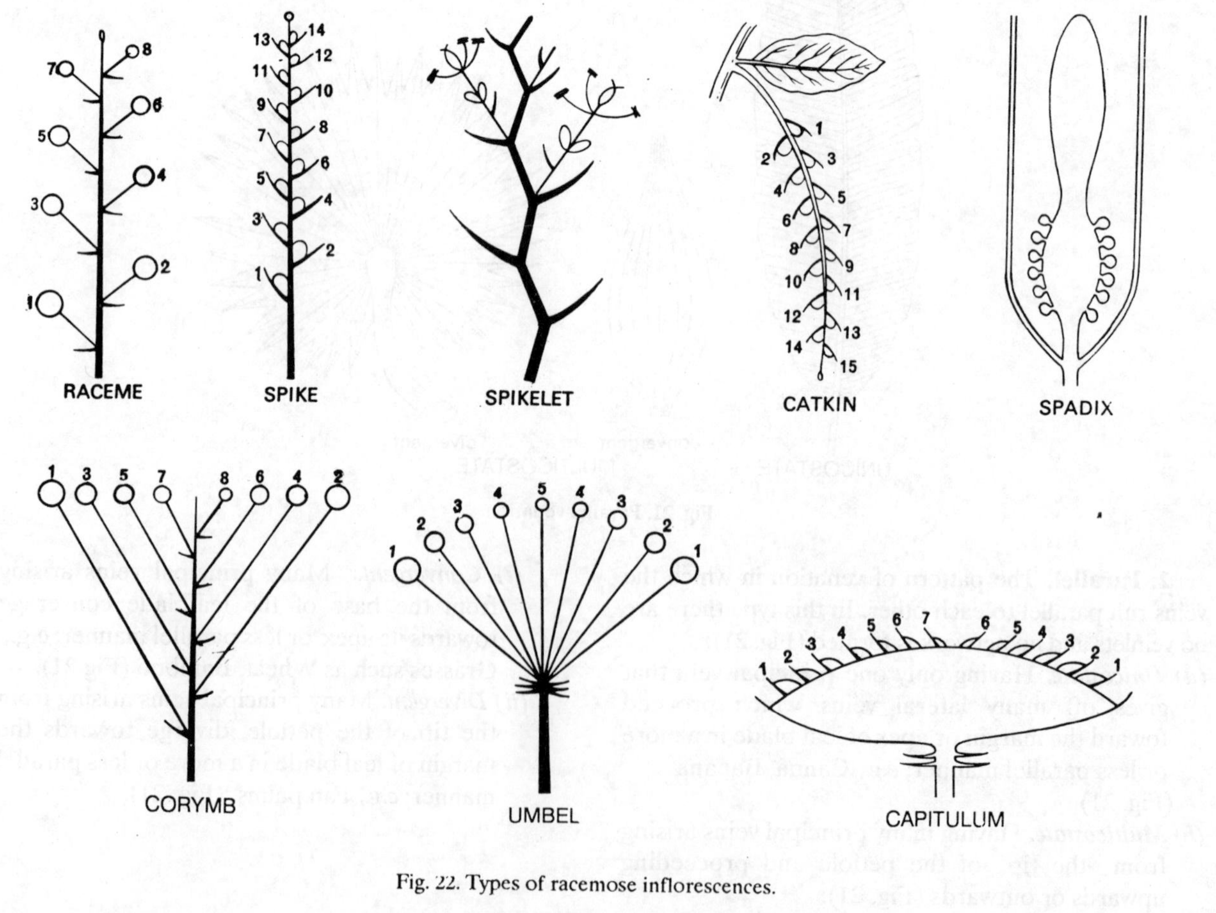

Fig. 22. Types of racemose inflorescences.

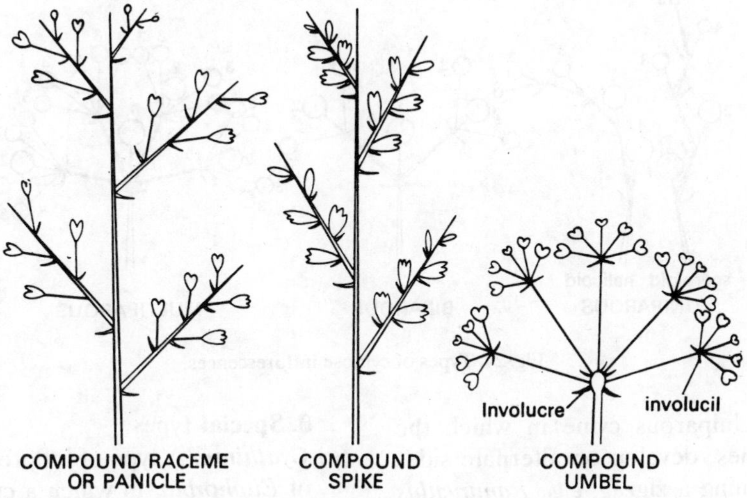

Fig. 23. Compound racemose inflorescences.

Meaning of Alternative Terms

1. Racemose. An inflorescence where the main axis does not terminate in a flower, but it continues to grow and gives off flowers laterally in acropetal succession.

(a) ***Raceme.*** A simple, elongated, indeterminate inflorescence with stalked flowers, *e.g.,* Radish, Mustard, *Crotalaria, Delphinium,* etc. (Fig. 22).

(b) ***Panicle.*** When axis of raceme is branched, it is called a panicle; *e.g.,* Gold Mohur (Fig. 23).

(c) ***Spike.*** Usually unbranched, elongated, simple, indeterminate inflorescence whose flowers are sessile; *e.g., Adhatoda, Piper longum* (Fig. 22).

(d) ***Compound spike.*** Axis is branched and the flowers are arranged in a spike-like manner on the branches; *e.g., Amaranthus,* (Fig. 23).

(e) ***Strobile.*** Type of spike in which each flower is borne in the axil of a persistent membranous bract; *e.g., Humulus lupulus.*

(f) ***Spikelet.*** The unit of the compound inflorescence of the grasses; composed of a cluster of one or more flowers and their associated bracts; *e.g.,* Grasses (Fig. 22).

(g) ***Catkin.*** A pendant spike of unisexual flowers found only in woody plants; *e.g., Morus, Salix,* (Fig. 22).

(h) ***Spadix.*** A thick or fleshy spike subtended or surrounded by a spathe; *e.g.,* Maize or Corn (Fig. 22).

(i) ***Corymb.*** Indeterminate inflorescence with shortened main axis, in which the lower flowers have much longer pedicels than the upper so that flowers are brought more or less to the same level *e.g.,* Candytuft (Fig. 22).

(j) ***Compound corymb.*** A branched corymb; *e.g., Pyrus torminalis.*

(k) ***Umbel.*** An inflorescence in which the flower stalks of more or less equal length, arise from the same point, like the ribs of an umbrella at the base of flower stalks, there is whorl of bracts forming an involucre; *e.g., Hydrocotyle asiatica* (Fig. 22).

(l) ***Compound umbel.*** An umbel with branched axis and the branches bearing the flowers. These are known as umbellules; *e.g.,* Coriander (Fig. 23).

(m) ***Capitate.*** When a large number of sessile flowers arise from a suppressed axis forming a globose structure as in *Acacia, Mimosa*. It differs from capitulum in the absence of a receptacle.

(n) ***Capitulum.*** A dense inflorescence comprising an aggregation of usually sessile flowers arranged on a convex receptacle formed by the axis, and having one or more whorls of bracts forming involucre; *e.g.,* Compositae family (Fig. 22).

2. Cymose. An inflorescence where the growth of the main axis is soon checked by the development of a flower its apex, and the lateral axix which develops below the terminal flower also ends in a flower, thus its growth is also checked (Fig. 24).

(a) ***Uniparous.*** (Monochasial). The main axis ending in a flower producing only one lateral branch at a time ending in a flower (Fig. 24).

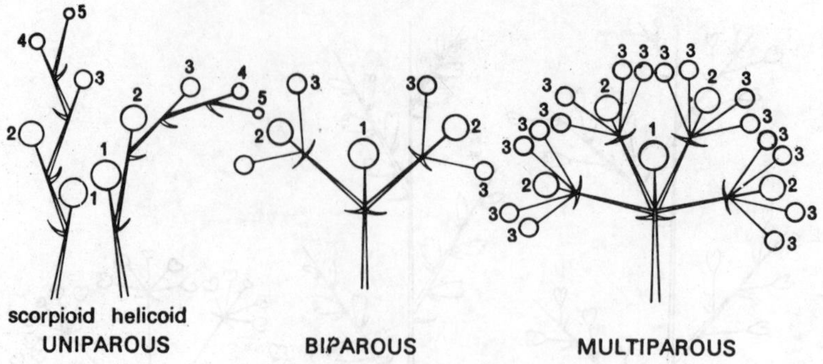

Fig. 24. Types of cymose inflorescences.

(i) *Scorpioid.* Uniparous cyme in which the lateral branches develop on alternate sides evidently forming a zigzag; *e.g., Ranunculus bulbosus* (Fig. 24).

(ii) *Helicoid.* Uniparous cyme in which the lateral branches develop successively on the same side, evidently forming a sort of helix; *e.g., Juncus, Begonia, Heliotropium* (Fig. 24).

(b) Biparous (Dichasial). A determinate inflorescence in which the main axis ends in a flower after producing two daughter axes of flowers; *e.g., Ixora, Saponaria, Mussaenda,* etc. (Fig. 24).

(c) Multiparous (Polychasial). A determinate inflorescence in which the main axis ends in a flower after producing a number of daughter axes or flowers around. This inflorescence looks like an umbel but can be distinguished from umbel by the opening of the middle flower first; *e.g., Calotropis.*

3. Special types

(a) Cyathium. A type of inflorescence characteristic of *Euphorbia,* in which a cup-shaped involucre, often provided with nectary, encloses a single female flower (reduced to pistil) in the centre and a number of male flowers (each reduced to a solitary stamen) around it (Fig. 25).

(b) Thyrsus. A panicle-like cluster with main axis indeterminate and the lateral axes determinate; *e.g.,* Lilacs, (Fig. 25).

(c) Verticillaster. It consists of a series of nodes. At each node there is a condensed dichasial cyme with a cluster of almost sessile flowers arranged opposite one another in the axils of opposite bracts or leaves; *e.g., Ocimum* (Fig. 25).

(d) Hypanthodium. The fleshy receptacle forms a cup like cavity with an apical opening (ostiole) guarded by scales and bearing flowers on the inner wall of the cavity; *e.g.,* Fig, Peepul, (Fig. 25).

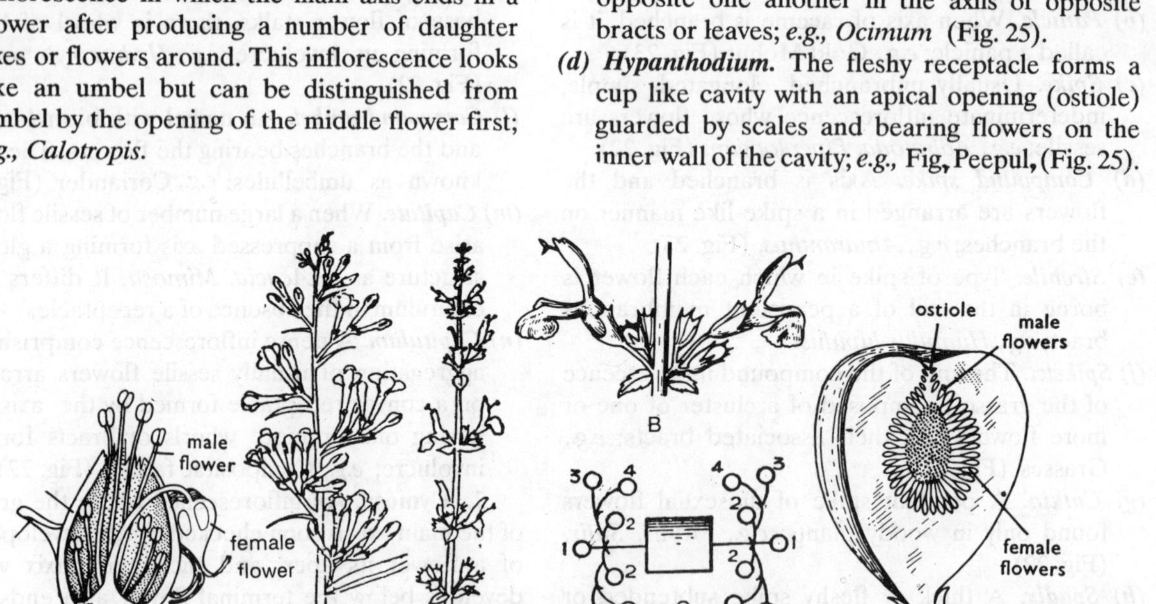

Fig. 25. Special types of inflorescences.

SOLITARY TERMINAL

SOLITARY AXILLARY

Fig. 26. Types of solitary flowers.

4. Solitary flower. Borne singly or alone.

(a) Solitary terminal. Borne singly at the apex; *e.g.,* Lily, Poppy, *Paris* (Fig. 26).

(b) Solitary axillary. Borne singly in the axil of a leaf; *e.g., Cucurbita,* China rose (Fig. 26).

6. FLOWER

Flower. Modified shoot, meant essentially for reproduction of the plant.

[I] Bract and Bracteoles

1. Bract. A modified, usually reduced leaf-like structure at the base of the flower.

(a) Involucral bracts. Bracts present at the base of an umbel.

(b) Involucels. Bracts present at the base of umbellule (secondary umbel).

2. Bracteole. Bracts occurring on secondary axis i.e. pedicel of flower.

Alternative Terms

Ebracteate/ Bracteate/ if bracteate whether Bracteolate or not.

Meaning of Alternative Terms

Ebracteate. Without bracts; *e.g., Solanum.*

Bracteate. With bract, *e.g., Adhatoda.*

Bracteolate. With bracteoles; *e.g., Adhatoda.*

Epicalyx. Whorl of bracteoles developing at the base of the calyx, *e.g.,* China rose.

[II] Attachment of Flower

Pedicel. Stalk of an individual flower.

Peduncle. The stalk of an inflorescence.

Alternative Terms

Sessile/ Pedicellate

Meaning of Alternative Terms

1. Sessile. Without a stalk; *e.g., Adhatoda, Morus,* etc.

2. Pedicellate. Having a stalk; *e.g., Dianthus.*

[III] Presence of Floral Whorls

Alternative Terms

Complete/ Incomplete

Meaning of Alternative Terms

1. Complete. A flower with four whorls of floral parts; pistil, stamens, sepals and petals; *e.g., Solanum.*

2. Incomplete. A flower lacking one or more of the four kinds of floral whorls sepals, petals, stamens or pistils; *e.g., Euphorbia.*

[IV] Symmetry

Alternative Terms

Actinomorphic/Zygomorphic

Meaning of Alternative Terms

1. Actinomorphic. (Regular). Applied to a flower in which the parts of each whorl are similar in shape;

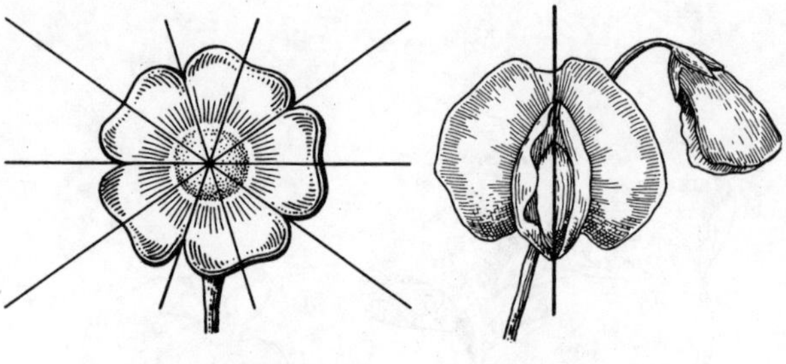

Fig. 27. Symmetry of the flower.

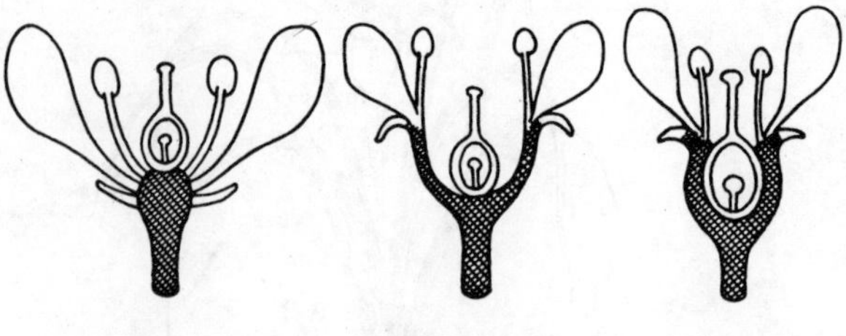

Fig. 28. Position of floral organs on thalamus.

the flower can be divided into two equal halves along more than one median longitudinal plane; *e.g., Dianthus, Ipomoea, etc*. (Fig. 27).

2. Zygomorphic. Term applied to a flower in which the members of some or all of the floral whorls are unequal. Most irregular flowers can be divided longitudinally into two equal halves in only one vertical plane; *e.g.,* Pea, *Adhatoda,* etc. (Fig. 27).

[V] Presence of Reproductive Organs

Alternaive Terms

Hermaphrodite/ Unisexual

If **unisexual** whether staminate or pistillate.

Meaning of Alternative Terms

1. Hermaphrodite. (Bisexual). A flower in which both stamens and pistils are present; *e.g.,* China rose.

2. Unisexual. A flower having only one sex; *e.g., Morus.*

(a) Staminate. A unisexual flower with stamens.

(b) Pistillate. A unisexual flower with a pistil.

[VI] Number of Floral Parts

Alternative Terms

Dimerous / Trimerous / Tetramerous Pentamerous.

Meaning of Alternative Terms

1. Dimerous. Two-merous, the parts in two's or multiple of 2 ; *e.g.,* Poppy.

2. Trimerous. Three-merous, the parts in three's or multiple of 3 ; *e.g., Argemone.*

3. Tetramerous. Four-merous, the parts in four's or multiple of 4. *e.g.,* Mustard.

4. Pentamerous. Five-merous, the parts in five's or multiple of 5; *e.g., Solanum.*

(B-15)

[VII] Position of Floral Organs on Thalamus

Alternative Terms

Hypogynous/Perigynous/ Epigynous.

Meaning of Alternative Terms

1. Hypogynous. A flower in which the ovary is superior and all other floral organs are situated below its level; *e.g., Citrus* (Fig. 28).

2. Perigynous. The floral organs borne and arising from around the ovary and not beneath it; *e.g.,* Peach, Plum (Fig. 28).

3. Epigynous. Used for a flower when the ovary is inferior and other floral organs arise above it; *e.g., Coriandrum* (Fig. 28).

[VIII] Arrangement of Floral Organs

Alternative Terms

Acyclic/ Spirocyclic/ Cyclic.

Meaning of Alternative Terms

1. Acyclic. Arranged in spirals and not in whorls; *e.g., Ranunculus.*

2. Spirocyclic. Half cyclic; *e.g., Ranunculus.*

3. Cyclic. Arranged in definite whorls; *e.g., Solanum.*

[IX] Colour

[X] Other Special Characters

If any one of the following structure is present, it should be mentioned.

1. Anthophore. Elongated portion of thalamus between calyx and corolla; *e.g., Silene saxifraga.*

2. Androphore. Elongated portion of thalamus between corolla and androecium; *e.g.,* Passion flower.

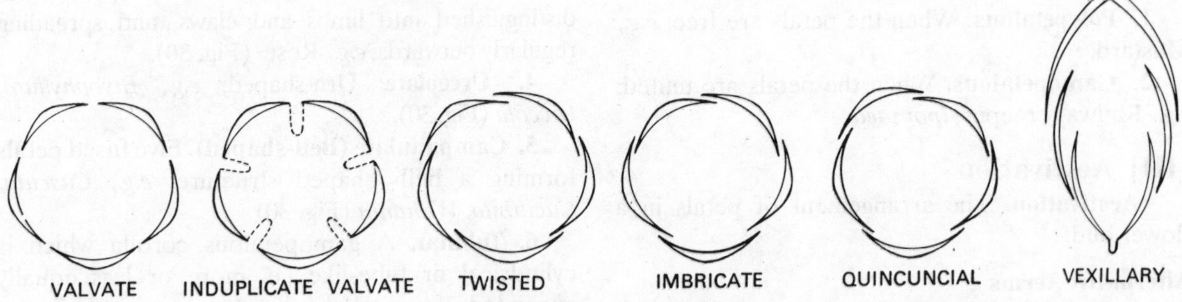

Fig. 29. Types of aestivation.

3. Gynophore. Elongated portion of thalamus between androecium and gynoecium; *e.g., Cleome, Bauhinia.*

4. Androgynophore. A gynophore associated with the androphore ; *e.g., Cleome gynandra (= Gynandropsis gynandra).*

7. CALYX

Calyx. The outer or first whorl of flower, consisting of sepals.

Sepal. One of the separate parts of a calyx, usually green and foliaceous.

[I] Number of sepals

Mention the number of sepals *e.g.,* 4 sepals.

[II] Cohesion

Alternative Terms

Polysepalous/ Gamosepalous.

Meaning of Alternative Terms

1. Polysepalous. When the sepals are free; *e.g., Geranium.*

2. Gamosepalous. When the sepals are fused; *e.g., Dianthus.*

[III] Aestivation

Aestivation. The arrangement of floral parts (sepals in this case) in bud.

Alternative Terms

Valvate/Twisted/ Imbricate/Quincuncial.

Meaning of Alternative Terms

1. Valvate. Sepals meeting by the edges without overlapping; *e.g., Solanum* (Fig. 29).

2. Twisted. (Contorted). One margin of the sepal overlaps that of the next one, and the other margin is overlapped by the third one (Fig. 29).

3. Imbricate. Out of the five sepals one is internal, one external and the other three partly internal, partly external; *e.g., Iberis amara, Cleome* (Fig. 29).

4. Quincuncial. A form of imbricate where there are five sepals, two internal, two external and one partly internal, partly external, *e.g., Stellaria, Dianthus* (Fig. 29).

[IV] Duration of Calyx

Alternative Terms

Caducous/Deciduous/Persistent-Marcescent/ Accrescent.

Meaning of Alternative Terms

1. Caducous. (Fugacious). Falling off early, or prematurely; *e.g.,* Poppy.

2. Deciduous. Falling off along with the petals just after fertilization; *e.g.,* Mustard, etc.

3. Persistent. Remaining attached in the fruit also; *e.g., Solanum, Datura.* There are two types.

(a) Marcescent. A persistent calyx assuming a shrivelled, dried up appearance; *e.g.,* Guava.

(b) Accrescent. A persistent calyx growing in size along with the fruit; *e.g., Physalis, Shorea.*

8. COROLLA

Corolla. Second whorl of flower made of petals.

Petal. One of the separate parts of corolla usually coloured and more or less showy.

[I] Number of Petals

Mention the number of petals, e.g., 4 petals.

[II] Cohesion

Alternative Terms

Polypetalous/Gamopetalous/

Meaning of Alternative Terms

1. Polypetalous. When the petals are free; *e.g.,* Mustard.

2. Gamopetalous. When the petals are united; *e.g.,* Railway creeper, *Ipomoea.*

[III] Aestivation

Aestivation. The arrangement of petals in a flower bud.

Alternative Terms

Valvate/Induplicate valvate/ Twisted/ Imbricate/ Quincuncial/Vexillary.

Meaning of Alternative Terms

1. Valvate. Petals meeting by the edges without overlapping; *e.g., Solanum* (Fig. 29).

2. Induplicate valvate. A form of valvate in which the margins of the petals are folded inwards on themselves; *e.g., Ipomoea* (Fig. 29).

3. Twisted (Contorted). One margin of the petal overlaps that of the next one, and the other margin is overlapped by the third one; *e.g.,* China rose (Fig. 29).

4. Imbricate. Out of the five petals one is internal, one external and the other three partly internal, partly external; *e.g., Callistemon* (Fig. 29).

5. Quincuncial. A form of imbricate where there are five petals, two internal, two external, and one partly internal, partly external; *e.g., Melia, Murraya* (Fig. 29).

6. Vexillary. Out of the five petals the posterior one is the largest and covers the two lateral petals and the latter in their turn overlap the two anterior and smallest petals; characteristic of papilionaceae (Fig. 29).

[IV] Shape of the Corolla

Alternative Terms

Cruciform/ Caryophyllaceous/ Rosaceous/ Urceolate/ Campanulate (bell-shaped)/ Tubular/ Infudibuliform (funnel-shaped)/ Hypocrateriform/ (salver-form)/ Rotate (wheel-shaped)/ Papilionaceous (butterfly-like) / Bilabiate (two-lipped)/Personate (masked)/ Ligulate (strap-shaped).

Meaning of Alternative Terms

1. Cruciform. Four free petals arranged in the form of a cross and each differentiated into a claw and a limb; *e.g.,* Mustard (Fig. 30).

2. Caryophyllaceous. Five petals with comparatively longer claws and with limbs placed at right angles to the claws; *e.g., Dianthus* (Fig. 30).

3. Rosaceous. Five or more free petals, not distinguished into limbs and claws, and spreading regularly outwards; *e.g.,* Rose (Fig. 30).

4. Urceolate. Urn-shaped; *e.g., Bryophyllum, Urceola* (Fig. 30).

5. Campanulate (Bell-shaped). Five fused petals forming a bell- shaped structure; *e.g., Cuscuta, Cucurbita, Withania* (Fig. 30).

6. Tubular. A gamopetalous corolla which is cylindrical or tube-like i.e. more or less equally expanded from the base to apex; *e.g.,* Sunflower (Fig. 30).

7. Infundibuliform (Funnel-shaped). A gamopetalous corolla shaped like the mouth of the gramophone (or Funnel-shaped); *e.g., Ipomoea, Petunia* (Fig. 30).

8. Hypocrateriform (Salver-form). A gamopetalous corolla with a long slender tube and an abruptly expanded flat limb; *e.g., Mussaenda, Ixora,* (Fig. 30).

9. Rotate (Wheel-shaped). A gamopetalous corolla with a flat and circular limb at right angles to the short or obsolete tube *cf.* hypocrateriform; *e.g., Nerium, Solanum,* Brinjal (Fig. 30).

10. Papilionaceous (Butterfly-like). A zygomorhic, polypetalous corolla with one large posterior **standard,** two lateral **wings** and two innermost and smallest petals apparently united, known as **keels**: *e.g.,* Pea (Fig. 30).

11. Bilabiate (Two-lipped). A zygomorphic, gamopetalous corolla divided into two lips-upper and lower with the mouth gaping wide open; *e.g., Ocimum, Leucas, etc.* (Fig. 30).

12. Personate (Masked). A zygormorphic, gamopetalous corolla like the aforesaid one; but in this case, the lips are placed so near to each other that they close the mouth of the corolla; *e.g.,* Dog flower *(Antirrhinum)* (Fig. 30).

13. Ligulate (Strap-shaped). A zygomorphic, gamopetalous corolla forming a short, narrow tube below but flattened above like a strap; *e.g., Sonchus* (Fig. 30).

[V] Colour of Corolla

[VI] Appendages of Corolla

Altternative Terms

Spur/Nectary/Corona.

Meaning of Alternative Terms

1. Spur. A tubular or sac-like projection from a bottom, as of a petal and usually containing a

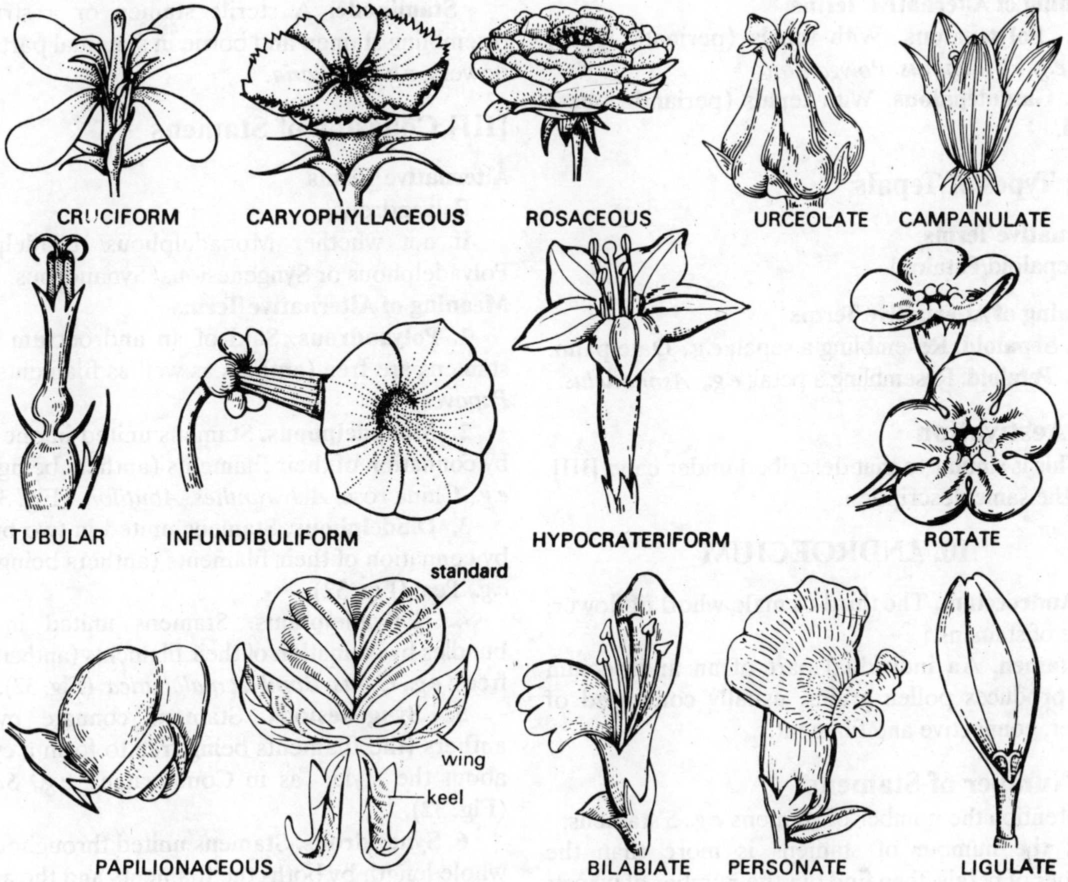

Fig. 30. Shapes of corolla.

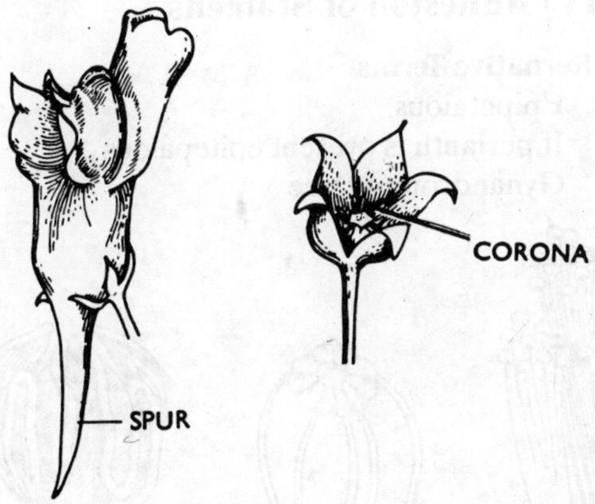

Fig. 31. Appendages of corolla.

nectar-secreting gland; *e.g., Delphinium* (Larkspur) (Fig. 30).

2. Nectary. A nectar - secreting gland, often appearing as a protuberance, scale or pit; *e.g., Salvia.*

3. Corona. Any appendage or extrusion that stands between the corolla and stamens, or on the corolla; *e.g.,* Madar, *Asclepias* (Fig. 30).

9. PERIANTH

Perianth. Sometimes calyx and corolla are not distinguishable from one another and the outer whorl is thus called perianth.

Tepal. One of the separate parts of perianth.

[I] Number of Tepals.

Mention the number of tepals; e.g. 6 tepals

[II] Number of Whorls

Mention the number of whorls, e.g. 6 tepals in two whorls of three each.

[III] Cohesion

Alternative Terms

Polytepalous/Gamotepalous.

Meaning of Alternative Terms

1. Polytepalous. With tepals (perinath lobes) free; *e.g.,Phyllanthus, Polygonum.*

2. Gamotepalous. With tepals (perianth lobes) fused.

[IV] Types of Tepals

Alternative Terms

Sepaloid/Petaloid

Meaning of Alternative Terms

1. Sepaloid. Resembling a sepal; *e.g.,* Date palm.

2. Petaloid. Resembling a petal; *e.g., Asphodelus.*

[V] Aestivation

This is similar to that described under calyx [III]. Use the same description.

10. ANDROECIUM

Androecium. The third or male whorl of flower; made of stamens.

Stamen. An individual part of an androecium that produces pollen grains, usually composed of anther, connective and filament.

[I] Number of Stamens

Mention the number of stamens *e.g.,* 5 stamens.

If the number of stamens is more than the number of petals, then find out the number of whorls in which these are distributed- in one whorl, two or more whorls or the number is indefinite.

[II] Fertility

Note if all the stamens are fertile or some of these are reduced to staminodes.

Staminode. A sterile stamen or a structure resembling stamen and borne in staminal part of the flowers; *e.g., Stellaria*.

[III] Cohesion of Stamens

Alternative Terms

Polyandrous/

If not whether Monadelphous/ Diadelphous/ Polyadelphous or Syngenesious/ Synandrous.

Meaning of Alternative Terms

1. Polyandrous. Said of an androecium whose stamens are free (anthers as well as filaments); *e.g., Papaver.*

2. Monadelphous. Stamens united in one group by connation of their filaments (anthers being free); *e.g.,* China rose, *Achyranthes, Abutilon* (Fig. 32).

3. Diadelphous. Stamens united in two bundles by connation of their filaments (anthers being free); *e.g.,* Pea (Fig. 32).

4. Polyadelphous. Stamens united in many bundles by connation of their filaments (anthers being free); *e.g., Citrus, Bombax malabarica* (Fig. 32).

5. Syngenesious. Stamens connate by their anthers (the filaments being free to form a cylinder about the style, as in Compositae); *e.g., Sonchus* (Fig. 32).

6. Synandrous. Stamens united throughout their whole length by both- the filaments and the anthers; *e.g., Cucurbita* (Fig.32).

[IV] Adhesion of Stamens

Alternative Terms

Epipetalous,

If perianth is present epitepalous,

Gynandrous or free

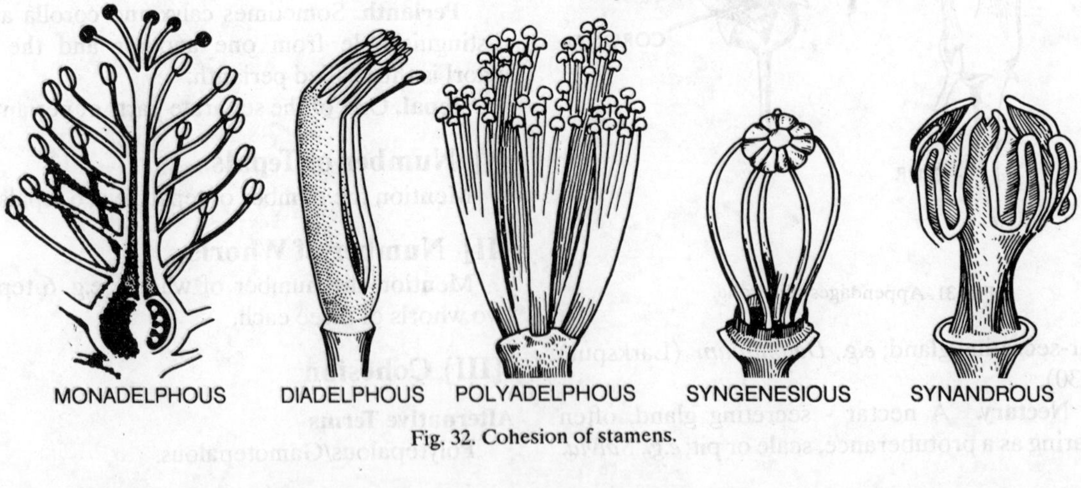

Fig. 32. Cohesion of stamens.

Meaning of Alternative Terms

1. Epipetalous. Stamens adhering to the corolla wholly or partially by their filaments (anthers remaining free); ***e.g., Ocimum, Solanum.***

2. Epitepalous. Stamens adhering to the perianth in the aforesaid manner; ***e.g., Asphodelus.***

3. Gynandrous. Stamens adhering to the carpels either throughout their whole length or by their anthers only; ***e.g., Calotropis.***

[V] Sequence of Staminal Whorls

Alternative Terms

If in more than one whorl then note whether the stamens of the outer whorl alternate with the petals or, opposite i.e. obdiplostemonous.

Meaning of Alternative Terms

1. Diplostemonous. With the stamens in two alternating whorls and those of the outer whorl alternate with the petals; ***e.g., Murraya*** **(Fig. 32).**

2. Obdiplostemonous. With the stamens in two alternating whorls and those of the outer whorl lying opposite the petals; ***e.g., Geranium, Stellaria*** **(Fig. 33).**

[VI] Length of Filaments

Alternative Terms

Whether filament is long or short, also see whether all the filaments are equal in length or didynamous (2 long and 2 short) or tetradynamous (4 long and 2 short).

Meaning of Alternative Terms

1. Didynamous. Out of the four stamens two are long and two short; *e.g., Ocimum* (Fig.34).

2. Tetradynamous. Out of the six stamens four inner are long and two outer short; *e.g* Mustard (Fig. 34).

[VII] Position of Stamens

Alternative Terms

Inserted /Exerted

Meaning of Alternative Terms

1. Inserted. Stamens shorter than the corolla tube remaining included within it; ***e.g., Mussaenda, Tabernaemontana, Catharanthus.***

2. Exserted. Stamens longer than the corolla tube, protruding outwards ***e.g.,*** Passion flower.

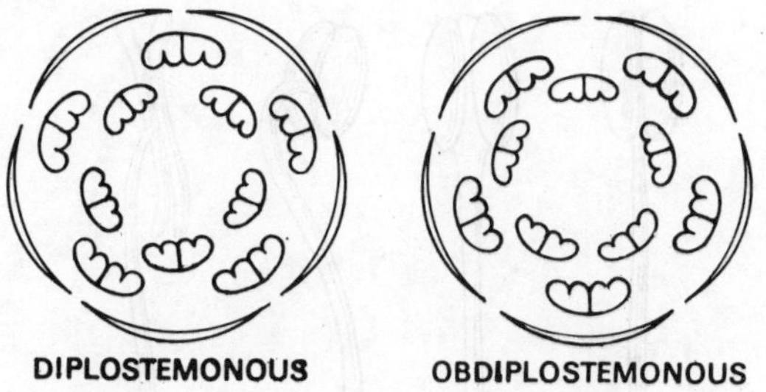

Fig. 33. Position of staminal whorls with reference to petals.

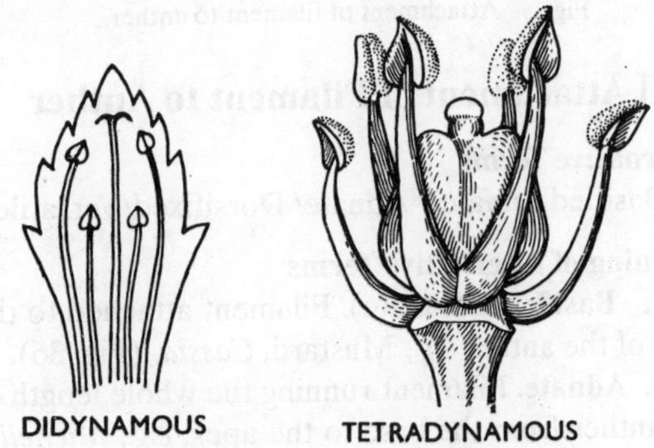

Fig. 34. Length of stamens.

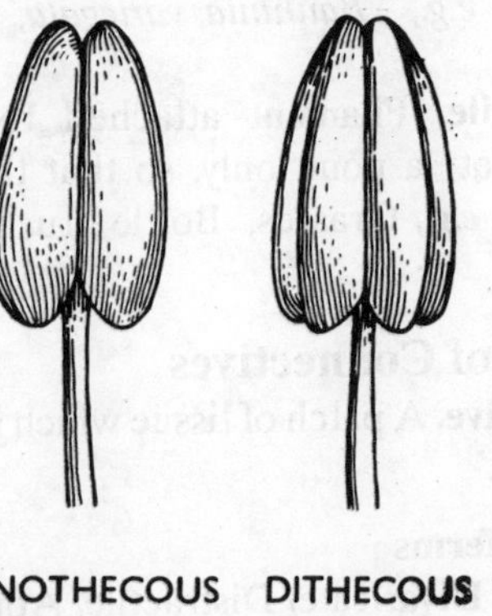

Fig. 35. Monothecous and dithecous stamens.

[VIII] Number of Locules

Alternative Terms

Dithecous/ Monothecous

Meaning of Alternative Terms

1. Dithecous. A two celled anther; ***e.g., Citrus*** **(Fig. 35).**

2. Monothecous. A one-celled anther; ***e.g., Phyllanthus,Ricinus,*** **China Rose (Fig. 35).**

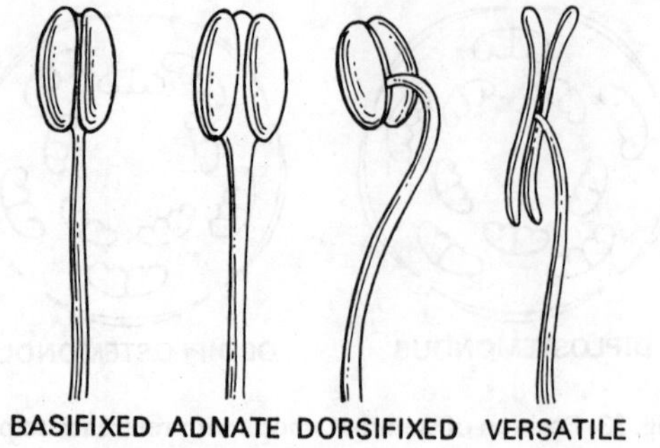

Fig. 36. Attachment of filament to anther.

[IX] Attachment of Filament to Anther

Alternative Terms

Basified (innate)/ Adnate/ Dorsifixed/Versatile.

Meaning of Alternative Terms

1. Basifixed. (Innate). Filament attached to the base of the anther *e.g.,* Mustard, *Cassia,* (Fig. 36).

2. Adnate. Filament running the whole length of the anther from the base to the apex; *e.g., Michelia, Verbena* (Fig. 36).

3. Dorsifixed. Filament attached to the back of the anther; *e.g., Bauhinia variegata, Citrus,* Pink (Fig. 36).

4. Versatile. Filament attached to the back of the anther at a point only, so that the latter can swing freely; *e.g.,* Grasses, Bottle brush, *Eucalyptus* (Fig. 36).

[X] Types of Connectives

Connective. A patch of tissue which joins the two anther lobes.

Alternative Terms

Discrete/ Divaricate/ Distractile/ Appendiculate.

Meaning of Alternative Terms

1. Discrete. When the connective is very small or absent; *e.g.,* Many species of *Euphorbia* (Fig. 37A).

2. Divaricate. When the connective develops in such a way that the two anther lobes get separated from one another; *e.g., Tilia, Justicia gandarussa* (Fig. 37B).

3. Distractile. When the connective is very much elongated and placed more or less on the filament separating the sterile and fertile lobes of the anther; *e.g., Salvia* (Fig. 37C).

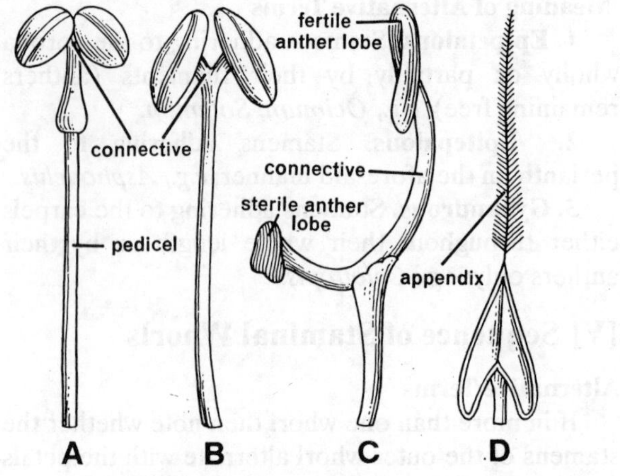

Fig. 37. Various types of connectives. A. Discrete, B. Divaricate, C. Distractile, D. Appendiculate.

4. Appendiculate. When the connective is prolonged into a feathery appendix beyond the anthers; *e.g., Nerium odorum* (Fig. 37D).

[XI] Dehiscence of Anther

Alternative Terms

Introrse/ Extrorse.

Meaning of Alternative Terms

1. Introrse. An anther dehiscing towards the centre of the flower; *e.g., Dianthus, Citrus.*

2. Extrorse. An anther dehiscing towards the periphery of the flower; *e.g., Argemone,* Poppy.

11. GYNOECIUM OR PISTIL

Gynoecium. The fourth or female whorl composed of one or more carpels.

Pistillode. A sterile Gynoecium or pistil.

Carpels. A leaf-like organ bearing ovules along the margins, the unit structure of a compound pistil.

[I] Number of Carpels

Alternative Terms

Simple or monocarpellary/ Compound

If compound Bicarpellary/ Tricarpellary/ Tetracarpellary/ Pentacarpelllary/ Multicarpellary.

Meaning of Alternative Terms

1. Simple or monocarpellary gynoecium. When the gynoecium is made up of only one carpel; *e.g.,* Pea (Fig. 38).

2. Compound gynoecium. When the gynoecium is made up of two or more carpels (Fig. 38).

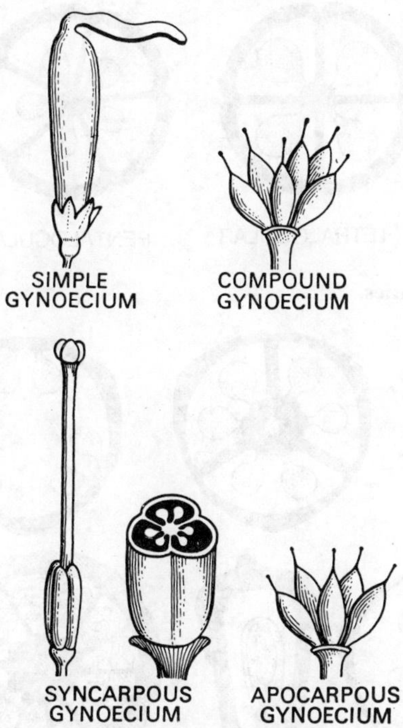

Fig. 38. Types of gynoecium.

(a) ***Bicarpellary.*** With two carpels; *e.g., Fumaria.*
(b) ***Tricarpellary.*** With three carpels; *e.g., Stellaria.*
(c) ***Tetracarpellary.*** With four carpels; *e.g., Datura.*
(d) ***Pentacarpellary.*** With five carpels; *e.g., Melia.*
(e) ***Multicarpellary.*** With many carpels; *e.g., Papaver.*

[II] Cohesion of Carpels

Alternative Terms

Apocarpous/ Syncarpous.

Meaning of Alternative Terms

1. Apocarpous. A pistil of two or more carpels which are free; *e.g., Clematis* (Fig. 38).

2. Syncarpous. A pistil of two or more carpels which are fused; *e.g., Melia* (Fig. 38).

[III] Position of Ovary

Alternative Terms

Superior/ Semi-inferior/ Inferior.

Meaning of Alternative Terms

1. Superior. When the ovary occupies highest position on thalamus and stamens, petals and sepals are successively inserted below it; *e.g., Citrus, Stellaria* (Fig. 39).

2. Semi-inferior. When the thalamus grows around the ovary to form a cup, and bears sepals, petals, and stamens on the rim of the cup; *e.g.,* Peach, Plum, Rose (Fig. 39).

3. Inferior. When the thalamus completely covers the ovary getting fused with it, and bears sepals, petals and stamens on the top of the ovary; *e.g., Coriandrum, Mussaenda, Cucurbita,* Guava (Fig. 39).

[IV] Number of Locules

Locule. Chamber or compartment of ovary.

Alternative Terms

Find out if it is uni-/ Bi-/ Tri-/ Tetra-/ Penta-/ Multilocular.

Meaning of Alternative Terms

1. Unilocular. With one chamber, *e.g., Stellaria* (Fig. 40).

2. Bilocular. With two chambers; *e.g., Solanum* (Fig. 40).

3. Trilocular. With three chambers; *e.g., Asphodelus* (Fig. 40).

4. Tetralocular. With four chambers; *e.g., Ocimum* (Fig. 40).

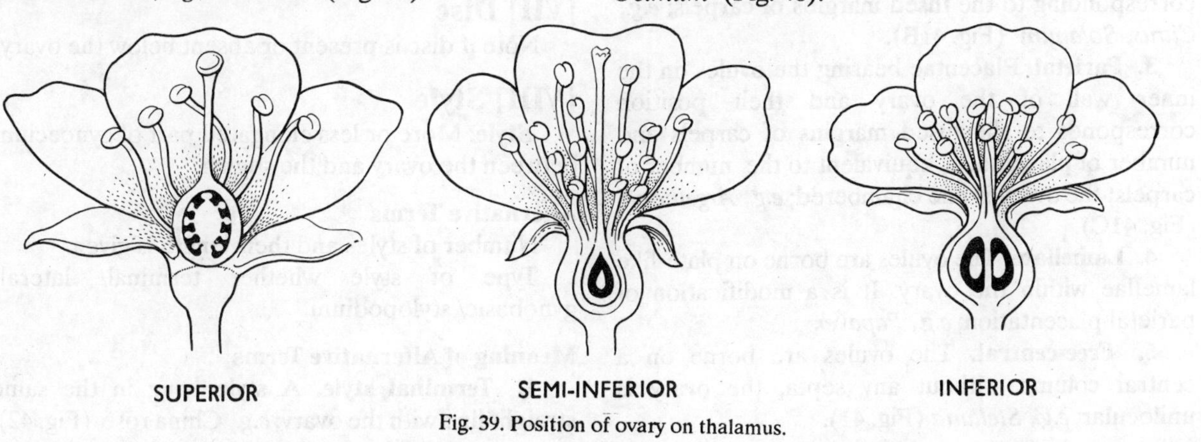

Fig. 39. Position of ovary on thalamus.

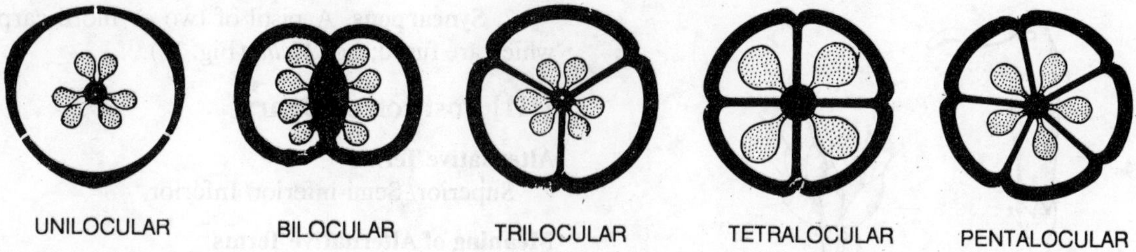

Fig. 40. One to five chambered ovaries.

5. Pentalocular. With five chambers; *e.g., Geranium* (Fig. 40).

6. Multilocular. With many chambers; *e.g., Citrus.*

[V] Number of Ovules

Find out the number of ovules in each locule. This can be done by observing the T. s. of ovary.

[VI] Placentation

Placentation. Arrangement of placentae and ovules in the ovary.

Placenta. The region or area of the ovary to which ovule or ovules are attached.

Ovule. The body which encloses embryo sac or female gametophyte and becomes seed after fertilization.

Alternative Terms

Marginal / Axile / Parietal / Lamellate / Free-central / Basal / Superficial.

Meaning of Alternative Terms

1. Marginal. Placentae developing along the junction of the two margins of the carpel in monocarpellary and one chambered ovary; *e.g.,* pea (Fig. 41A).

2. Axile. Placentae bearing the ovules developed from the central axis of a compound ovary, corresponding to the fused margins of carpels; *e.g., Citrus, Solanum* (Fig. 41B).

3. Parietal. Placentae bearing the ovules on the inner wall of the ovary and their position corresponds to the fused margins of carpels and number of placentae is equivalent to the number of carpels; the ovary is one chambered; *e.g., Argemone* (Fig. 41C).

4. Lamellate. The ovules are borne on plate-like lamellae within the ovary. It is a modification of parietal placentation; *e.g., Papaver.*

5. Free-central. The ovules are borne on a central column without any septa, the ovary is unilocular; *e.g., Stellaria* (Fig. 41).

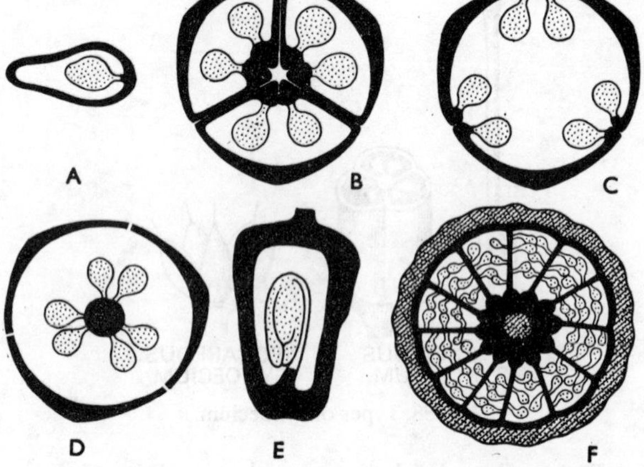

Fig. 41. Various types of placentation. A. Marginal, B. Axile, C. Parietal, D. Free-central, E. Basal, F. Superficial.

6. Basal. The ovules are a few, reduced to one and are borne at the base of the ovary, the ovules when solitary often filling the cavity, the ovary is unilocular; *e.g., Sonchus* (Fig. 41E).

7. Superficial. Ovary is multilocular, carpels being numerous as in axile type but placenate in this case develop all round the inner surface of partition wall; *e.g.,* Water lily (Fig. 41F).

[VII] Disc

Note if disc is present or absent below the ovary.

[VIII] Style

Style. More or less elongated part of gynoecium between the ovary and the stigma.

Alternative Terms

Number of styles and their length is given.

Type of style whether terminal/ lateral/ gynobasic/ stylopodium.

Meaning of Alternative Terms

1. Terminal style. A style lying in the same straight line with the ovary; *e.g.,* China rose (Fig. 42).

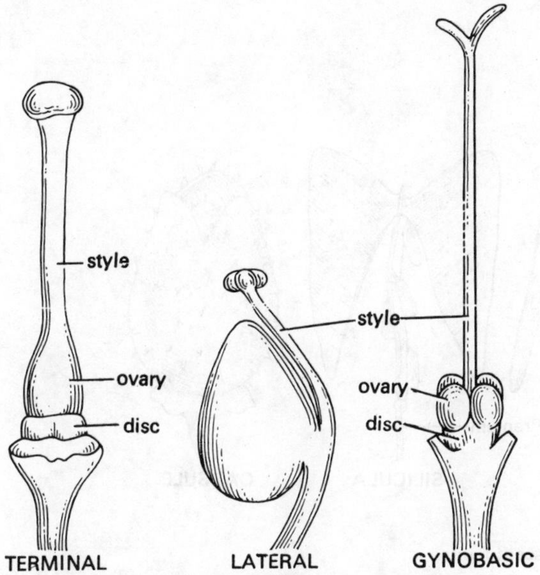

Fig. 42. Various types of styles.

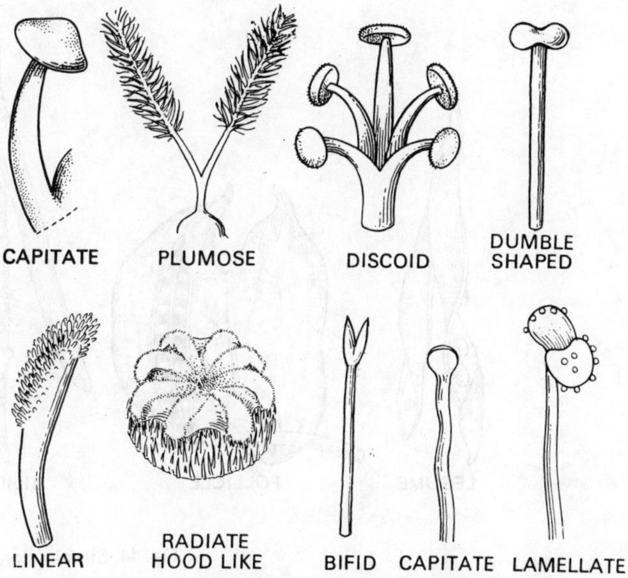

Fig. 43. Various types of stigmas.

2. Lateral style. A style which is seen to arise from the side of the ovary; *e.g.,* Strawberry (Fig. 42).

3. Gynobasic style. A style arising from the depression in the centre of the ovary or directly from thalamus; *e.g., Ocimum* (Fig. 42).

4. Stylopodium. When the base of the style is swollen to form a pad-like structure; *e.g., Coriandrum.*

[IX] Stigma

Stigma. Terminal part of gynoecium that receives pollen grains.

Alternative Terms

Number and shape of stigma-

Capitate/ Plumose/Discoid/ Dumb-bell shaped/ Linear / Radiate hood- like / Bifid / Knob-like / Lamellate/ Sticky.

Meaning of Alternative Terms

1. Capitate. Shaped like a cap; *e.g., Cleome, Citrus* (Fig.43).

2. Plumose. Feather-like stigma; *e.g.,* Grasses (Fig. 43).

3. Discoid. Disc-shaped; *e.g., Melia,* China rose (Fig. 43).

4. Dumb-bell shaped. Like a dumb-bell; *e.g., Ipomoea fistulosa* (Fig. 43).

5. Linear. Long and narrow (Fig. 43).

6. Radiate hood- like. A hood-like stigma with radiating septae; *e.g.,* Poppy (Fig. 43).

7. Bifid. Forked into two; *e.g., Ixora, Sonchus* (Fig. 43).

8. Knob-like. Shaped like a knob; *e.g., Cryptostegia, Justicia, Achyranthes.*

9. Lamellate. Provided with many fin like blades; *e.g., Mazus* (Fig. 43).

10. Sticky. A stigma producing a sticky liquid for catching pollen grains; *e.g., Cleome viscosa.*

12. FRUITS

Fruit. It is a mature or ripened ovary.

Types of Fruits

Alternative Terms

Simple/ Aggregate/Composite

[I] If **simple** whether dry or fleshy.

1. If **dry** whether dehiscent / indehiscent / schizocarpic

(a) If **dehiscent** whether Legume/ Follicle/Siliqua/ Silicula/ Capsule/ Pyxis/ Utricle.

Type of dehiscence- Sutural/ Loculicidal/ Septicidal/ Septifragal/ Poricidal/ Circumscissile.

(b) If **indehiscent** whether Caryopsis/ Achene/ Cypsela/ Samara/ Nut.

(c) If **schizocarpic** whether Lomentum/ Cremocarp/ Regma/ Carcerulus.

2. If **fleshy** whether Drupe/Pome/ Berry/ Pepo/ Hesperidium/ Balausta/ Amphisarca.

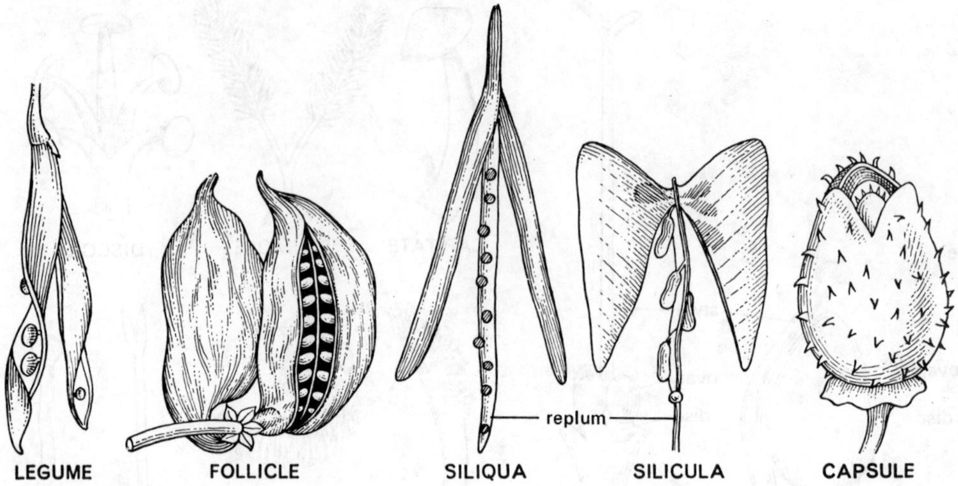

Fig. 44. Simple, dry, dehiscent fruits.

[II] If **aggregate** whether Etaerio of Drupes/ Etaerio of Achenes/ Etaerio of Follicles/ Etaerio of Berries.

[III] If **composite** whether sorosis/ syconus.

Meaning of Alternative Terms

Simple fruit

A single fruit developing from a single ovary of a single flower with or without accessory parts.

1. Dry fruits

(a) ***Dehiscent or capsular fruits.*** Which burst automatically on ripening and discharge their seeds. These are of following 7 types.

(i) Legume. A type of dry fruit developed from a simple, superior and one chambered pistil and opening along both the sutures; *e.g.*, Peas, Beans, etc. (Fig. 44).

(ii) Follicle. A dry fruit derived from a superior and one chambered pistil and opening along ventral suture only; *e.g., Calotropis, Catharanthus roseus,* (Fig. 44).

(iii) Siliqua. A dry two chambered long, narrow, many-seeded fruit developing from a bicarpellary, syncarpous, superior ovary and dehiscing from below upwards by both the sutures and seeds remaining attached to replum; *e.g.,* Mustard (Fig. 44).

(iv) Silicula. A much shorter and flattened siliqua containing only a few seeds; *e.g.,* candytuft, *Capsella* (Fig.44).

(v) Capsule. A many seeded dry fruit that develops from a compound, generally superior, one to many chambered pistil and opens in various ways, allowing the seeds to escape; *e.g., Datura*, Cotton, Lady's finger, (Fig. 44).

(vi) Pyxis. A capsule with circumscissile dehiscence; *e.g., Celosia cristata, Plantago,*

(vii) Utricle. A one seeded fruit with a thin wall, often dehiscent by a lid; *e.g., Amaranthus, Chenpodium.*

Dehiscence types. The process of opening of a fruit.

1. Sutural. When dehiscence takes place along one or both the sutures; *e.g.,* Pea, *Calotropis,* Mustard (Fig. 45).

2. Loculicidal. When each locule splits along the middle of the back and separates into as many valves as the number of locules; *e.g.,* Malvaceae and Acanthaceae (Fig.45).

3. Septicidal. When it opens at the point of union of septum or partition to the side wall in such a way that carpels separate; *e.g., Linum; Ricinus* (Fig. 45).

4. Septifragal. When the dehiscence is loculicidal or septicidal but the valves fall off, leaving the seeds attached to the central column, *e.g., Datura* (Fig. 45).

5. Poricidal. When it opens by means of pores whose valves are often flap-like, *e.g.,* Poppy (Fig. 45).

6. Circumscissile. When the dehiscence is transverse and the tip valve comes off as a lid, *e.g., Celosia cristata, Plantago, Eucalyptus,* (Fig. 45).

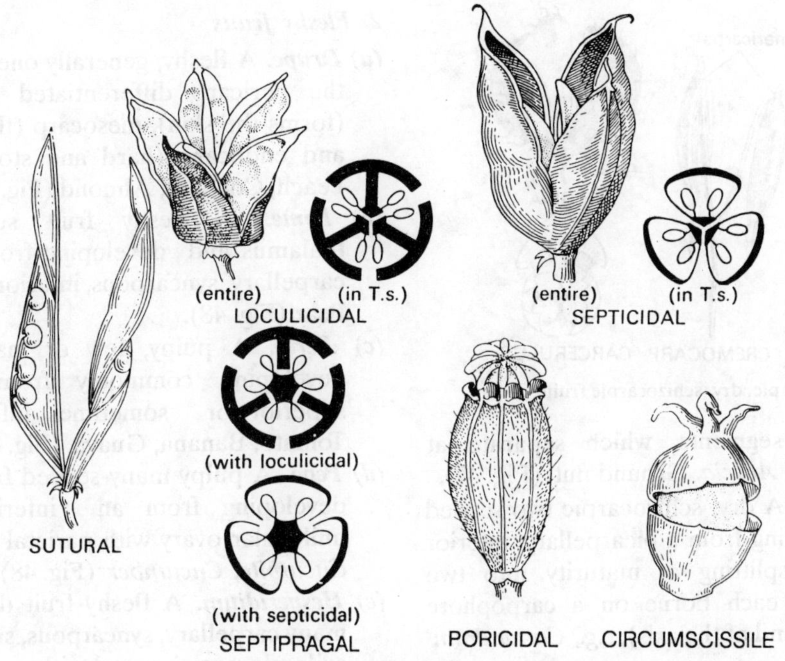

Fig. 45. A few dehiscence types.

(b) ***Indehiscent or achenial fruits.*** Which do not split open at maturity and thus the seeds are liberated only by the destruction of pericarp. These are of following five types.

(i) Caryopsis. A very small dry, indehiscent, one-seeded fruit developing from a monocarpellary, superior ovary, with the pericarp fused with the seed coat; *e.g.,* Wheat (Fig. 46).

(ii) Achene. A small, indehiscent, one seeded fruit developing from a monocarpellary, superior ovary, and in which the seed coat is not fused with to the pericarp; *e.g. Mirabilis, Fagopyrum* (Fig. 46).

(iii) Cypsela. A dry, indehiscent, one-seeded fruit developing from a bicarpellary, syncarpous, inferior unilocular ovary, with the pericarp and seed coat free; *e.g., Sonchus* (Fig. 46).

(iv) Nut. A dry, indehiscent, one-seeded fruit, developing from a superior, bi-or polycarpellary ovary and in which the fruit wall is hard, stony or woody at maturity; *e.g.,* Chestnut, Cashewnut, Oak, Water Chestnut, Litchi (Fig. 46).

(v) Samara. A dry, indehiscent, one or two-seeded, winged fruit developing from a superior ovary; *e.g., Hiptage, Acer, Holoptia* (Fig. 46).

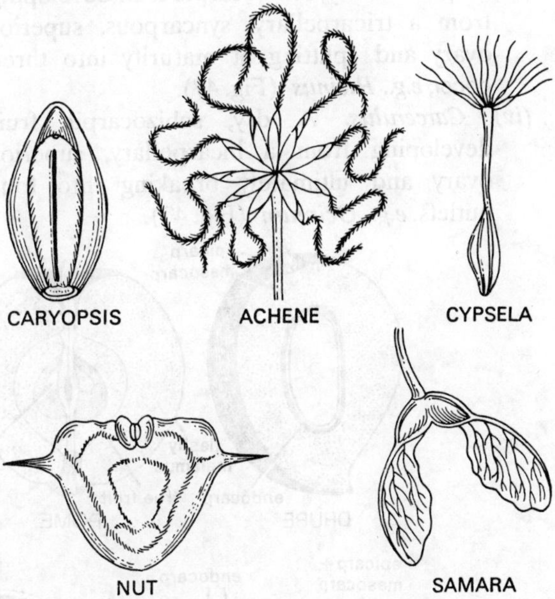

Fig. 46. Simple, dry, indehiscent fruits.

*(c) **Schizocarpic or splitting fruits.*** Intermediate between dehiscent and indehiscent. The fruit breaks up into one or more seeded units. Sometimes the seeds are liberated only after the decay of pericarp. These are of following 4 types.

(i) Lomentum. A dry schizocarpic leguminous fruit, constricted between the seeds to form

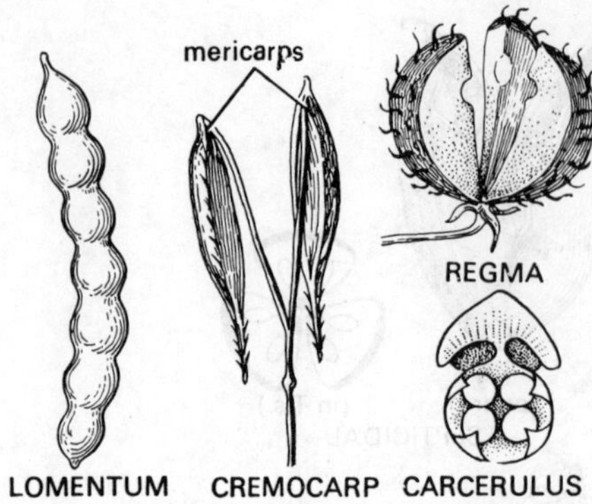

Fig. 47. Simple, dry, schizocarpic fruits.

one-seeded segments, which separate at maturity; *e.g., Acacia,* Ground nut (Fig. 47).

(ii) *Cremocarp.* A dry, schizocarpic two seeded fruit developing from a bicarpellary, inferior ovary and splitting at maturity into two mericaprps, each borne on a carpophore (prolonged end of the axis); *e.g., Coriandrum* (Fig. 47).

(iii) *Regma.* A dry, schizocarpic fruit developing from a tricarpellary, syncarpous, superior ovary and splitting at maturity into three cocci, *e.g., Ricinus* (Fig. 47).

(iv) *Carcerulus.* A dry, schizocarpic fruit developing from a bicarpellary, superior ovary and ultimately breaking into four nutlets, *e.g., Ocimum* (Fig. 47).

2. *Fleshy fruits*

(a) *Drupe.* A fleshy, generally one-seeded fruit with the pericarp differentiated into the epicarp (forms the skin), mesocarp (flesyhy and edible) and endocarp (hard and stony); *e.g.,* Mango, Peach, Coconut, Almond (Fig. 48).

(b) *Pome.* A fleshy fruit surrounded by the thalamus and developing from a two or more carpellary, syncarpous, inferior ovary; *e.g,* Apple, Pear (Fig. 48).

(c) *Berry.* A pulpy, few or many-seeded fruit developing commonly from a syncarpous, superior or sometimes inferior ovary; *e.g.,* Tomato, Banana, Guava (Fig. 48).

(d) *Pepo.* A pulpy many-seeded fruit like berry but developing from an inferior, tricarpellary, unilocular ovary with parietal placentation; *e.g., Cucurbita, Cucumber* (Fig. 48).

(e) *Hesperidium.* A fleshy fruit developing from a many carpellary, syncarpous, superior ovary with axile placentation and with endocarp projecting inwards forming distinct chambers, and the epicarp and mesocarp fused together forming the rind of the fruit; *e.g.,* Lemon, Orange etc. (Fig. 48).

(f) *Balausta.* A many chamberd and many seeded, inferior fruit like the berry. Pericarp is tough with two rows of carpels one above the other bearing seeds irregularly. Calyx is persistent

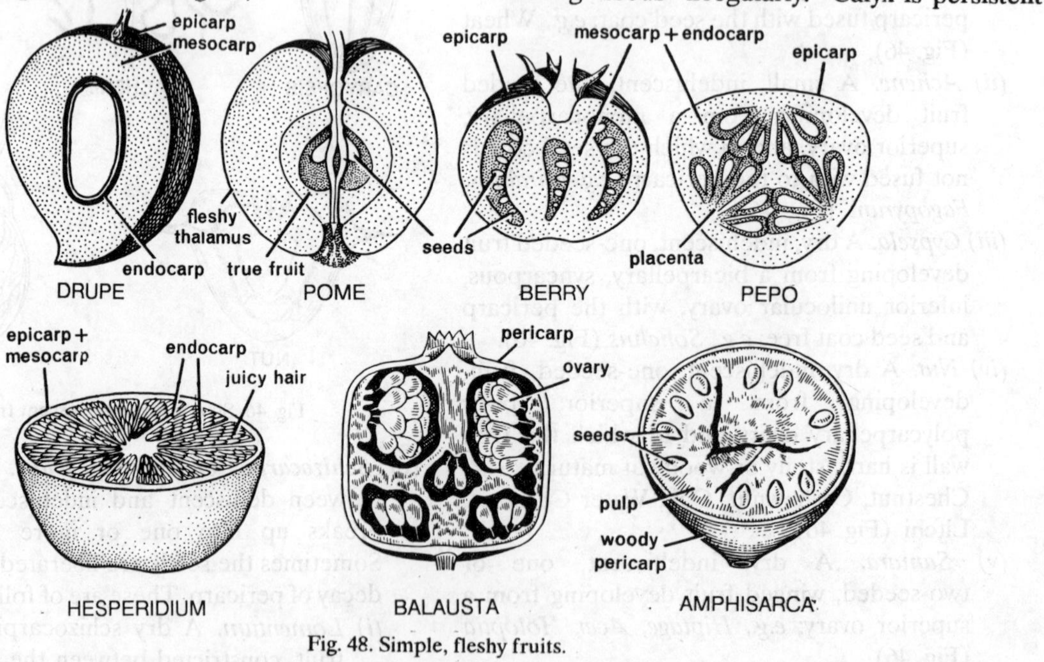

Fig. 48. Simple, fleshy fruits.

Fig. 49. Aggregate fruits, (A. Surface view, B. L. s.).

and succulent testa is edible; *e.g.,* Pomegranate (Fig. 48).

(g) Amphisarca. A fleshy fruit with a woody pericarp developing from a syncarpous, superior, many seeded ovary. The edible portion is the placenta and the inner pulpy layers of pericarp; *e.g., Aegle marmelos* (Fig. 48).

Aggregate fruit

Fruit developed from a flower having a number of free carpels, all of which ripen together, and are more or less coherent at maturity.

1. Etaerio of drupes. An aggregate of drupes; *e.g., Rubus,* (Fig. 49A&B).

2. Etaerio of achenes. An aggregate of achenes; *e.g.,* Strawberry, *Naravelia* (Fig. 49C).

3. Etaerio of follicles. An aggregate of follicles; *e.g., Michelia champaca, Magnolia* (Fig. 49D).

4. Etaerio of berries. An aggregate of berries; *e.g., Artabotrys, Anona squamosa* (Fig. 49E).

Multiple of composite fruit

Fruit composed of a number of closely associated fruits, derived from entire inflorescence and forming one body at maturity; *e.g.,* Jack fruit.

1. Sorosis. A fruit developing from spike or spadix in which the flowers fuse by their succulent tepals and axis bearing them becomes fleshy or woody thus forming a compact mass; *e.g.,* Pineapple, Mulberry, Jack fruit (Fig. 50).

2. Syconus. A fruit developing from hypanthodium inflorescence, characteristically having a hollow, pear shaped fleshy receptacle; *e.g.,* Fig (Fig. 50).

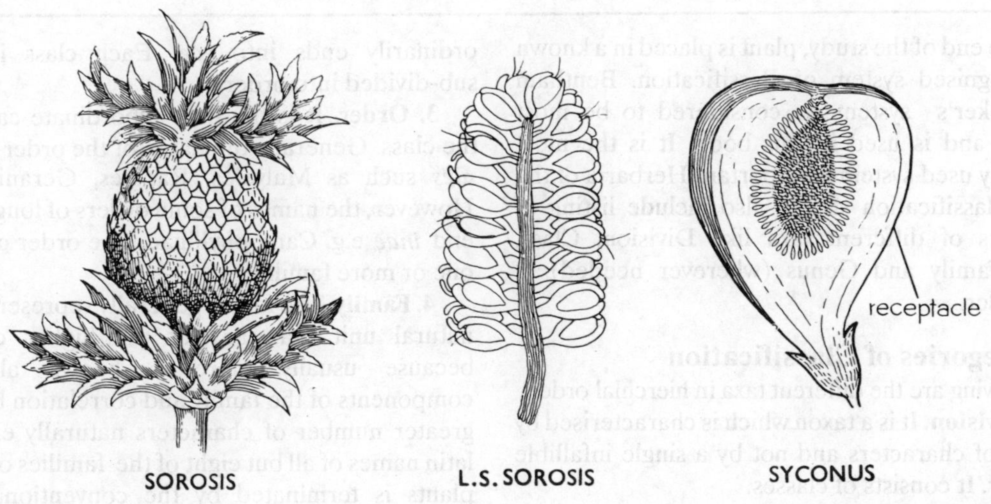

Fig. 50. Multiple or composite fruits.

III. Floral Formula

Once the description of the plant is completed, major characters of a flower are written in a special way where a few signs and letters are used. This formula is useful in knowing major characters of a flower at one glance. In this method characters of bracts, symmetry, sex, calyx, corolla (or perianth), androecium and gynoecium are denoted in this order. Some of the commonly used denotations are given below. Choose those or modify according to the need amongst the following few.

1. Bracts and Epicalyx

Br	Bracteate
Ebr	Ebracteate
Brl	Bracteolate
E	Epicalyx

2. Symmetry

⊕	Actinomorphic
⦶ or %	Zygomorphic

3. Sex

♂	Staminate flower
♀	Pistillate flower
⚥	Hermaphrodite

4. Calyx

K	Calyx
K_4	Four free sepals (polysepalous)
$K_{(4)}$	Four fused sepals (gamosepalous)

5. Corolla

C	Corolla
C_4	Four free petals (polypetalous)
$C_{(4)}$	Four fused petals (gamopetalous)

6. Perianth

P	Perianth
P_6	Six free tepals (polytepalous)
$P_{(6)}$	Six fused tepals (gamotepalous)
P_{3+3}	Six tepals in two whorls of three each

7. Androecium

A	Androecium
A_5	Five free stamens (polyandrous)
$A_{(5)}$	Five fused stamens (monadelphous or syngenesious or synandrous)
A_{5+5}	Ten stamens in two whorls of five each
A_0	Stamens absent
A_α	Stamens idefinite in number
$\overset{\frown}{C\ A}$	Stamens epipetalous
$\overset{\frown}{P\ A}$	Stamens epiphyllous (epitepalous)

8. Gynoecium

G	Gynoecium
G_2	Two free carpels (apocarpous)
$G_{(2)}$	Two fused carpels (syncarpous)
G_0	Carpels absent
$\underline{G}_{(2)}$	Bicarpellary,syncarpous, superior ovary
$G_{(2)}-$	Bicarpellary, syncarpous, semi-inferior ovary
$\overline{G}_{(2)}$	Bicarpellary, syncarpous, inferior ovary.

IV. Classification and Identification

At the end of the study, plant is placed in a known and recognised system of classification. Bentham and Hooker's system is considered to be most practical and is used in this book. It is the most commonly used system in important Herbaria of the world. Classification should also include listing of characters of different taxa like Division, Class, Order, Family and Genus (wherever needed) in serial order.

[I] Categories of Classification

Following are the different taxa in hierchial order.

1. Division. It is a taxon which is characterised by a group of characters and not by a single infallible character. It consists of classes.

2. Class. It is the next full category, subordinate in rank to the division. The name of the class ordinarily ends into *eae.* Each class is further sub-divided into orders.

3. Order. It is the next subordinate category to the class. Generally the name of the order ends into *ales* such as Malvales, Ranales, Geraniales, etc. However, the names of some orders of long standing end *inae* e.g. Caryophyllinae. The order consists of one or more families.

4. Family. The family generally represents a more natural unit than any of the higher categories because usually more is known about the components of the family and correlation between a greater number of characters naturally exists. The latin names of all but eight of the families of vascular plants is terminated by the conventional ending *aceae,* e.g. Ranunculaceae.

5. Genus. The genus is subordinate to the family and in one family there may be several genera. The generic name of the plant is the first of the two words which comprise a binomial viz. *Ranunculus scleratus*-*Ranunculus* being the generic name. The latin names of the genera are always adjectives used as such and are singular names starting with capital letter without uniform endings. Genus is subdivided into one or many species.

6. Species. A species is the basic unit of classification. A species indicates or specifies only one kind of a plant such as sweet pea, wild pea, etc. All the species are related i.e. they have descended from the same ancestor or ancestors. Individual plants belonging to the same speices are similar in fundamental structure and other characters and moreover these important features are maintained in nature through innumerable generations.

The above categories are further sub-divided whenever needed. This sub-classification includes-sub-kingdom, sub-division, sub-class, sub-order (ending in *ineae*), sub-family (ending in *oideae*), sub-genus and sub-species or variety.

[II] Systems of Classification

Many different systems of classification have been proposed from time and again. All these systems have been placed into three categories.

1. Artificial. It is an arbitrary arrangement of groups based on incomplete knowledge or simple inconvenience.

2. Natural. It is based on the true or supposed relationship of the plants.

3. Phylogenetic. It is based on the phylogeny or evolutionary trends of the plants.

For practical purposes system of **Bentham** and **Hooker** (1862-1883) is followed being used by the different well-known herbaria of the world. This system was published in *Genera plantarum* in three volumes in Latin language. The classification of the seed plants numbering 97,205 only, was described. The system in essence is a refinement over the system of A.P. de Candolle. The refinements are to be noted in Polypetalae where a new series Disciflorae has been incorporated between Thalamiflorae and Calyciflorae and in the revision of the classification of Monochlamydeae which is an apetalous taxa. The Gymnosperms were given a status parallel in rank to Dicotyledons and Monocotyledons, and were placed between them. One of the most important contributions of this work is the descriptions of taxa of all levels. Thus, this originality of **Bentham** and **Hooker's** work has elevated it, to a level of its own, since all subsequent systems of classification are compilations from this literature.

An outline classification of **Bentham** and **Hooker** along with important characters of various units is given below.

(For the sake of convenience it is slightly modified and only those families are listed which are described in the subsequent text).

[III] Classification of Bentham and Hooker

CLASS 1. DICOTYLEDONAE

1. Venation reticulate.
2. Flowers pentamerous.

Sub-Class I. Polypetalae

1. Petals free.

Series I. Thalamiflorae

1. Thalamus dome-shaped.
2. Flowers hypogynous and ovary superior.

Order 1. Ranales

1. Stamens indefinite.
2. Carpels free or immersed in torus; very rarely united.

Family 1. Ranunculaceae

1. Usually herbs, often with divided leaves.
2. Flowers hemicyclic, with one to many generally free carpels.
3. Stamens indefinite and extrorse.
4. Fruit follicle or capsule.

Family 2. Magnoliaceae

1. Trees or shrubs with alternate, exstipulate, simple leaves.
2. Flowers spiral or spirocyclic with convex or elongated floral axis.
3. Stamens and carpels numerous and free.
4. Fruits, in etaerio : individual fruit is follicle or samara or berry.

Family 3. Anonaceae

1. Trees or shrubs with alternate, exstipulate, simple leaves.
2. Flowers usually trimerous.
3. Stamens and carpels usually many.
4. Fruit etaerio of berries.

Order 2. Parietales

1. Carpels united to form an unilocular ovary with parietal placentation.

Family 1. Papaveraceae
1. Herbs with alternate exstipulate leaves and latex.
2. Calyx caducous.
3. Flower actinomorphic and dimerous or trimerous with extrorse stamens.
4. Gynoecium 2-16 carpellary; fruit capsule.

Family 2. Fumariaceae
1. Herbs with alternate exstipulate leaves and latex.
2. Calyx caducous.
3. Flower transversely zygomorphic and dimerous with extrorse stamens.
4. Gynoecium 1-2 carpellary; fruit capsule or nut.

Family 3. Cruciferae (Brassicaceae)
1. Herbs with alternate extipulate leaves and latex.
2. Regular, bisexual flowers arranged in a raceme.
3. Corolla cruciform.
4. Stamens tetradynamous.
5. Ovary bicarpellary, syncarpous, unilocular but becomes bilocular due to the development of a false septum ; fruit siliqua.

Family 4. Capparidaceae
1. Leaves alternate.
2. Floral axis usually elongated below and roecium or gynoecium to form androphore or gynophore.
3. Fruit capsule, berry or drupe.

Order 3. Caryophyllineae
1. Stamens 5 or 10.
2. Ovary unilocualr or rarely imperfectly 2-5 locular.
3. Placentation free-cental or rarely axile.
4. Embryo curved.

Family 1. Caryophyllaceae
1. Herbs with opposite decussate leaves.
2. Actinomorphic and hermaphrodite flowers in cymose panicles.
3. Gynoecium 2-5 carpellary, syncarpous, superior.
4. Ovary unilocular with free-central placentation; fruit capsule or berry.

Order 4. Malvales
1. Stamens usually indefinite and monadelphous.
2. Ovary 3-8 carpellary with axile placentation.

Family 1. Malvaceae
1. Leaves stipulate.
2. Calyx often with an epicalyx.
3. Stamens monothecous and reniform.
4. Ovary of five to many fused carpels, each with one to many ovules.
5. Fruit capsule or schizocarp.

Family 2. Tiliaceae
1. Usually woody plants with alternate stipulate leaves.
2. Stamens many or rarely 10, free or in bundles with dithecous anthers.
3. Ovary of 2-8 fused carpels and 2-8 locular.

Series II Disciflorae
1. A disc is usually present below the ovary.
2. Ovary superior and flowers hypogynous.

Order 1. Geraniales
1. Disc usually annular, adnate to the stamens or reduced to glands.
2. Ovary multicarpellary, syncarpous with axile placentation.
3. Ovules ascending or pendulous and raphe usually ventral.

Family 1. Rutaceae
1. Leaves exstipulate and containing aromatic oil glands.
2. Stamens 2-5 or many and obdiplostemonous.
3. Disc annular.
4. Fruit hesperidium.

Family 2. Meliaceae
1. Leaves pinnately compound and exstipulate.
2. Flowers in cymose panicles.
3. Stamens obdiplostemonous and form a staminal tube.
4. Seeds often winged.

Series III Calyciflorae
1. Thalamus cup-shaped.
2. Ovary inferior.

Order 1. Rosales
1. Alternate stipulate leaves.
2. Carpels one or more.

Family 1. Papilionaceae
1. Flowers zygomorphic.
2. Gynoecium usually one.
3. Corolla papilionaceous with descending imbricate aestivation.
4. Stamens diadelphous.

Family 2. Caesalpiniaceae
1. Flowers zygomorphic.
2. Gynoecium usually one.
3. Corolla with ascending imbricate aestivation.

Family 3. Mimosaceae
1. Flowers actinomorphic.

2. Gynoecium usually one.
3. Corolla valvate.
4. Stamens indefinite.

Family 4. Rosaceae

1. Corolla rosaceous.
2. Thalamus convex, flat or hollowed.
3. Stamens bent in bud condition, usually many.

Order 2. Myrtales

1. Leaves simple and entire.
2. Ovary syncarpous, usually inferior.
3. Placentation axile.

Family 1. Myrtaceae

1. Woody with opposite or alternate exstipulate leaves.
2. Stamens indefinite, sometimes in bundles.
3. Carpels 2, 5 or 8.

Order 3. Passiflorales

1. Tendril climbers.
2. Ovary usually inferior, syncarpous, unilocular with parietal placentation.

Family 1. Cucurbitaceae

1. Flowers usually unisexual.
2. Stamens five, free or each two united or all the five in a central synandrium.
3. Carpels usually three, stigmas forked.
4. Fruit a pepo.

Order 4. Umbellales

1. Inflorescence umbel.
2. Ovary inferior with 1, 2 or 8 fused carpels and as many locules.
3. Ovules solitary, pendulous in each locule.

Family 1. Umbelliferae

1. Stems fistular.
2. Leaves alternate, exstipulate, usually much dissected with sheathing leaf base.
3. Carpels two, fused with two styles on swollen style base (stylopodium).
4. Fruit schizocarp splitting into two mericarps.

Sub-class II. Gamopetalae

1. Petals fused.

Series I Inferae

1. Ovary inferior.
2. Stamens usually as many as corolla lobes.

Order 1. Rubiales

1. Leaves opposite.
2. Stamens epipetalous.
3. Ovary 2-8 locular.

Family 1. Rubiaceae

1. Opposite, decussate, entire leaves with interpetiolar stipules.
2. Flowers in cymes.
3. Gynoecium bicarpellary, syncarpous, ovary inferior, bilocular, each with 1-8 ovules.
4. Placentum T-shaped.

Order 2. Asterales

1. Stamens epipetalous.
2. Ovary unilocular with one ovule.

Family 1. Compositae (Asteraceae)

1. Leaves generally alternate.
2. Inflorescence capitulum.
3. Calyx reduced to hairy pappus.
4. Stamens epipetalous and syngenesious.

Series II Heteromerae

1. Ovary superior, carpels more than two.

Series III Bicarpellatae

1. Ovary usually superior.
2. Carpels two.

Order 1. Gentianales

1. Leaves opposite.
2. Flowers actinomorphic.
3. Stamens epipetalous.

Family 1. Apocynaceae

1. Inflorescence cymose.
2. Latex present.
3. Stamens not gynandrous.
4. Number of ovules one or two in each locule.
5. Ovaries two, free but united by the style.

Family 2. Asclepiadaceae

1. Flowers solitary or in cymose umbels.
2. Petals usually convolute.
3. Stamens gynandrous; pollen usually in pollinia with translators.
4. Ovaries two, free but united by the style.

Order 2. Polemoniales

1. Leaves alternate, exstipulate.
2. Flower actinomorphic.

Family 1. Convolvulaceae

1. Gynoecium bicarpellary, syncarpous with two basal ovules in each locule on axile placentae.
2. Fruit capsule.

Family 2. Solanaceae

1. Flowers solitary terminal or cymosely umbelled.
2. The septum is oblique and placentae are highly swollen.
3. Fruit berry or capsule.

Order 3. Personales

1. Flowers zygomorphic.
2. Corolla bilabiate personate.
3. Stamens usually 4, didynamous or two.
4. Ovary uni,-bi-or rarely tetralocular, ovules indefinite.

Family 1. Scrophulariaceae

1. Flowers never terminal.
2. Gynoecium bicarpellary, syncarpous, bilocular.
3. Ovules many on axile placentae.

Family 2. Acanthaceae

1. Herbs or shrubs with opposite leaves.
2. Flowers in spikes, racemes or cymose umbels.
3. Anthers are situated at unequal heights.
4. Gynoecium bilocular, each locule with indefinite to two ovules.
5. Jaculators are present between the seeds.

Order 4. Lamiales

1. Flowers zygomorphic.
2. Corolla bilipped.
3. Stamens 4, didynamous or two.
4. Ovary 2-4 locular.
5. Ovule one in each locule, rarely more.

Family 1. Verbenaceae

1. Opposite or whorled leaves.
2. Flowers in cymose umbels.
3. Gynoecium is usually tetracarpellary by formation of secondary septa.
4. Fruit drupe or schizocarp.

Family 2. Labiatae (Lamiaceae)

1. Stem quadrangular.
2. Decussate or whorled exstipulate leaves.
3. Inflorescence verticillaster.
4. Gynoecium generally bilocular with two ovules in each locule. Sometimes tetralocular with one ovule in each locule.
5. Style gynobasic.
6. Fruit carcerulus.

Sub-Class III. Monochlamydeae

1. Flowers usually with one whorl of perianth, commonly sepaloid or none.

Series I Curvembryeae

1. Embryo curved.

Family 1. Amaranthaceae

1. Opposite or alternate exstipulate leaves.
2. Flowers small, haplochlamydous, usually hermaphrodite and actinomorphic.
3. Tepals 4 or 5, usually sepaloid.
4. Stamens 1-5, anteposed.
5. .Gynoecium 2-3 carpellary, syncarpous, superior, unilocular with indefinite to one ovule.

Family 2. Chenopodiaceae

1. Leaves alternate, often fleshy.
2. Flowers small, haplochlamydous, actinomophic and either hermaphrodite or unisexual.
3. Tepals five or sometimes less, fused.
4. Stamens as many and anteposed, bent inwards in bud condition.
5. Gynoecium superior and unilocular with usually one basal erect ovule.

Series II Multiovulatae Aquaticae

Series III Multiovulatae Terrestres

Series IV Microembryeae

Series V Daphnales

Series VI Achlamydosporae

Series VII Unisexuales

1. Flowers unisexual.
2. Perianth sepaloid or much reduced or absent.
3. Ovules one or two per carpel.

Family 1. Euphorbiaceae

1. Alternate stipulate leaves with latex.
2. Perianth usually in one whorl or absent.
3. Stamens one to indefinite, free or united or branched.
4. Gynoecium tricapellary, syncarpous, ovary trilocular with one or two ovules in each locule.
5. Styles three.

Family 2. Moraceae

1. Leaves stipulate with latex.
2. Cymes often head-like.
3. Tepals usually four or absent.
4. Stamens as many and opposite the tepals.
5. Gynoecium bicarpellary, syncarpous, ssuperior, unilocular with usually one pendulous ovule.

Series VIII Ordines Anomali

CLASS 2. MONOCOTYLEDONAE

1. Venation parallel.
2. Flowers trimerous.

Series I Microspermae

1. Overy inferior.
2. Seeds very small.

Family 1. Orchidaceae

1. Flowers hermaphrodite, zygomorphic, often resupinated.

2. Perianth in two whorls of 3 each.
3. Stamen one or two united with the style to form column.
4. Gynoecium tricarpellary, syncarpous, ovary inferior with indefinite ovules.
5. Stigmas 3, the third usually rudimentary or forming a rostellum.

Series II Epigynae

1. Perianth partly peraloid.
2. Ovary usually inferior.

Family 1. Scitamineae (Musaceae)

1. Compound inflorescence with large petaloid bracts.
2. Flowers zygomorphic, hermaphrodite or unisexual.
3. Perianth in two whorls and petaloid.
4. Gynoecium tricarpellary, syncarpous, trilocular, with one to indefinite ovules.
5. Fruit berry or capsule.

Series III Coronarieae

1. Inner perianth petaloid.
2. Ovary superior.

Family 1. Liliaceae

1. Inflorescence usually scapiferous racemose type.
2. Perianth in two whorls and petaloid.
3. Stamens also in two whorls and epiphyllous.
4. Gynoecium 2-5 locular and placentation axile.

Series IV Calycineae

1. Perianth sepaloid, herbaceous or membranous.
2. Ovary superior.

Family 1. Palmae

1. Tree-like plants with fan leaves.
2. Flowers actinomorphic, unisexual and in spikes.
3. Perianth in two whorls and sepaloid.
4. Stamens 3 + 3, or 3, 9 or 8.
5. Gynoecium tricarpellary, trilocular with one ovule in each locule.
6. Fruit berry or drupe.

Series V Nudiflorae

Series VI Apocarpae

Series VII Glumaceae

1. Flowers solitary, sessile in the axile of bracts.
2. Perianth of scales or none.
3. Ovary usually unilocular and one ovuled.

Family 1. Cyperaceae

1. Herbs with usually 3 angled stem and 3-ranked leaves with closed sheaths.
2. Flowers in spikelets, naked, hermaphrodite or unisexual.
3. Stamens three to one.
4. Gynoecium 2-3 carpellary, syncarpous, ovary superior, unilocular with one basal anatropous ovule.

Family 2. Gramineae (Poaceae)

1. Jointed stems with alternate 2-ranked leaves with split sheath and ligule.
2. Inflorescence spikelet and each begins with one or two empty glumes, then palae with axillary flowers.
3. Stamens usually three.
4. Gynoecium superior with one ovule.
5. Fruit caryopsis.

V The Diagrams

The diagrams should also be given equal emphasis. Only the outline diagrams are drawn with a sharp, firm pencil. The lines of the diagrams should be continuous and shading be done only wherever necessary (as in the diagrams of a twig). The different parts of a diagram should be labelled neatly. The caption of the sketch should be given below it. Generally the following diagrams are drawn.

(1) **A flowering twig** showing all the details such as the details of the stem, the phyllotaxy, shape, etc. of the leaf, the inflorescence, etc.

(2) **Longitudinal section of the flower** should be cut with the help of a sharp blade from below upwards. In case of *zygomorphic flowers* it is cut along the plane of a *symmetry*. In such a diagram, the relationship of the parts must be carefully represented and all heavy shading be avoided.

(3) **A stamen** must show the length of the filament and the fixation of the anther.

(4) **Gynoecium** must show the ovary, style and stigma as seen externally. Also draw, if there is any disc below the ovary.

(5) **T. s. of the ovary** must clearly indicate the number of carpels, locules and the number of ovules in each locule. The type of placentation is also to be shown clearly and carefully.

(6) **Floral diagram** must be good enough to represent all the floral parts in a perfect manner.

VI Floral Diagram

The floral diagram is an ideal ground plan of a flower. It is a method with which many of the characteristics of its parts and symmetry can be expressed in a graphic form.

Firstly, the floral diagram is always circular and the differences in floral symmetry are shown by difference in the size and form of the individual parts in the diagram. The floral whorls are represented in concentric circles, sepals on the outside, then petals, stamens and carpels towards inner sides respectively. If the flowers are spiral, then spiral arragnement is drawn inwards to the centre.

Secondly, the parts are represented by sections, drawn in, upon the respective circles at position corresponding to their actual position. An observation fo the relationship of the flower to the inflorescence ascertains the positions. Above the diagram a small circle is drawn to represent the mother axis. Mother axis is not drawn is case of terminal flowers, in others it is denoted in the following way –

(1) If flower is zygomorphic ⦶
(2) If flower is actinomorphic ⊕

If there is bract, draw its section below the diagram. The bracteoles if present, are drawn on the sides. Now, note whether a sepal or a space between two sepals, stands towards mother axis. Begin with this sepal and mark the other sepals to correspond with the number, relative size and position of the actual sepals. In case of odd number of sepals, the odd sepal would either be anterior or posterior to the flower i.e., opposite the bract or opposite the mother axis respectively. Petals are also to be drawn likewise but should alternate the sepals. In case of zygomorphic flowers, the petals and sometimes the sepals also, are of unequal sizes. If any portion of sepal or petal has a spur, this may be shown by drawing a loop at the back of the organ.

Next, if parts of the same whorl are fused, draw lines to connect their edges together. In case, the parts of different whorls are joined viz. stamens to petals, draw linking lines between the parts concerned.

Stamens are marked by transverse sections of the anthers. It is carefully seen whether they are in one or more whorls. If they are obdiplostemonous, the stamens of the outer whorl are drawn opposite to the petals. Extrorse anthers are to be faced towards the petals and the introrse ones towards the gynoecium. Staminodes are represented either by a cross (X) or asterisk (*). The gynoecium is represented by a transverse section of the ovary. In case the parts are spirally arranged, care should be taken to count their number in one complete turn of the spiral and mark them on the diagram at corresponding intervals.

OUTLINES OF THE SYSTEM OF CLASSIFICATION PROPOSED BY BENTHAM & HOOKER*

SEED PLANTS OR PHANEROGAMS

Class I DICOTYLEDONAE

Sub-class 1. Polypetalae

Series I
Thalamiflorae
Order 1.
Ranales
Families
Ranunculaceae
Magnoliaceae
Anonaceae
(5 other families)
Order 2.
Parietales
Families
Papaveraceae
Cruciferae
Capparidaceae
(6 other families)
Order 3.
Polygalineae
(4 families)
Order 4.
Caryophyllineae
Family
Caryophyllaceae
(3 other families)
Order 5.
Guttiferales
(6 families)
Order 6.
Malvales
Families
Malvaceae
Tiliaceae
(1 more family)

Series II
Disciflorae
Order 1.
Geraniales
Families
Rutaceae
Meliaceae
(9 other families)
Order 2.
Olacales
(3 families)
Order 3.
Celastrales
(4 familes)
Order 4.
Sapindales
(5 families)

Series III
Calyciflorae
Order 1.
Rosales
Families
Leguminosae
Rosaceae
(7 other families)
Order 2.
Myrtales
Family
Myrtaceae
(5 other families)
Order 3.
Passiflorales
Family
Cucurbitaceae
(6 other families)
Order 4.
Ficoidales
(2 families)
Order 5.
Umbellales
Family
Umbelliferae
(2 other families)

Sub-class 2. Gamopetalae

Series I
Inferae
Order 1.
Rubiales
Family
Rubiaceae
(1 more familiy)
Order 2.
Asterales
Family
Compositae
(3 other families)
Order 3.
Campanales
(3 families)

Series II
Heteromerae
Order 1.
Ericales
(6 families)
Order 2.
Primulales
(3 families)
Order 3
Ebenales
(3 families)

Series III
Bicarpellatae
Order 1.
Gentianales
Families
Apocynaceae
Asclepiadaceae
(4 other families)
Order 2.
Polemoniales
Families
Convolvulaceae
Solanaceae
(3 other families)
Order 3.
Personales
Families
Scrophulariaceae
Acanthaceae
(6 other families)
Order 4.
Lamiales
Families
Verbenaceae
Labiatae
(3 other families)

Sub-class 3. Monochlamydeae

Series 1.
Curvembryeae
Family
Amaranthaceae
Chenopodiaceae
Polygonaceae
(4 other families)
Series 2.
Multiovulatae aquaticae
(1 family)
Series 3.
Multiovulatae terrestres
(3 families)
Series 4.
Microembryeae
(4 families)
Series 5.
Daphnales
(5 families)
Series 6.
Achlamydosporeae
(3 families)
Series 7.
Unisexuales
Families
Euphlorbiaceae
Urticaceae
(7 other families)
Series 8.
Ordines anomali
(4 families)

Class II GYMNOSPERMAE

Class III MONOCOTYLEDONAE

Series 1
Microspermae
(3 families)
Family
Orchidaceae
Series 2.
Epigynae
Family
Scitamineae
(6 other families)
Series 3.
Coronarieae
Family
Liliaceae
(7 other families)
Series 4
Calycineae
Family
Palmae
(2 other familes)
Series 5.
Nudiflorae
(5 families)
Series 6.
Apocarpae
(3 families)
Series 7.
Glumaceae
Families
Cyperaceae
Gramineae
(4 other families)

*Names of only those families are listed which are described in the subsequent text.

3

Description of Plant

RANUNCULACEAE*

Ranunculus scleratus Linn.

Habit. Herb.
Root. Tap, branched.
Stem. Herbaceous, aerial, erect, angular, fistular, smooth, nodes and internodes very prominent, green in colour.
Leaf. Cauline and ramal, alternate, exstipulate, simple, petiolate, leaf base cheaving, lamina much dissected, each lobe is ovate, entire, obtuse, glabrous, multicostate reticulate.
Inflorescence. Dichasial cyme.
Flower. Bracteate, bracteolate, pedicellate, complete, actinomorphic, hermaphrodite, pentamerous, hypogynous, thalamus prominent and convex, spirocyclic and yellow.
Calyx. Sepals 5, polysepalous, quincuncial, slightly petaloid and boat shaped.
Corolla. Petals 5, polypetalous, imbricate, yellow, each petal at its base has a pocket-shaped nectary.
Androecium. Stamens indefinite, polyandrous, spirally arranged, filament long, dithecous, basifixed, extrorse.
Gynoecium. Polycarpellary, apocarpous, ovary superior, unilocular, one ovule in each locule, placentation basal, style absent, stigma simple and sticky.
Fruit. Etaerio of achenes.
Floral formula. Br, brl, $\oplus$, ⚥ , K_5, C_5, A_∞, $\underline{G}_\infty$.
Classification and identification.

Class. *Dicotyledonae*
1. Venation reticulate.
2. Flowers pentamerous.

Sub-Class. *Polypetalae*
1. Petals free.

Series. *Thalamiflorae*
1. Thalamus dome-shaped.
2. Flowers hypogynous and ovary superior.

Orders. *Ranales*
1. Stamens indefinite.
2. Carpels free or immersed in torus.

Family. *Ranunculaceae*
1. Usually herbs often with divided leaves.
2. Flowers hemicyclic with one to many generally free carpels.
3. Stamens indefinite and extrorse.

***1. English name.** Crowfoot family
2. Systematic position in other systems of classification.

Rendle (1925)	**Engler and Prantl** (1931)	**Hutchinson** (1959)
Dicotyledons	Dicotyledoneae	Dicotyledons
Dialypetalae	Archichlamydeae	Herbaceae
Ranales	Ranales	Ranales
Ranunculaceae	Ranunculaceae	Ranunculaceae

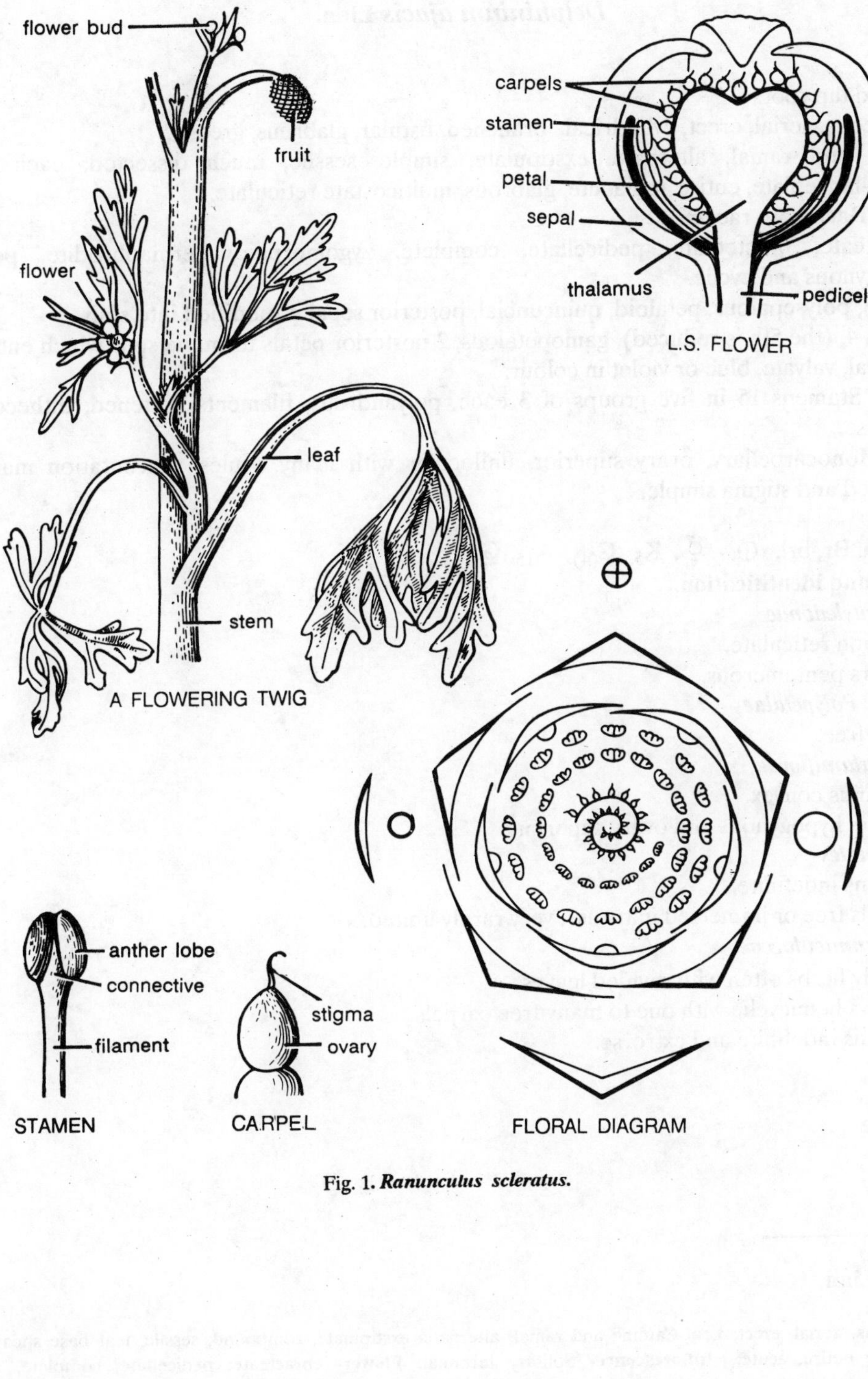

Fig. 1. ***Ranunculus scleratus.***

---

1. English name. Butter cup or water crowfoot.
2. Vernacular names. Shim, Jaldhania.
3. Economic importance. The leaves are used as vesicant.

Delphinium ajacis Linn.

Habit. Herb.

Root. Branched tap root.

Stem. Herbaceous, aerial, erect, cylindrical, branched, fistular, glabrous, green.

Leaf. Cauline and ramal, alternate, exstipulate, simple, sessile, much dissected, each segment is linear-lanceolate, entire and acute, glabrous, multicostate reticulate.

Inflorescence. Racemose raceme.

Flower. Bracteate, bracteolate, pedicellate, complete, zygomorphic, hermaphrodite, pentamerous, hypogynous and cyclic.

Calyx. Sepals 5, polysepalous, petaloid, quincuncial, posterior sepal is modified into spur.

Corolla. Petals 4, (the 5th is reduced), gamopetalous, 2 posterior petals form the spur which enters the spur of sepal, valvate, blue or violet in colour.

Androecium. Stamens 15 in five groups of 3 each, polyandrous, filaments flattened, dithecous, adnate, extrorse.

Gynoecium. Monocarpellary, ovary superior, unilocular with many ovules, placentation marginal, style reduced and stigma simple.

Fruit. Follicle.

Floral formula. Br, brl, ⦶ , ⚥, K_5, $C_{(4)}$, A_{15}, $\underline{G}_1$.

Classification and identification.

Class. ***Dicotyledonae***

1. Venation reticulate.
2. Flowers pentamerous.

Sub-Class. ***Polypetalae***

1. Petals free.

Series. ***Thalamiflorae***

1. Thalamus convex.
2. Flowers hypogynous and ovary superior.

Order. ***Ranales***

1. Stamens indefinite.
2. Carpels free or immersed in torus ; very rarely united.

Family. ***Rannuculaceae***

1. Usually herbs often with divided leaves.
2. Flowers hemicyclic with one to many free carpels.
3. Stamens indefinite and extrorse.

Nigella sativa Linn.

Stem- Herbaceous, aerial, erect; **Leaf**-Cauline and ramal, alternate, exstipulate, compound, sessile, leaf base sheathing, ultimate segments linear, entire, acute; **Inflorescence**- Solitary terminal; **Flower**- ebracteate, pedicellate, complete, actinomorphic, hermaphrodite, pentamerous, hypogynous and spirocyclic; **Calyx**- Sepals 5, polysepalous, imbricate, greenish white ;**Corolla**-Represented by generally 8, bifid, greenish white honey glands; **Androecium** - Stamens indefinite, polyandrous, spirally arranged,filaments slender, dithecous, adnate, introrse; **Gynoecium**-5-12 carpellary, syncarpous, ovary superior, 5-12 locular with many ovules in each locule, placentation axile, style and stigma as many as carpels; **Fruit** - Capsule;

Floral formula - Ebr, ⊕ , ⚥ , K_5, C_8, A_∞, $\underline{G}_{(5\text{-}12)}$.

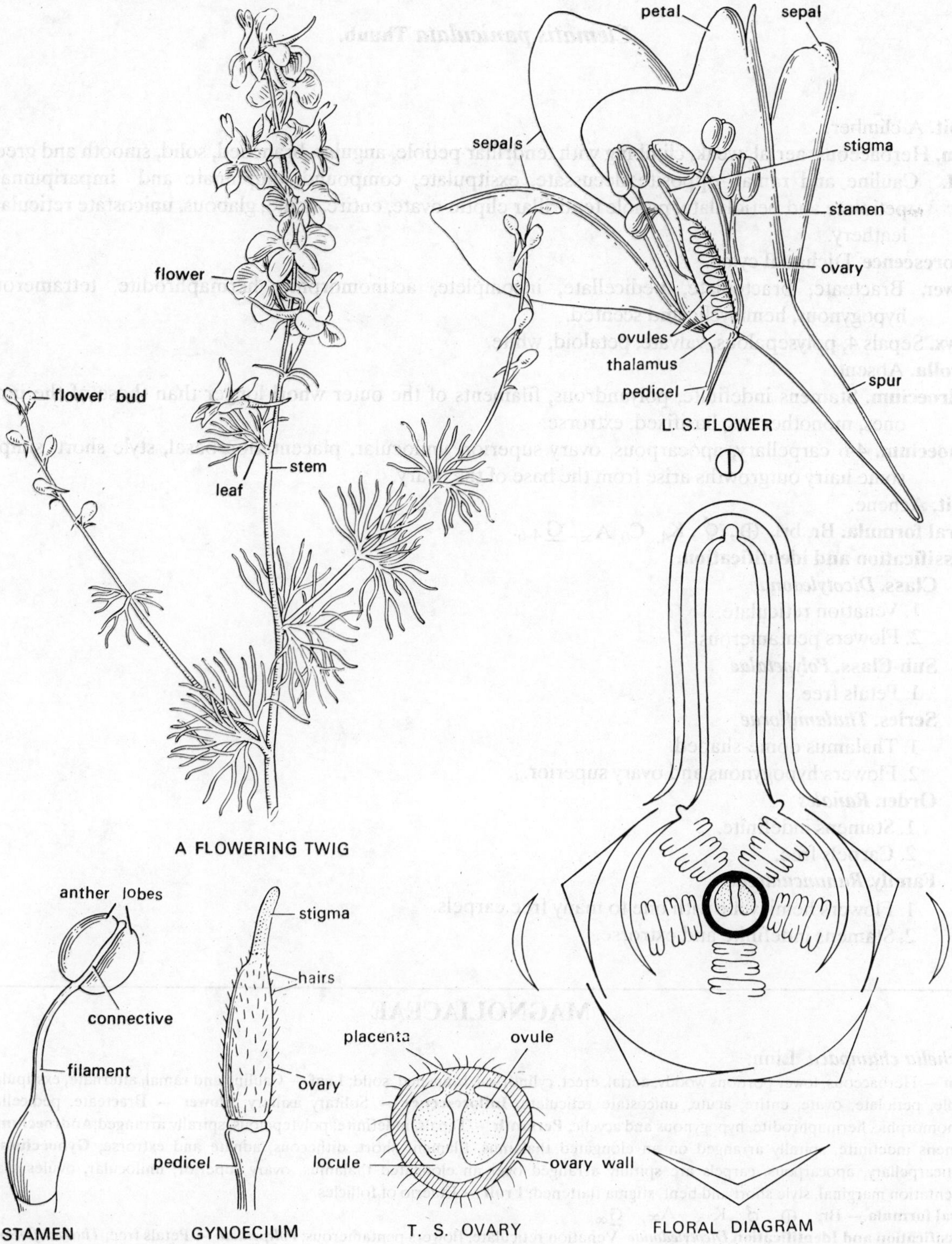

Fig. 2. ***Delphinium ajacis.***

---

1. English name. Rocket larkspur.

2. Economic importance. Grown as ornamental plant. The seeds are insecticidal.

Clematis paniculata Thunb.

Habit. A climber.

Stem. Herbaceous, aerial, weak, climbing with tendrillar petiole, angular, branched, solid, smooth and green.

Leaf. Cauline and ramal, opposite decussate, exsitpulate, compound, unipinnate and imparipinnate, petiolate and petiolulate, petiole tendrillar eliptic-ovate, entire, acute, glabous, unicostate reticulate, leathery.

Inflorescence. Dichasial cyme.

Flower. Bracteate, bracteolate, pedicellate, incomplete, actinomorphic, hermaphrodite, tetramerous, hypogynous, hemicyclic and scented.

Calyx. Sepals 4, polysepalous, valvate, petaloid, white.

Corolla. Absent.

Androecium. Stamens indefinite, polyandrous, filaments of the outer whorl longer than those of the inner ones, monothecous, basifixed, extrorse.

Gynoecium. 4-6 carpellary, apocarpous, ovary superior, unilocular, placentation basal, style short, simple, some hairy outgrowths arise from the base of the ovary.

Fruit. Achene.

Floral formula. Br, brl, ⊕, ⚥, K_4, C_0, A_∞, $\underline{G}_{4\text{-}6}$.

Classification and identification.

Class. ***Dicotyledonae***

1. Venation reticulate.
2. Flowers pentamerous.

Sub-Class. ***Polypetalae***

1. Petals free.

Series. ***Thalamiflorae***

1. Thalamus dome-shaped.
2. Flowers hypogynous and ovary superior.

Order. ***Ranales***

1. Stamens indefinite.
2. Carpels free.

Family. ***Ranunculaceae***

1. Flowers hemicyclic with one to many free carpels.
2. Stamens indefinite and extrorse.

MAGNOLIACEAE

Michelia champaca Linn.

Stem – Herbaceous, lower portions woody, aerial, erect, cylindrical, branched, soild; **Leaf** – Cauline and ramal, alternate, exstipulate, simple, petiolate, ovate, entire, acute, unicostate reticulate; **Inflorescence** – Solitary axillary; **Flower** – Bracteate, pedicellate, actinomorphic, hermaphrodite, hypogynous and acyclic; **Perianth** – Tepals indefinite, polytepalous, spirally arranged; **Androecium** – Stamens indefinite, spirally arranged on an elongated thalamus, filament short, dithecous, adnate and extrorse; **Gynoecium** – Multicarpellary, apocarpous, carpels are spirally arranged over an elongated thalamus, ovary superior, unilocular, ovules many placentation marginal, style short and bent, stigma flattened; **Fruit** – Etaerio of follicles.

Floral formula – Br, ⊕, ⚥, K_∞, A_∞, $\underline{G}_\infty$.

Classification and Identification. ***Dicotyledonae*** Venation reticulate, flowers pentamerous; ***Polypetalae*** – Petals free; ***Thalamiflorae*** – Thalamus dome--shaped, and ovary superior; ***Ranales*** – Stamens indefinite, carpels free; ***Magnoliaceae*** – Flower spiral or spirocyclic with elongated floral axis, stamens and carpels numerous and free.

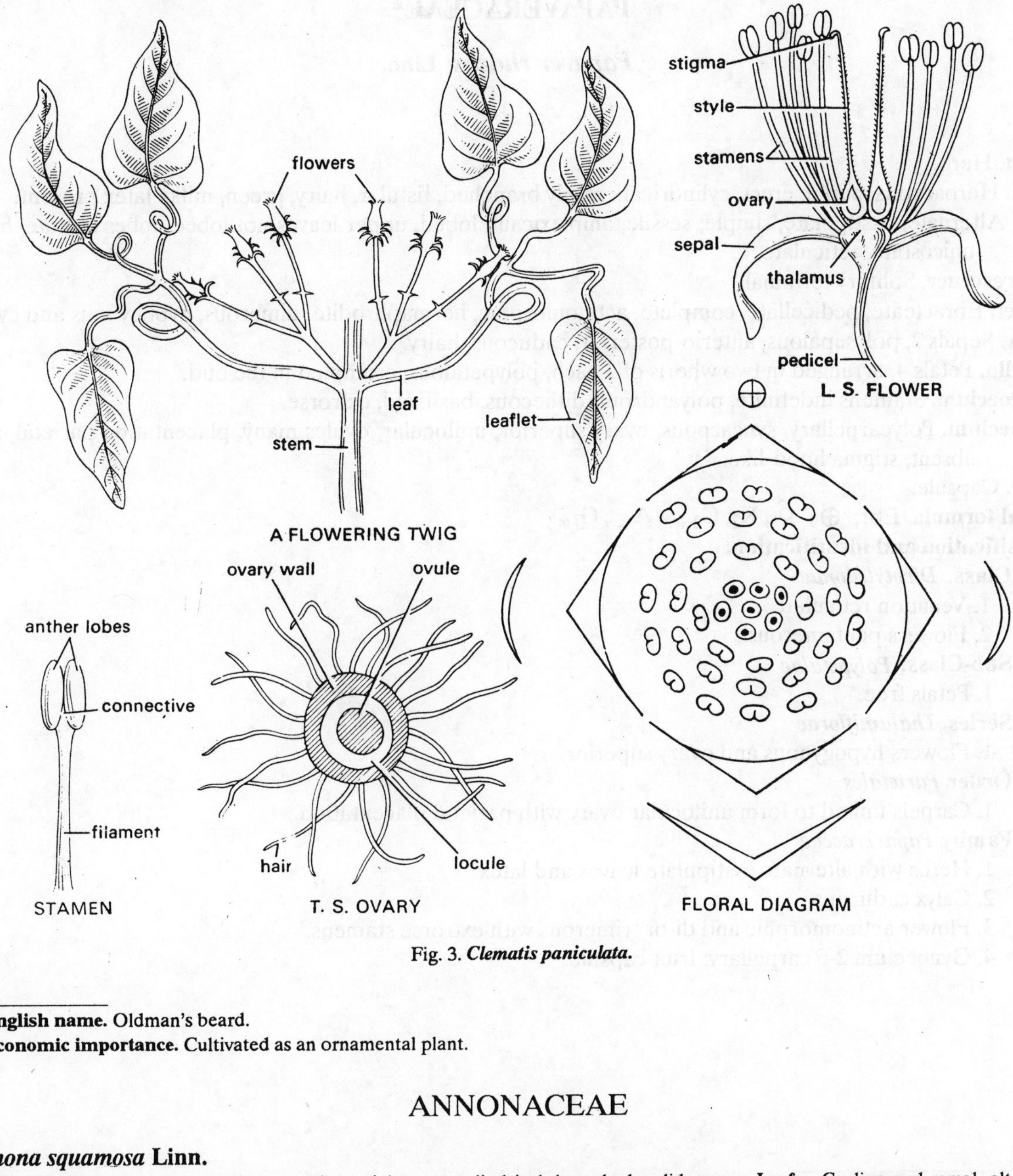

Fig. 3. ***Clematis paniculata.***

---

1. English name. Oldman's beard.

2. Economic importance. Cultivated as an ornamental plant.

ANNONACEAE

Annona squamosa Linn.

Stem— Herbaceous, lower portions woody, aerial, erect, cylindrical, branched, solid, green; **Leaf**— Cauline and ramal, alternate, exstipulate, simple, elliptic-lanceolate, entire, obtuse, glabrous, unicostate reticulate; **Inflorescence**— Dichasial cyme or solitary axillary; **Flower**— Bracteate, pedicellate, complete, actinomorphic, hermaphrodite trimerous, hypogynous and spirocyclic, **Calyx**— Sepals 3, gamosepetalous, connate at the base, valvate; **Corolla**— Petals 3, polypetalous, valvate; **Androecium**— Stamens indefinite, spirally arranged on an elongated thalamus, filament short, dithecous, adnate, extrorse; **Gynoecium**—Multicarpellary, apocarpous, carpels spirally arranged on an elongated thalamus, ovary superior, unilocular, basal placentation, style short, stigma long and papillose; **Fruit**— Etaerio of berries:

Floral formula – Br, $\oplus$, ♀, $K_{(3)}$ C_3, A_∞, $\underline{G}_\infty$

Classification and identification. *Dicotyledonae*— Venation reticulate, flowers pentamerous; ***Polypetalae***— Petals free; ***Thalamiflorae***— Thalamus dome shaped, ovary superior; ***Ranales***— Stamens indefinite, carpels free; ***Annonaceae***—Flowers usually trimerous, stamens and carpels usually many, fruit etaerio of berries.

PAPAVERACEAE*

Papaver rhoeas Linn.

Habit. Herb.

Stem. Herbaceous, aerial, erect, cylindrical, rarely branched, fistular, hairy, green, milky latex present.

Leaf. Alternate, exstipulate, simple, sessile, amplexicaul, lobed, upper leaves not lobed, lobes serrate, hairy, unicostate, reticulate.

Inflorescence. Solitary terminal.

Flower. Ebracteate, pedicellate, complete, actinomorphic, hermaphrodite, dimerous, hypogynous and cyclic.

Calyx. Sepals 2, polysepalous, anterio-posterior, caducous, hairy.

Corolla. Petals 4, arranged in two whorls of 2 each, polypetalous, crumpled in the bud.

Androecium. Stamens indefinite, polyandrous, dithecous, basifixed, extrorse.

Gynoecium. Polycarpellary, syncarpous, ovary superior, unilocular, ovules many, placentation parietal, style absent, stigma hood-like.

Fruit. Capsule.

Floral formula. Ebr, ⊕, ⚥, K_2, C_{2+2}, $A_\propto$, $\underline{G}_{(\propto)}$

Classification and identification.

Class. ***Dicotyledonae***

1. Venation reticulate.
2. Flowers pentamerous.

Sub-Class. ***Polypetalae***

1. Petals free.

Series. ***Thalamiflorae***

1. Flowers hypogynous and ovary superior.

Order. ***Parietales***

1. Carpels united to form unilocular ovary with parietal placentation.

Family. ***Papaveraceae***

1. Herbs with alternate exstipulate leaves and latex.
2. Calyx caducous.
3. Flower actinomorphic and di-or trimerous with extrorse stamens.
4. Gynoecium 2-6 carpellary; fruit capsule.

***1. English name. Poppy family.**

2. Systematic position in other systems of classification.

Rendle (1925)	Engler and Prantl (1931)	Hutchinson (1959)
Dicotyledons	Dicotyledoneae	Dicotyledons
Dialypetalae	Archichlamydeae	Herbaceae
Rhoeadales	Rhoeadales	Rhoeadales
Papaveraceae	Papaveraceae	Papaveraceae

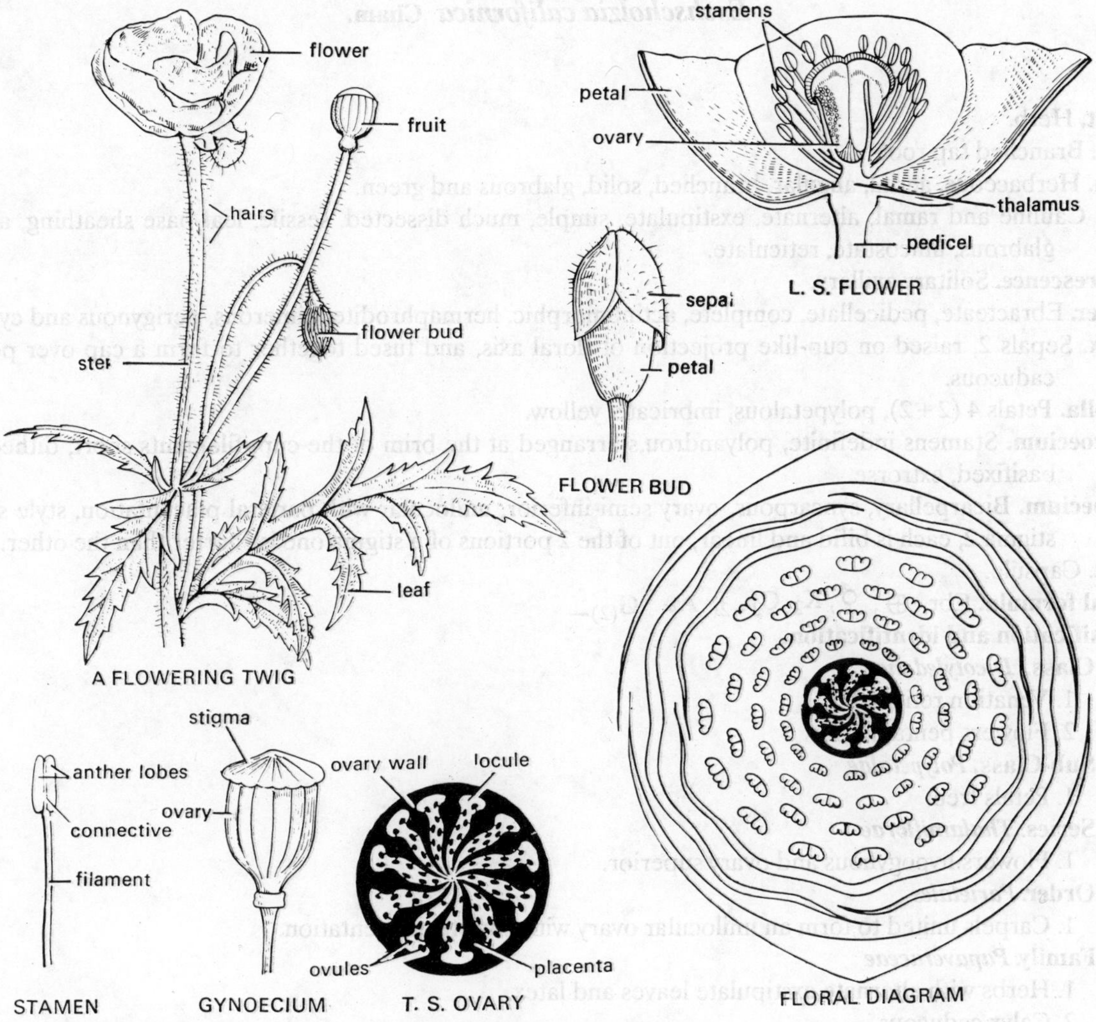

Fig. 4. ***Papaver rhoeas.***

---

1. English name. Corn poppy.

2. Vernacular name. Lal post.

3. Economic importance. Besides being grown as an ornamental, the milk of the fruits is narcotic and light sedative.

Eschscholzia californica Cham.

Habit. Herb.

Root. Branched tap root.

Stem. Herbaceous, aerial, angular, branched, solid, glabrous and green.

Leaf. Cauline and ramal, alternate, exstipulate, simple, much dissected, sessile, leaf-base sheathing, acute, glabrous, unicostate, reticulate.

Inflorescence. Solitary axillary.

Flower. Ebracteate, pedicellate, complete, actinomorphic, hermaphrodite, dimerous, perigynous and cyclic.

Calyx. Sepals 2, raised on cup-like projection of floral axis, and fused together to form a cap over petals, caducous.

Corolla. Petals 4 (2 + 2), polypetalous, imbricate, yellow.

Androecium. Stamens indefinite, polyandrou,s arranged at the brim of the cup, filaments short, dithecous, basifixed, extrorse.

Gynoecium. Bicarpellary, syncarpous, ovary semi-inferior, unilocular with parietal placentation, style short, stigma 2, each is bifid and linear; out of the 2 portions of a stigma one is shorter than the other.

Fruit. Capsule.

Floral formula. Ebr, $\oplus$, ⚥, K_2, C_{2+2}, A_∞, $G_{(2)}$—

Classification and identification.

Class. *Dicotyledonae*

1. Venation reticulate.
2. Flowers pentamerous.

Sub-Class. *Polypetalae*

1. Petals free.

Series. *Thalamiflorae*

1. Flowers hypogynous and ovary superior.

Order. *Parietales*

1. Carpels united to form an unilocular ovary with parietal placentation.

Family. *Papaveraceae*

1. Herbs with alternate exstipulate leaves and latex.
2. Calyx caducous.
3. Flowers actinomorphic and di-or trimerous with extrorse stamens.
4. Gynoecium 2-16 carpellary; fruit capsule.

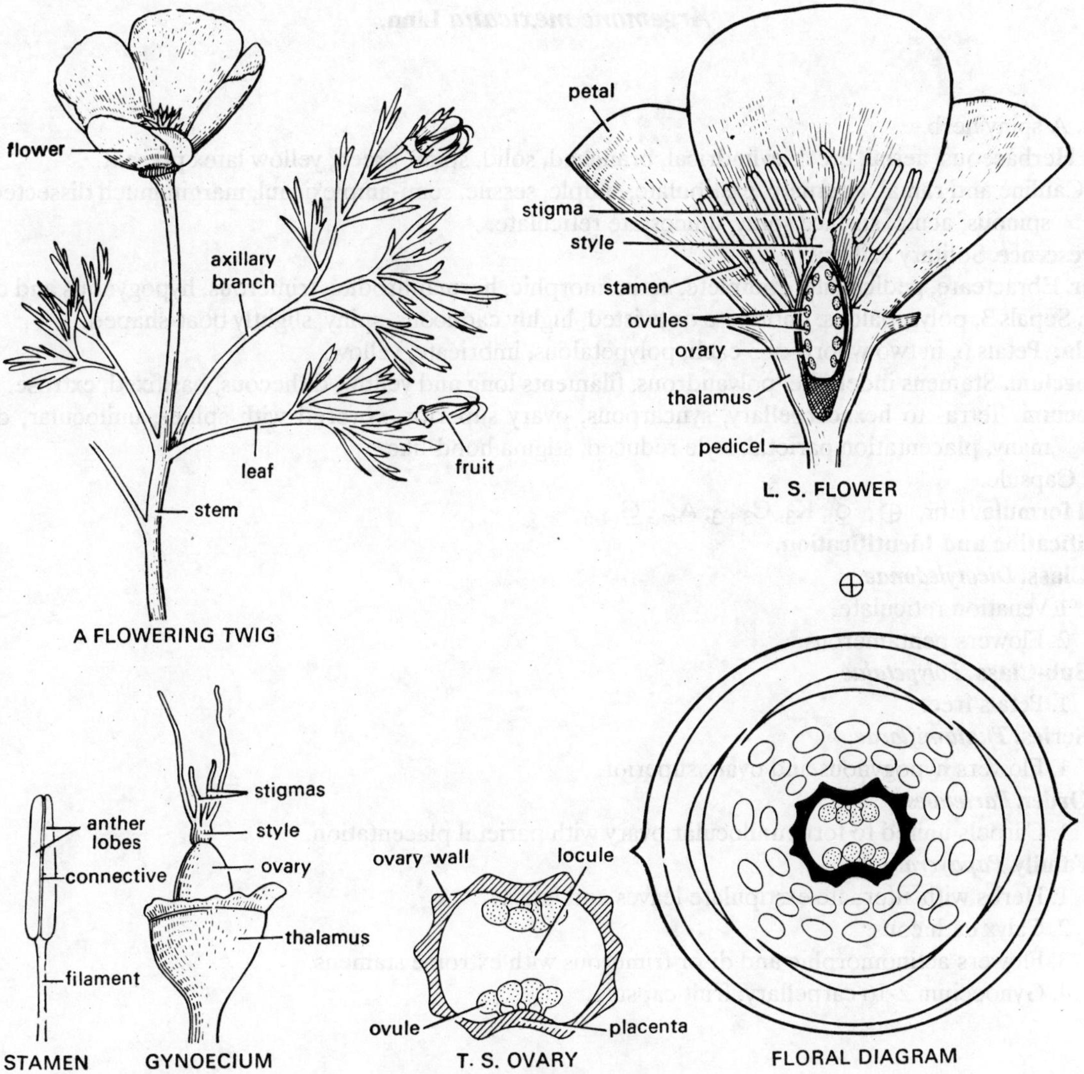

Fig. 5. ***Eschscholzia californica.***

1. English name. California poppy.

2. Vernacular name. Peeli poppy.

3. Economic importance. Grown as an ornamental.

Argemone mexicana Linn.

Habit. A spiny herb.

Stem. Herbaceous, aerial, erect, cylindrical, branched, solid, spiny, green, yellow latex present.

Leaf. Cauline and ramal, alternate, exstipulate, simple, sessile, semi-amplexicaul, margin much dissected and spinous, acute, surface spiny, unicostate reticulate.

Inflorescence. Solitary axillary.

Flower. Ebracteate, pedicellate, complete, actinomorphic, hermaphrodite, trimerous, hypogynous and cyclic.

Calyx. Sepals 3, polysepalous, imbricate or twisted, highly caducous, spiny, slightly boat-shaped.

Corolla. Petals 6, in two whorls of 3 each, polypetalous, imbricate, yellow.

Androecium. Stamens indefinite, polyandrous, filaments long and yellow, dithecous, basifixed, extrose.

Gynoecium. Tetra- to hexacarpellary, syncarpous, ovary superior, covered with spines, unilocular, ovules many, placentation parietal, style reduced, stigma hood-like.

Fruit. Capsule.

Floral formula. Ebr, ⊕, ⚥, K_3, C_{3+3}, A_∞, $\underline{G}_{(4\text{-}6)}$

Classification and Identification.

Class. ***Dicotyledonae***

1. Venation reticulate.
2. Flowers pentamerous.

Sub-Class. ***Polypetalae***

1. Petals free.

Series. ***Thalamiflorae***

1. Flowers hypogynous and ovary superior.

Order. ***Parietales***

1. Carpels united to form unilocular ovary with parietal placentation.

Family. ***Papaveraceae***

1. Herbs with alternate exstipulate leaves and latex.
2. Calyx caducous.
3. Flowers actinomorphic and di-or trimerous with extrorse stamens.
4. Gynoecium 2-16 carpellary; fruit capsule.

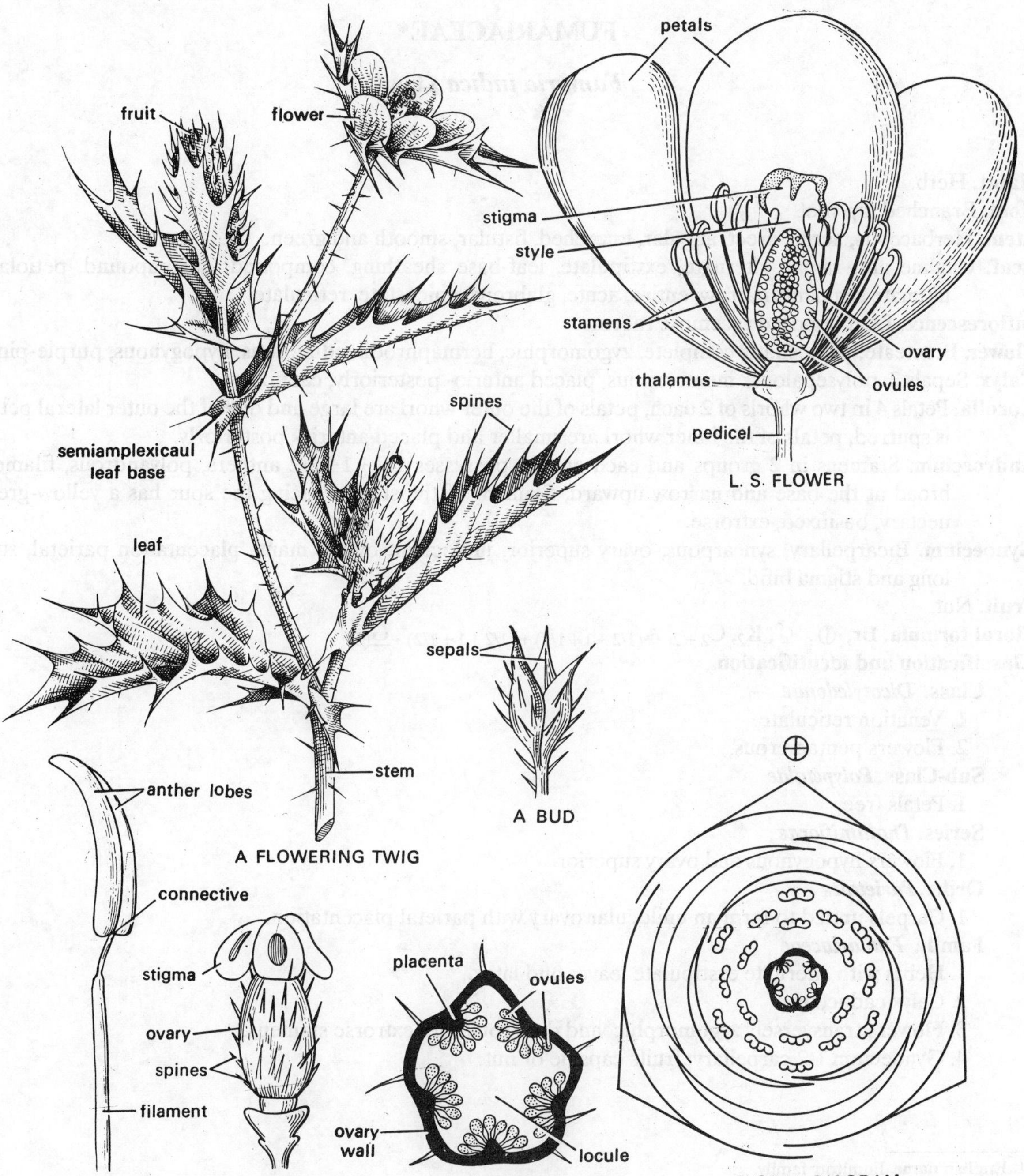

Fig. 6. ***Argemone mexicana.***

---

1. **English names.** Mexican prickly poppy, Mexican thistle.
2. **Vernacular names.** Peeli Kataili, Bharbhanda, Shailkanta.
3. **Economic importance.** The seeds yield an oil which is illuminant and lubricant, often used as an adulterant to mustard oil. The toxic properties of oil are harmful to man. In U.P. the plant is being used to reclaim 'usar' land.

FUMARIACEAE*

Fumaria indica Linn.

Habit. Herb.

Root. Branched tap root.

Stem. Herbaceous, aerial, erect, angular, branched, fistular, smooth and green.

Leaf. Cauline and ramal, alternate, exstipulate, leaf-base sheathing, compound, decompound, petiolate, ultimate segments narrow, entire, acute, glabrous, unicostate, reticulate.

Inflorescence. Leaf opposed racemose raceme.

Flower. Bracteate, pedicellate, complete, zygomorphic, hermaphrodite, dimerous, hypogynous, purple-pink.

Calyx. Sepals 2, polysepalous, membranous, placed anterio- posteriorly, caducous.

Corolla. Petals 4 in two whorls of 2 each, petals of the outer whorl are large and one of the outer lateral petals is spurred, petals of the inner whorl are smaller and placed anterio- posteriorly.

Androecium. Stamens in 2 groups and each groups possesses 1/2 + 1 + 1/2 anthers, polyandrous, filament broad at the base and narrow upward, filament of the stamen facing the spur has a yellow-green nectary, basifixed, extrorse.

Gynoecium. Bicarpellary, syncarpous, ovary superior, unilocular, ovules many, placentation parietal, style long and stigma bifid.

Fruit. Nut.

Floral formula. Br, ⦶, ⚥, K_2, C_{2+2}, $A_{(1/2+1+1/2)+(1/2+1+1/2)}$, $\underline{G}_{(2)}$.

Classification and identification.

Class. ***Dicotyledonae***

1. Venation reticulate.
2. Flowers pentamerous.

Sub-Class. ***Polypetalae***

1. Petals free.

Series. ***Thalamiflorae***

1. Flowers hypogynous and ovary superior.

Order. ***Parietales***

1. Carpels united to form an unilocular ovary with parietal placentation.

Family. ***Fumariaceae***

1. Hebrs with alternate exstipulate leaves and latex.
2. Calyx caducous.
3. Flowers transversely zygomorphic and dimerous with extrorse stamens.
4. Gynoecium 1-2 carpellary; fruits capsule or nut.

***1. English name.** Fumitory family.

2. Systematic position in other systems of classification.

Rendle (1925)	**Engler and Prantl (1931)**	**Hutchinson (1959)**
Dicotyledons	Dicotyledoneae	Dicotyledons
Dialypetalae	Archichlamydeae	Herbaceae
Rhoeadales	Rhoeadales	Rhoeadales
Papaveraceae	Papaveraceae	Fumariaceae
Fumarioideae (Sub. Fam.)	Fumarioideae (Sub. Fam.)	

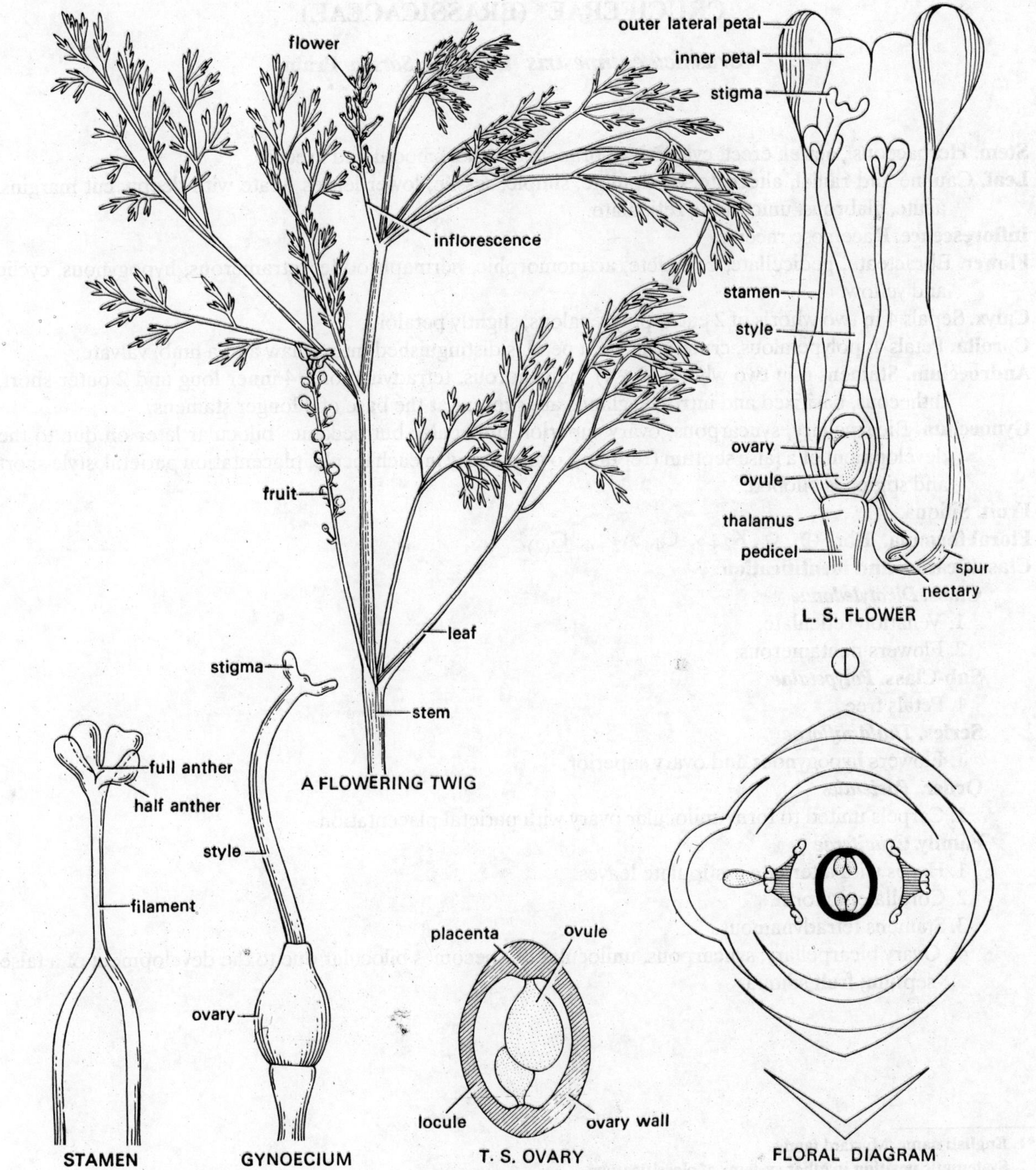

Fig. 7. ***Fumaria indica.***

---

1. Vernacular name. Pit-papara.

2. Economic importance. The dried plant is used as an anthelmintic, diuretic and diaphoretic.

CRUCIFERAE* (BRASSICACEAE)

Brassica campestris Linn. Var. *Sarson* Prain

Stem. Herbaceous , aerial, erect, cylindrical, branched, solid, smooth and green.

Leaf. Cauline and ramal, alternate, exstipulate, simple, sessile, lower leaves lyrate with deeply cut margins, acute, glabrous, unicostate, reticulate.

Inflorescence. Racemose raceme.

Flower. Ebracteate, pedicellate, complete, actinomorphic, hermaphrodite, tetramerous, hypogynous, cyclic and yellow.

Calyx. Sepals 4 in two whorls of 2 each, polysepalous, slightly petaloid.

Corolla. Petals 4, polypetalous, cruciform, each petal is distinguished into a claw and a limb, valvate.

Androecium. Stamens 6 in two whorls (2 + 4), polyandrous, tetradynamous, 4 inner long and 2 outer short, dithecous, basifixed and introrse, glands are present at the base of 4 longer stamens.

Gynoecium. Bicarpellary, syncarpous, ovary superior, unilocular but becomes bilocular later on due to the development of a false septum (replum), ovules many in each locule, placentation parietal, style short and stigma is bilobed.

Fruit. Siliqua.

Floral formula. Ebr, $\oplus$, ⚥, K_{2+2}, C_4, A_{2+4}, $\underline{G}_{(2)}$.

Classification and identification.

Class. ***Dicotyledonae***

1. Venation reticulate.
2. Flowers pentamerous.

Sub-Class. ***Polypetalae***

1. Petals free.

Series. ***Thalamiflorae***

1. Flowers hypogynous and ovary superior.

Order. ***Parietales***

1. Carpels united to form unilocular ovary with parietal placentation.

Family. ***Cruciferae***

1. Herbs with alternate exstipulate leaves.
2. Corolla cruciform.
3. Stamens tetradynamous.
4. Ovary bicarpellary, syncarpous, unilocular but becomes bilocular due to the development of a false septum; fruit siliqua.

***1. English name.** Mustard family.

2. Systematic position in other systems of classification.

Rendle (1925)	**Engler and Prantl (1931)**	**Hutchinson (1959)**
Dicotyledons	Dicotyledoneae	Dicotyledons
Dialypetalae	Archichlamydeae	Herbaceae
Rhoeadales	Rhoeadales	Cruciales
Cruciferae	Cruciferae	Cruciferae

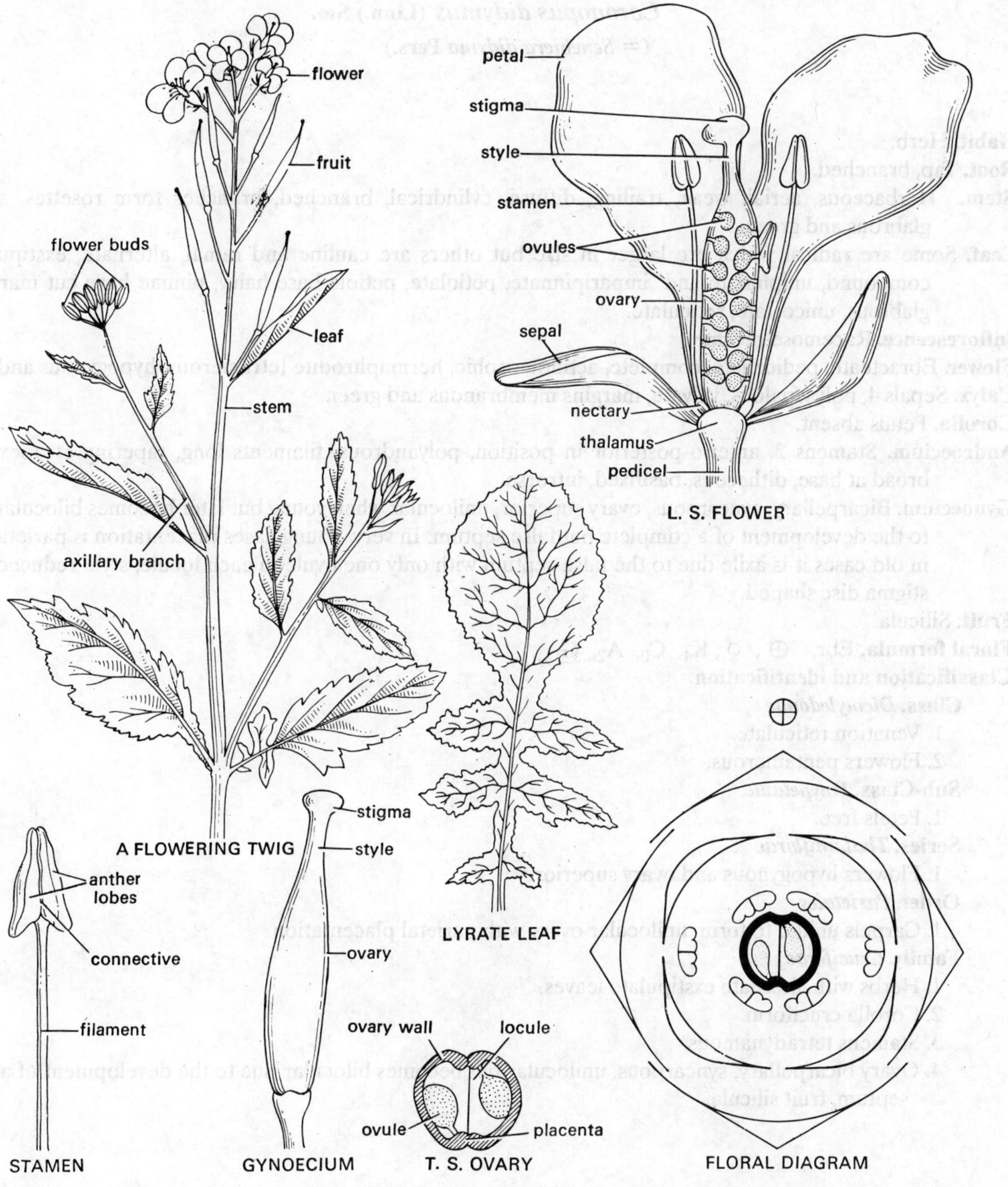

Fig. 8. ***Brassica campestris.***

---

1. **English name.** Indian Colza, Yellow mustard.
2. **Vernacular name.** Sarson.
3. **Economic importance.** The seeds yield an oil used for cooking and anointing the body. The oil cake is a good cattle feed. The tender leaves and shoots are used as vegetable.

Coronopus didymus (Linn.) Sm.

(= *Senebiera didyma* Pers.)

Habit. Herb.

Root. Tap, branched.

Stem. Herbaceous, aerial, weak, trailing, diffuse, cylindrical, branched, branches form rosettes, solid, glabrous and green.

Leaf. Some are radical which are larger in size but others are cauline and ramal, alternate, exstipulate, compound, unipinnate and imparipinnate, petiolate, petiole base hairy, pinnae have cut margins, glabrous, unicostate, reticulate.

Inflorescence. Racemose raceme.

Flower. Ebracteate, pedicellate, complete, actinomorphic, hermaphrodite tetramerous, hypogynous and cyclic.

Calyx. Sepals 4, polysepalous, valvate, margins membranous and green.

Corolla. Petals absent.

Androecium. Stamens 2, anterio-posterior in position, polyandrous, filaments long, tapering at apex and broad at base, dithecous, basifixed, introrse.

Gynoecium. Bicarpellary, syncarpous, ovary superior, unilocular when young but later becomes bilocular due to the development of a complete but false septum. In very young cases placentation is parietal but in old cases it is axile due to the false septum with only one ovule in each locule, style reduced and stigma disc shaped.

Fruit. Silicula.

Floral formula. Ebr, ⊕, ⚥, K_4, C_0, A_2, $\underline{G}_{(2)}$.

Classification and identification.

Class. ***Dicotyledonae***

1. Venation reticulate.
2. Flowers pentamerous.

Sub-Class. ***Polypetalae***

1. Petals free.

Series. ***Thalamiflorae***

1. Flowers hypogynous and ovary superior.

Order. ***Parietales***

1. Carpels united to form unilocular ovary with parietal placentation.

Family. ***Cruciferae***

1. Herbs with alternate exstipulate leaves.
2. Corolla cruciform.
3. Stamens tetradynamous.
4. Ovary bicarpellary, syncarpous, unilocular but becomes bilocular due to the development of a false septum, fruit silicula.

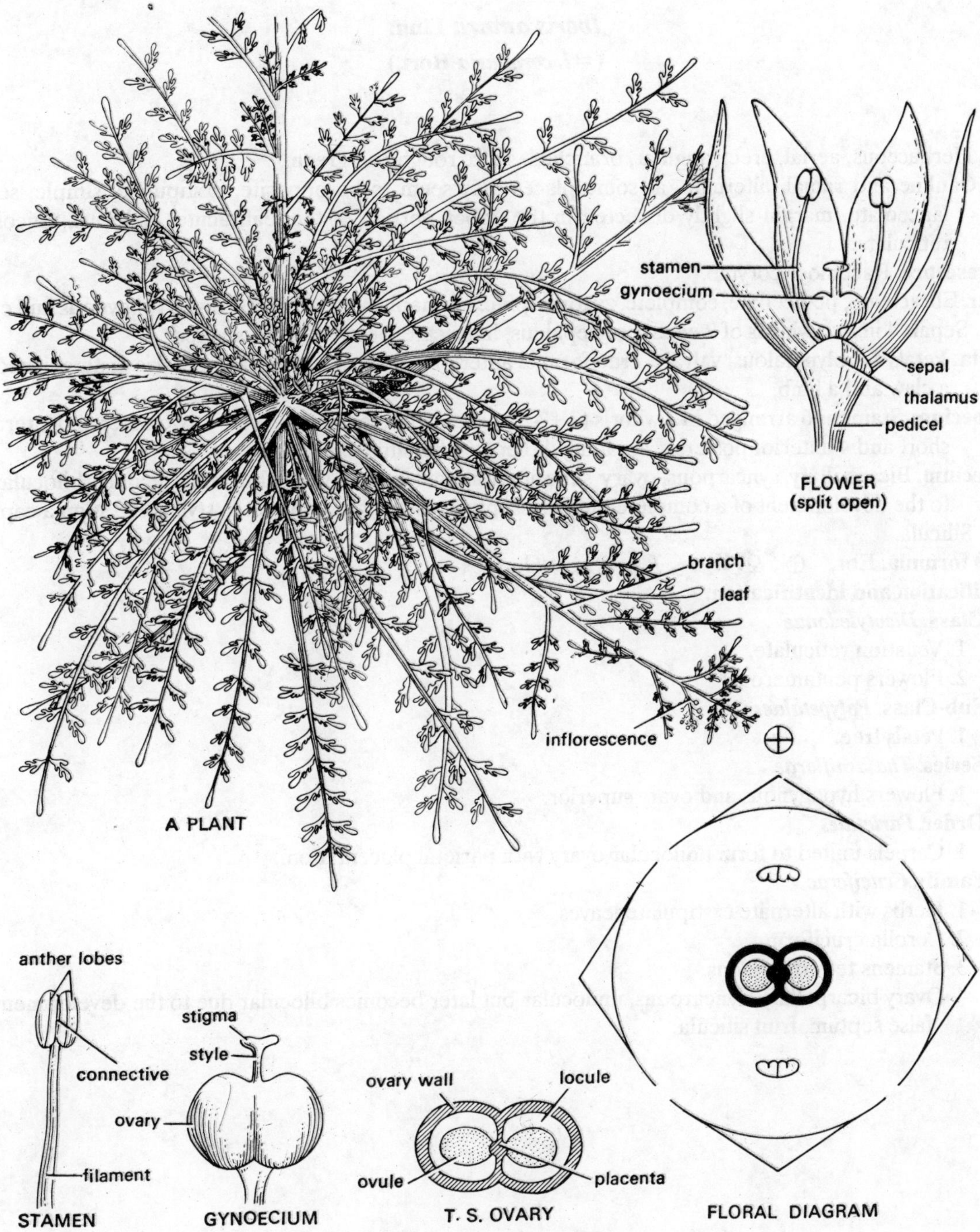

Fig. 9. ***Coronopus didymus.***

1. English name. Lesser wart-cress.

Iberis amara Linn.
(=*I. coronaria* Hort.)

Stem. Herbaceous, aerial, erect, angular, branched, solid, rough and green.

Leaf. Cauline and ramal, alternate, at some places they seem to be opposite, exstipulate, simple, sessile, lanceolate, margin slightly dissected in the upper portion of the leaf, acute, glabrous, unicostate, reticulate.

Inflorescence. Racemose corymb.

Flower. Ebracteate, pedicellate, complete, zygomorphic, hermaphrodite, tetramerous, hypogynous and cyclic.

Calyx. Sepals 4 in two whorls of 2 each, polysepalous, imbricate, petaloid, boat-shaped.

Corolla. Petals 4, polypetalous, valvate, cruciform, 2 anterior petals are large, each petal is distinguished into a claw and a limb.

Androecium. Stamens 6 arranged in 2 whorls (2+4), polyandrous, tetradynamous – two outer and lateral are short and 4 anterio- posterior are long, dithecous, dorsifixed, introrse.

Gynoecium. Bicarpellary, syncarpous, ovary superior, unilocular when young but later becomes bilocular due to the development of a complete but false septum, placentation parietal, style long, stigma capitate.

Fruit. Silicula.

Floral formula. Ebr, ⦶, ⚥, K_{2+2}, C_4, A_{2+4}, $\underline{G}_{(2)}$.

Classification and identification.

Class. ***Dicotyledonae***
1. Venation reticulate.
2. Flowers pentamerous.

Sub-Class. ***Polypetalae***
1. Petals free.

Series. ***Thalamiflorae***
1. Flowers hypogynous and ovary superior.

Order. ***Parietales***
1. Carpels united to form unilocular ovary with parietal placentation.

Family. ***Cruciferae***
1. Herbs with alternate exstipulate leaves.
2. Corolla cruciform.
3. Stamens tetradynamous.
4. Ovary bicarpellary, syncarpous, unilocular but later becomes bilocular due to the development of a false septum, fruit silicula.

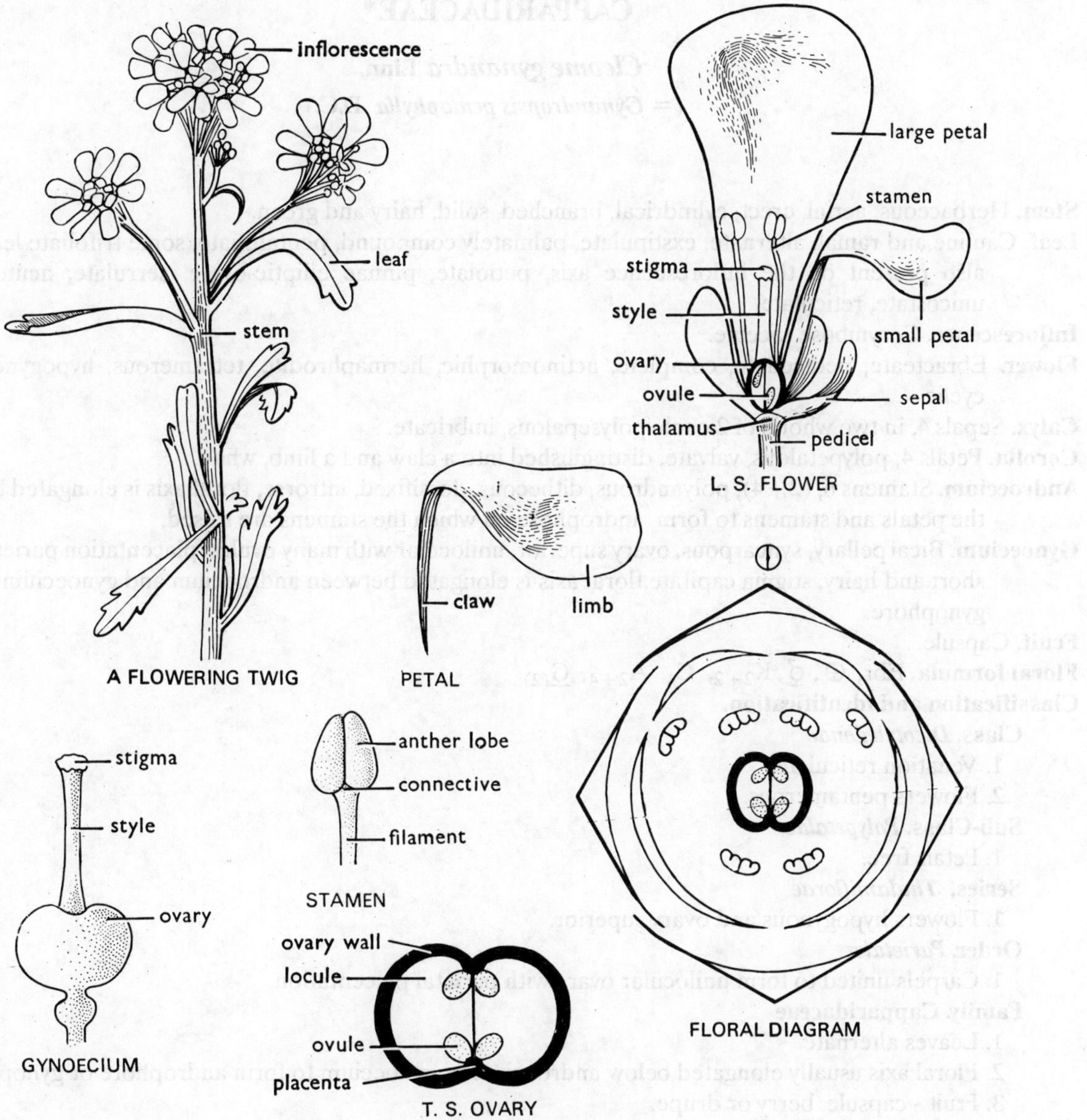

Fig. 10. ***Iberis amara.***

---

1. English name. Rocket Candytuft.

2. Economic importance. Cultivated as an ornamental.

CAPPARIDACEAE*

Cleome gynandra Linn.

(= *Gynandropsis pentaphylla* D.C.)

Stem. Herbaceous, aerial, erect, cylindrical, branched, solid, hairy and green.

Leaf. Cauline and ramal, alternate, exstipulate, palmately compound, pentafoliate, some trifoliate leaves are also present on the inflorescence axis, petiolate, pinnae elliptic-ovate, serrulate, acute, hairy, unicostate, reticulate.

Inflorescence. Corymbose raceme.

Flower. Ebracteate, pedicellate, complete, actinomorphic, hermaphrodite, tetramerous, hypogynous and cyclic.

Calyx. Sepals 4, in two whorls of 2 each, polysepalous, imbricate.

Corolla. Petals 4, polypetalous, valvate, distinguished into a claw and a limb, white.

Androecium. Stamens 6, (2+4), polyandrous, dithecous, dorsifixed, introrse, floral axis is elongated between the petals and stamens to form androphore on which the stamens are raised.

Gynoecium. Bicarpellary, syncarpous, ovary superior, unilocular with many ovules, placentation parietal, style short and hairy, stigma capitate,floral axis is elongated between androecium and gynoecium to form gynophore.

Fruit. Capsule.

Floral formula. Ebr, ⊕, ⚥, K_{2+2}, C_4, A_{2+4}, $\underline{G}_{(2)}$.

Classification and identification.

Class. ***Dicotyledonae***

1. Venation reticulate.
2. Flowers pentamerous.

Sub-Class. ***Polypetalae***

1. Petals free.

Series. ***Thalamiflorae***

1. Flowers hypogynous and ovary superior.

Order. ***Parietales***

1. Carpels united to form unilocular ovary with parietal placentation.

Family. Capparidaceae

1. Leaves alternate.
2. Floral axis usually elongated below androecium or gynoecium to form androphore or gynophore.
3. Fruit - capsule, berry or drupe.

***1. English name.** Caper family.

2. Systematic position in other systems of classification.

Rendle (1925)	**Engler and Prantl (1931)**	**Hutchinson (1959)**
Dicotyledons	Dicotyledoneae	Dicotyledons
Dialypetalae	Archichlamydeae	Lignosae
Rhoeadales	Rhoeadales	Capparidales
Capparidaceae	Capparidaceae	Capparidaceae

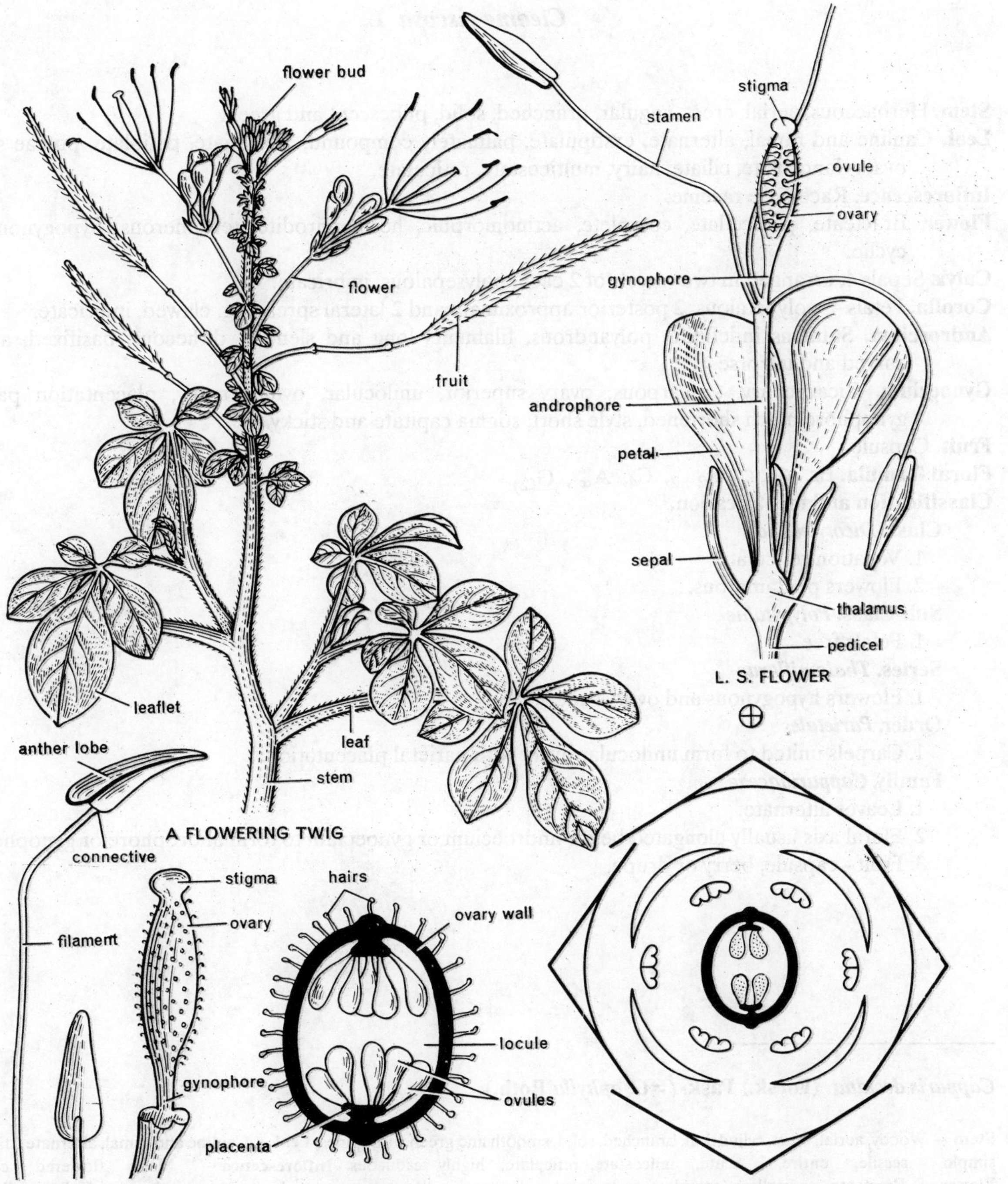

Fig. 11. ***Cleome gynandra*** (= *Gynandropsis pentaphylla*).

---

1. Vernacular name. Hul-hul.

2. Economic importance. The leaves are used in rheumatism. The plant is also used as an antidote to snake bite and scorpion sting.

Cleome viscosa L.

Stem. Herbaceous, aerial, erect, angular, branched, solid, pubescent and green.
Leaf. Cauline and ramal, alternate, exstipulate, palmately compound, 3-5 foliate, petiolate, pinnae sessile, ovate- lanceolate, ciliate, hairy, multicostate, reticulate.
Inflorescence. Racemose raceme.
Flower. Bracteate, pedicellate, complete, actinomorphic, hermaphrodite, tetramerous, hypogynous and cyclic.
Calyx. Sepals 4, arranged in two whorls of 2 each, polysepalous, imbricate.
Corolla. Petals 4, polypetalous, 2 posterior approximate and 2 lateral spreading, clawed, imbricate.
Androecium. Stamens indefinite, polyandrous, filaments long and slender, dithecous, basifixed, anthers curved and introrse.
Gynoecium. Bicarpellary, syncarpous, ovary superior, unilocular, ovules many, placentation parietal, gynophore much shortened, style short, stigma capitate and sticky.
Fruit. Capsule.
Floral formula. Br, $\oplus$, ⚥, K_{2+2}, C_4, A_∞, $\underline{G}_{(2)}$.
Classification and identification.

Class. ***Dicotyledonae***
1. Venation reticulate.
2. Flowers pentamerous.

Sub-Class. ***Polypetalae***
1. Petals free.

Series. ***Thalamiflorae***
1. Flowers hypogynous and ovary superior.

Order. ***Parietales***
1. Carpels united to form unilocular ovary with parietal placentation.

Family. ***Capparidaceae***
1. Leaves alternate.
2. Floral axis usually elongated below androecium or gynoecium to form androphore or gynophore.
3. Fruit - capsule, berry or drupe.

Capparis decidua (Forsk.) Pask. (=*C. aphylla* Roth.).

Stem – Woody, aerial, erect, cylindrical, branched, solid, smooth and green with spines; **Leaf** – Cauline and ramal, alternate, stipulate, simple, sessile, entire, acute, unicostate, reticulate, highly caducous: **Inflorescence** – Many flowered corymb; **Flower** – Bracteate, pedicellate, complete, zygomorphic, hermaphrodite, tetramerous, hypogynous and cyclic; **Calyx** – Sepals 4 arranged in two whorls of two each, inner sepal saccate, imbricate; **Corolla** – Petals 4, polypetalous, imbricate, scarlet; **Androecium** – Stamens indefinite, polyandrous, present at the base of the gynophore, filaments long, dithecous, dorsifixed, introrse; **Gynoecium** – Bicarpellary, syncarpous, ovary superior, unilocular, placentation parietal, style and stigma simple, a long gynophore present; **Fruit** – Berry;

Floral formula – Br, $\oplus$, ⚥, K_{2+2}, C_4, A_∞, $\underline{G}_{(2)}$.

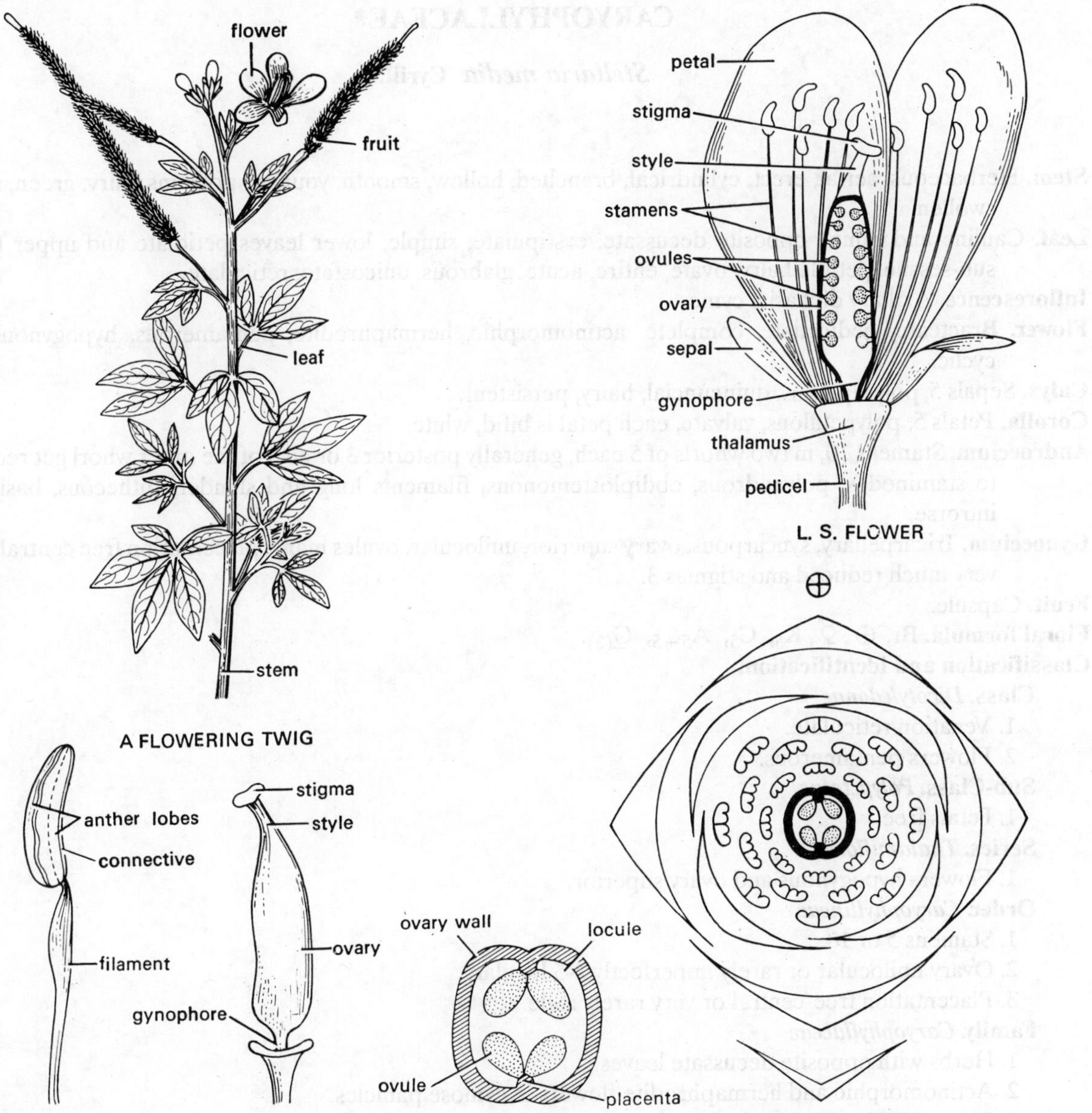

Fig. 12. ***Cleome viscosa.***

---

1. **English name.** Sticky cleome.
2. **Vernacular names.** Hurhur, Arkakanta.
3. **Economic importance.** Seeds are used as carminative and are also used in curries.

CARYOPHYLLACEAE*

Stellaria media Cyrill.

Stem. Herbaceous, aerial, erect, cylindrical, branched, hollow, smooth, younger portions hairy, green, nodes swollen.

Leaf. Cauline and ramal, opposite decussate, exstipulate, simple, lower leaves petiolate and upper leaves sub-sessile, petiole hairy, ovate, entire, acute, glabrous, unicostate, reticulate.

Inflorescence. Axillary dichasial cyme.

Flower. Bracteate, pedicellate, complete, actinomorphic, hermaphrodite, pentamerous, hypogynous and cyclic.

Calyx. Sepals 5, polysepalous, quincuncial, hairy, persistent.

Corolla. Petals 5, polypetalous, valvate, each petal is bifid, white.

Androecium. Stamens 10, in two whorls of 5 each, generally posterior 3 or all 5 of the outer whorl get reduced to staminodes, polyandrous, obdiplostemonous, filaments long and slender, dithecous, basifixed, introrse.

Gynoecium. Tricarpellary, syncarpous, ovary superior, unilocular, ovules many, placentation free central, style very much reduced and stigmas 3.

Fruit. Capsule.

Floral formula. Br, $\oplus$, ⚥, K_5, C_5, A_{5+5}, $\underline{G}_{(3)}$.

Classification and identification.

Class. ***Dicotyledonae***

1. Venation reticulate.
2. Flowers pentamerous.

Sub-Class. ***Polypetalae***

1. Petals free.

Series. ***Thalamiflorae***

1. Flowers hypogynous and ovary superior.

Order. ***Caryophyllineae***

1. Stamens 5 or 10.
2. Ovary unilocular or rarely imperfectly 2-5 locular.
3. Placentation free-central or very rarely axile.

Family. ***Caryophyllaceae***

1. Herbs with opposite decussate leaves.
2. Actinomorphic and hermaphrodite flowers in cymose panicles.
3. Ovary 2-5 carpellary, syncarpous, unilocular with free- central placentation.
4. Fruit - capsule or berry.

***1. English name.** Pink family.

2. Systematic position in other systems of classification.

Rendle (1925)	Engler and Prantl (1931)	Hutchinson (1959)
Dicotyledons	Dicotyledoneae	Dicotyledons
Monochlamydeae	Archichlamydeae	Herbaceae
Centrospermae	Centrospermae	Caryophyllales
Caryophyllaceae	Caryophyllaceae	Caryophyllaceae

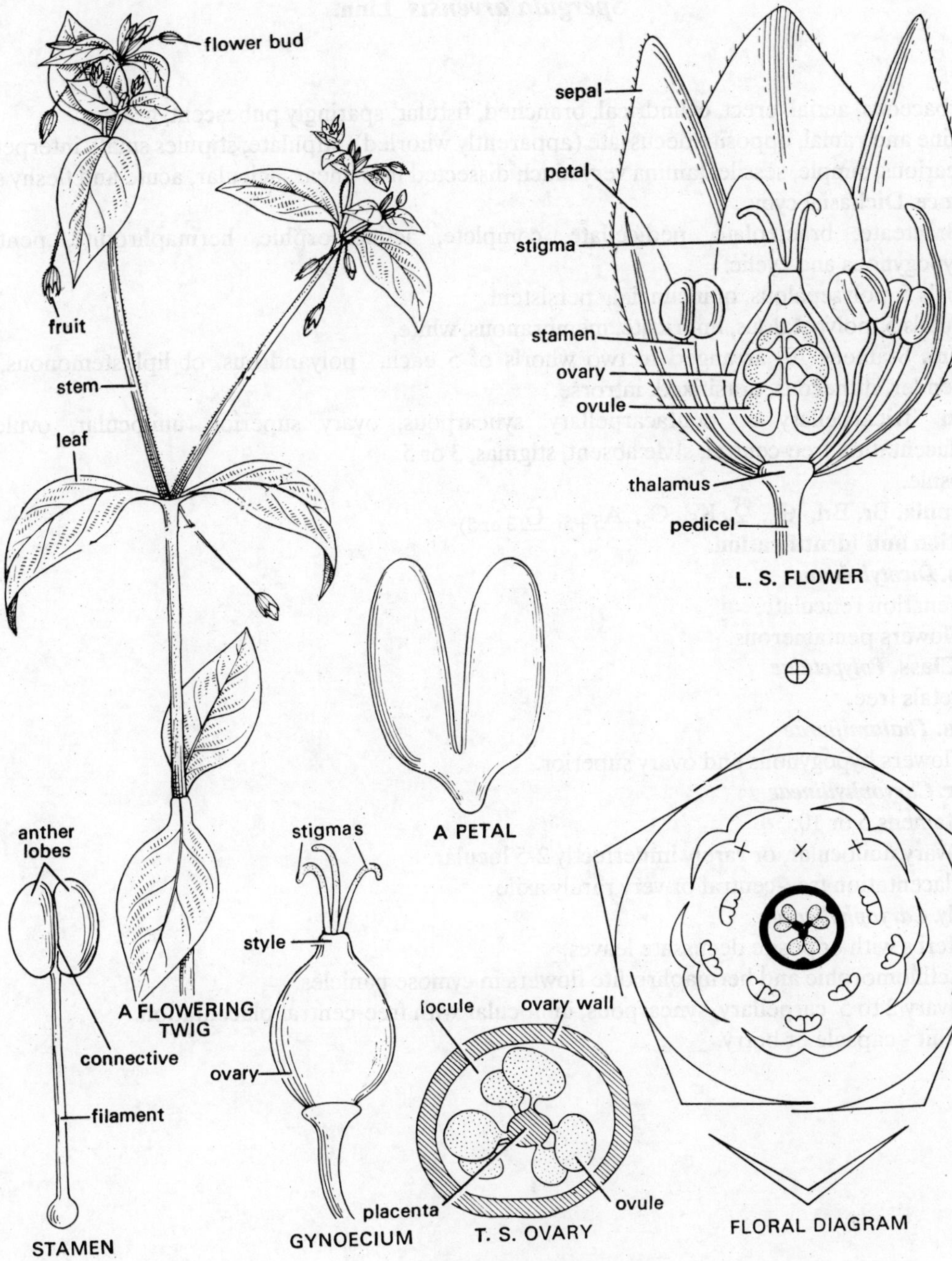

Fig. 13. ***Stellaria media.***

---

1. English name. Common chickweed.

Spergula arvensis Linn.

Stem. Herbaceous, aerial, erect, cylindrical, branched, fistular, sparingly pubescent, green.

Leaf. Cauline and ramal, opposite decussate (apparently whorled), stipulate, stipules small, interpetiolar and scarious, simple, sessile, lamina very much dissected into linear, acicular, acute and fleshy segments.

Inflorescence. Dichasial cyme.

Flower. Bracteate, bracteolate, pedicellate, complete, actinomorphic, hermaphrodite, pentamerous, hypogynous and cyclic.

Calyx. Sepals 5, polysepalous, quincuncial, persistent.

Corolla. Petals 5, polypetalous, imbricate, membranous, white.

Androecium. Stamens 10, arranged in two whorls of 5 each, polyandrous, obdiplostemonous, filament slender, dithecous, dorsifixed, introrse.

Gynoecium. Tricarpellary or pentacarpellary, syncarpous, ovary superior, unilocular, ovules many, placentation free-central, stvle absent, stigmas, 3 or 5.

Fruit. Capsule.

Floral formula. Br, Brl, ⊕, ⚥, K_5, C_5, A_{5+5}, $\underline{G}_{(3 \text{ or } 5)}$.

Classification and identification.

Class. ***Dicotyledonae***

1. Venation reticulate.
2. Flowers pentamerous.

Sub-Class. ***Polypetalae***

1. Petals free.

Series. ***Thalamiflorae***

1. Flowers hypogynous and ovary superior.

Order. ***Caryophyllineae***

1. Stamens 5 or 10.
2. Ovary unilocular, or rarely imperfectly 2-5 locular.
3. Placentation free-central or very rarely axile.

Family. ***Caryophyllaceae***

1. Herbs with opposite decussate leaves.
2. Actinomorphic and hermaphrodite flowers in cymose panicles.
3. Ovary 2 to 5 carpellary, syncarpous, unilocular with free-central placentation.
4. Fruit - capsule or berry.

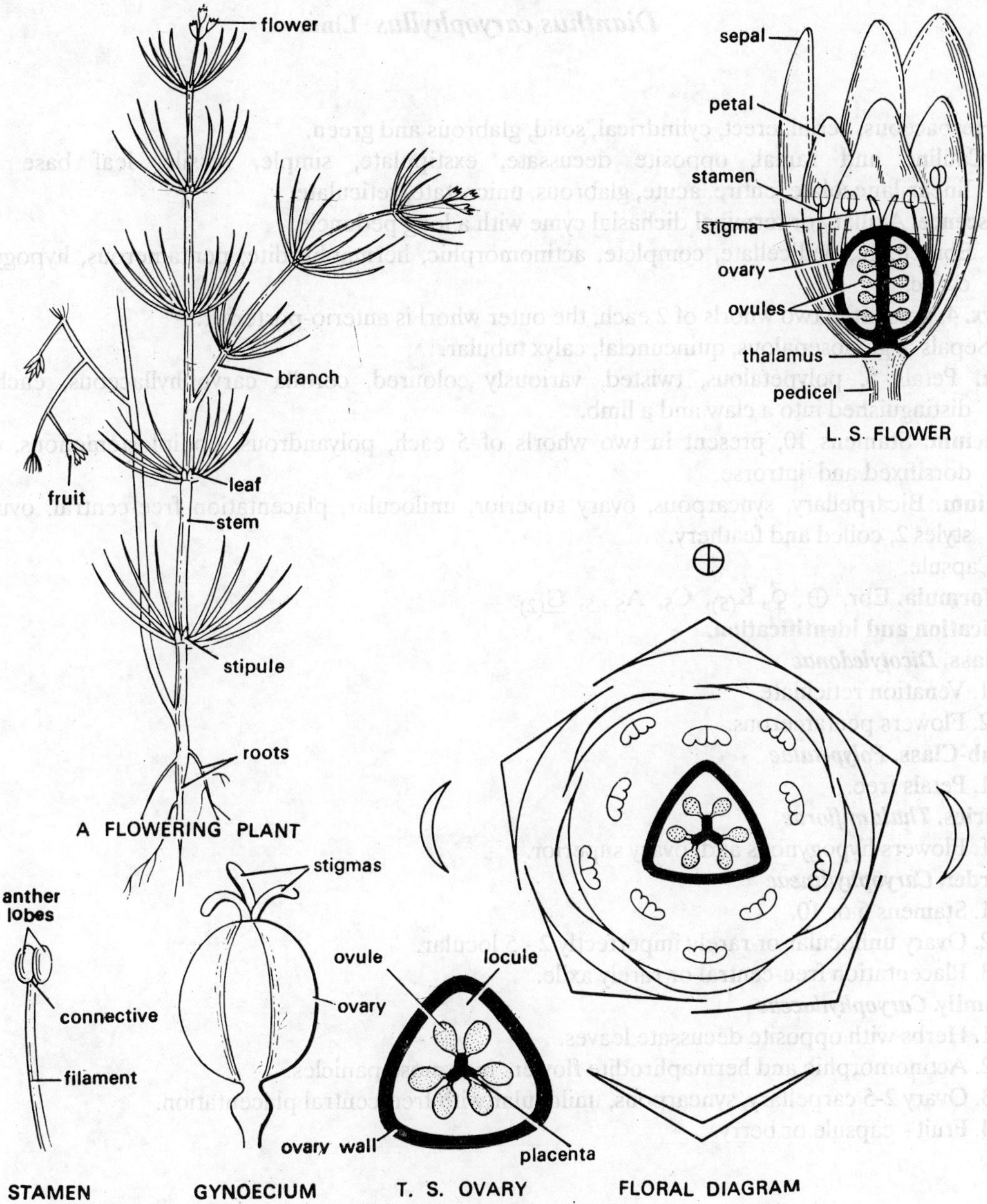

Fig. 14. ***Spergula arvensis.***

1. **English name.** Corn spurrey.
2. **Economic importance.** It is grown in Europe as a fodder plant. In Columbia it is used as a diuretic.

Dianthus caryophyllus Linn.

Stem. Herbaceous, aerial, erect, cylindrical, solid, glabrous and green.

Leaf. Cauline and ramal, opposite decussate, exstipulate, simple, sessile, leaf base sheathing, linear-lanceolate, entire, acute, glabrous, unicostate, reticulate.

Inflorescence. Axillary or terminal dichasial cyme with a long peduncle.

Flower. Ebracteate, pedicellate, complete, actinomorphic, hermaphrodite, pentamerous, hypogynous and cyclic.

Epicalyx. 4, present in two whorls of 2 each, the outer whorl is anterio-posterior.

Calyx. Sepals 5, gamosepalous, quincuncial, calyx tubular.

Corolla. Petals 5, polypetalous, twisted, variously coloured, corolla caryophyllaceous, each petal is distinguished into a claw and a limb.

Androecium. Stamens 10, present in two whorls of 5 each, polyandrous, obdiplostemonous, dithecous, dorsifixed and introrse.

Gynoecium. Bicarpellary, syncarpous, ovary superior, unilocular, placentation free-central, ovules many, styles 2, coiled and feathery.

Fruit. Capsule.

Floral formula. Ebr, ⊕, ⚥, $K_{(5)}$, C_5, A_{5+5}, $\underline{G}_{(2)}$.

Classification and identification.

Class. ***Dicotyledonae***

1. Venation reticulate.
2. Flowers pentamerous.

Sub-Class. ***Polypetalae***

1. Petals free.

Series. ***Thalamiflorae***

1. Flowers hypogynous and ovary superior.

Order. ***Caryophyllineae***

1. Stamens 5 or 10.
2. Ovary unilocular or rarely imperfectly 2 - 5 locular.
3. Placentation free-central or rarely axile.

Family. ***Caryophyllaceae***

1. Herbs with opposite decussate leaves.
2. Actinomorphic and hermaphrodite flowers in cymose panicles.
3. Ovary 2-5 carpellary, syncarpous, unilocular with free-central placentation.
4. Fruit - capsule or berry.

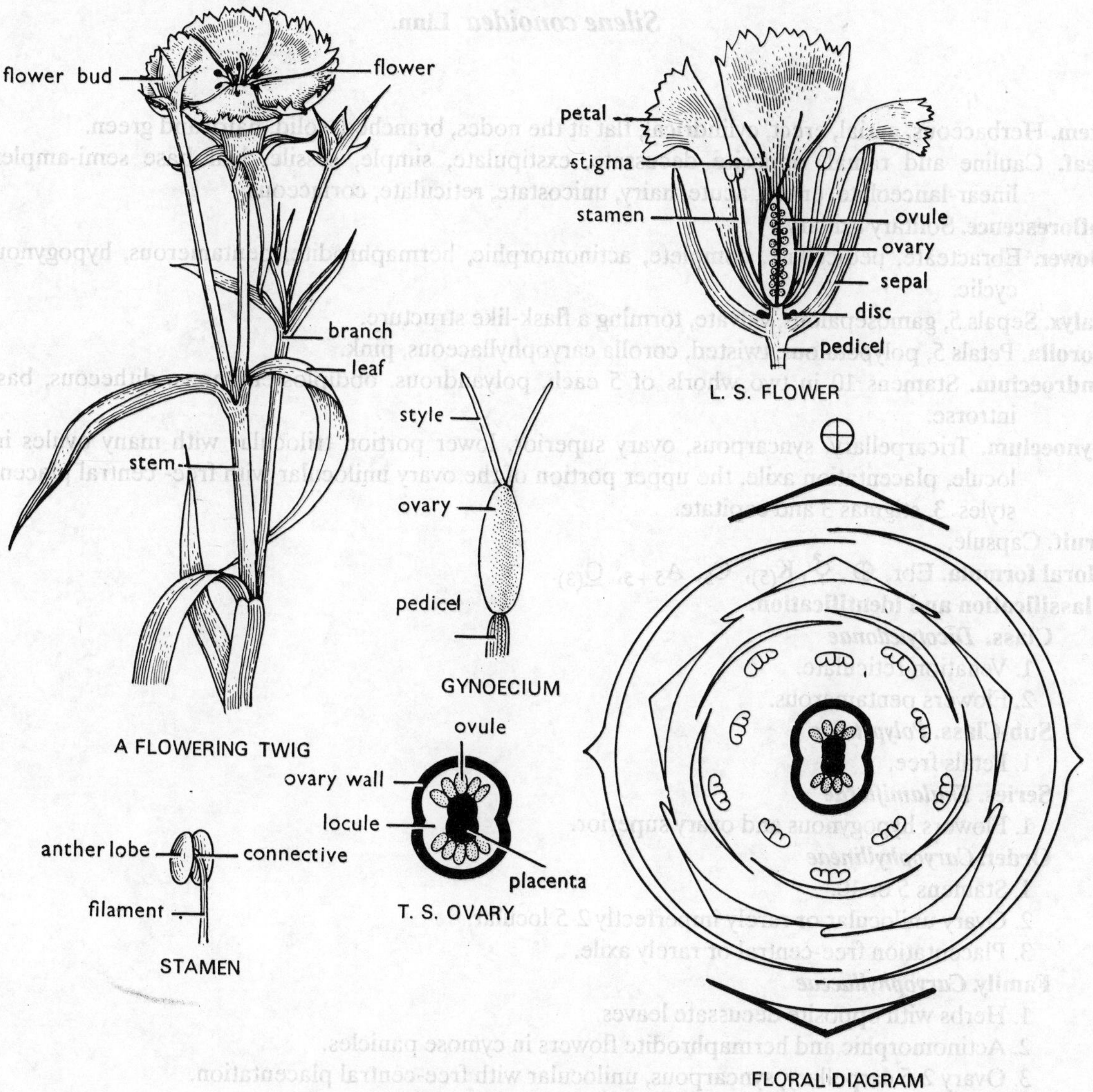

Fig. 15. ***Dianthus caryophyllus.***

1. **English name.** Carnation.
2. **Economic importance.** Grown as an ornamental.

Silene conoidea Linn.

Stem. Herbaceous, aerial, erect, cylindrical, flat at the nodes, branched, solid, hairy and green.

Leaf. Cauline and ramal, opposite decussate, exstipulate, simple, sessile, leaf base semi-amplexicaul, linear-lanceolate, entire, acute, hairy, unicostate, reticulate, coriaceous.

Inflorescence. Solitary axillary.

Flower. Ebracteate, pedicellate, complete, actinomorphic, hermaphrodite, pentamerous, hypogynous and cyclic.

Calyx. Sepals 5, gamosepalous, valvate, forming a flask-like structure.

Corolla. Petals 5, polypetalous, twisted, corolla caryophyllaceous, pink.

Androecium. Stamens 10 in two whorls of 5 each, polyandrous, obdiplostemonous, dithecous, basifixed, introrse.

Gynoecium. Tricarpellary, syncarpous, ovary superior, lower portion trilocular with many ovules in each locule, placentation axile, the upper portion of the ovary unilocular with free- central placentation, styles 3, stigmas 3 and capitate.

Fruit. Capsule.

Floral formula. Ebr, $\oplus$, ⚥, $K_{(5)}$, C_5, A_{5+5}, $\underline{G}_{(3)}$.

Classification and identification.

Class. ***Dicotyledonae***

1. Venation reticulate.
2. Flowers pentamerous.

Sub-Class. ***Polypetalae***

1. Petals free.

Series. ***Thalamiflorae***

1. Flowers hypogynous and ovary superior.

Order. ***Caryophyllineae***

1. Stamens 5 or 10.
2. Ovary unilocular or rarely imperfectly 2-5 locular.
3. Placentation free-central or rarely axile.

Family. ***Caryophyllaceae***

1. Herbs with opposite decussate leaves.
2. Actinomorphic and hermaphrodite flowers in cymose panicles.
3. Ovary 2-5 carpellary, syncarpous, unilocular with free-central placentation.
4. Fruit - capsule or berry.

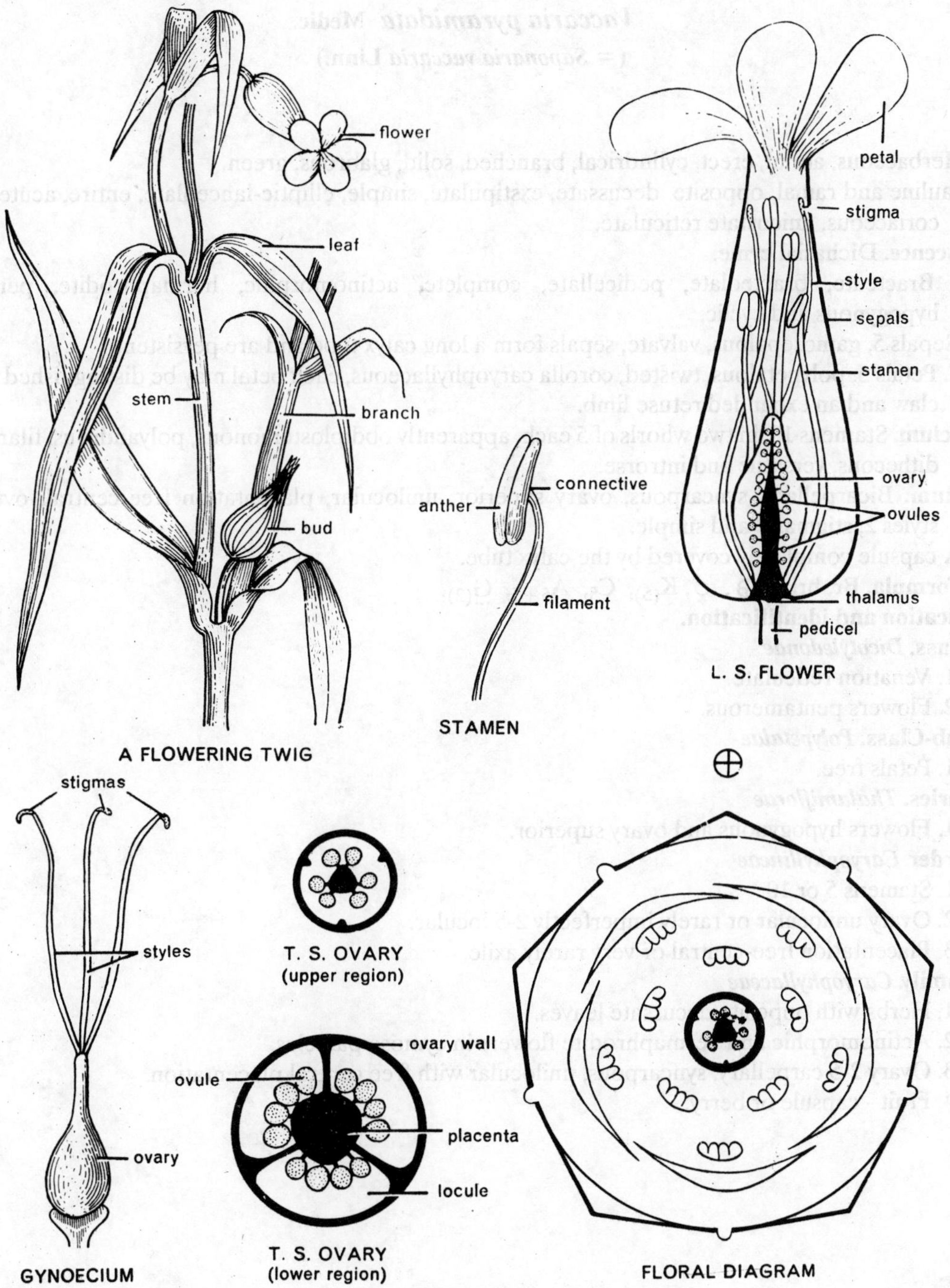

Fig. 16. ***Silene conoidea.***

---

1. Economic importance. The plant is used for fomentation.

Vaccaria pyramidata Medic.
(= *Saponaria vaccaria* Linn.)

Stem. Herbaceous, aerial, erect, cylindrical, branched, solid, glabrous, green.

Leaf. Cauline and ramal, opposite decussate, exstipulate, simple, elliptic-lanceolate, entire, acute, glabrous, coriaceous, unicostate reticulate.

Inflorescence. Dichasial cyme.

Flower. Bracteate, bracteolate, pedicellate, complete, actinomorphic, hermaphrodite, pentamerous, hypogynous and cyclic.

Calyx. Sepals 5, gamosepalous, valvate, sepals form a long calyx tube and are persistent.

Corolla. Petals 5, polypetalous, twisted, corolla caryophyllaceous, each petal may be distinguished into a long claw and an expanded retuse limb.

Androecium. Stamens 10, in two whorls of 5 each, apparently obdiplostemonous, polyandrous, filaments long, dithecous, versatile and introrse.

Gynoecium. Bicarpellary, syncarpous, ovary superior, unilocular, placentation free-central, ovules many, styles 2, stigmas 2 and simple.

Fruit. A capsule completely covered by the calyx tube.

Floral formula. Br, brl, ⊕, ⚥, $K_{(5)}$, C_5, A_{5+5}, $\underline{G}_{(2)}$.

Classification and identification.

Class. ***Dicotyledonae***

1. Venation reticulate.
2. Flowers pentamerous.

Sub-Class. ***Polypetalae***

1. Petals free.

Series. ***Thalamiflorae***

1. Flowers hypogynous and ovary superior.

Order. ***Caryophyllineae***

1. Stamens 5 or 10.
2. Ovary unilocular or rarely imperfectly 2-5 locular.
3. Placentation free-central or very rarely axile.

Family. ***Caryophyllaceae***

1. Herbs with opposite decussate leaves.
2. Actinomorphic and hermaphrodite flowers in cymose panicles.
3. Ovary 2-5 carpellary, syncarpous, unilocular with free central placentation.
4. Fruit - capsule or berry.

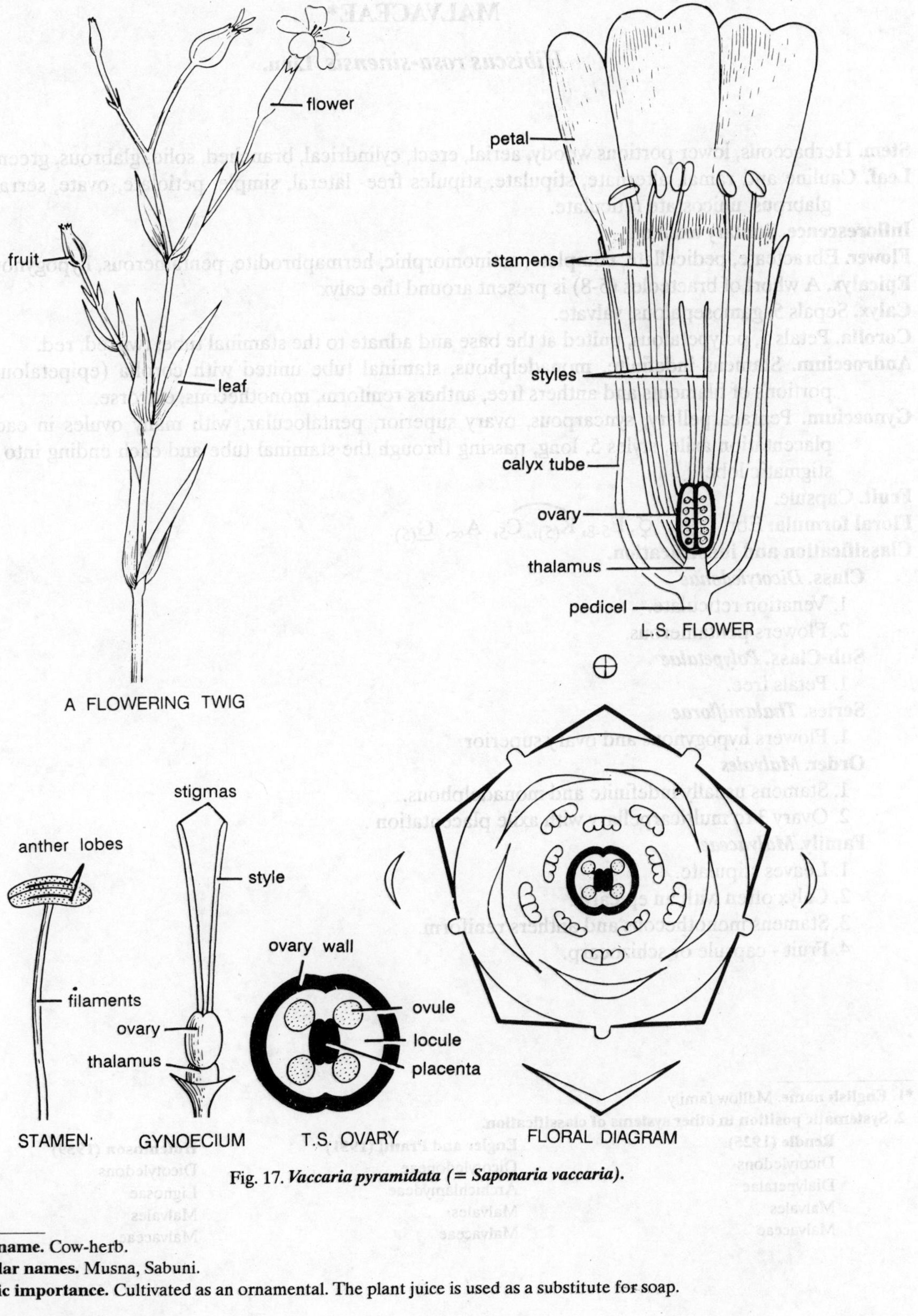

Fig. 17. ***Vaccaria pyramidata* (= *Saponaria vaccaria*).**

---

1. English name. Cow-herb.

2. Vernacular names. Musna, Sabuni.

3. Economic importance. Cultivated as an ornamental. The plant juice is used as a substitute for soap.

MALVACEAE*

Hibiscus rosa-sinensis Linn.

Stem. Herbaceous, lower portions woody, aerial, erect, cylindrical, branched, solid, glabrous, green.

Leaf. Cauline and ramal, alternate, stipulate, stipules free- lateral, simple, petiolate, ovate, serrate, acute, glabrous, unicostate reticulate.

Inflorescence. Solitary axillary.

Flower. Ebracteate, pedicellate, complete, actinomorphic, hermaphrodite, pentamerous, hypogynous, cyclic.

Epicalyx. A whorl of bracteoles (5-8) is present around the calyx.

Calyx. Sepals 5, gamosepalous, valvate.

Corolla. Petals 5, polypetalous, united at the base and adnate to the staminal tube, twisted, red.

Androecium. Stamens indefinite, monadelphous, staminal tube united with corolla (epipetalous), upper portions of filaments and anthers free, anthers reniform, monothecous, extrorse.

Gynoecium. Pentacarpellary, syncarpous, ovary superior, pentalocular, with many ovules in each locule, placentation axile, styles 5, long, passing through the staminal tube and each ending into a discoid stigmatic lobe.

Fruit. Capsule.

Floral formula. Ebr, ⊕, ⚥, $E_{5\text{-}8}$, $\widehat{K_{(5)}, C_5}$, A_{∞}, $\underline{G}_{(5)}$.

Classification and identification.

Class. ***Dicotyledonae***

1. Venation reticulate.
2. Flowers pentamerous.

Sub-Class. ***Polypetalae***

1. Petals free.

Series. ***Thalamiflorae***

1. Flowers hypogynous and ovary superior.

Order. ***Malvales***

1. Stamens usually indefinite and monadelphous.
2. Ovary 3 to multicarpellary with axile placentation .

Family. ***Malvaceae***

1. Leaves stipulate.
2. Calyx often with an epicalyx.
3. Stamens monothecous and anthers reniform.
4. Fruit - capsule or schizocarp.

***1. English name.** Mallow family.

2. Systematic position in other systems of classification.

Rendle (1925)	**Engler and Prantl (1931)**	**Hutchinson (1959)**
Dicotyledons	Dicotyledoneae	Dicotyledons
Dialypetalae	Archichlamydeae	Lignosae
Malvales	Malvales	Malvales
Malvaceae	Malvaceae	Malvaceae

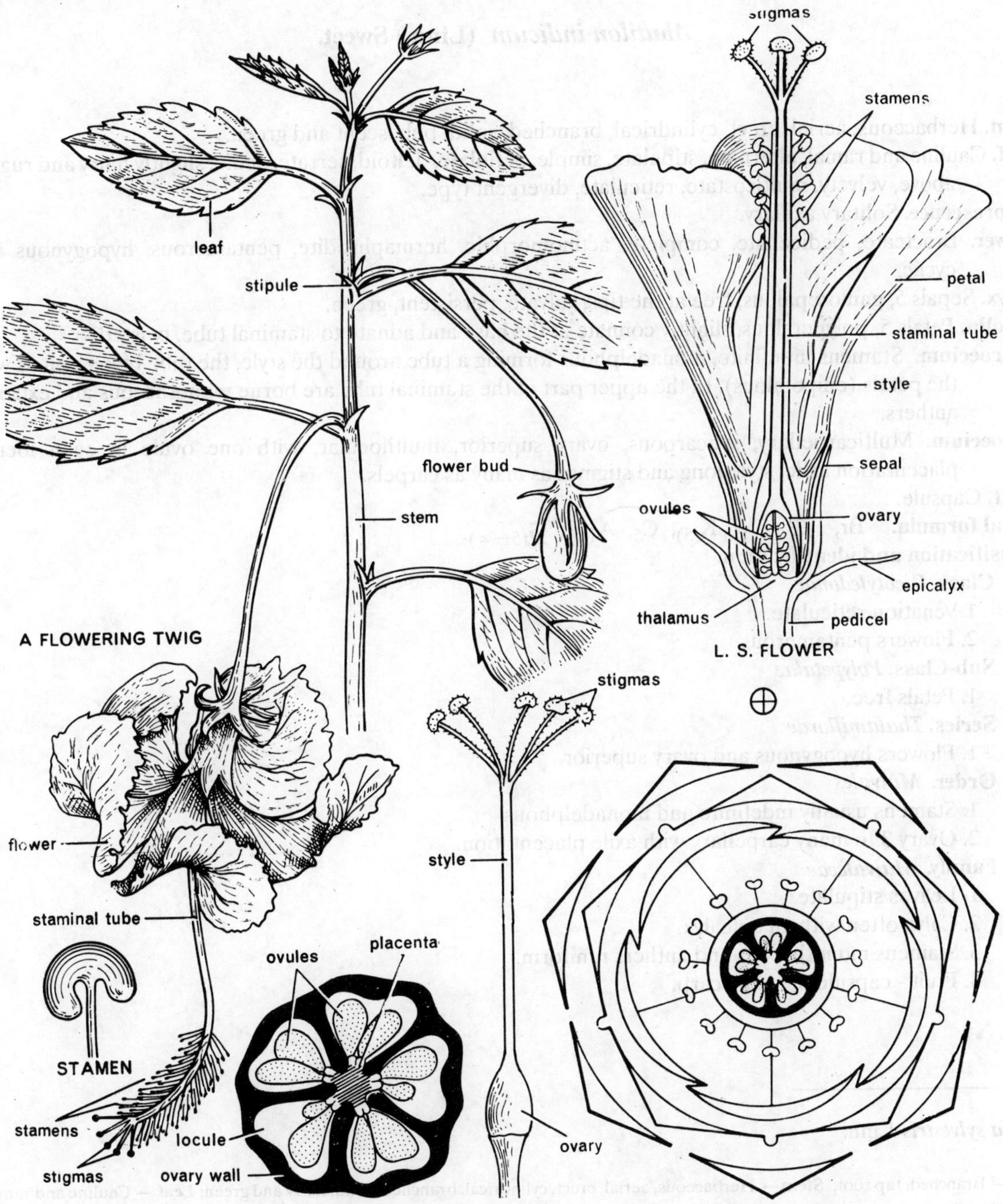

Fig. 18. ***Hibiscus rosa-sinensis.***

---

1. **English names.** Chinese shoe-flower, Rose-of-China.
2. **Vernacular names.** Gurhal, Jasum.
3. **Economic importance.** The flowers yield a dark purplish dye used for making shoe polishes. The decoction of flowers is also used in bronchial catarrh.

Abutilon indicum (Linn.) Sweet.

Stem. Herbaceous, aerial, erect, cylindrical, branched, solid, pubescent and green.

Leaf. Cauline and ramal, alternate, stipulate, simple, petiolate, deltoid, serrate, acute, slightly hairy and rugose above, velvety, multicostate, reticulate, divergent type.

Inflorescence. Solitary axillary.

Flower. Bracteate, pedicellate, complete, actinomorphic, hermaphrodite, pentamerous, hypogynous and cyclic.

Calyx. Sepals 5, gamosepalous, free at the tips, valvate, persistent, green.

Corolla. Petals 5, polypetalous, slightly connate at the base and adnate to staminal tube, twisted.

Androecium. Stamens indefinite, monadelphous forming a tube around the style, the tube being united with the petals (epipetalous). In the upper part of the staminal tube are borne monothecous and extrorse anthers.

Gynoecium. Multicarpellary, syncarpous, ovary superior, multilocular, with one ovule in each locule, placentation axile, style long and stigmas as many as carpels.

Fruit. Capsule.

Floral formula. Br, ⊕, ⚥, $K_{(5)}$, $\widehat{C_5, A_{(\infty)}}$, $\underline{G}_{(5-\infty)}$.

Classification and identification.

Class. ***Dicotyledonae***

1. Venation reticulate.
2. Flowers pentamerous.

Sub-Class. ***Polypetalae***

1. Petals free.

Series. ***Thalamiflorae***

1. Flowers hypogynous and ovary superior.

Order. ***Malvales***

1. Stamens usually indefinite and monadelphous.
2. Ovary 3 to many carpellary with axile placentation.

Family. ***Malvalceae***

1. Leaves stipulate.
2. Calyx often with an epicalyx.
3. Stamens monothecous and anthers reniform.
4. Fruit - capsule or schizocarp.

Malva sylvestris Linn.

Root – Branched, tap root; **Stem**— Herbaceous, aerial, erect, cylindrical, branched, solid, hairy and green; **Leaf** – Cauline and ramal, alternate, stipulate, simple, petiolate, cordate, crenate, obtuse, upper surface glabrous and lower hairy, multicostate reticulate; **Inflorescence** – Axillary cyme; **Flower** — Bracteate, bracteolate, bracteoles 3, pedicellate, complete, actinomorphic, hermaphrodite, pentamerous, hypogynous and cyclic; **Calyx** – Sepals 5, gamosepalous, valvate, persistent; **Corolla** – Petals 5, polypetalous, basifixed, extrorse; **Androecium** – Stamens indefinite, monoadelphous forming a staminal tube around the style, epipetalous, anthers reniform, monotheous, basifixed, extrorse; **Gynoecium** – Multicarpellary, syncarpous, ovary superior, multilocular, placentation axile, style and stigma as many as carpels; **Fruit** – Capsule.

Floral formula - Br, brl, ⊕, ⚥, $K_{(5)}$, $\widehat{C_5, A(\infty)}$, $\underline{G}_{(5)}$.

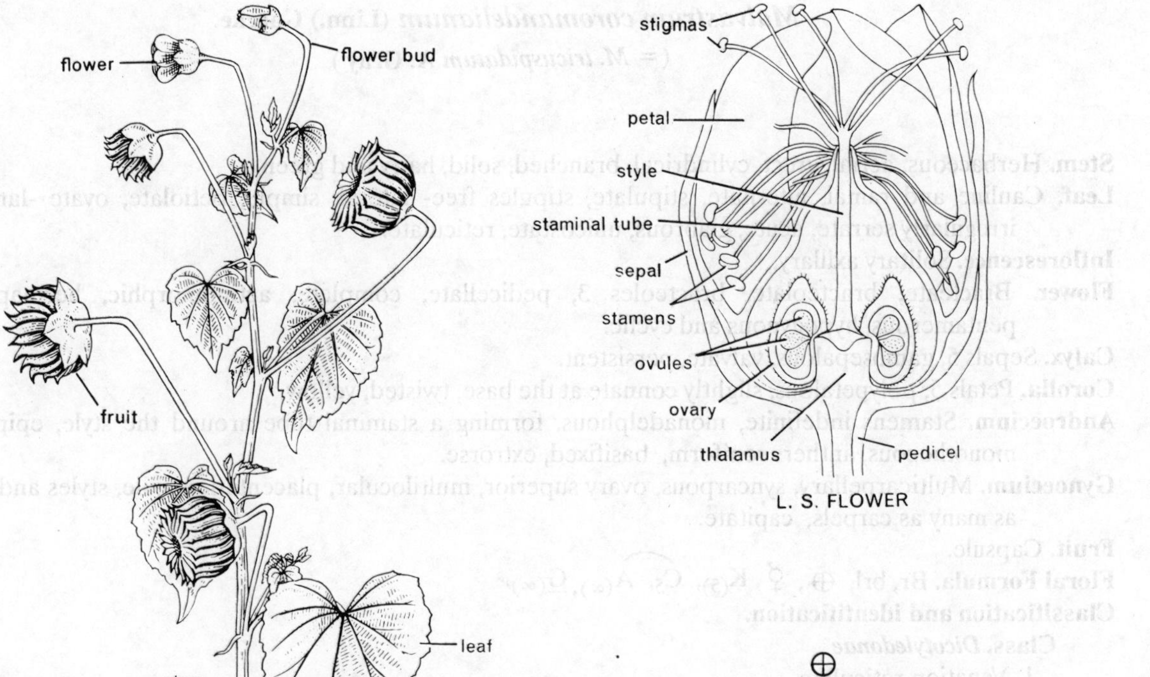

Fig. 19. ***Abutilon indicum.***

---

1. English names. Country mallow, Indian Abutilon.

2. Vernacular name. Kanghi.

3. Economic importance. The stems on retting, yield a fibre which is used for making ropes.

Malvastrum coromandelianum (Linn.) Garcke.
(= *M. tricuspidatum* A. Gray)

Stem. Herbaceous, aerial, erect, cylindrical, branched, solid, hairy and green.
Leaf. Cauline and ramal, alternate, stipulate, stipules free- lateral, simple, petiolate, ovate -lanceolate, irregularly serrate, acute, glabrous, unicostate, reticulate.
Inflorescence. Solitary axillary.
Flower. Bracteate, bracteolate, bracteoles 3, pedicellate, complete, actinomorphic, hermaphrodite, pentamerous, hypogynous and cyclic.
Calyx. Sepals 5, gamosepalous, valvate, persistent.
Corolla. Petals 5, polypetalous, slightly connate at the base, twisted, yellow.
Androecium. Stamens indefinite, monadelphous, forming a staminal tube around the style, epipetalous, monothecous, anthers reniform, basifixed, extrorse.
Gynoecium. Multicarpellary, syncarpous, ovary superior, multilocular, placentation axile, styles and stigmas as many as carpels, capitate.
Fruit. Capsule.
Floral Formula. Br, brl, ⊕, ⚥, $K_{(5)}$, $\overparen{C_5, A_{(\infty)}}$, $\underline{G}_{(\infty)}$.
Classification and identification.

Class. *Dicotyledonae*
1. Venation reticulate.
2. Flowers pentamerous.

Sub-Class. *Polypetalae*
1. Petals free.

Series. *Thalamiflorae*
1. Flowers hypogynous and ovary superior.

Order. *Malvales*
1. Stamens usually indefinite and monadelphous.
2. Ovary 3 carpellary with axile placentation.

Family. *Malvaceae*
1. Leaves stipulate.
2. Calyx often with an epicalyx.
3. Stamens monothecous and anthers reniform.
4. Fruit - capsule or schizocarp.

Sida cordifolia Linn.

Stem- Herbaceous, aerial, erect, cylindrical, branched, solid, puberulous, green; **Leaf** — Cauline and ramal, alternate, stipulate, cordate, serrate, acute, pubescent, unicostate reticulate; **Inflorescence** - Solitary axillary; **Flower** — Bracteate, pedicellate, complete, actinomorphic, hermaphrodite, pentamerous, hypogynous and cyclic; **Calyx** — Sepals 5, gamosepalous, deeply partite, valvate; **Corolla**— Petals 5, polypetalous, connate at the base, twisted, yellow; **Androecium** — Stamens indefinite, monoadelphous forming a staminal tube around the style, epipetalous, anthers reniform , monotheous, basifixed, extrorse; **Gynoecium** — Multicarpellary, syncarpous, ovary superior, mlultilocular, placentation axile, style passing through the staminal tube, stigmas as many as the carpels and capitate; **Fruit** — Schizocarp;

Floral formula- Br, ⊕, ⚥, $K_{(5)}$, $\overparen{C_5, A_{(\infty)}}$, $\underline{G}_{(\infty)}$.

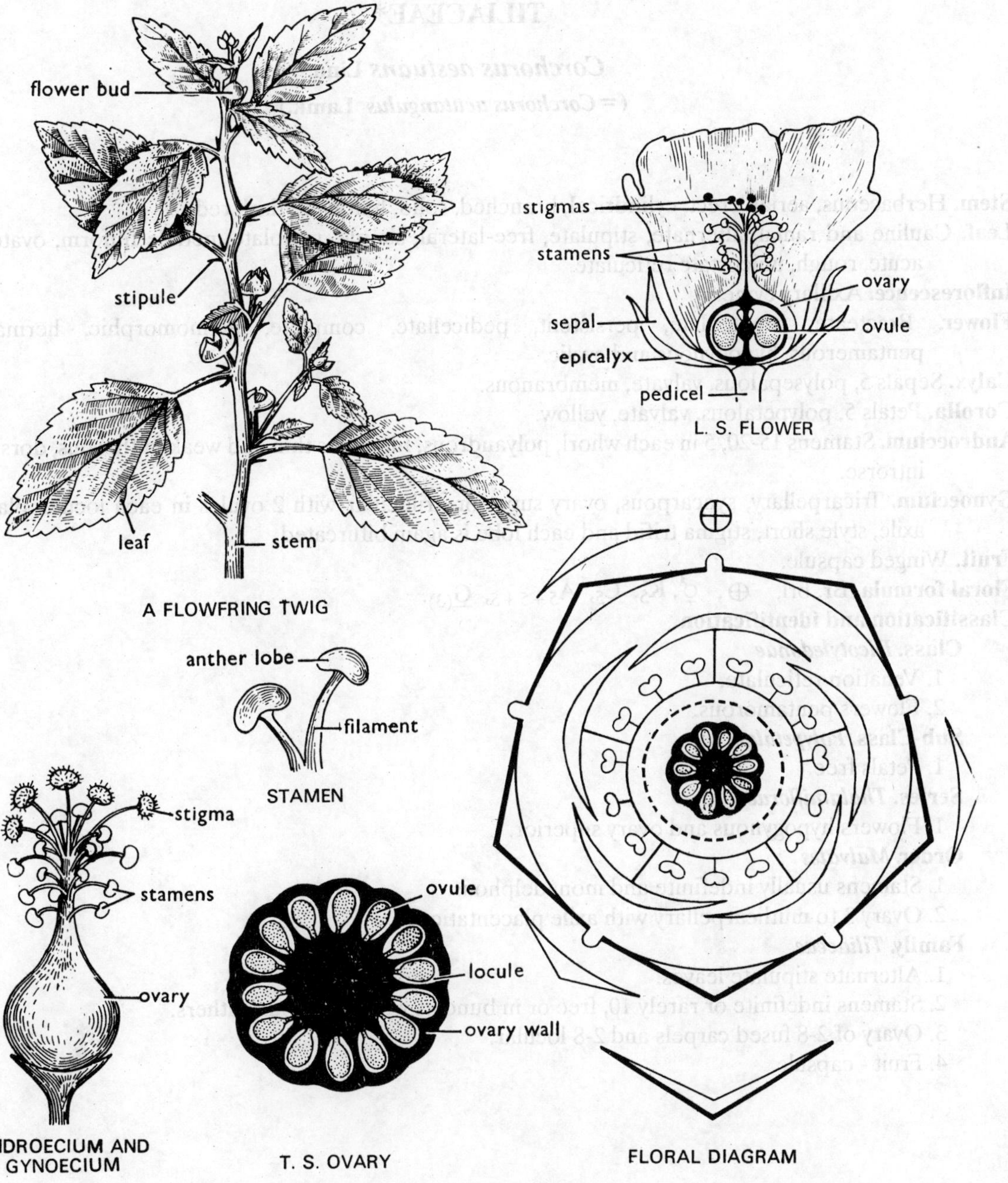

Fig. 20. ***Malvastrum coromandelianum.***

---

1. Economic importance. Leaves are applied to inflammed sores and wound for cooling and healing. Decoction is given in dysentry. Stem fibre is used for making brooms.

TILIACEAE*

Corchorus aestuans Linn.

(= *Corchorus acutangulus* Lamk.)

Stem. Herbaceous, aerial, erect, cylindrical, branched, solid, hairy and dark red.

Leaf. Cauline and ramal, alternate, stipulate, free-lateral, simple, petiolate, petiole filiform, ovate, serrate, acute, rough, unicostate reticulate.

Inflorescence. Axillary cyme.

Flower. Bracteate, bracteolate, persistent, pedicellate, complete, actinomorphic, hermaphrodite, pentamerous, hypogynous and cyclic.

Calyx. Sepals 5, polysepalous, valvate, membranous.

Corolla. Petals 5, polypetalous, valvate, yellow.

Androecium. Stamens 15-20, 5 in each whorl, polyandrous, filaments thin and weak, dithecous, dorsifixed and introrse.

Gynoecium. Tricarpellary, syncarpous, ovary superior, trilocular with 2 ovules in each locule, placentation axile, style short, stigma trifid and each lobe is again bifurcated.

Fruit. Winged capsule.

Floral formula. Br, brl, $\oplus$, ⚥, K_5, C_5, A_{5+5+5}, $\underline{G}_{(3)}$.

Classification and identification.

Class. ***Dicotyledonae***

1. Venation reticulate.
2. Flowers pentamerous.

Sub-Class. ***Polypetalae***

1. Petals free.

Series. ***Thalamiflorae***

1. Flowers hypogynous and ovary superior.

Order. ***Malvales***

1. Stamens usually indefinite and monadelphous.
2. Ovary 3 to mutlicarpellary with axile placentation.

Family. ***Tiliaceae***

1. Alternate stipulate leaves.
2. Stamens indefinite or rarely 10, free or in bundles with dithecous anthers.
3. Ovary of 2-8 fused carpels and 2-8 locular.
4. Fruit - capsule.

***1. English name.** Linden family.

2. Systematic position in other systems of classification.

Rendle (1925)	**Engler and Prantl (1931)**	**Hutchinson (1959)**
Dicotyledons	Dicotyledoneae	Dicotyledons
Dialypetalae	Archichlamydeae	Lignosae
Malvales	Malvales	Tiliales
Tiliaceae	Tiliaceae	Tiliaceae

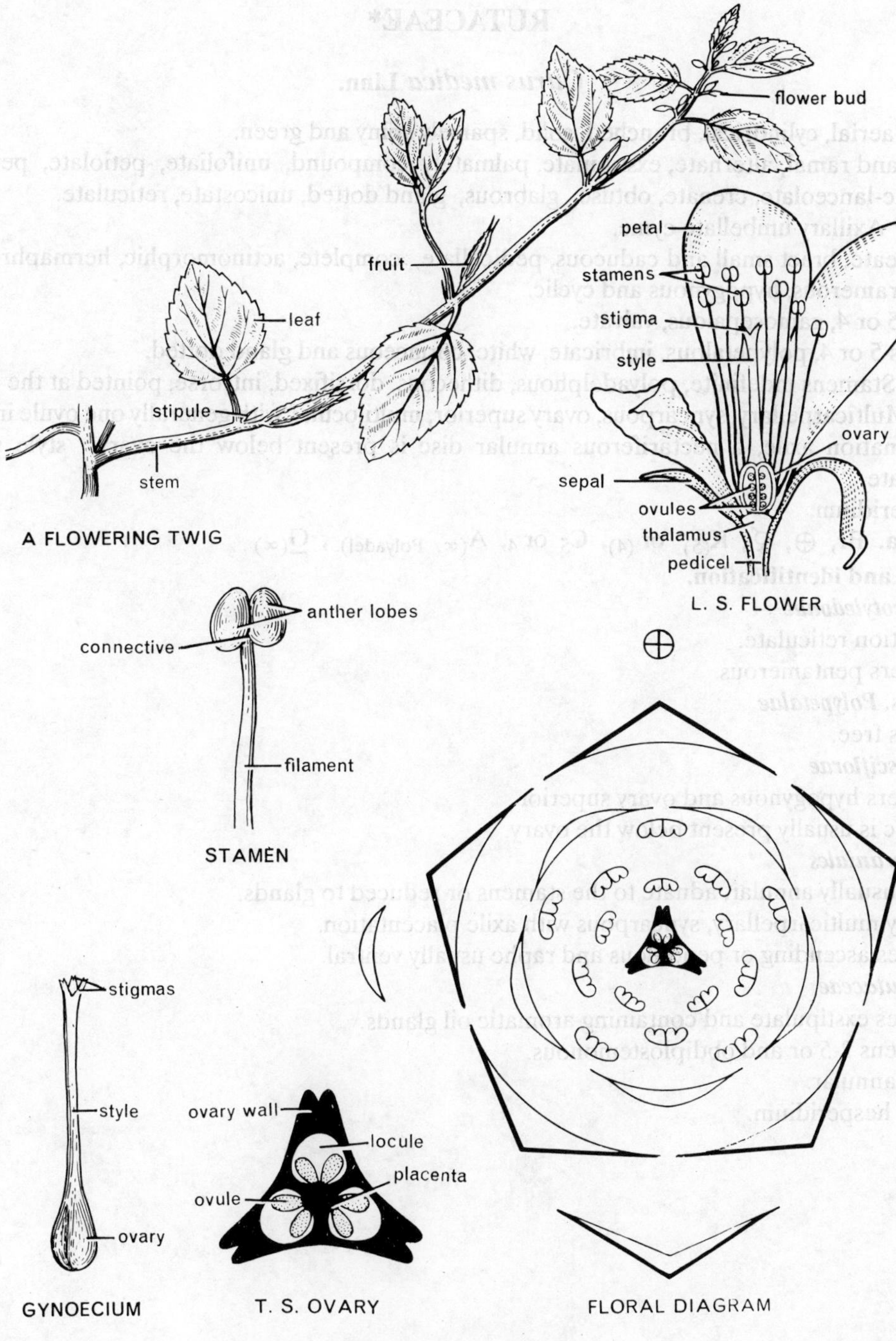

Fig. 21. ***Corchorus aestuans.***

RUTACEAE*

Citrus medica Linn.

Stem. Woody, aerial, cylindrical, branched, solid, sparsely spiny and green.

Leaf. Cauline and ramal, alternate, exstipulate, palmately compound, unifoliate, petiolate, petiole winged, elliptic-lanceolate, crenate, obtuse, glabrous, gland dotted, unicostate, reticulate.

Inflorescence. Axillary umbellate cyme.

Flower. Bracteate, bract small and caducous, pedicellate, complete, actinomorphic, hermaphrodite, penta- or tetramerous, hypogynous and cyclic.

Calyx. Sepals 5 or 4, gamosepalous, valvate.

Corolla. Petals 5 or 4, polypetalous, imbricate, white, coriaceous and gland dotted.

Androecium. Stamens indefinite, polyadelphous, dithecous, dorsifixed, introrse, pointed at the apex.

Gynoecium. Multicarpellary, syncarpous, ovary superior, multilocular with generally one ovule in each locule, placenation axile, a nectariferous annular disc is present below the ovary, style stout, stigma capitate.

Fruit. A hesperidium.

Floral formula. Br, ⊕, ⚥, $K_{(5)}$ or $_{(4)}$, C_5 or $_4$, $A_{(\infty,\ \text{Polyadel}).}$, $\underline{G}_{(\infty)}$.

Classification and identification.

Class. ***Dicotyledonae***

1. Venation reticulate.
2. Flowers pentamerous.

Sub-Class. ***Polypetalae***

1. Petals free.

Series. ***Disciflorae***

1. Flowers hypogynous and ovary superior.
2. A disc is usually present below the ovary.

Order. ***Geraniales***

1. Disc usually annular, adnate to the stamens or reduced to glands.
2. Ovary multicarpellary, syncarpous with axile placentation.
3. Ovules ascending or pendulous and raphe usually ventral.

Family. ***Rutaceae***

1. Leaves exstipulate and containing aromatic oil glands.
2. Stamens 2-5 or and obdiplostemonous.
3. Disc annular.
4. Fruit hesperidium.

***1. English name.** Rue family.

2. Systematic position in other systems of classification.

Rendle (1925)	**Engler and Prantl** (1931)	**Hutchinson** (1959)
Dicotyledons	Dicotyledoneae	Dicotyledons
Dialypetalae	Archichlamydeae	Lignosae
Rutales	Geraniales	Rutales
Rutaceae	Rutaceae	Rutaceae

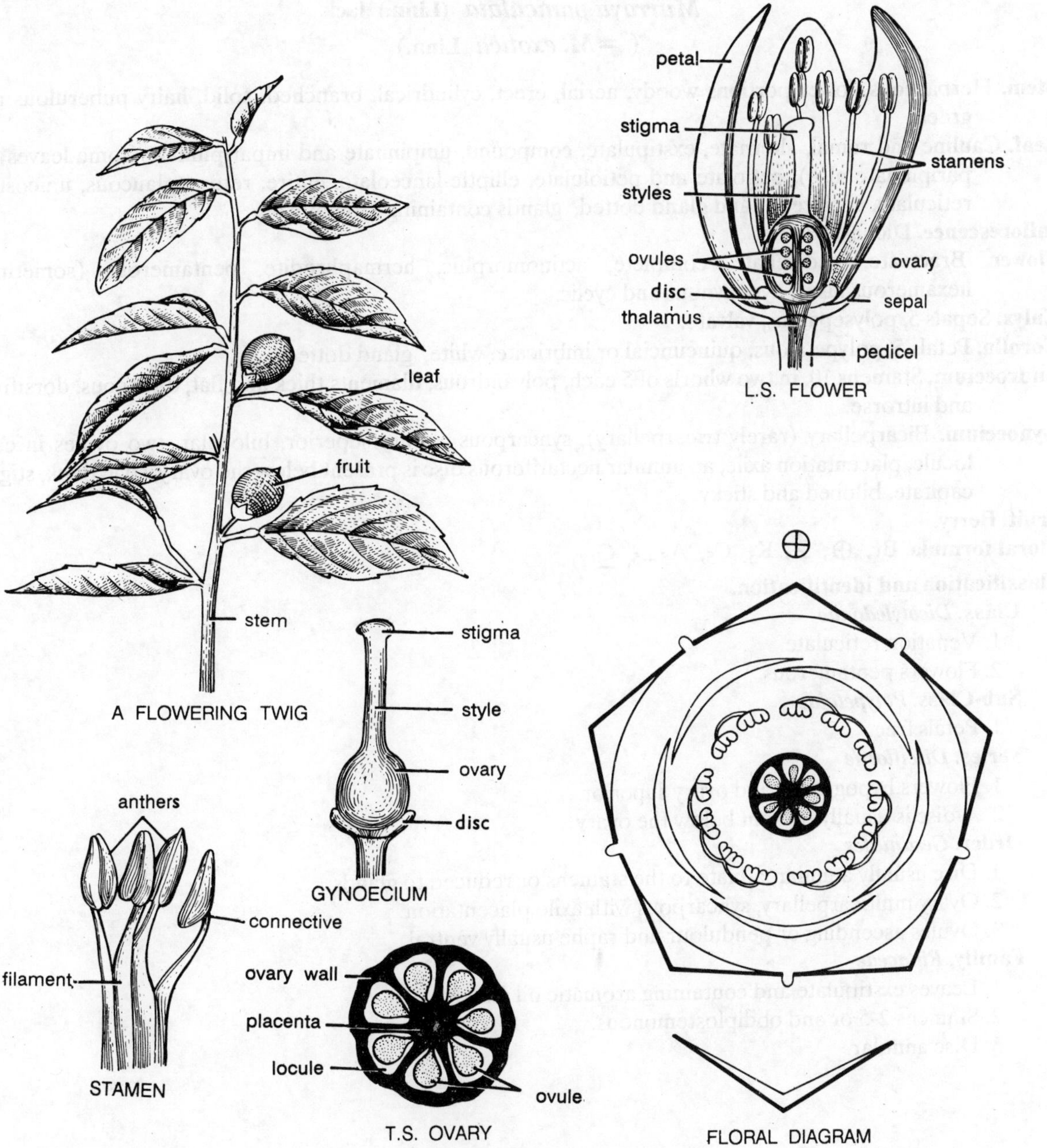

Fig. 22. ***Citrus medica.***

---

1. English name. Citron.
2. Vernacular names. Bara Nimbu, Bijawara.
3. Economic importance. The fruit juice is rich in vitamin c which is an astringent. The fruits are pickled.

Murraya paniculata (Linn.) Jack.
(=*M. exotica* Linn.)

Stem. Herbaceous, lower portions woody, aerial, erect, cylindrical, branched, solid, hairy puberulous and green.

Leaf. Cauline and ramal, alternate, exstipulate, compound, unipinnate and imparipinnate (some leaves are paripinnate also), petiolate and petiolulate, elliptic-lanceolate, entire, retuse, glaucous, unicostate reticulate, coriaceous and gland dotted, glands containing aromatic oil.

Inflorescence. Dichasial cyme.

Flower. Bracteate, pedicellate, complete, actinomorphic, hermaphrodite, pentamerous (sometimes hexamerous also), hypogynous and cyclic.

Calyx. Sepals 5, polysepalous, valvate.

Corolla. Petals 5, polypetalous, quincuncial or imbricate, white, gland dotted.

Androecium. Stamens 10, in two whorls of 5 each, polyandrous, filaments thick and flat, dithecous, dorsifixed and introrse.

Gynoecium. Bicarpellary (rarely tricarpellary), syncarpous , ovary superior, bilocular, two ovules in each locule, placentation axile, an annular nectariferous disc is present below the ovary, style thick, stigma capitate, bilobed and sticky.

Fruit. Berry.

Floral formula. Br, $\oplus$, ⚥, K_5, C_5, A_{5+5}, $\underline{G}_{(2)}$.

Classification and identification.

Class. *Dicotyledonae*

1. Venation reticulate.
2. Flowers pentamerous.

Sub-Class. *Polypetalae*

1. Petals free.

Series. *Disciflorae*

1. Flowers hypogynous and ovary superior.
2. A disc is usually present below the ovary.

Order. *Geraniales*

1. Disc usually annular, adnate to the stamens or reduced to glands.
2. Ovary multicarpellary, syncarpous with axile placentation.
3. Ovules ascending or pendulour and raphe usually ventral.

Family. *Rutaceae*

1. Leaves exstipulate and containing aromatic oil glands.
2. Stamens 2-5 or and obdiplostemonous.
3. Disc annular.

Murraya koenigii **(Spreng)**

Stem - Herbaceous, lower portions woody, aerial, erect, cylindrical, branched, solid and green; **Leaf** - Cauline and ramal , alternate, exstipulate, compound, unipinnate, ovate, entire, retuse, unicostate reticulate, glabrous; **Inflorescence** - Panicle cyme;, **Flower** - Bracteate, bracteolate, pedicellate, complete, actinomorphic, hermaphrodite, pentamerous, hypogynous and cyclic; **Calyx** - Sepals 5, polysepalous, slightly connate at the base, valvate; **Corolla** - Petals 5, polypetalous, imbricate, gland dotted; **Androecium** - Stamens 10, in two whorls of 5 each, polyandrous, filaments broad, dithecous, dorsifixed, introrse; **Gynoecium** - Bicarpellary, syncarpous, ovary superior, bilocular, two ovules in each locule, placentation axile, a hypogynous nectariferous disc present, style long, stigma capitate; **Fruit** - Berry;

Floral formula. Br, brl, $\oplus$, ⚥, K_5, C_5, A_{5+5}, $\underline{G}_{(2)}$.

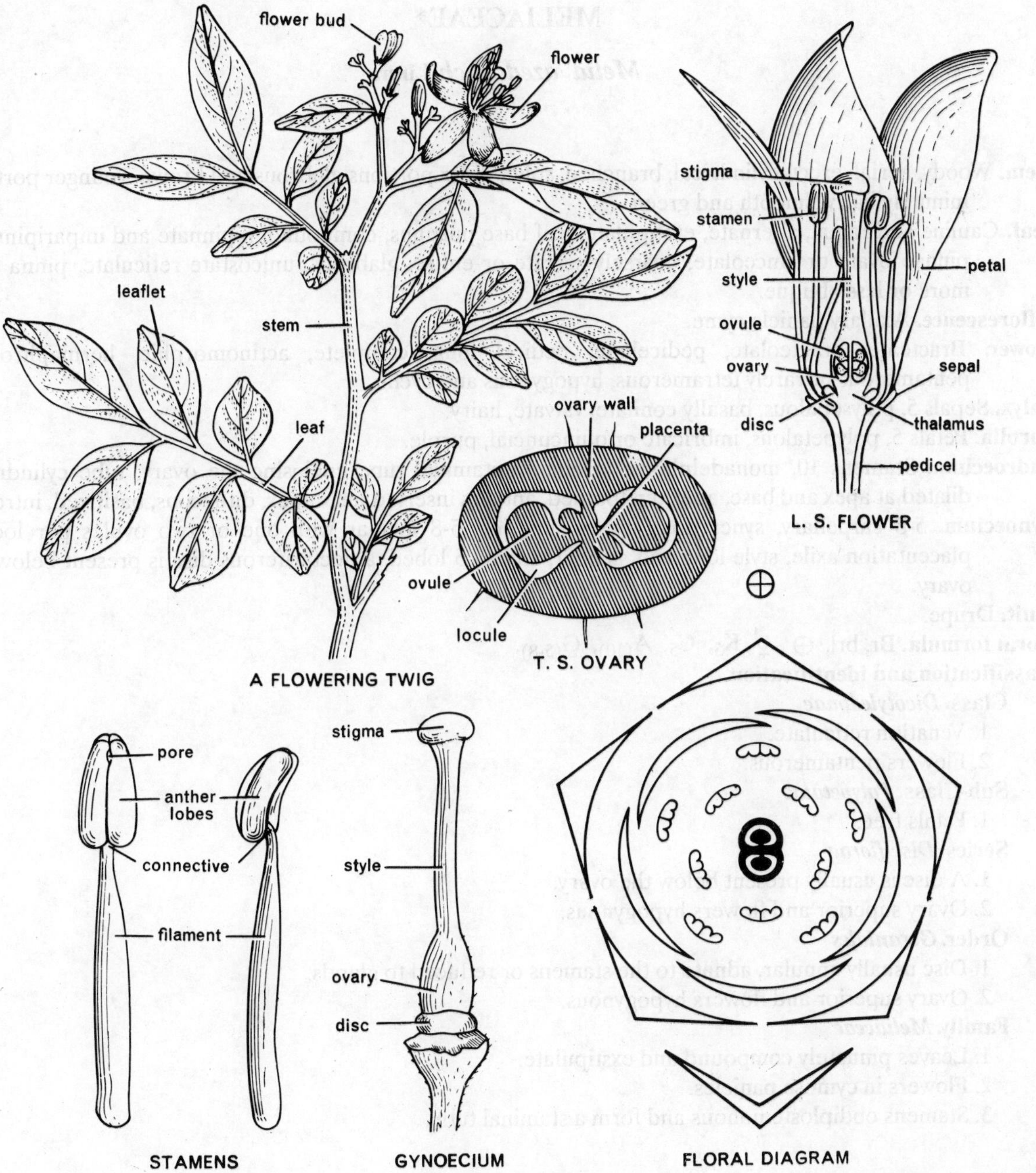

Fig. 23. ***Murraya paniculata.***

---

1. English name. Orange-jessamine.
2. Vernacular names. Kamini, Bisar.
3. Economic importance. The plant is cultivated for its fragrant flowers. The leaves are astringent and are used in dysentery.

MELIACEAE*

Melia azedarach Linn.

Stem. Woody, aerial, erect, cylindrical, branched, solid, older portions glabrous and brown, younger portions minutely hairy, smooth and green.

Leaf. Cauline and ramal, alternate, exstipulate, leaf base pulvinus, compound, bipinnate and imparipinnate, pinnae ovate or lanceolate, coarsely serrate or entire, glabrous, unicostate reticulate, pinna base more or less oblique.

Inflorescence. Axillary panicle cyme.

Flower. Bracteate, bracteolate, pedicellate, pedicel long, complete, actinomorphic, hermaphrodite, pentamerous or rarely tetramerous, hypogynous and cyclic.

Calyx. Sepals 5, polysepalous, basally connate, valvate, hairy.

Corolla. Petals 5, polypetalous, imbricate or quincuncial, purple.

Androecium. Stamens 10, monadelphous, forming a staminal tube enclosing the ovary, tube cylindrical, dilated at apex and base, apex ten toothed, anthers inserted near apex, dithecous, basifixed, introrse.

Gynoecium. 5-8 carpellary, syncarpous, ovary superior, 5-8 locular with one or two ovules per locule, placentation axile, style long and slender, stigma 5 lobed, a nectariferous disc is present below the ovary.

Fruit. Drupe.

Floral formula. Br, brl, $\oplus$, ⚥, K_5, C_5, $A_{(10)}$, $\underline{G}_{(5\text{-}8)}$.

Classification and identification.

Class. *Dicotyledonae*

1. Venation reticulate.
2. Flowers pentamerous.

Sub-Class. *Polypetalae*

1. Petals free.

Series. *Disciflorae*

1. A disc is usually present below the ovary.
2. Ovary superior and flowers hypogynous.

Order. *Geraniales*

1. Disc usually annular, adnate to the stamens or reduced to glands.
2. Ovary superior and flowers hypogynous.

Family. *Meliaceae*

1. Leaves pinnately compound and exstipulate.
2. Flowers in cymose panicles.
3. Stamens obdiplostemonous and form a staminal tube.

---

*1. **English name.** Melia family.

2. **Systematic position in other systems of classification.**

Rendle (1925)	**Engler and Prantl (1931)**	**Hutchinson (1959)**
Dicotyledons	Dicotyledoneae	Dicotyledons
Dialypetalae	Archichlamydeae	Lignosae
Rutales	Geraniales	Meliales
Meliaceae	Meliaceae	Meliaceae

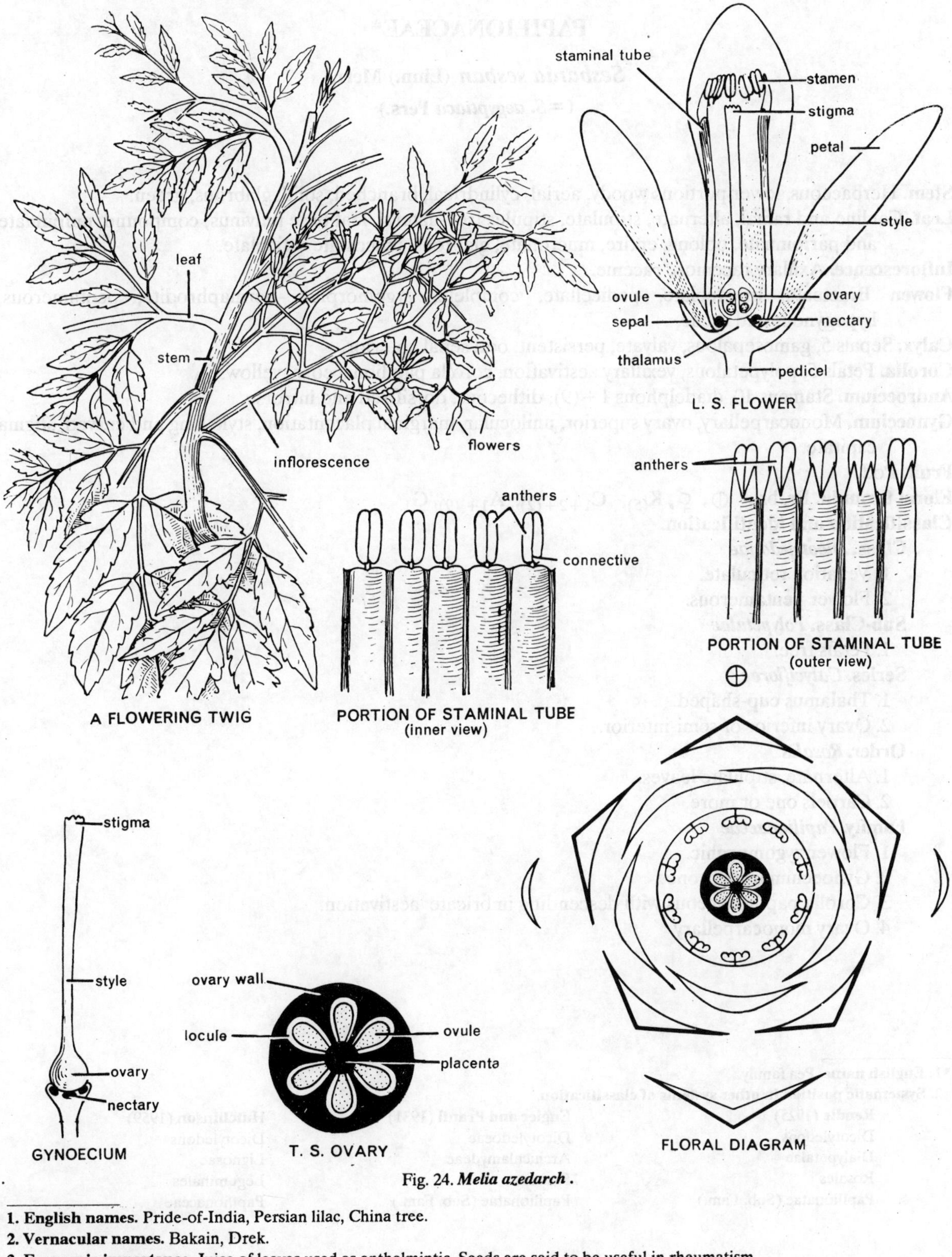

Fig. 24. ***Melia azedarch*** .

1. English names. Pride-of-India, Persian lilac, China tree.

2. Vernacular names. Bakain, Drek.

3. Economic importance. Juice of leaves used as anthelmintic. Seeds are said to be useful in rheumatism.

PAPILIONACEAE*

Sesbania sesban (Linn.) Merr.

(=*S. aegyptiaca* Pers.)

Stem. Herbaceous, lower portions woody, aerial, cylindrical, branched, solid, glabrous, green.

Leaf. Cauline and ramal, alternate, stipulate, stipules free- lateral, leaf base pulvinus, compound, unipinnate and paripinnate, oblong, entire, mucronate, glabrous, unicostate reticulate.

Inflorescence. Axillary racemose raceme.

Flower. Bracteate, bracteolate, pedicellate, complete, zygomorphic, hermaphrodite, pentamerous, hypogynous and cyclic.

Calyx. Sepals 5, gamosepalous, valvate, persistent, odd sepal anterior.

Corolla. Petals 5, polypetalous, vexillary aestivation, corolla papilionaceous, yellow.

Androecium. Stamens 10, diadelphous 1 + (9), dithecous, dorsifixed and introrse.

Gynoecium. Monocarpellary, ovary superior, unilocular, marginal placentation, style long and curved, stigma capitate.

Fruit. Pod.

Floral formula. Br, brl, ⦶, ⚥, $K_{(5)}$, $C_{1+2+(2)}$, $A_{1+(9)}$, $\underline{G_1}$.

Classification and identification.

Class. ***Dicotyledonae***
1. Venation reticulate.
2. Flower pentamerous.

Sub-Class. ***Polypetalae***
1. Petals free.

Series. ***Calyciflorae***
1. Thalamus cup-shaped.
2. Ovary inferior or semi-inferior.

Order. ***Rosales***
1. Alternate, stipulate leaves.
2. Carpels one or more.

Family. ***Papilionaceae***
1. Flower zygomorphic.
2. Gynoecium usually one.
3. Corolla papilionaceous with descending imbricate aestivation.
4. Ovary monocarpellary.

***1. English name.** Pea family.

2. Systematic position in other systems of classification.

Rendle (1925)	**Engler and Prantl** (1931)	**Hutchinson** (1959)
Dicotyledons	Dicotyledoeae	Dicotyledons
Dialypetalae	Archichlamydeae	Lignosae
Rosales	Rosales	Leguminales
Papilionatae (Sub. Fam.)	Papilionatae (Sub. Fam.)	Papilionaceae

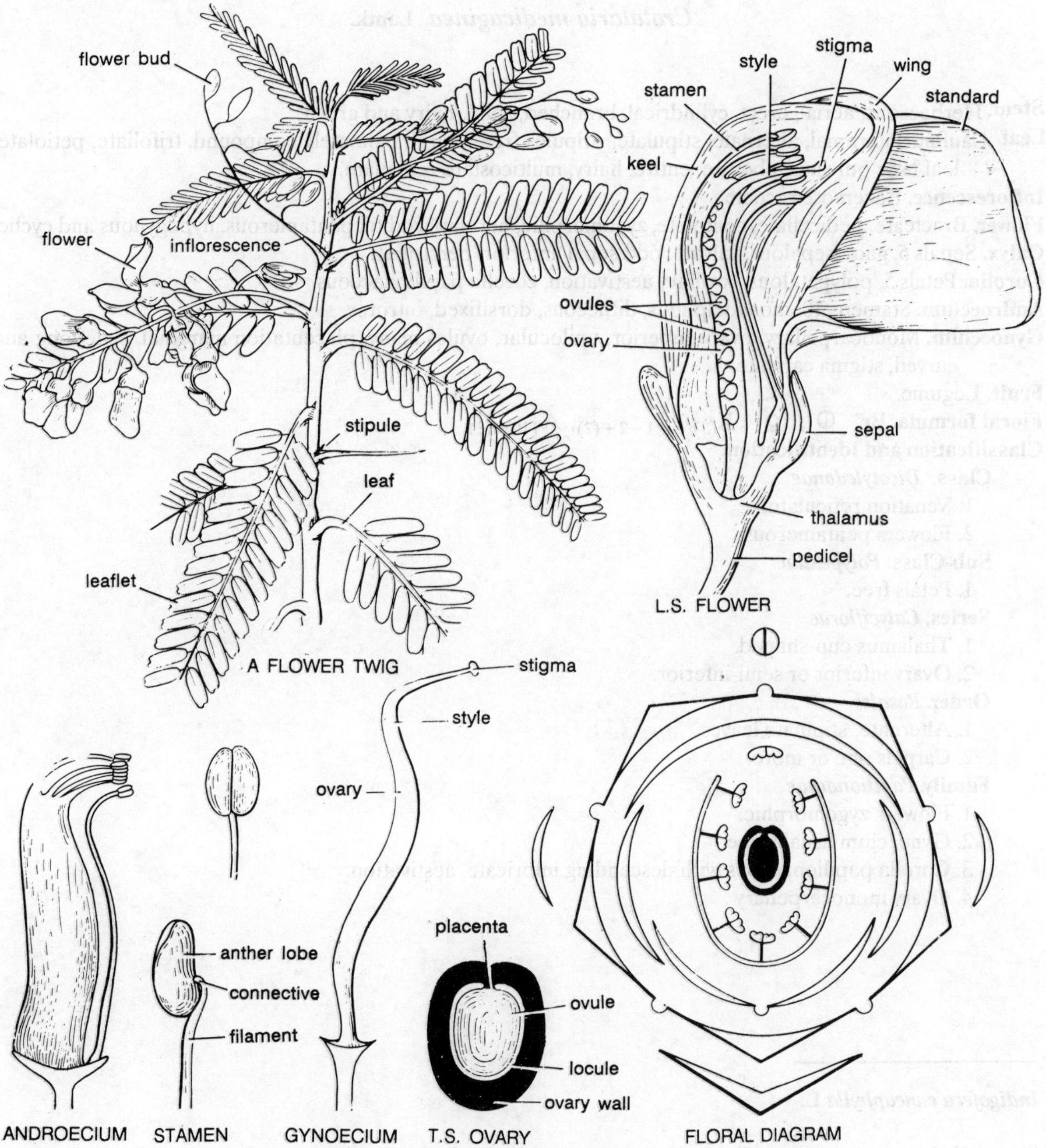

Fig. 25. ***Sesbania sesban.***

---

1. Vernacular names. Balmota, Jait, Jayanti.

2. Economic importance. The plant is used as a windbreak. The stem fibre is used for making ropes. The medicinal properties of seeds are useful in treating diarrhoea and excessive menstrual flow.

Crotalaria medicaginea Lamk.

Stem. Herbaceous, aerial, erect, cylindrical, branched, solid, hairy and green.

Leaf. Cauline and ramal, alternate, stipulate, stipules free-lateral, palmately compound, trifoliate, petiolate, leaf base pulvinus, obovate, entire, hairy, multicostate reticulate.

Inflorescence. Racemose raceme.

Flower. Bracteate, pedicellate, complete, zygomorphic, hermaphrodite, pentamerous, hypogynous and cyclic.

Calyx. Sepals 5, gamosepalous, valvate, odd sepal anterior, persistent.

Corolla. Petals 5, polypetalous, vexillary aestivation, corolla papilionaceous.

Androecium. Stamens 10, monadelphous, dithecous, dorsifixed, introrse.

Gynoecium. Monocarpellary, ovary superior, unilocular, ovules many, placentation marginal, style long and curved, stigma capitate.

Fruit. Legume.

Floral formula. Br, $\oplus$, ⚥, $K_{(5)}$, $C_{1+2+(2)}$, $A_{(10)}$, $\underline{G}_1$.

Classification and identification.

Class. ***Dicotyledonae***
1. Venation reticulate.
2. Flowers pentamerous.

Sub-Class. ***Polypetalae***
1. Petals free.

Series. ***Calyciflorae***
1. Thalamus cup-shaped.
2. Ovary inferior or semi-inferior.

Order. ***Rosales***
1. Alternate, stipulate leaves.
2. Carpels one or more.

Family. ***Papilionaceae***
1. Flowers zygomorphic.
2. Gynoecium usually one.
3. Corolla papilionaceous with descending imbricate aestivation.
4. Ovary monocarpellary .

Indigofera enneaphylla L.

Stem – Herbaceous, aerial, erect, cylindrical, branched, solid and green; **Leaf** – Cauline and ramal, alternate, stipulate, free lateral, compound, unipinnate and imparipinnate, petiolate, leaf base pulvinus, pinnae oblanceolate, entire, mucronate, unicostate reticulate; **Inflorescence** – Racemose spike; **Flower** – Bracteate, pedicellate, complete, zygomorphic, hermaphrodite, pentamerous, hypogynous and cyclic; **Calyx** – Sepals 5, gamosepalous, deeply partite, odd sepal anterior, valvate; **Corolla** – Petals 5, polypetalous, papilionaceous, vexillary; **Androecium** – Stamens 10, diadelphous 1 + (9), **Gynoecium** – Monocarpellary, ovary superior, unilocular, ovule's two placentation marginal, style curved, stigmas simple; **Fruit** – Pod.

Floral formula – Br, $\oplus$, ⚥, $K_{(5)}$, $C_{1+2+(2)}$, $A_{1+(9)}$, $\underline{G}_1$.

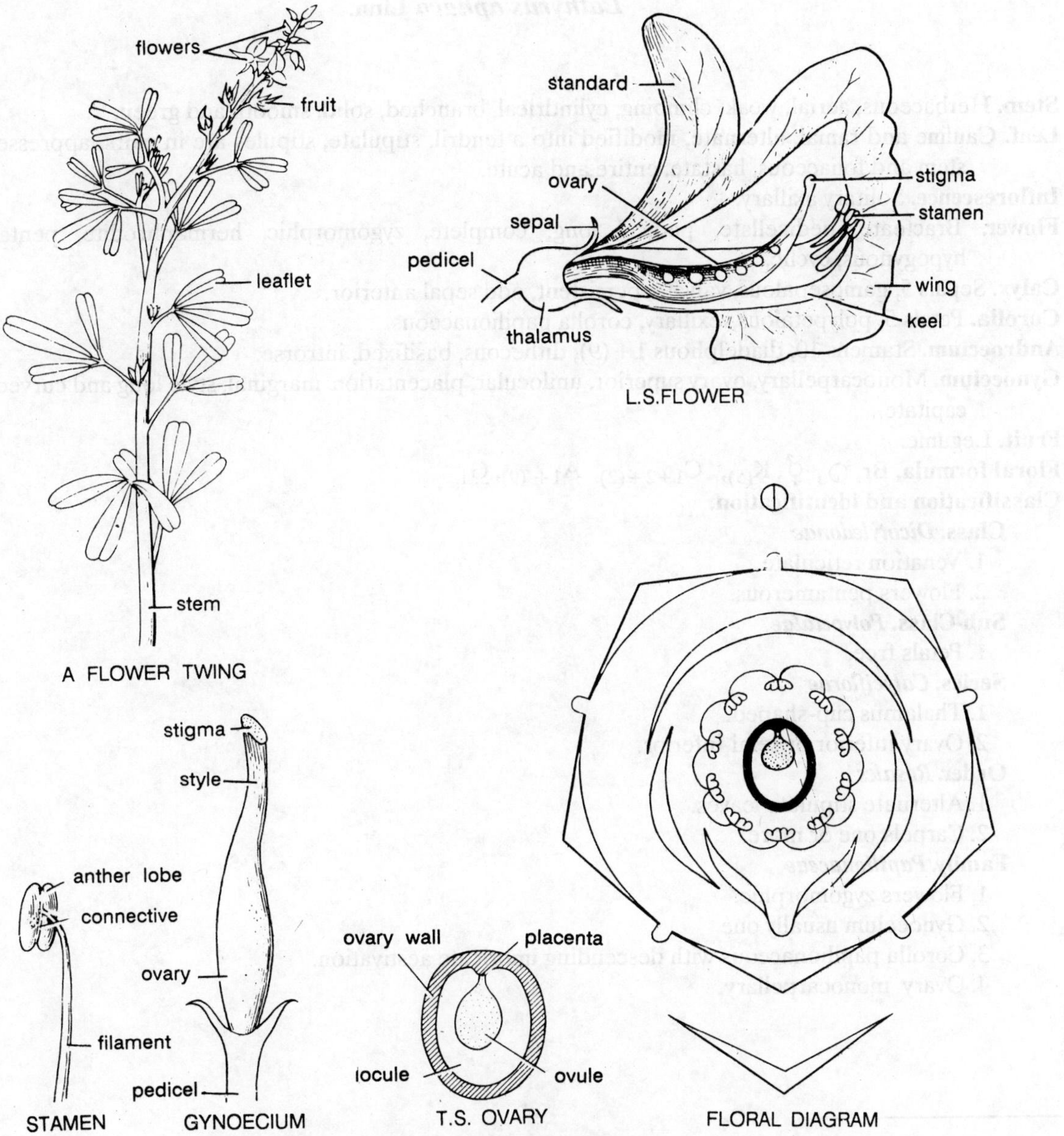

Fig. 26. ***Crotalaria medicaginea.***

---

1. Vernacular name. Gulabi;

2. Economic importance. Besides fodder, the plant is medicinally used in Punjab.

Lathyrus aphaca Linn.

Stem. Herbaceous, aerial, weak, climbing, cylindrical, branched, solid, smooth and green.

Leaf. Cauline and ramal, alternate, modified into a tendril, stipulate, stipules are in pairs, appressed to the stem and foliaceous, hastate, entire and acute.

Inflorescence. Solitary axillary.

Flower. Bracteate, pedicellate, pedicel long, complete, zygomorphic, hermaphrodite, pentamerous, hypogynous, cyclic.

Calyx. Sepals 5, gamosepalous, valvate, persistent, odd sepal anterior.

Corolla. Petals 5, polypetalous,vexillary, corolla papilionaceous.

Androecium. Stamens 10, diadelphous 1 + (9), dithecous, basifixed, introrse.

Gynoecium. Monocarpellary, ovary superior, unilocular, placentation marginal, style long and curved, stigma capitate.

Fruit. Legume.

Floral formula. Br, ϕ, ⚥, $K_{(5)}$, $C_{1+2+(2)}$, $A_{1+(9)}$, $\underline{G}_1$.

Classification and identification.

Class. ***Dicotyledonae***

1. Venation reticulate.
2. Flowers pentamerous.

Sub-Class. ***Polypetalae***

1. Petals free.

Series. ***Calyciflorae***

1. Thalamus cup-shaped.
2. Ovary inferior or semi-inferior.

Order. ***Rosales***

1. Alternate stipulate leaves.
2. Carpels one or more.

Family. ***Papilionaceae***

1. Flowers zygomorphic.
2. Gynoecium usually one.
3. Corolla papilionaceous with descending imbricate aestivation.
4. Ovary monocarpellary.

Melilotus indica (L.) All.

Stem — Herbaceous, aerial, erect, cylindrical, branched, soild, glabrous and green; **Leaf** — Cauline and ramal, alternate, stipulate, compound, trifoliate, petiolate, pinnae sub- sessile, obovate, serrate, mucronate, unicostate reticulate; **Inflorescence** — Racemose raceme; **Flower** — Bracteate, pedicellate, complete, zygomorphic, hermaphrodite, pentamerous, hypogynous and cyclic; **Calyx-** Sepals 5, gamosepalous, valvate, odd sepal anterior; **Corolla** — Petals 5, polypetalous, vexillary, papilionaceous, yellow; **Androceium** — Stamens 10, diadelphous 1 + (9), dithecous, dorsifixed, introrse; **Gynoecium** — Monocarpellary,ovary superior, unilocular, placentation marginal, style curved and stigma simple; **Fruit** - Pod;

Floral formula — Br, ϕ, ⚥, $K_{(5)}$, $C_{1+2+(2)}$, $A_{1+(9)}$, $\underline{G}_1$.

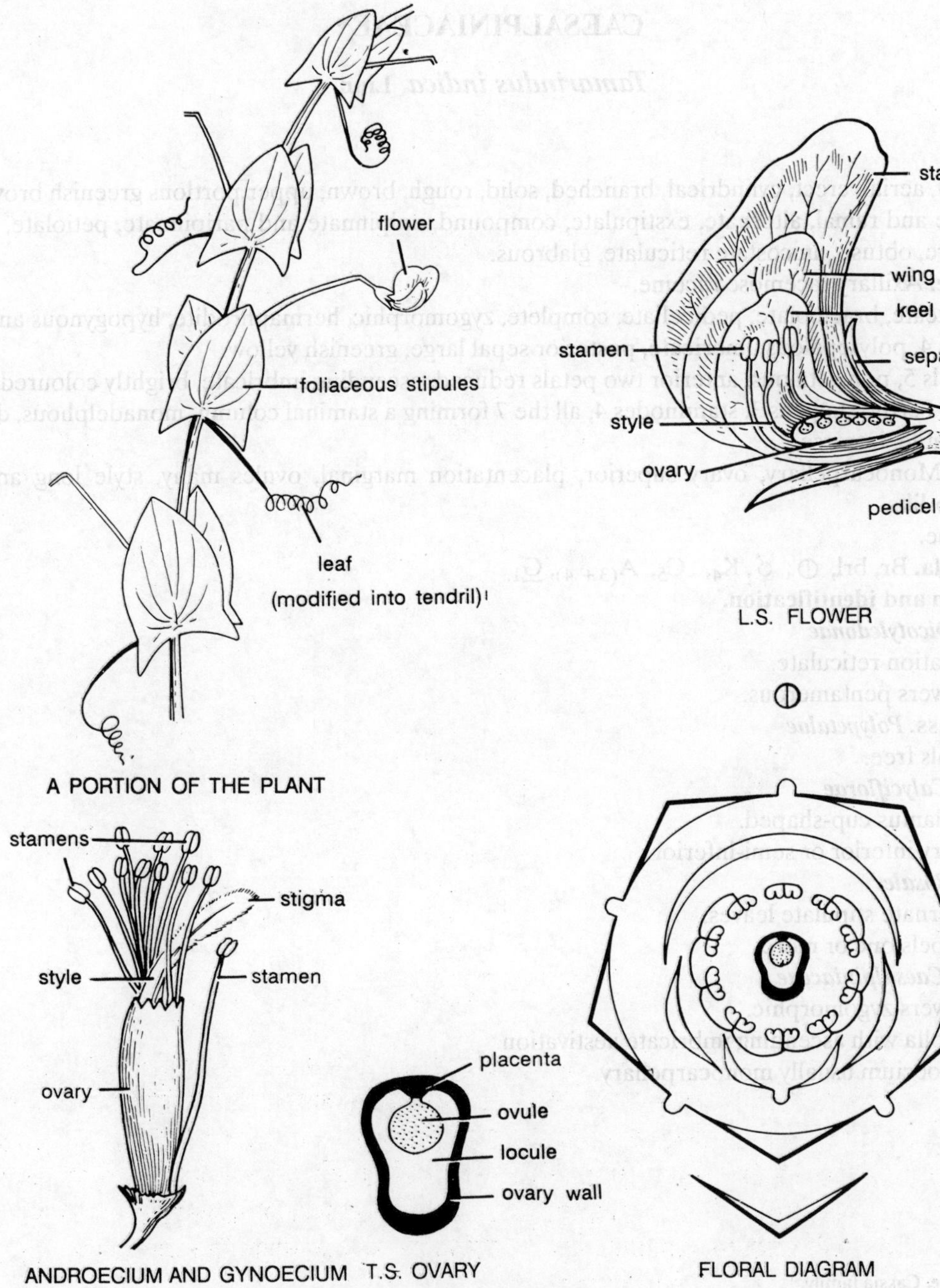

Fig. 27. ***Lathyrus aphaca.***

---

1. English names. Yellow vetchling, Wild Pea.

2. Vernacular name. Jangli-matar.

3. Economic importance. The plant is used as a cattle fodder.

CAESALPINIACEAE*

Tamarindus indica Linn.

Stem. Woody, aerial, erect, cylindrical, branched, solid, rough, brown, upper portions greenish brown.
Leaf. Cauline and ramal, alternate, exstipulate, compound, unipinnate and paripinnate, petiolate, elliptical, entire, obtuse, unicostate reticulate, glabrous.
Inflorescence. Axillary racemose raceme.
Flower. Bracteate, bracteolate, pedicellate, complete, zygomorphic, hermaphrodite, hypogynous and cyclic.
Calyx. Sepals 4, polysepalous, imbricate, posterior sepal large, greenish yellow.
Corolla. Petals 5, polypetalous, anterior two petals reduced, ascending imbricate, brightly coloured.
Androecium. Fertile stamens 3, staminodes 4, all the 7 forming a staminal column, monadelphous, dithecous, versatile, introrse.
Gynoecium. Monocarpellary, ovary superior, placentation marginal, ovules many, style long and stigma knob-like.
Fruit. Legume.
Floral formula. Br, brl, ⊕, ⚥, K_4, C_5, $A_{(3+4)}$, $\underline{G}_1$.
Classification and identification.

Class. ***Dicotyledonae***
1. Venation reticulate.
2. Flowers pentamerous.

Sub-Class. ***Polypetalae***
1. Petals free.

Series. ***Calyciflorae***
1. Thalamus cup-shaped.
2. Ovary inferior or semi-inferior.

Order. ***Rosales***
1. Alternate stipulate leaves.
2. Carpels one or more.

Family. ***Caesalpiniaceae***
1. Flowers zygomorphic.
2. Corolla with ascending imbricate aestivation.
3. Gynoecium usually monocarpellary.

***1. English name.** Cassia family.
2. Systematic position in other systems of classification.

Rendle(1925)	Engler and Prantl (1931)	Hutchinson(1959)
Dicotyledons	Dicotyledoneae	Dicotyledons
Dialypetalae	Archichlamydeae	Lignosae
Rosales	Rosales	Leguminales
Leguminosae	Leguminosae	Caesalpiniaceae
Caesalpinioideae (Sub.Fam.)	Caesalpinioideae (Sub Fam.)	

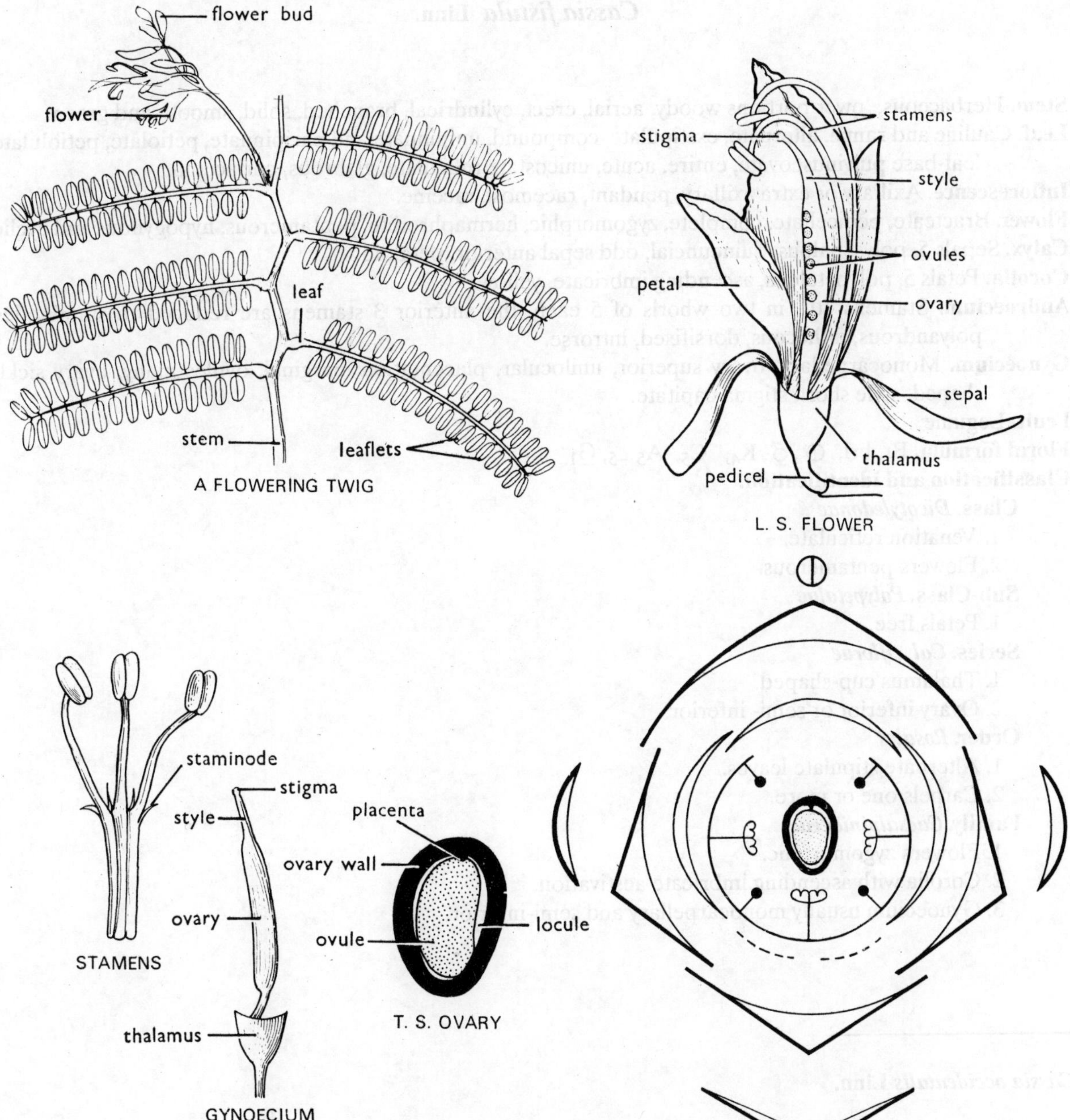

Fig. 28. ***Tamarindus indica.***

1. **English names.** Tamarind, Tamarindo.
2. **Vernacular names.** Imli, Tentul.
3. **Economic importance.** The fruits are edible and are also used medicinally as carminative and laxative. The unripe fruits are rich source of tartaric acid. The seeds yield jellose and polyose. Whereas the former is used as a sizing material in cotton mills, the latter is a substitute for fruit pectins.

Cassia fistula Linn.

Stem. Herbaceous, 'ower portions woody, aerial, erect, cylindrical, branched, solid, smooth and green.
Leaf. Cauline and ramal, alternate, exstipulate, compound, unipinnate and paripinnate, petiolate, petiolulate, leaf-base pulvinus, ovate, entire, acute, unicostate reticulate, glabrous, coriaceous.
Inflorescence. Axillary or extra axillary, pendant, racemose raceme.
Flower. Bracteate, pedicellate, complete, zygomorphic, hermaphrodite, pentamerous, hypogynous and cyclic.
Calyx. Sepals 5, polysepalous, quincuncial, odd sepal anterior, petaloid.
Corolla. Petals 5, polypetalous, ascending imbricate, yellow.
Androecium. Stamens 10, in two whorls of 5 each, the anterior 3 stamens are reduced to staminodes, polyandrous, dithecous, dorsifixed, introrse.
Gynoecium. Monocarpellary, ovary superior, unilocular, placentation marginal, ovules many, ovary sickle shaped, style short, stigma capitate.
Fruit. Legume.
Floral formula. Br, brl, Φ, ⚥, K_4, C_5, A_{5+5}, $\underline{G}_1$.
Classification and identification.

Class. *Dicotyledonae*
1. Venation reticulate.
2. Flowers pentamerous.

Sub-Class. *Polypetalae*
1. Petals free.

Series. *Calyciflorae*
1. Thalamus cup-shaped.
2. Ovary inferior or semi- inferior.

Order. *Rosales*
1. Alternate stipulate leaves.
2. Carpels one or more.

Family. *Caesalpiniaceae*
1. Flowers zygomorphic.
2. Corolla with ascending imbricate aestivation.
3. Gynoecium usually monocarpellary and semi-inferior.

Cassia occidentalis Linn.

Stem – Herbaceous, aerial, erect, cylindrical, branched, solid, glabrous and red; **Leaf** – Cauline and ramal, alternate, stipulate, free-lateral, compound, unipinnate and paripinnate, petiolate, petiolulate, a single gland present at the base of the petiole, elliptic-lanceolate, entire, acute, pubescent, unicostate reticulate; **Inflorescence** – Axillary cyme; **Flower** – Bracteate, pedicellate, complete, zygomorphic, hermaphrodite, pentamerous, hypogynous and cyclic; **Calyx** – Sepals 5, polysepalous, odd sepal anterior, quincuncial, boat- shaped; **Corolla** – Petals 5, polypetalous, ascending imbricate, yellow; **Androecium** – Stamens 10 in two whorls of 5 each, in outer whorl two posterior and one anterior stamen, and in the inner whorl one posterior stamen, are reduced to staminodes, rest stamens are fertile, 2 anterior stamens of inner whorl are large, polyandrous, filaments short, dithecous, basifixed, dehisce by apical pores; **Gynoecium** – Monocarpellary, ovary superior, unilocular, ovules many, placentation marginal, style curved, **Fruit** - Legume

Floral formula – Br, Φ, ⚥, K_4, C_5, A_{5+5}, $\underline{G}_1$.

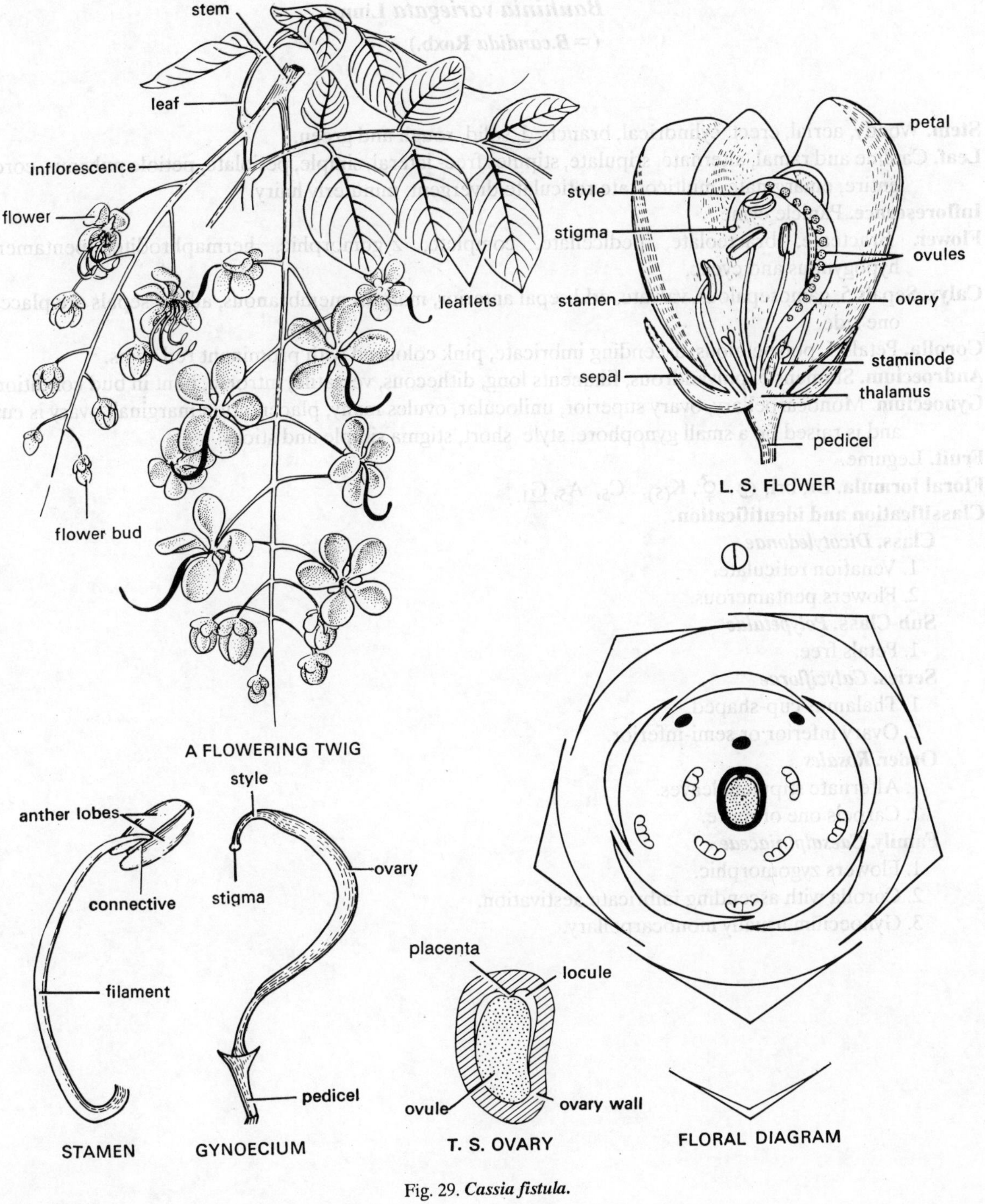

Fig. 29. ***Cassia fistula.***

---

1. **English names.** Indian laburnum, Golden shower.
2. **Vernacular names.** Amaltas, Bandarlauri, Gurmala.
3. **Economic importance.** Cultivated as an ornamental and the tree looks extremely handsome when in flower. The sweet, black pulp of the fruit is used as a purgative. The bark is used in dyeing and tanning.

Bauhinia variegata Linn.
(=*B.candida* Roxb.)

Stem. Woody, aerial, erect, cylindrical, branched, solid, rough and green.

Leaf. Cauline and ramal, alternate, stipulate, stipules free- lateral, simple, petiolate, petiole pulvinus, cordate, entire, emarginate, multicostate reticulate divergent, minuterly hairy.

Inflorescence. Panicle cyme.

Flower. Bracteate, bracteolate, pedicellate, complete, zygomorphic, hermaphrodite, pentamerous, hypogynous and cyclic.

Calyx. Sepals 5, gamosepalous, valvate, odd sepal anterior, margins membranous, all the sepals are placed on one side.

Corolla. Petals 5, polypetalous, ascending imbricate, pink coloured with prominent red veins.

Androecium. Stamens 5, polyandrous, filaments long, dithecous, versatile, introrse, bent in bud condition.

Gynoecium. Monocarpellary, ovary superior, unilocular, ovules many, placentation marginal, ovary is curved and is raised on a small gynophore, style short, stigma simple and sticky.

Fruit. Legume.

Floral formula. Br, brl, ⊕, ⚥, $K_{(5)}$, C_5, A_5, $\underline{G}_1$.

Classification and identification.

Class. ***Dicotyledonae***

1. Venation reticulate.
2. Flowers pentamerous.

Sub-Class. ***Polypetalae***

1. Petals free.

Series. ***Calyciflorae***

1. Thalamus cup-shaped.
2. Ovary inferior or semi-inferior.

Order. ***Rosales***

1. Alternate stipulate leaves.
2. Carpels one or more.

Family. ***Caesalpiniaceae***

1. Flowers zygomorphic.
2. Corolla with ascending imbricate aestivation.
3. Gynoecium usually monocarpellary.

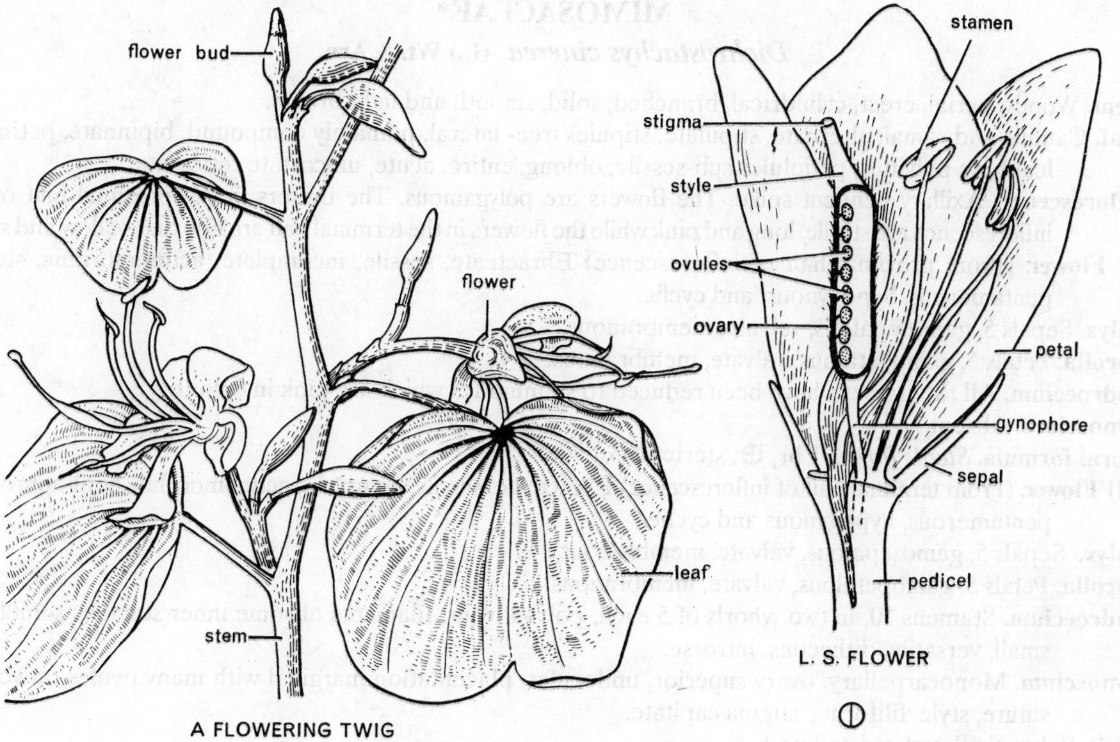

Fig. 30. ***Bauhinia variegata.***

1. English names. Mountain ebony, Variegated Bauhinia.

2. Vernacular names. Kachnar.

3. Economic importance. The flower buds are eaten as vegetable. The bark is used for dyeing and tanning. The plant is cultivated as an ornamental.

MIMOSACEAE*

Dichrostachys cinerea (L.) Wt. & Arn.

Stem. Woody, aerial, erect, cylindrical, branched, solid, smooth and light brown.

Leaf. Cauline and ramal, alternate, stipulate, stipules free- lateral, pinnately compound, bipinnate, petiolate, leaf base pulvinus, petiolules sub-sessile, oblong, entire, acute, unicostate reticulate.

Inflorescence. Axillary pendent spike. The flowers are polygamous. The flowers in the proximal half of the inflorescence are sterile, long and pink while the flowers in the terminal half are bisexual, yellow and short.

[I] Flower. (From proximal half of inflorescence) Ebracteate, sessile, incomplete, actinomorphic, sterile, pentamerous, hypogynous and cyclic.

Calyx. Sepals 5, gamosepalous, valvate, membranous.

Corolla. Petals 5, gamopetalous, valvate, membranous.

Androecium. All the stamens have been reduced to staminodes which are pink in colour.

Gynoecium. Absent.

Floral formula. *Sterile flower.* Ebr, ⊕, sterie, $K_{(5)}$, $C_{(5)}$, A_0, G_0

[II] Flower. (From terminal half of inflorescence) Ebracteate, sessile, complete, actinomorphic, hermaphrodite, pentamerous, hypogynous and cyclic.

Calyx. Sepals 5, gamosepalous, valvate, membranous.

Corolla. Petals 5, gamopetalous, valvate, membranous.

Androecium. Stamens 10, in two whorls of 5 each, polyandrous, filaments of some inner stamens sometimes small, versatile, dithecous, introrse.

Gynoecium. Monocarpellary, ovary superior, unilocular, placentation marginal with many ovules on ventral suture, style filiform , stigma capitate.

Fruit. Sub-articulated, twisted pod.

Floral formula. *Fertile flower.* Ebr, ⊕ , ⚥ , $K_{(5)}$, A_{5+5}, $\underline{G_1}$

Classification and identification.

Class. ***Dicotyledonae***

1. Venation reticulate.
2. Flowers pentamerous.

Sub-Class. ***Polypetalae***

1. Petals free.

Series. ***Calyciflorae***

1. Alternate stipulate leaves.
2. Carpels one or more.

Order. ***Rosales***

1. Thalamus cup-shaped.
2. Ovary usually inferior or semi-inferior.

Family. ***Mimosaceae***

1. Flowers actinomorphic.
2. Gynoecium usually one and superior. 3. Corolla valvate. 4. Fruit generally lomentum.

***1. English name.** Acacia family.

2. Systematic position in other systems of classification.

Rendle (1925)	**Engler and Prantl (1931)**	**Hutchinson (1959)**
Dicotyledons	Dicotyledoneae	Dicotyledons
Dialypetalae	Archichlamydeae	Lignosae
Rosales	Rosales	Leguminales
Leguminosae	Leguminosae	Mimosaceae
Mlmosoideae (sub. fam.)	Mimosoideae (sub.Fam.)	

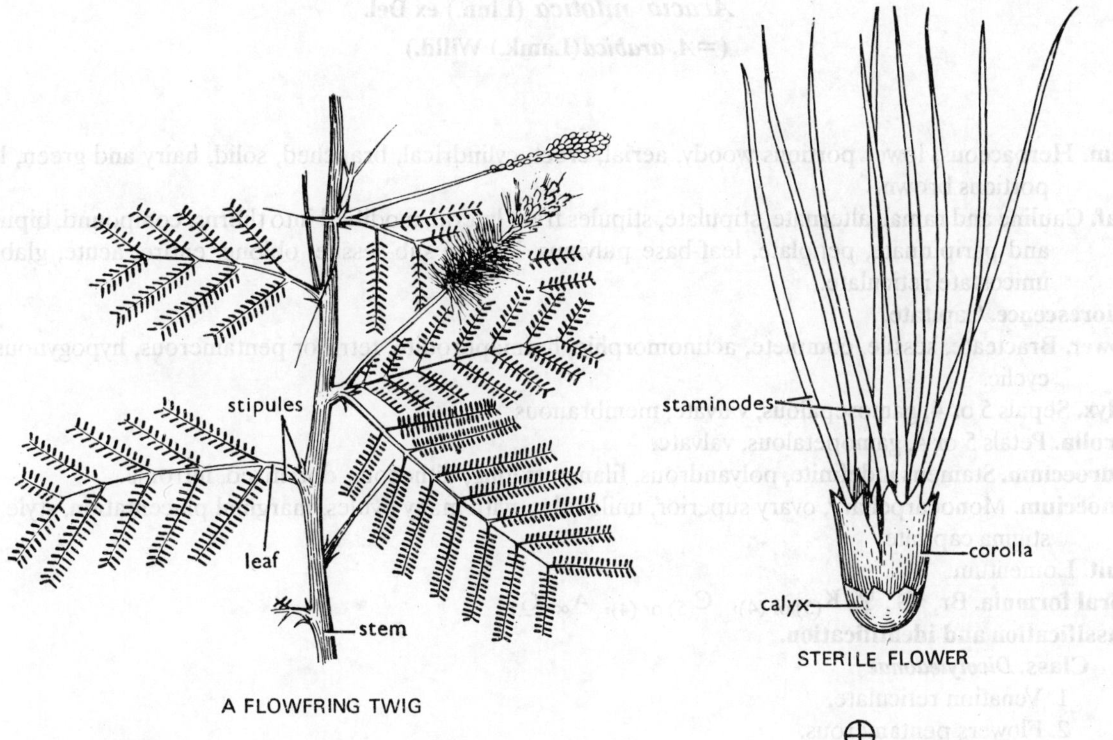

Fig. 31. ***Dichrostachys cinerea.***

1. Vernacular names. Vertuli, Kunlai.

2. Economic importance. The bark is used for tanning and the root in rheumatism and renal troubles.

Acacia nilotica (Linn.) ex Del.
(=*A. arabica*(Lamk.) Willd.)

Stem. Herbaceous, lower portions woody, aerial, erect, cylindrical, branched, solid, hairy and green, lower portions brown.

Leaf. Cauline and ramal, alternate, stipulate, stipules free- lateral, modified into thorns, compound, bipinnate and paripinnate, petiolate, leaf-base pulvinus, leaflets sub-sessile, oblong, entire, acute, glabrous, unicostate reticulate.

Inflorescence. Capitate.

Flower. Bracteate, sessile, complete, actinomorphic, hermaphrodite, tetra-or pentamerous, hypogynous and cyclic.

Calyx. Sepals 5 or 4, gamosepalous, valvate, membranous

Corolla. Petals 5 or 4, gamopetalous, valvate.

Androecium. Stamens indefinite, polyandrous, filaments long, dithecous, dorsifixed, introrse.

Gynoecium. Monocarpellary, ovary superior, unilocular, with many ovules, marginal placentation, style long, stigma capitate.

Fruit. Lomentum.

Floral formula. Br, $\oplus$, ⚥, $K_{(5)\text{ or }(4)}$, $C_{(5)\text{ or }(4)}$, A_{∞}, $\underline{G}_1$.

Classification and identification.

Class. ***Dicotyledonae***
1. Venation reticulate.
2. Flowers pentamerous.

Sub-Class. ***Polypetalae***
1. Petals free.

Series. ***Calyciflorae***
1. Alternate stipulate leaves.
2. Carpels one or more.

Order. ***Rosales***
1. Thalamus cup-shaped.
2. Ovary usually inferior or semi-inferior

Family. ***Mimosaceae***
1. Flowers actinomorphic.
2. Gynoecium usually one and ovary superior.
3. Corolla valvate.
4. Fruit generally lomentum.

Mimosa pudica Linn.

Stem – Herbaceous, lower portions woody, aerial, diffuse, cylindrical, branched, solid, hairy; **Leaf** – Cauline and ramal, alternate,stipulate, free -lateral, compound, bipinnate, petiolate, leaf base pulvinus, pinnae 10-20 pairs, sessile, oblong., entire, acute, hairy, unicostate, reticulate, sensitive to touch; **Inflorescence** – Axillary capitate; **Flower** – Bracteate, sessile, complete, actinomorphic, hermaphrodite, tetramerous, hypogynous and cyclic; **Calyx** – Sepals 4, gamosepalous, valvate; **Corolla** – Petals 4, gamopetalous, valvate; **Androecium** – Stamens 4, polyandrous, filament long, dithecous, dorsifixed, introrse, **Gynoecium** – Monocarpellary, ovary superior, unilocular, ovules many, placentation marginal, style long and stigma simple; **Fruit** – Lomentum:

Floral formula – Br, $\oplus$, ⚥, $K_{(4)}$, $C_{(4)}$, A_4, $\underline{G}_1$.

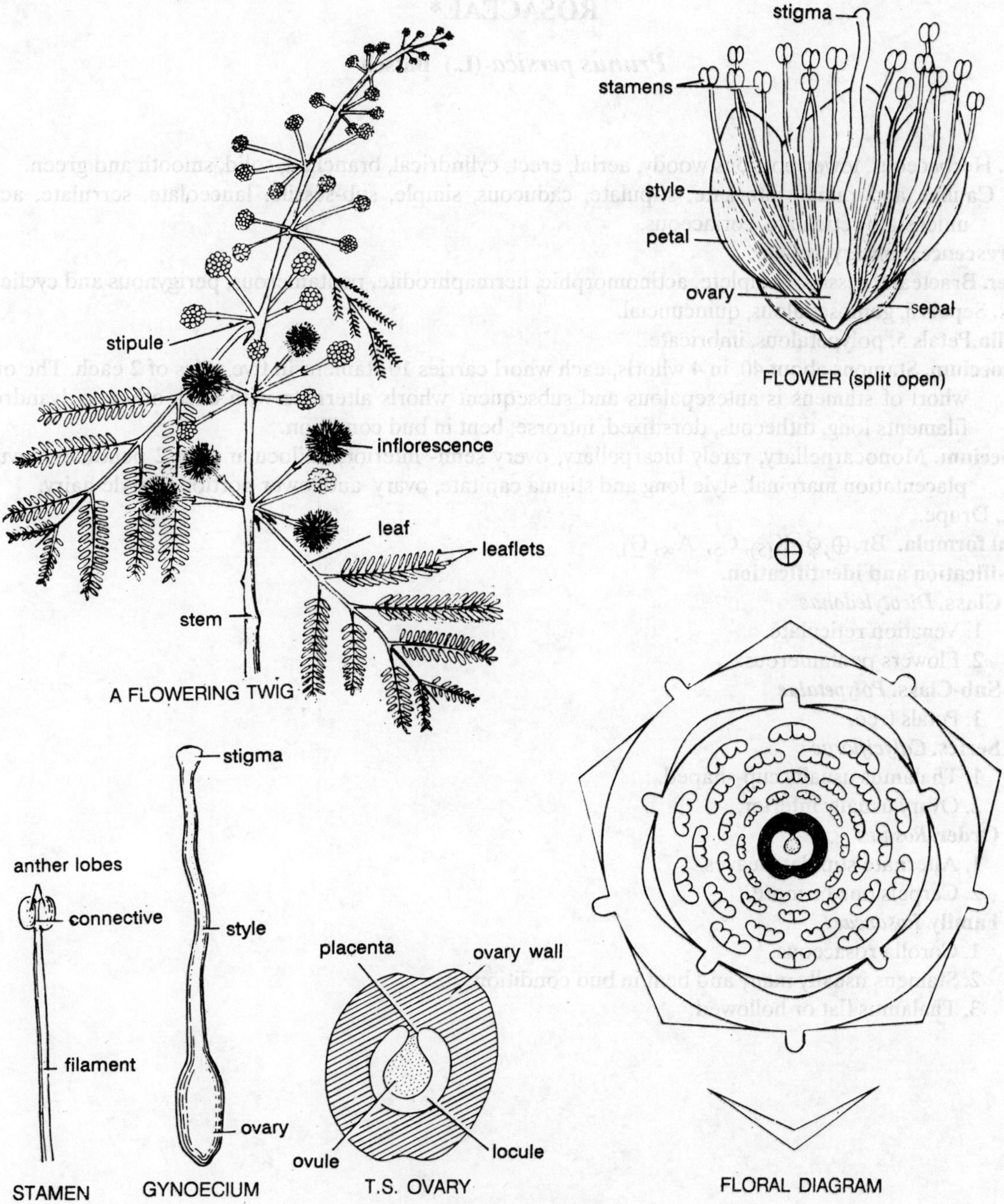

Fig. 32. ***Acacia nilotica.***

---

1. English name. Babool Acacia.

2. Vernacular names. Babool, Kikar.

3. Economic importance. Gum obtained from the stems is used medicinally in dysentry. The bark is used as a tan.

ROSACEAE*

Prunus persica (L.) Batsch

Stem. Herbaceous, lower portions woody, aerial, erect, cylindrical, branched, solid, smooth and green.

Leaf. Cauline and ramal, alternate, stipulate, caducous, simple, sub-sessile, lanceolate, serrulate, acute, unicostate reticulate, coriaceous,

Inflorescence. Solitary axillary.

Flower. Bracteate, sessile, complete, actinomorphic, hermaphrodite, pentamerous, perigynous and cyclic.

Calyx. Sepals 5, gamosepalous, quincuncial.

Corolla. Petals 5, polypetalous, imbricate.

Androecium. Stamens about 40, in 4 whorls, each whorl carries 10 stamens in five pairs of 2 each. The outer whorl of stamens is antesepalous and subsequent whorls alternate with each other, polyandrous, filaments long, dithecous, dorsifixed, introrse, bent in bud condition.

Gynoecium. Monocarpellary, rarely bicarpellary, overy semi- inferior, unilocular with 2 pendulous ovules, placentation marginal, style long and stigma capitate, ovary and lower portion of style hairy.

Fruit. Drupe.

Floral formula. $Br, \oplus, ⚥, K_{(5)}, C_5, A_{\infty}, \underline{G}_1.$

Classification and identification.

Class. ***Dicotyledonae***

1. Venation reticulate.
2. Flowers pentamerous.

Sub-Class. ***Polypetalae***

1. Petals free.

Series. ***Calyciflorae***

1. Thalamus usually cup-shaped.
2. Ovary usually inferior.

Order. ***Rosales***

1. Alternate stipulate leaves.
2. Carpels one or more.

Family. ***Rosaceae***

1. Corolla rosaceous.
2. Stamens usually many and bent in bud condition.
3. Thalamus flat or hollowed.

***1. English name.** Rose family.

2. Systematic position in other systems of classification.

Rendle (1925)	**Engler and Prantl (1931)**	**Hutchinson (1959)**
Dicotyledons	Dicotyledoneae	Dicotyledons
Dialypetalae	Archichlamydeae	Lignosae
Rosales	Rosales	Rosales
Rosaceae	Rosaceae	Rosaceae

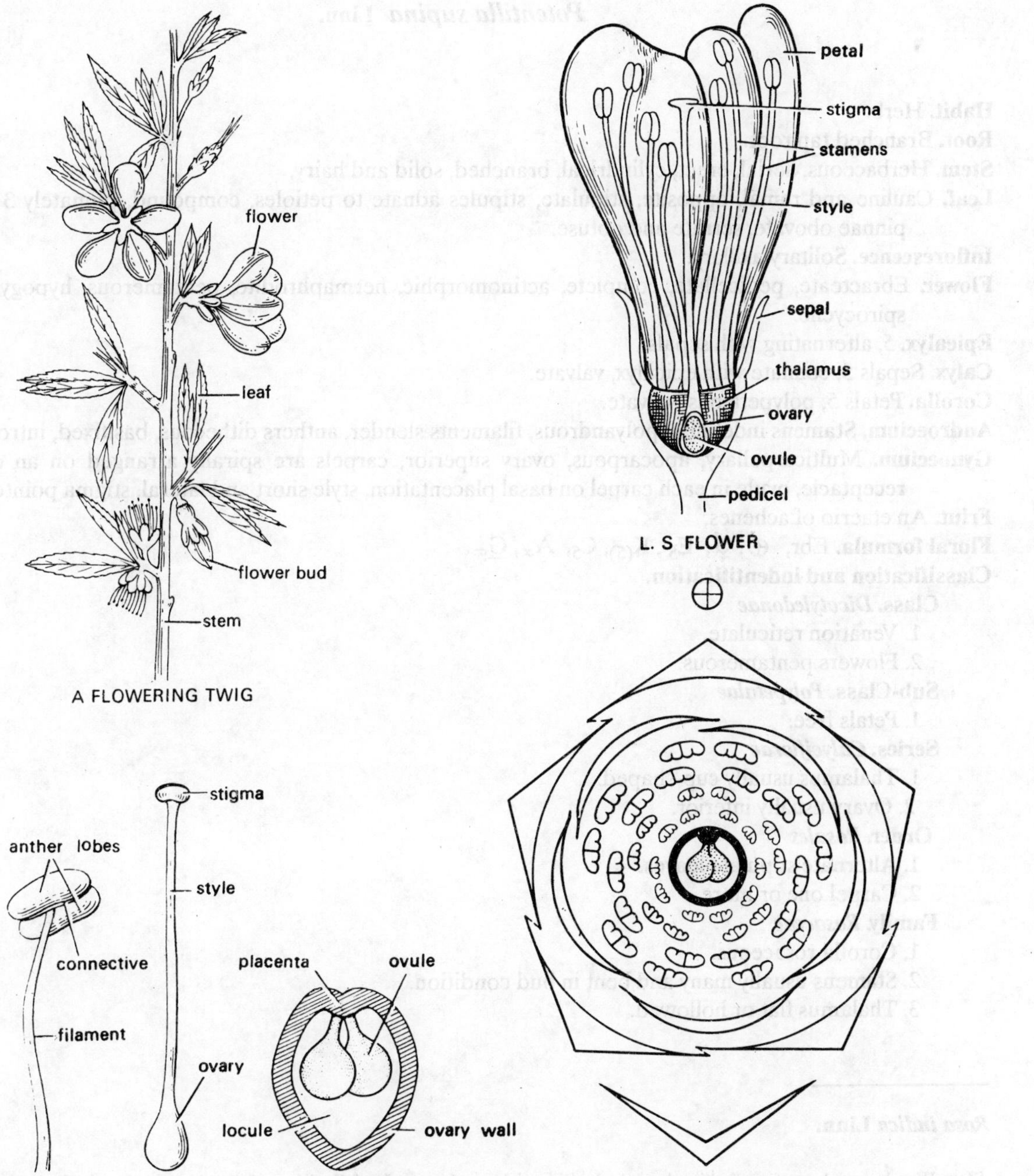

Fig. 33. ***Prunus persica.***

---

1. English name. Peach.

2. Vernacular name. Aru.

3. Economic importance. This plant is grown for its edible fruits which are antiscorbutic.

Potentilla supina Linn.

Habit. Herb.
Root. Branched tap root.
Stem. Herbaceous, aerial, erect, cylindrical, branched, solid and hairy.
Leaf. Cauline and ramal, opposite, stipulate, stipules adnate to petioles, compound, pinnately 3-9 foliate, pinnae obovate, serrate and obtuse.
Inflorescence. Solitary axillary.
Flower. Ebracteate, pedicellate, complete, actinomorphic, hermaphrodite, pentamerous, hypogynous and spirocyclic.
Epicalyx. 5, alternating with sepals.
Calyx. Sepals 5, connate with epicalyx, valvate.
Corolla. Petals 5, polypetalous, valvate.
Androecium. Stamens indefinite, polyandrous, filaments slender, anthers dithecous, basifixed, introrse.
Gynoecium. Multicarpellary, apocarpous, ovary superior, carpels are spirally arranged on an elongated receptacle, ovule in each carpel on basal placentation, style short and lateral, stigma pointed.
Friut. An etaerio of achenes.
Floral formula. Ebr, ⊕, ⚥, E_5, $K_{(5)}$, C_5, A_∞, $\underline{G}_\infty$.
Classification and indentification.

Class. ***Dicotyledonae***
1. Venation reticulate.
2. Flowers pentamerous.

Sub-Class. ***Polypetalae***
1. Petals free.

Series. ***Calyciflorae***
1. Thalamus usually cup-shaped.
2. Ovary usually inferior.

Order. ***Rosales***
1. Alternate stipulate leaves.
2. Carpel one or more.

Family. ***Rosaceae***
1. Corolla rosaceous.
2. Stamens usually many and bent in bud condition.
3. Thalamus flat or hollowed.

Rosa indica Linn.

Stem-Woody, aerial, erect or climbing, branched, solid, prickly and green: **Leaf**-Cauline and ramal, alternate, stipulate, stipules adnate, compound, unipinnate and imparipinnate, petiolate, petiolulate, ovate, serrate, acute, unicostate, reticulate; **Inflorescence**-Flowers solitary or in terminal pairs or sometimes in clusters; **Flower**- Ebracteate, pedicellate, complete, actinomorphic, hermaphrodite, epigynous, and cyclic; **Calyx**-Sepals 5, gamosepalous, quincuncial, persistent and hairy; **Corolla**-Petals 5 or more, polypetalous, imbricate, rosaceous, variously coloured; **Androecium**-Stamens indefinite, polyandrous, filaments slender and unequal, dithecous, dorsifixed, introrse; **Gynoecium**-Polycarpellary, apocarpous, ovary inferior, enclosed in calyx tube, basal placentation, style short, stigma capitate; **Fruit**- Etaerio of achenes;

Floral formula- Ebr, ⊕, ⚥, E_5, $K_{(5)}$, C_5, A_∞, $\underline{G}_\infty$

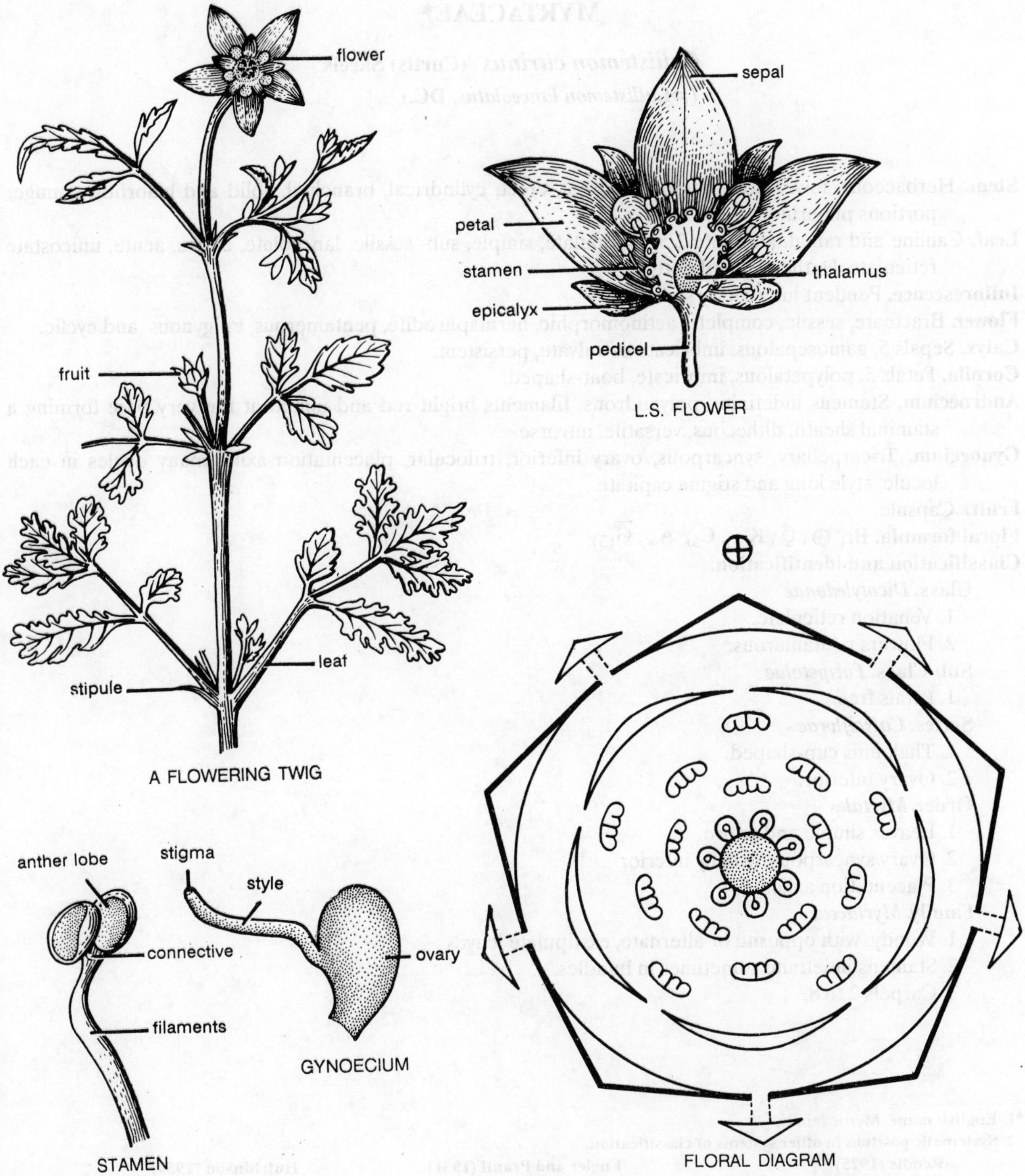

Fig. 34. ***Potentilla supina.***

MYRTACEAE*

Callistemon citrinus (Curtis) Skeels
(=*Callistemon lanceolatus*, DC.)

Stem. Herbaceous, lower portion woody, aerial, erect, cylindrical, branched, solid and glabrous, younger portions puberulous, brown.

Leaf. Cauline and ramal, alternate 2/5, exstipulate, simple, sub- sessile, lanceolate, entire, acute, unicostate reticulate, leathery, gland dotted.

Inflorescence. Pendent intercalary spike.

Flower. Bracteate, sessile, complete, actinomorphic, hermaphrodite, pentamerous, epigynous and cyclic.

Calyx. Sepals 5, gamosepalous, imbricate or valvate, persistent.

Corolla. Petals 5, polypetalous, imbricate, boat-shaped.

Androecium. Stamens indefinite, polyandrous, filaments bright red and united at the very base forming a staminal sheath, dithecous, versatile, introrse.

Gynoecium. Tricarpellary, syncarpous, ovary inferior, trilocular, placentation axile, many ovules in each locule, style long and stigma capitate.

Fruit. Capsule.

Floral formula. Br, $\oplus$, ⚥, $K_{(5)}$, C_5, A_∞, $\overline{G}_{(3)}$.

Classification and identification.

Class. ***Dicotyledonae***
1. Venation reticulate.
2. Flowers pentamerous.

Sub-Class. ***Polypetalae***
1. Petals free.

Series. ***Calyciflorae***
1. Thalamus cup-shaped.
2. Ovary inferior.

Order. ***Myrtales***
1. Leaves simple and entire.
2. Ovary syncarpous, usually inferior.
3. Placentation axile.

Family. ***Myrtaceae***
1. Woody, with opposite or alternate, exstipulate leaves.
2. Stamens indefinite sometimes in bundles.
3. Carpels 2 to 8.

---

*1. **English name**. Myrtle family.

2. **Systematic position in other systems of classification.**

Rendle (1925)	Engler and Prantl (1931)	Hutchinson (1959)
Dicotyledons	Dicotyledoneae	Dicotyledons
Dialypetalae	Archichlamydeae	Lignosae
Myrtiflorae	Myrtiflorae	Myrtales
Myrtaceae	Myrtaceae	Myrtaceae

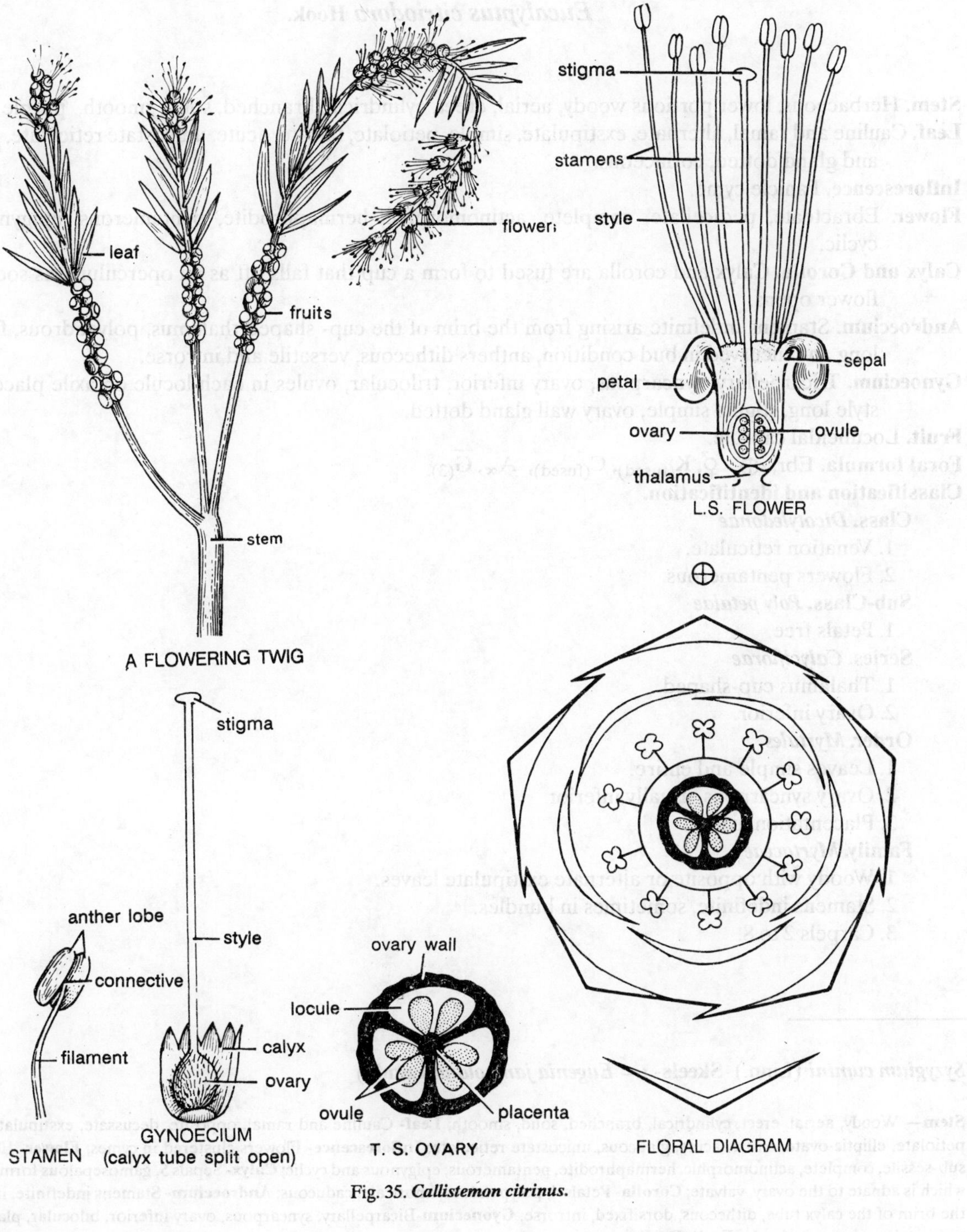

Fig. 35. ***Callistemon citrinus.***

---

1. **English names.** Bottle-brush.
2. **Vernacular name.** Laal botal brush.
3. **Economic importance.** The plant is largely cultivated as an ornamental and looks extremely beautiful when in flower.

Eucalyptus citriodora Hook.

Stem. Herbaceous, lower portions woody, aerial, erect, cylindrical, branched, solid, smooth, purple brown.
Leaf. Cauline and ramal, alternate, exstipulate, simple, petiolate, falcate, acute, unicostate reticulate, glabrous and gland dotted, coriaceous.
Inflorescence. Panicle cyme.
Flower. Ebracteate, pedicellate, complete, actinomorphic, hermaphrodite, pentamerous, epigynous and cyclic.
Calyx and Corolla. Calyx and corolla are fused to form a cup that falls off as an operculum as soon as the flower opens.
Androecium. Stamens indefinite arising from the brim of the cup- shaped thalamus, polyandrous, filaments long and incurved in bud condition, anthers dithecous, versatile and introrse.
Gynoecium. Tricarpellary, syncarpous, ovary inferior, trilocular, ovules in each locule on axile placentation, style long, stigma simple, ovary wall gland dotted.
Fruit. Loculicidal capsule.
Foral formula. Ebr, $\oplus$, ⚥, $K_{(fused)}$, $C_{(fused)}$, A_{∞}, $\overline{G}_{(3)}$.
Classification and identification.

Class. ***Dicotyledonae***
1. Venation reticulate.
2. Flowers pentamerous.

Sub-Class. ***Poly petalae***
1. Petals free.

Series. ***Calyciflorae***
1. Thalamus cup-shaped.
2. Ovary inferior.

Order. ***Myrtales***
1. Leaves simple and entire.
2. Ovary syncarpous, usually inferior
3. Placentation axile.

Family. ***Myrtaceae***
1. Woody with opposite or alternate exstipulate leaves.
2. Stamens indefinite, sometimes in bundles.
3. Carpels 2 to 8.

Syzygium cumini (Linn.) Skeels- (= *Eugenia jambolana* Lamk.)

Stem— Woody, aerial, erect, cylindrical, branched, solid, smooth; **Leaf-** Cauline and ramal, opposite, decussate, exstipulate, simple, petiolate, elliptic-ovate, entire, acute, glaucous, unicostate reticulate; **Inflorescence-** Flowers clustered in cymes; **Flower-** Ebracteate, sub-sessile, complete, actinomorphic, hermaphrodite, pentamerous, epigynous and cyclic; **Calyx-** Sepals 5, gamosepalous forming a tube which is adnate to the ovary, valvate; **Corolla-** Petals 4, polypetalous, imbricate, caducous; **Androecium-** Stamens indefinite, inserted at the brim of the calyx tube, dithecous, dorsifixed, introrse; **Gyonecium**-Bicarpellary, syncarpous, ovary inferior, bilocular, placentation axile, style and stigma simple; **Fruit-** Drupe;

Floral formula.- Ebr, $\oplus$, ⚥, $K_{(5)}$, C_4, A_{∞}, $\overline{G}_{(3)}$

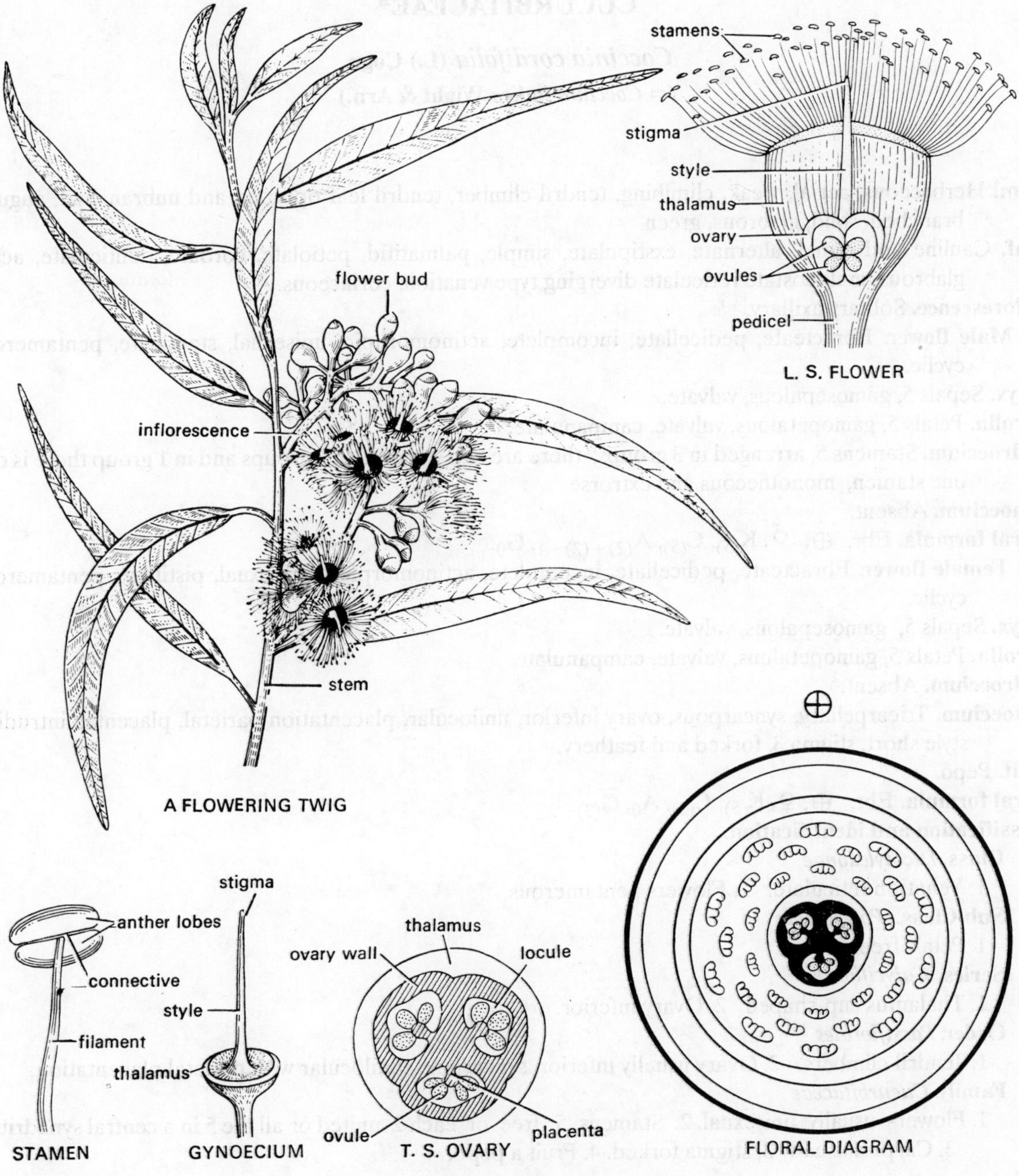

Fig. 36. ***Eucalyptus citriodora.***

---

1. English names. Lemon-scented gum, Eucalyptus.

2. Vernacular name. Safeda.

3. Economic importnce. The leaves yield an essential oil which is used in perfumery. Now-a- days the pulp from stem is being used in the manufacture of paper.

CUCURBITACEAE*

Coccinia cordifolia (L.) Cogn.

(= *Coccinia indica* Wight & Arn.)

Stem. Herbaceous, aerial, weak, climibing, tendril climber, tendril leaf opposed and unbranched, angular, branched, solid, glabrous, green.

Leaf. Cauline and ramal, alternate, exstipulate, simple, palmatifid, petiolate, cordate, denticulate, acute, glabrous, multicostate reticulate diverging type venation, coriaceous.

Inflorescence. Solitary axillary.

[I] Male flower. Ebracteate, pedicellate, incomplete, actinomorhpic, unisexual, staminate, pentamerous, cyclic.

Calyx. Sepals 5, gamosepalous, valvate.

Corolla. Petals 5, gamopetalous, valvate, campanulate.

Androecium. Stamens 5, arranged in 3 groups, there are two stamens in 2 groups and in 1 group there is only one stamen, monothecous and extrorse.

Gynoecium. Absent.

Floral formula. Ebr, ⊕, ♂, $K_{(5)}$, $C_{(5)}$, $A_{(2)+(2)+1}$, G_0.

[II] Female flower. Ebracteate, pedicellate, incomplete, actinomorphic, unisexual, pistillate, pentamerous, cyclic.

Calyx. Sepals 5, gamosepalous, valvate.

Corolla. Petals 5, gamopetalous, valvate, campanulate.

Androecium. Absent.

Gynoecium. Tricarpellary, syncarpous, ovary inferior, unilocular, placentation parietal, placentae intruding, style short, stigma 3, forked and feathery.

Fruit. Pepo.

Floral formula. Ebr, ⊕, ♀, $K_{(5)}$, $C_{(5)}$, A_0, $\overline{G}_{(3)}$.

Classification and identification.

Class. ***Dicotyledonae***

1. Venation reticulate. 2. Flowers pentamerous.

Sub-Class. ***Polypetalae***

1. Petals free.

Series. ***Calyciflorae***

1. Thalamus cup-shaped. 2. Ovary inferior.

Order. ***Passiflorales***

1. Tendril climbers. 2. Ovary usually inferior, syncarpous, unilocular with parietal placentation.

Family. ***Cucurbitaceae***

1. Flowers usually unisexual. 2. Stamens 5, free or each 2 united or all the 5 in a central synadrium. 3. Carpels usually 3, stigma forked. 4. Fruit a pepo.

***1. English name.** Gourd family.

2. Systematic position in other systems of classification.

Rendle (1925)	Engler and Prantl (1931)	Hutchinson (1959)
Dicotyledons	Dicotyledoneae	Dicotyledons
Dialypetalae	Sympetalae	Lignosae
Peponiferae	Cucurbitales	Cucurbitales
Cucurbitaceae	Cucurbitaceae	Cucurbitaceae

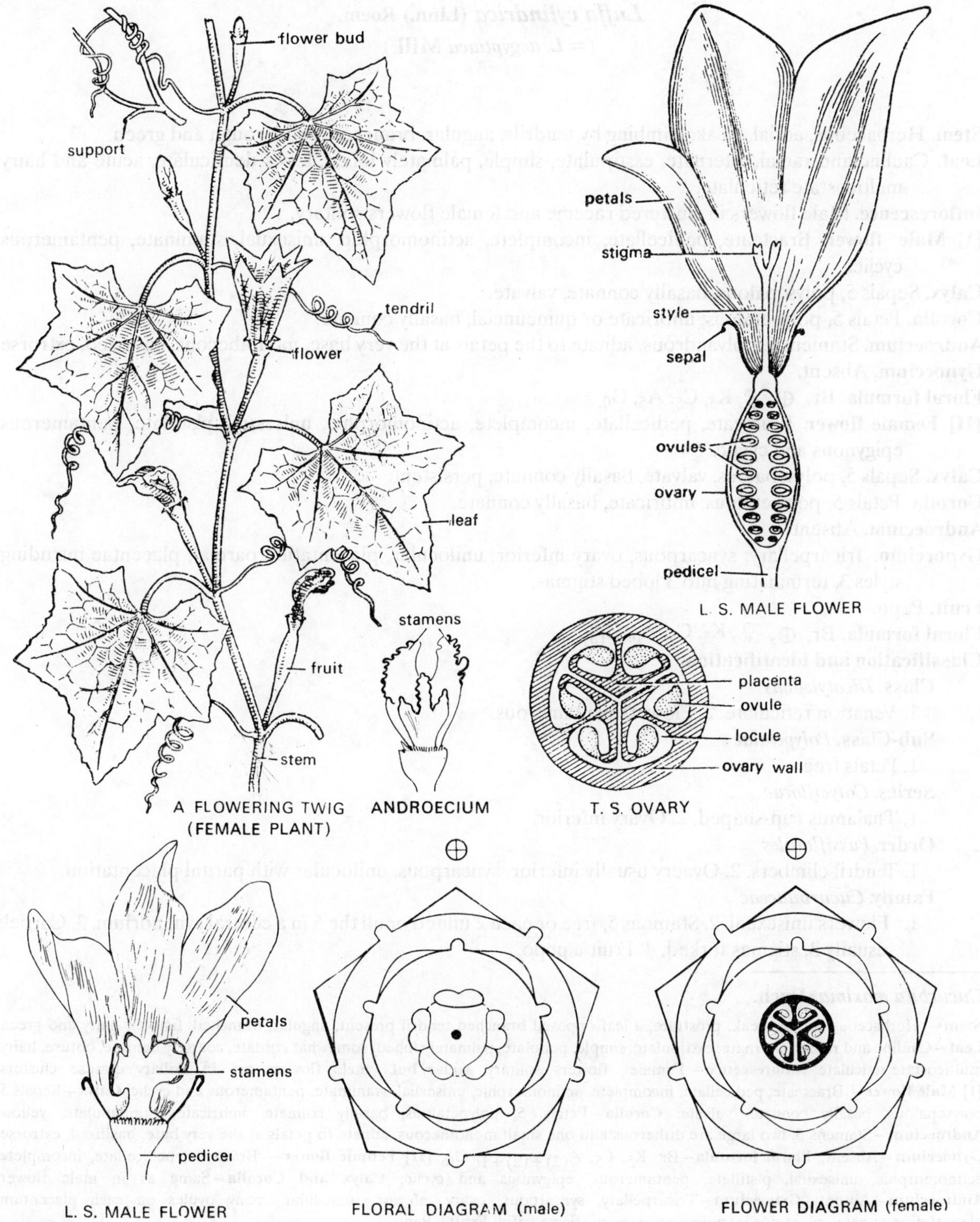

Fig. 37. ***Coccinia cordifolia.***

---

1. English name. Kovai fruit.

2. Vernacular names. Kanduri, Kudroom.

3. Economic importance. Plant is dioecious. The fruits are used as vegetable.

Luffa cylindrica (Linn.) Roem.
(= *L. aegyptiaca* Mill.)

Stem. Herbaceous, aerial, weak, climbing by tendrils, angular, branched, solid, rough and green.

Leaf. Cauline and ramal, alternate, exstipulate, simple, palmately lobed, lobes denticulate, acute and hairy, multicostate reticulate.

Inflorescence. Male flowers in clustered raceme and female flowers solitary.

[I] Male flower. Bracteate, pedicellate, incomplete, actinomorphic, unisexual, staminate, pentamerous, cyclic.

Calyx. Sepals 5, polysepalous, basally connate, valvate.

Corolla. Petals 5, polypetalous, imbricate or quincuncial, basally connate.

Androecium. Stamens 5, polyandrous, adnate to the petals at the very base, monothecous, basifixed, extrorse.

Gynoecium. Absent.

Floral formula. Br, ⊕, ♂, K_5, C_5, A_5, G_0.

[II] Female flower. Bracteate, pedicellate, incomplete, actinomorphic, unisexual, pistillate, pentamerous, epigynous and cyclic.

Calyx. Sepals 5, polysepalous, valvate, basally connate, persistent.

Corolla. Petals 5, polypetalous, imbricate, basally connate.

Androecium. Absent

Gynoecium. Tricarpellary, syncarpous, ovary inferior, unilocular, placentation paretal, placentae intruding, styles 3, terminating into 3 lobed stigmas.

Fruit. Pepo.

Floral formula. Br, ⊕, ♀, K_5, C_5, A_0, $G_{(3)}$.

Classification and identification.

Class. ***Dicotyledons***

1. Venation reticulate. 2. Flowers pentamerous.

Sub-Class. ***Polypetalae***

1. Petals free.

Series. ***Calyciflorae***

1. Thalamus cup-shaped. 2. Ovary inferior.

Order. ***Passiflorales***

1. Tendril climbers. 2. Ovaery usually inferior, syncarpous, unilocular with parital placentation.

Family. ***Cucurbitaceae***

1. Flowers unisexual. 2. Stamens 5, free or each 2 united or all the 5 in a central synandrium. 3. Carpels usually 3, stigmas forked. 4. Fruit a pepo.

Cucurbita maxima Duch.

Stem— Herbaceous, aerial, weak, prostrate, a leaf-opposed branched tendril present, angular, branched, fistular, hairy and green; **Leaf**—Cauline and ramal, alternate, exstipulate, simple, petiolate, palmately lobed, somewhat cordate, coarsely dentate, obtuse, hairy, multicostate reticulate; **Inflorescence**— Female flowers solitary axillary but male flowers are in axillary cymose clusters; **[I] Male flower**— Bracteate, pedicellate, incomplete, actinomorphic, unisexual, staminate, pentamerous and cyclic; **Calyx**—Sepals 5, polysepalous, basally connate, valvate; **Corolla**—Petals, 5, polypetalous, basally connate, imbricate, campanulate, yellow; **Androecium**—Stamens 3, two large are dithecous and one small monothecous, adnate to petals at the very base, basifixed, extrorse; **Gynoecium**—Absent; **Floral formula**—Br, K_5, C_5, $A_{(2)+(2)+1}$, G_0; **[II] Female flower**— Bracteate, pedicellate, incomplete, actinomorphic, unisexual, pistillate, pentamerous, epigynous and cyclic; **Calyx and Corolla**—Same as in male flower; **Androecium**—Absent; **Gynoecium**—Tricarpellary, syncarpous, ovary inferior, unilocular, many ovules on each placentum, placentation parietal, placentae intruding, style short, stigma trifid; **Fruit**—Pepo.

Floral formula—Br, ⊕, ♀, K_5, C_5, A_0, $\overline{G}_{(3)}$

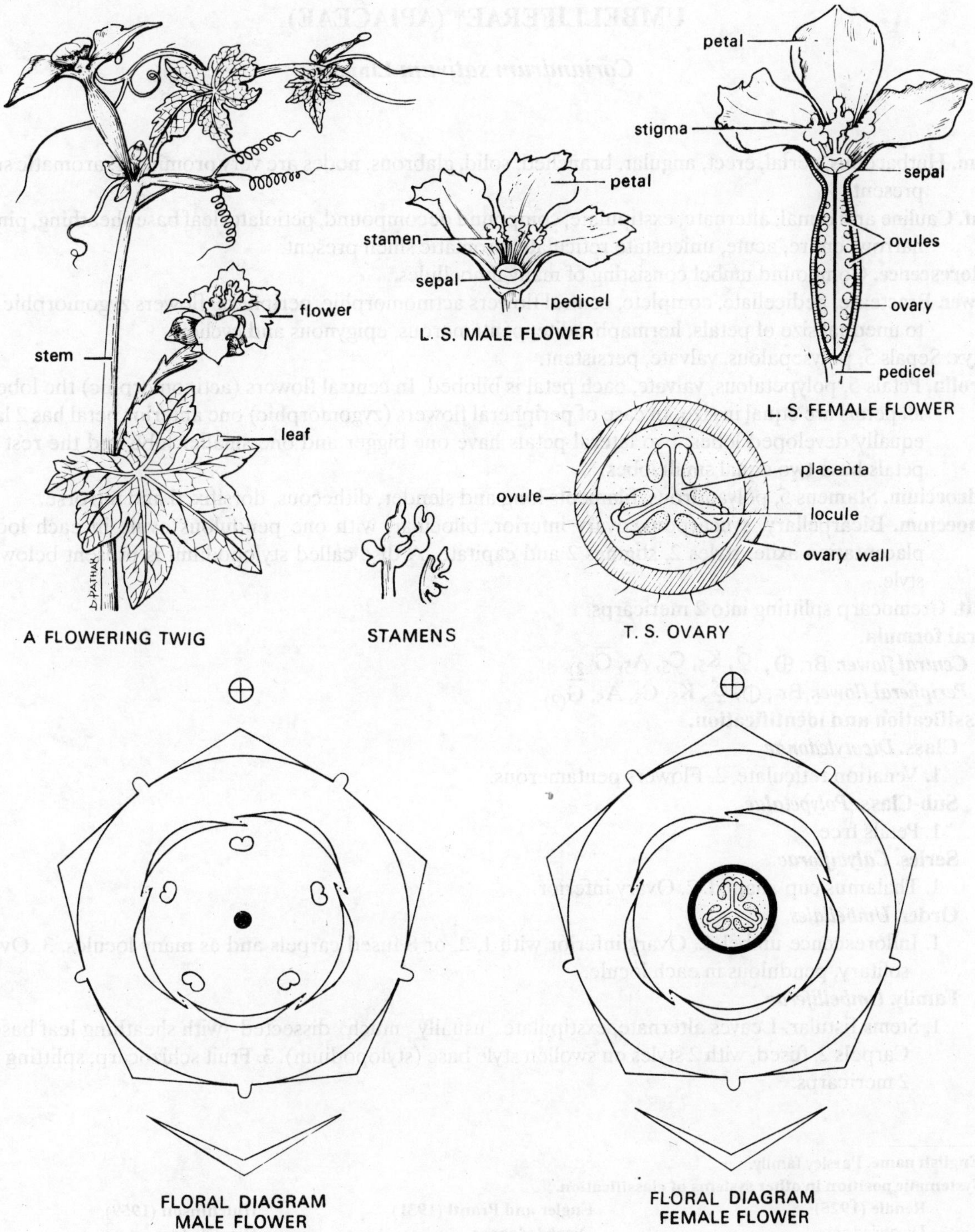

Fig. 38. ***Luffa cylindrica.***

---

1. English names. Vegetable sponge, Dishcloth gourd.

2. Vernacular name. Ghia tori.

3. Economic importance. Cultivated for its fruits which are used as vegetable. Dried fruits yield sponge.

UMBELLIFERAE* (APIACEAE)

Coriandrum sativum Linn.

Stem. Herbaceous, aerial, erect, angular, branched, solid, glabrous, nodes are very prominent, aromatic smell present.

Leaf. Cauline and ramal, alternate, exstipulate, compound decompound, petiolate, leaf base sheathing, pinnae narrow, entire, acute, unicostate reticulate, aromatic smell present.

Inflorescence. Compound umbel consisting of many umbellules.

Flower. Bracteate, pedicellate, complete, central flowers actinomorphic, peripheral flowers zygomorphic due to unequal size of petals, hermaphrodite, pentamerous, epigynous and cyclic.

Calyx. Sepals 5, polysepalous, valvate, persistent.

Corolla. Petals 5, polypetalous, valvate, each petal is bilobed. In central flowers (actinomorphic) the lobes of all petals are equal in size. In case of peripheral flowers (zygomorphic) one anterior petal has 2 large equally developed lobes, two lateral petals have one bigger and one smaller lobe and the rest two petals have two equal small lobes.

Androecium. Stamens 5, polyandrous, filaments long and slender, dithecous, dorsifixed and introrse.

Gynoecium. Bicarpellary, syncarpous, ovary inferior, bilocular, with one pendulous ovule in each locule, placentation axile, styles 2, stigmas 2 and capitate. A disc called stylopodium is present below the style.

Fruit. Cremocarp splitting into 2 mericarps.

Floral formula.

(a) Central flower. Br, ⊕, ⚥, K_5, C_5, A_5, $\overline{G}_{(2)}$.

(b) Peripheral flower. Br, ⦶, ⚥, K_5, C_5, A_5, $\overline{G}_{(2)}$.

Classification and identification.

Class. ***Dicotyledonae***

1. Venation reticulate. 2. Flowers pentamerous.

Sub-Class. ***Polypetalae***

1. Petals free.

Series. ***Calyciflorae***

1. Thalamus cup-shaped. 2. Ovary inferior.

Order. ***Umbellales***

1. Inflorescence umbel. 2. Ovary inferior with 1, 2, or 8 fused carpels and as many locules. 3. Ovules solitary, pendulous in each locule.

Family. ***Umbelliferae***

1. Stems fistular. Leaves alternate, exstipulate usually much dissected with sheathing leaf base. 2. Carpels 2, fused, with 2 styles on swollen style base (stylopodium). 3. Fruit schizocarp, splitting into 2 mericarps.

***1. English name.** Parsley family.

2. Systematic position in other systems of classification.

Rendle (1925)	**Engler and Prantl (1931)**	**Hutchinson (1959)**
Dicotyledons	Dicotyledoneae	Dicotyledons
Dialypetalae	Archichlamydeae	Herbaceae
Umbelliflorae	Umbelliflorae	Umbellales
Umbelliferae	Umbelliferae	Umbelliferae

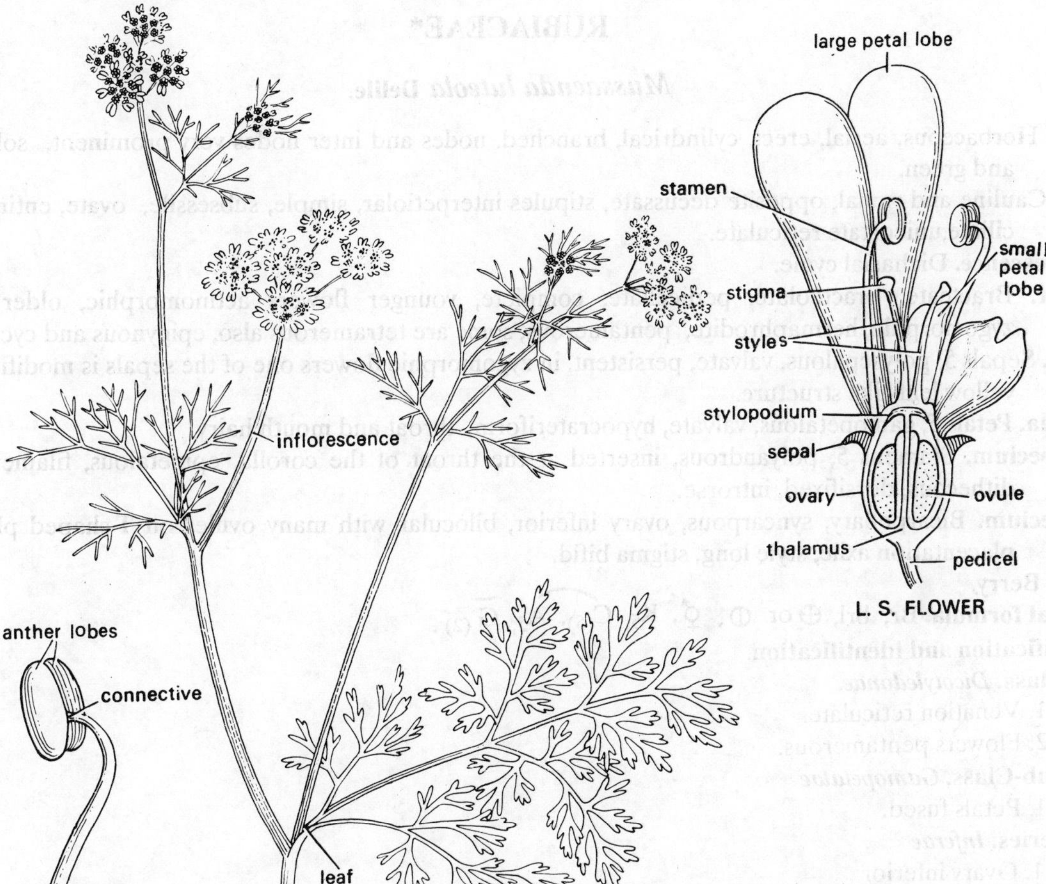

Fig. 39. ***Coriandrum sativum.***

---

1. **English name.** Coriander.
2. **Vernacular name.** Dhania.
3. **Economic importance.** The leaves and fruits are used as condiment and flavouring material.

RUBIACEAE*

Mussaenda luteola Delile.

Stem. Herbaceous, aerial, erect, cylindrical, branched, nodes and inter nodes very prominent, solid, hairy and green.

Leaf. Cauline and ramal, opposite decussate, stipules interpetiolar, simple, subsessile, ovate, entire, acute, ciliate,unicostate reticulate.

Inflorescence. Dichasial cyme.

Flower. Bracteate, bracteolate, pedicellate, complete, younger flowers actinomorphic, older flowers zygomorphic, hermaphrodite, pentamerous, some are tetramerous also, epigynous and cyclic.

Calyx. Sepals 5, polysepalous, valvate, persistent, in zygomorphic flowers one of the sepals is modified into a yellow leaf-like structure.

Corolla. Petals 5, gamopetalous, valvate, hypocrateriform, throat and mouth hairy.

Androecium. Stamens 5, polyandrous, inserted at the throat of the corolla, epipetalous, filament short, dithecous, dorsifixed, introrse.

Gynoecium. Bicarpellary, syncarpous, ovary inferior, bilocular with many ovules on T-shaped placentae, placentation axile, style long, stigma bifid.

Fruit. Berry.

Floraal formula. Br, brl, ⊕ or ⦶, ⚥, K_5, $\overset{\frown}{C_{(5)}, A_5}$, $\overline{G}_{(2)}$.

Classification and identification.

Class. ***Dicotyledonae.***
1. Venation reticulate.
2. Flowers pentamerous.

Sub-Class. ***Gamopetalae***
1. Petals fused.

Series. ***Inferae***
1. Ovary inferior.
2. Stamens usually as many as corolla lobes.

Order. ***Rubiales***
1. Leaves opposite.
2. Stamens epipetalous.
3. Ovary 2-8 locular.

Family. ***Rubiaceae***
1. Opposite decussate, entire leaves with interpetiolar stipules.
2. Flowers in cymes.
3. Gynoecium bicarpellary, syncarpous, inferior, each locule with 1-8 ovules.
4. Placentum T-shaped.

***1. English name.** Madder family

2. Systematic position in other systems of classification.

Rendle (1925)	**Engler and Prantl** (1931)	**Hutchinson** (1959)
Dicotyledons	Dicotyledoneae	Dicotyledons
Sympetalae	Sympetalae	Lignosae
Tetracyclicae	Rubiales	Rubiales
Inferae	Rubiaceae	Rubiaceae
Rubiales		
Rubiaceae		

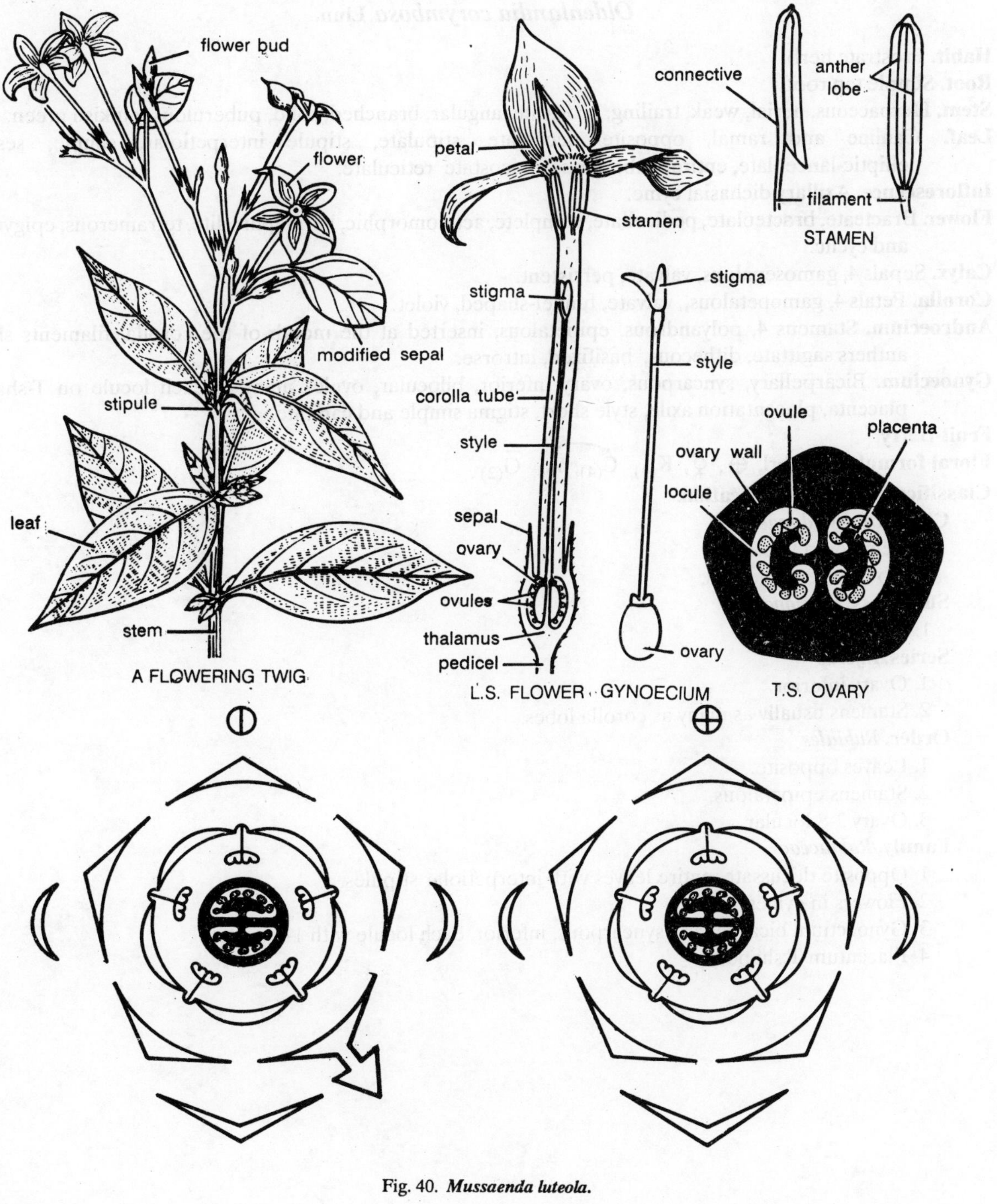

Fig. 40. ***Mussaenda luteola.***

---

1. Economic importance. The plant is grown asanornamental.

Oldenlandia corymbosa Linn.

Habit. Prostrate herb.

Root. Simple tap root.

Stem. Herbaceous, aerial, weak, trailing, prostrate, angular, branched, solid, puberulous, pinkish green.

Leaf. Cauline and ramal, opposite decussate, stipulate, stipule interpetiolar, simple, sessile, elliptic-lanceolate, entire, puberulous, unicostate reticulate.

Inflorescence. Axillary dichasial cyme.

Flower. Bracteate, bracteolate, pedicellate, complete, actinomorphic, hermaphrodite, tetramerous, epigynous and cyclic.

Calyx. Sepals 4, gamosepalous, valvate, persistent.

Corolla. Petals 4, gamopetalous, valvate, funnel-shaped, violet.

Androecium. Stamens 4, polyandrous, epipetalous, inserted at the mouth of the corolla, filaments short, anthers sagittate, dithecous, basifixed, introrse.

Gynoecium. Bicarpellary, syncarpous, ovary inferior, bilocular, ovules many in each locule on T-shaped placenta, placentation axile, style short, stigma simple and capitate.

Fruit-Berry.

Floral formula. Br, brl, $\oplus$, ⚥, $K_{(4)}$, $\overparen{C_{(4)}, A_{4}}$, $\overline{G}_{(2)}$.

Classification and identification.

Class. ***Dicotyledonae***

1. Venation reticulate.
2. Flowers pentamerous.

Sub-Class. ***Gamopetalae***

1. Petals fused.

Series. ***Inferae***

1. Ovary inferior.
2. Stamens usually as many as corolla lobes.

Order. ***Rubiales***

1. Leaves opposite.
2. Stamens epipetalous.
3. Ovary 2-8 locular.

Family. ***Rubiaceae***

1. Opposite decussate, entire leaves with interpetiolar stipules.
2. Flowers in cymes.
3. Gynoectium bicarpellary, syncarpous, inferior, each locule with 1-8 ovules.
4. Placentum T.shaped.

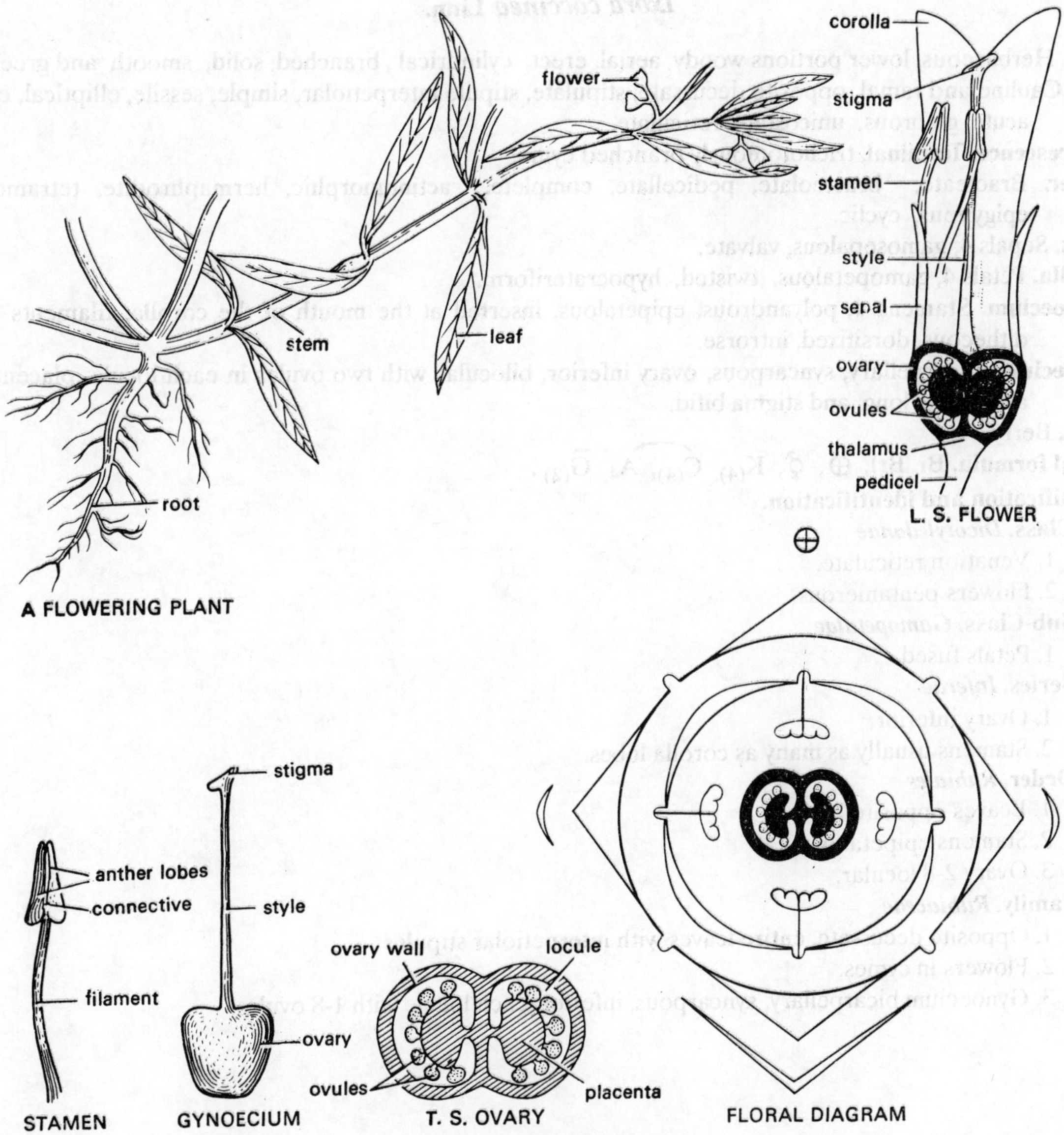

Fig. 41. ***Oldenlandia corymbosa.***

---

1. English name. Daman-paper.

2. Economic importance. The decoction of the plant is used as a cure for bilious attacks, dysentry and cholera.

Ixora coccinea Linn.

Stem. Herbaceous, lower portions woody, aerial, erect, cylindrical, branched, solid, smooth and green.

Leaf. Cauline and ramal, opposite decussate, stipulate, stipule interpetiolar, simple, sessile, elliptical, entire, acute, glabrous, unicostate, reticulate.

Inflorescence. Terminal, trichotomously branched cyme.

Flower. Bracteate, bracteolate, pedicellate, complete, actinomorphic, hermaphrodite, tetramerous, epigynous, cyclic.

Calyx. Sepals 4, gamosepalous, valvate.

Corolla. Petals 4, gamopetalous, twisted, hypocrateriform.

Androecium. Stamens 4, polyandrous, epipetalous, inserted at the mouth of the corolla, filaments short, dithecous, dorsifixed, introrse.

Gynoecium. Bicarpellary, syncarpous, ovary inferior, bilocular with two ovules in each locule, placentation axile, style long and stigma bifid.

Fruit. Berry.

Floral formula. Br, Brl, ⊕, ⚥, $K_{(4)}$, $\overparen{C_{(4)}, A_4}$, $\overline{G}_{(2)}$.

Classification and identification.

Class. *Dicotyledonae*

1. Venation reticulate.
2. Flowers pentamerous.

Sub-Class. *Gamopetalae*

1. Petals fused.

Series. *Inferae*

1. Ovary inferior.
2. Stamens usually as many as corolla lobes.

Order. *Rubiales*

1. Leaves opposite,
2. Stamens epipetalous.
3. Ovary 2-8 locular.

Family. *Rubiaceae*

1. Opposite decussate, entire leaves with interpetiolar stipules.
2. Flowers in cymes.
3. Gynoecium bicarpellary, syncarpous, inferior, each locule with 1-8 ovules.

Spermadictyon suaveolens Roxb. (=*Hamiltonia suaveolens* Roxb.)

Stem- Herbaceous, lower portions woody, aerial, erect, cylindrical, branched, solid, green, **Leaf-** Cauline and ramal, opposite decussate, stipulate, interpetiolar, simple, sub- sessile, elliptic- lanceolate, entire, acute, puberulous, unicostate reticulate; **Inflorescence-** Umbellate cyme; **Flower-** Bracteate, bracteolate, subsessile, complete, actinomorphic , hermaphrodite, pentamerous, epigynous and cyclic; **Calyx** - Sepals 5, gamosepalous, valvate; **Corolla-** Petals 5, gamopetalous, valvate, trumpet shaped; **Androecium-** Stamens 5, polyandrous, epipetalous, inserted at the throat of the corolla, filament short, dithecous, basifixed, introrse; **Gynoecium** - Pentacarpellary, (sometimes hexacarpellary), syncarpous, inferior, pentalocular (sometimes hexalocular) with one ovule in each locule, placentation axile, style filiform, stigmas as many as carpels and linear; **Fruit** - Capsule;

Floral formula - Br, brl, ⊕, ⚥, $K_{(5)}$, $\overparen{C_{(5)}, A_5}$, $\overline{G}_{(2)}$.

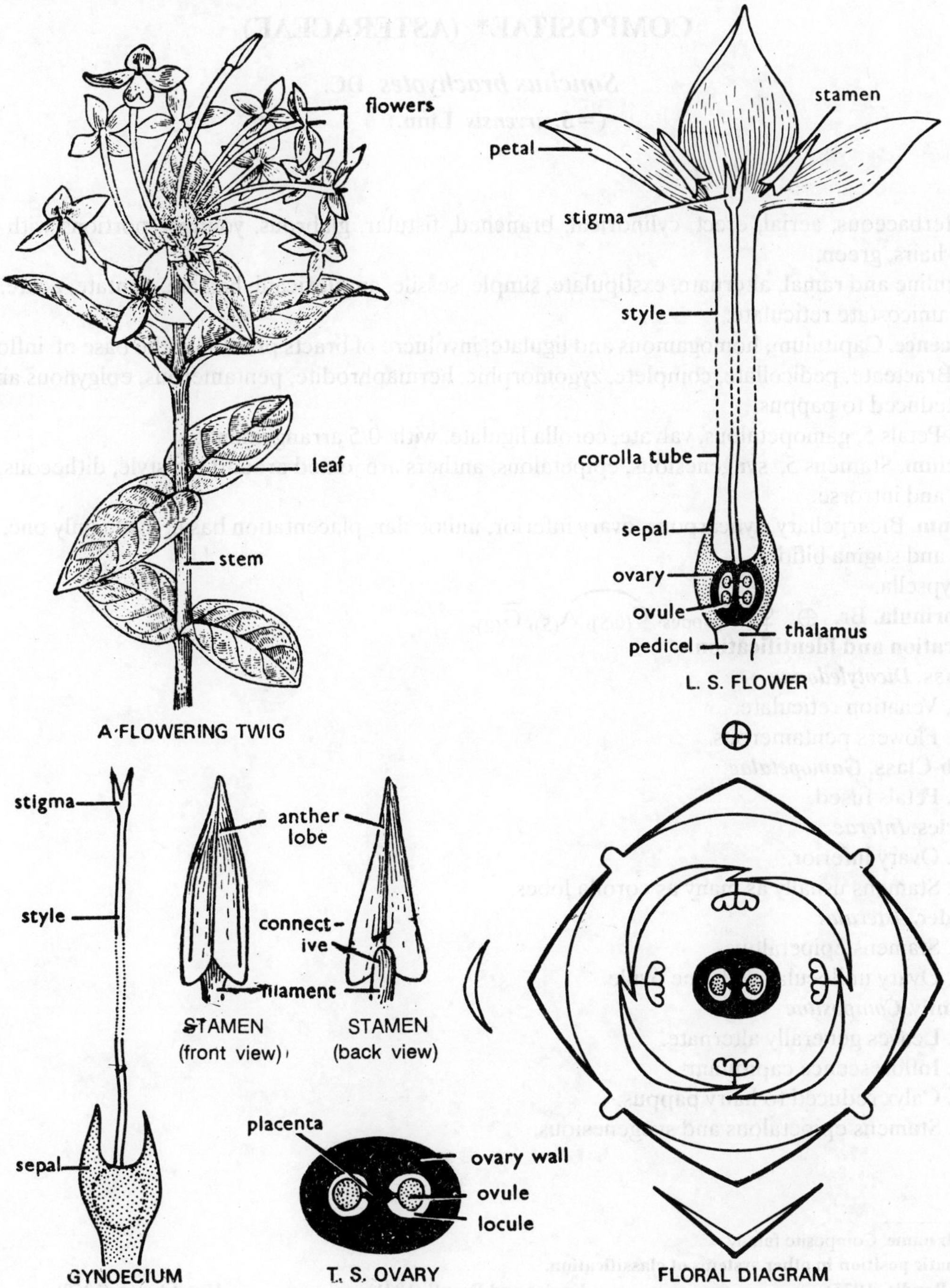

Fig. 42. *Ixora coccinea.*

---

1. **English names.** Jungle flame, Ixora.
2. **Vernacular names.** Rangan, Rookmini, Rajana.
3. **Economic importance.** The plant is grown as an ornamental.

COMPOSITAE* (ASTERACEAE)

Sonchus brachyotes DC.

(=*S. arvensis* Linn.)

Stem. Herbaceous, aerial, erect, cylindrical, branched, fistular, glabrous, younger portions with glandular hairs, green.

Leaf. Cauline and ramal, alternate, exstipulate, simple, sessile, amplexicaul, hastate, dentate, acute, glabrous, unicostate reticulate.

Inflorescence. Capitulum, homogamous and ligulate, involucre of bracts present at the base of inflorescence.

Flower. Bracteate, pedicellate, complete, zygomorphic, hermaphrodite, pentamerous, epigynous and cyclic.

Calyx. Reduced to pappus.

Corolla. Petals 5, gamopetalous, valvate, corolla ligulate, with 0/5 arrangement..

Androecium. Stamens 5, syngenesious, epipetalous, anthers are joined around the style, dithecous, basifixed and introrse.

Gynoecium. Bicarpellary, syncarpous, ovary inferior, unilocular, placentation basal, ovule only one, style long and stigma bifid.

Fruit. Cypsella.

Floral formula. Br, $\oplus$, ⚥, K_{pappus}, $\overset{\frown}{C_{(0/5)}, A_{(5)}}$, $\overline{G}_{(2)}$.

Classification and identification.

Class. ***Dicotyledonae***

1. Venation reticulate.
2. Flowers pentamerous.

Sub-Class. ***Gamopetalae***

1. Petals fused.

Series. ***Inferae***

1. Ovary inferior.
2. Stamens usually as many as corolla lobes.

Order. ***Asterales***

1. Stamens epipetalous.
2. Ovary unilocular with one ovule.

Family. ***Compositae***

1. Leaves generally alternate.
2. Inflorescence capitulum.
3. Calyx reduced to hairy pappus.
4. Stamens epipetalous and syngenesious.

---

*1. **English name.** Composite family.

2. **Systematic position in other systems of classification.**

Rendle (1925)	**Engler and Prantl (1931)**	**Hutchinson (1959)**
Dicotyedons	Dicotyledoneae	Dicotyledons
Sympetalae	Sympetalae	Herbaceae
Tetracyclicae	Campanulatae	Asterales
Inferae	Compositae	Compositae
Campanulales		
Compositae		

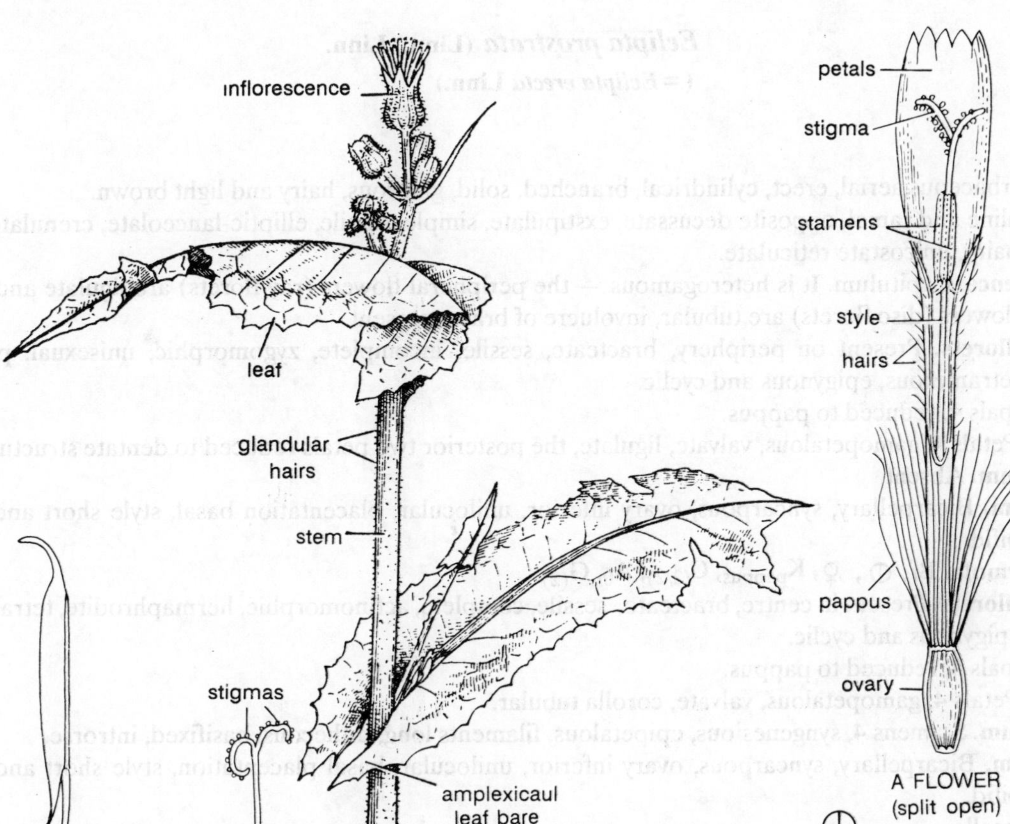

Fig. 43. ***Sonchus arvensis.***

1. Economic importance. The plant is used medicinally in many parts of this country.

Eclipta prostrata (Linn.) Linn.
(= *Eclipta erecta* Linn.)

Stem. Herbaceous,aerial, erect, cylindrical, branched, solid, glabrous, hairy and light brown.

Leaf. Cauline and ramal, opposite decussate, exstipulate, simple, sessile, elliptic-lanceolate, crenulate, acute, hairy, unicostate reticulate.

Inflorescence. Capitulum. It is heterogamous – the peripheral flowers (ray florets) are ligulate and central flowers (disc florets) are tubular, involucre of bracts present.

[I] Ray florets. Present on periphery, bracteate, sessile, incomplete, zygomorphic, unisexual, pistillate, tetramerous, epigynous and cyclic.

Calyx. Sepals 4, reduced to pappus.

Corolla. Petals 4, gamopetalous, valvate, ligulate, the posterior two petals reduced to dentate structures.

Androecium. Absent.

Gynoecium. Bicarpellary, syncarpous, ovary inferior, unilocular, placentation basal, style short and stigma bifid.

Floral formula. Br, ⦶ , ♀, K_{pappus}, $C_{(2/2)}$, A_0, $\overline{G}_{(2)}$.

[II] Disc florets. Present in centre, bracteate, sessile, complete, actinomorphic, hermaphrodite, tetramerous, epigynous and cyclic.

Calyx. Sepals 4, reduced to pappus.

Corolla. Petals 4, gamopetalous, valvate, corolla tubular.

Androecium. Stamens 4, syngenesious, epipetalous, filaments long, dithecous, basifixed, introrse.

Gynoecium. Bicarpellary, syncarpous, ovary inferior, unilocular, basal placentation, style short and stigma bifid.

Fruit. Cypsella.

Floral formula. Br, ⊕, ⚥, K_{pappus}, $\overgroup{C_{(4)}, A_{(4)}}$, $\overline{G}_{(2)}$.

Classification and identification.

Class. ***Dicotyledonae***
1. Venation reticulate.
2. Flowers pentamerous.

Sub-Class. ***Gamopetalae***
1. Petals fused.

Series. ***Inferae***
1. Ovary inferior.
2. Stamens usually as many as corolla lobes.

Order. ***Asterales***
1. Stamens epipetalous.
2. Ovary unilocular with one ovule.

Family. ***Compositae***
1. Leaves generally alternate.
2. Inflorescence capitulum.
3. Calyx reduced to hairy pappus.
4. Stamens epipetalous and syngenesious.

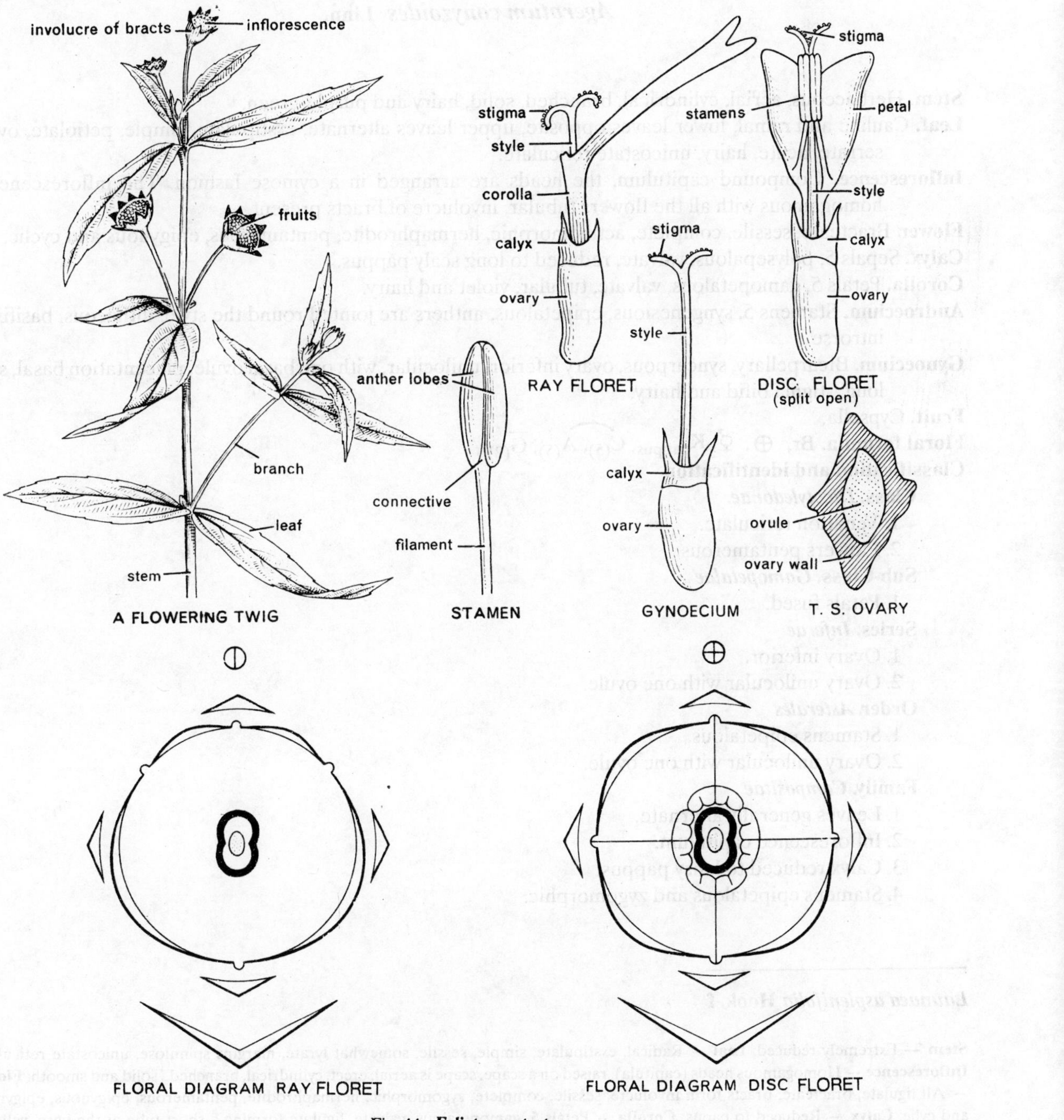

Fig. 44. ***Eclipta prostrata.***

1. **Vernacular name.** Bhangra.
2. **Economic importance.** The juice of the plant is used in cases of spleen enlargement. In Bengal the fresh leaves are employed in tatooing the skin.

Ageratum conyzoides Linn.

Stem. Herbaceous, aerial, cylindrical, branched, solid, hairy and purple-green.

Leaf. Cauline and ramal, lower leaves opposite, upper leaves alternate, exstipulate, simple, petiolate, ovate, serrate, acute, hairy, unicostate reticulate.

Inflorescence. Compound capitulum, the heads are arranged in a cymose fashion. The inflorescence is homogamous with all the flowers tubular, involucre of bracts present.

Flower. Bracteate, sessile, complete, actinomorphic, hermaphrodite, pentamerous, epigynous and cyclic.

Calyx. Sepals 5, polysepalous, valvate, reduced to long scaly pappus.

Corolla. Petals 5, gamopetalous, valvate, tubular, violet and hairy.

Androecium. Stamens 5, syngenesious, epipetalous, anthers are jointed round the style, dithecous, basifixed, introrse.

Gynoecium. Bicarpellary, syncarpous, ovary inferior, unilocular, with one basal ovule, placentation basal, style long, stigma bifid and hairy.

Fruit. Cypsella.

Floral formula. Br, $\oplus$, ⚥, K_{pappus}, $\overbrace{C_{(5)}, A_{(5)}}$, $\overline{G}_{(2)}$.

Classification and identification

Class. ***Dicotyledonae.***

1. Venation reticulate.
2. Flowers pentamerous.

Sub-Class. ***Gamopetalae***

1. Petals fused.

Series. ***Inferae***

1. Ovary inferior.
2. Ovary unilocular with one ovule.

Order. ***Asterales***

1. Stamens epipetalous.
2. Ovary unilocular with one ovule.

Family. ***Compositae***

1. Leaves generally alternate.
2. Inflorescence capitulum.
3. Calyx reduced to hairy pappus.
4. Stamens epipetalous and zygomorphic.

Launaea asplenifolia Hook. f

Stem — Extremely reduced; **Leaf** – Radical, exstipulate, simple, sessile, somewhat lyrate, margins spinulose, unicostate reticulate; **Inflorescence** – Homogamous heads (capitula), raised on a scape, scape is aerial, erect, cylindrical, branched., solid and smooth; **Flower** – All ligulate, bracteate, bracts form involucre, sessile, complete, zygomorphic, hermaphrodite, pentamerous, epigynous, epigynous and cylic; **Calyx** – Reduced to papus; **Corolla** – Petals 5, gamopetalous, valvate, ligulate forming a short tube at the base, yellow ; **Androecium** – Stamens 5, syngenesious, epipetalous, anthers joined around the style, dithecous, basifixed, introrse; **Gynoecium**– Bicarpellary, syncarpous, ovary inferior, unilocular, with one ovule, placentation basal, style long, stigmas two and plumose; **Fruit** – Cypsella.

Floral formula - Br, ⌽, ⚥, K_{pappus}, $\overbrace{C_{(5)}, A_{(5)}}$, $\overline{G}_{(2)}$.

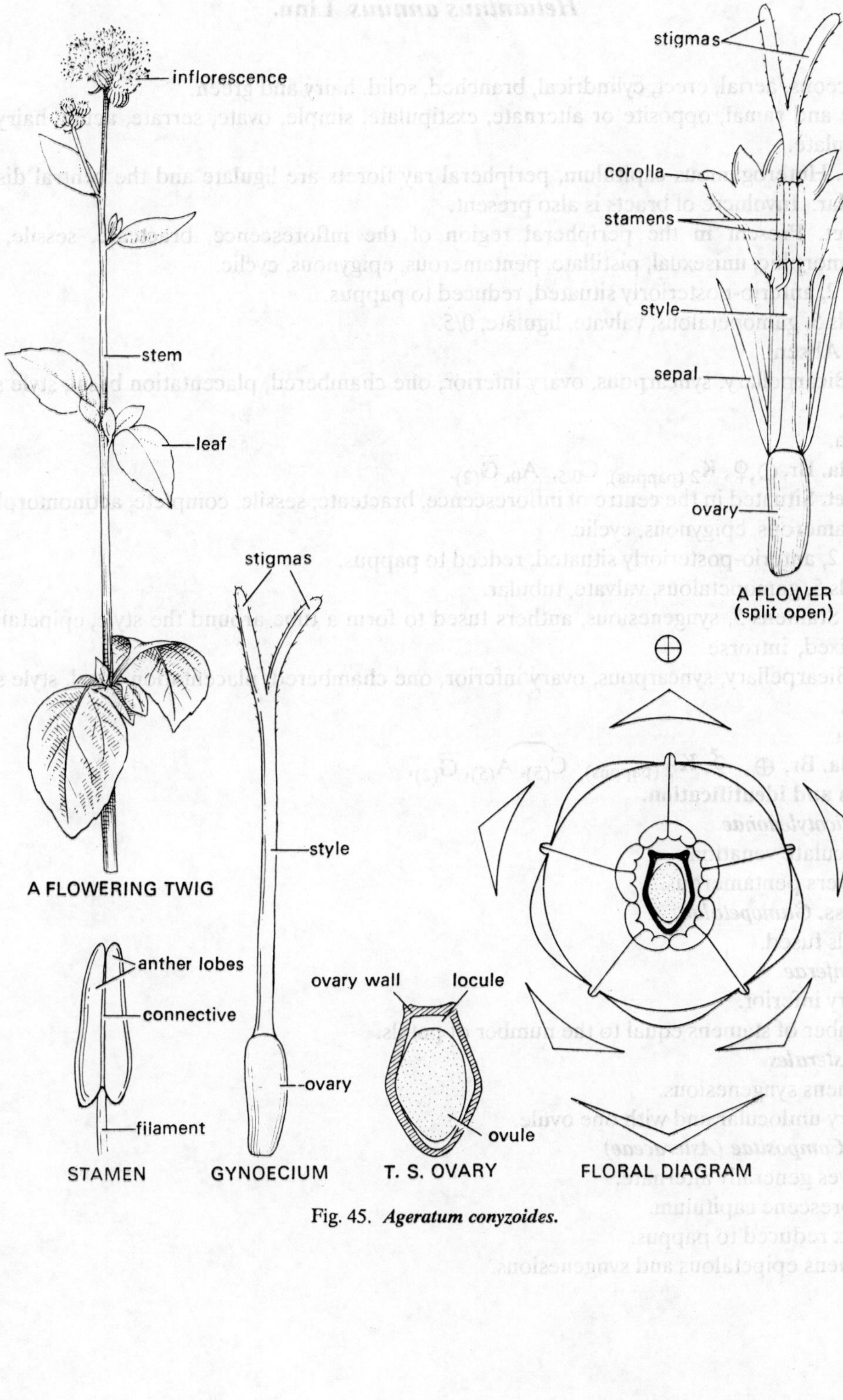

Fig. 45. ***Ageratum conyzoides.***

Helianthus annuus Linn.

Stem. Herbaceous, aerial, erect, cylindrical, branched, solid, hairy and green.

Leaf. Cauline and ramal, opposite or alternate, exstipulate, simple, ovate, serrate, acute, hairy, unicostate, reticulate.

Inflorescence. Heterogamous capitulum, peripheral ray florets are ligulate and the central disc florets are tubular. Involucre of bracts is also present.

[I] Ray floret. Present in the peripheral region of the inflorescence, bracteate, sessile, incomplete, zygomorphic, unisexual, pistillate, pentamerous, epigynous, cyclic.

Calyx. Sepals 2, anterio-posteriorly situated, reduced to pappus.

Corolla. Petals 5, gamopetalous, valvate, ligulate, 0/5.

Androecium. Absent.

Gynoecium. Bicarpellary, syncarpous, ovary inferior, one chambered, placentation basal, style short, stigma bifid.

Fruit. Cypsela.

Floral formula. Br, ⦶, ♀, $K_{2\ (pappus)}$, $C_{0/5}$, A_0, $\overline{G}_{(2)}$.

[II] Disc floret. Situated in the centre of inflorescence, bracteate, sessile, complete, actinomorphic, bisexual, pentamerous, epigynous, cyclic.

Calyx. Sepals 2, anterio-posteriorly situated, redced to pappus.

Corolla. Petals 5, gamopetalous, valvate, tubular.

Androecium. Stamens 5, syngenesious, anthers fused to form a tube around the style, epipetalous dithecous, basifixed, introrse.

Gynoecium. Bicarpellary, syncarpous, ovary inferior, one chambered, placentation basal, style short, stigma bifid.

Fruit. Cypsela.

Floral formula. Br, ⊕, ⚥, $K_{2\ (pappus)}$, $\widehat{C_{(5)}, A_{(5)}}$, $\overline{G}_{(2)}$.

Classification and identification.

Class. ***Dicotyledonae***

1. Reticulate venation.
2. Flowers pentamerous.

Sub-Class. ***Gamopetalae***

1. Petals fused.

Series. ***Inferae***

1. Ovary inferior.
2. Number of stamens equal to the number of petals.

Order. ***Asterales***

1. Stamens syngenesious.
2. Ovary unilocular and with one ovule.

Family. ***Compositae (Asteraceae)***

1. Leaves generally alternate.
2. Infloresc ene capitulum.
3. Calyx reduced to pappus.
4. Stamens epipetalous and syngenesious.

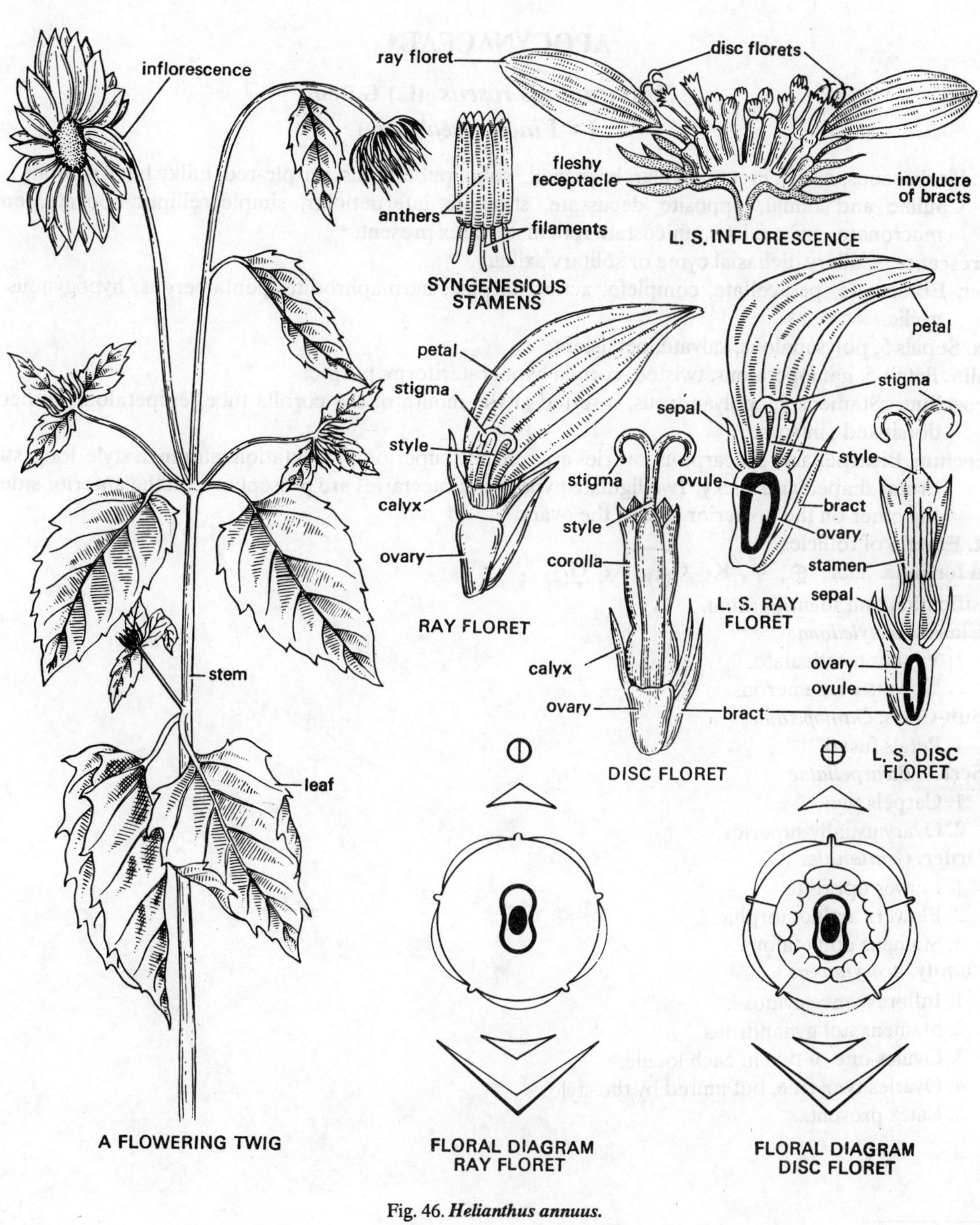

Fig. 46. ***Helianthus annuus.***

---

1. English name. Sunflower.

2. Vernacular name. Suraj mukhi

3. Economic importance. Fatty oil extracted from the seeds, is used in cooking.

APOCYNACEAE*

Catharanthus roseus (L.) G.Don

(= *Vinca rosea* Linn.)

Stem. Herbaceous, aerial, erect, angular, branched, solid, puberulous, purple-red, milky latex present.

Leaf. Cauline and ramal, opposite decussate, stipulate interpetiolar, simple, elliptic-obovate, entire, mucronate, puberulous, unicostate reticulate, latex present.

Inflorescence. Axillary dichasial cyme or solitary axillary.

Flower. Ebracteate, pedicellate, complete, actinomorphic, hermaphrodite, pentamerous, hypogynous and cyclic.

Calyx. Sepals 5, polysepalous, valvate, persistent.

Corolla. Petals 5, gamopetalous, twisted, corolla hypocrateriform, purple.

Androecium. Stamens 5, polyandrous, inserted at the mouth of the corolla tube, epipetalous, dithecous, dorsifixed , introrse.

Gynoecium. Bicarpellary, syncarpous, ovaries are free and superior, placentation marginal, style long, stigma drum- shaped and sticky. Two ligulate hypogynous nectaries are present one on the anterior side and the other on the posterior side of the ovary.

Fruit. Etaerio of follicles.

Flora formula. Ebr, ⊕, ⚥, K_5, $\overparen{C_{(5)}, A_5}$, $\underline{G}_{(2)}$.

Classification and identification.

Class. *Dicotyledonae*

1. Venation reticulate.
2. Flowers pentamerous.

Sub-Class. *Gamopetalae*

1. Petals fused.

Series. *Bicarpellatae*

1. Carpels two
2. Ovary usually superior.

Order. *Gentianales*

1. Leaves opposite.
2. Flowers actinomorphic.
3. Stamens epipetalous.

Family. *Acocynaceae*

1. Inflorescence cymose.
2. Stamens not gynandrous.
3. Ovules one or two in each locule.
4. Ovaries two, free, but united by the style.
5. Latex present.

---

*1. **English name.** Dogbane family.

2. **Systematic position in other systems of classification.**

Rendle (1925)	**Engler and Prantl** (1931)	**Hutchinson** (1959)
Dicotyledons	Dicotyledoneae	Dicotyledons
Sympetalae	Sympetalae	Lignosae
Tetracyclicae	Contortae	Apocynales
Superae	Apocynaceae	Apocynaceae
Contortae		
Apocynaceae		

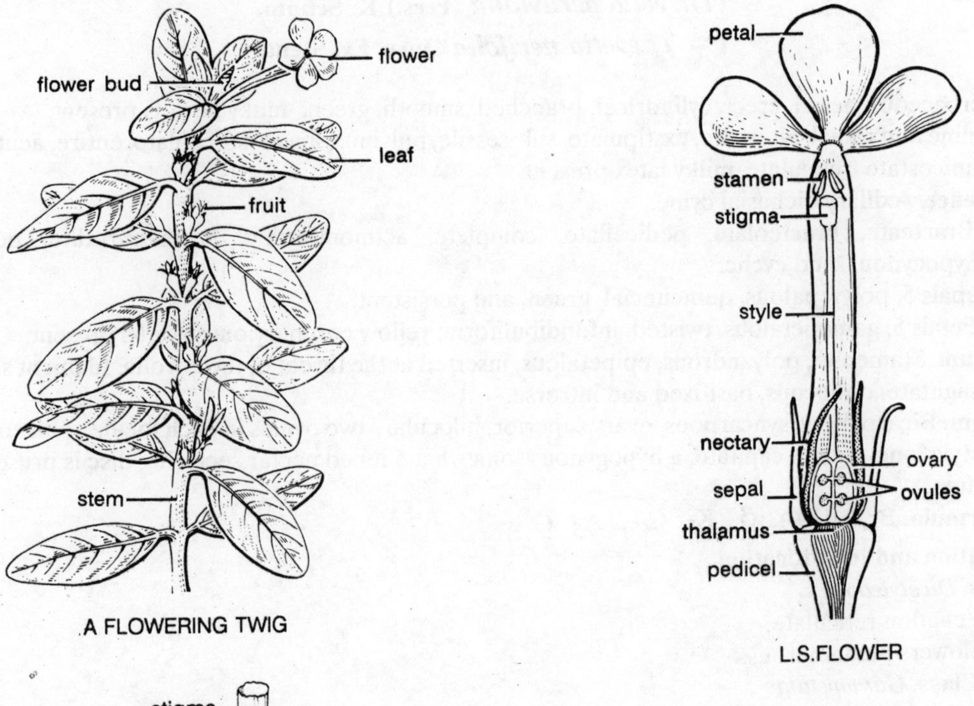

Fig. 47. ***Catharanthus roseus.***

---

1. English name. Madagascar periwinkle.

2. Vernacular names. Sada Sawagan, Sadabahar.

3. Economic importance. The plant is grown as an ornamental.

Thevetia peruviana (Pers.) K. Schum.
(= *Thevetia nerifolia* Juss. Ex. Steud.)

Stem. Herbaceous, aerial, erect, cylindrical, branched, smooth, green, milky latex is present.

Leaf. Cauline and ramal, alternate, exstipulate, sub-sessile, pulvinus, linear-lanceolate, entire, acute, glabrous, unicostate reticulate, milky latex present.

Inflorescence. Axillary dichasial cyme.

Flower. Bracteate, bracteolate, pedicellate, complete, actinomorphic, hermaphrodite, pentamerous, hypogynous and cyclic.

Calyx. Sepals 5, polysepalous, quincuncial, green and persistent.

Corolla. Petals 5, gamopetalous, twisted, infundibuliform, yellow coronary outgrowths present.

Androecium. Stamens 5, polyandrous, epipetalous, inserted at the throat of the corolla, filament short, anther sagittate, dithecous, basifixed and introrse.

Gynoecium. Bicarpellary, syncarpous, ovary superior, bilocular, two ovules in each locule, placentation axile, style long, stigma capitate, a hypogynous somewhat 5 lobed nectar secreting disc is present.

Fruit. Drupe.

Floral formula. Br, brl, $\oplus$, ⚥, K_5, $\overset{\frown}{C_{(5)}, A_5}$, $\underline{G}_{(2)}$

Classification and identification.

Class. *Dicotyledons*

1. Venation reticulate.
2. Flowers pentamerous.

Sub-Class. *Gamopetalae*

1. Petals fused.

Series. *Bicarpellatae*

1. Carpels two.
2. Ovary usually superior.

Order. *Gentianales*

1. Leaves opposite.
2. Flowers actinomorphic.
3. Stamens epipetalous.

Family. *Apocynaceae*

1. Inflorescence cymose.
2. Stamens not gynandrous.
3. Ovules one or two in each locule.
4. Ovaries two, free, but united by the style.
5. Latex present

Nerium indicum Mill. (= *N. odorum Soland; N. oleander* Blanco)

Stem - Herbaceous, lower portion woody, aerial, erect, cylindrical, branched, solid, rough, nodes swollen, hyaline latex present; **Leaf**-Cauline and ramal, whorled with 3 leaves in each whorl, exstipulate, simple, subsessile, leaf base pulvinus, lanceolate, entire, spiny, acute, glabrous, unicostate reticulate, latex present; **Inflorescence** - Terminal dichasial cyme or panicled cyme; **Flower** - Bracteate, bracteolate, pedicellate, complete, actinomorphic, hermaphrodite,pentamerous, hypogynous and cyclic; **Calyx** - Sepals 5, polysepalous, twisted, purple red; **Corolla** - Petals 5, gamopetalous, twisted, rotate, coronary outgrowths present at the throat of the corolla, red or white; **Androecium** - Stamens 5, polyandrous, epipetalous, situated at the throat of corolla, filament short, anthers sagittate, dithecous, introrse, connective appediculate and all of them twist to form a thread- like structure; **Gynoecium** - Bicarpellary, syncarpous, ovary superior, bilocular with many ovules in each locule, placentation axile.

Floral formula - Br, brl, $\oplus$, ⚥, K_5, $\overset{\frown}{C_{(5)}, A_5}$, $\underline{G}_{(2)}$.

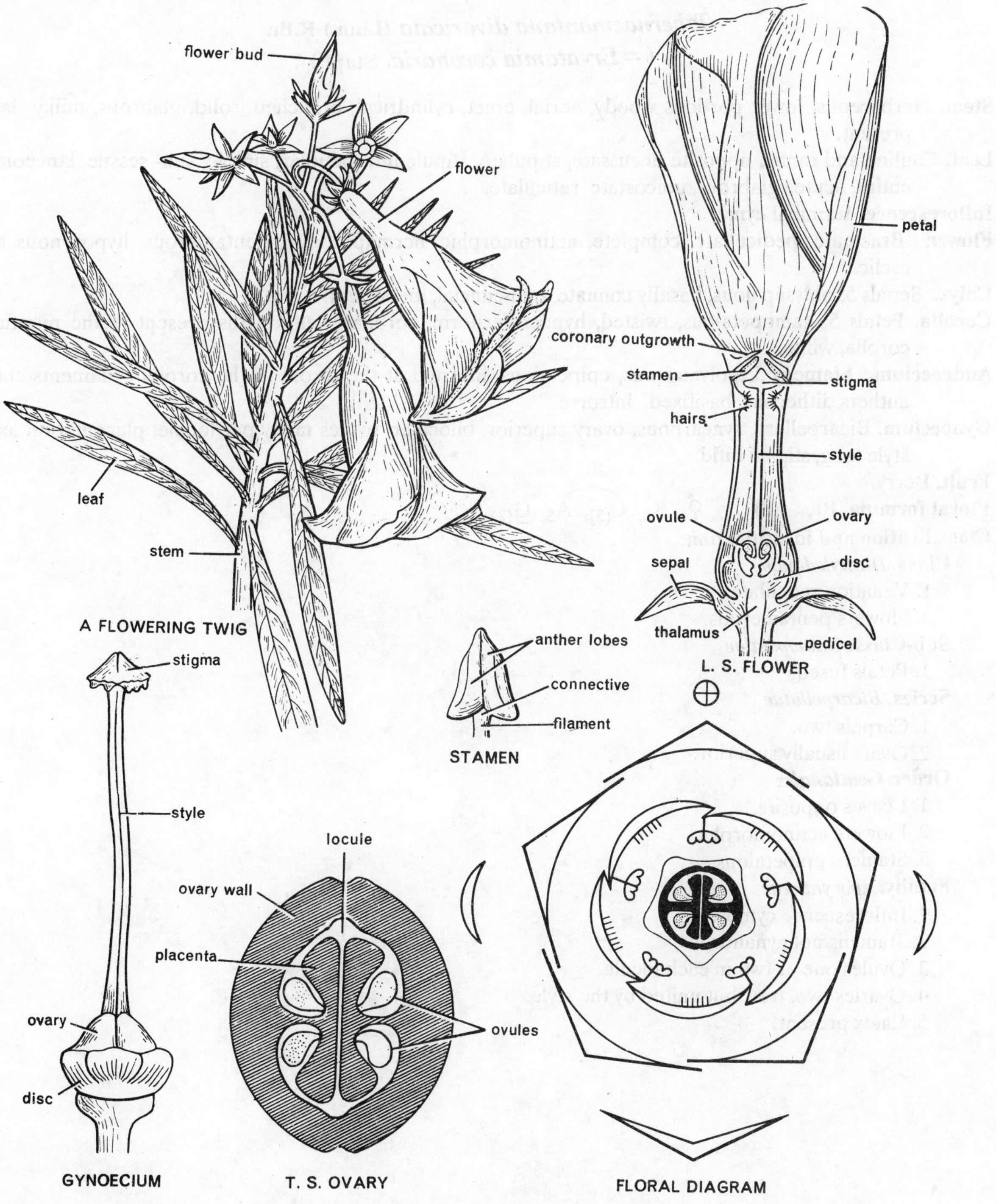

Fig. 48. ***Thevetia peruviana.***

---

1. English name. Yellow oleander.

2. Vernacular name. Peeli kaner.

3. Economic importance. Bark is used in different kinds of intermittent fevers.

Tabernaemontana divaricata (Linn.) R.Br. (=*Ervatamia coronaria*, Stapf.)

Stem. Herbaceous, lower portions woody, aerial, erect, cylindrical, branched, solid, glabrous, milky latex present.

Leaf. Cauline and ramal, opposite decussate, stipulate, stipule intrapetiolar, simple, sub- sessile, lanceolate, entire, acute, glabrous, unicostate reticulate.

Inflorescence. Terminal cyme.

Flower. Bracteate, pedicellate, complete, actinomorphic, hermaphrodite, pentamerous, hypogynous and cyclic.

Calyx. Sepals 5, polysepalous, basally connate, quincuncial, persistent.

Corolla. Petals 5, gamopetalous, twisted, hypocrateriform, coronary outgrowths present at the mouth of corolla, white.

Androecium. Stamens 5, polyandrous, epipetalous, inserted at the throat of the corolla , filaments short, anthers dithecous, basifixed, introrse.

Gynoecium. Bicarpellary, syncarpous, ovary superior, bilocular, ovules many per locule, placentation axile, style long, stigma bifid.

Fruit. Berry.

Floral formula. Br, ⊕, ⚥, K_5, $\overset{\frown}{C_{(5)}, A_5}$, $\underline{G}_{(2)}$.

Classification and identification.

Class. ***Dicotyledonae***
1. Venation reticulate.
2. Flowers pentamerous.

Sub-Class. ***Gamopetalae***
1. Petals fused.

Series. ***Bicarpellatae***
1. Carpels two.
2. Ovary usually superior.

Order. ***Gentianales***
1. Leaves opposite.
2. Flowers actinomorphic.
3. Stamens epipetalous.

Family. ***Apocynaceae***
1. Inflorescence cymose.
2. Stamens not gynandrous.
3. Ovules one or two in each locule.
4. Ovaries two, free, but united by the style.
5. Latex present.

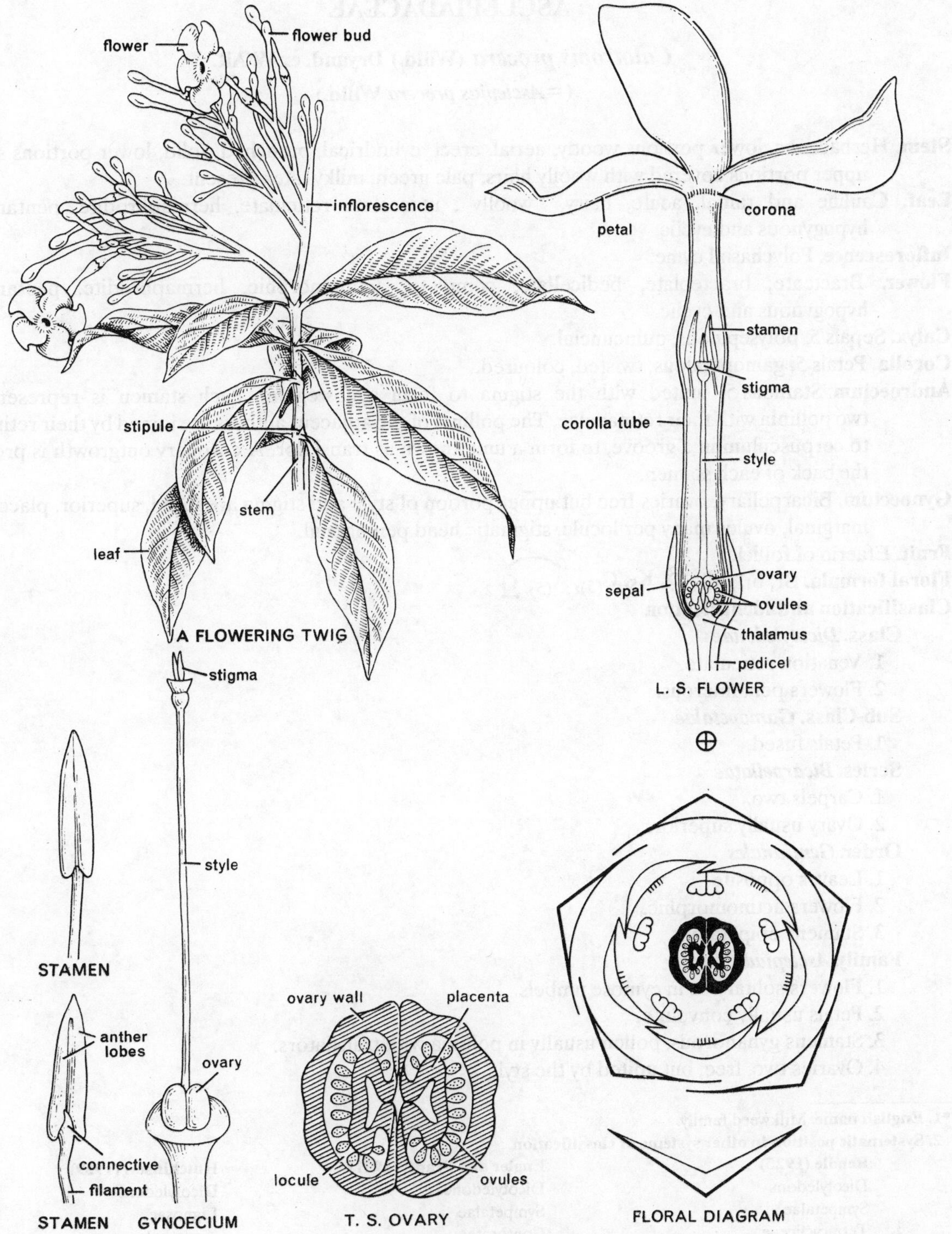

Fig. 49. ***Tabernaemontana divaricata.***

---

1. English name. Crape-jasmine.

2. Vernacular names. Chandni, Chamela, Tagar.

3. Economic importance. Plant is grown as an ornamental. Red pulp around seeds is used as a dye.

ASCLEPIADACEAE*

Calotropis procera (Willd.) Dryand. ex W. Ait.

(=*Asclepias procera* Willd.)

Stem. Herbaceous, lower portions woody, aerial, erect, cylindrical, branched, solid, lower portions smooth, upper portions covered with woolly hairs, pale green, milky latex present.

Leaf. Cauline and ramal, acute, hairy, woolly , unicostate reticulate, hermaphrodite, pentamerous, hypogynous and cyclic.

Inflorescence. Polychasial cyme.

Flower. Bracteate, bracteolate, pedicellate, complete, actinomorphic, hermaphrodite, pentamerous, hypogynous and cyclic.

Calyx. Sepals 5, polysepalous, quincuncial.

Corolla. Petals 5, gamopetalous, twisted, coloured.

Androecium. Stamens 5, united with the stigma to form gynostegium, each stamen is represented by two pollinia with their retinaculae. The pollinia of the adjacent anthers are joined by their retinaculae to corpusculum in a groove, to form a unit known as translator. A coronary outgrowth is present at the back of each stamen.

Gynoecium. Bicarpellary, ovaries free but upper portion of style and stigma are fused, superior, placentation marginal, ovules many per locule, stigmatic head pentagonal.

Fruit. Etaerio of follicle.

Floral formula. Br, brl, ⊕, ⚥, K_5, $C_{(5)}$, $\overparen{A_{(5)}, \underline{G}_2}$.

Classification and identification

Class. ***Dicotyledonae***

1. Venation reticulate.
2. Flowers pentamerous.

Sub-Class. ***Gamopetalae***

1. Petals fused.

Series. ***Bicarpellatae***

1. Carpels two.
2. Ovary usually superior.

Order. ***Gentianales***

1. Leaves opposite.
2. Flowers actinomorphic.
3. Stamens epipetalous.

Family. ***Asclepiadaceae***

1. Flowers solitary or in cymose umbels.
2. Petals usually convolute.
3. Stamens gynandrous, pollen usually in pollinia with translators.
4. Ovaries two, free, but united by the style.

***1. English name.** Milkweed family.

2. Systematic position in other systems of classification.

Rendle (1925)	Engler and Prantl (1931)	Hutchinson (1959)
Dicotyledons	Dicotyledoneae	Dicotyledons
Sympetalae	Sympetalae	Lignosae
Tetracycliceae	Contorate	Apocynales
Superae	Ascelpiadaceae	Asclepiadaceae
Asclepiadaceae		

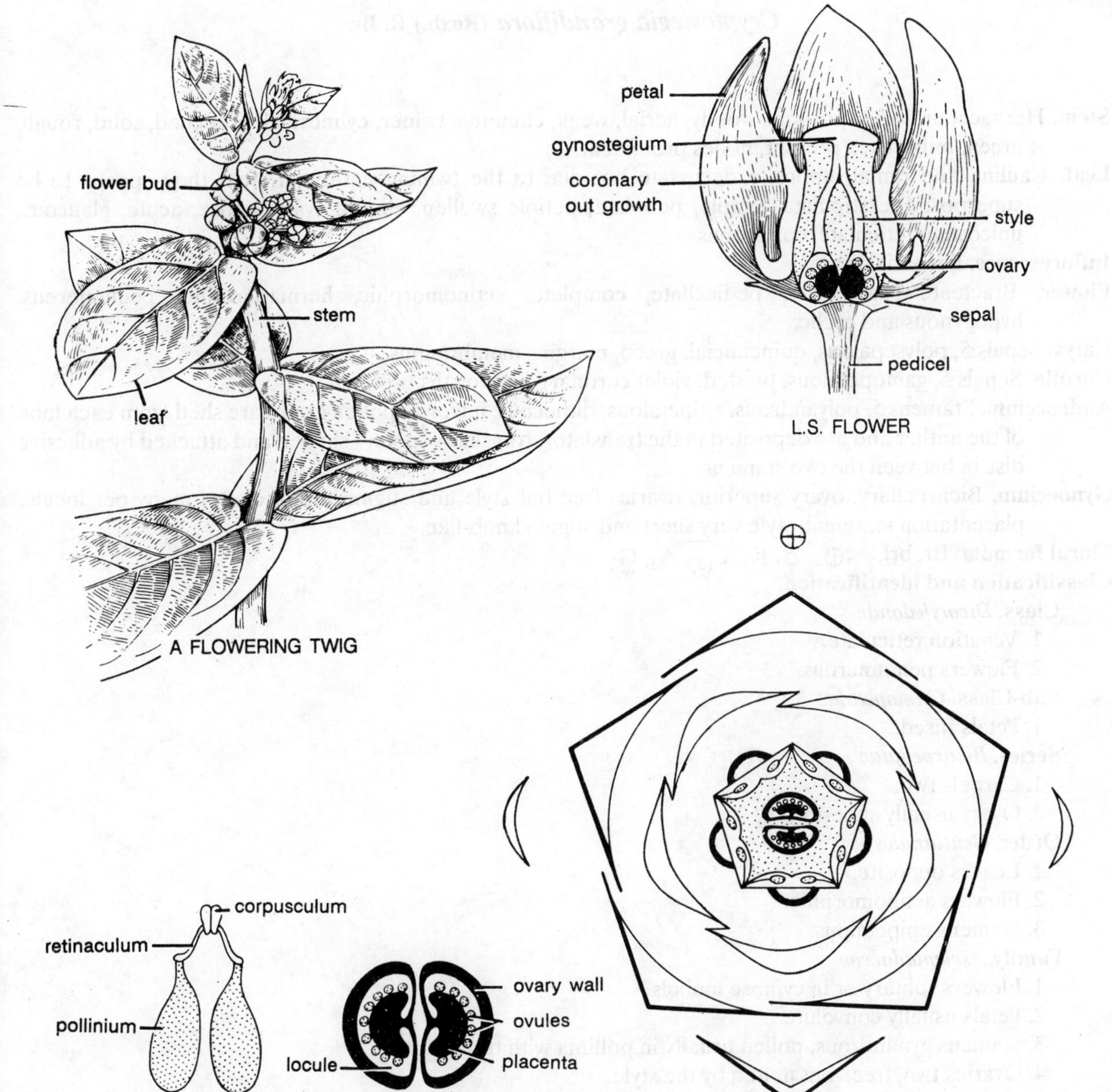

Fig. 50. ***Calotropis procera.***

---

1. English name. Akund, Swallow-wart.

2. Vernacular name. Aak, Madar, Spalmai, Akada.

3. Economic importance. Madar fiber extracted from stem is made into cordage. Floss from seeds is used as stuffing material. Milky juice is used as an infanticide and abortifacient. The leaves are insecticidal and are also used in fomentation.

Cryptostegia grandiflora (Roxb.) R. Br.

Stem. Herbaceous, lower portions woody, aerial, weak, climbing, twiner, cylindrical, branched, solid, rough, green, milky latex present, nodes prominent.

Leaf. Cauline and ramal, opposite decussate but due to the twining nature of stem they appear to be superposed, exstipulate, simple, petiolate, petiole swollen, elliptic-ovate, entire, acute, glaucous, unicostate reticulate, coriaceous.

Inflorescence. Dichasial cyme.

Flower. Bracteate bracteolate, pedicellate, complete, actinomorphic, hermaphrodite, pentamerous, hypogynous and cyclic.

Calyx. Sepals 5, polysepalous, quincuncial, green, margins membranous.

Corolla. Sepals 5, gamopetalous, twisted, violet coronary outgrowths present.

Androceium. Stamens 5, polyandrous, epipetalous, dithecous, introrse, pollen grains are shed from each lobe of the anther and are deposited in the translator, translator spoon - shaped and attached by adhesive disc in between the two stamens.

Gynoecium. Bicarpellary, ovary superior, ovaries free but style and stigma fused, ovules many per locule, placentation marginal, style very short and stigma knob-like.

Floral formula. Br, brl, $\oplus$, ⚥, K_5, $\widehat{C_{(5)}, A_5}$, $\underline{G}_2$.

Classification and identification.

Class. ***Dicotyledonae***

1. Venation reticulate.
2. Flowers pentamerous.

Sub-Class. ***Gamopetalae***

1. Petals fused.

Series. ***Bicarpellatae***

1. Carpels two.
2. Ovary usually superior

Order. ***Gentianales***

1. Leaves opposite.
2. Flowers actinomorphic.
3. Stamens epipetalous.

Family. ***Asclepiadaceae***

1. Flowers solitary or in cymose umbels.
2. Petals usually convolute.
3. Stamens gynandrous; pollen usually in pollinia with translators.
4. Ovaries two, free, but united by the style.

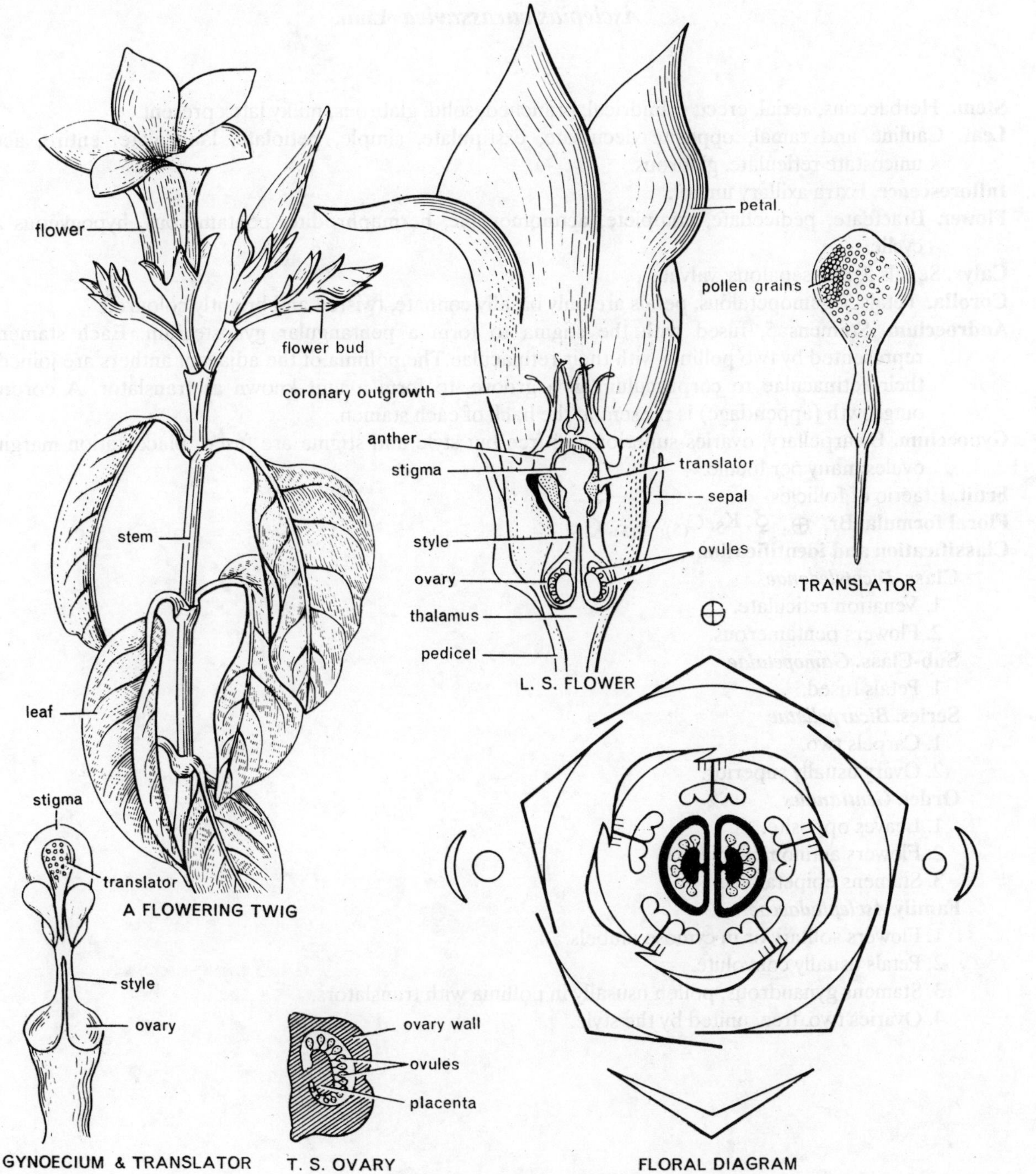

Fig. 51. ***Cryptostegia grandiflora.***

---

1. English name. Rubber vine.

2. Vernacular name. Vilayti Vakhandi.

3. Economic importance. Cultivated as an ornamental for its violet flowers. The floss from fruits is useful in making vegetable parchment paper, kraft and tissue paper.

Asclepias curassavica Linn.

Stem. Herbaceous, aerial, erect, cylindrical, branched, solid, glabrous, milky latex present.

Leaf. Cauline and ramal, opposite decussate, exstipulate, simple, petiolate, lanceolate, entire, acute, unicostate reticulate, glabrous.

Inflorescence. Extra axillary umbel.

Flower. Bracteate, pedicellate, complete, actinomorphic, hermaphrodite, pentamerous, hypogynous and cyclic.

Calyx. Sepals 5, polysepalous, valvate.

Corolla. Petals 5, gamopetalous, petals are only basally connate, twisted and brightly coloured.

Androecium. Stamens 5, fused with the stigma to form a pentangular gynostegium. Each stamen is represented by two pollinia with their retinaculae.The pollinia of the adjacent anthers are joined by their retinaculae to corpusculum in a groove, to form a unit known as translator. A coronary outgrowth (appendage) is present at the back of each stamen.

Gynoecium. Bicarpellary, ovaries superior and free but style and stigma are fused, placentation marginal, ovules many per locule.

Fruit. Etaerio of follicles

Floral formula. Br, $\oplus$, ⚥, K_5, $C_{(5)}$, $\overset{\frown}{A_{(5)}, \underline{G}_2}$.

Classification and identification.

Class. ***Dicotyledonae***

1. Venation reticulate.
2. Flowers pentamerous.

Sub-Class. ***Gamopetalae***

1. Petals fused.

Series. ***Bicarpellatae***

1. Carpels two.
2. Ovary usually superior.

Order. ***Gentianales***

1. Leaves opposite.
2. Flowers actinomorphic.
3. Stamens epipetalous.

Family. ***Asclepiadaceae***

1. Flowers solitary or in cymose umbels.
2. Petals usually convolute.
3. Stamens gynandrous; pollen ususally in pollinia with translators.
4. Ovaries two, free, united by the style.

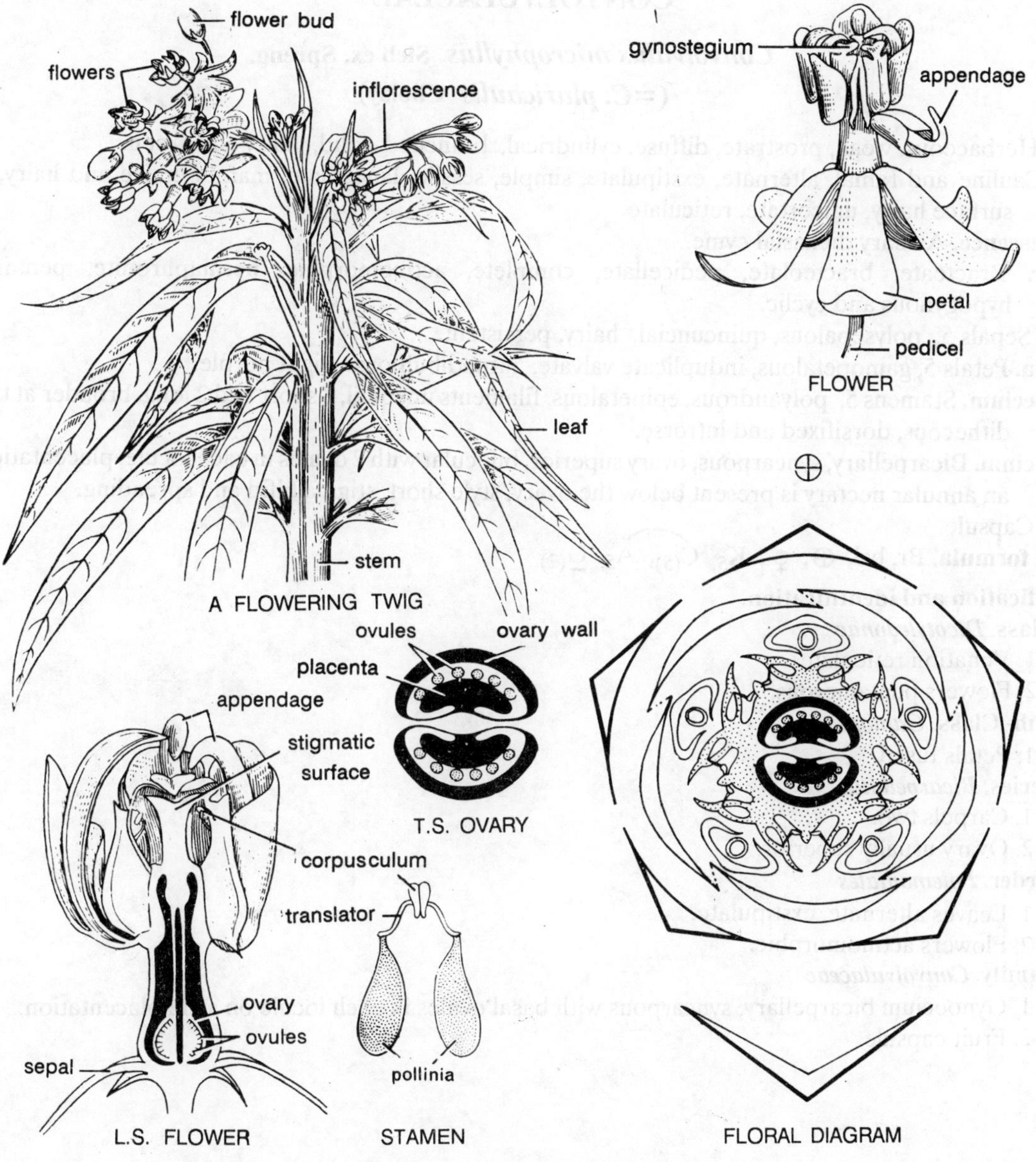

Fig. 52. ***Asclepias curassavica.***

---

1. English name. False ipecac, Blood flower.
2. Vernacular name. Kakatundi, Kaura-dodi.
3. Economic importance. Cultivated as an ornamental. The root is used as a purgative and also in curing piles and gonorrhoea.

CONVOLVULACEAE*

Convolvulus microphyllus Sieb ex. Spreng.
(=*C. pluricaulis* Choisy)

Stem. Herbaceous, weak, prostrate, diffuse, cylindrical, branched, solid, hairy and green.

Leaf. Cauline and ramal, alternate, exstipulate, simple, sessile, lanceolate, margin entire and hairy, acute, surface hairy, unicostate, reticulate.

Inflorescence. Axillary dichasial cyme.

Flower. Bracteate, bracteolate, pedicellate, complete, actinomorphic, hermaphrodite, pentamerous, hypogynous and cyclic.

Calyx. Sepals 5, polysepalous, quincuncial, hairy, persistent.

Corolla. Petals 5, gamopetalous, induplicate valvate, infundibuliform, light purple.

Androecium. Stamens 5, polyandrous, epipetalous, filaments unequal, 3 short and 2 long, broader at the base, dithecous, dorsifixed and introrse.

Gynoecium. Bicarpellary, syncarpous, ovary superior, bilocular with 2 ovules in each locule, placentation axile, an annular nectary is present below the ovary, style short, stigma bifid and spreading.

Fruit. Capsule.

Floral formula. Br, brl, $\oplus$, ⚥, K_5, $\widehat{C_{(5)}, A_5}$, $\underline{G}_{(2)}$.

Classification and identification.

Class. *Dicotyledonae*
1. Venation reticulate.
2. Flowers pentamerous.

Sub- Class. *Gamopetalae*
1. Petals fused.

Series. *Bicarpellatae*
1. Carpels two.
2. Ovary usually superior.

Order. *Polemoniales*
1. Leaves alternate, exstipulate.
2. Flowers actinomorphic.

Family. *Convolvulaceae*
1. Gynoecium bicarpellary, syncarpous with basal ovules in each locule on axile placentation.
2. Fruit capsule.

---

*1. **English name.** Morning Glory family.

2. **Systematic position in other systems of classification.**

Rendle (1925)	**Engler and Prantl** (1931)	**Hutchinson** (1959)
Dicotyledons	Dicotyledoneae	Dicotyledons
Sympetalae	Sympetalae	Herbaceae
Tetracylicae	Tubiflorae	Solanales
Superae	Convolvulaceae	Convolvulaceae
Convolvulales		
Convolvulaceae		

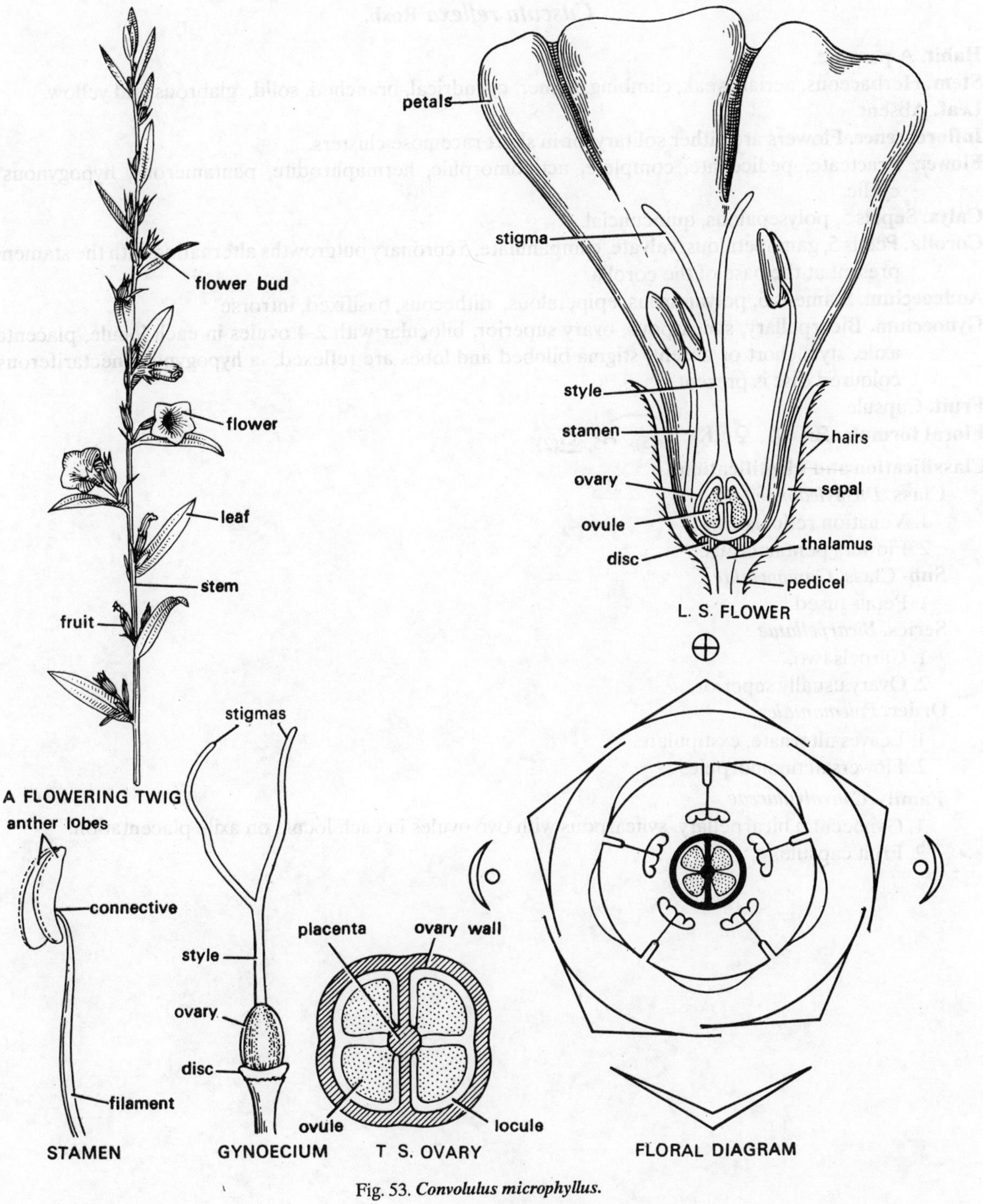

Fig. 53. ***Convolulus microphyllus.***

---

1. Vernacular name. Sankh Pushpi.

2. Economic importance. A drug is extracted from leaves which is used as a brain tonic.

Cuscuta reflexa Roxb.

Habit. A parasite.

Stem. Herbaceous, aerial, weak, climbing, twiner, cylindrical, branched, solid, glabrous and yellow.

Leaf. Absent.

Inflorescence. Flowers are either solitary or in short racemose clusters.

Flower. Bracteate, pedicellate, complete, actinomorphic, hermaphrodite, pentamerous, hypogynous and cyclic.

Calyx. Sepals 5, polysepalous, quincuncial.

Corolla. Petals 5, gamopetalous, valvate, campanulate, 5 coronary outgrowths alternating with the stamens are present at the base of the corolla.

Androecium. Stamens 5, polyandrous, epipetalous, dithecous, basifixed, introrse.

Gynoecium. Bicarpellary, syncarpous, ovary superior, bilocular with 2-4 ovules in each locule, placentation axile, style short or absent, stigma bilobed and lobes are reflexed, a hypogynous nectariferous red coloured disc is present.

Fruit. Capsule.

Floral formula. Br, $\oplus$, ⚥, K_5, $\overbrace{C_{(5)}, A_5}$, $\underline{G}_{(2)}$.

Classification and identification.

Class. *Dicotyledonae*

1. Venation reticulate.
2. Flowers pentamerous.

Sub- Class. *Gamopetalae*

1. Petals fused.

Series. *Bicarpellatae*

1. Carpels two.
2. Ovary usually superior.

Order. *Polemoniales*

1. Leaves alternate, exstipulate.
2. Flowers actinomorphic.

Family. *Convolvulaceae*

1. Gynoecium bicarpellary, syncarpous with two ovules in each locule on axile placentation.
2. Fruit capsule.

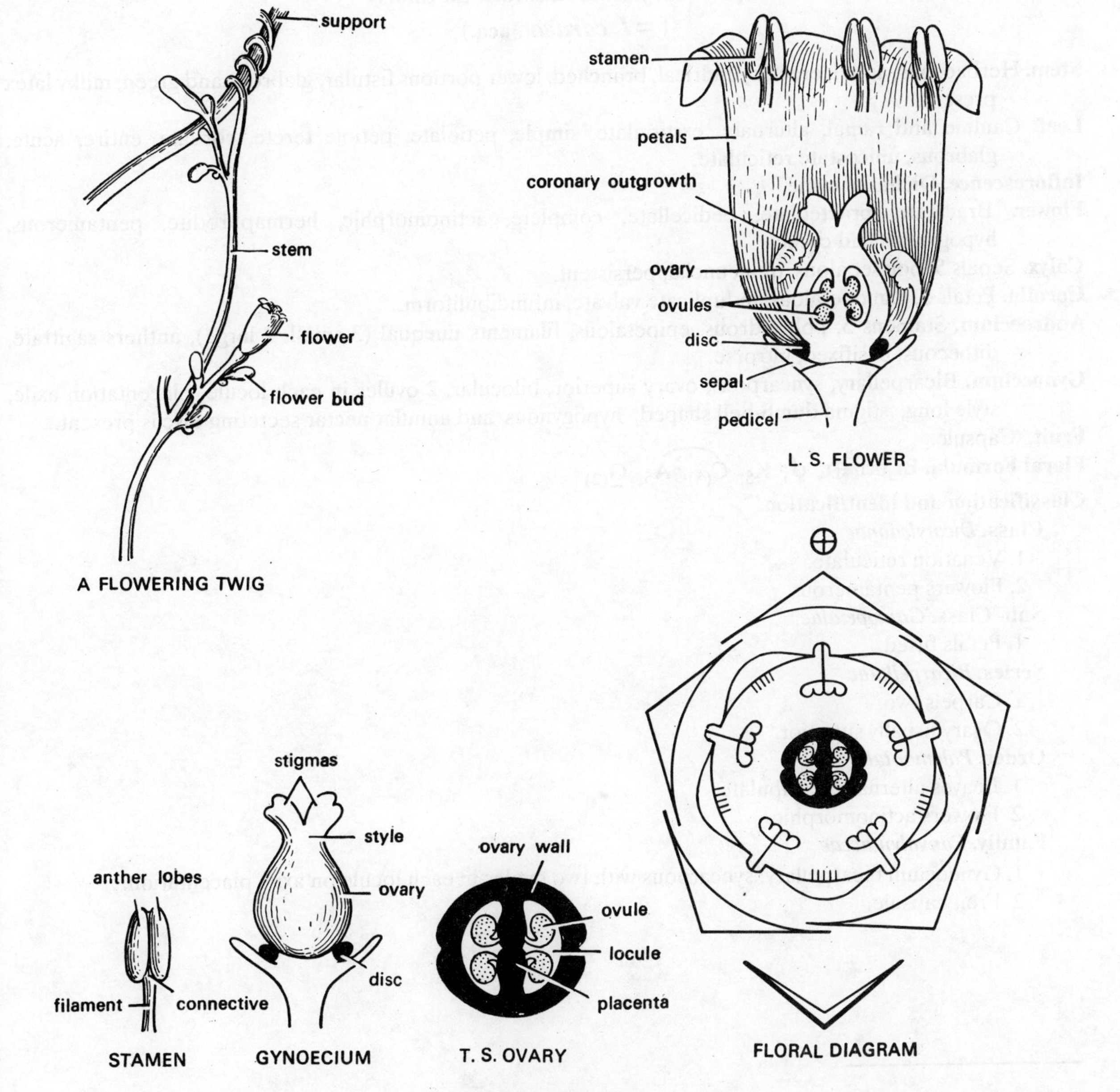

Fig. 54. ***Cuscuta reflexa.***

1. **English name.** Dodder.
2. **Vernacular names.** Amarbel, Aakashbel.
3. **Economic importance.** Seeds are carminative. The stem is used in bileous disorders.

Ipomoea fistulosa Mart. ex. Choisy
(= *I. carnea* Jacq.)

Stem. Herbaceous, aerial, erect, cylindrical, branched, lower portions fistular, glabrous and green, milky latex present.

Leaf. Cauline and ramal, alternate, exstipulate, simple, petiolate, petiole terete, cordate, entire, acute, glabrous, unicostate reticulate.

Inflorescence. Dichasial cyme.

Flower. Bracteate, bracteolate, pedicellate, complete, actinomorphic, hermaphrodite, pentamerous, hypogynous and cyclic.

Calyx. Sepals 5, polysepalous, quincuncial, persistent.

Corolla. Petals 5, gamopetalous, induplicate valvate, infundibuliform.

Androecium. Stamens 5, polyandrous, epipetalous, filaments unequal (3 small, 2 large), anthers sagittate, dithecous, basifixed, introrse.

Gynoecium. Bicarpellary, syncarpous, ovary superior, bilocular, 2 ovules in each locule, placentation axile, style long, stigma dumb-bell shaped, hypogynous and annular nectar secreting disc is present.

Fruit. Capsule.

Floral Formula. Br,brl, $\oplus$, ⚥, K_5, $\overparen{C_{(5)}, A_5}$, $\underline{G}_{(2)}$.

Classification and identification.

Class. *Dicotyledonae*
1. Venation reticulate.
2. Flowers pentamerous.

Sub- Class. *Gamopetalae*
1. Petals fused.

Series. *Bicarpellatae*
1. Carpels two.
2. Ovary usually superior.

Order. *Polemoniales*
1. Leaves alternate, exstipulate.
2. Flowers actinomorphic.

Family. *Convolvulaceae*
1. Gynoecium bicarpellary, syncarpous with two ovules in each locule on axile placentation.
2. Fruit capsule.

Ipomoea cairica (Linn.) Sweet (= *I.palmata* Forsk.)

Stem - Herbaceous, aerial, weak, climbing, cylindrical, branched, solid, glabrous and green; **Leaf-** Cauline and ramal, alternate, exstipulate, palmately compound, divided into 5-7 segments, petiolate , segments somewhat elliptic -ovate, entire, obtuse, glabrous, multicostate reticulate; **Inflorescence** - Axillary dichasial cyme or solitary; **Flower** - Bracteate, pedicellate, pedicel long, complete, actinomorphic, hermaphrodite,pentamerous, hypogynous and cyclic; **Calyx-** Sepals 5, polysepalous, quincuncial; **Corolla** - Petals 5, gamopetalous, induplicate valvate, corolla infundibiliform; **Androecium** - Stamens 5, polyandrous, epipetalous, filaments of 2 long and 3 short, anthers sagittate, dithecous, basifixed, introrse; **Gynoecium**-- Bicarpellary, syncarpous, ovary superior, bilocular with 2 ovules in each locule, axile placentation, a hypogynous nectariferous disc is present which is somewhat five partite, style long, stigma dumb-bell shaped. **Fruit**-Capsule.

Floral formula. Br, $\oplus$, ⚥, K_5, $\overparen{C_{(5)}, A_5}$, $\underline{G}_{(2)}$.

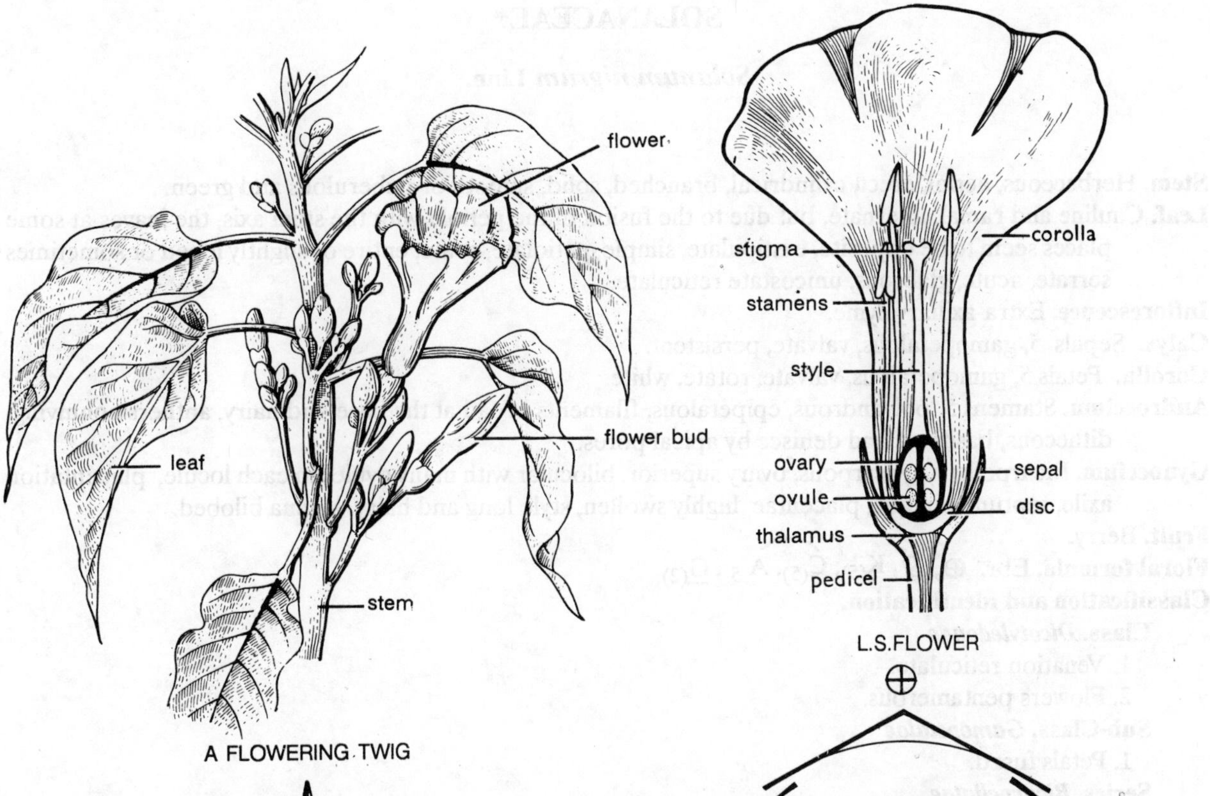

Fig. 55. ***Ipomoea fistulosa.***

---

1. Vernacular name. Ubchak.

2. Economic importance. The plant is used as a hedge on boundaries to protect the cultivated plants from animal grazing.

SOLANACEAE*

Solanum nigrum Linn.

Stem. Herbaceous, aerial, erect, cylindrical, branched, solid, smooth or puberulous and green.

Leaf. Cauline and ramal, alternate, but due to the fusion of the petiole with the stem axis, the leaves at some places seem to be opposite, exstipulate, simple, petiolate, ovate, entire or slightly lobed or sometimes serrate, acute, glabrous, unicostate reticulate.

Inflorescence. Extra-axillary cyme.

Calyx. Sepals 5, gamopetalous, valvate, persistent.

Corolla. Petals 5, gamopetalous, valvate, rotate, white.

Androecium. Stamens 5, polyandrous, epipetalous, filaments broad at the base and hairy, anthers conniving, dithecous, basifixed and dehisce by apical pores.

Gynoecium. Bicarpellary, syncarpous, ovary superior, bilocular with many ovules in each locule, placentation axile, septum oblique, placentae highly swollen, style long and hairy, stigma bilobed.

Fruit. Berry.

Floral formula. Ebr, $\oplus$, ⚥, $K_{(5)}$, $\overset{\frown}{C_{(5)}, A_{5}}$, $\underline{G}_{(2)}$.

Classification and identification.

Class. ***Dicotyledonae***
1. Venation reticulate.
2. Flowers pentamerous.

Sub-Class. ***Gamopetalae***
1. Petals fused.

Series. ***Bicarpellatae***
1. Carpels two.
2. Ovary usually superior.

Order. ***Polemoniales***
1. Alternate, exstipulate leaves.
2. Flowers actinomorphic.

Family. ***Solanaceae***
1. Flowers solitary terminal or cymosely umbelled.
2. Septum is oblique and the placentae are highly swollen.
3. Fruit - berry or capsule.

---

*1. **English name.** Nightshade family.

2. **Systematic position in other systems of classification.**

Rendle (1925)	Engler and Prantl (1931)	Hutchinson (1959)
Dicotyledons	Dicotyledonae	Dicotyledons
Sympetalae	Sympetalae	Herbaceae
Tetracyclicae	Tubiflorae	Solanales
Superae	Solanaceae	Solanaceae
Tubiflorae		
Solanineae		
Solanaceae		

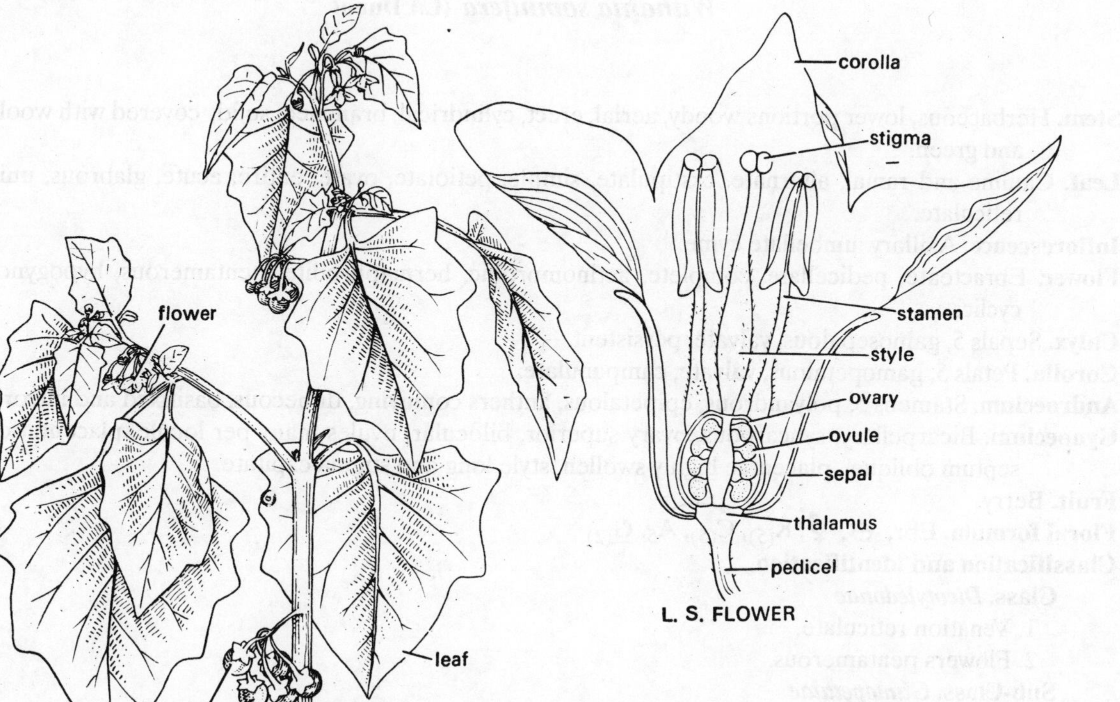

Fig. 56. ***Solanum nigrum.***

---

1. English name. Black nightshade.

2. Vernacular name. Makoi.

3. Economic importance. Berries are edible. The juice of the plant is given in chronic enlargement of liver.

Withania somnifera (L.) Dunal

Stem. Herbaceous, lower portions woody, aerial, erect, cylindrical, branched, solid, covered with woolly hairs and green.

Leaf. Cauline and ramal, alternate, exstipulate, simple, petiolate, ovate, entire, acute, glabrous, unicostate reticulate.

Inflorescence. Axillary umbellate cyme.

Flower. Ebracteate, pedicellate, complete, actinomorphic, hermaphrodite, pentamerous, hypogynous and cyclic.

Calyx. Sepals 5, gamosepalous, valvate, persistent.

Corolla. Petals 5, gamopetalous, valvate, campanulate.

Androecium. Stamens 5, polyandrous, epipetalous, anthers conniving, dithecous, basifixed and introrse.

Gynoecium. Bicarpellary, syncarpous, ovary superior, bilocular, ovules many per locule, placentation axile, septum oblique, placentae highly swollen, style long and stigma capitate.

Fruit. Berry.

Floral formula. Ebr, $\oplus$, ⚥, $K_{(5)}$, $\overparen{C_{(5)}, A_5}$, $\underline{G}_{(2)}$.

Classification and identification.

Class. ***Dicotyledonae***

1. Venation reticulate.
2. Flowers pentamerous.

Sub-Class. ***Gamopetalae***

1. Petals fused.

Series. ***Bicarpellatae***

1. Carpels two.
2. Ovary usually superior.

Order. ***Polemoniales***

1. Alternate exstipulate leaves.
2. Flowers actinomorphic.

Family. ***Solanaceae***

1. Flowers solitary, terminal or cymosely umbelled.
2. Septum is oblique and the placentae are highly swollen.
3. Fruit berry or capsule.

Datura stramonium Linn.

Stem – Herbaceous, aerial, erect, cylindrical, branched, pubescent, green; **Leaf** – Cauline and ramal, alternate or sub- opposite, exstipulate, simple, petiolate, fused with the axis to some distance, ovate, entire, acute, pubescent, unicostate reticulate; **Inflorescence** – Solitary axillary or extra- axillary; **Flower** – Ebracteate, pedicellate, complete, actinomorphic, hermaphrodite, pentamerous, hypogynous and cyclic; **Calyx** – Sepals 5, gamosepalous, twisted, persistent; **Corolla** – Petals 5, gamopetalous, twisted, trumpet-shaped, white; **Androecium** – Stamens 5, polyandrous, epipetalous, anthers conniving, dithecous, basifixed, introrse; **Gynoecium** – Bicarpellary, syncarpous, ovary superior, bilocular at the apex and tetralocular at the base due to the false septum, ovules many per locule, placentation axile, septum oblique, placentae highly swollen, style long and stigma dome-shaped; **Fruit** – A septifragal capsule.

Floral formula – Ebr, $\oplus$, ⚥, $K_{(5)}$, $\overparen{C_{(5)}, A_5}$, $\underline{G}_{(2)}$.

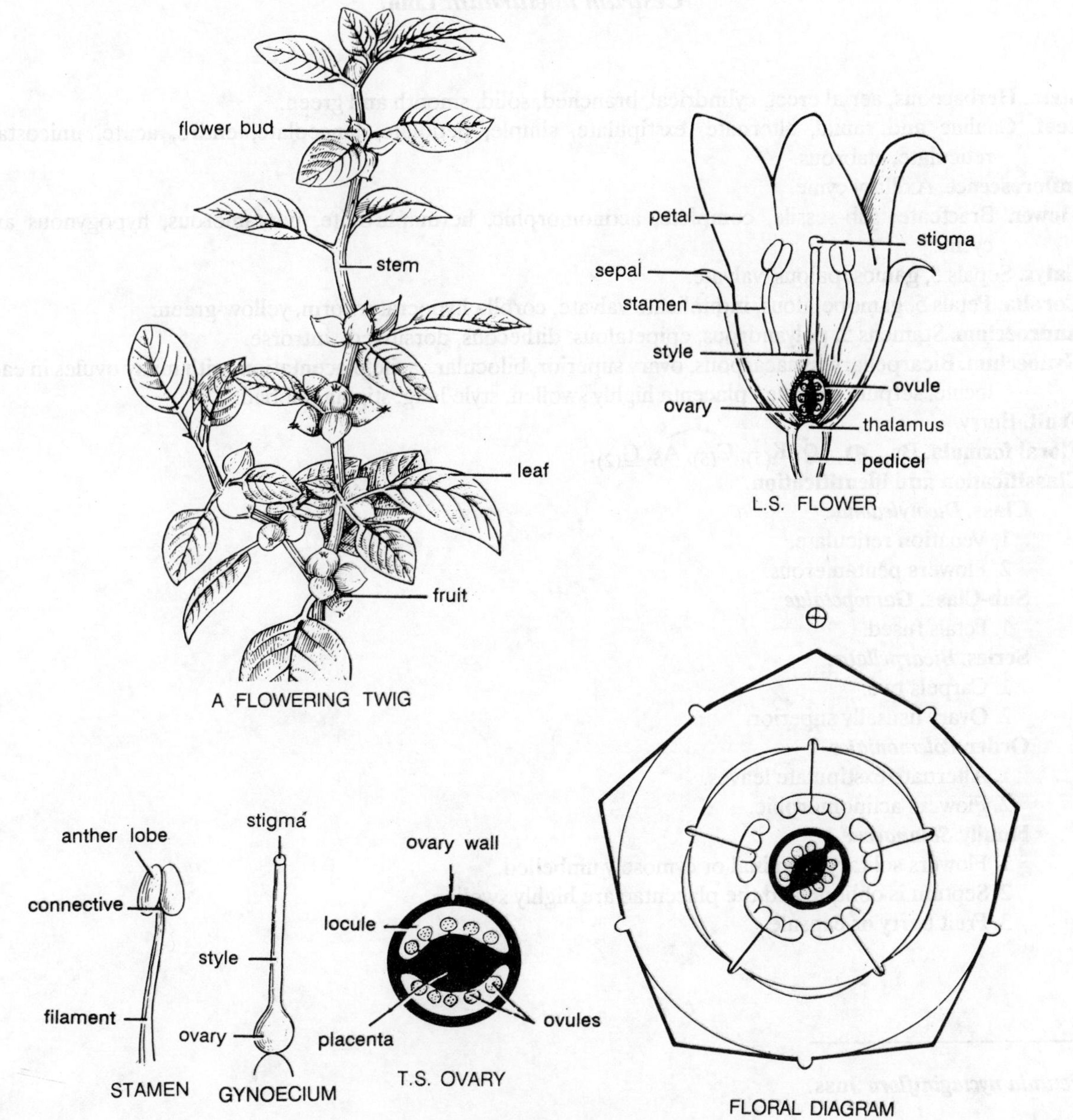

Fig. 57. ***Withania somnifera.***

---

1. Vernacular names. Asgand, Punir.

2. Economic importance. The plant contains substances with narcotic and soparific properties. Roots and leaves possess antibiotic and antibacterial activities.

Cestrum nocturnum Linn.

Stem. Herbaceous, aerial erect, cylindrical, branched, solid, smooth and green.

Leaf. Cauline and ramal, alternate, exstipulate, simple, petiolate, lanceolate, entire, acute, unicostate reticulate, glabrous.

Inflorescence. Axillary cyme.

Flower. Bracteate, sub-sessile, complete, actinomorphic, hermaphrodite, pentamerous, hypogynous and cyclic.

Calyx. Sepals 5, gamosepalous, valvate.

Corolla. Petals 5, gamopetalous, induplicate valvate, corolla hypocrateriform, yellow-green.

Androecium. Stamens 5, polyandrous, epipetalous, dithecous, dorsifixed, introrse.

Gynoecium. Bicarpellary, synacarpous, ovary superior, bilocular, axile placentation, with many ovules in each locule, setpum oblique, placenta highly swollen, style long, stigma bilobed.

Fruit. Berry.

Floral formula. Br, $\oplus$, ⚥, $K_{(5)}, \overparen{C_{(5)}, A_5}, \underline{G}_{(2)}$.

Classification and identification.

Class. ***Dicotyledonae***

1. Venation reticulate.
2. Flowers pentamerous.

Sub-Class. ***Gamopetalae***

1. Petals fused.

Series. ***Bicarpellatae***

1. Carpels two.
2. Ovary ususally superior.

Order. ***Polemoniales***

1. Alternate exstipulate leaves.
2. Flowers actinomorphic.

Family. ***Solanaceae***

1. Flowers solitary, terminal or cymosely umbelled.
2. Septum is oblique and the placentae are highly swollen.
3. Fruit berry or capsule.

Petunia nyctaginiflora Juss.

Stem —Herbaceous, aerial, erect, cylindrical, branched, solid, hairy and green; **Leaf** — Cauline and ramal, alternate in the lower region but opposite decussate in upper region, exstipulate, simple, sessile, elliptic-ovate, entire, acute, hairy, unicostate reticulate, coriaceous; **Inflorescence** — Axillary dichasial cyme; **Flower** — Bracteate, pedicellate, complete, actinomorphic, hermaporodite, pentamerous, hypogynous and cyclic; **Calyx** — Sepals 5, gamosepalous, deeply partite, persistent and hairy; **Corolla** — Petals 5, gamopetalous, induplicate valvate, infundibuliform, varioursly coloured; **Androecium** — Stamens 5, polyandrous, epipetalous, filaments unequal, dithecous, basifixed, introrse; **Gynoecium** — Bicarpellary, syncarpous, ovary superior, bilocular, with many ovules in each locule, placentation axile, septum oblique, placentae highly swollen, style long, stigma capitate and sticky a disc below the ovary; **Fruit** — Capsule.

Floral formula Br, $\oplus$, ⚥, $K_{(5)}, \overparen{C_{(5)}, A_5}, \underline{G}_{(2)}$.

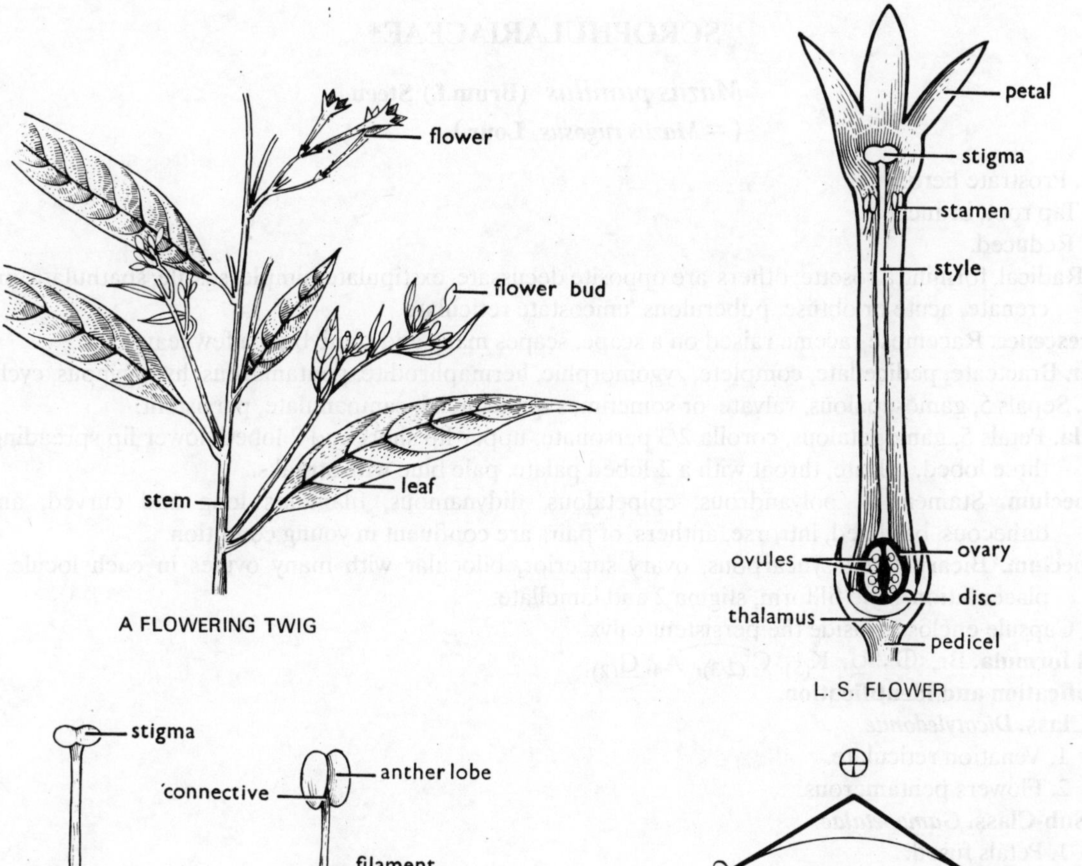

Fig. 58. ***Cestrum nocturnum.***

---

1. English name. Night jessamine.

2. Vernacular name. Raat-ki-rani.

3. Economic importance. Grown for its flowers which emit fragrance at night.

SCROPHULARIACEAE*

Mazus pumilus (Brum.f.) Steen.
(=*Mazus rugosus* Lour.)

Habit. Prostrate herb.

Root. Tap root, branched.

Stem. Reduced.

Leaf. Radical, forming a rosette; others are opposite decussate, exstipulate, simple, sessile, spathulate, margin crenate, acute or obtuse, puberulous, unicostate reticulate.

Inflorescence. Racemose raceme raised on a scape, scapes many and some bear a few leaves.

Flower. Bracteate, pedicellate, complete, zygomorphic, hermaphrodite, pentamerous, hypogynous, cyclic.

Calyx. Sepals 5, gamosepalous, valvate or sometimes quincuncial, campanulate, persistent.

Corolla. Petals 5, gamopetalous, corolla 2/3 personate, upper lip short and 2 lobed, lower lip spreading and three lobed, valvate, throat with a 2-lobed palate, pale blue with streaks.

Androecium. Stamens 4, polyandrous, epipetalous, didynamous, filaments long and curved, anthers dithecous, basifixed, introrse, anthers of pairs are confluent in young condition.

Gynoecium. Bicarpellary, syncarpous, ovary superior, bilocular with many ovules in each locule, axile placentation, style filiform, stigma 2 and lamellate.

Fruit. Capsule enclosed inside the persistent calyx.

Floral formula. Br, ⊕, ⚥, $K_{(5)}$, $\overbrace{C_{(2/3)}, A_4}$, $\underline{G}_{(2)}$.

Classification and identification.

Class. ***Dicotyledonae***

1. Venation reticulate.
2. Flowers pentamerous.

Sub-Class. ***Gamopetalae***

1. Petals fused.

Series. ***Bicarpellatae***

1. Carpels two,
2. Ovary usually superior.

Order. ***Personales***

1. Flowers zygomorphic.
2. Corolla personate.
3. Stamens usually 4, didynamous or 2.
4. Ovary uni-bi-or rarely tetralocular; ovules usually indefinite.

Family. ***Scrophulariaceae***

1. Flowers never terminal.
2. Gynoecium bicarpellary, syncarpous, bilocular.
3. Ovules many on axile placentation.

***1. English name.** Figwort family.

2. Systematic position in other systems of classification.

Rendle (1925)	**Engler and Prantl (1931)**	**Hutchinson (1959)**
Dicotyledons	Dictyledoneae	Dicotyledons
Sympetalae	Sympetalae	Herbaceae
Tetracyclicae	Tubiflorae	Personales
Superae	Scrophulariaceae	Scrophulariaceae
Tubiflorae		
Solanineae		
Scrophulariaceae		

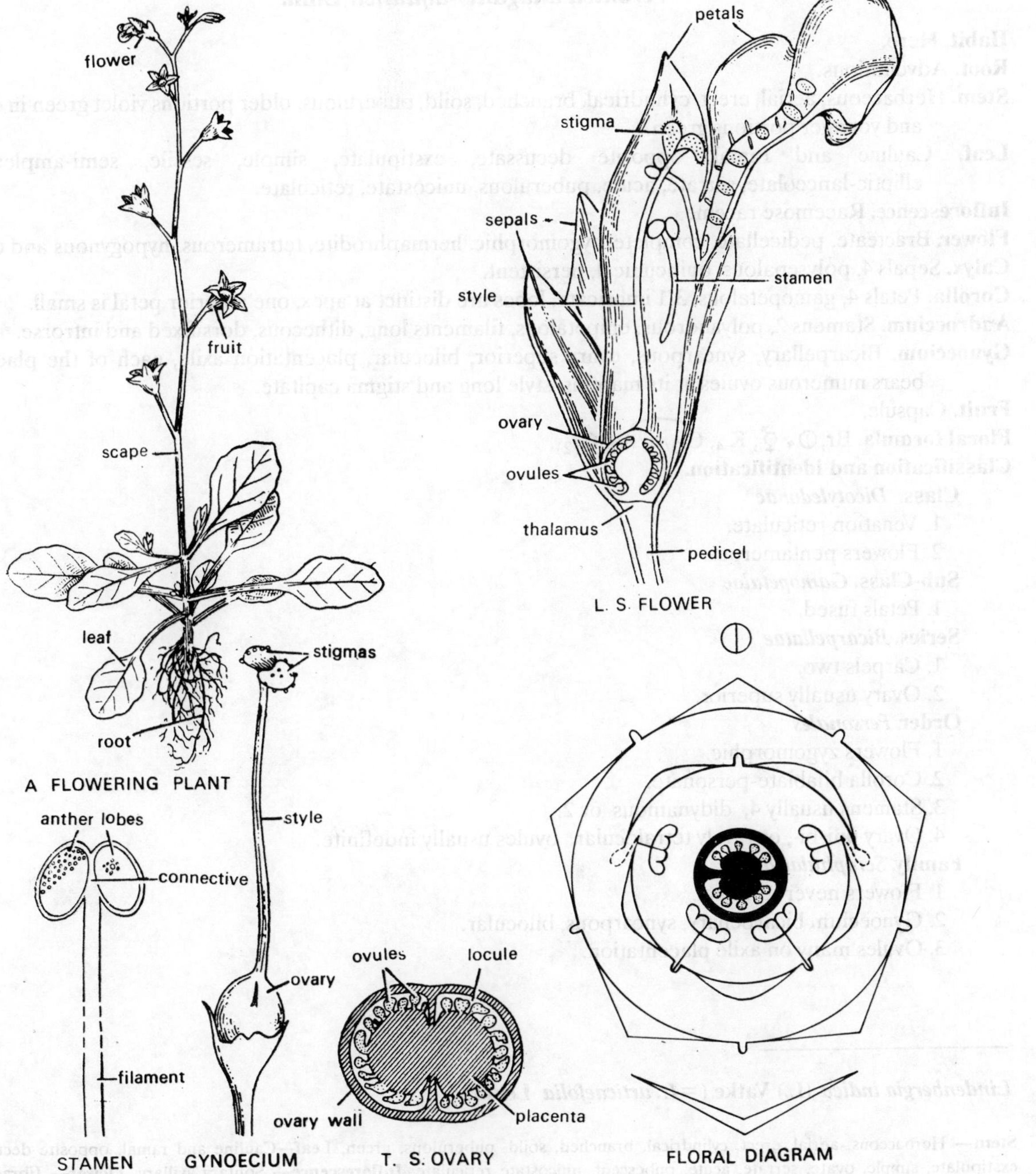

Fig. 59. *Mazus pumilus.*

1. Economic importance. An infusion of plants is given as tonic.

Veronica anagallis-aquatica Linn.

Habit. Herb.

Root. Adventitious.

Stem. Herbaceous, aerial, erect, cylindrical, branched, soild, puberulous, older portions violet green in colour and younger portions green.

Leaf. Cauline and ramal, opposite decussate, exstipulate, simple, sessile, semi-amplexicaul, elliptic-lanceolate, serrate, acute, puberulous, unicostate, reticulate.

Inflorescence. Racemose raceme.

Flower. Bracteate, pedicellate, complete, zygomorphic, hermaphrodite, tetramerous, hypogynous and cyclic.

Calyx. Sepals 4, polysepalous, quincunical, persistent.

Corolla. Petals 4, gamopetalous, 3/1 imbricate, lobes are distinct at apex, one anterior petal is small.

Androecium. Stamens 2, polyandrous, epipetalous, filaments long, dithecous, dorsifixed and introrse.

Gynoecium. Bicarpellary, syncarpous, ovary superior, bilocular, placentation axile, each of the placentae bears numerous ovules at its margins, style long and stigma capitate.

Fruit. Capsule.

Floral formula. Br, ⦶, ⚥, K_4, $\widehat{C_{(3/1)}, A_2}$, $\underline{G}_{(2)}$.

Classification and identification.

Class. *Dicotyledonae*

1. Venation reticulate.
2. Flowers pentamerous.

Sub-Class. *Gamopetalae*

1. Petals fused.

Series. *Bicarpellatae*

1. Carpels two.
2. Ovary usually superior.

Order. *Personales*

1. Flowers zygomorphic.
2. Corolla bilabiate-personate.
3. Stamens usually 4, didynamous or 2.
4. Ovary uni-bi-, or rarely tetralocular, ovules usually indefinite.

Family. *Scrophulariaceae*

1. Flowers never terminal.
2. Gynoecium bicarpellary, syncarpous, bilocular.
3. Ovules many on axile placentation.

Lindenbergia indica (L.) Vatke (=*L. urticaefolia* Lehm.)

Stem— Herbaceous, aerial, erect, cylindrical, branched, soild, puberulous, green; **Leaf**—Cauline and ramal, opposite decussate, exstipulate, simple, ovate, serrate, acute, pubescent, unicostate reticulate; **Inflorescence**— Solitary axillary; **Flower**— Ebracteate, sub-sessile, complete, zygomorphic, hermaphrodite, pentamerous, hypogynous and cyclic; **Calyx**— Sepals 5, gamosepalous, imbricate, hairy; **Corolla**— Petals 5, gamopetalous, corolla 2/3 bilabiate personate, imbricate; **Androecium**— Stamens 4, polyandrous. epipetalous, didynamous, anthers are separated from one another by the elongation of the connective, dithecous, introrse; **Gynoecium**— Bicarpellary, syncarpous, ovary superior, bilocular with many ovules in each locule, placentation axile, style long, stigma fimbriate; **Fruit**— Capsule;

Floral formula— Ebr, ⦶, ⚥, $K_{(5)}$, $\widehat{C_{(2/3)}, A_{2+2}}$, $\underline{G}_{(2)}$.

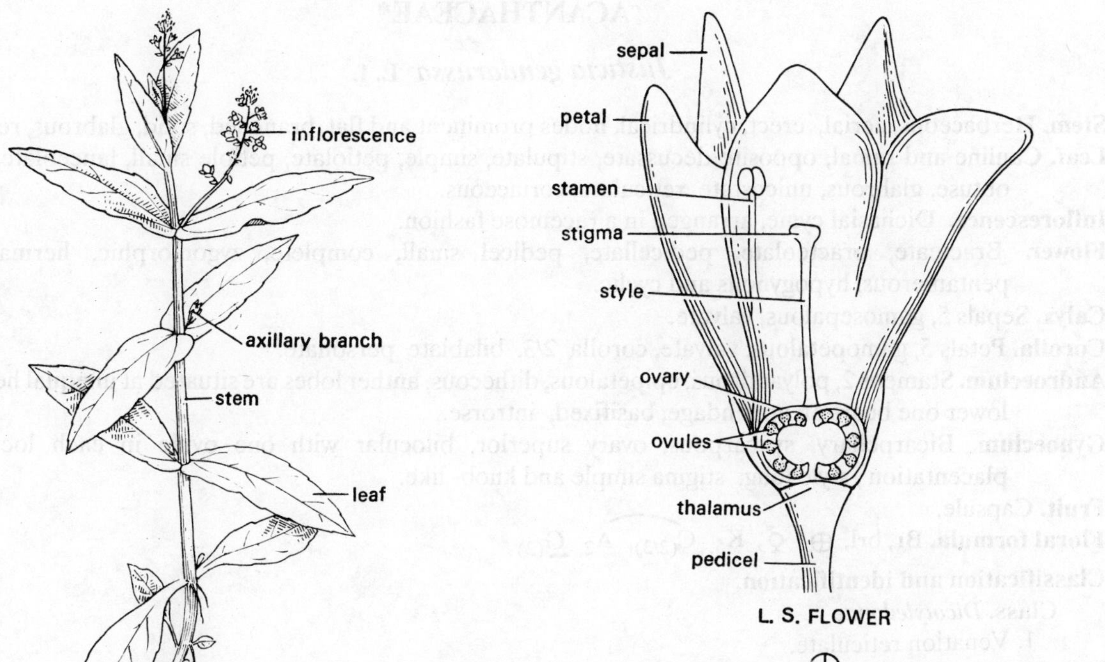

Fig. 60. ***Veronica anagallis-aquatica.***

---

1. Economic importance. The herb is used as a blood purifer and also cures skin diseases.

ACANTHACEAE*

Justicia gendarussa L. f.

Stem. Herbaceous, aerial, erect, cylindrical, nodes prominent and flat, branched, solid, glabrous, red-brown.

Leaf. Cauline and ramal, opposite decussate, stipulate, simple, petiolate, petiole small, lanceolate, crenate, obtuse, glabrous, unicostate reticulate, coriaceous.

Inflorescence. Dichasial cyme, arranged in a racemose fashion.

Flower. Bracteate, bracteolate, pedicellate, pedicel small, complete, zygomorphic, hermaphrodite, pentamerous, hypogynous and cyclic.

Calyx. Sepals 5, gamosepalous, valvate.

Corolla. Petals 5, gamopetalous, valvate, corolla 2/3, bilabiate personate.

Androecium. Stamens 2, polyandrous, epipetalous, dithecous, anther lobes are situated at unequal heights and lower one bears an appendage, basifixed, introrse.

Gynoecium. Bicarpellary, syncarpous, ovary superior, bilocular with one ovule in each locule, axile placentation , style long, stigma simple and knob- like.

Fruit. Capsule.

Floral formula. Br, brl, ⊕, ⚥, K_5, $\overbrace{C_{(2/3)}, A_2}$, $\underline{G}_{(2)}$.

Classification and identification.

Class. *Dicotyledonae*

1. Venation reticulate.
2. Flowers pentamerous.

Sub- Class. *Gamopetalae*

1. Petals fused.

Series. *Bicarpellatae*

1. Carpels two.
2. Ovary usually superior.

Order. *Personales*

1. Flowers zygomorphic.
2. Corolla bilabiate personate.
3. Stamens usually 4 didynamous, or two.
4. Ovary uni-,bi-or tetralocular, ovules usually indefinite.

Family. *Acanthaceae*

1. Herbs or shrubs with opposite leaves.
2. Flowers in spikes, racemes or cymose umbels.
3. Anthers are situated at unequal heights.
4. Gynoecium bilocular, each locule with indefinite to two ovule
5. Jaculators are present between the seeds.

***1. English name.** Acanthus family.

2. Systematic position in other systems of classification.

Rendle (1925)	**Engler and Prantl** (1931)	**Hutchinson** (1959)
Dicotyledons	Dicotyledoneae	Dicotyledons
Sympetalae	Sympetalae	Herbaceae
Tetracylicae	Tubiflorae	Personales
Superae	Acanthaceae	Acanthaceae
Tubiflorae		
Solanineae		
Acanthaceae		

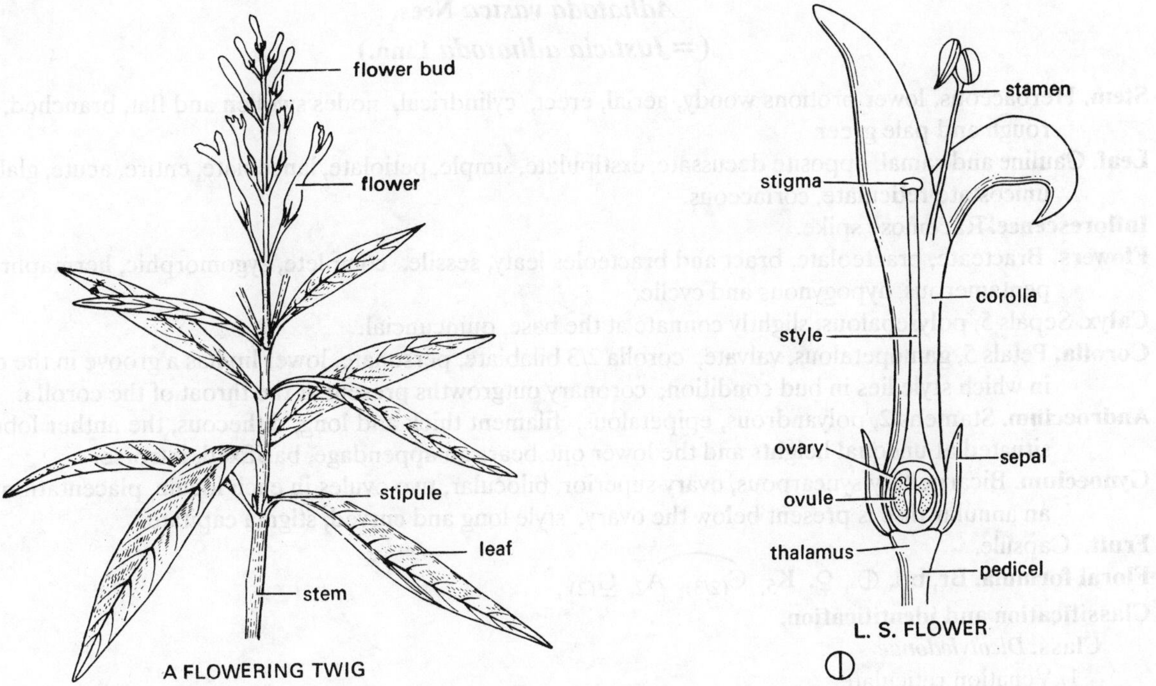

Fig. 61. ***Justicia gendarussa.***

1. Vernacular name. Nili-nargandi.

2. Economic importance. It is used as a hedge plant.

Adhatoda vasica Nees
(=*Justicia adhatoda* Linn.)

Stem. Herbaceous, lower protions woody, aerial, erect, cylindrical, nodes swollen and flat, branched, solid, rough and pale green.

Leaf. Cauline and ramal, opposite decussate, exstipulate, simple, petiolate, lanceolate, entire, acute, glabrous, unicostate reticulate, coriaceous.

Inflorescence. Racemose spike.

Flowers. Bracteate, bracteolate, bract and bracteoles leafy, sessile, complete, zygomorphic, hermaphrodite, pentamerous, hypogynous and cyclic.

Calyx. Sepals 5, polysepalous, slightly connate at the base, quincuncial.

Corolla. Petals 5, gamopetalous, valvate, corolla 2/3 bilabiate, personate, lower lip has a groove in the centre in which style lies in bud condition, coronary outgrowths present at the throat of the corolla.

Androecium. Stamens 2, polyandrous, epipetalous, filament thick and long, dithecous, the anther lobes are situated at unequal heights and the lower one bears an appendage, basifixed, introrse.

Gynoecium. Bicarpellary syncarpous, ovary superior, bilocular, two ovules in each locule, placentation axile, an annular disc is present below the ovary, style long and curved, stigma capitate.

Fruit. Capsule.

Floral formula. Br, brl, ⊕, ⚥, K_5, $\overset{\frown}{C_{(2/3)}, A_2}$, $\underline{G}_{(2)}$.

Classification and identification.

Class. ***Dicotyledonae***

1. Venation reticulate.
2. Flowers pentamerous.

Sub- Class. ***Gamopetalae***

1. Petals fused.

Series. ***Bicarpellatae***

1. Carpels two.
2. Ovary usually superior.

Order. ***Personales***

1. Flowers zygomorphic.
2. Corolla bilabiate-personate.
3. Stamens usually 4 didynamous, or 2
4. Ovary uni-bi-, or tetralocular, ovules usually indefinite.

Family. ***Acanthaceae***

1. Herbs or shrubs, with opposite leaves.
2. Flowers in spikes, racemes or cymose umbels.
3. Anthers are situated at unequal heights.
4. Gynoecium bilocular, each locule with indefinite to two ovules.
5. Jaculators are present between the seeds.

Dipterocanthus prostratus (Poir.) Nees (=*Ruellia prostrata* Lamk.)

Stem -Herbaceous, lower portions woody, aerial, erect, quadrangular, branched, solid, glabrous and green; **Leaf** - Cauline and ramal, opposite, decussate, exstipulate, simple, sessile, leaf-base chaeving, linear-lanceolate, lamina slightly oblique, sinuate, acute, unicostate, reticulate, coriaceous; **Inflorescence** - Axillary dichasial cyme; **Flower** - Bracteate, bracteolate, pedicellate, complete, slightly zygomorphic, hermaphrodite, pentamerous, hypogynous and cyclic; **Calyx** - Sepals 5, gamosepalous, deeply partite, valvate, persistent; **Corolla** - Petals 5, corolla 2/3, gamopetalous, twisted, corolla infundibuliform, purple; **Androecium** - Stamens 2+2, polyandrous, epipetalous, didynamous, dithecous, anther lobes slightly unequally situated, basifixed, introrse; **Gynoecium** - Bicarpellary, syncarpous, ovary superior, bilocular, with one big ovule in each locule, axile placentation, style long and stigma bifid; **Fruit** - Capsule. Each seed has a jaculator at its base.

Floral formula - Br, brl, ⊕, ⚥, $K_{(5)}$, $\overset{\frown}{C_{(2/3)}, A_{2+2}}$, $\underline{G}_{(2)}$.

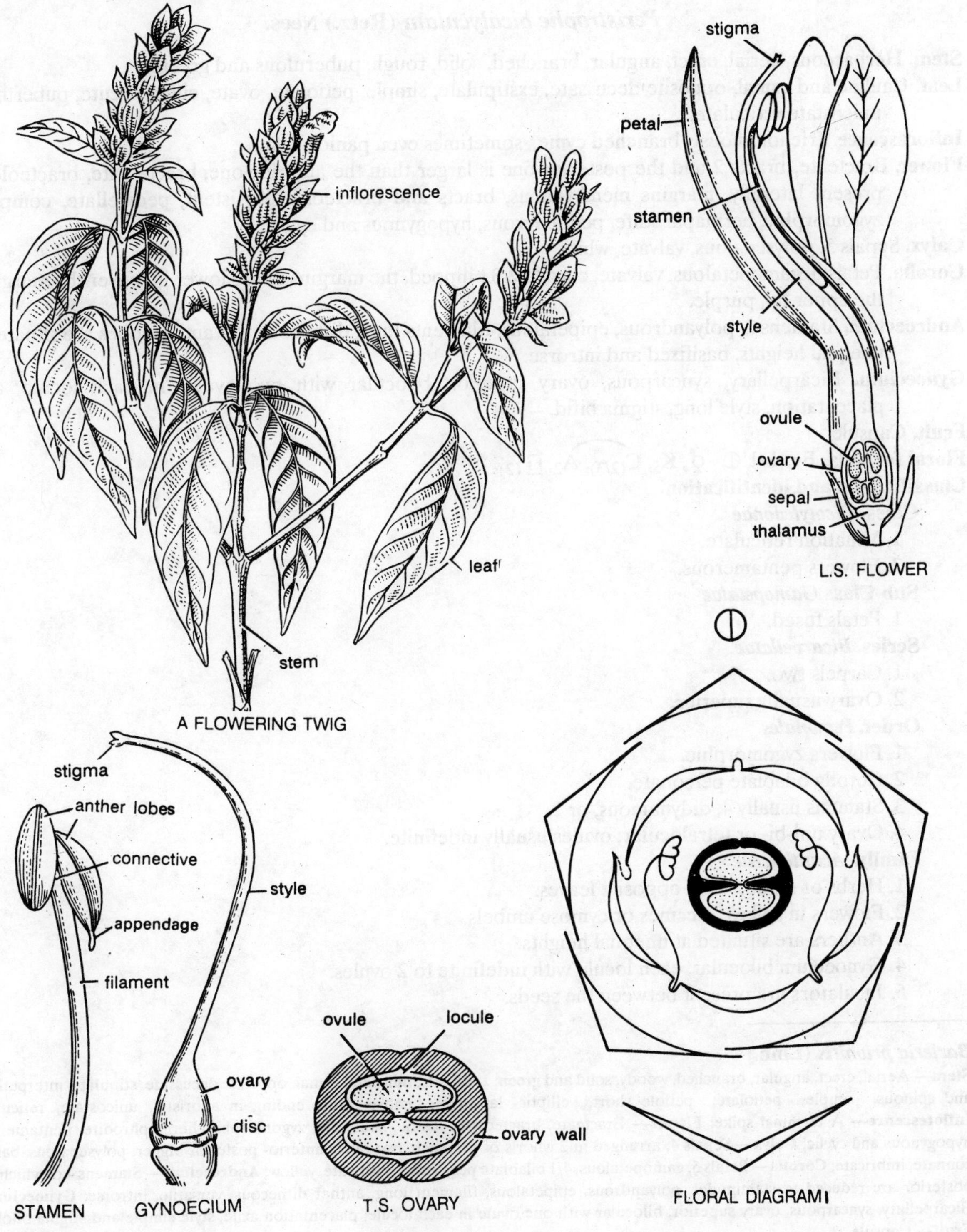

Fig. 62. ***Adhatoda vasica.***

---

1. English name. Malabar nut.

2. Vernacular names. Adulasa, Basak, Safed bansa.

3. Economic importance. Leaves are used as Ayurvedic drug, used as an expectorant and relieves cough.

Peristrophe bicalyculata (Retz.) Nees.

Stem. Herbaceous, aerial, erect, angular, branched, solid, rough, puberulous and green.

Leaf. Cauline and ramal, opposite decussate, exstipulate, simple, petiolate, ovate, ciliate, acute, puberulous, unicostate reticulate.

Inflorescence. Trichotomously branched cyme, sometimes even panicle cyme.

Flower. Bracteate, bracts 2 and the posterior one is larger than the anterior one, bracteolate, bracteoles 4, present laterally, margins membranous, bracts and bracteoles persistent, pedicellate, complete, zygomorphic, hermaphrodite, pentamerous, hypogynous and cyclic.

Calyx. Sepals 5, polysepalous, valvate, white.

Corolla. Petals 5, gamopetalous, valvate, corolla 2/3 bilipped, the margins of the lower lip cover the margin of the upper lip, purple.

Androecium. Stamens 2, polyandrous, epipetalous, filaments long, dithecous, the anther lobes are situated at unequal heights, basifixed and introrse.

Gynoecium. Bicarpellary, syncarpous, ovary superior, bilocular with two ovules in each locule, axile placentation, style long, stigma bifid.

Fruit. Capsule.

Floral formula. Br, brl, ⏀ ⚥, K_5, $\overparen{C_{(2/3)}, A_2}$, $\underline{G}_{(2)}$.

Classification and identification.

Class. ***Dicotyledonae***

1. Venation reticulate.
2. Flowers pentamerous.

Sub-Class.*Gamopetalae*

1. Petals fused.

Series. ***Bicarpellatae***

1. Carpels two.
2. Ovary usually superior.

Order. ***Personales***

1. Flowers zygomorphic.
2. Corolla bilabiate personate.
3. Stamens usually 4, didynamous, or 2.
4. Ovary uni-bi- or tetralocular; ovules usually indefinite.

Family. ***Acanthaceae***

1. Herbs or shrubs, with opposite leaves.
2. Flowers in spikes, racemes or cymose umbels.
3. Anthers are situated at unequal heights.
4. Gynoecium bilocular, each locule with indefinite to 2 ovules.
5. Jaculators are present between the seeds.

Barleria prionitis **(Linn.)**

Stem— Aerial, erect, angular, branched, woody, solid and green; **Leaf**— Cauline and ramal, opposite decussate, stipulate, interpetiolar and spinous, simple, petiolate, petiole short, elliptic- lanceolate, entire, acute ending in a bristle, unicostate, reticulate; **Inflorescence**— A terminal spike; **Flower**— Bracteate, bracteolate, sessile, complete, zygomorphic, hermaphrodite, pentamerous, hypogynous and cyclic; **Calyx**— Sepals 4, arranged in 2 whorls of two each, two outer anterio- posterior bigger, polysepalous, basally connate, imbricate; **Corolla**— Petals 5, gamopetalous, 4/1 bilabiate personate, imbricate, yellow; **Androecium**— Stamens 4 of which two posterior are reduced to staminodes, polyandrous, epipetalous, filament long, anther dithecous, versatile, introrse; **Gynoecium**— Bicarpellary, syncarpous, ovary superior, bilocular with one ovule in each locule, placentation axile, style simple and stigma bilobed; **Fruit**— Capsule.

Floral formula. Br, brl, ⊕ ⚥, K_{2+2}, $\overparen{C_{(4/2)}, A_4}$, $\underline{G}_{(2)}$.

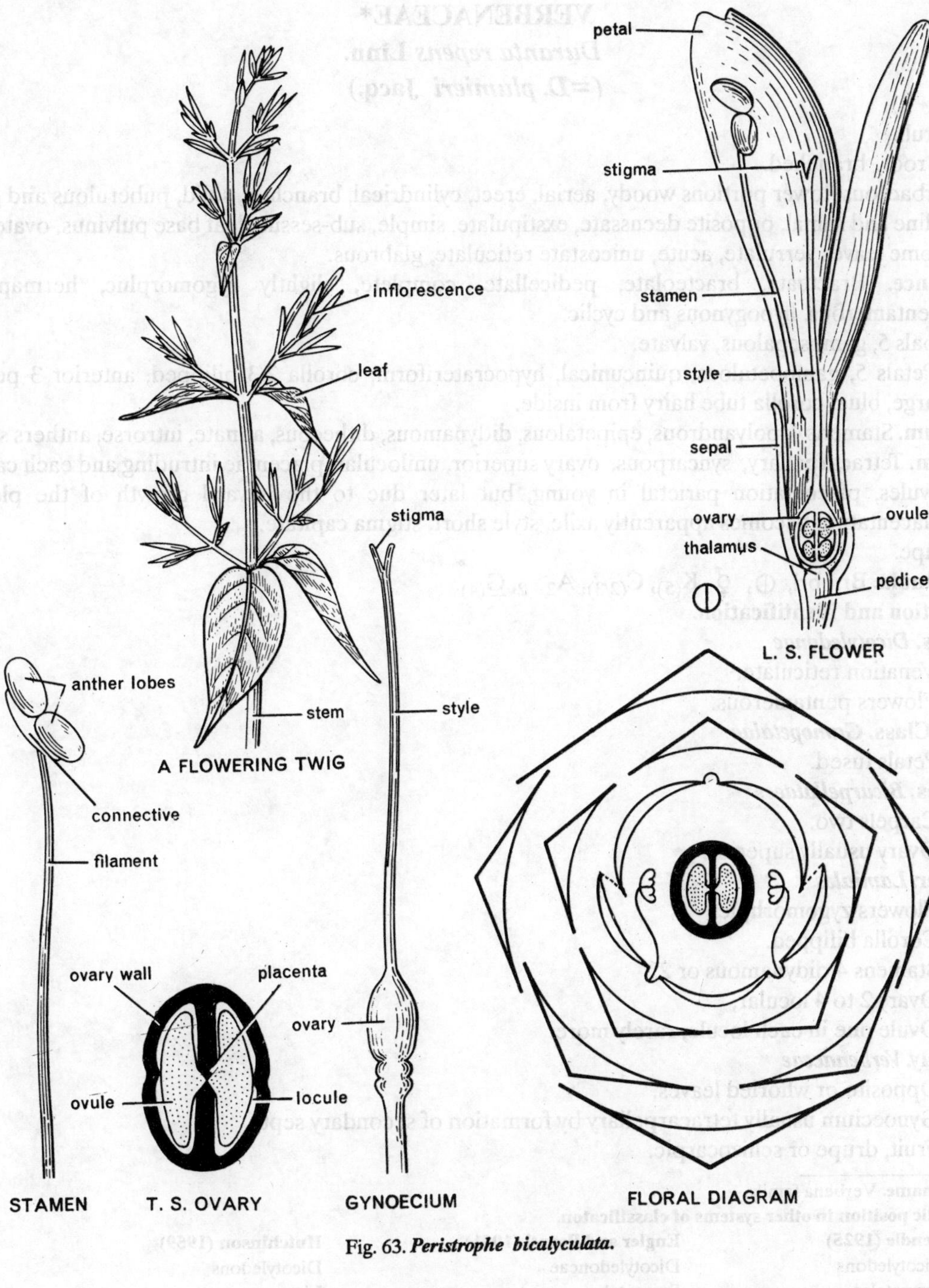

Fig. 63. ***Peristrophe bicalyculata.***

1. Vernacular name. Atrilal

2. Economic importance. The plant is considered by the natives as a remedy for snake-bites.

VERBENACEAE*

Duranta repens Linn.
(=*D. plumieri* Jacq.)

Habit. Shrub.

Root. Tap root, branched.

Stem. Herbaceous, lower portions woody, aerial, erect, cylindrical, branched, solid, puberulous and green.

Leaf. Cauline and ramal, opposite decussate, exstipulate, simple, sub-sessile, leaf base pulvinus, ovate, entire, some leaves serrulate, acute, unicostate reticulate, glabrous.

Inflorescence. Bracteate, bracteolate, pedicellate, complete, slightly zygomorphic, hermaphrodite, pentamerous, hypogynous and cyclic.

Calyx. Sepals 5, gamosepalous, valvate.

Corolla. Petals 5, gamopetalous, quincunical, hypocrateriform, corolla 2/3 bilipped, anterior 3 petals are large, blue, corolla tube hairy from inside.

Androecium. Stamens 4, polyandrous, epipetalous, didynamous, dithecous, adnate, introrse, anthers sagittate.

Gynoecium. Tetracarpellary, syncarpous, ovary superior, unilocular, placentae intruding and each carrying 2 ovules, placentation parietal in young, but later due to the inward growth of the placentae, placentation becomes apparently axile, style short, stigma capitate.

Fruit. Drupe.

Floral formula. Br, brl, ⊕, ⚥, $K_{(5)}$, $C_{(2/3)}$, A_{2+2}, $\underline{G}_{(4)}$.

Classification and identification.

Class. ***Dicotyledonae***
1. Venation reticulate.
2. Flowers pentamerous.

Sub-Class. ***Gamopetalae***
1. Petals fused.

Series. ***Bicarpellatae***
1. Carpels two.
2. Ovary usually superior.

Order. ***Lamiales***
1. Flowers zygomorhpic.
2. Corolla bilipped.
3. Stamens 4 didynamous or 2.
4. Ovary 2 to 4 locular,
5. Ovule one in each locule, rarely more.

Family. ***Verbenaceae***
1. Opposite or whorled leaves.
2. Gynoecium usually tetracarpellary by formation of secondary septa.
3. Fruit, drupe or schizocarpic.

***1. English name.** Verbena family.

2. Systematic position in other systems of classificaton.

Rendle (1925)	**Engler and Prantl (1931)**	**Hutchinson (1959)**
Dicotyledons	Dicotyledoneae	Dicotyledons
Sympetalae	Sympetalae	Lignosae
Tetracyclicae	Tubiflorae	Verbenales
Superae	Verbenaceae	Verbenaceae
Tubiflorae		
Verbenineae		
Verbenaceae		

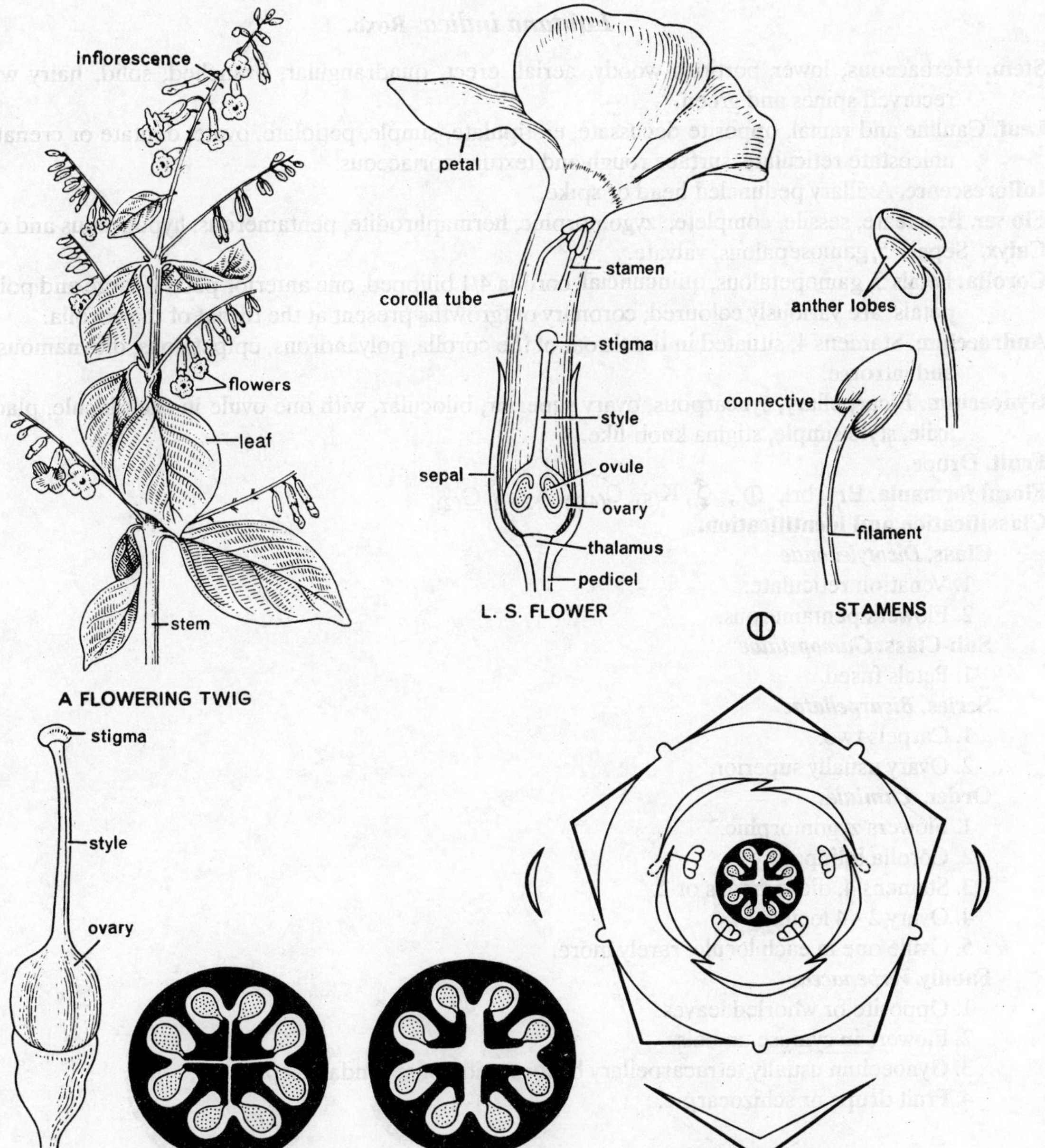

Fig. 64. ***Duranta repens.***

---

1. English names. Golden dew drop, Pigeon berry.

2. Economic importance. Grown as a hedge plant.

Lantana indica Roxb.

Stem. Herbaceous, lower portions woody, aerial, erect, quadrangular, branched, solid, hairy with some recurved spines and green.

Leaf. Cauline and ramal, opposite decussate, exstipulate, simple, petiolate, ovate, dentate or crenate, acute, unicostate reticulate, surface rough and texture coriaceous.

Inflorescence. Axillary peduncled head or spike.

Flower. Bracteate, sessile, complete, zygomorphic, hermaphrodite, pentamerous, hypogynous and cyclic.

Calyx. Sepals 5, gamosepalous, valvate.

Corolla. Petals 5, gamopetalous, quincuncial, corolla 4/1 bilipped, one anterior petal is large and pointed, the petals are variously coloured, coronary outgrowths present at the throat of the corolla.

Androecium. Stamens 4, situated in the throat of the corolla, polyandrous, epipetalous, didynamous, adnate, and introrse.

Gynoecium. Bicarpellary, syncarpous, ovary superior, bilocular, with one ovule in each locule, placentation axile, style simple, stigma knob-like.

Fruit. Drupe.

Floral formaula. Br, brl, ⦶, ⚥, $K_{(5)}$, $\overset{\frown}{C_{(4/1)}, A_{2+2}}$, $\underline{G}_{(2)}$.

Classification and identification.

Class. ***Dicotyledonae***

1. Venation reticulate.
2. Flowers pentamerous.

Sub-Class. ***Gamopetalae***

1. Petals fused.

Series. ***Bicarpellatae***

1. Carpels two.
2. Ovary usually superior.

Order. ***Lamiales***

1. Flowers zygomorphic.
2. Corolla bilipped.
3. Stamens 4, didynamous or 2.
4. Ovary 2 - 4 locular.
5. Ovule one in each locule, rarely more.

Family. ***Verbenaceae***

1. Opposite or whorled leaves.
2. Flowers in cymose umbels.
3. Gynoecium usually tetracarpellary by formation of secondary septae.
4. Fruit drupe or schizocarpic.

Clerodendrum inerme (L.) Gaertn. (= *Volkameria inermis* L.)

Stem.— Herbaceous, aerial, erect, somewhat angular, branched, solid, puberulous, green; **Leaf**— Cauline and ramal, opposite decussate, exstipulate, simple, petiolate, elliptical, entire, obtuse, pubescent, unicostate, reticulate; **Inflorescence**— Axillary dichasial cyme; **Flower**— Bracteate, bracteolate, pedicellate, complete, actinomorphic, hermaphrodite, pentamerous, hypogynous and cyclic; **Calyx**—Sepals 5, gamosepalous, valvate; **Corolla**— Petals 5, gamopetalous, imbricate, hypocrateriform; **Androecium**—Stamens 4, polyandrous, epipetalous, didynamous, filaments long, dithecous, dorsifixed, introrse; **Gynoecium**— Bicarpellary, syncarpous, ovary superior, unilocular, placentae T-shaped and very much intruding, each with two ovules, placentation parietal, style long and stigma bifid; **Fruit**— Drupe;

Floral formula— Br, brl, ⊕, ⚥, $K_{(5)}$, $\overset{\frown}{C_{(5)}, A_{2+2}}$, $\underline{G}_{(2)}$.

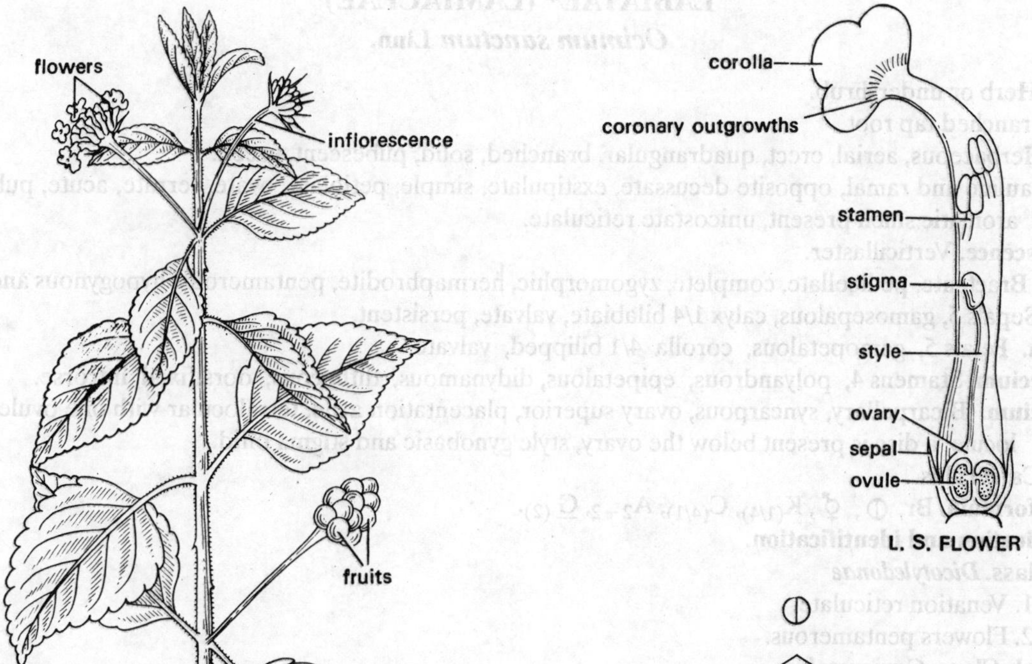

Fig. 65. ***Lantana indica.***

---

1. Vernacular name. Kuri.

2. Economic importance. Leaves are said to be used as an antidote for snake bites.

LABIATAE* (LAMIACEAE)

Ocimum sanctum Linn.

Habit. Herb or undershrub.
Root. Branched tap root.
Stem. Herbaceous, aerial, erect, quadrangular, branched, solid, pubescent, green.
Leaf. Cauline and ramal, opposite decussate, exstipulate, simple, petiolate, ovate, serrate, acute, pubescent, aromatic smell present, unicostate reticulate.
Inflorescence. Verticillaster.
Flower. Bracteate, pedicellate, complete, zygomorphic, hermaphrodite, pentamerous, hypogynous and cyclic.
Calyx. Sepals 5, gamosepalous, calyx 1/4 bilabiate, valvate, persistent.
Corolla. Petals 5, gamopetalous, corolla 4/1 bilipped, valvate.
Androecium. Stamens 4, polyandrous, epipetalous, didynamous, dithecous, dorsifixed, introrse.
Gynoecium. Bicarpellary, syncarpous, ovary superior, placentation axile, tetralocular with one ovule in each locule, a disc is present below the ovary, style gynobasic and stigma bifid.
Fruit. Carcerulus.
Floral formula. Br, ⊕, ⚥, $K_{(1/4)}$, $C_{(4/1)}$, $\overset{\frown}{A}_{2+2}$, $\underline{G}_{(2)}$.
Classification and identification.

Class. ***Dicotyledonae***
1. Venation reticulate.
2. Flowers pentamerous.

Sub-Class. ***Gamopetalae***
1. Petals fused.

Series. ***Bicarpellatae***
1. Carpels two.
2. Ovary usually superior.

Order. ***Lamiales***
1. Flowers zygomorphic.
2. Corolla bilipped.
3. Stamens 4, didynamous or 2.
4. Ovary 2 - 4 locular.
5. Fruit drupe or schizocarpic.

Family. ***Labiatae***
1. Stem quadrangular. 2. Decussate or whorled exstipulate leaves. 3. Inflorescence verticillaster.
4. Gynoecium generally bilocular with 2 ovules in each locule, sometimes tetralocular with one ovule in each locule. 5. Style gynobasic. 6. Fruit carcerulus.

---

*1. **English name.** Mint family.
2. **Systematic position in other systems of classification.**

Rendle (1925)	Engler and Prantl (1931)	Hutchinson (1959)
Dicotyledons	Dicotyledoneae	Dicotyledons
Sympetalae	Sympetalae	Herbaceae
Tetracyclicae	Tubiflorae	Lamiales
Superae	Labiatae	Labiatae
Tubiflorae		
Verbenineae		
Labiatae		

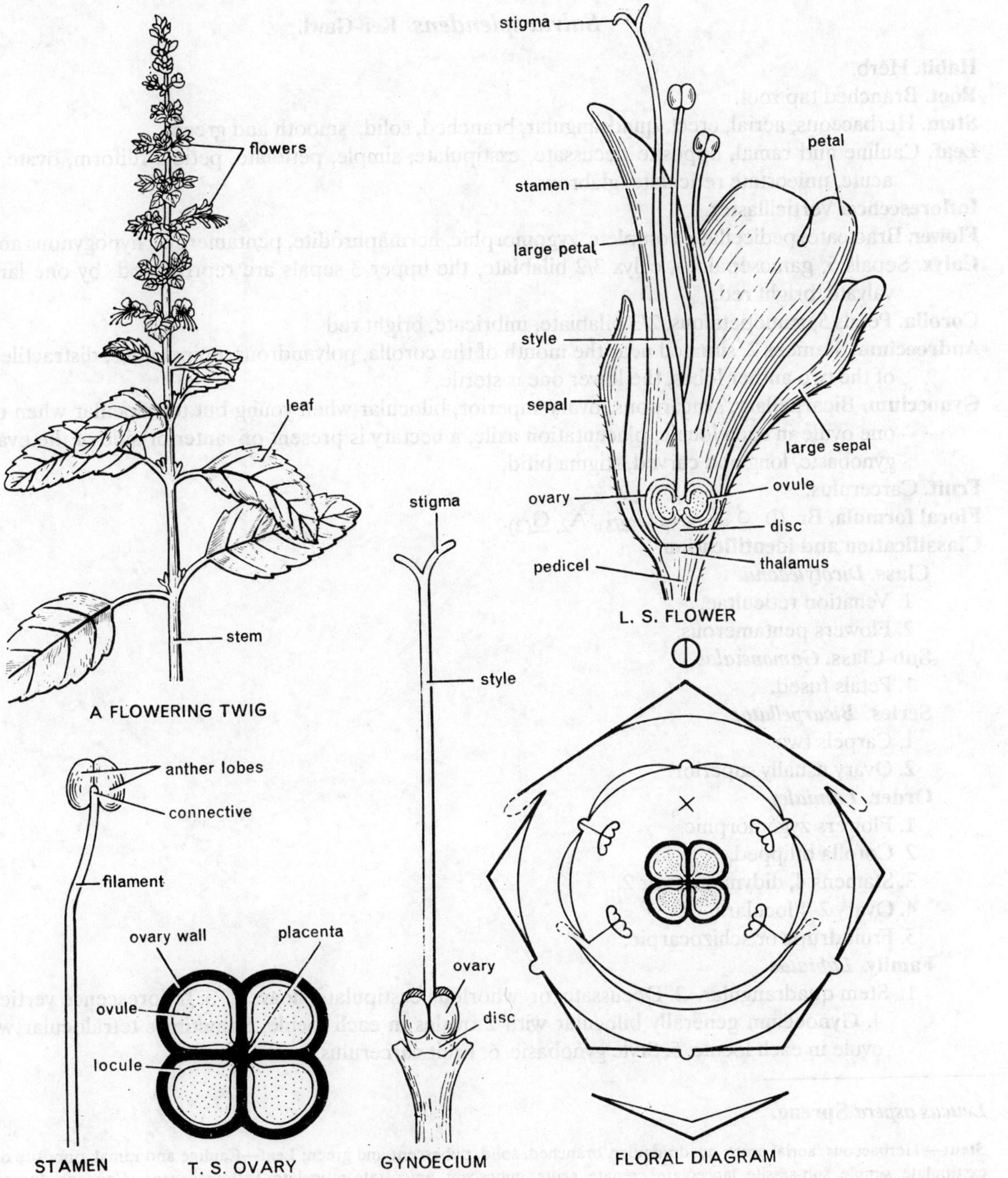

Fig. 66. ***Ocimum sanctum.***

---

1. English name. Sacred Basil, Holy Basil.

2. Vernacular name. Tulsi.

3. Economic importnace. The seeds are used in chronic diarrhoea and dysentery. Deccoction of the leaves is said to be useful in cold.

Salvia splendens Ker-Gawl.

Habit. Herb.

Root. Branched tap root.

Stem. Herbaceous, aerial, erect, quadrangular, branched, solid, smooth and green.

Leaf. Cauline and ramal, opposite decussate, exstipulate, simple, petiolate, petiole filiform, ovate, serrate, acute, unicostate reticulate, glabrous.

Inflorescence. Verticillaster.

Flower. Bracteate, pedicellate, complete, zygomorphic, hermaphrodite, pentamerous, hypogynous and cyclic.

Calyx. Sepals 5, gamosepalous, calyx 3/2 bilabiate, the upper 3 sepals are represented by one large lobe, valvate, bright red.

Corolla. Petals 5, gamopetalous, 2/3 bilabiate, imbricate, bright red.

Androecium. Stamens 2, situated near the mouth of the corolla, polyandrous, epipetalous, distractile and out of the two anther lobes, the lower one is sterile.

Gynoecium. Bicarpellary, syncarpous, ovary superior, bilocular when young but tetralocular when old, with one ovule in each locule, placentation axile, a nectary is present on anterior side of the ovary, style gynobasic, long and curved, stigma bifid,

Fruit. Carcerulus.

Floral formula. Br, ⊕ ⚥, $K_{(3/2)}$, $\overset{\frown}{C_{(2/3)}, A_2}$, $\underline{G}_{(2)}$.

Classification and identification.

Class. ***Dicotyledonae***

1. Venation reticultae.
2. Flowers pentamerous.

Sub-Class. ***Gamopetalae***

1. Petals fused.

Series. ***Bicarpellatae***

1. Carpels two.
2. Ovary usually superior.

Order. ***Lamiales***

1. Flowers zygomorphic.
2. Corolla bilipped.
3. Stamens 4, didynamous or 2.
4. Ovary 2-4 locular.
5. Fruit drupe or schizocarpic.

Family. ***Labiatae***

1. Stem quadrangular. 2. Decussate or whorled, exstipulate leaves. 3. Inflorescence verticillaster. 4. Gynoecium generally bilocular with 2 ovules in each locule. Sometimes tetralocular with one ovule in each locule. 5. Style gynobasic. 6. Fruit carcerulus.

Leucas aspera Spreng.

Stem— Herbaceous, aerial erect, quadrangular, branched, solid, pubescent and green; **Leaf**—Cauline and ramal, opposite decussate, exstipulate, simple, sub-sessile, lanceolate, crenate, acute, pubescent, unicostate reticulate; **Inflorescence**— Condensed verticillaster; **Flower**— Bracteate, sub-sessile, complete, zygomorphic, hermaphrodite, pentamerous, hypogynous and cyclic; **Calyx**— Sepals 10, gamosepalous, valvate; **Corolla**— Petals 5, gamopetalous, corolla 2/3 bilipped, imbricate, white; **Androecium**— Stamens 4, polyandrous, epipetalous, didynamous, filaments long, anther dithecous, dorsifixed and introrse; **Gynoecium**— Bicarpellary, syncarpous, ovary superior, bilocular becoming tetralocular later on due to the developement of a false septum, ovule one in each locule, placentation axile, a disc is present below the ovary, style long and gynobasic, bifid; **Fruit**— Carcerulus.

Floral formula— Br, ⊕, ⚥, $K_{(10)}$, $\overset{\frown}{C_{(2/3)}, A_{2+2}}$, $\underline{G}_{(2)}$.

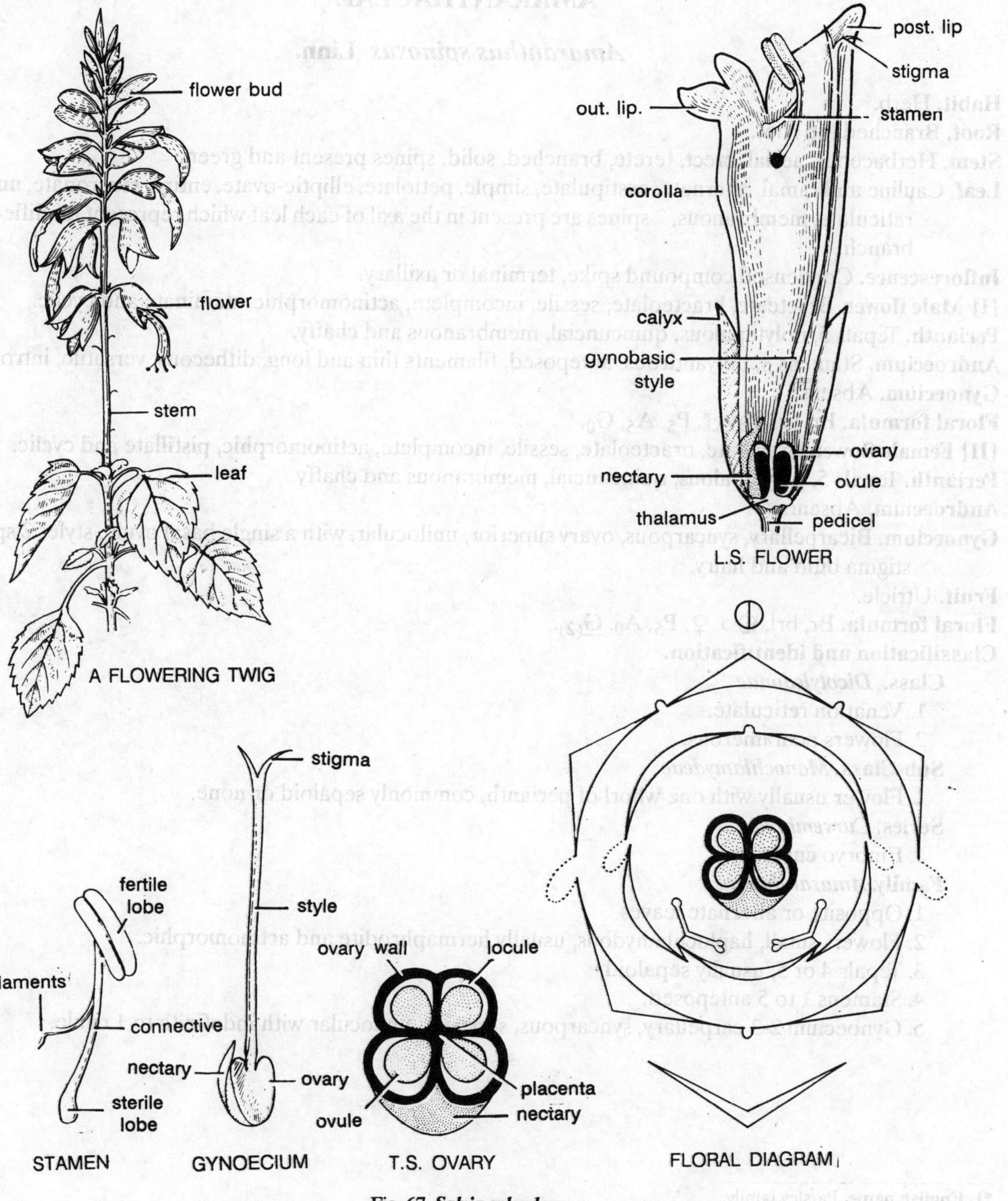

Fig. 67. ***Salvia splendens.***

---

1. English name. Scarlet sage.

2. Vernacular name. Salbia sefakuss, Sesti.

3. Economic importance. Grown as an ornamental.

AMARANTHACEAE*

Amaranthus spinosus Linn.

Habit. Herb.
Root. Branched tap root.
Stem. Herbaceous, aerial, erect, terete, branched, solid, spines present and green.
Leaf. Cauline and ramal, alternate, exstipulate, simple, petiolate, elliptic-ovate, entire, mucronate, unicostate, reticulate, membranous, 2 spines are present in the axil of each leaf which represent modified axillary branch.
Inflorescence. Condensed compound spike, terminal or axillary.
[I] Male flower. Bracteate, bracteolate, sessile, incomplete, actinomorphic, staminate and cyclic.
Perianth. Tepals 5, polytepalous, quincuncial, membranous and chaffy.
Androecium. Stamens 5, polyandrous, anteposed, filaments thin and long, dithecous, versatile, introrse.
Gynoecium. Absent.
Floral formula. Br, brl, ⊕, ♂, P_5, A_5, G_0.
[II] Female flower. Bracteate, bracteolate, sessile, incomplete, actinomorphic, pistillate and cyclic.
Perianth. Tepals 5, polytepalous, quincuncial, membranous and chaffy.
Androecium. Absent.
Gynoecium. Bicarpellary, syncarpous, ovary superior, unilocular, with a single basal ovule, styles 2 spreading, stigma bifid and hairy.
Fruit. Utricle.
Floral formula. Br, brl, ⊕, ♀, P_5, A_0, $\underline{G}_{(2)}$.
Classification and identification.

Class. *Dicotyledonae*
1. Venation reticulate.
2. Flowers pentamerous.

Sub-Class. *Monochlamydeae*
1. Flower usually with one whorl of perianth, commonly sepaloid or none.

Series. *Curvembryae*
1. Embryo curved.

Family. *Amaranthaceae*
1. Opposite or alternate leaves.
2. Flowers small, haplochlamydous, usually hermaphrodite and actinomorphic.
3. Tepals 4 or 5, usually sepaloid.
4. Stamens 1 to 5 anteposed.
5. Gynoecium 2-3 carpellary, syncarpous, superior, unilocular with indefinite to 1 ovule.

***1. English name.** Parsley family.
2. Systematic position in other systems of classification.

Rendle (1925)	Engler and Prantl (1931)	Hutchinson (1959)
Dicotyledons	Dicotyledoneae	Dicotyledons
Monochlamydeae	Archichlamydeae	Herbaceae
Centrospermae	Centrospermae	Chenopodiales
Amarantaceae	Amarantaceae	Amarantaceae

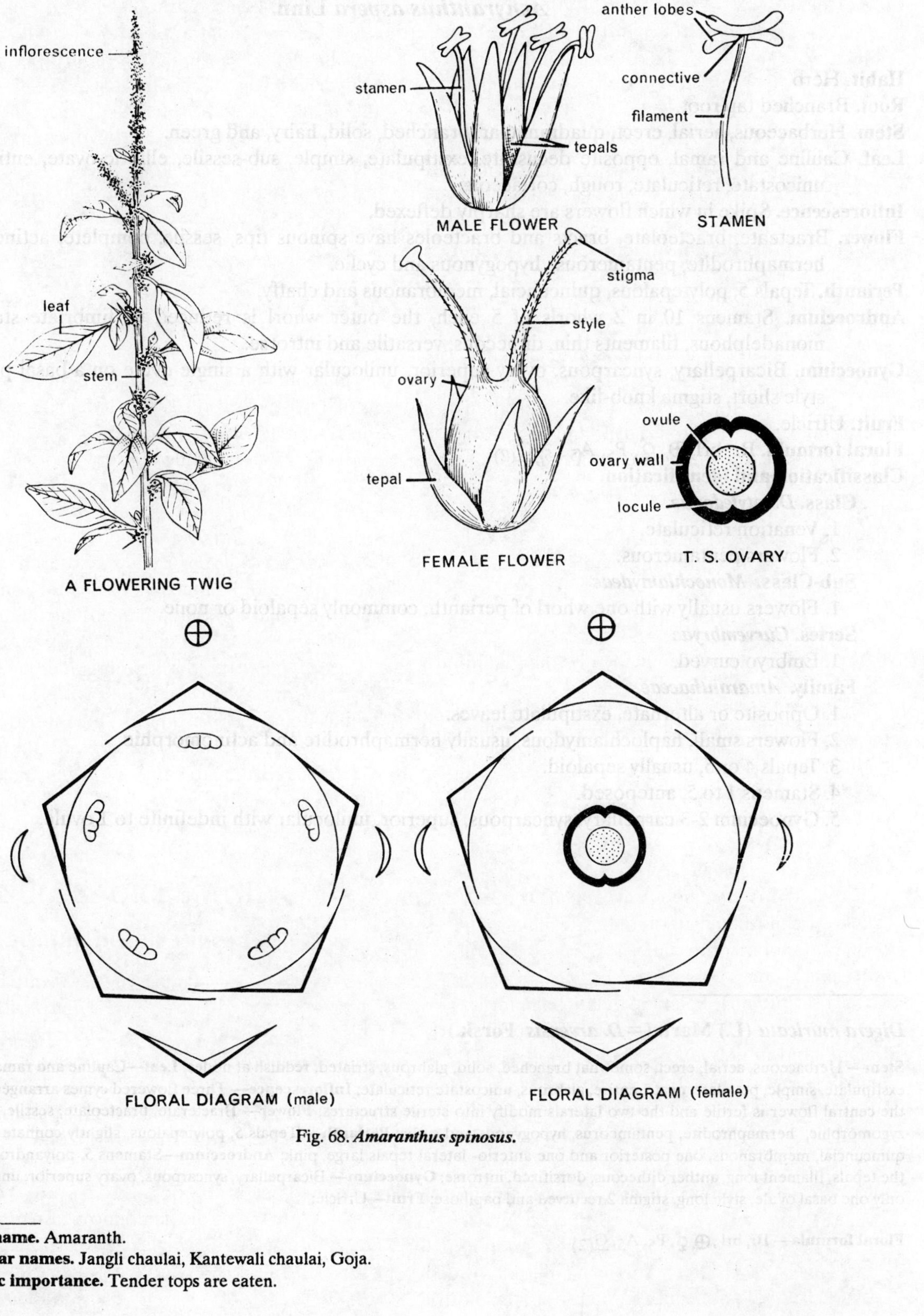

Fig. 68. *Amaranthus spinosus.*

---

1. English name. Amaranth.

2. Vernacular names. Jangli chaulai, Kantewali chaulai, Goja.

3. Economic importance. Tender tops are eaten.

Achyranthus aspera Linn.

Habit. Herb.

Root. Branched tap root.

Stem. Herbaceous, aerial, erect, quadrangular, branched, solid, hairy, and green.

Leaf. Cauline and ramal, opposite decussate, exstipulate, simple, sub-sessile, elliptic-ovate, entire, acute, unicostate, reticulate, rough, coriaceous.

Inflorescence. Spike in which flowers are sharply deflexed.

Flower. Bracteate, bracteolate, bracts and bracteoles have spinous tips, sessile, complete, actinomorphic, hermaphrodite, pentamerous, hypogynous and cyclic.

Perianth. Tepals 5, polytepalous, quincuncial, membranous and chaffy.

Androecium. Stamens 10 in 2 whorls of 5 each, the outer whorl is reduced to fimbriate staminodes, monadelphous, filaments thin, dithecous, versatile and introrse.

Gynoecium. Bicarpellary, syncarpous, ovary superior, unilocular with a single ovule on a basal placentum, style short, stigma knob-like.

Fruit. Utricle.

Floral formula. Br, brl, ⊕, ⚥, P_5, $A_{(5+5)}$, $\underline{G}_{(2)}$.

Classification and identification.

Class. *Dicotyledonae*

1. Venation reticulate.
2. Flowers pentamerous.

Sub-Class. *Monochlamydeae*

1. Flowers usually with one whorl of perianth, commonly sepaloid or none.

Series. *Curvembryae*

1. Embryo curved.

Family. *Amaranthaceae*

1. Opposite or alternate, exstipulate leaves.
2. Flowers small, haplochlamydous, usually hermaphrodite and actinomorphic.
3. Tepals 4 or 5, usually sepaloid.
4. Stamens 1 to 5, anteposed.
5. Gynoecium 2-3 carpellary, syncarpous, superior, unilocular with indefinite to 1 ovule.

Digera muricata (L.) Mart. (=*D. arvensis* Forsk.)

Stem— Herbaceous, aerial, erect, somewhat branched, solid, glabrous, striated, reddish at nodes; **Leaf**—Cauline and ramal, alternate, exstipulate, simple, petiolate, ovate, entire, glabrous, unicostate reticulate; **Inflorescence**— Three flowered cymes arranged in a spike, the central flower is fertile and the two laterals modify into sterile structures; **Flower**— Bracterate, bracteolate, sessile, incomplete, zygomorphic, hermaphrodite, pentameorus, hypogynous and cyclic; **Perianth**— Tepals 5, polytepalous, slightly connate at the base, quincuncial, membranous, one posterior and one anterio- lateral tepals large, pink; **Androecium**—Stamens 5, polyandrous, opposite the tepals, filament long, anther dithecous, dorsifixed, introrse; **Gynoecium**— Bicarpellary, syncarpous, ovary superior, unilocular with only one basal ovule, style long, stigma 2 recurved and papillose; **Fruit**—Utricle;

Floral formula— Br, brl , ⊕, ⚥, P_5, A_5, $\underline{G}_{(2)}$.

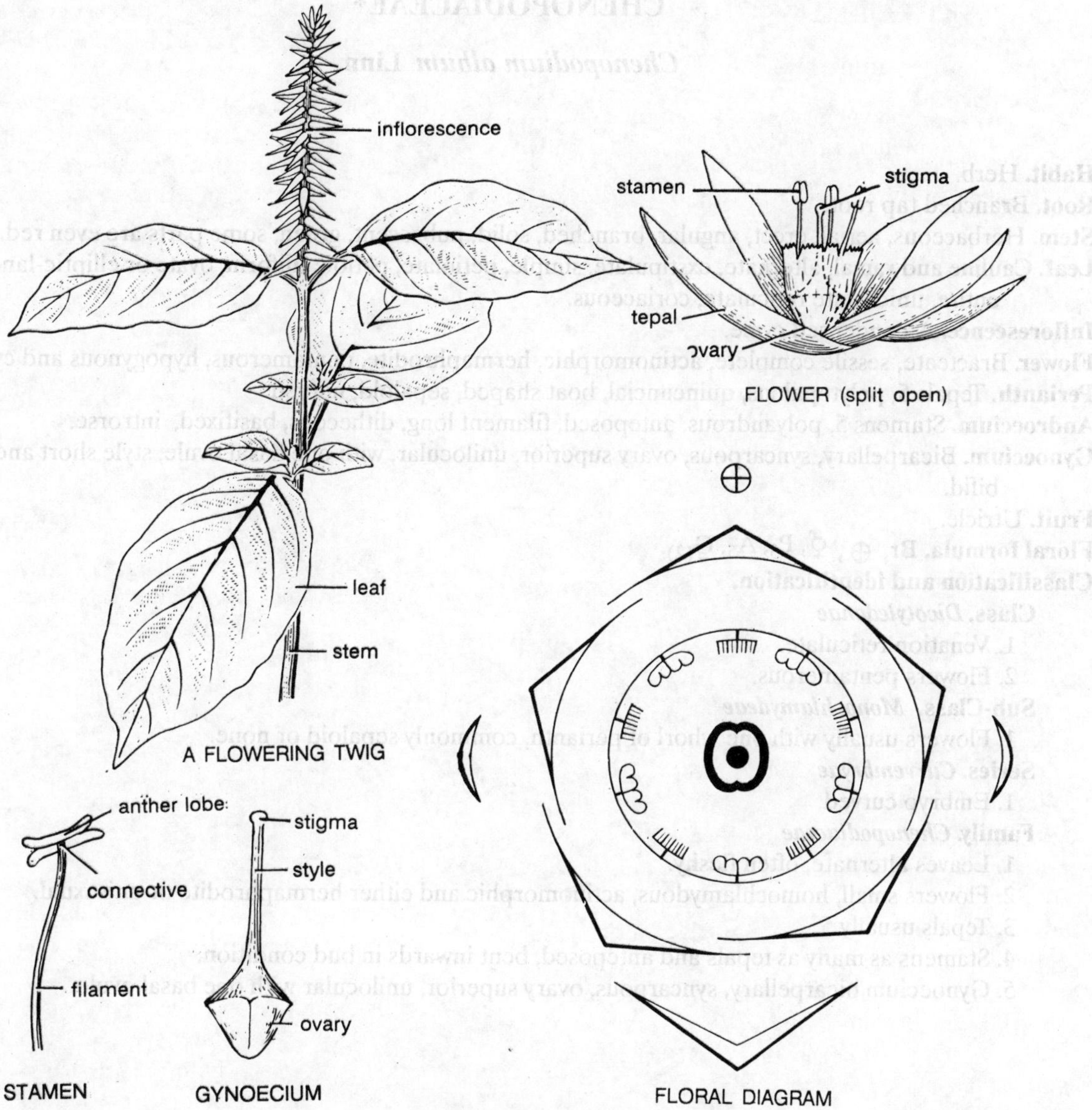

Fig. 69. ***Achyranthus aspera.***

1. Vernacular name. Latjeera. Chirchita, Puthkunda.

2. Economic importance. The plant is used in treatment of piles, boils, skin erruptions, renal dropsy and bronchial infection.

CHENOPODIACEAE*

Chenopodium album Linn.

Habit. Herb.
Root. Branched tap root.
Stem. Herbaceous, aerial, erect, angular, branched, solid, pubescent, green, some parts are even red.
Leaf. Cauline and ramal, alternate, exstipulate, simple, petiolate, petiole filiform, ovate or elliptic-lanceolate, entire, unicostate reticulate, coriaceous.
Inflorescence. A condensed cyme.
Flower. Bracteate, sessile complete, actinomorphic, hermaphrodite, pentamerous, hypogynous and cyclic.
Perianth. Tepals 5, polytepalous, quincuncial, boat shaped, sepaloid, nerved.
Androecium. Stamens 5, polyandrous, anteposed, filament long, dithecous, basifixed, introrse.
Gynoecium. Bicarpellary, syncarpous, ovary superior, unilocular, with one basal ovule, style short and stigma bifid.
Fruit. Utricle.
Floral formula. Br, ⊕, ⚥, P_5, A_5, $\underline{G}_{(2)}$.
Classification and identification.

Class. ***Dicotyledonae***
1. Venation reticulate.
2. Flowers pentamerous.

Sub-Class. ***Monochlamydeae***
1. Flowers usually with one whorl of perianth, commonly sepaloid or none.

Series. ***Curvembryae***
1. Embryo curved.

Family. ***Chenopodiaceae***
1. Leaves alternate, often fleshy.
2. Flowers small, homochlamydous, actinomorphic and either hermaphrodite or unisexual.
3. Tepals usually 5.
4. Stamens as many as tepals and anteposed, bent inwards in bud condition.
5. Gynoecium bicarpellary, syncarpous, ovary superior, unilocular with one basal ovule.

***1. English name.** Goosefoot family.
2. Systematic position in other systems of classification.

Rendle (1925)	Engler and Prantl (1931)	Hutchinson(1959)
Dicotyledons	Dicotyledoneae	Dicotyledons
Monochlamydeae	Archichlamydeae	Herbaceae
Centrospermae	Centrospermae	Chenopodiales
Chenopodiaceae	Chenopodiaceae	Chenopodiaceae

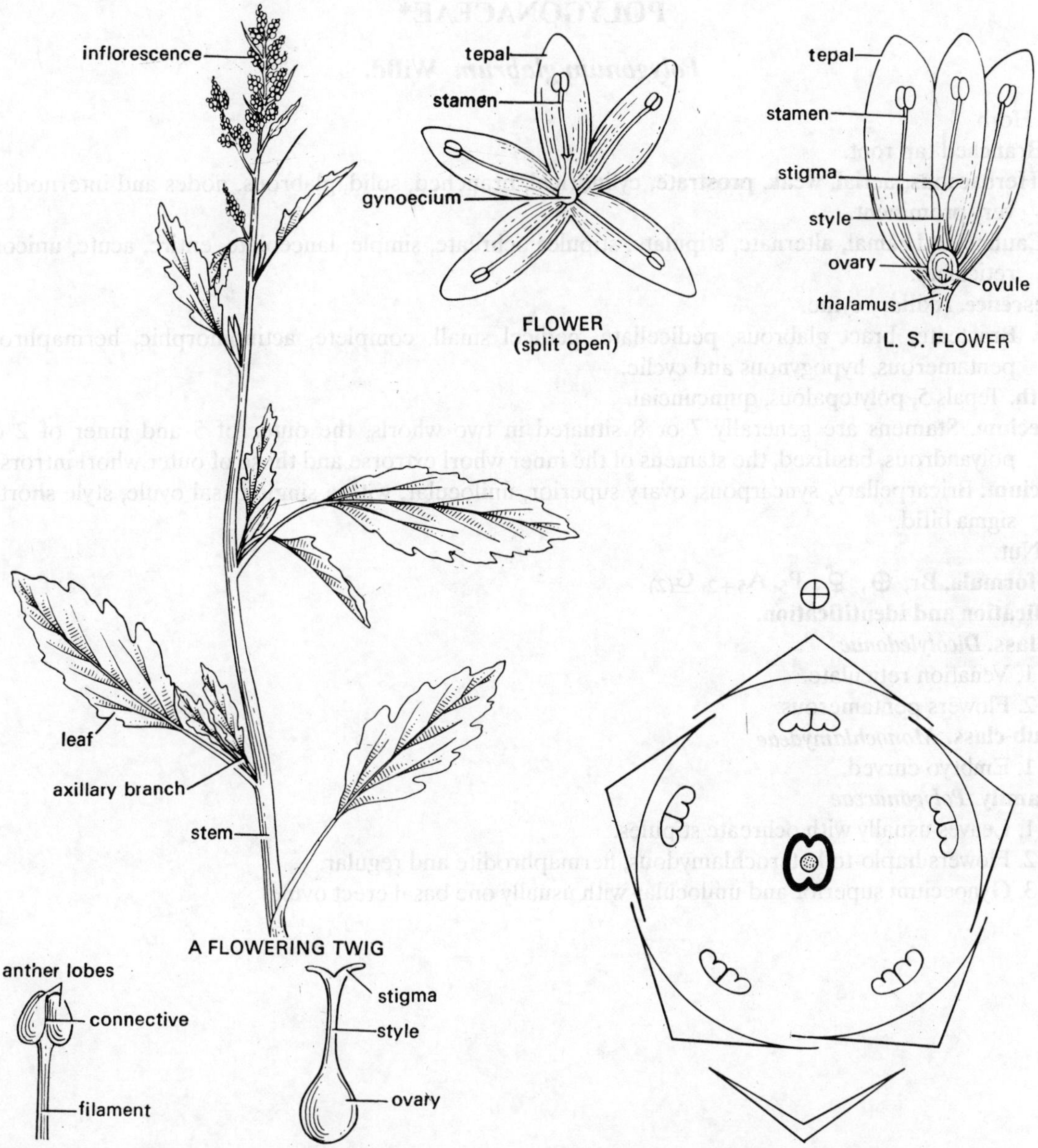

Fig. 70. ***Chenopodium album.***

---

1. English name. Pigweed, Lambs-quarters.

2. Vernacular name. Bathua.

3. Economic importance. Leaves and tender twigs are used as vegetable and fodder.

POLYGONACEAE*

Polygonum glabrum Willd.

Habit. Herb.

Root. Branched tap root.

Stem. Herbaceous, aerial, weak, prostrate, cylindrical, branched, solid, glabrous, nodes and internodes are very prominent.

Leaf. Cauline and ramal, alternate, stipulate, stipules ochreate, simple, lanceolate, entire, acute, unicostate reticulate.

Inflorescence. Axillary cyme.

Flower. Bracteate, bract glabrous, pedicellate, pedicel small, complete, actinomorphic, hermaphrodite, pentamerous, hypogynous and cyclic.

Perianth. Tepals 5, polytepalous, quincuncial.

Androecium. Stamens are generally 7 or 8 situated in two whorls, the outer of 5 and inner of 2 or 3, polyandrous, basifixed, the stamens of the inner whorl extrorse and those of outer whorl introrse.

Gynoecium. Bricarpellary, syncarpous, ovary superior, unilocular, with a single basal ovule, style short and sigma bifid.

Fruit. Nut.

Floral formula. Br, $\oplus$, ⚥, P_5, A_{5+2}, $\underline{G}_{(2)}$.

Classification and identification.

Class. ***Dicotyledonae***

1. Venation reticulate.
2. Flowers pentamerous.

Sub-class. ***Monochlamydeae***

1. Embryo curved.

Family. ***Polygonaceae***

1. Leaves usually with ochreate stipules.
2. Flowers haplo-to heterochlamydous, hermaphrodite and regular.
3. Gynoecium superior and unilocular with usually one basal erect ovule.

***1. English name.** Buckwheat family.

2. Systematic position in other systems of classification.

Rendle (1925)	**Engler and Prantl (1931)**	**Hutchinson (1959)**
Dicotyledons	Dicotyledoneae	Dicotyledons
Monochlamydeae	Archichlamydeae	Herbaceae
Polygonales	Polygonales	Polygonales
Polygonaceae	Polygonaceae	Polygonaceae

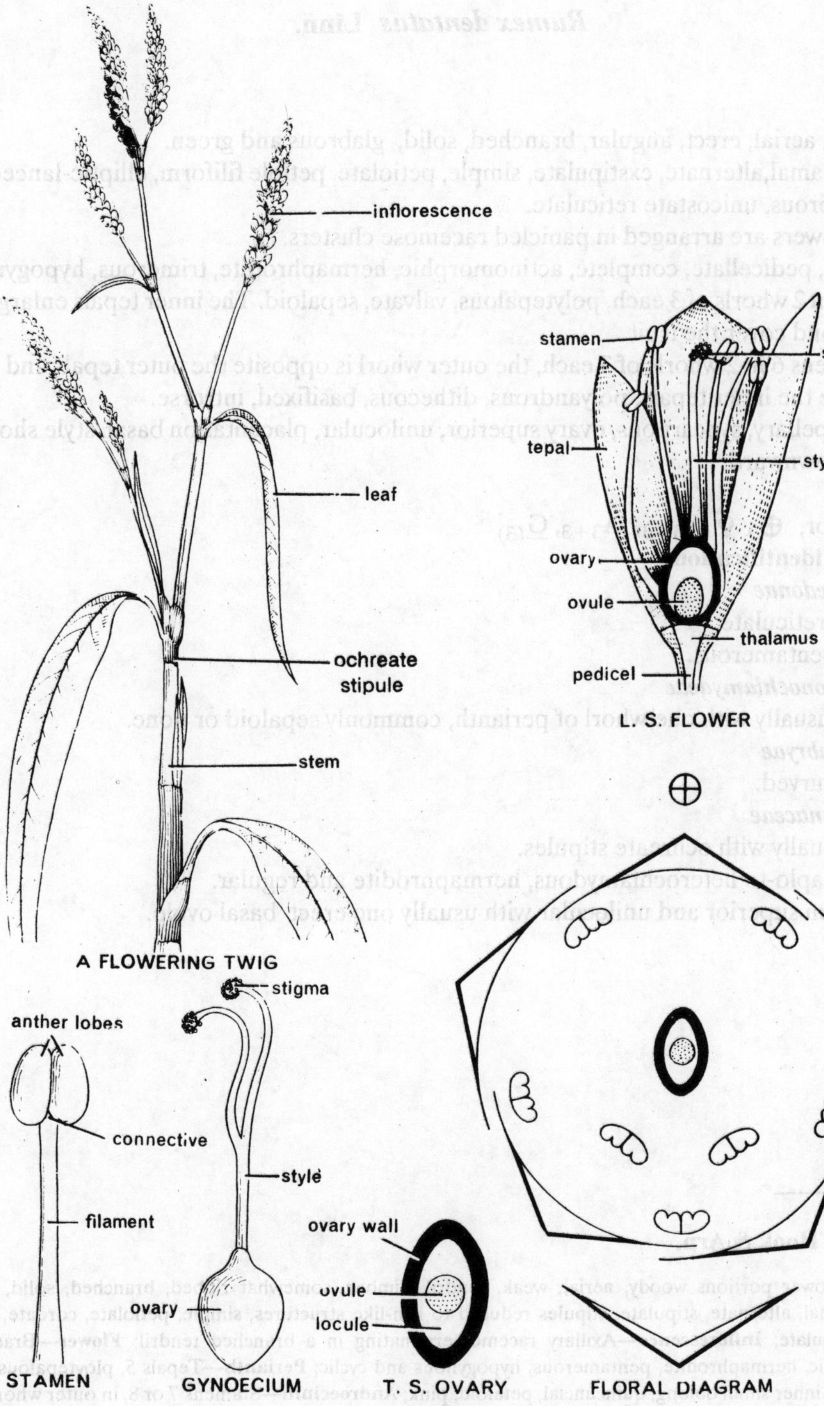

Fig. 71. ***Polygonum glabrum.***

1. Vernacular names. Nali, Bihangni, Atlaria.

2. Economic imprtance. The infusion of leaves is used in colic pain.

Rumex dentatus Linn.

Stem. Herbaceous, aerial, erect, angular, branched, solid, glabrous and green.

Leaf. Cauline and ramal,alternate, exstipulate, simple, petiolate, petiole filiform, elliptic-lanceolate, undulate, acute, glabrous, unicostate reticulate.

Inflorescensce. Flowers are arranged in panicled racemose clusters.

Flower. Ebracteate, pedicellate, complete, actinomorphic, hermaphrodite, trimerous, hypogynous and cyclic.

Perianth. Tepals 6 in 2 whorls of 3 each, polytepalous, valvate, sepaloid. The inner tepals enlarge in the fruiting conditon and cover the fruit.

Androecium. Stamens 6 in 2 whorls of 3 each, the outer whorl is opposite the outer tepals and the inner whorl is opposite the inner tepals, polyandrous, dithecous, basifixed, introrse.

Gynoecium. Tricarpellary, syncarpous, ovary superior, unilocular, placentation basal, style short, stigma 3 and hanging downward.

Fruit. Nut.

Floral formula. Ebr, ⊕, ⚥, P_{3+3}, A_{3+3}, $\underline{G}_{(3)}$.

Classification and identification.

Class. ***Dicotyledonae***

1. Venation reticulate.
2. Flowers pentamerous.

Sub-Class. ***Monochlamydeae***

1. Flowers usually with one whorl of perianth, commonly sepaloid or none.

Series. ***Curvembryae***

1. Embryo curved.

Family. ***Polygonaceae***

1. Leaves usually with ochreate stipules.
2. Flowers haplo-to heterochlamydous, hermaphrodite and regular.
3. Gynoecium superior and unilocular with usually one erect basal ovule.

Antigonon leptopus Hook & Arn.

Stem– Herbaceous, lower portions woody, aerial, weak, tendril climber, somewhat ribbed, branched, solid, rough and green; **Leaf**—Cauline and ramal, alternate, stipulate, stipules reduced to rim-like structures, simple, petiolate, cordate, entire, acuminate, rough, unicostate reticulate; **Inflorescence**—Axillary raceme terminating in a branched tendril; **Flower**—Bracteate, pedicellate, incomplete, zygomorphic, hermaphrodite, pentamerous, hypogynous and cyclic; **Perianth**—Tepals 5, ploytepalous, three outer large and ovate- cordate, two inner small oblong, quincuncial, petaloid, pink; **Androecium**—Stamens 7 or 8, in outer whorl which is opposite the tepals, there are 5 stamens and in the inner whorl 2 or 3 stamens, monadelphous at the base, filament papillose, anther dithecous, dorsifixed and introrse; **Gynoecium**—Tricarpellary, syncarpous, ovary superior, unilocular with only one basal ovule, hypogynous nectary is present, styles 3 recurved, stigma3, capitate; **Fruit**— Single seeded nut;

Floral formula—Br, ⌽, ⚥, P_5, $A_{(5+2 \text{ or } 3)}$, $\underline{G}_{(3)}$.

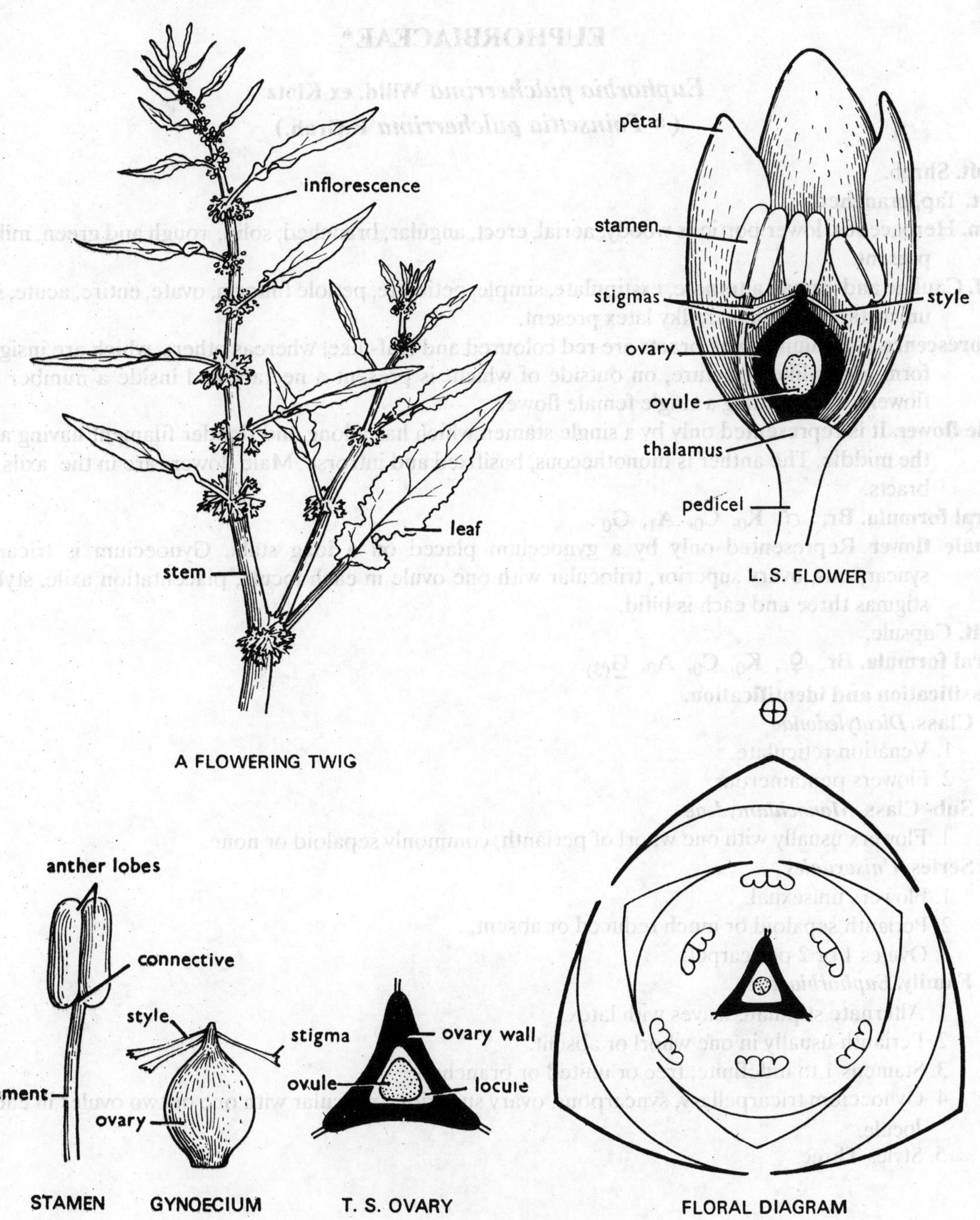

Fig. 72. ***Rumex dentatus.***

---

1. Vernacular names. Lalbibi, Khat-Palak, Ambarah.

2. Economic importance. The roots are the sources of a red dye. Leaves are eaten as vegetable.

EUPHORBIACEAE*

Euphorbia pulcherrima Willd. ex Klotz.
(=*Poinsettia pulcherrima* R.Grah.)

Habit. Shrub.

Root. Tap, branched.

Stem. Herbaceous, lower portions woody, aerial, erect, angular, branched, solid, rough and green, milky latex present.

Leaf. Cauline and ramal, alternate, exstipulate, simple, petiolate, petiole filiform, ovate, entire, acute, smooth, unicostate reticulate, milky latex present.

Inflorescence. Cyathium, some bracts are red coloured and leaf- like, whereas others, which are insignificant form a cup-like structure, on outside of which is present a nectary and inside a number of male flowers, surrounding a single female flower.

Male flower. It is represented only by a single stamen which has a long and slender filament having a joint in the middle. The anther is monothecous, basifixed and introrse. Male flowers are in the axils of scaly bracts.

Floral formula. Br, ♂, K_0, C_0, A_1, G_0.

Female flower Represented only by a gynoecium placed on a long stalk. Gynoecium is tricarpellary, syncarpous, ovary superior, trilocular with one ovule in each locule, placentation axile, style short, stigmas three and each is bifid.

Fruit. Capsule.

Floral formula. Br, ♀, K_0, C_0, A_0, $\underline{G}_{(3)}$.

Classification and identification.

Class. *Dicotyledonae*
1. Venation reticulate.
2. Flowers pentamerous.

Sub- Class. *Monochlamydeae*
1. Flowers usually with one whorl of perianth, commonly sepaloid or none.

Series. *Unisexuales*
1. Flowers unisexual.
2. Perianth sepaloid or much reduced or absent.
3. Ovules 1 or 2 per carpel.

Family. *Euphorbiaceae*
1. Alternate stipulate leaves with latex.
2. Perianth usually in one whorl or absent.
3. Stamens 1 to indefinite, free or united or branched.
4. Gynoecium tricarpellary, syncarpous, ovary superior, trilocular with one or two ovules in each locule.
5. Styles Three.

***1. English name.** Spurge family.

2. Systematic position in other systems of classification.

Rendle (1925)	**Engler and Prantl** (1931)	**Hutchinson** (1959)
Dicotyledons	Dicotyledoneae	Dicotyledons
Dialypetalae	Archichlamydeae	Lignosae
Tricoccae	Geraniales	Euphorbiales
Euphorbiaceae	Euphorbiaceae	Euphorbiaceae

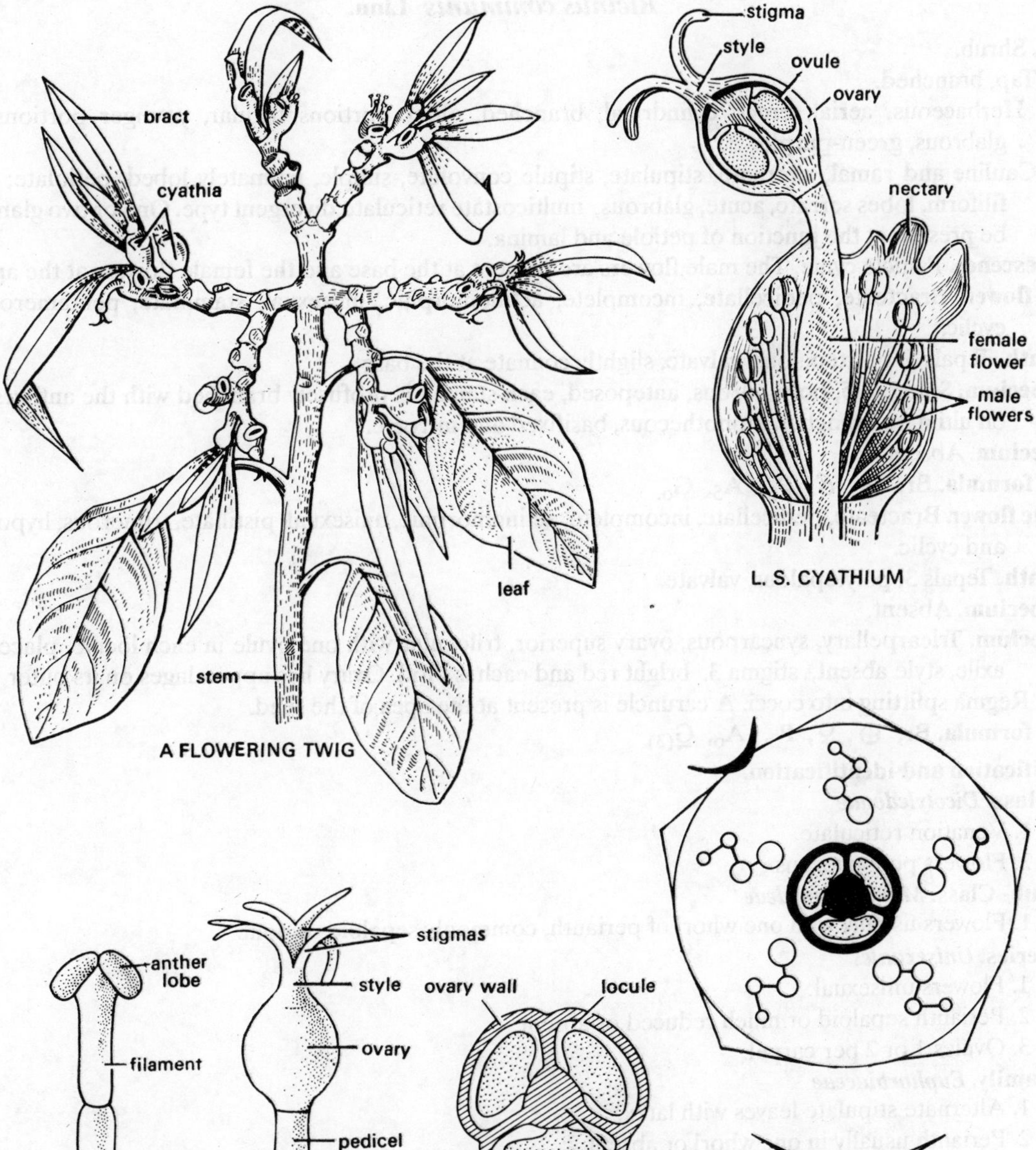

Fig. 73. ***Euphorbia pulcherrima.***

1. English name. Poinsettia.

2. Vernacular name. Laal patta.

3. Economic importance. Grown as an ornamental.

Ricinus communis Linn.

Habit. Shrub.
Root. Tap, branched.
Stem. Herbaceous, aerial, erect, cylindrical, branched, older portions fistular, younger portions solid, glabrous, green-purple.
Leaf. Cauline and ramal, alternate, stipulate, stipule convolute, simple, palmately lobed, petiolate; petiole filiform, lobes serrate, acute, glabrous, multicostate reticulate,divergent type. One or two glands may be present at the junction of petiole and lamina.
Inflorescence. Panicle cyme. The male flowers are present at the base and the female flowers at the apex.
Male flower. Bracteate, pedicellate, incomplete, actinomorphic, unisexual, staminate, pentamerous and cyclic.
Perianth. Tepals 5, polytepalous, valvate, slightly connate at the base.
Androecium. Stamens 5, polyandrous, anteposed, each stamen is profusely branched with the anthers borne on ultimate branches, monothecous, basifixed and introrse.
Gynoecium. Absent.
floral formula. Br, ⊕, ♂, P_5, A_5, G_0.
Female flower. Bracteate, pedicellate, incomplete, actinomorphic, unisexual, pistillate, trimerous, hypogynous and cyclic.
Perianth. Tepals 3, polytepalous, valvate.
Androecium. Absent.
Gynoecium. Tricarpellary, syncarpous, ovary superior, trilocular with one ovule in each locule, placentation axile, style absent, stigma 3, bright red and each is bifid. Ovary has appendages on its outer wall.
Fruit. Regma splitting into cocci. A caruncle is present at the apex of the seed.
floral formula. Br, ⊕, ♀, P_3, A_0, $\underline{G}_{(3)}$.
Classification and identification.

Class. *Dicotyledonae*
1. Venation reticulate.
2. Flowers pentamerous.

Sub- Class. *Monochlamydeae*
1. Flowers usually with one whorl of perianth, commonly sepaloid or none.

Series. *Unisexuales*
1. Flowers unisexual.
2. Perianth sepaloid or much reduced or absent.
3. Ovules 1 or 2 per carpel.

Family. *Euphorbiaceae*
1. Alternate stipulate leaves with latex.
2. Perianth usually in one whorl or absent.
3. Stamens 1 to indefinite, free or united or branched.
4. Gynoecium tricarpellary, syncarpous, superior, trilocular with one or two ovules in each locule.
5. Style three.

Euphorbia hirta Linn.

Stem - Herbaceous, aerial, erect, cylindrical, branched, solid, puberulous, green, milky latex present; **Leaf** - Cauline and ramal, opposite superposed, exstipulate, simple, subsessile, oblique, serrulate, retuse , acute, puberulous, unicostate reticulate; **Inflorescence** - Cyathium aggregated in axillary clusters, each cyathium consists of 5 involucre of bracts, fused to form a cup. On the inner side of each bract,a gland is present. In the centre of cyathium there is a single female flower surrounded by many male flowers; **Male flower**- Represented by a single stamen, which is separated from the pedicel by a joint, dithecous, introrse; **Female flower** - Represented by gynoecium raised on a long pedicel, tricarpellary, syncarpous, ovary superior, trilocular, style absent or short, stigma 3, each is bifurcated; **Fruit** - Regma splitting into 3 cocci;

Floral formula-male flower - Br, ⊕, ♂, K_0, C_0, A_1, G_0.
Floral formula-female flower - Br, ⊕, ♀, K_0, C_0, A_0, $\underline{G}_{(3)}$

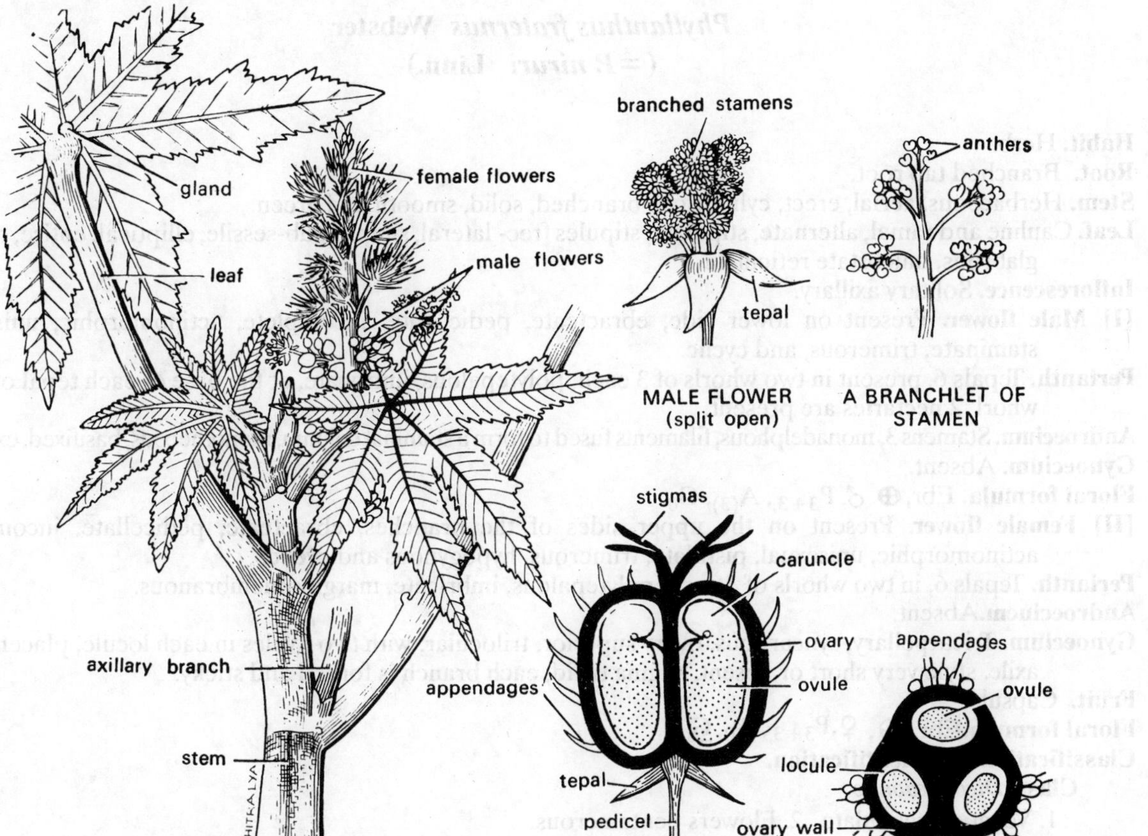

Fig. 74. ***Ricinus communis.***

---

1. **English name.** Castor bean.
2. **Verancular name.** Arandi.
3. **Economic importance.** The seeds are the source of castor oil, used mainly as a lubricant and as a purgative. The oil cake is a good fertilizer.

Phyllanthus fraternus Webster
(=*P. niruri* Linn.)

Habit. Herb.
Root. Branched tap root.
Stem. Herbaceous, aerial, erect, cylindrical, branched, solid, smooth and green.
Leaf. Cauline and ramal, alternate, stipulate, stipules free- lateral, simple, sub-sessile, elliptical, entire, obtuse, glabrous, unicostate reticulate.
Inflorescence. Solitary axillary.
[I] Male flower. Present on lower side, ebracteate, pedicellate, incomplete, actinomorphic, unisexual, staminate, trimerous, and cyclic.
Perianth. Tepals 6, present in two whorls of 3 each, polytepalous, imbricate, at the base of each tepal of inner whorl 2 nectaries are present.
Androecium. Stamens 3, monadelphous, filaments fused to form a staminal column, monothecous, basifixed, extrorse.
Gynoecium. Absent.
Floral formula. Ebr, ⊕ ♂, P_{3+3},, $A_{(3)}$, G_0.
[II] Female flower. Present on the upper sides of the branches, ebracteate, pedicellate, incomplete, actinomorphic, unisexual, pistillate, trimerous, hypogynous and cyclic.
Perianth. Tepals 6, in two whorls of 3 each, polytepalous, imbricate, margins membranous.
Androeciucm. Absent.
Gynoecium. Tricarpellary, syncarpous, ovary superior, trilocular, with two ovules in each locule, placentation axile, style very short or absent, stigma trifid, each branch is forked and sticky.
Fruit. Capsule.
Floral formula. Ebr, ⊕, ♀,P_{3+3},, A_0, $\underline{G}_{(3)}$.
Classification and identification.

Class. ***Dicotyledonae***

1. Venation reticulate. 2. Flowers pentamerous.

Sub-Class. ***Monochlamydeae***

1. Flowers usually with one whorl of perianth, commonly sepaloid or none.

Series. ***Unisexuales***

1. Flowers unisexual. 2. Perianth sepaloid or much reduced or absent. 3. Ovules 1 or 2 per carpel.

Family. ***Euphorbiaceae***

1. Alternate stipulate leaves with latex. 2. Perianth usually in one whorl or absent. 3. Stamens 1 to indefinite, free or united or branched. 4. Gynoecium tricarpellary syncarpous, superior, trilocular with one or two ovules in each locule.

Croton bonplandianum Ball.

Habit— Herb; **Stem**— Herbaceous, aerial, erect, angular, branched, solid, rough and green; **Leaf**— Cauline and ramal, alternate, exstipulate, simple, petiolate, ovate, serrate, acute, glabrous, unicostate reticulate; **Inflorescence**— Racemose, female flowers below and usually solitary, male flowers above and usually in dichasial cymes; **Male flower**— Bracteate, pedicellate, incomplete, actinomorphic, unisexual, staminate, pentamerous and cyclic; **Calyx**— Sepals 5, polysepalous, imbricate; **Corolla**— Petals 5, polypetalous valvate; **Androecium**—Stamens indefinite, filaments connate below, monothecous, adnate, introrse; **Gynoecium**— Absent; **Female flower**— Bracteate, pedicellate, incomplete, actinomorphic, unisexual, pistillate, pentamerous, hypogynous and cyclic; **Calyx**— Sepals 5, polysepalous, valvate, persistent, a gland is present opposite each sepal; **Corolla**—Absent; **Androecium**— Absent; **Gynoecium**— Tricarpellary, syncarpous, ovary superior, trilocular, one ovule in each locule, placentation axile, style short and 3, stigmas 3 and each is bifid; **Fruit**— Regma splitting into 3 coccit.

Floral formula- male flower— Br, ⊕ , ♂, K_5, A_∞, G_0
Floral formula. female flower— Br, ⊕ , ♀, K_5, C_0, A_0, $\underline{G}_{(3)}$.

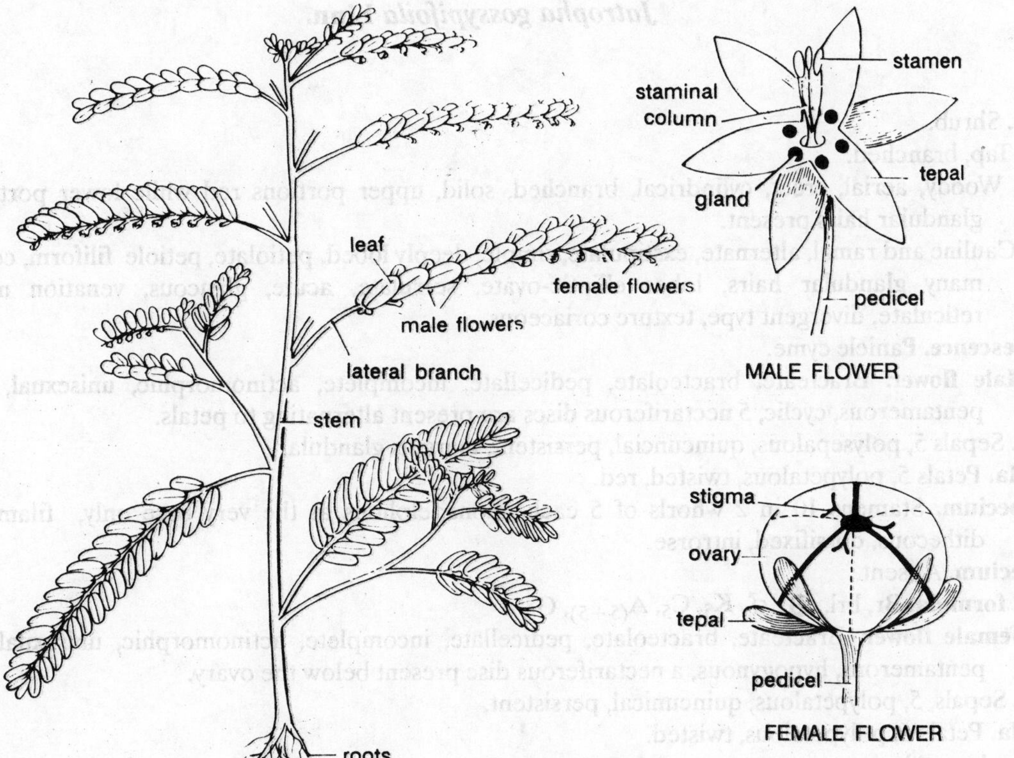

Fig. 75. ***Phyllanthus fraternus.***

---

1. Vernacular names. Jaramala, Jangli amli, Bhuinanvalah.

2. Economic importance. The plant is supposed to be diurectic and astringent. Fresh roots are used for jaundice.

Jatropha gossypifoila Linn.

Habit. Shrub.

Root. Tap, branched.

Stem. Woody, aerial, erect, cylindrical, branched, solid, upper portions red while lower portions green, glandular hairs present.

Leaf. Cauline and ramal, alternate, exstipulate, simple, deeply lobed, petiolate, petiole filiform, covered with many glandular hairs, lobes elliptic-ovate, serrulate, acute, glaucous, venation multicostate reticulate, divergent type, texture coriaceous.

Inflorescence. Panicle cyme.

[I] Male flower. Bracteate, bracteolate, pedicellate, incomplete, actinomorphic, unisexual, staminate, pentamerous, cyclic, 5 nectariferous discs are present alternating to petals.

Calyx. Sepals 5, polysepalous, quincuncial, persistent, margins glandular.

Corolla. Petals 5, polypetalous, twisted, red.

Androecium. Stamens 10 in 2 whorls of 5 each, monadelphous at the very base only, filaments short, dithecous, dorsifixed, introrse.

Gynoecium. Absent.

Floral formula. Br, brl, ⊕, ♂, K_5, C_5, $A_{(5+5)}$, G_0.

[II] Female flower. Bracteate, bracteolate, pedicellate, incomplete, actinomorphic, unisexual, pistillate, pentamerous, hypogynous, a nectariferous disc present below the ovary.

Calyx. Sepals, 5, polypetalous, quincunical, persistent.

Corolla. Petals 5, polypetalous, twisted.

Androecium. Absent.

Gynoecium. Tricarpellary, syncarpous, ovary superior, trilocular, placentation axile with one ovule in each locule, styles 3, stigma 3 and each is bifid.

Fruit. Regma splitting into 3 cocci.

Floral formula. Br, brl, ⊕, ♀, K_5, C_5 A_0, $\underline{G}_{(3)}$.

Classification and identification.

Class. ***Dicotyledonae***

1. Venation reticulate.
2. Flowers pentamerous.

Sub-Class. ***Monochlamydeae***

1. Flowers usually with one whorl of perianth, commonly sepaloid or none.

Series. ***Unisexuales***

1. Flowers unisexual.
2. Perianth sepaloid or much reduced or absent.
3. Ovules 1 or 2 per carpel.

Family. ***Euphorbiaceae***

1. Alternate stipulate leaves with latex.
2. Perianth usually in one whorl or absent.
3. Stamens 1 to indefinite, free or united or branched.
4. Gynoecium tricarpellary, syncarpous, superior, trilocular with one or two ovules in each locule.
5. Styles three.

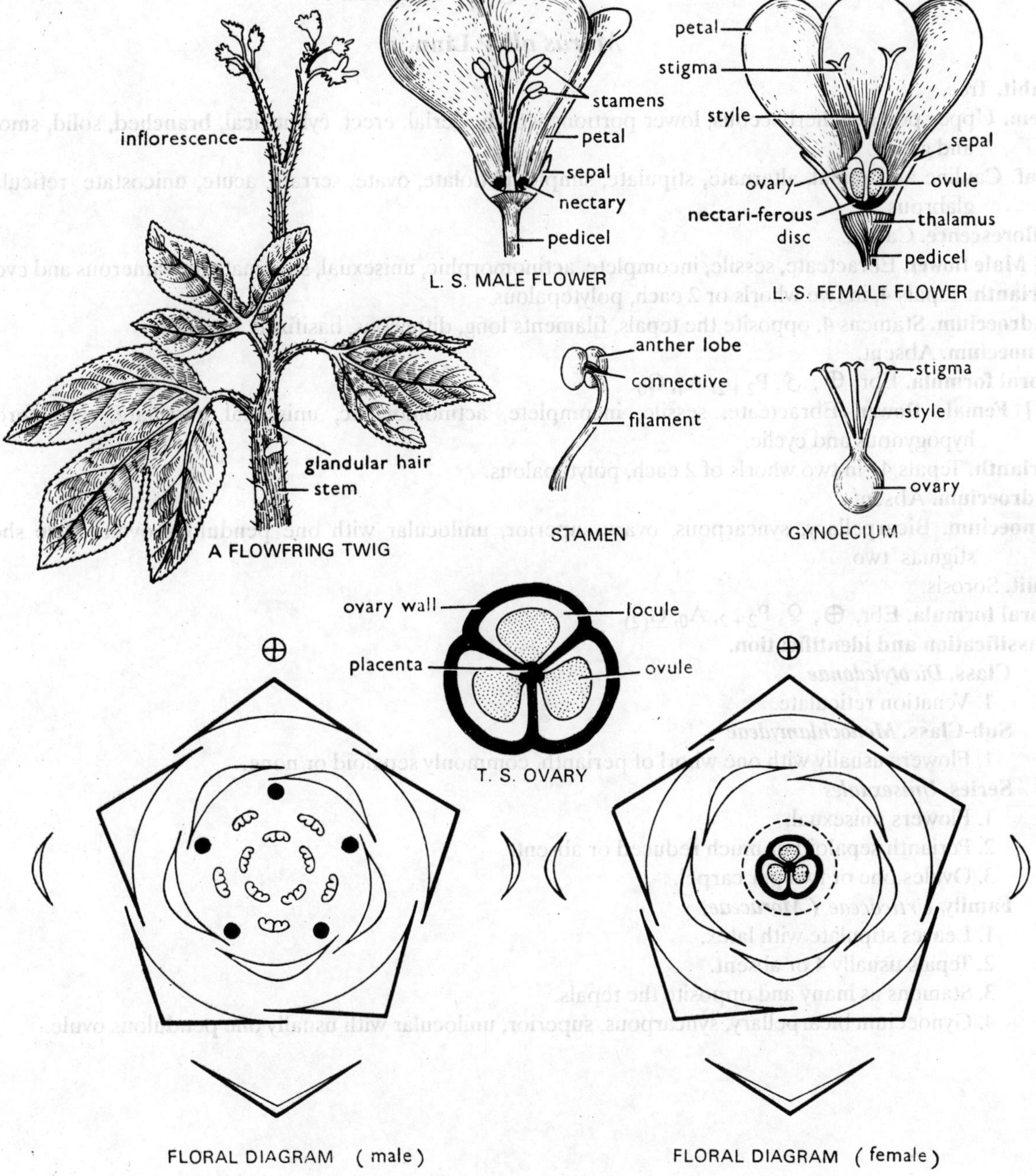

Fig. 76. ***Jatropha gossypifolia.***

---

1. English name. Bellyache bush.

2. Vernacular name. Bherenda.

3. Economic importance. Cultivated as an ornamental. Ether extract of shoots has antibiotic activity against *E. coli.*

URTICACEAE (MORACEAE)*

Morus alba Linn.

Habit. Tree.

Stem. Upper portions herbaceous, lower portions woody, aerial, erect, cylindrical, branched, solid, smooth and green.

Leaf. Cauline and ramal, alternate, stipulate, simple, petiolate, ovate, serrate, acute, unicostate reticulate, glabrous.

Inflorescence. Catkin.

[I] Male flower. Ebracteate, sessile, incomplete, actinomorphic, unisexual, staminate, tetramerous and cyclic.

Perianth. Tepals 4, in two whorls or 2 each, polytepalous.

Androecium. Stamens 4, opposite the tepals, filaments long, dithecous, basifixed, introrse.

Gynoecium. Absent.

Floral formula. Ebr, ⊕, ♂, P_{2+2}, A_4, G_0.

[II] Female flower. Ebracteate, sessile, incomplete, actinomorphic, unisexual, pistillate, tetramerous, hypogynous and cyclic.

Perianth. Tepals 4, in two whorls of 2 each, polytepalous.

Androecium. Absent.

Gynoecium. Bicarpellary, syncarpous, ovary superior, unilocular with one pendulous ovule, style short, stigmas two.

Fruit. Sorosis.

Floral formula. Ebr, ⊕, ♀, P_{2+2}, A_0, $\underline{G}_{(2)}$.

Classification and identification.

Class. ***Dicotyledonae***

1. Venation reticulate.

Sub-Class. ***Monochlamydeae***

1. Flowers usually with one whorl of perianth, commonly sepaloid or none.

Series. ***Unisexuales***

1. Flowers unisexual.
2. Perianth sepaloid or much reduced or absent.
3. Ovules one or two per carpel.

Family. ***Urticaceae (Moraceae)***

1. Leaves stipulate with latex.
2. Tepals usually 4 or absent.
3. Stamens as many and opposite the tepals.
4. Gynoecium bicarpellary, syncarpous, superior, unilocular with usually one pendulous ovule.

***1. English name.** Mulberry family.

2. Systematic position in other systems of classification.

Rendle (1925)	Engler and Prantl (1931)	Hutchinson (1959)
Dicotyledons	Dicotyledoneae	Dicotyledons
Monochlamydeae	Archichlamydeae	Lignosae
Urticiflorae	Uriticales	Urticales
Moraceae	Moraceae	Moraceae

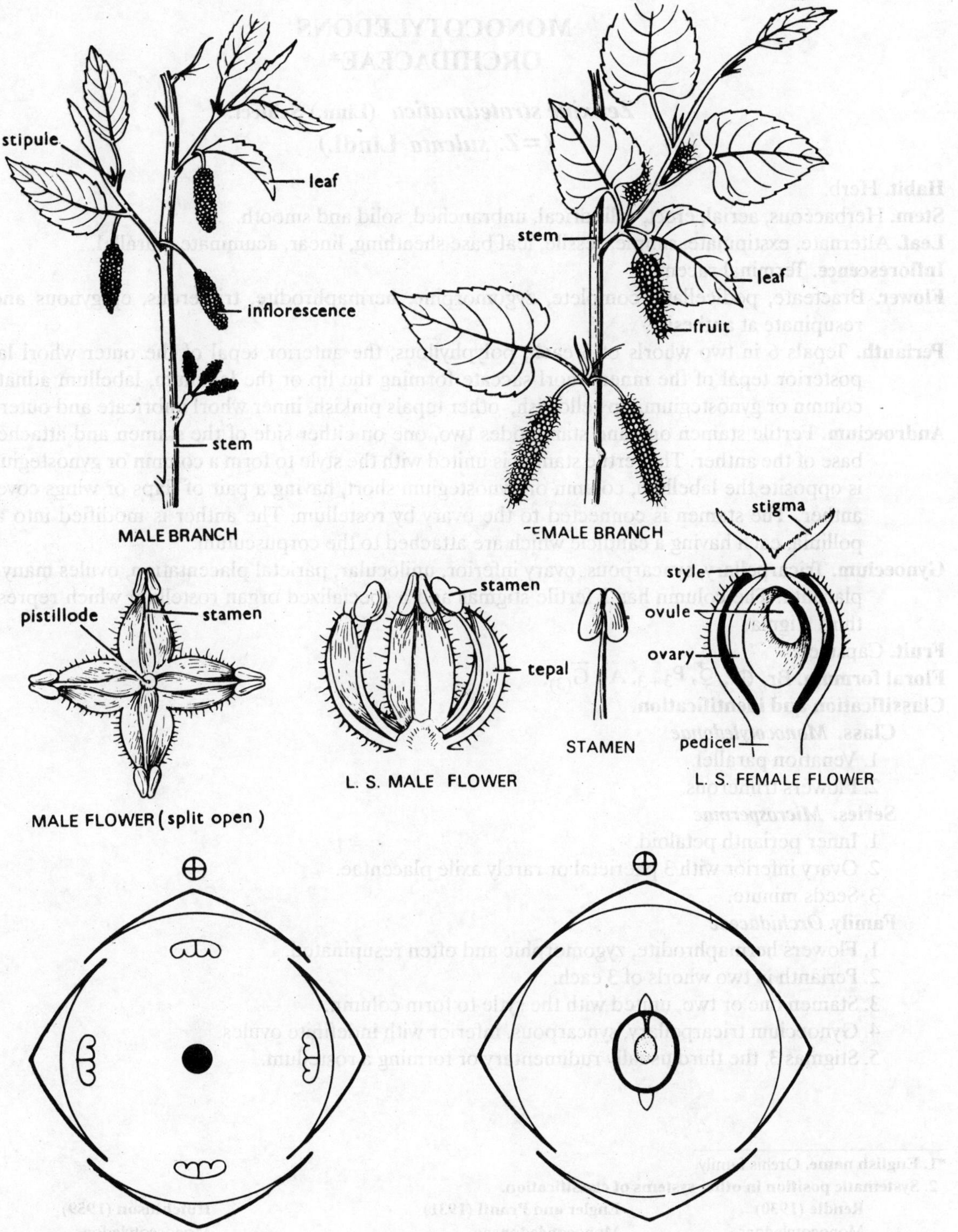

Fig. 77. ***Morus alba.***

---

1. English name. White mulberry.

2. Vernacular names. Tut,Tul,Shehtoot.

3. Economic importance. The fruits are edible and the wood is used for making hockey-sticks.

MONOCOTYLEDONS
ORCHIDACEAE*

Zeuxine strateumatica (Linn.) Schlect.
(=*Z. sulcata* Lindl.)

Habit. Herb.
Stem. Herbaceous, aerial, erect, cylindrical, unbranched, solid and smooth.
Leaf. Alternate, exstipulate, simple, sessile, leaf base sheathing, linear, acuminate, parallel.
Inflorescence. Terminal raceme.
Flower. Bracteate, pedicellate, complete, zygomorphic, hermaphrodite, trimerous, epigynous and cyclic, resupinate at anthesis.
Perianth. Tepals 6 in two whorls of 3 each, polyphyllous, the anterior tepal of the outer whorl large; the posterior tepal of the inner whorl saccate forming the lip or the labellum, labellum adnate to the column or gynostegium, lip yellowish, other tepals pinkish, inner whorl imbricate and outer valvate.
Androecium. Fertile stamen one and staminodes two, one on either side of the stamen and attached to the base of the anther. The fertile stamen is united with the style to form a column or gynostegium which is opposite the labellum, column or gynostegium short, having a pair of flaps or wings covering the anther. The stamen is connected to the ovary by rostellum. The anther is modified into a pair of pollinia, each having a caudicle which are attached to the corpusculum.
Gynoecium. Tricarpellary, syncarpous, ovary inferior, unilocular, parietal placentation, ovules many on each placenta. The column has 2 fertile stigmas and a specialized organ rostellum which represents the third stigma.
Fruit. Capsule.
Floral formula. Br, ⦶, ⚥, P_{3+3}, A_1, $\overline{G}_{(3)}$.
Classification and identification.

Class. ***Monocotyledonae***
1. Venation parallel.
2. Flowers trimerous.

Series. ***Microspermae***
1. Inner perianth petaloid.
2. Ovary inferior with 3 paerietal or rarely axile placentae.
3. Seeds minute.

Family. ***Orchidaceae***
1. Flowers hermaphrodite, zygomorphic and often resupinated.
2. Perianth in two whorls of 3 each.
3. Stamen one or two, united with the sytle to form column.
4. Gynoecium tricarpellary, syncarpous, inferior with indefinite ovules.
5. Stigmas 3, the third usually rudimentary or forming a rostellum.

***1. English name.** Orchis family.
2. Systematic position in other systems of classification.

Rendle (1930)	**Engler and Prantl (1931)**	**Hutchinson (1959)**
Monocotyledons	Monocotyledoneae	Monoccotyledons
Microspermae	Microspermae	Corolliferae
Orchidaceae	Orchidaceae	Orchidales
		Orchidacae

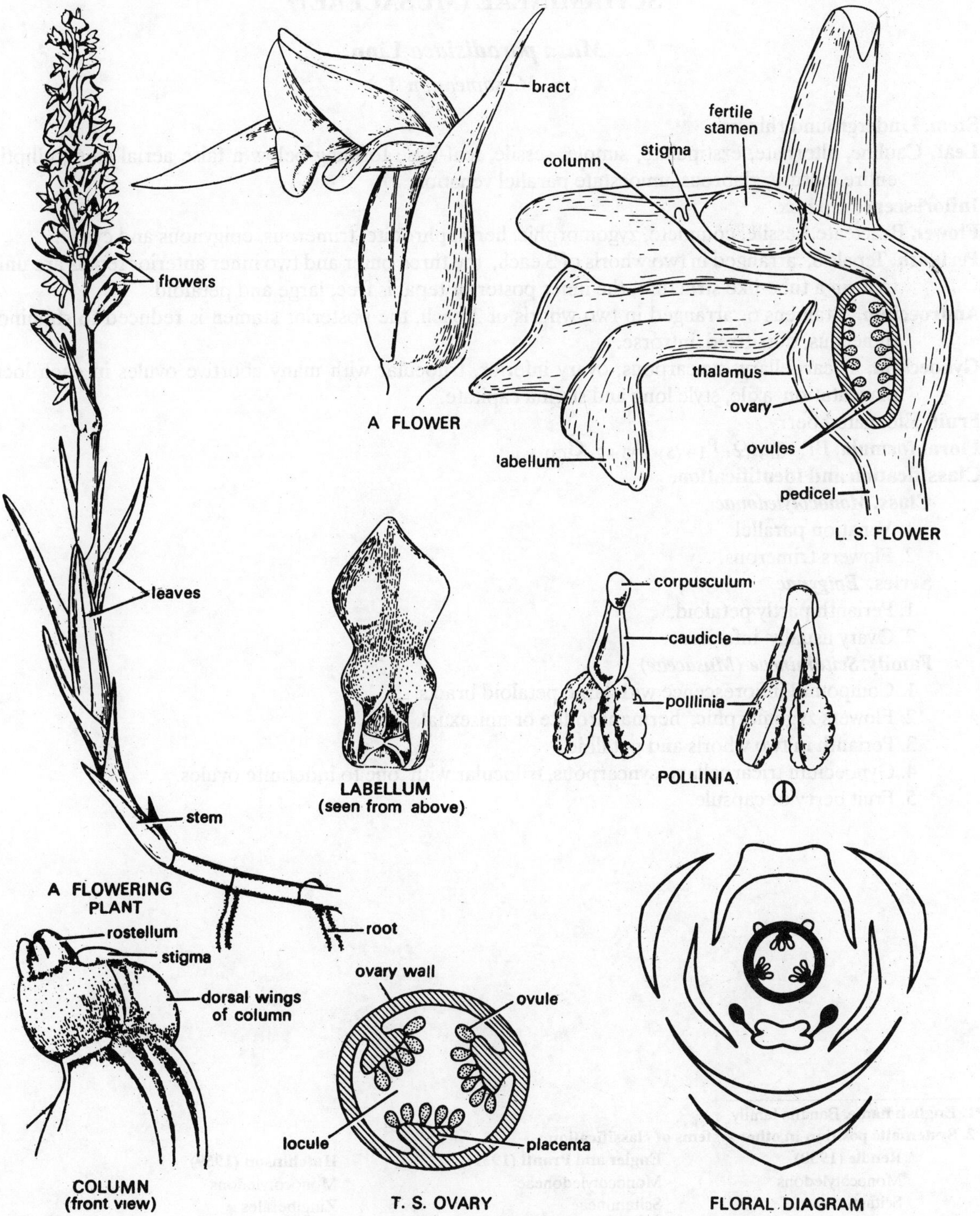

Fig. 79. ***Zeuxine strateumatica.***

SCITAMINEAE (MUSACEAE)*

Musa paradisiaca Linn.

(= *M. sapientum* L.)

Stem. Underground rhizome.

Leaf. Cauline, alternate, exstipulate, simple, sessile, leaf-base forming below a false aerial stem, elliptical, entire, obtuse, glabrous, uniocstate parallel venation.

Inflorescence. Spadix.

Flower. Bracteate, sessile, complete, zygomorphic, hermaphrodite, trimerous, epigynous and cyclic.

Perianth. Tepals 6, arranged in two whorls of 3 each, the three outer and two inner anterior tepals are united to form a tube-like structure, the inner posterior tepal is free, large and petaloid.

Androecium. Stamens 6 arranged in two whorls of 3 each, the posterior stamen is reduced to staminode, dithecous, dorsifixed, introrse.

Gynoecium. Tricarpellary, syncarpous, ovary inferior, trilocular with many abortive ovules in each locule, placentation axile, style long and stigma capitate.

Fruit. Elongated berry.

Floral formula. Br, Φ, ⚥, $P_{1+(5)}$, A_{3+2}, $\overline{G}_{(3)}$.

Classification and identification.

Class. ***Monocotyledonae***

1. Venation parallel.
2. Flowers trimerous.

Series. ***Epigynae***

1. Perianth partly petaloid.
2. Ovary usually inferior.

Family. ***Scitamineae (Musaceae)***

1. Compound inflorescence with large petaloid bracts.
2. Flowers zygomorphic, hermaphrodite or unisexual.
3. Perianth in two whorls and petaloid.
4. Gynoecium tricarpellary, syncarpous, trilocular with one to indefinite ovules.
5. Fruit berry or capsule.

***1. English name.** Banana family.

2. Systemaitc position in other systems of classification.

Rendle (1930)	**Engler and Prantl (1931)**	**Hutchinson (1959)**
Monocotyledons	Monocotyledoneae	Monocotyledons
Scitamineae	Scitamineae	Zingiberales
Musaceae	Musaceae	Musaceae

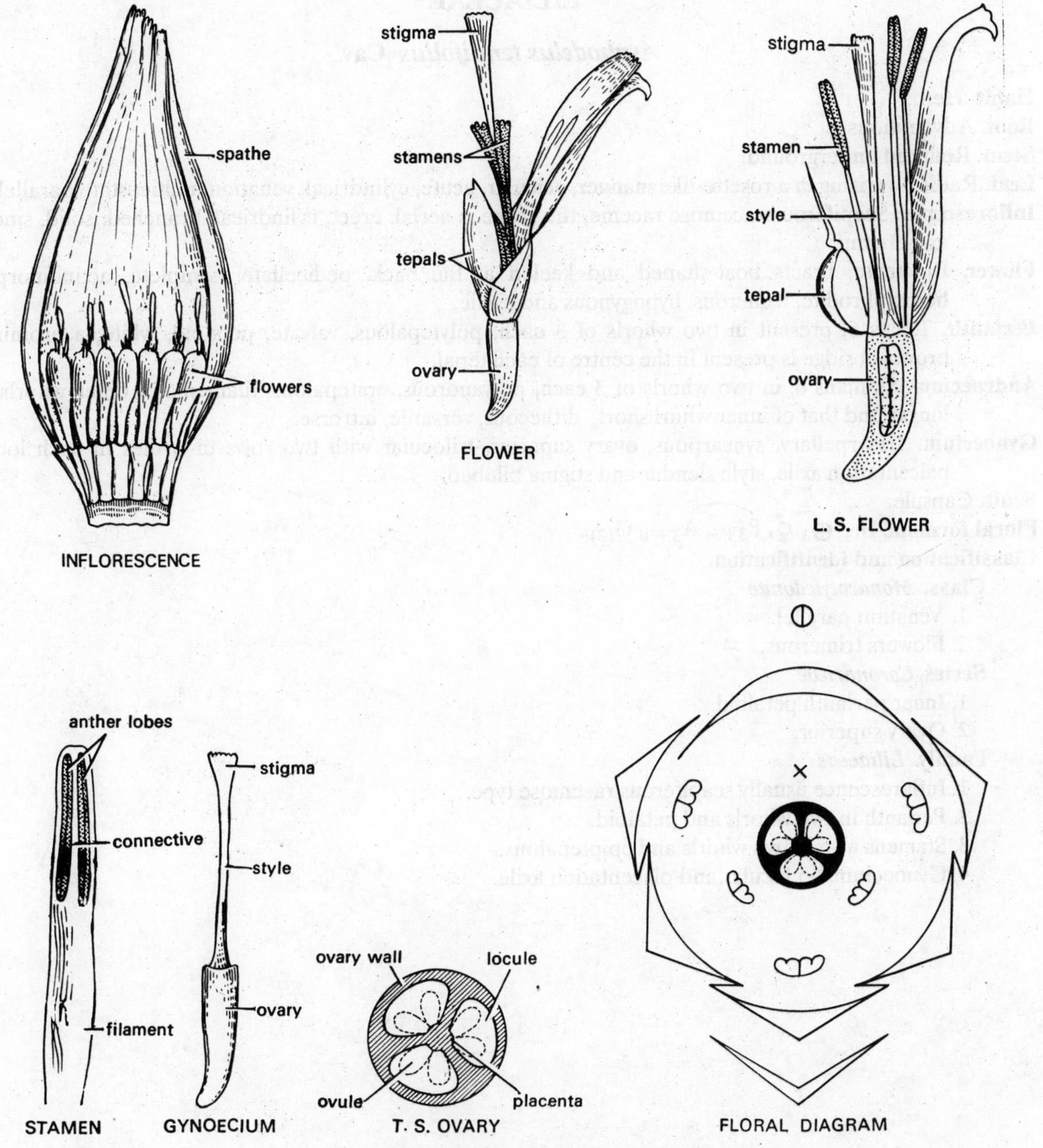

Fig. 80. ***Musa paradisiaca.***

---

1. English name. Banana.
2. Vernacular name. Kela.
3. Economic importance. Fruits are edible. Banana stem is a good source of starch.

LILIACEAE*

Asphodelus tenuifolius Cav.

Habit. Herb.
Root. Adventitious.
Stem. Reduced underground.
Leaf. Radical. arising in a rosette-like manner, acicular, acute, cylindrical, venation multicostate parallel.
Inflorescence. Scapiferous racemose raceme, the scape is aerial, erect, cylindrical, branched, solid, smooth and green.
Flower. Bracteate, bracts boat-shaped and keeled at the back, pedicellate, complete, actinomorphic, hermaphrodite, trimerous, hypogynous and cyclic.
Perianth. Tepals 6, present in two whorls of 3 each, polytepalous, valvate, petaloid, white, a prominent brownish ridge is present in the centre of each tepal.
Androecium. Stamens 6, in two whorls of 3 each, polyandrous, epitepalous, filaments of outer whorls are longer and that of inner whorl short, dithecous, versatile, introrse.
Gynoecium. Tricarpellary, syncarpous, ovary superior, trilocular with two rows of ovules in each locule, palcentation axile, style slender and stigma bilobed.
Fruit. Capsule.
Floral formula. Br, $\oplus$, ⚥, $\overset{\frown}{P_{3+3}, A_{3+3}}$, $\underline{G}_{(3)}$.
Classification and identification.

Class. *Monocotyledonae*
1. Venation parallel.
2. Flowers trimerous.

Series. *Coronarieae*
1. Inner perianth petaloid.
2. Ovary superior.

Family. *Liliaceae*
1. Inflorescence usually scapiferous racemose type.
2. Perianth in two whorls and petaloid.
3. Stamens also in two whorls and epiptepalous.
4. Gynoecium 2-5 locular and placentation axile.

***1. English name.** Lily family.
2. Systematic position in other systems of classification.

Rendle (1930)	**Engler and Prantl (1931)**	**Hutchinson (1959)**
Monocotyledons	Monocotyledoneae	Monocotyledons
Liliflorae	Liliflorae	Liliales
Liliaceae	Liliaceae	Liliaceae

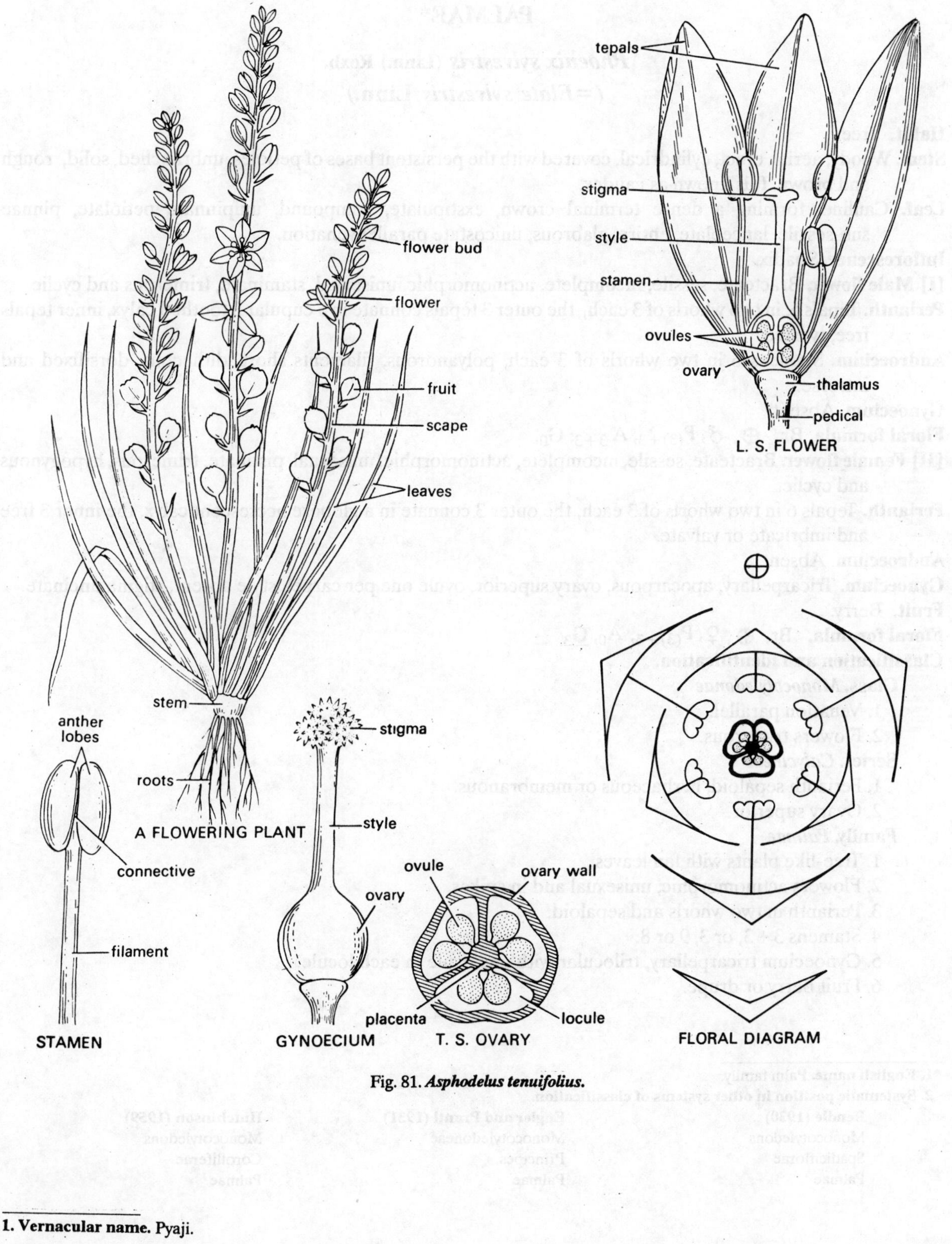

Fig. 81. ***Asphodelus tenuifolius.***

---

1. Vernacular name. Pyaji.

PALMAE*

Phoenix sylvestris (Linn.) Roxb.

(=*Elate sylvestris* Linn.)

Habit. Tree.

Stem. Woody, aerial, erect, cylindrical, covered with the persistent bases of petioles, unbranched, solid, rough and brown. It is known as caudex.

Leaf. Cauline, forming a dense terminal crown, exstipulate, compound, unipinnate petiolate, pinnae sub-sessile, lanceolate, entire, glabrous, unicostate parallel venation.

Inflorescence. Spadix.

[I] Male flower. Bracteate, sessile, incomplete, actinomorphic, unisexual, staminate, trimerous and cyclic.

Perianth. Tepals 6, in two whorls of 3 each, the outer 3 tepals connate in a cupular 3 toothed calyx, inner tepals free, twisted.

Androecium. Stamens 6 in two whorls of 3 each, polyandrous, filaments short, dithecous, dorsifixed and introrse.

Gynoecium. Absent.

Floral formula. Br, ⊕, ♂, $P_{(3)+3}$, A_{3+3}, G_0.

[II] Female flower. Bracteate, sessile, incomplete, actinomorphic, unisexual, pistillate, trimerous, hypogynous and cyclic.

Perianth. Tepals 6 in two whorls of 3 each, the outer 3 connate in a globose accrescent calyx, the inner 3 free and imbricate or valvate.

Androecium. Absent.

Gynoecium. Tricarpellary, apocarpous, ovary superior, ovule one per carpel, style absent, stigma uncinate.

Fruit. Berry.

Floral formula. Br, ⊕, ♀, $P_{(3)+3}$, A_0, $\underline{G_3}$.

Classification and identification.

Class. ***Monocotyledonae***

1. Venation parallel.
2. Flowers trimerous.

Series. ***Calycineae***

1. Perianth sepaloid, herbaceous or membranous.
2. Ovary superior.

Family. ***Palmae***

1. Tree-like plants with fan leaves.
2. Flowers actinomorphic, unisexual and in spikes.
3. Perianth in two whorls and sepaloid.
4. Stamens 3+3, or 3, 9 or 8.
5. Gynoecium tricarpellary, trilocular with one ovule in each locule.
6. Fruit berry or drupe.

***1. English name.** Palm family.

2. Systematic position in other systems of classification.

Rendle (1930)	**Engler and Prantl (1931)**	**Hutchinson (1959)**
Monocotyledons	Monocotyledoneae	Monocotyledons
Spadiciflorae	Principes	Corolliferae
Palmae	Palmae	Palmae

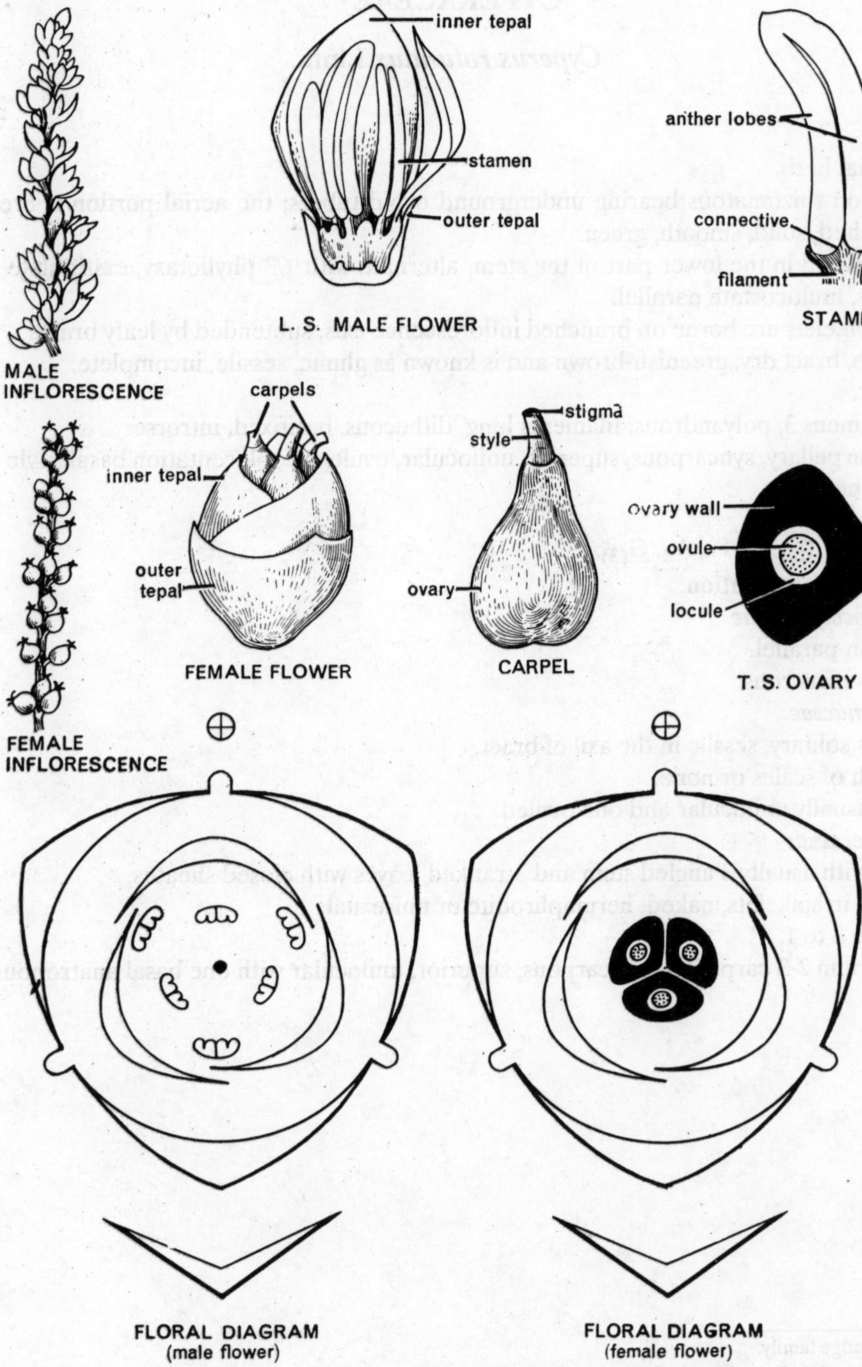

Fig. 82. *Phoenix sylvestris.*

---

1. English name. Wild date.

2. Vernacular name. Khajur.

3. Economic importance. The ripe fruits are edible.

CYPERACEAE*

Cyperus rotundus Linn.

Habit. A perennial herb.

Stem. Basal region rhizomatous bearing underground ovoid tubers; the aerial portion is erect, triangular, unbranched, solid, smooth, green.

Leaf. Leaves crowded in the lower part of the stem, alternate with 1/3 phyllotaxy, exstipulate, entire, acute, glabrous, multicostate parallel.

Inflorescence. Spikelets are borne on branched inflorescence axis, subtended by leafy bracts.

Flower. Bracteate, bract dry, greenish-brown and is known as glume, sessile, incomplete.

Perianth. Absent.

Androecium. Stamens 3, polyandrous, filaments long, dithecous, basifixed, introrse.

Gynoecium. Tricarpellary, syncarpous, superior, unilocular, ovule one, placentation basal, style one, stigmas 3 and feathery.

Fruit. Achene.

Floral formula. Br, $\oplus$, ⚥, P_0, A_3, $\underline{G}_{(3)}$.

Classification and identification.

Class. ***Monocotyledonae***

1. Venation parallel.
2. Flowers trimerous.

Series. ***Glumaceae***

1. Flowers solitary, sessile in the axil of bract.
2. Perianth of scales or none.
3. Ovary usually unilocular and one ovuled.

Family. ***Cyperaceae***

1. Herbs with usually 3 angled stem and 3-ranked leaves with closed sheaths.
2. Flowers in spikelets, naked, hermaphrodite or unisexual.
3. Stamens 3 to 1.
4. Gynoecium 2-3 carpellary, syncarpous, superior, unilocular with one basal anatropous ovule.

***1. English name.** Sedge family.

2. Systematic position in other systems of classification.

Rendle (1930)	Engler and Prantl (1931)	Hutchinson (1959)
Monocotyledons	Monocotyledoneae	Monocotyledons
Glumiflorae	Glumiflorae	Glumiflorae
Cyperaceae	Cyperaceae	Cyperaceae

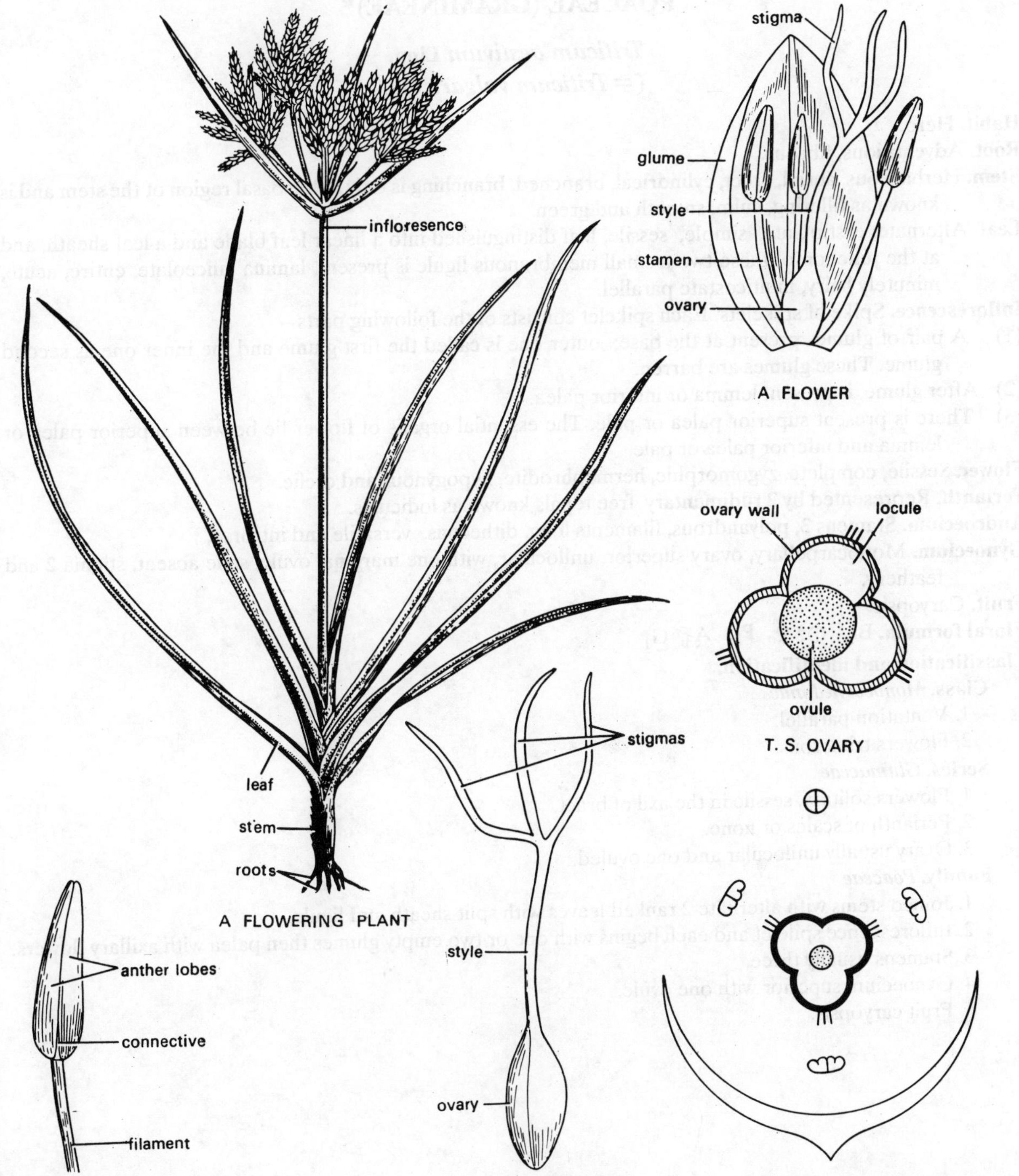

Fig. 83. ***Cyperus rotundus.***

---

1. **English name.** Sedge.
2. **Vernacular name.** Motha.

POACEAE (GRAMINEAE)*

Triticum aestivum Linn.
(= *Triticum vulgare* Vill.)

Habit. Herb.

Root. Adventitious, fibrous.

Stem. Herbaceous, aerial, erect, cylindrical, branched, branching is only at the basal region of the stem and is known as tillering, culm, smooth and green.

Leaf. Alternate, exstipulate, simple, sessile, leaf distinguished into a linear leaf blade and a leaf sheath, and at the junction of these two a small membranous ligule is present, lamina lanceolate, entire, acute, minutely hairy, multicostate parallel.

Inflorescence. Spike of spikelets. Each spikelet consists of the following parts—

(1) A pair of glumes present at the base; outer one is called the first glume and the inner one as second glume. These glumes are barren.

(2) After glume, is present lemma or inferior palea.

(3) There is present superior palea or pale. The essential organs of flower lie between superior palea or lemma and inferior palea or pale.

Flower. Sessile, complete, zygomorphic, hermaphrodite, hypogynous and cyclic.

Perianth. Represented by 2 rudimentary free tepals known as lodicules.

Androecium. Stamens 3, polyandrous, filaments long, dithecous, versatile and introrse.

Gynoecium. Monocarpellary, ovary superior, unilocular, with one marginal ovule, style absent, stigma 2 and feathery.

Fruit. Caryopsis.

Floral formula. Br, ⦶, ⚥, P_2, A_3, $\underline{G_1}$.

Classification and identification.

Class. *Monocotyledonae*

1. Ventation parallel.
2. Flowers trimerous.

Series. *Glumaceae*

1. Flowers solitary, sessile in the axil of bract.
2. Perianth of scales or none.
3. Ovary usually unilocular and one ovuled.

Family. *Poaceae*

1. Joined stems with alternate 2 ranked leaves with split sheath and ligule.
2. Inflorescence spilelet and each begins with one or two empty glumes then palea with axillary flowers.
3. Stamens usually three.
4. Gynoecium superior with one ovule.
5. Fruit caryopsis.

***1. English name.** Grass family.

2. Systematic position in other systems of classification.

Rendle (1930)	**Engler and Prantl** (1931)	**Hutchinson** (1959)
Monocotyledons	Monocotyledoneae	Monocotyledons
Glumiflorae	Glumiflorae	Glumiflorae
Gramineae	Gramineae	Gramineae

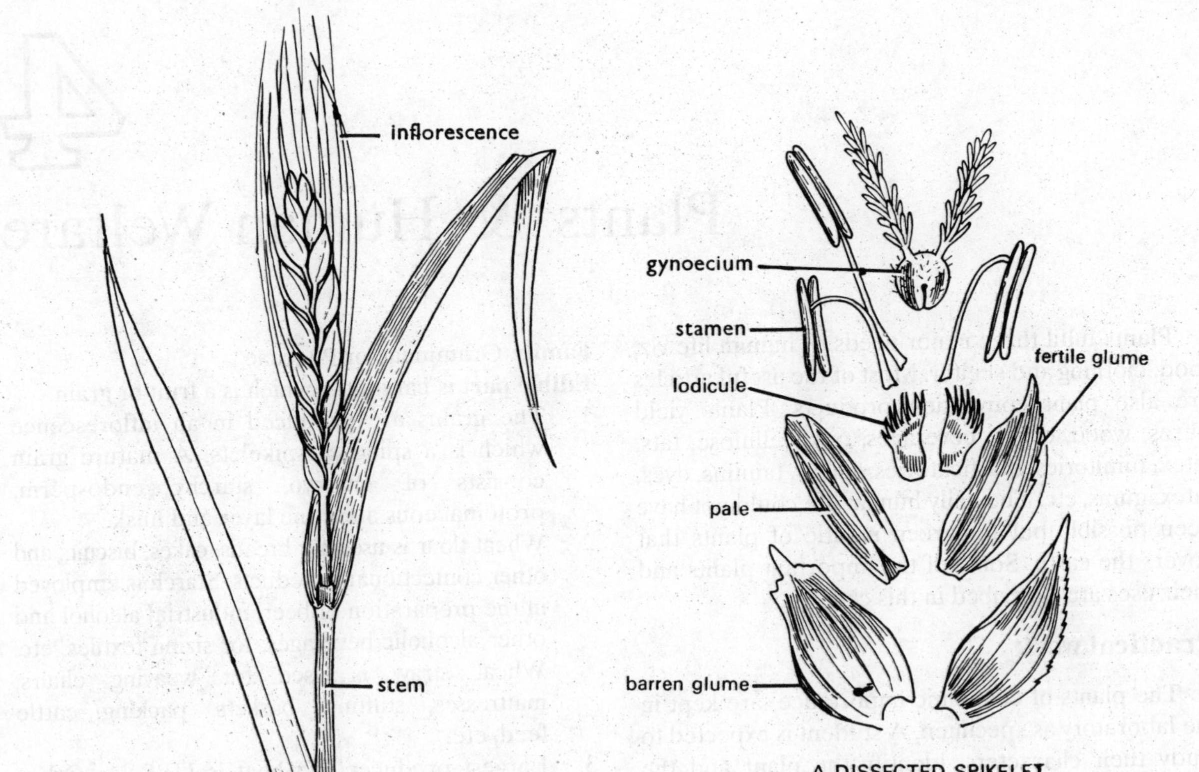

Fig. 84. ***Triticum aestivum.***

---

1. **English name.** Wheat.
2. **Vernacular names.** Gehun, Kanak.
3. **Economic importance.** Cultivated as a food crop. The wheat straw is used as a cattle feed and in the manufacture of paper.

4

Plants & Human Welfare

Plants fulfil three major needs of human life viz, food, clothing and shelter. Most of the useful articles are also plant conversion products. Plants yield fibres, wood, drugs, beverages, oils, cellulose, fats, latex, fumitories, masticatories, spices, tannins, dyes, latex, gums, etc. The daily human life could not have been possible but for green mantle of plants that covers the earth. Some of the important plants and their uses are described in this chapter.

Practical work

The plants of economic importance are kept in the laboratory as specimen. A student is expected to study their characters, identify the plant and the useful plant parts. A student should also be informed about different uses of the plant, cultivation, production and marketing statistics, etc. Therefore, comments written in practical record should include the following sequence.

1. Botanical name of the plant
2. Common English/ Hindi / vernacular name
3. Family
4. Part/parts of the plant used
5. Characters of the plant/ plant part
6. Cultivation, harvesting and processing
7. Uses of the plant part/parts
8. World production
9. Production in India

Practical record should also include diagrams of typical plant or plant part which is economically useful.

I. PLANTS OF ECONOMIC IMPORTANCE

CEREALS

1. Wheat

Botanical name. ***Triticum aestivum***
Hindi name. Gehoon, Kanak
Family. Gramineae or Poaceae
Edible part is caryopsis which is a fruit or grain.

1. The grains are produced in an inflorescence which is a spike of spikelets. A mature grain consists of embryo, starchy endosperm, proteinaceous aleurone layer and husk.
2. Wheat flour is used for breads, cakes, biscuits and other confectionary products. Starch is employed in the preparation of beer, industrial alcohol and other alcoholic beverages, for sizing textiles, etc. Wheat straw is used for weaving chairs, mattresses, stuffing, baskets, packing, cattle feed, etc.
3. Largest producer of wheat is U. S. A. Other wheat producing countries are Russia, China, Canada, Australia, India, etc.
4. In India it is a major cereal and covers 12% of the total area under cereals and 76% of that under winter cereals. It is mainly cultivated in U.P., Haryana, Punjab and M.P.
5. Various species used include *T. aestivum, T. durum, T. dicoccum, T. sphaerococum,* etc.

2. Rice

Botanical name. ***Oryza sativa***
Hindi name. Chawal, Dhan
Family. Gramineae or Poaceae
Edible part is caryopsis which is a fruit called grain.

1. Half the world's population, mostly the densely populated regions of the world, use this cereal as a staple food.
2. Plant is a large annual grass. The inflorescence is a panicle, its branches ending into a grain, covered by a husk.
3. The plant grows in hot, moist tropics. The area should be flooded with water during early stages.

4. The grains are used after removal of the husk and are very nutritious. Grain contains considerable amount of proteins, fat and starch. It also forms a raw material for alcoholic beverages. The stems are used as hat fibres and straw for mushroom cultivation.
5. China produces about 32% of the worlds rice, India following with 21%. The highest yield in India comes from West Bengal and Bihar.

3. Maize or Corn

Botanical name. *Zea mays*
Hindi name. Makka, Bhutta
Family. Gramineae or Poaceae
Edible part is caryopsis which is a fruit called grain.

1. The plant is annual grass. It possesses both male and female flowers on the same plant. Grains are fruits (caryopsis) which contain proteins besides starchy endosperm.
2. Maize is used as a food for livestock; flour is used in the preparation of corn bread. Other uses include corn flakes, corn starch, syrup, corn oil, dextrins, industrial alcohol. Fibres are also obtained from the main plant for making paper, yarn and as pith. Zein-the maize protein is useful in the manufacture of artificial fibres.
3. U. S. A. produces half the world's output. Other corn producing countries include China, Argentina, Brazil, India, Mexico, etc.
4. In India, maize was introduced by East India company in 12th century. It is now chiefly cultivated in U. P., Bihar, Rajasthan, M. P., Punjab, A. P., etc.

PULSES OR LEGUMES

1. Cajan pea or Pigeon pea

Botanical name. *Cajanus cajan*
Hindi name. Arhar
Family. Papilionaceae
Edible part is the seed produced in pod or legume (fruit).

1. This annual plant is 6-7 feet tall. The leaves are trifoliate and flowers are borne in an axillary raceme.
2. It is grown as a mixed crop with jowar, bajra, ragi, cotton, maize, ground nut, etc.
3. Cajan pea is extensively used as *dal;* the green leaves and tops as animal feed and also as a green manure.
4. It is chiefly grown in U.P., Rajasthan, Orissa, Maharashtra, Bihar, M.P., etc. India also export small quantities to U. K., France, Sri Lanka, Burma, etc.

2. Soyabean

Botanical name. *Glycine max*
Hindi name. Soyabean
Family. Papilionaceae
Edible part is the seed produced in pod or legume.

1. It is a small, bushy, erect or prostrate annual that grows from 1-6 feet. Each pod contains 3-4 seeds.
2. It is grown alone or mixed with maize or sorghum; in fertile loam or sandy loam soils.
3. Soyabean contains 32-42% proteins and has the highest lysine content (3.8%).
4. Besides being used variously as a food article, soyabean flour, oil and milk are also extensively used.
5. Manchuria leads the production followed by Korea, Japan, China and Indonesia. India also grows a small amount of this crop.

3. Black gram

Botanical name. *Vigna mungo(= Phaseolus mungo)*
Hindi name. Urd
Family. Papilionaceae
Edible part is the seed produced in pod or legume.

1. It is a herbaceous annual with procumbent branches, wooly in appearance. The leaves are trifoliate and the flowers are borne in clusters of five to six.
2. It is grown as a mixed crop in loamy or heavy soils in warm climate with good amount of rain.
3. It is highly prized for its high phosphoric contents. It is preferred in the preparation of *papars, kachoris,* etc. The seeds are eaten raw, germinated, salted or boiled. They are also used as *dal.* Straw is fed to the cattle.
4. The major areas of production in India include M.P., U.P., Punjab, Maharashtra, West Bengal, A.P. and Karnataka.

4. Green gram

Botanical name. *Vigna radiata (= Phaseolus radiatus)*
Hindi name. Moong
Family. Papilionaceae
Edible part is a seed produced in pod or legume.

1. This small herbaceous annual grows to a height of 1-3 feet. The leaves are trifoliate and the yellow flowers are produced in clusters.
2. It grows on loams as well as on red and black soils as a kharif crop. It requires rainfall between 25-35 inches distributed throughout the year.
3. The green pods are used as vegetable, seeds as a pulse and straw and husk as fodder for cattle. Seeds are eaten as whole, as *dal*, parched, salted, germinated or boiled.
4. It is widely cultivated in India. The major states are M.P., U.P., Punjab, Maharashtra, Rajasthan, Karnataka, Tamil Nadu, Bihar and A.P.

5. Chick peas, Gram peas or Bengal gram

Botanical name. *Cicer arietinum*
Hindi name. Chana
Family. Papilionaceae
Edible part is a seed produced in pod or legume.

1. The plant is branched, about 2 feet tall, leaves are pinnately compound and the fruit contains 1-3 seeds.
2. It is a dry crop grown in rabi season. It is best suited to areas of moderate rainfall with mild cold weather in water retentive clay loams and black cotton soils.
3. Gram is eaten raw, boiled or cooked. Green foliage is also used as a vegetable. It is used as a *dal* and gram flour or *besan* is used in various preparations.
4. It is rich in proteins, carbohydrates and contains varied amounts of vitamin A, B, and C. It also contains useful quantities of minerals.
5. In india it is mainly cultivated in U.P., Punjab, Rajasthan, M.P., Bihar, Maharashtra, A.P., West Bengal, Tamil Nadu and Karnataka.

TIMBERS

1. Shisham

Botanical name. *Dalbergia sisso*
Hindi name. Shisham
Family. Papilionaceae
Part of the plant used is heartwood which is a valuable timber.

1. It is a large tree reaching a height of 30 m and a girth of 2.4 m.
2. The heartwood is brownish in colour with darker streaks. It is hard and moderately heavy to very heavy.
3. It is diffuse porous. Growth rings are indistinct and ripple marks are present.
4. The wood can be seasoned without much difficulty. It can last for about 288 months.
5. The tree occurs throughout the sub -Himalayan tract from Indus to Assam. It has also been extensively cultivated in many parts of the country especially Punjab, U.P., West Bengal and Assam.
6. Shisham is very commonly used for building purposes, furniture, carriages, carving, etc.

2. Sal

Botanical name. *Shorea robusta*
Hindi name. Sal
Family. Dipterocarpaceae
Part of the plant used is heartwood which is a valuable timber.

1. It is a large deciduous tree reaching a height of about 37 m (up to 46 m) and a girth of about 3.7 m.
2. The sapwood and heart wood are distinct. The sapwood is white with brownish tinge and heart wood is brown to reddish brown. The wood is dull hard to very hard and usually heavy to very heavy.
3. It is difffuse porous to ring porous. The annual rings are indistinct to absent. Ripple marks are normally absent.
4. The wood is difficult to season. It develops cracks during seasoning. It remains in good condition even after 20 years of contact with the ground.
5. This most popular wood is used as a structural timber used for doors, windows, beams, planks, etc. It is also useful as railway sleepers.

3. Teak

Botanical name. *Tectona grandis*
Hindi name. Teak or sagwan
Family. Verbenaceae
Part of the plant used is heart wood as timber.

1. It is a large deciduous tree with outer bark peeling off in long thin flakes.
2. The wood is moderately hard, strongly and characteristically scented. It contains an oil which is easily perceptible to touch. The oil acts as preservative against white ants.

3. Heart wood is dark brown and turns almost black with age. Annual rings are distinct, marked with regularly arranged pores.
4. Teak wood is used for construction purposes, furniture and cabinet work.
5. The tree grows in western Ghats, Tamil Nadu, M.P., Orissa, Mysore and Bihar.

SUGAR & STARCH

1. Sugarcane

Botanical name. ***Saccharum officinarum***
Hindi name. Ganna
Family. Gramineae or Poaceae
Part of the plant used is stem for sugar extraction.

1. This perennial grass grows 8 to 12 feet tall and is supported by stilt roots.
2. It grows best in warm humid weather.
3. The juice extracted from stem by expression is crystallised to manufacture sugar. The bagasse, molasses and filter mud which are by-products of sugar extraction are also used variously.
4. Chief cane sugar producing countries include Brazil, Cuba, India, China, Australia, etc.
5. Eighty per cent sugar cane in India is grown in north India with U.P. leading the list

2. Potato

Botanical name. ***Solanum tuberosum***
Hindi name. Aalu
Family. Solanaceae
Part of the plant used is underground stem tuber.

1. It is rich in starch and forms one of the most commonly used vegetable
2. Plant, a native of South America, is about foot tall, spreading annual. The undergound branches swell at the tip to form tubers.
3. It grows over a wide range of soil and climatic conditions.
4. It is a universal table food and is also used for sizing cotton and paper, production of dextrins, alcohol, adhesives, etc.
5. About 90% production comes from Europe. In India it is largely cultivated in U.P., H.P., Punjab, M.P., etc.

MEDICINAL PLANTS

1. Belladona

Botanical name. ***Atropa belladonna***
Hindi names. Sag-angur, Angurshefa
Family. Solanaceae
Part of the plant used is the root for extraction of a drug atropine.

1. Drug is applied externally to relieve pain, taken internally to check excessive perspiration, whooping coughs, as sedatives, antispasmodic, mydriatic in diseases of eye, to dilate pupil during eye testing, antidote in poisoning by opium and in asthma.
2. Plant grows abundantly in Himalayas and is cultivated in Europe and America.

2. Poppy (Opium)

Botanical name. ***Papaver somniferum***
Hindi names. Afim, post
Family. Papaveraceae
Part of plant used is unripe capsule from which latex based drug morphine is extracted.

1. The dried juice or latex obtained from unripe capsules is used.
2. The incisions are made on the unripe capsules, shortly after the fall of petals. The crude latex contains resins, oils and alkaloids including morphine and codeine.
3. The latex has narcotic and soothing properties and is used as a nervous stimulant to induce sleep and relieve spasms. Large quantities are injurious or even lethal. Oils from the poppy seeds are medicinally used.
4. The herb is a native of West Asia and is grown in India, China and Asia Minor. In India, the plants are cultivated in U.P., Punjab, Rajasthan and M.P.

3. Rauvolfia

Botanical name. ***Ravolfia serpentina***
Hindi names. Sarpa gandha, Chota chand
Family. Apocynaceae
Part of the plant used is root from which drug is extracted.

1. This plant is being used since ancient times. Root and bark contain many alkaloids including serpentine and reserpine.
2. It is used in the treatment of epileptic fits, snake bites, high blood pressure and has hypnotic, sedative and tranquilising effects.
3. Plant grows in tropcial Himalayas and in plains near the foot hills. The best growth occurs in north and south Kanara along the western ghats. It is grown in West Bengal, Bihar and U.P.

4. Quinine

Botanical name. *Cinchona officinalis* (also ***C. calisaya, C. succirubra***)
Hindi name. Cinchona
Family. Rubiaceae
Part of the plant used is bark for extraction of antimalarial drug quinine.

1. Twelve year old bark of the tree, is used to extract quinine – a white granular substance with a bitter taste. It contains about 20 or so alkaloids of which cinchonidine, cinchonine and quinidine are useful as medicine.
2. Medicinally it is used against malaria, as a tonic, antiseptic and in the treatment of fever.
3. The plant is distributed in India, Java, some parts of Europe and central and south America.

5. Datura

Botanical name. *Datura stramonium*
Hindi name. Dhatura
Family. Solanaceae
Parts of the plant used are leaves, flowering tops and seeds for the extraction of a drug useful in asthma.

1. The active principles are alkaloids e.g. hyoscyamine, atropine and scopalamine.
2. It is used for relaxing bronchial muscles in asthma, as intoxicant, emetic and digestive.
3. Datura seeds are smoked for asthma.
4. Plant is native of Asia, and grows as a weed in India, particularly in temperate climate.

BEVERAGES

1. Tea

Botanical name. *Camellia sinensis* (= *Thea sinensis*)
Hindi name. Chai
Family. Ternstroemiaceae

Parts of plant used are leaves which give a popular beverage called tea.

1. Plant is a shurb. Three to four feet tall. It grows at an altitude of about 5000′ above MSL on steep slopes.
2. Tea contains 2.5% theine, 13-18% tannin, volatile oils and a small amount of caffeine.
3. The leaves are plucked and cured and an infusion in boiled water yields most popular of the beverages.
4. India is one of the leading producers and exporters of tea. About 73% of the total output comes from south-east region, especially Assam and West Bengal.

2. Coffee

Botanical name. *Coffea arabica* (also ***C. robusta, C. liberica***)
Hindi name. Kafi
Family. Rubiaceae
Parts of the plant used are seeds which are used for the preparation of a beverage called coffee.

1. The plant grows in hot, moist climate. These are raised from seeds or seedlings and come into bearing in the third year.
2. The fruits are berries and the skin is removed. The seeds are then roasted to develop aroma, flavour and colour. Seeds contain 0.75 to 1.5% caffeine, a volatile oil caffeol, glucose, dextrin, proteins and fatty oils.
3. Arabian coffee (*C. arabica*) is a source of 90% of the world supply. Brazil tops the world production. U.S.A. leads in per capita consumption.
4. In India, coffee is cultivated in Karnataka, Tamil Nadu and Kerala.

OILS

1. Sesame

Botanical name. *Sesamum indicum*
Hindi name. Til
Family. Tiliaceae
Part of the plant used are seeds for extraction of oil.

1. It yields one of the most important semi-drying oils. The oil content varies from 46.0 to 52.0 per cent. The oil is extracted by cold pressure.
2. The finer grades of oil are nearly colourless and tasteless. It is used in cooking, medicine, as a

substitute for olive oil, etc. The poorer grades are used for soaps, perfumery, lubricants, and as rubber substitutes. The oil cake is used as cattle feed while the seeds are used in confectionary and baking.

3. In India sesame is grown in U.P., Rajasthan, M.P., and A.P. The maximum yield comes from Uttar Pradesh. It is grown alone or mixed with bajra, millets, pulses, castor, etc.

2. Groundnut

Botanical name. ***Arachis hypogaea***
Hindi name. Moongphali
Family. Papilionaceae
Part of the plant used are seeds from which oil is extracted.

1. Seeds are an important source of vegetable non-drying oil.
2. The oil is expressed by hydraulic presses and expellers.
3. The filtered and refined oil is edible, and is used as salad oil, making margarine, shortening, etc. Poorer grades are used for soap making, as lubricants and illuminants. The residual oil cake is a good cattle feed and is also used as a fertilizer.
4. The major ground nut producing countries are India, China, West Africa, U.S.A., etc.

3. Castor

Botanical name. ***Ricinus communis***
Hindi name. Arandi
Family. Euphorbiaceae
Part of the plant used are seeds which are used for oil extraction.

1. It yields one of the most important non-drying oils. The oil contents of seeds vary from 35 to 58%. It is green in colour. Oil is collected from the seeds by solvent extraction or expression.
2. Castor oil is used as purgative. Being water resistant, it is used for making fabrics, for protective covering of air-planes, insulations, etc. It is also used in soap manufacture, inks, plastics, paints, varnishes, leather preservation, etc. Oil cake is poisonous and can not be used as cattle feed. However, it is an excellent fertilizer.
3. In India A.P., Tamil Nadu, Maharashtra and Karnataka are chief castor seed growing states.

4. Sarsoon

Botanical name. ***Brassica campestris*** (also ***B. juncea***, ***B. napus***)
Hindi name. Sarson
Family. Cruciferae
Part of the plant used are seeds for extraction of oil.

1. It yields one of the most important edible oils. The oil content varies between 30-48%.
2. It is mostly grown alongwith rabi crops. *Altemaria* blight is the common disease.
3. Oil contains glycerides and erucic acid.
4. The seed and oil are used as condiments in the preparation of pickles and for flavouring curries and vegetables. Oil is also used in lamps, in tempering steel, in oiling wooden goods, in making soaps, etc. The oil cake is used as a cattle feed. The leaves of young plants are used as green vegetable.
5. India is the first both with regard to acreage and production in the world. It is chiefly grown in Bihar, M.P., West Bengal, Orissa and U.P.

5. Linseed

Botanical name. ***Linum usitatissimum***
Hindi name. Alsi
Family. Linaceae
Parts of the plant used are (a) seeds for oil extraction and (b) stem for extraction of fibres.

1. **Oil.** The seeds contain about 32 to 40% of drying oil which is expressed mechanically. It is chiefly used in the preparation of paints and varnishes because it dries into thin elastic film when exposed due to absorption of oxygen from the atmosphere. It is also used in the preparation of soaps, manufacture of printing ink and linoleum, oil cloth, water proof fabrics, and as edible oil in some areas. The residue oilcake is a valuable cattle feed and manure.
2. **Fibres.** The pericyclic fibres are separated from the stem. These are very tough, wiry strands of long and thick (cellulose) cells. Fibres possess great tensile strength, fineness and durability. It is used in the manufacture of linen cloth, thread, canvas, writing and cigarette papers and insulating materials.
3. The major linseed growing countries are U.S.A., Canada, Argentina, Russia and India.

4. In India *Linum* is chiefly grown for its oil and fibres in M.P., U. P. and Maharashtra as rabi crop.

SPICES

1. Cardamom

Botanical name. ***Elettaria cardamomum***
Hindi name. Choti elaichi
Family. Zingiberaceae
Parts of the plant used are fruits which are valuable as a spice.

1. The plant is native of India, indigenous to moist, evergreen forests of South India. It is grown either as a pure plantation crop or as subsidiary to coffee and areca nut. It is also found as a natural undergrowth in some forest tracts.
2. The fruits are triangular capsules and seeds have delicate flavour. It is used for flavouring curries, cakes and pickles. The seeds contain 2 to 8% of strongly aromatic volatile oil with a pleasant cooling taste.
3. The crop is cultivated in hilly forest regions of entire Western Ghats, Mysore, Kerala, Assam and Tamil Nadu.

2. Pepper

Botanical name. ***Piper nigrum***
Hindi name. Kali mirch
Family. Piperaceae
Part of the plant used are fruits used as a spice.

1. Seeds yield an oil of aromatic odour. The pungent taste is due to the presence of an oleoresin. It stimulates the flow of saliva and gastric juices and has a cooling effect.
2. It is chiefly cultivated in India, Malayasia and Indonesia. In India, most of the pepper comes from Kerala, other states being Karnataka, Tamil Nadu, Maharashtra and Assam.

3. Coriander

Botanical name. ***Coriandrum sativum***
Hindi name. Dhania
Family. Umbelliferae
Parts of the plant used are fruits as flavouring agent and a spice.

1. It is a small perennial plant. This herb with decompound leaves bears an umbel inflorescence. The fruit is a cremocarp, splitting into two mericarps.
2. It is used as a common flavouring agent for its pleasant aroma. It also has stimulant, carminative and antiseptic properties. Oil of coriander is used to flavour beverages such as gin, whiskey, etc.
3. It is a native of Mediterranean region. Coriander is now extensively grown in Europe, Morocco, India and South Africa.

FIBRES

1. Jute

Botanical name. ***Corchorus capsularis*** (also ***C. olitorius***)
Hindi names. Pat, Titapat.
Family. Tiliaceae
Parts of plant used are fibres from phloem (bast fibres) of stem.

1. The plant is an annual shrub and is grown from seeds. It is best grown in humid regions with moderate rains, on light, sandy, deltaic loams.
2. The fibres are obtained from the secondary phloem by retting the stem. The stems are beaten and fibres separated.
3. The fibre is used for manufacturing packing cloth, hessian, bags for transport and storage, rugs, curtains, upholstry, linings, ropes, twines, etc.
4. This is the most important cash crop of north-east India, especially valleys of Ganges and Brahamputra in Assam, West Bengal, Bihar and Orissa. About 67% of the products are consumed at home while the rest are exported to U.S.A., U.K., Australia, Canada, Argentina, etc. Other major jute producing country is Bangla Desh.

2. Sannhemp

Botanical name. ***Crotalaria juncea***
Hindi name. Sann
Family. Papilionaceae
Parts of the plant used are bast (phloem) fibres from the stem.

1. The plant is an annual herb of Asiatic origin. Besides bast (phloem) fibres, it is also grown as a green manure. Fibres are light coloured, coarse, strong and durable.
2. The fibre is used for making ropes, mats, cordage, tissue and cirgarette paper and cellulose for wrapping paper while plant stalks and leaves are cattle feed.
3. It is grown throughout India, especially in Maharashtra, Tamil Nadu, West Bengal and U.P. and is exported to U.K., Italy, France and Belgium.

3. Cotton

Botanical names. ***Gossypium arboreum, G. herbaceum, G. hirsutum, G. barbadense***

Hindi name. Kapas

Family. Malvaceae

Parts of the plant used are

(a) seeds for oil extraction and

(b) seed hair as cotton fibres.

1. This plant is an important fibre and oil seed crop. Both oil and fibres are obtained from the seeds. The fibres are epidermal hair, while oil is expressed from the seeds.
2. Plant is a perennial shurb or a small tree which grows on sandy damp soil of humid regions. Black alluvial soil of the Deccan plateau is considered the best.
3. (a) **Oil** obtained from the seeds is used as salad and cooking oil, preparation of oleomargarine, oil residue as raw material for soap, washing powders, roofing tar, glycerine, etc. Oil cake is used as food for cattle.

(b) **Seed hairs** are used as fibres. The fibres are collected from seeds and after processing bales are made into varied products. It is an important constituent of cotton fabrics, rubber tyre fabrics, carpets, blankets, cordage, etc. Raw cotton is used for stuffing.

4. Cotton is cultivated in U.S. A., India, Pakistan, Egypt and Brazil.
5. In India, it is grown in Maharashtra, Karnataka, Punjab, Assam, Gujarat, Madhya Pradesh and Uttar Pradesh. There are 657 cotton mills in the country and cotton textiles are being exported from India.

4. Hemp

Botanical name. ***Cannabis sativa***

Hindi names. Ganja, Bhang, Charas

Family. Cannabinaceae

Parts of the plant used are

(a) stems for bast fibres

(b) seeds for oil and

(c) inflorescence for narcotic drug

1. (a) White fibres are formed in the pericycle. The best quality fibre is obtained from male plants. Fibres are long, strong and durable. These are less elastic and flexible because walls are lignified.

(b) Seeds yield a drying oil and

(c) narcotic drugs are obtained from flowering tops, aerial part and leaves.

(i) *Gaanja* which is used as a fumitory and smoked alone or along with tobacco is obtained from dried flowering tops.

(ii) *Charas* is a resinous exudation from the aerial parts of the plant and

(iii) *Bhang* is an infusion of the dried leaves and flowering shoots.

2. (a) Fibres are used for ropes, twines, carpets, sail cloth, sacks, bags, etc.

(b) the oil is used for its drying properties and

(c) the narcotic drugs are of medicinal value in small doses.

3. Russia U.S.A., Italy and Chile grow this crop.

5. Coconut (Coir)

Botanical name. ***Cocos nucifera***

Hindi name. Nariyal

Family. Palmae

Parts of the plant used are

(a) mesocarp of the fruit for fibres and

(b) endosperm of the seed for extraction of oil.

1. This tall palm tree bears fruits in bunches on the tree. The fruit is a three sided drupe consisting of a smooth rind or exocarp, a reddish brown fibrous mesocarp and a hard stony endocarp or shell enclosing the seed. The well known coconut meat and milk are actually the endosperm of the seed.
2. Coconut has manifold uses —

(a) The fibrous husk is used for the manufacture of coir which is used for the cordage, mats, foot rugs, brushes, stuffing, etc.

(b) The shells are used as containers and as fuel.
(c) The milk (watery endosperm) is a refreshing drink.
(d) The meat (the cellular endosperm) is eaten raw or dried to form copra from which oil is extracted. Coconut oil is used in the manufacture of margarine, vegetable ghee and hard soaps.
(e) Unopened inflorescence yields palm sugar and
(f) Leaves are used for thatching.
(3) Indonesia leads the production followed by Philippines, India and Sri Lanka.

FUMITORY

Tobacco

Botanical name. *Nicotiana tabacum*
Hindi name. Tambaku
Family. Solanaceae
Parts of the plant used are leaves which are smoked as tobacco.

1. The plant is a native of West Indies and is grown under varying conditions in almost every country.
2. The leaves are removed one by one as they mature. Later these are cured (dry fermentation) to develop aroma, harshness and other desirable qualities.
3. Tobacco has narcotic and soothing properties due to the presence of an alkaloid nicotine. The aroma and flavour is due to essential oils and other aromatic substances developed during processing.
4. Before use, tobacco leaves of various grades are blended. It is used for cigars, cigarettes, chewing purposes, for hookah and snuff. It is said to produce pulmonary emphysema and incidence of cancer and cardiac diseases among tobacco smokers is higher.
5. U.S.A. leads the world production. In India it is grown in parts of Punjab, Haryana, Jammu and Kashmir, Himachal Pradesh, Andhra Pradesh and Karnataka.

RUBBER

Rubber

Botancial name. *Hevea brasiliensis*
Family. Euphorbiaceae
Part of the plant used is the latex from stem.

1. Latex occurs in special cells of the bark, leaves and other soft parts of the tree. The latex cells are distributed in between phloem. The latex from the lower parts of the tree is usually commercially important.
2. The tree is a native of Amazon. It is 60 to 140 feet in height.
3. Rubber is elastic, flexible, air tight, water proof, long lasting and a good insulator of heat and electricity.
4. Latex rubber contains 92 to 94 per cent rubber hydrocarbon, 3 per cent resin, 2 per cent proteins and 0.2 per cent ash.
5. In India rubber is extracted on commercial scale in Kerala, Tamil Nadu, Karnataka, Assam, Andaman and West Bengal.

II. MICROCHEMICAL TESTS

1. Cellulose

Purpose : To detect the presence of cellulose.

Materials

Microscope, slides, cover glasses, iodine solution, sulphuric acid 75%, water, paper or cotton fibres, etc.

Procedure

1. Tear the paper or cotton in a way so that fibres are exposed.
2. Place the fibres in a drop of water on a slide.
3. Add a few drops of iodine and allow the fibres to take stain.
4. The fibres turn brown.
5. Add a drop of 75% sulphuric acid and then wash with water.
6. The colour of the fibres changes.

Results

The fibres turn blue.

Conclusion

The change into blue indicates the presence of cellulose in the wall thickenings.

This is because cellulose dissolves in cold concentrated sulphuric acid and is precipitated as amyloid on dilution.

2. Cutin

Purpose : To detect the presence of cutin.

Materials

Microscope, slides, cover glasses, razor or blade, watch glasses, water, potassium hydroxide (KOH), *Ficus or Nerium* leaf, etc.

Procedure

1. Cut the section of the leaf and place in water.
2. Treat the section with KOH solution.
3. Observe the colour of the outermost deposit on epidermis.

Results and conclusion

The yellow colour of the deposition on epidermis indicates that it is composed of cutin – a fat-like subtance.

3. Suberin

Purpose : To detect the presence of suberin.

Materials

Bottle cork/natural cork, Sudan IV (alcoholic), alcohol 50%, slides, cover glasses, water, glycerine, etc.

Procedure

1. Cut thin slice of the material.
2. Leave the fresh section in Sudan IV to take stain for about 20 minutes.
3. Wash the excess of stain with 50% alcohol.
4. Transfer the section to water and mount in glycerine.
5. Observe the colour under the microscope.

Results and conclusion

The suberised portions become red stained indicating the presence of suberin in the wall.

4. Lignin

Purpose : To detect the presence of lignin.

Materials

Match shavings/match sticks/ wood shavings, phloroglucin (1% alcoholic), hydrochloric acid (25%), 1% neutral aqueous potassium permanganate, ammonium hydroxide (sodium bicarbonate), slides, cover glasses, water, etc.

Procedure

Follow any of the two methods given below.

1. **Method 1.** Prepare thin slices of the material. Place them in 1% alcoholic phloroglucin. Cover the section with coverglass. Allow 25% hydrochloric acid to diffuse along the edges of coverglass.
2. **Method 2.** Treat the section with 1% aq. neutral potassium permanganate for about 15-20 minutes. Wash with 2% hydrochloric acid followed by repeated washings with water. Add a few drops of either ammoium hydroxide or sodium bicarbonate.

Results and conclusion

1. In the first case red violet colour is taken by lignified walls.
2. In the second method, deep red colour develops in the lignified elements of the deciduous plants.

5. Mucilage

Purpose : To detect the presence of mucilage.

Materials

Linseed testa, copper sulphate (10%), potassium hydroxide (10%), water, slides, cover glasses, glycerine, etc.

Procedure

1. Cut thin section of linseed testa.
2. Soak the sections in 10% copper sulphate solution for 20 minutes.
3. Wash the section in water and transfer to 10% potassium hydroxide.
4. Mount the section in glycerine and observe the colour.

Results and conclusion

The cells with mucilage are stained bright blue indicating that the material possesses mucilage.

6. Latex

Purpose : To detect the presence of latex.

Materials

Latex from *Calotropis*/members of Euphorbiaceae/ Apocynaceae, sucrose, alcohol conc: sulphuric acid, test tubes, test tube holder, water, etc.

Procedure

1. Prepare an alcoholic extract of latex.
2. Add an equal amount conc. sulphuric acid and sucrose to the latex extract.

Results and conclusion

The colour turns pinkish-purple indicating the presence of latex.

7. Hemicellulose

Purpose : To test for the presence of hemicellulose.

Materials

Soyabean seeds, iodine, water, slides, cover glasses, glycerine, etc.

Procedure

1. Cut a thin section of the seed.
2. Observe the section under microsocpe.
3. Treat the section with iodine for a few minutes.
4. Observe the colour of the section.

Results and conclusion

The colour turns blue indicating the presence of hemicelluloses.

8. Glucose (Reducing sugars)

Purpose : To test for the reducing sugar: glucose (grape-sugar).

Materials

Fehling's solution, Benedict's solution, test tubes, test tube holder, spirit lamp, water, glucose (grape-sugar), etc.

Procedure

There are two tests to detect the presence of glucose. These are given below.

(a) Fehling's test. 1. Take about 5 ml of Fehling solution in a test tube.

2. Add few drops of glucose solution and boil.

(b) Benedict's test. 1. Take about 5 ml of Benedict's solution in a test tube.

2. Add a few drops of glucose solution and boil.

Results

1. The Fehling's solution gives brownish red precipitate.
2. Benedict's test gives red yellow or green precipitate.

Conclusion

The tests reveal the presence of glucose.

Sugar when treated with alkali undergoes enolization to produce enediols. These being highly reactive reducing agents, are capable of reducing oxidising Cu^{++} ions. Both Fehling's and Benedict's solutions contain soluble Cu^{++} ions in soluble form as complexes with citrate or tartrate. On coming in contact with enediols Cu^{++} (cupric) ions are reduced to Cu^{+} (cuprous) ions which later combine to precipitate yellow cuprous hydroxide. Yellow precipitate of cuprous hydroxide on heating, gets converted to reddish cuprous oxide.

$$\text{sugar} \xrightarrow[\text{enediols}]{\text{alkali}} \text{enediols}$$

$$Cu^{++} \longrightarrow Cu^{+}$$

$$Cu^{+} + OH \longrightarrow CuOH\ (\text{yellow})$$

$$2CuOH \longrightarrow Cu_2O\ (\text{Red}) + H_2O$$

Overall reaction :

$$\underset{\text{(Glucose)}}{C_6H_{16}O_6} + 2Cu(OH)_2 \xrightarrow{\text{Boil}} \underset{\text{(Gluconic acid)}}{C_6H_{12}O_7} + \underset{\text{(Cuprous oxide)}}{Cu_2O} + H_2O$$

9. Sucrose (Non-reducing sugars)

Purpose : To test for starch/sucrose (non-reducing sugars).

Materials

Sucrose/starch/beet root, Fehling's solution, Benedict's solution, hydrochloric acid, sodium carbonate/sodium bicarbonate, test tubes, test tube holder, spirit lamp, etc.

Procedure

1. Add to sugar equal volume of concentrated hydrochloric acid.
2. Boil the mixtrue for about five minutes.
3. Neutralise the resulting solution with sodium carbonate or bicarbonate.
4. Then subject the solution to the test of reducing sugars by adding Fehling's or/and Benedict's solutions.

Results

1. Fehling's solution gives brownish red precipitate.
2. Benedict's solution gives yellow red or green precipitate.

Conclusion

The test reveals the presence of non-reducing sugars.

Sucrose occurs widely in plants. It is formed by condensation of one molecule of glucose with one molecule of fructose. On hydrolysis these are formed once again and then give the same results as reducing sugars when subjected to Fehling's and Benedict's solution.

$C_6H_{12}O_6 + C_6H_{12}O_6 \longrightarrow C_{12}H_{22}O_{11} + H_2O$
(Glucose) (Fructose) (Sucrose)

10. Proteins

Purpose : To test the presence of proteins.

Materials

Gram flour/legumes/soya bean, Millon's reagent a and b, nitric acid, ammonium hydroxide, sodium hydroxide (20%), copper sulphate (1%), test tubes, test tube holder, water, spirit lamp, etc.

Procedure

There are two methods for testing the presence of proteins.

(a) ***Xanthoproteic test.*** 1. Treat the suspension of tissue in water. Add concentated nitric acid. A white precipitate is formed.
2. Heat the solution. Yellow colour is developed.
3. Now add a few drops of concentated ammonium hydroxide. Observe the change in colour. The colour deepens to orange.

(b) ***Biuret test.*** 1. Prepare a suspension of material in water.
2. Add 1 ml of sodium hydroxide (20%) and a drop of copper sulphate to the suspension.
3. Observe the developing colour. Add Millons reagent (a or b). Mix thoroughly and boil.
4. Note the change in colour in both cases – Millons reagent 'a' and/or 'b'.

Results

(a) ***Xanthoproteic test.*** The yellow colour changes to orange.

(b) ***Biurete test.*** The colour developed is violet. On addition of Millon's reagent 'a' it turns to red on heating and with Millon's reagent 'b' it turns reddish on heating.

Conclusion

The colour changes indicate the presence of protein.

Biurete develops violet colour when treated with dilute $CuSO_4$ solution. This reaction is also shown by compounds containing – $CONH_2$ groups joined directly or by C or N atoms. Proteins also give this reaction because they possess CO – NH – C – CO – NH – peptide bond architecture.

In Xanthoproteic reaction nitration of phenyl rings occurs to yield yellow substitution products which turn orange upon the addition of alkali (salt formation).

11. Fats or oils

Purpose : To test for the presence of fats/oils.

Materials

Seed of almonds/soyabean/ground nut, Sudan III (alcoholic), water, osmic acid 1%, test tubes, test tube holders, glycerine, microscope, slides, coverglasses, etc.

Procedure

Any of the two following methods could be followed.

1. **Method 1.** Cut thin sections of the material. Place the section in Sudan III for about 10 minutes. Wash the sections with 50% alcohol. Mount in glycerine after repeated washes with water. Observe the colour under microscope.
2. **Method 2.** Add a few drops of osmic acid to the material in the test tube. Observe the developing colour.

Results

1. The oil drops take red stain
2. Black colour is developed.

12. Starch

Purpose : To test the presence of starch.

Materials

Starch, test tube, test tube holder, spirit lamp, iodine, HCl, Benedicts solution, Na OH (or Na_2CO_3) etc.

Procedure

Follow any one of the two methods given below.

1. **Method 1.** Take a pinch of starch and add water. Add a few drops of iodine.
2. **Method 2.** Take a pinch of starch and add water. Boil it by adding HCl. Make this solution alkaline by adding NaOH or Na_2CO_3. Test with Benedicts solution.

Results

1. Black colour appears.
2. Red precipitate is formed.

Conclusions

The tests indicate the presence of starch.

Table 1. **Methods to detect food adulteration**

FOOD STUFFS	ADULTERANT	METHOD OF DETECTION
1. Cereals and pulses	(a) Foreign matter	Take a known quantity (50 g)and pick up all foreign matter by hand or forceps. Weigh the amount and calculate the percentage (it should not exceed 4%).
	(b) Insect infection	(i) Take a known quantity (50 gm). Pick up all the damaged grains. Calculate percentage (it should not exceed 1%). (ii) Put the grains in water. Infested grains float on the surface. Calculate the percentage.
2. Pulses (arhar, masoor and chana)	Khesari dal	Pick up the Khesari dal (triangular and gray coloured seeds) and calculate percentage as before (it should not exceed 1%).
3. Turmeric (Haldi)	Lead chromate	Weigh 2 g of Haldi powder, reduce it to white ash in crucible (600C for 4 hours). Cool. Add 5 ml of 1:7: dil. H_2SO_4 and filter. Add a few drops of 0.2% diphenyl carbazide (alcoholic), Pink colour indicates the presence of lead chromate.
4. Milk	(a) Water added or fat removed	(a) Specific gravity determination of milk by lactometer.
	(b) Starch	(b) Iodine test.
5. Tea leaves	Arificial colour	(i) Place the leaves on white paper. The appearance of yellow or reddish colour over the paper will show the presence of artificially added colour. (ii) Spread a little slaked lime on glass plate. Sprinkle a little tea dust on the lime. Any colour (*e.g* red, orange, etc.) other than greenish yellow (due to pressence of naturally occurring chlorophyll) indicates the presence of coal tar dye.
6. Chillies	Coloured saw dust, brick powder, talcum powder.	Ash a spoonful of chillies. Abundant amount of ash indicates adulteration.
7. Oil	(a) Mineral oil	(a) Take 2 ml of sample. Add an equal amount of N/2 alcoholic potash. Heat for 15 minutes in boiling water bath. Cool and add about 10 ml of water. Presence of turbidity indicates presence of mineral oil.
	(b) Argemone oil	(b) Add nitric acid. If red colour appears, it indicates the presence of argemone oil.

8. Pure ghee	**Vanaspati ghee**	**Bodoudouin test (for the presence of sesame oil). To 5 ml of melted ghee add 0.1 g of sucrose dissolved in 5 ml of dilute HCl. Shake well and keep for 15 minutes. A permanent pink colour indicates the presence of sesame oil.**
9. Sweets	**Metanil yellow**	**Dissolve a little sample in water, shake and transfer the water extract to another tube. Add dilute HCl. A violet red colouration indicates the presence of metanil yellow.**

5

Embryology of Angiosperms

Reproduction in angiosperms occurs within the flowers. The essential organs include anthers and ovules wherein all reprodctive processes take place. Basically these are sporophytic structures. The sporogenous tissue and later spore mother cells formed within these organs undergo meiotic division and the gametophytic phase ensues. This results in formation of pollen tetrads or microspores and megaspore tetrad, the processes being called as micro – and megasporogenesis respectively. The microspore further develops partly inside the microsporangium and after dispersal germinates on the stigma to produce pollen tube. Inside the pollen tube are two male gametes. The formation of male gametes is called microgametogenesis and the transference of pollen grains from the anther to the stigma as pollination. Inside the ovules, out of the four megaspores of a tetrad, generally the chalazal one remains functional to form an embryo sac or female gametophyte. The process is called as megagametogenesis.

An embryo sac is generally 8 nucleate (polygonum type) in large number of angiosperms, consisting of two synergids and egg at the micropylar end, two polar nuclei in the centre and three antipodals at the chalazal end. One of the male gametes, fuses with the egg and another with 2 polar nuclei; the former process is called true fertilization and the latter as triple fusion. These together are known as double fertilization.

The zygote thus formed due to fertilization ultimately produces an embryo. The processes involved are known as embryogeny. Double fertilization results into triploid endosperm, characteristic of angiosperms.

ANTHER

1 Structure of young anther

Study the slide showing T.s. of young anther.

Observations

The section shows following characters.

1. The section appears slightly lobed.
2. The outermost is a single layered epidermis. The cells are cuticularised.
3. At four corners of the anther, the derivatives formed as a result of archesporial cells are present.
4. Of these, wall layers are situated below the epidermis and mass of sporogenous cells near the centre of the lobe.
5. The epidermis is followed by a layer or two of parenchymatous wall layers. The innermost wall layer is called tapetum. It is nutritive in function.

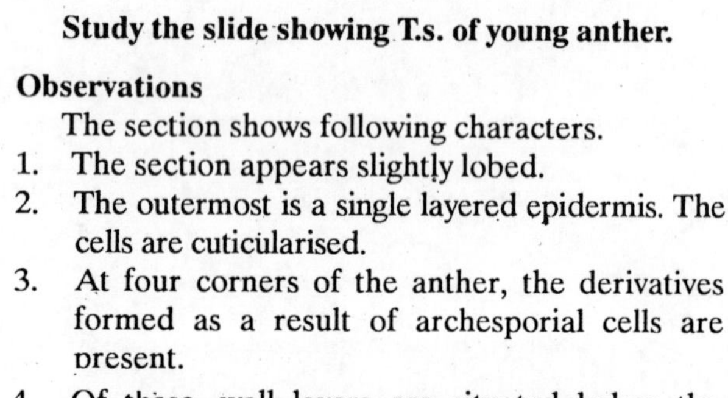

Fig. 1. Anther : T.s. Developing anther.

6. The sporogenous cells lie inside the wall. These act as pollen or microspore mother cells and divide meiotically.
7. In the middle of the anther lobe, procambial strand is present.

2. Structure of mature anther

Study the slide showing T.s. of mature anther.

Observations

It shows following characters.

1. An organized anther is four chambered in a transection.
2. The wall consists of an outer epidermis, an endothecium, one to three middle layers and an innermost tapetum.
3. The tapetum at maturity is multinucleate and contains dense cytoplasm which is finally used up by the developing microspores.
4. Prior to dehiscence, the tapetum and also the middle layers degenerate. The cells of the endothecium are radially elongated and exhibit, characteristic fibrous thickenings.
5. The microspores or pollen grains, are at first arranged in tetrads, (as a result of reduction division of the microspore mother cell). Later, these separate and occur as individual pollen grains, dispersed throughout the chamber. Each shows characteristic shape, size and structure.

POLLEN GRAINS

1. Characters of pollen grains for study

Following characters of the pollen grains are observed.

1. Polarity. The pollen grains are often formed in tetrads. While in tetrad, one end of the individual grain is noted (Fig. 3A).

(a) Proximal pole. The end of the pollen grain directed towards the centre of the tetrad (Fig. 3A).

(b) Distal pole. The end of the pollen grain directed away from the centre of the tetrad (Fig. 3A).

Accordingly following are the axes.

(a) Polar axis. Hypothetical line connecting the two poles (Fig. 3B).

(b) Equatorial axis. Hypothetical line that lies perpendicular to the polar axis (Fig. 3B).

2. Symmetry. The pollen grains may be

(a) Symmetric- bilateral or radial.

(b) Asymmetric-without any symmetry.

3. Apertures. The exine of the pollen grains is often provided with apertures which are thin, more or less distinctly delimited areas formed only of a hyaline membrane. The following are the major types.

(a) Inaperturate-aperture absent.

(b) Aperturate-aperture present.

The shape of aperture. On the basis of shape these can be further divided.

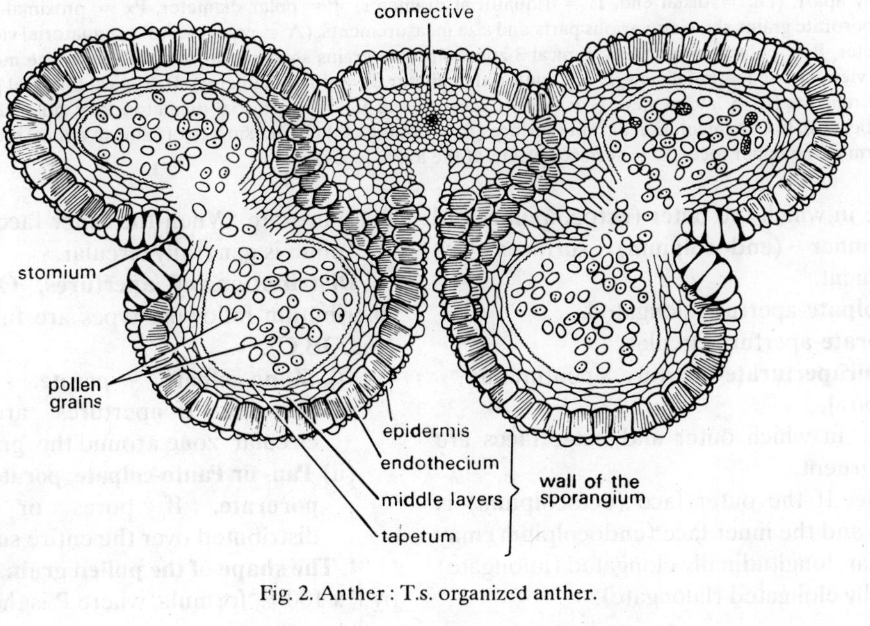

Fig. 2. Anther : T.s. organized anther.

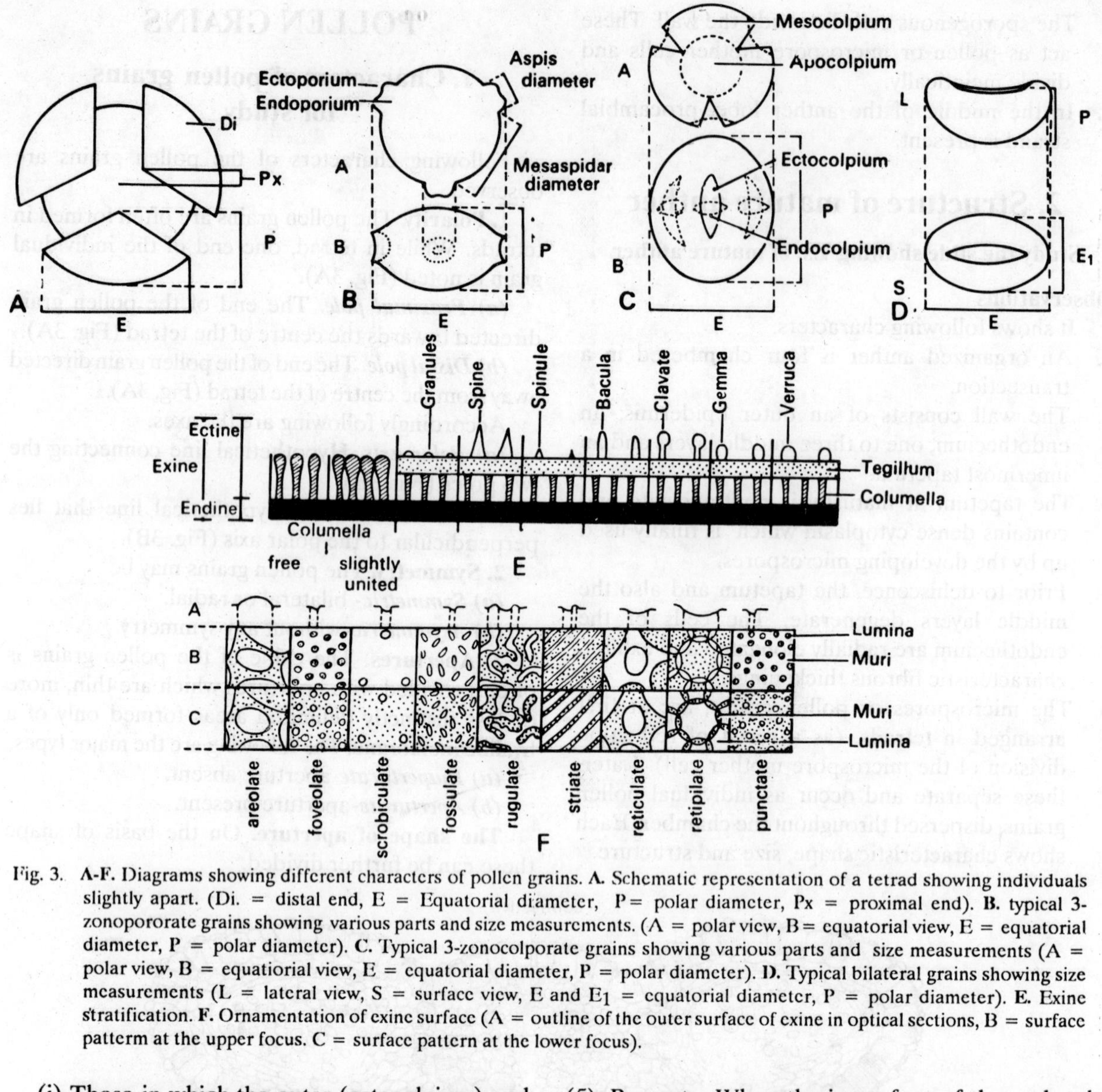

Fig. 3. **A-F. Diagrams showing different characters of pollen grains. A. Schematic representation of a tetrad showing individuals slightly apart. (Di. = distal end, E = Equatorial diameter, P = polar diameter, Px = proximal end). B. typical 3-zonopororate grains showing various parts and size measurements. (A = polar view, B = equatorial view, E = equatorial diameter, P = polar diameter). C. Typical 3-zonocolporate grains showing various parts and size measurements (A = polar view, B = equatiorial view, E = equatorial diameter, P = polar diameter). D. Typical bilateral grains showing size measurements (L = lateral view, S = surface view, E and E_1 = equatorial diameter, P = polar diameter). E. Exine stratification. F. Ornamentation of exine surface (A = outline of the outer surface of exine in optical sections, B = surface patterm at the upper focus. C = surface pattern at the lower focus).**

(i) Those in which the outer (ectocolpium) and the inner (endocolpium) surfaces are congruent.

(1) **Colpate**-aperture elongated.

(2) **Porate**-aperture circular.

(3) **Spiraperturate**-aperture a continuous spiral.

(ii) Those in which outer and inner faces are incongruent.

(4) Colporate. If the outer face (ectocolpium) is elongate and the inner face (endocolpium) may be circular, longitudinally elongated (lolongate) or laterally elongated (lalongate).

(5) Pororate. When the inner face of the endocolpium is generally circular.

Distribution of apertures. On the basis of distribution following types are further recognised (Fig. 3B,C).

(i) **Zono-colpate, - porate. - colporate or - pororate.** If apertures are arranged in a circular zone around the grain.

(ii) **Pan- or Panto-colpate, porate, - colporate or - pororate.** If pores or apertures are distributed over the entire surface.

4. The shape of the pollen grain. It is determined by P x 100/E formula, where P is the polar diameter and E the equatorial diameter. Some of the shapes are Perbolate, Oblate, Sub-oblate, Oblate-Spheroidal Prolate – spheroidal, Sub-prolate, Prolate, Perprolate, etc.

5. Exine stratification. The wall is made of intine and exine (Fig. 3 E). The intine is colourless and disappears during the slide preparation. Exine consists of two layers - the inner homogenous layer, the endine (= nexine) and the outer heterogenous layer, the ectine (= sexine). The ectine is composed of radial rods, the columellae, which are either free at their tips or are united to form a layer called tegillum (= tectum).

6. Exine ornamentation. (Fig. 3F). The following are some of the patterns.

(1) The columellae forming the ectine produce **pilate** pattern with bright and dark areas.

(2) In some other cases columellae are arranged regularly and are fused to produce areas or **lumina,** the intervening areas between lumina being called **muri.**

(3) When a network is produced the pattern is **reticulate** which may be **retipilate** with incomplete fusion of columellae, **foveolate** with circular closely placed lumina, **scrobiculate** with circular but distantly placed lumina, or **fossulate** with elongated lumina.

(4) When lumina are parallel the pattern is called **striate** and when reticulate it is **rugulate.**

(5) A network with raised areas is called **areolate.**

(6) In some cases excrescenes such as minute granules are present on the tegillum, the pattern is **granulose,** as **spinulose** with pointed or blunt ends, if rounded warts it is **gemmate, verrucate** if base of the warts is not constricted, **tuberculate** when tubercles are present, **spinose** if they are pointed, **baculate** if rod shaped and **clavate** if club shaped.

2. Preparation of pollen grains for study

Following are the steps in the preparation of slides for pollen study.

Collection of material

1. The polliniferous material (anthers) is collected fresh or herbarium sheets can also be used.
2. The anthers are picked by a clean forceps.

Preparation of material

1. The anthers are tapped by needles or glass rod on a clean slide to obtain a mass of pollen grains.
2. This mass of pollen grains is picked up by the flat end of the forceps and transferred to the centre of another clean microscopic slide.

Pre-treatment

1. A drop of alcohol is added to the pollen grains. This releases oily and resinous substances in the form of a ring around pollen. Upto 3 or 4 drops of alcohol can be used.
2. The ring is wiped clean with cotton moistened with alcohol.

Mounting

1. A small pellet of glycerine jelly prestained with methyl green is taken. It is placed over the mass of pollen grains. Coverslip is also placed over the pellet.
2. A small piece of paraffin wax (melting point 60-70°C) is placed close to the coverslip.
3. Both, jelly and wax are warmed over the flame of the spirit lamp in such a way that while the jelly spreads a little, the remaining vacant space below the coverslip is occupied by wax.

3. The study of pollen grains of some common plants

1. *Arachis hypogaea* Linn. (Fam. Papilionaceae; Vern. Mungphali).

Grains 3-zonocolpate, subprolate (37 x 28 μ) or prolate (23-41 x 20-25 μ), colpus membrane crustate (operculate); ecto-exine thinner than endo-exine, surface foveolate (Fig. 4A)

2. *Argemone mexicana* Linn. (Fam. Papaveraceae; Vern. Pili Kateli).

Grains 3-colpate, subprolate (36 x 29μ; range 33- 24 x 24- 33 μ). Colpi with rounded ends. Ectine slightly thinner than endine, distinctly reticulate with simplibacculate muri, colpus membrane granulate.

3. *Canna indica* L. (Fam. Cannaceae; vern. keli). Inaperturate, spheroidal (diamete r 68 μ; range 62-71 μ). Ectine and endine not clearly differentiated; columella obscure. Ectine surface spinulate; spinule ends pointed.(Fig. 4C)

4. *Cleome viscosa* Linn. (Fam. Cleomaceae; Vern. Hurhur).

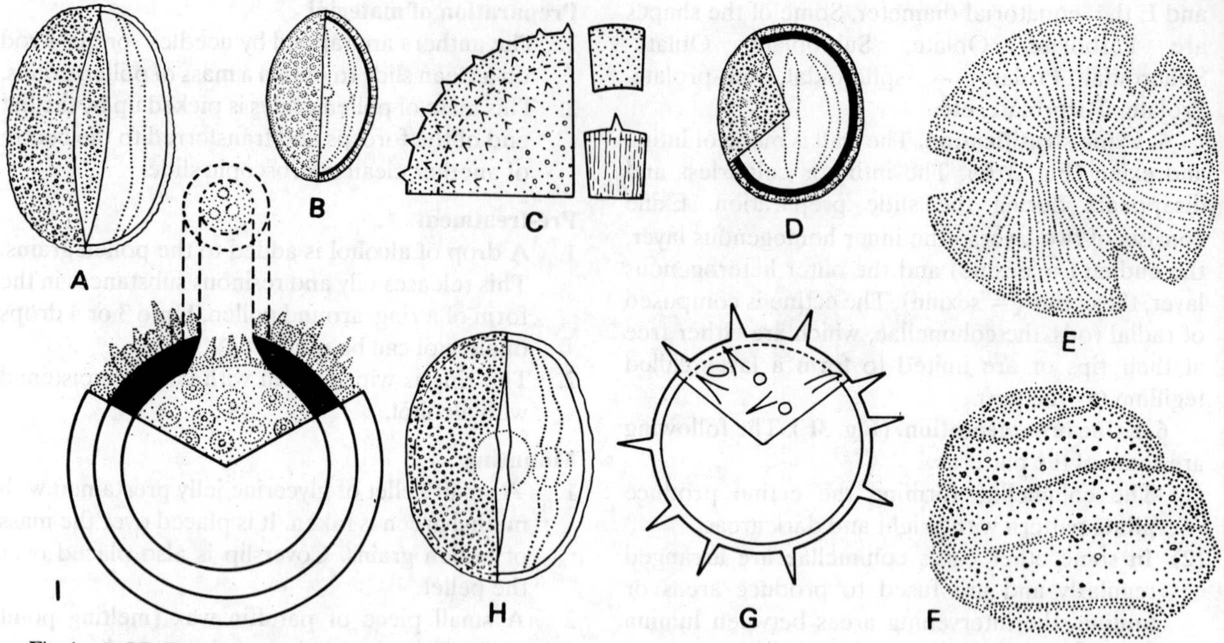

Fig. 4. **A - I Pollen grains** of some common plants. **A.** *Arachis hypogaea*, **B.** *Argemone mexicana*, **C.** *Canna indica*, **D.** *Cleome viscosa*, **E.** *Datura stramonium*, **F.** *Eriocaulon decangulare*, **G.** *Hibiscus esculentus*, **H.** *Lathyrus odoratus*, **I.** *Mirabilis jalapa*.

Grains 3-colporate, prolate (34. 4 x 22; range 33 - 40.7 x 18.5 - 25. 9 μ). Ectine thicker than endine, reticulate (muri distinctly simplibacculate). Colpi almost running from pole to pole, coarsely granulate.

5. *Datura stramonium* Linn. (Fam. Solanaceae, Vern. Dhatura).

Grains 3-zonocolporate, spheroidal, size 46 x 47μ (range 43-49 x 43- 52 μ). Colpi short, tips acute, Ectine thicker than endine, tegillate. Exine surface striated, in some reticulate.(Fig. 4E)

6. *Eriocaulon decangulare* Linn. (Fam. Eriocaulaceae)

Spiraperturate (pantoaperturate), size 32 μ (range at aperture margins). Endine very thin. Ectine surface spinulose. Spinules minute and sparse (Fig. 4F)

7. *Hibiscus esculentus* Linn. (Fam. Malvaceae, Vern. Bhindi) (Fig. 4G)

Grains pantoporate, spheroidal, pore size 10μ, surface spiniferous, interspinal areas reticulate.

8. *Lathyrus odoratus* Linn. (Fam. Papilionaceae; Eng. Sweet Pea)

Grains 3-zonocolporate, subprolate (37-44 x 30-33 μ) or prolate, ecto-exine thicker than endo-exine, surface reticulate (Fig. 4H)

9. *Mirabilis jalapa* Linn. (Fam. Nyctaginaceae; Vern. Gulabbas)

Grains pantoporate, spheroidal, diameter 225 μ; (range 162 - 238 μ). Membrane provided with one or few spinules. Ectine thicker than endine, subtegillate, punctate, spionse, spines of various heights(Fig. 4I)

Distribution in aperture classes

1. **Zonocolpate:** *Argemone, Arachis*
2. **Zonocolporate:** *Cleome, Lathyrus*
3. **Zonoporate:** *Datura*
4. **Pantoporate:** *Hibiscus, Mirabilis*
5. **Spiraperturate:** *Eriocaulon*
6. **Inaperturate:** *Canna*

4. Germination of pollen grains

Materials

Anthers of *Antirrhinum* (snap dragon), *Catharanthus roseus* (Periwinkle; Sada bahar), *Papaver somniferum* (Poppy; Afim) or any other easily available plant; sugar, boron, cavity slides, cover slips, microscope, water, etc.

Procedure

1. Prepare 15% sugar solution by dissolving 1.5 gm sugar in 100 ml of water.
2. Add a pinch of boron to sugar solution.
3. Clean the cavity slide and place a drop of this solution in the cavity.

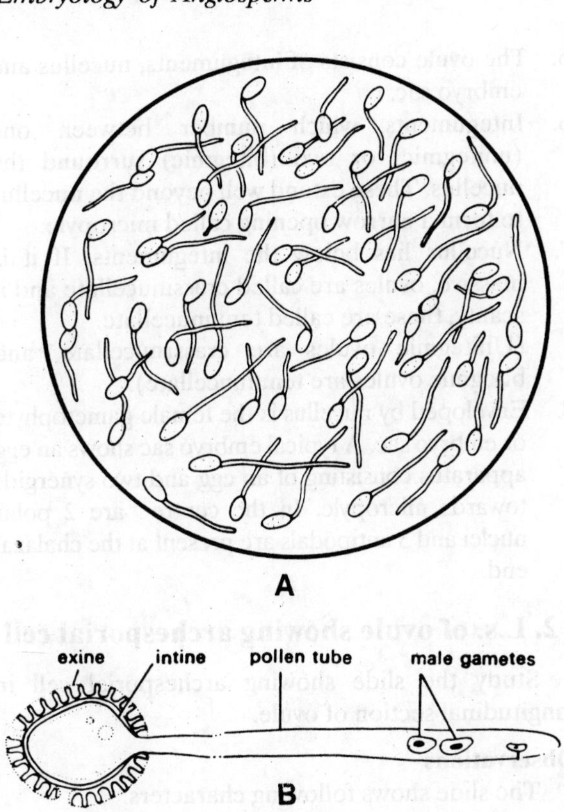

Fig. 5. **Pollen grains.** Germination of pollen grains. A. As seen under the light microscope, B. Details of the structure.

4. Remove mature anthers from fresh flowers. Crush them on a slide. Collect the pollen grains with a brush from the crushed anthers. Dust the brush free of anthers in the cavity filled with solution.
5. Place a cover slip over the cavity.
6. Allow the slide to remain as such for a few hours or overnight.
7. Remove the coverslip slowly and gradually. Mount the coverslip on a fresh and clean slide in a drop of safranin. The lower side of the coverslip with germinated pollen grains should be in contact with safranin.
8. Observe the slide.

Observations

The following characters are observed.

1. Numerous germinated pollen grains are seen.
2. A pollen grain has a distinct ornamented exine with germ pores.
3. Intine lies internal to exine. It is thin and uniform.

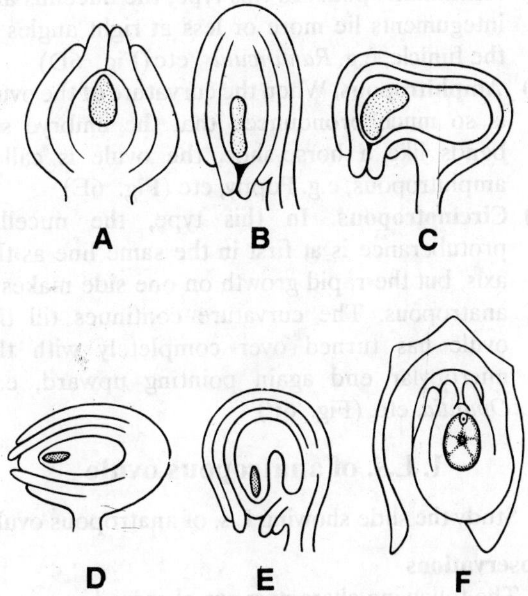

Fig. 6. **Ovule:** Different types of ovules.

4. Intine forms a pollen tube that comes out through one of the germ pores.
5. Pollen tube shows a vegetative nucleus and two small male gametes.

OVULE

Ovule is defined as integumented megasporangium. It encloses embryo sac which is the female gametophyte of angiosperms. Following are the types of ovules.

Types of ovules

(1) **Atropous or Orthotropous.** The ovule is straight, so that the micropyle lies on the same vertical axis with the funicle and chalaza, e.g., *Polygonum, Piper,* etc (Fig. 6A)

(2) **Anatropous.** In this type, the body of the ovule becomes completely inverted, so that the micropyle and hilum come to lie very close to each other. The micropyle and the chalaza lie on the same vertical axis but not funicle, e.g., *Helianthus,* Castor, etc.(Fig. 6B)

(3) **Campylotropous.** When the ovule is curved in such a way, so that the micropyle and chalaza do not lie on the same straight line, it is called campylotropous, e.g. Pea, Mustard, etc.

(4) **Hemianatropous.** In this type, the nucellus and integuments lie more or less at right angles to the funicle, e.g. *Ranunculus,* etc (Fig. 6D)

(5) **Amphitropous.** When the curvature of the ovule is so much pronounced that the embryo sac bends like a horse-shoe, the ovule is called amphitropous, e.g. Poppy, etc.(Fig. 6E)

(6) **Circinotropous.** In this type, the nucellar protuberance is at first in the same line as the axis, but the rapid growth on one side makes it anatropous. The curvature continues till the ovule has turned over completely with the micropylar end again pointing upward, e.g. *Opuntia,* etc. (Fig. 6F)

1. L.s. of anatropous ovule

Study the slide showing L.s. of anatropous ovule.

Observations

The following characters are observed.

1. Anatropous ovule is most common among angiosperms.
2. The ovule is a rounded structure attached to the placenta by a stalk, the funicle. The place of attachment of funicle to the body of the ovule is known as hilum.
3. The basal region of the ovule, where from integuments arise, is known as chalaza.
4. In anatropous ovules, the funicle extends above, along the body of the ovule to form a ridge, known as raphe.

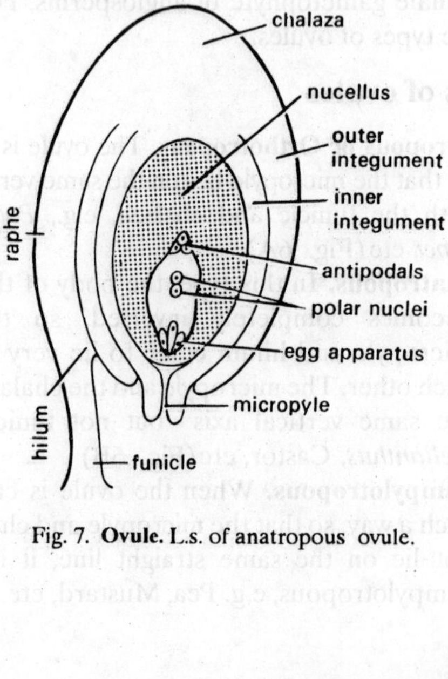

Fig. 7. **Ovule.** L.s. of anatropous ovule.

5. The ovule consists of integuments, nucellus and embryo sac.
6. Integuments which number between one (unitegmic) or two (bitegmic) surround the nucellus. These extend well beyond the nucellus to form a narrow opening called micropyle.
7. Nucellus lies below the integuments. If it is massive, ovules are called crassinucellate and if scanty, these are called tenuinucellate. (Unitegmic ovules are crassinucellate and bitegmic ovules are tenuinucellate).
8. Enveloped by nucellus is the female gametophyte or embryo sac. A typical embryo sac shows an egg apparatus consisting of an egg and two synergids towards micropyle. In the centre are 2 polar nuclei and 3 antipodals are present at the chalazal end.

2. L.s. of ovule showing archesporial cell

Study the slide showing archesporial cell in longitudinal section of ovule.

Observations

The slide shows following characters.

1. The ovule is attached to the placenta with its stalk called funicle.
2. The ovule is poorly differentiated and shows only integuments and nucellus.
3. Archesporial cell originates from nucellar hypodermis.
4. It is identified by its large size, dense cytoplasm and prominent nucleus.
5. Archesporial initial may directly behave as megaspore mother cell or it may cut off some parietal tissue.

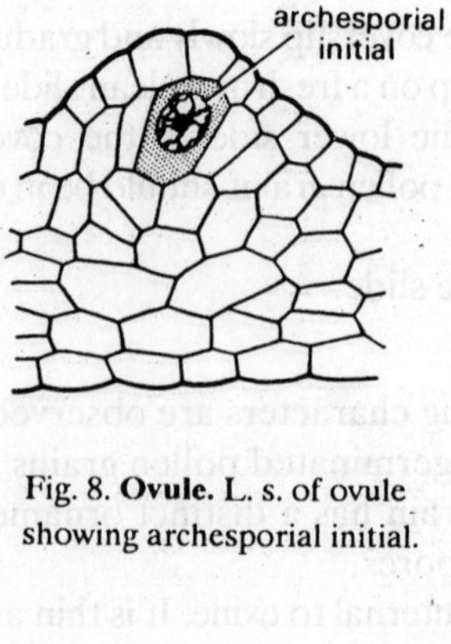

Fig. 8. **Ovule.** L. s. of ovule showing archesporial initial.

3. L.s. of ovule showing megaspore tetrad

Study the slide of longitudinal section of ovule showing megaspore tetrad.

Observations

It shows following characters.

1. The ovule is attached to the placenta by its funicle.
2. The ovule consists of integuments and the nucellus.
3. Outermost are two integuments which cover the ovule.
4. In the nucellus, a few cells below the nucellar epidermis lies a linear tetrad of megaspore.
5. The lowermost or chalazal megaspore is functional while the three upper or micropylar megaspores are non-functional and, therefore, degenerate.
6. The functional megaspore is large in size. The protoplasm is dense and the nucleus is prominent.

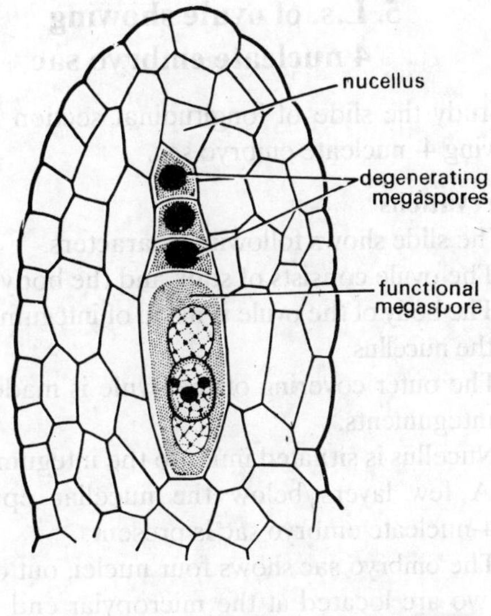

Fig. 9. **Ovule.** L.s. ovule showing megaspore tetrad.

4. L. s. of ovule showing binucleate embryo sac

Study the slide of longitudinal section of ovule showing binucleate embryo sac.

Observations

The slide shows following characters.

1. The ovule is attached to the placenta by a stalk called funicle.
2. The ovule is made of integuments and the nucellus.
3. Outermost part of the ovule is made of two integuments.
4. Inner to the integuments lies nucellus.
5. A few layers below the nucellar epidermis, binucleate embryo sac is situated.
6. At the top of the sac, three degenerating megaspores can still be seen.
7. The embryo sac has two nuclei, one at each pole, separated by a large vacuole.

Fig. 10. **Ovule.** L.s. ovule showing binucleate embryo sac.

5. L.s. of ovule showing 4 nucleate embryo sac

Study the slide of longitudinal section of ovule showing 4- nucleate embryo sac.

Observations

The slide shows following characters.

1. The ovule consists of stalk and the body.
2. The body of the ovule is made of integuments and the nucellus.
3. The outer covering of the ovule is made of two integuments.
4. Nucellus is situated inner to the integuments.
5. A few layers below the nucellar epidermis, 4-nucleate embryo sac is present.
6. The embryo sac shows four nuclei, out of which two are located at the micropylar end and the rest two at the chalazal end.
7. The nuclei at two ends are separated by large vacuole in the centre.

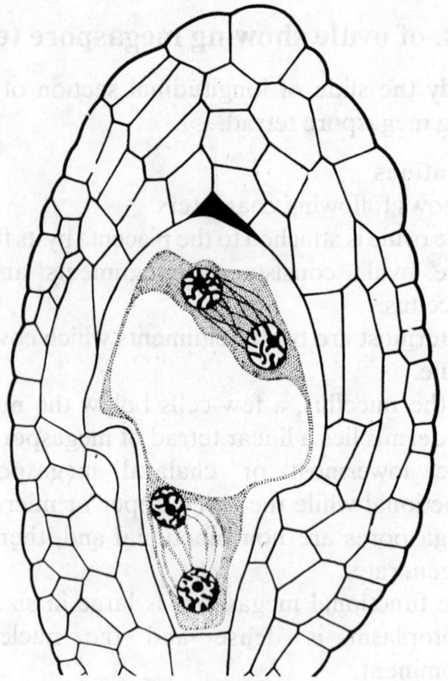

Fig. 11. **Ovule.** L.s. ovule showing 4-nucleate embryo sac.

6. L.s. of ovule showing 8-nucleate polygonum type of embryo sac

Study the slide of longitudinal section of ovule showing 8- nucleate Polygonum type of embryo sac.

Observations

Following characters are observed.

1. The ovule shows stalk and the body.
2. The body consists of integuments, nucellus and the embryo sac.
3. There are two integuments which form the outermost covering of the ovule.
4. A small amount of nucellus is present between the integuments and the embryo sac.
5. Embryo sac is present deep into the tissue of nucellus.
6. Organised 8-nucleate Polygonum-type embryo sac has an egg apparatus, two polar nuclei and three antipodals.
7. Egg apparatus is situated at the micropylar end. It consists of centrally placed egg cell with two synergids, one on each side of the egg.
8. An egg cell has a large vacuole towards its micropylar end while synergids have a small vacuole toward its chalazal end.
9. Each synergid has a beak-like structure on its lateral side and filiform apparatus at its micropylar end.

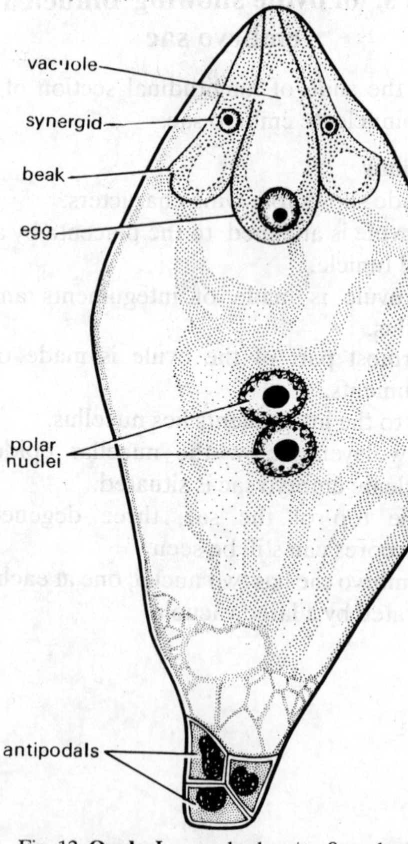

Fig. 12. **Ovule.** L.s. ovule showing 8-nucleate polygonum-type embryo sac.

10. Two polar nuclei are located in the centre of the embryo sac. These later fuse to form the secondary nucleus.
11. Three antipodal cells are located at the chalazal end. These degenerate soon, either before or just after fertilization.
12. Since this embryo sac develops from a single megaspore, it is known as monosporic, 8-nucleate Polygonum-type embryo sac.

ENDOSPERM

Endosperm, in angiosperms provides nutrition to the developing embryo. It is formed as a result of divisions of the primary endosperm nucleus, which is triploid.

The primary endosperm nucleus (3n) is formed due to the fusion of second male gamete (n) with the two polar nuclei (n and n) or their fusion product, the secondary nucleus (2n). Thus, the endosperm, in angiosperms, is a triploid tissue formed after fertilization.

On the basis of development, the endosperm is divided into 3 types. Type of endosperm is determined by the behaviour of first and subsequent divisions of primary endosperm nucleus. In quite advanced stage of development, all the types endosperms become cellular.

1. L.s. of ovule showing nuclear endosperm

Study the slide of longitudinal section of ovule and observe the endosperm.

Observations

It shows following characters.

1. The ovule is made of stalk and the body.
2. The body consists of integuments, nucellus, embryo and the endosperm.
3. There are two integuments which form the outermost covering of ovule.
4. A small amount of nucellus lies inner to integuments.
5. The major and the central part of ovule is occupied by a large amount of endosperm. It surrounds a small embryo present near the micropylar end.
6. The endosperm is nuclear endosperm. In this type the primary endosperm nucleus divides amitotically to form many free nuclei. The division of the nucleus is not followed by wall formation. This type of division is also known as free nuclear division.
7. Many free nuclei formed by this method lie towards the periphery in the cytoplasm.

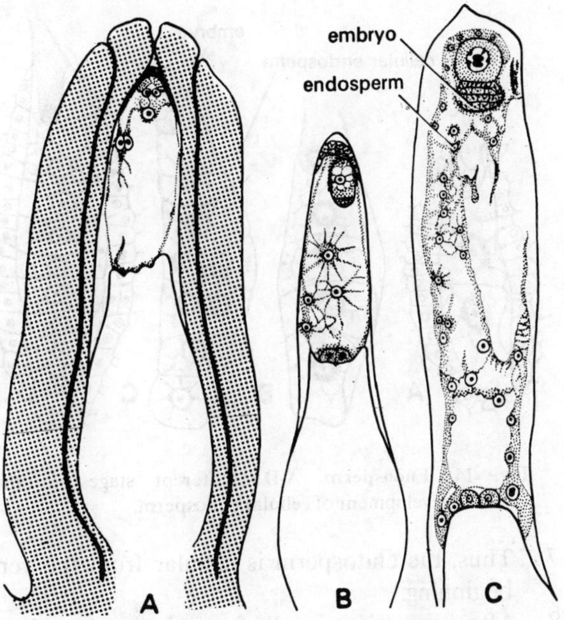

Fig. 13. **Endosperm. A.** to **C.** Different stages in the development of nuclear endosperm.

2. L.s. of ovule showing cellular endosperm

Study the slide of longitudinal section of ovule and observe the endosperm.

Observations

It shows the following characters.

1. The ovule is made of stalk and the body.
2. The body consists of integuments, nucellus, embryo and the endosperm.
3. There are two integuments which form the outermost covering of the ovule.
4. A small amount of nucellus lies inner to integuments.
5. Most of the central region of ovule is filled with cellular endosperm.
6. In this type of endosperm formation, the first and subsequent divisions of the primary endosperm nucleus are followed by wall formation.

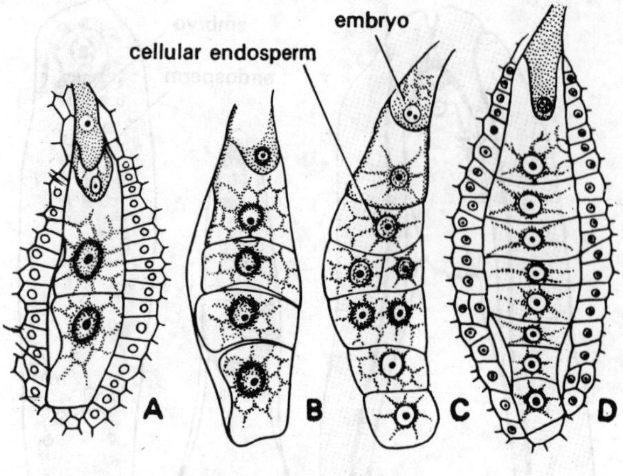

Fig. 14. **Endosperm. A-D.** Different stages in the development of cellular endosperm.

7. Thus, the endosperm is cellular from the very beginning.
8. After sometime, wall formation starts from periphery towards centre and ultimately the whole endosperm becomes cellular.

3. L.s. of ovule showing helobial endosperm

Study the slide of longitudinal section of ovule and observe the following characters.

Observations

The following characters are seen.

1. The ovule shows stalk and the body.
2. The body consists integuments, nucellus, zygote and the endosperm.
3. There are two integuments which form the outermost covering of the ovule.
4. Endosperm is present in the central part of the ovule and occupies a very large part.
5. It shows helobial endosperm which is intermediate between nuclear and cellular type.
6. It is named as helobial after the tribe Helobiae (monocots) where it is predominently found.
7. After the first division of the primary endosperm nucleus, a transverse wall is formed. Thus, the embryo sac is divided into two chambers, the micropylar chamber and the chalazal chamber.
8. Later on, free-nuclear divisions take place in both the chambers.

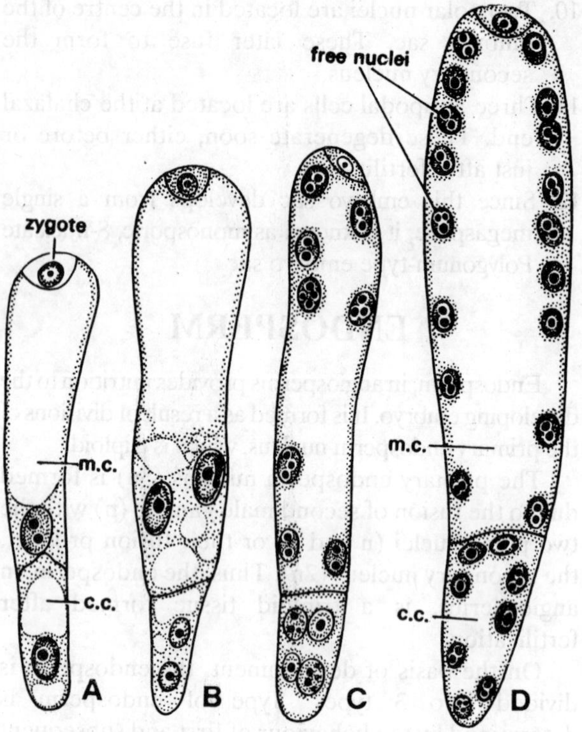

Fig. 15. **Endosperm. A-D.** Different stages in the development of Helobial endosperm.

EMBRYO

After fertilization i.e. fusion between male gamete and the female gamete, a series of changes occur in the ovule resulting in the formation of seed. The seed is, therefore, a fertilized ovule, consisting of seed coat and an embryo. There may also be remnant part of nucellus called perisperm and also the endosperm. Embryo consists of suspensor situated near the micropyle, cotyledons towards chalaza and a small embryonal axis called tigellum.

Dissection of embryo

Seeds of mustard, *Petunia* tomata, etc. are used to dissect out the embryo.

The following is the procedure.

1. Place the seed on the stage of dissecting microscope or binocular.
2. Locate the micropyle which appears like a small opening.

3 Remove the seed coat from this point, carefully with the help two sharply pointed needles.
4. Once the seed coat is removed, embryo could be seen clearly between the cotyledons.
5. Place this embryo on a slide in a drop of water and study the structure.

1. To dissect out globular embryo

Take a very small sized seed e.g. mustard. Locate the micropyle and remove the seed coat. A small embryo can be seen under the microscope.

Observations

It shows following characters.

1. Globular embryo consists of a suspensor and a globular mass of 16 cells.
2. The suspensor is a uniseriate (single) row of 8-10 (more) cells.
3. The uppermost cell of the suspensor is slightly swollen and is known as vesicular cell.
4. The lowermost cell of the suspensor is the hypophysis. It contributes to the formation of root.
5. The globular mass of 16 cells is the embryo itself. Of these, 8 outer cells form the dermatogen and the 8 inner cells form periblem and plerome.

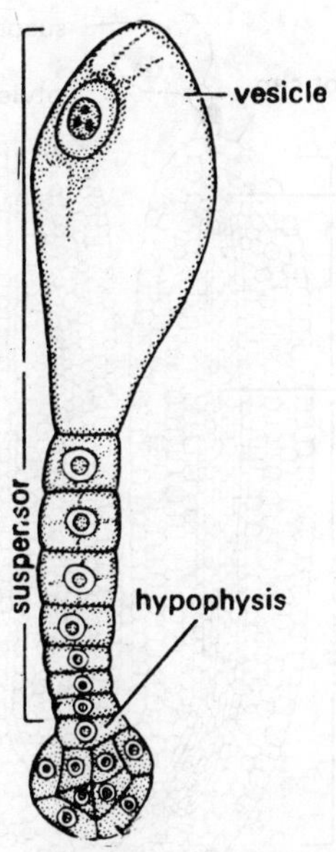

Fig. 16. **Embryo.** Globular embryo.

2. To dissect out heart-shaped embryo

Take a small seed of mustard. Locate the micropyle under the dissecting microscope. Remove the seed coat starting from this point. A small white to yellowish coloured embryo can be seen under the microscope.

Observations

It shows following characters.

1. Heart-shaped embryo consists of a suspensor and a heart-shaped mass of cells.
2. The suspensor is a row of cells arranged in a single series.
3. The uppermost cell of suspensor lies closer to micropyle. It is swollen and is known as vesicular cell.
4. The lowermost cell of suspensor lies close to the embryo proper. It is known as hypophysis.
5. Heart-shaped embryo is formed as a result of cell divisions in globular embryo at places where cotyledons develop.

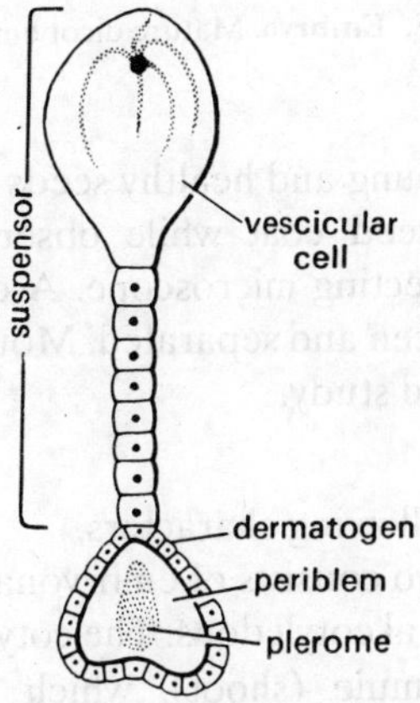

Fig. 17. **Embryo. Heart shaped embryo.**

6. Heart-shaped embryo is differentiated into outer dermatogen, middle periblem and innermost plerome.

3. To remove mature dicot embryo

Crucifer embryo is typical of dicotyledons. *Capsella bursa- pastoris* is the commonest example. However, mustard seeds would equally be useful.

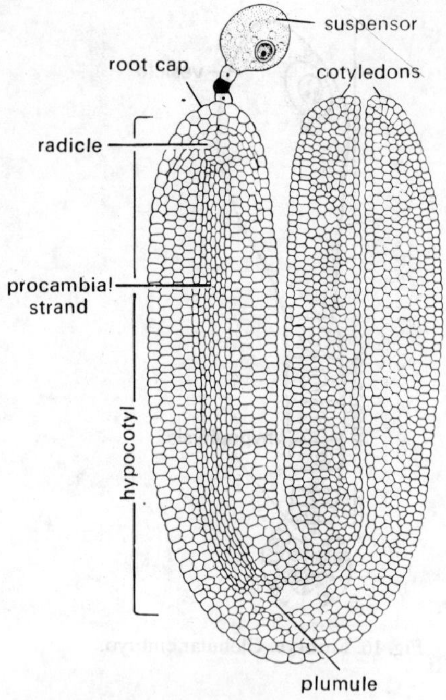

Fig. 18. **Embryo.** Mature dicot embryo.

Procedure

Take out young and healthy seeds from the fruit. Remove the seed coat while observing the seed under the dissecting microscope. A curved embryo can be easily seen and separated. Mount the embryo in glycerine and study.

Observations

It shows following characters.

1. The embryo consists of embryonal axis with two large lateral cotyledons. The cotyledons cover a small plumule (shoot), which is terminal in position.
2. At the other end is the swollen suspensor.
3. The portion of embryonal axis which is above the level of cotyledons is called epicotyl and the portion below the level of cotyledons is called the hypocotyl.
4. The epicotyl forms the plumule (embryonic shoot) and lower end of hypocotyl forms the radicle (embryonic root).
5. In the hypocotyl region, the central cells become somewhat elongated and form the procambial strand.
6. The pronounced curvature of the cotyledons is due to their own enlargement and also of the hypocotyl.

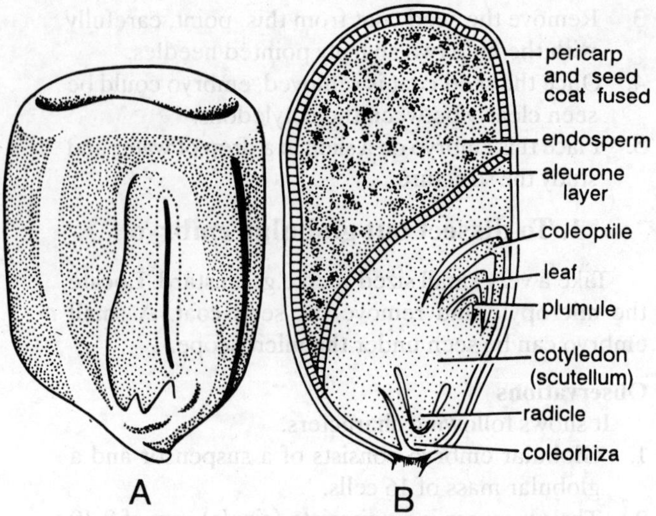

Fig. 19. **Embryo.** L.s. of maize grain showing monocot embryo.

4. L. s. of maize grain showing monocot embryo

Study the slide of longitudinal section of monocot (maize) seed.

Observations

It shows following characters.

1. It is a fruit-caryopsis where fruit wall is fused with seed coat. The grain consists of seed coat, fruit wall, endosperm, cotyledon, plumule and radicle.
2. Outermost covering is made of seed coat and fruit wall fused together.
3. The grain shows two regions-the larger portion is endosperm and the smaller portion is embryo.
4. The endosperm is a nutritive tissue which stores large amount of starch. It is separated from the embryo by epithelial layer.
5. The embryo consists of
   (a) shield shaped cotyledon called scutellum and
   (b) the embryonal axis.
6. In the grass family, cotyledon is known as scutellum. It absorbs food material from the endosperm which is supplied to the growing embryo.
7. The embryonal axis consists of plumule and the radicle.
8. Plumule is lateral in position and is surrounded by a leaf- sheath called coleoptile.
9. Radicle is surrounded by a root-sheath called coleorhiza.

6

Anatomy

The plants are made of organs. There are only three fundamental organs – stem, root and leaves. All these organs are made of tissue systems. These are the groups of different types of tissues but perform only one function. The tissues constituting the tissue system are derived from meristematic tissues. These are situated only at a few places called meristems. There are various types of meristems. One of these is the shoot apical meristem. It is responsible for growth of plant in length and the formation of primary permanent tissues. Another type of meristematic tissue is the cambium. It produces secondary permanent tissues which increase girth of the plants.

The tissues are classified into two major groups- simple tissues and the complex tissues. The simple tissues are made of only one type cells. These include parenchyma, sclerenchyma, collenchyma, etc. The complex tissues are made of more than one type of cells. Complex tissues include xylem and phloem. The xylem consists of cell types such as tracheids, vessels, xylem fibres and xylem parenchyma. The phloem is composed of sieve cells, sieve tubes, companion cells, phloem fibres and phloem parenchyma.

Groups of some of these different types of tissues together perform a common function and are called tissue system. There are three tissue systems- epidermal tissue system, ground or fundamental tissue system and vascular tissue system.

Each plant organ shows a typical organization of these three tissue systems. These are so characteristic that it is possible to distinguish one organ from the other.

The primary organization of a plant is due to activity of shoot apical organization and general structural pattern of an organ remains basically similar in all types of plants.

In dicotyledons, the stem and the root both grow once again after the plant acquires primary structure. This growth is known as secondary growth. It occurs due to the activity of a secondary meristem that occupies the lateral position the i. e. vascular cambium. The plants become woody and the girth increases. The tissues added by the vascular cambium are secondary xylem (wood) and secondary phloem.

I. Meristems

There are two major types of meristems which can be studied. These include shoot apical meristem and root apical meristem. The organization of meristems shows regions contributing to the formation of different parts of the plant body.

Work to be done

[I] Study the slide showing L.s. of the shoot apex.
[II] Study the slide showing L. s. of the root apex.

Practical Work and study

[I] Study of the slide showing L.s. of the shoot apex

1. The stem apex or the shoot apex is hemispherical to slightly flattened in longitudinal plane.
2. It remains protected by the covering of young and developing leaves.
3. The shoot apex shows an apical promeristem. It consists of tunica and corpus.
4. Tunica is the outermost covering. It is one to two layered. The cells of the tunica divide in anticlinal plane and increase surface area of the shoot apex.
5. Corpus is the mass of randomly dividing cells. It lies immediately below the tunica. Sometimes the initial layer of the corpus gets regularly arranged and appears similar to tunica.
6. In the centre, just below the corpus; is present rib meristem. The cells of this region are arranged in regular files. This region gives rise to pith.

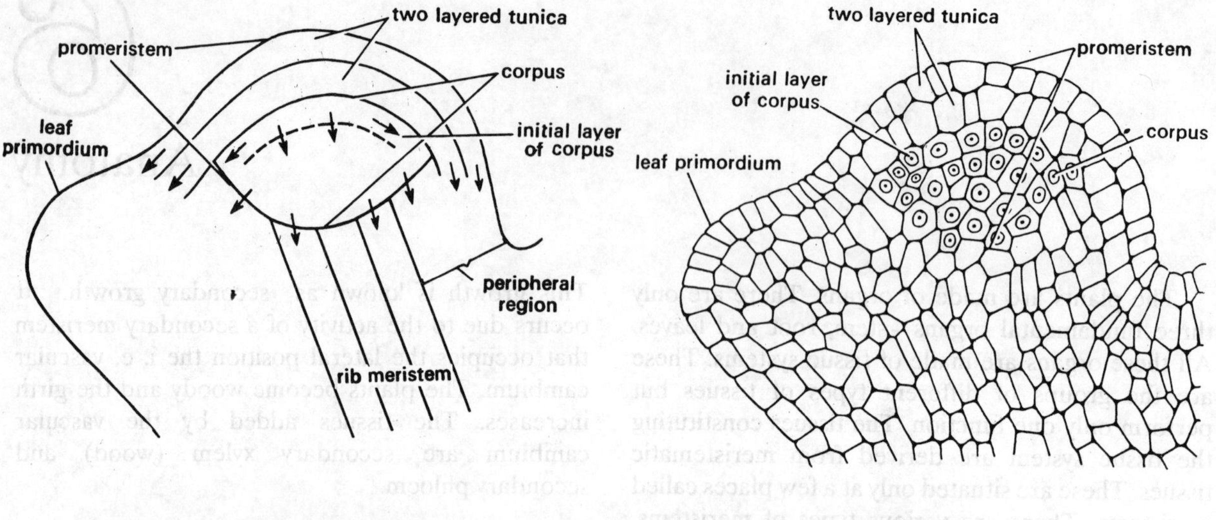

Fig. 1. L.s. shoot apex, A. Outlines showing major regions, B. Cellular details.

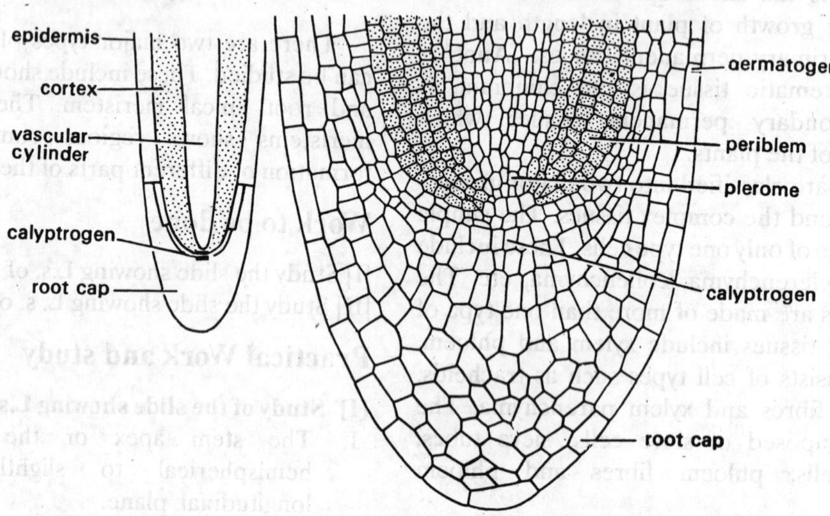

Fig. 2. L.s. root apex, A. Outlines showing major regions, B. Cellular details.

7. Near the periphery, surrounding the rib meristem lies the peripheral or flank meristem. This region shows actively dividing cells and lateral organs like leaf and branches arise from these cells.

[II] Study of the slide showing L. s. of the root apex

1. The longitudinal section of the root apex appears gradually tapering.
2. It is the terminal portion of the root covered by root cap.
3. Calyptrogen follows root cap and lies closer to the root apex. It gives rise to the tissue of the root cap.
4. Inside the calyptrogen lies the root apex which is subterminal in position. The cells in this region are actively dividing and contribute to the tissues of the root.
5. Three regions based on structure and growth of the root apex are recognised. These are plerome, periblem and dermatogen.
6. Dermatogen is single layered. It gives rise to the outermost layer or epiblema.
7. Periblem is single layered at the apex and becomes many layered higher up. It forms middle region or the cortex of the root.

8. Plerome gives rise to pericycle, medullary or pith rays, pith and the vascular bundles. Some procambial strands give rise to bundles of xylem and others to the bundles of phloem in an alternating manner.

II. Cells and Tissues

Tissue is a group of cells which may be similar or (simple tissue) or dissimilar in character (complex tissue) and is specialised for a particular function. Characteristics functions and distribution of some of these plant tissues are given below.

***Table 1.* Characteristic features, functions and distribution of plant tissues.**

Tissue	Living or dead	Wall Material	Cell Shape	Main Functions	Distribution
1. Parenchyma	Living	Cellulose, pectins and hemicelluloses	Usually isodiametric, sometimes elongated	Packing tissue. Support in herbaceous plants. Metabolically active. Intercellular air spaces allow gaseous exchange. Food storage. Transport of materials through cells or cell walls.	Cortex, pith, medullary rays and packing tissue in xylem and phloem.
2. Modified parenchyma					
(a) Epidermis	Living	Cellulose, pectins and hemicelluloses, and covering of cutin	Elongated and flattened	Protection from desiccation and infection. Hairs and glands may have additional functions.	Single layer of cells covering entire primary plant body.
(b) Mesophyll	Living	Cellulose, pectins and hemicelluloses	Isodiametric chlorenchyma, irregular or column-shaped depending on location	Photosynthesis (contains chloroplasts). Storage of starch.	Between upper and lower epidermis of leaves.
(c) Endodermis	Living	Cellulose, pectins and hemicellouloses, and deposits of suberin (Casparian strips)	As epidermis	Selective barrier to movement of water and mineral salts (between cortex and xylem) in roots. Starch sheath with possible role in geotropic response in stems.	Around vascular tissue. (innermost layer of cortex)
(d) Pericycle	Living	Cellulose, pectins and hemicelluloses	As parenchyma	In roots, it retains meristematic activity producing lateral roots and contributing to secondary growth if this occurs.	In roots between central vascular tissue and endodermis.
3.Collenchyma	Living	Cellulose, pectins and hemicelluloses	Elongated and polygonal with tapering ends	Support (a mechanical function).	Outer regions of cortex, e.g. angles of stems, midrib of leaves.
4. Sclerenchyma					
(a) Fibres	Dead	Mainly lignin. Cellulose, pectins and hemi-celluloses also present.	Elongated and polygonal with tapering interlocking ends.	Support (purely mechanical).	Outer regions of cortex, pericycle of stems, xylem and phloem
(b)Sclereids	Dead	As fibres	Roughly isodiametric, though variations occur	Support or mechanical protection	Cortex, pith, phloem, shells and stones of fruits, seed coats.

5. Xylem. Mixture fo living and dead cells. Xylem also contains fibres and parenchyma.					
(a) Tracheids.	Dead	Mainly lignin. Cellulose, pectins and hemicelluloses also present.	Elongated and tubular	Translocation of water and mineral salts. Support.	Vascular system
(b) Vessels.	Dead	Mainly lignin. Cellulose, pectins and hemicelluloses also present	Elongated but broad and cylindrical	Translocation of water and mineral salts. Support	Vascular system
5. Phloem. Mixture of living and dead cells. Phloem also contains fibres and sclereids.					
(a) Sieve tubes.	Living	Cellulose, pectins and hemicelluloses.	Elongated and tubular	Translocation of organic solutes (food)	Vascular system
(b) Companion cells.	Living	Cellulose, pectins and hemicelluloses.	Elongated and narrow	Work in association with sieve tubes	Vascular system

Work to be done

Maceration of various materials to study
[I] Parenchyma
[II] Collenchyma
[III] Sclerenchymatous fibres
[IV] Stone cells or sclereids
[V] Tracheids
[VI] Vessels

Practical work and study

Some of the types of cells can be studied individually by separating them from one another by a process called **maceration.** This process has been described on pages 8 and 9 of the 1st chapter ***Introduction to Laboratory.*** However, Schuttze's method which is most convenient and quick is repeated for the benefit of students.

1. Materials. The following is the list of materials recommended for use in maceration to study different types of cells.

(a) Parenchyma. Young stem of *Cucurbita*, pea, gram, marigold or any herbaceous plant.

(b) Collenchyma. The midrib of a young leaf of *Cucurbita* or any other dicotyledon.

(c) Sclerenchyma. Stem of *Xanthium,* sunflower, maize, *Pinus,* etc.

(d) Stone cells. Bark of a plant or pulp of pear.

(e) Xylem and phloem. Stem of *Cucurbita, Xanthium,* sunflower, etc.

(f) Tracheids and pits. Secondary xylem or wood of *Pinus,* match sticks or match boxes, etc.

2. The Technique. Schultze's method of maceration consists of following steps.

1. Cut the desired material into small pieces.
2. Place them in a test tube filled with water and boil for about 5 minutes.
3. Pour off the water. Fill the test tube with sufficient amount of concentrated nitric acid. Add a few crystals of potassium chlorate.
4. The tube is heated slowly over the spirit lamp. The acid is brought to boil gradually with care.
5. Careful boiling is continued till the material is bleached white.
6. The acid is drained out. The tube is filled with water again for washing the material. The care is taken not to allow the bleached material to come out of the test tube.
7. The material is now transferred to a slide and teased with needles or crushed with glass rod till individual cells get isolated. This can be ensured by observing the material under microscope.

3. The staining and mounting. Once the cells are separated, these are stained and a slide is prepared.

1. A small amount of macerated material is placed on a clean slide.
2. A drop of safranin is poured on the material. The slide is allowed to remain as such for a few minutes so that material takes up the stain.
3. Drop of stain is now drained off and a few drops off water are placed on the material to wash off excess of stain. This is done carefully so that isolated cells too are not drained away.
4. After a few washes of water, a drop of glycerine is placed on the material and coverslip is mounted.

4. The observations. Mostly sclerenchyma and tracheary elements get isolated and are seen clearly. The description of all the major types of cells given below is for convenience.

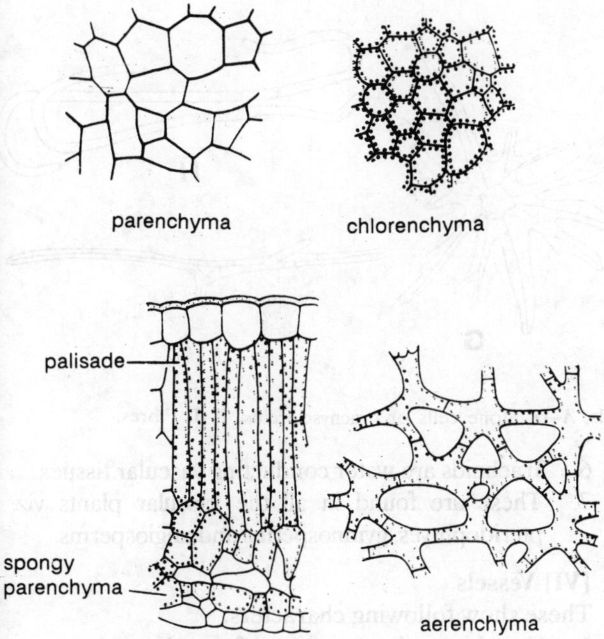

Fig. 3. Different types of parenchyma.

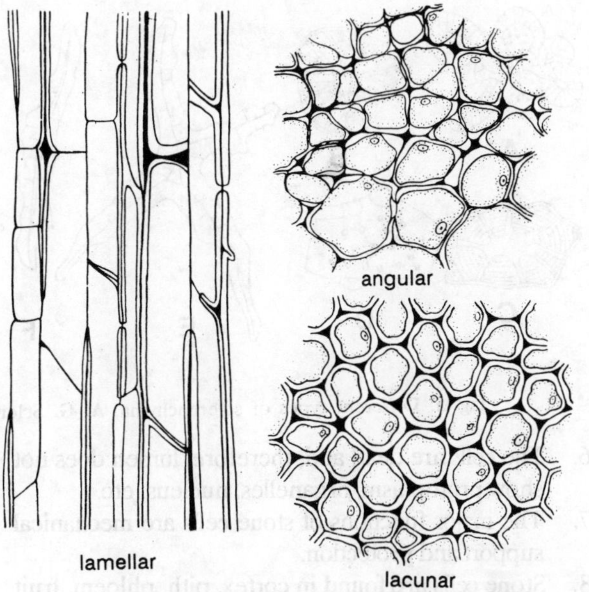

Fig. 4. Different types of collenchyma.

[I] Parenchyma

It shows following characters.

1. The cells are nearly isodiametric.
2. The cell walls are thin. These are made of cellulose, hemicellulose and pectic substances.
3. Parenchymatous cells are living and, therefore, contain cytoplasunic organelles and a nucleus.
4. These generally act as storage tissue and hence reserve foods are present.
5. Parenchyma forms a major part of the cortex and pith of roots and stems.

[II] Collenchyma

It shows following characters.

1. The cell shape varies from isodiametric to elongated.
2. The cell walls are unevenly thickened. The walls are made of cellulose, pectic and other wall substances but no lignin.
3. If the thickening occurs in the corners, these are called angular collenchyma. In some other cells, the thickening appears on the tangential walls. This type is called lamellar collenchyma.
4. Collenchymatous cells retain active protoplast at maturity and are capable of further growth and division.
5. Collenchyma performs both mechanical and vital functions. The cells are relatively soft and pliable and hence form a major mechanical tissue of herbs.

[III] Sclerenchymatous fibres

These show following characters.

1. Sclerenchymatous fibre is a long and thick cell, many times longer than broad.
2. The ends of the fibres taper into sharp points.
3. The cell walls are mainly made of lignin. Cellulose, pectins and hemicelluloses are also present.
4. The thick walls show many slit-like pits. Even bordered pits may be present.
5. The lumen or cell cavity is very narrow. There is no protoplasm, the cell being dead.
6. The fibres are mostly unicellular but may also be multicellular.

[IV] Stone cells or brachysclereids

These show following characters.

1. The cells are isodiametric or irregular in shape.
2. The secondary walls are very thick being highly lignified. Lignin occurs in concentric layers almost parallel to one another.
3. The primary cell wall is made of celluloses, hemicelluloses and pectins.
4. The lumen or cell cavity is very narrow.
5. The wall shows simple openings or pits.

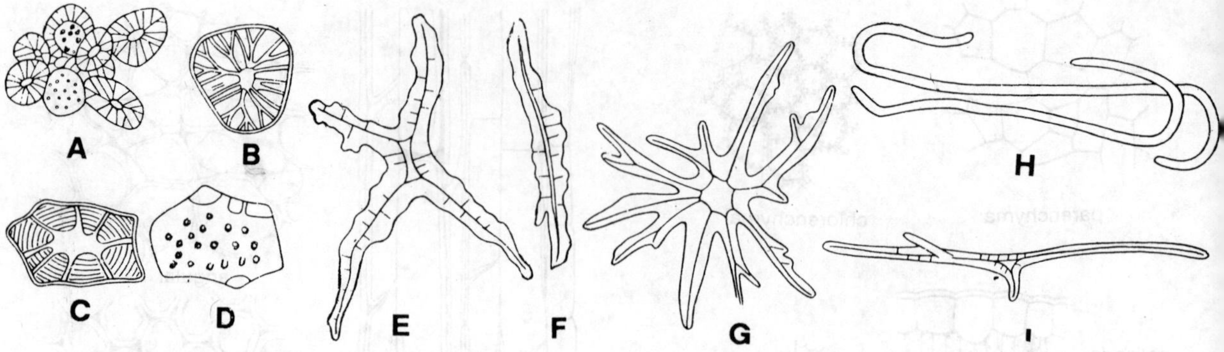

Fig. 5. Different types of sclerenchyma. **A.–G.** Sclereids, **A–D.** Stone cells or brachysclereids, **H–I.** Fibres.

6. The cells are dead and, therefore, lumen does not show protoplasm, organelles, nucleus, etc.
7. The major functions of stone cells are mechanical support and protection.
8. Stone cells are found in cortex, pith, phloem, fruit walls, seed coats, etc.

[V] Tracheids

1. These are narrow, elongated and tubular cells.
2. The primary cell wall deposits are cellulose, hemicellulose and pectins. The thick secondary wall is made of lignin.
3. Lignin deposition occurs in different forms viz. annular, spiral, scalariform, reliculate and pitted.
4. The cells are dead and are without any protoplasnic contents.
5. The ends of tracheids are narrow and tapering. The end walls are intact and the contact with the neighbouring tracheids is made through the common pits.
6. Tracheids are water conducting vascular tissues.
7. These are found in all the vascular plants viz. pteridophtyes, gymnosperms and angiosperms.

[VI] Vessels

These show following characters.

1. Vessel is made of a series of vessel members.
2. Vessel member is a more or less elongated cell, non-living at maturity. The secondary wall is highly lignified.
3. The end walls show variety of perforations. The perforated part of the end wall is called the perforation plate.
4. The secondary walls are pitted. The pits may be either simple or bordered pits may be present. The arrangement of pits varies from species to species.
5. The pits may be arranged in a single row (uniseriate) or may be present in two or more rows (multiseriate). The adjacent vessel members show common pit pairs.

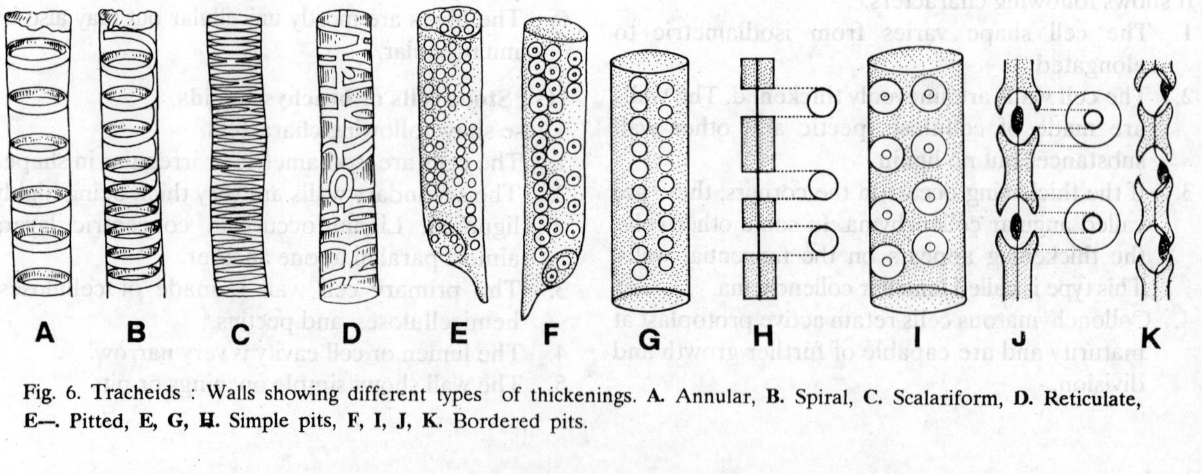

Fig. 6. Tracheids : Walls showing different types of thickenings. **A.** Annular, **B.** Spiral, **C.** Scalariform, **D.** Reticulate, **E–.** Pitted, **E, G, H.** Simple pits, **F, I, J, K.** Bordered pits.

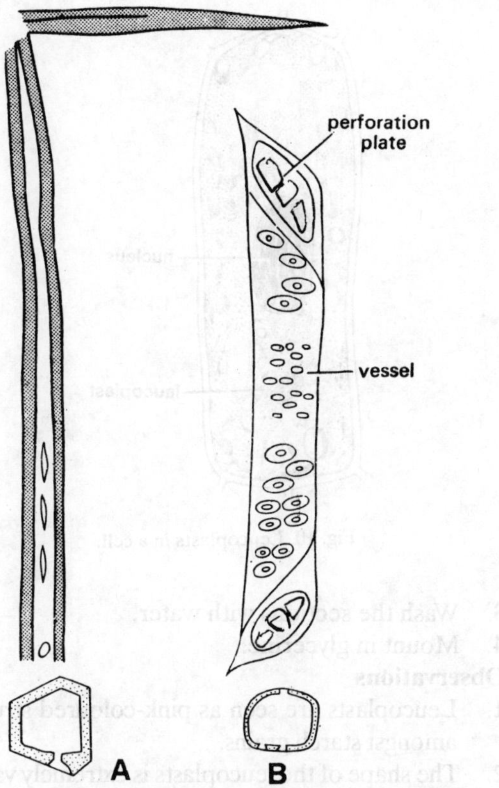

Fig. 7. Vessels. A. Vessel with a simple perforation plate, B. Vessel with multiperforate plate.

III.Cell Components

The cell is a unit of structure and function of an organism. It is made of three major parts-cell wall, protoplasm and vacuole. Protoplasm is the physical basis of life. It is further made of cytoplasm and nucleus. There are many organelles in the cytoplasm. Some of these take active part in the metabolic activities of the cell e.g. chloroplasts, mitochondria, golgi bodies. etc. These are known as protoplasmic inclusions. The other types are the reserve products or waste materials formed during activities of the cell, such as starch grains, aleurone grains, etc.

Work to be done

This part of the book includes the study of

[I] Chloroplasts
[II] Chromoplasts
[III] Leucoplasts
[IV] Starch grains
[V] Aleurone grains
[VI] Inulin
[VII] Raphides
[VIII] Cystolith

Practical work and study

Exercise 1

Purpose : To study chloroplasts.

Materials

Leaves of *Funaria* (moss), slides, coverslips, mircoscope, water, (leaves of spinach can also be successfully used to observe chloroplasts), etc.

Method

Separate the young leaves from the moss plant. Mount in water and study under the microscope.

Observations

1. Discoid or oval-flattened chloroplasts can be seen close to the cell wall.
2. Chloroplasts are green in colour due to the abundance of photosynthetic pigment-the chlorophyll.
3. Other pigments present in the chloroplast include xanthophylls and carotenes.
4. Chloroplasts are the seats of photosynthesis and therefore, end product in the form of starch grains is also seen.

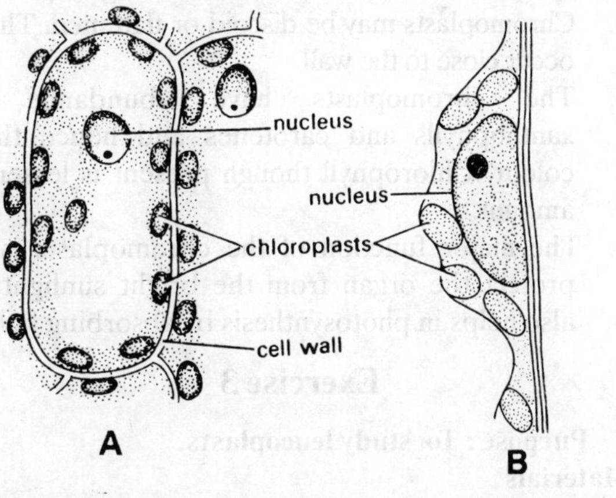

Fig. 8. Chloroplasts. A. Position in the cell. B. A part enlarged.

Exercise 2

Purpose : To study the chromoplasts

Materials

Fruits of tomato, slides, coverslips, microscope, water, etc.

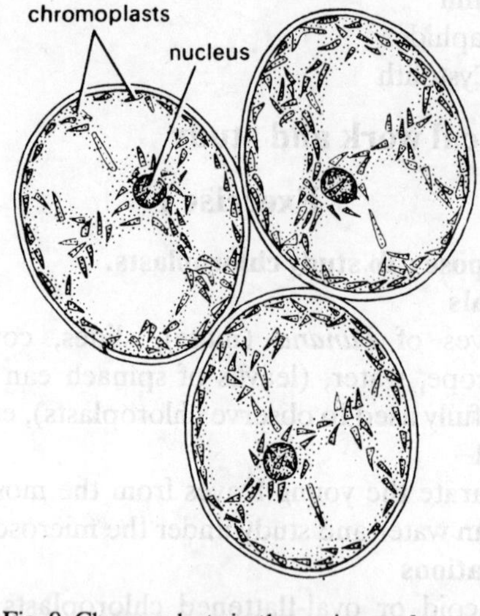

Fig. 9. Chromoplasts in the pericarp of tomato.

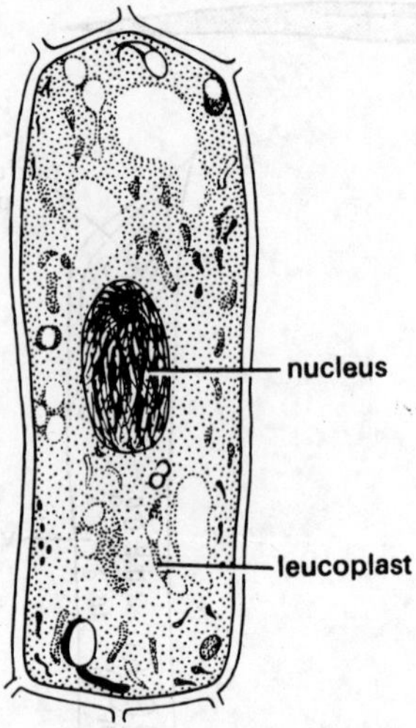

Fig. 10. Leucoplasts in a cell.

Method

Peel off a part of fruit wall with a small amount of pulp attached to it. Mount in a drop of water and observe under the microscope.

Observations

1. The cells are filled with numerous orange or red coloured chromoplasts.
2. In ripe fruits chromoplasts occur in groups.
3. Chromoplasts may be discoid or flattened. These occur close to the wall.
4. The chromoplasts have abundance of xanthophylls and carotenes and hence their colour. Chlorophyll though present is lesser in amount.
5. The major function of the chromoplasts is to protect the organ from the bright sunlight. It also helps in photosynthesis by absorbing light.

Exercise 3

Purpose : To study leucoplasts.

Materials

Potato tuber, slides, coverslips, microscope, acid fuchsin, glycerine, water, etc.

Method

1. Cut thin sections of potato tuber.
2. Place them in a watch glass containing 1% aqueous solution of acid fuchsin. Cover the watch glass with another but larger watch glass. Allow the sections to take stain for at least 3-4 hours.
3. Wash the sections with water.
4. Mount in glycerine.

Observations

1. Leucoplasts are seen as pink-coloured structures amongst starch grains.
2. The shape of the leucoplasts is extremely variable.
3. It is filled with numerous starch grains.
4. Leucoplasts are the storage plastids which generally store starch.

Exercise 4

Purpose : To study starch grains.

Materials

Potato tuber, seeds of pea, slides, coverslip, microscope, Iodine solution, glycerine, etc.

Method

1. Cut a thin sction of potato tuber or seed of pea.
2. Place the section on a slide and stain it with a drop of iodine.
3. Wash the section by pouring water and draining it off. Repeat till excess stain is washed off.
4. Mount the section on another clean slide using glycerine as a mounting medium.

Observations

1. Each starch grain has a hilum which is a point of origin of starch deposition.
2. Starch is deposited in layers around hilum.
3. In the starch grains of pea, hilum is located in the centre and the layers of starch are uniformly deposited around it. These starch grains are

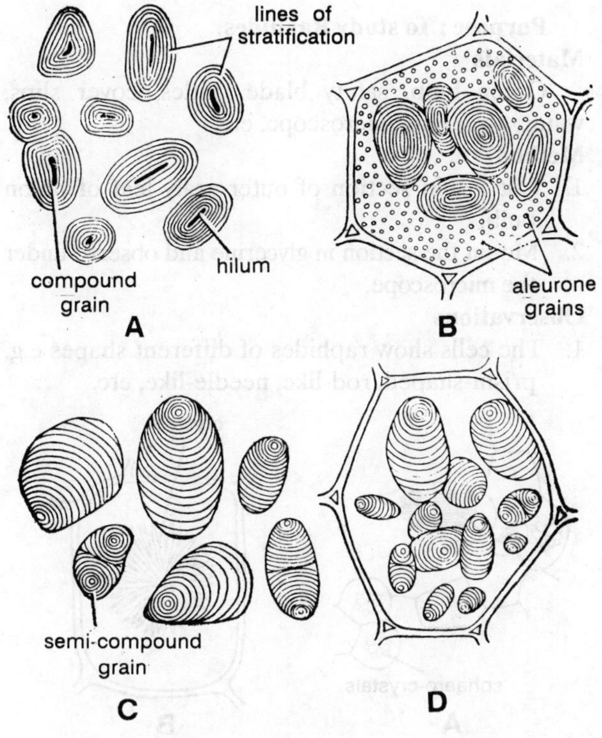

Fig. 11. Starch grains. **A.** and **B.** Starch grains in cotyledons of pea, **C.** and **D.** Starch grains in potato tuber.

called concentric and simple. Sometimes two or more starch grains get attached to one another. Such starch grains are called concentric and compound.

4. In the starch grains of potato, hilum is located in one corner and layers of starch are dposited eccentrically around it. Such starch grains are eccentric and simple. Sometimes two or more starch grains remain attached to one another. Such starch grains are called eccentric and compound.
5. The starch grains are characteristic of a particular plant and can be easily identified. The characters of starch grains of some of the common plants are listed below.

(a) Grains of wheat – simple, concentric, spherical and flattened.
(b) Grains of rice – simple, concentric, with many arms.
(c) Grains of maize – simple, concentric, angular.
(d) Seeds of pea – simple, concentric, spherical or elongated.
(e) Seeds of gram – simple, concentric, spherical or elongated.
(f) Tuber of potato – simple, eccentric, spherical or oval.
(g) Fruit of banana – simple, concentric, spherical.

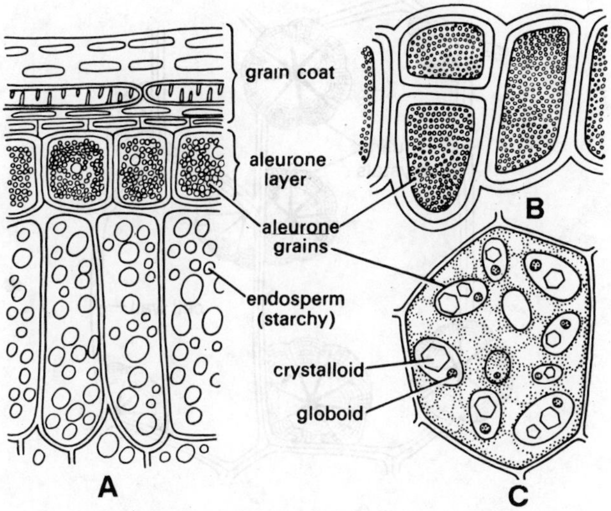

Fig. 12. Aleurone grains in A. Wheat, B.Maize, C. Castor.

Exercise 5

Purpose : To study Aleurone grains.

Materials

Seeds of castor, safety blade, slides, coverslips, microscope, water, glycerine, etc.

Method

1. Remove the seed coat from castor seeds.
2. Cut a thin section of the endosperm.
3. Mount the section in glycerine and observe under the microscope.

Observations

1. Each cell shows many spherical or oval, aleurone grains.
2. Each aleurone grain is made of crystalloid and globoid.
3. Crystalloid is large and has many angles. It is mostly made of proteins.
4. Globoid is a small globular or oval structure. It is made of calcium or magnesium diphosphate.
5. Aleurone grains are abundant in the aleurone layer found in grains of cereals like wheat, maize, rice, etc.

Exercise 6

Purpose : To study Inulin crystals.

Materials

Tuberous roots of *Dahlia*, safety blade, test tubes/specimen tubes, 95% alcohol, glycerine,

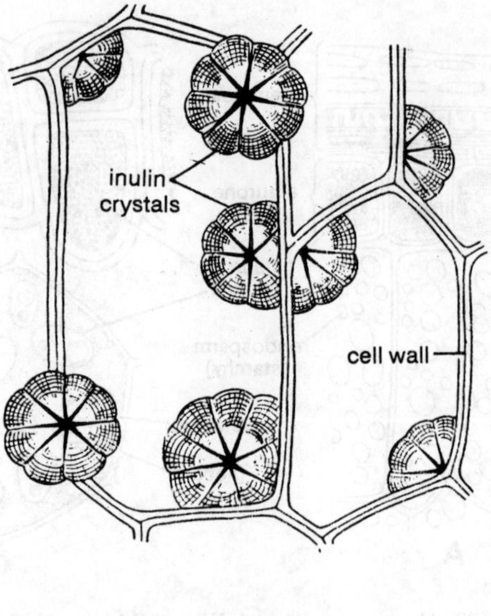

Fig. 13. Inulin crystals Deposits across the cell walls in roots of *Dahlia*.

orcein, sulphuric acid, water, slides, coverslips, microscope, etc.

Method

1. Cut thin sections of tuberous roots of *Dahlia.*
2. Place the sections in a specimen tube filled with 95% alcohol.
3. Allow the sections to remain in alcohol for 6 to 7 days.
4. Transfer the sections to saturated alcoholic solution of orcein Allow sections to take stain for about an hour.
5. Mount the sections in orein. Add a few drops of sulphuric acid to the stain before mounting a coverslip. (Alternatively sections are also mounted in glycerine and sulphuric acid is not required.)

Observations

1. Groups of inulin crystals are seen in the parenchymatous cells (mostly those closer to vascular bundles).
2. Inulin crystals are fan-shaped.
3. These are mostly attached to cell walls.
4. Inulin is a soluble carbohydrate and remains dissolved in the cell sap, before being deposited.
5. Inulin gets easily converted into sugar as and when required by the plant.

Exercise 7

Purpose : To study Raphides.

Materials

Onion bulb, safety blade, slides, cover slips, water, glycerine, microscope, etc.

Method

1. Cut a thin section of outer scaly leaf of onion bulb.
2. Mount the section in glycerine and observe under the microscope.

Observations

1. The cells show raphides of different shapes e.g. prism-shaped, rod-like, needle-like, etc.

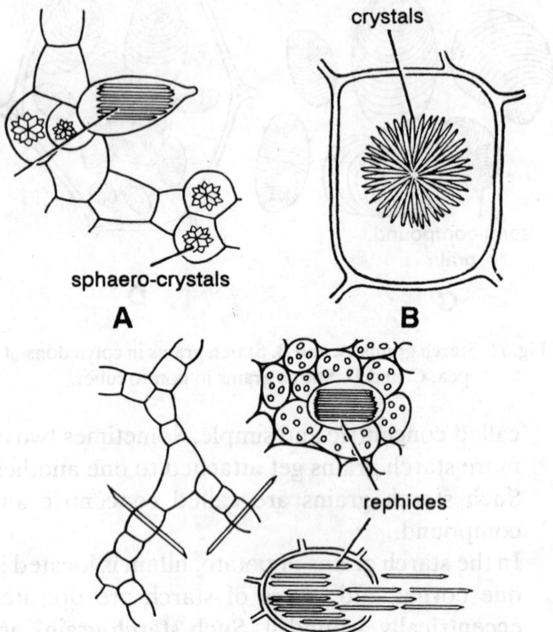

Fig. 14. Diffferent types of raphides. A. Water hyacinth,. B. Balsam or *Impatiens,* C. Sphaeroraphides in *Pistia*. D. Raphides in the scales of onion.

2. Raphides are the crystals of calcium oxalate.
3. These may be present either singly or in groups. When in groups these become star-shaped (sphaero-raphides) or form bundles.
4. Some of the plants in which raphides are found, are given below
(a) *Colocasia* (Eng-Taro; Hindi-Arvi, Kachalu) – petiole shows raphides, and sphaeroraphides.
(b) *Amorphophallus* (Eng.-Elephant-foot yam; Hindi- Jimikand)-needle shaped raphides in leaves.
(d) *Eichhornia* (Eng.-Water hyacinth; Hindi-Samundersonkh) – Raphides in the petiole.
(e) *Carica papaya* (Eng.-Papaya; Hindi-Papita) – Raphides in the petiole.
(f) *Impatiens* (Eng.-Garden balsam; Hindi-Gul-mehndi) – Raphides in the leaves
(g) *Chenopodium* (Eng.- Pigweed; Hindi-Bathua) – Sphaeroraphides in leaf.

Exercise 8

Purpose : To study Cystolith.

Materials

Leaves of *Ficus elastica* (India Rubber plant), safety blade, slides, coverslips, water, microscope, safranin, etc.

Method

1. Cut a thin section of the leaf.
2. Stain in safranin for about 10 miunutes.
3. Wash in water till proper destaining is obtained.
4. Mount in glycerine and study under the microscope.

Observations

1. The epidermis is made of many layers.
2. The cells of the innermost layer of multiple epidermis are elongated.
3. These cells show a peg-like ingrowth produced by the cell wall.
4. Many crystals of calcium carbonate are deposited on this ingrowth (stalk) to form grape - like cluster. This is known as cystolith.
5. Cystoliths are also found in
(a) Leaves of *Ficus benghalensis* (Eng.-Banyan; Hindi-Bargad).
(b) Leaves of *Momordica charantia* (Eng.- Bitter gourd; Hindi.-Karela).
(c) Leaves of *Ruellia tuberosa* (Eng.-Meno-weed).

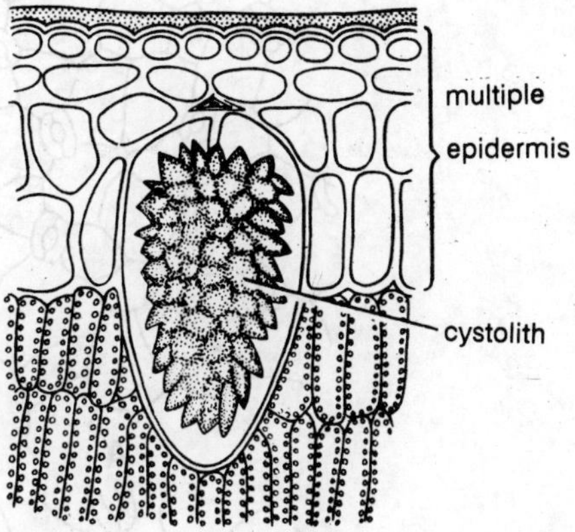

Fig. 15. Cystolith in the leaf of *Ficus elastica.*

IV. EPIDERMAL STUDIES

Epidermis is the outermost layer which forms a protective cover of different organs. Of these, leaf epidermis is functionally very important because it bears two important structures – stomata and the trichomes.

Stomata are concerned with gaseous exchange on which depend photosynthesis and respiration – the two principle metabolic processes of the plants. Stomata also allow transpiration which results in loss of excess of water absorbed from the soil.

Trichomes are epidemal appendages. These include glandular and non-glandular hairs, scales, papillae and the absorbing hairs of roots. Trichomes form a covering on all the plant parts. These insulate the plant from changes in the external environment. Trichomes also help to reduce the rate of transpiration.

Work to be done

[I] Study of different types of stomata.
[II] Study of trichomes.

Practical work and study

Exercise 1

Purpose : To Study different types of stomata

Materials

Leaves of *Citrullus*/ *Capsicum*/*Tridax*/*Tagetus*/ *Sedum*/ *Brassica*/ *Vigna*/ *Dianthus*/ *Ocimum,* etc,

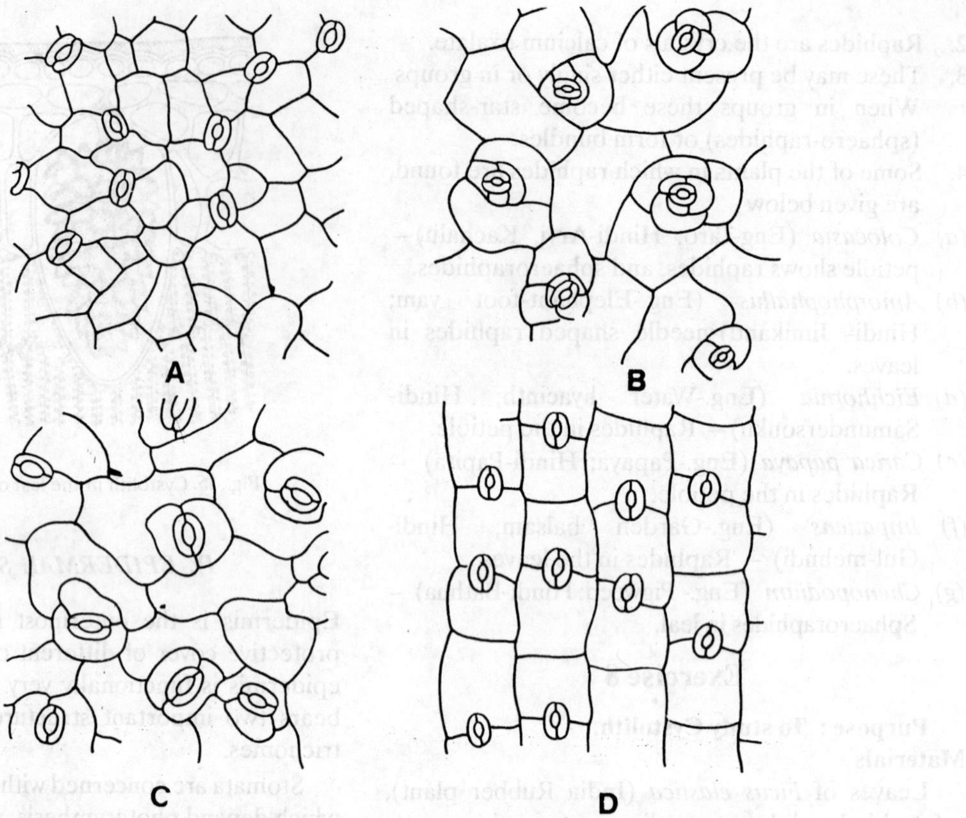

Fig. 16. Different types of stomata. A. Anomocytic. B. Anisocytic. C. Paracytic. D. Diacytic.

slides, coverslips, microscope, water, safranin, glycerine, needles, forceps, etc.

Method

1. Tear the leaf suddenly and with force with lower epidrmis upwards.
2. A thin membranous lower epidermis gets separated near the broken edges. Pull this into a strip with forceps or fingers.
3. The strip is stained with 1% aqueous safranin, washed in water and then mounted in glycerine.

Observations

1. The stomata are generally present on the lower leaf surface.
2. A typical dicotyledonous stomatal apparatus consists of ~uard cells and the surrounding accessory or subsidiary cells.
3. The guard cells are bean-shaped or kidney-shaped. The walls are unevenly thickened. The outer convex surface is thin and elastic while the inner concave surface is thick and non-elastic.
4. Each guard cell has a prominent nucleus. Chloroplasts are discoid and are arranged centrifugally (near the wall).
5. The subsidiary cells or accessory cells are epidermal cells associated with guard cells. These are generally morphologically distinct from the other epidermal cells.
6. On the basis of number and arrangement of subsidiary cells Metcalfe and Chalk (1950) proposed following four types of stomata in dicotyledons.

(a) Anomocytic. (Irregular-celled type; formerly Ranunculaceous type). Subsidiary cells are not present and several ordinary epidermal cells irregularly surround stomata, e.g. *Citrullus* (Eng. – Watermelon, Hindi – Tarbooz), *Capsicum* (Eng. – Chillies, Hindi – Hari mirch), *Tagetes* (Eng. – Marigold, Hindi – Genda), *Tridax*, etc.

(b) Anisocytic. (Unequal-celled type; formerly Cruciferous type). There are three subsidiary cells surrounding the stoma. Of these, one is distinctly smaller than the other two; e.g., *Brassica* (Eng. – Mustard, Hindi – Sarson), *Sedum*, etc.

(c) Paracytic (Parallel-celled type, formerly Rubiaceous type). In this type one or more subsidiary cells flank the stoma, parallel to the long

axis of the guard cells, e.g., *Vigna mungo* (Eng–Black gram, Hindi–urd), *Vigna radiata* (Eng–Green gram, Hindi–Mung), etc.

(d) Diacytic. (Cross-celled type, formerly Caryophyllaceous type). In this type a pair of subsidiary cells with their common walls is at right angles to the long axis of the guard cells, surrounds the stoma, e.g., *Dianthus* (Eng.–Carnation, Pink), *Ocimum* (Eng.–Basil, Hindi– Tulsi); etc.

Exercise 2

Purpose : To study Trichomes.

Materials

Plants of or stems and leaves of *Helianthus annuus, Parthenium, Calendula, Sonchus, Ocimum,* needles, safety blade, forceps, slides, coverslips, safranin, water, microscope, etc.

Method

1. Scrap the surface of the stem or leaf with safety blade.
2. Collect the scrapped material with forceps.
3. Place it on the slide and stain with safranin.
4. Mount in glycerine after spreading the material almost into individual cells. Observe different types of trichomes and draw them.

Observations

1. A mixture of different types trichomes is observed. Some of the types are described below.
2. *Helianthus annuus*. It is a vesicular filiform hair; made of a foot and body. The foot is simple. The body consists of 5-10 cells. It is uniseriate, filiform, cylindrical or slightly tapering above.
3. *Parthenium alpinum*. It is a capitate hair, made of foot and body. The foot is simple. The body is differentiated into stalk and the head. The stalk is 1 to 4-celled . The head is unicellular and swollen.
4. *Calendula officinalis*. It is a aseptate-flagellate hair. It consists of foot and body. The foot may be simple or compound. Body is differentiated into stalk and head. It is uniseriate. The stalk is 1 to 10 cells long. The head is unicellular, very long and flagellate.
5. *Sonchus oleraceus*. It is multiseriate capitate glandular hair. It is made of foot and body. The foot may either be simple or compound. The body is multiseriate and consists of stalk and head. Stalk is several times longer than head.

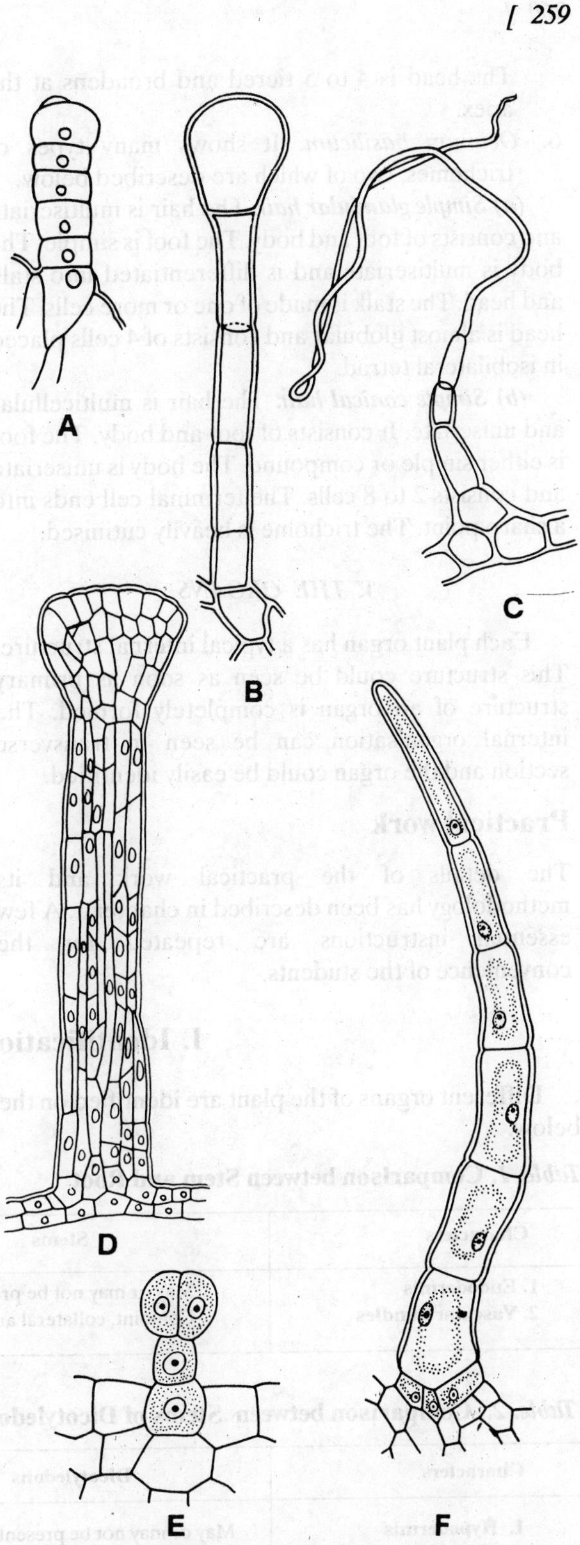

Fig. 17. Different types of trichomes. A. *Helianthus annuus*, B. *Parthenium alpinum*, C. *Calendula officinalis*, D. *Sonchus oleraceus*, E. and F. *Ocimum basilicum*.

The head is 4 to 5 tiered and broadens at the apex.

6. *Ocimum basilicum.* It shows many types of trichomes, two of which are described below.

(a) Simple glandular hair. The hair is multiseriate and consists of foot and body. The foot is simple. The body is multiseriate and is differentiated into stalk and head. The stalk is made of one or more cells. The head is almost globular and consists of 4 cells placed in isobilateral tetrad.

(b) Simple conical hair. The hair is multicellular and uniseriate. It consists of foot and body. The foot is either simple or compound. The body is uniseriate and consists 2 to 8 cells. The terminal cell ends into a sharp point. The trichome is heavily cutinised.

V. THE ORGANS

Each plant organ has a typical internal structure. This structure could be seen as soon as primary structure of an organ is completely formed. The internal organisation can be seen in transverse section and the organ could be easily identified.

Practical work

The details of the practical work and its methodology has been described in chapter 1. A few essential instructions are repeated for the convenience of the students.

1. Cut a transverse section of the material with a sharp razor.
2. Select a thin and uniformly cut section.
3. Stain the section either in safranin-fast green combination or crystal violet-erythrosine combination.
4. Mount a properly stained section in glycerine.
5. Observe the section under the microscope and study.
6. Once the observations are complete, draw two diagrams –
   (i) an outline diagram of the transverse section and
   (ii) a part of the section drawn to show different types of cells found in every part.
7. Label the diagrams neatly.
8. Write down the description, starting with
   (i) Epidermis
   (ii) Cortex / Ground Tissue
   (iii) Endodermis
   (iv) Pericycle
   (v) Vascular tissues
9. Identify the material
   (i) Root/ stem/ leaf
   (ii) Dicotyledonous/ Monocotyledonous
10. Give description of abnormalities or special characters if any.

I. Identification of Plant Organs

Different organs of the plant are identified on the basis of anatomy. These anatomical characters are listed below.

***Table. 1.* Comparison between Stem and Root**

Characters	Stems	Roots
1. Endodermis	May or may not be present.	Always very clearly marked.
2. Vascular bundles	Conjoint, collateral and endarch.	Radial and exarch.

***Table. 2.* Comparison between Stems of Dicotyledonous and Moncotyledonous Plants**

Characters	Dicotyledons	Monocotyledons
1. Hypodermis	May or may not be present, if present mostly collenchymatous.	Generally present, sclerenchymatous.
2. Cortex	A few layers of parenchyma extend up to the endodermis.	

3. Endodermis	Generally absent; mostly represented by endodermoid cells; if present, in the form of a ring.	The cells following hypodermis are not differentiated. They are generally parenchymatous and extend from hypodermis up to the centre of the axis. It is known as ground tiusse.
4. Pericycle	Present between the vascular tissue and cortex; either parenchymatous or sclerenchymatous, one to few layered.	
5. Medullary ray	A strip of parenchyma between the vascular bundles.	
6. Pith	A central and well marked out cylinder present; parenchymatous or sclerenchymatous.	Well marked pith can not be distinguished.
7. Vascular bundles	(a) Conjoint, collateral/bicollateral endarch, open. (b) Arranged in a ring. (c) Almost all of them are uniform in size. (d) Phloem parenchyma present. (e) Bundle sheath absent.	(a) Conjoint, collateral, endarch and closed. (b) Scattered throughout ground tissue. (c) Larger toward the centre and smaller outside. (d) Phloem parenchyma absent. (e) Well developed bundle sheath present.

***Table 3.* Comparison between Roots of Dicotyledons and Monocotyledons**

Characters	Dicotyledons	Monocotyledons
1. Vascular bundles	There are about 2-6 protoxylem groups (i.e. condition is diarch to hexarch); rarely more groups.	The number of protoxylem groups generally exceeds 2-6, therefore, the condition is polyarch; rarely only a few.
2. Pericycle	It generally gives rise to lateral roots, vascular cambium and cork cambium.	Only lateral roots are produced.
3. Cambium	It appears later to form a comlete ring between the xylem and phloem groups.	It is altogether absent.
4. Pith	Small or absent.	Large and well developed.

A Key for Identification

1. Vascular bundle conjoint, collateral (bicollateral)and endarch, endodermis not well developed. **Stem (2)**

1. Vascular bundle radial and exarch, endodermis conspicuous with casparian strips. **Root (3)**

2. (i) Epidermis, cortex and vascular tissues well differentiated;
(ii) vascular bundles conjoint, collateral (bicollateral) and open; arranged in a ring; and
(iii) pith well developed. **– Dicotyledonous stem.**

2. A. (i) Epidermis differentiated, presence of ground tissue;
(ii) vascular bundles conjoint, collateral and always closed, scattered in the ground tissue; and
(iii) pith not well marked. **– Monocotyledonous stem.**

3. (i) Protoxylem groups up to six in number;
(ii) pith small; and
(iii) secondary growth present. **– Dicotyledonous root**

3. A. (i) Protoxylem groups more than six in number;
(ii) pith well developed and
(iii) secondary growth absent. **– Monocotyledonous root.**

Luffa

T. s. Stem

Cut a transverse section of the material, stain in safranin and fast green combination and mount in glycerine.

[I] Observations

The outlines of the section show ridges and furrows.

Epidermis. It consists of single layer of cells. A few multicellular hairs are present. A thin cuticle covers epidermis.

Cortex. 1. It is few to many layered, consisting of (a) collenchyma and (b) chlorenchyma.

2. Collenchyma lies below the epidermis in the ridges. It is several layers deep. In the furrows, it is two to three layered or sometimes absent.
3. Chlorenchyma lies below the collenchyma in both ridges and furrows. This is two or three layered deep and the cells contain numerous chloroplasts.

Endodermis. (Starch sheath). This single layer separates cortex from the vascular tissues. The cells lack casparian strips but show starch. Thus it is called as starch sheath.

Pericycle. 1. It follows endodermis and is a few layers deep.

2. The cells are thick walled and sclerenchymatous due to lignification.

The ground tissue. 1. It extends from the pericycle to the centre of the section.

2. The cells are parenchymatous and large intercellular spaces are present.

Vascular bundles. 1. There are about ten vascular bundles arranged in two rows.

2. Each vascular bundle is conjoint, bicollateral, endarch and open.
3. Each ring consists of five vascular bundles. The outer ring is situated opposite the ridges and the vascular bundles are smaller in size. The inner ring is located opposite the furrows. The vascular bundles of this ring are larger in size.
(In a bicollateral vascular bundle xylem is centrally located. On both of its sides are cambial strips (inner and outer cambia) and on outer side of the cambia on either sides, phloem groups are present. These are called inner phloem and outer phloem
4. The xylem consists of wide and pitted vessels, tracheids, fibres and xylem parenchyma. The protoxylem faces inner cambium.
5. The inner and outer cambial layers are situated between phloem and xylem on either sides.
6. The phloem occupies both the ends of vascular bundle. It is composed of sieve tubes, companion cells and phloem parenchyma.

Pith. The central part of the section is occupied by parenchyma.

[II] Identification

1. Stem. 1. Vascular bundles are conjoint and bicollateral.

2. Protoxylem is endarch.

2. Dicotyledonous stem. 1. Cortex is well differentiated.

2. Endodermis and pericycle distinguishable.
3. Vascular bundles in a ring and open.
4. Pith well developed.

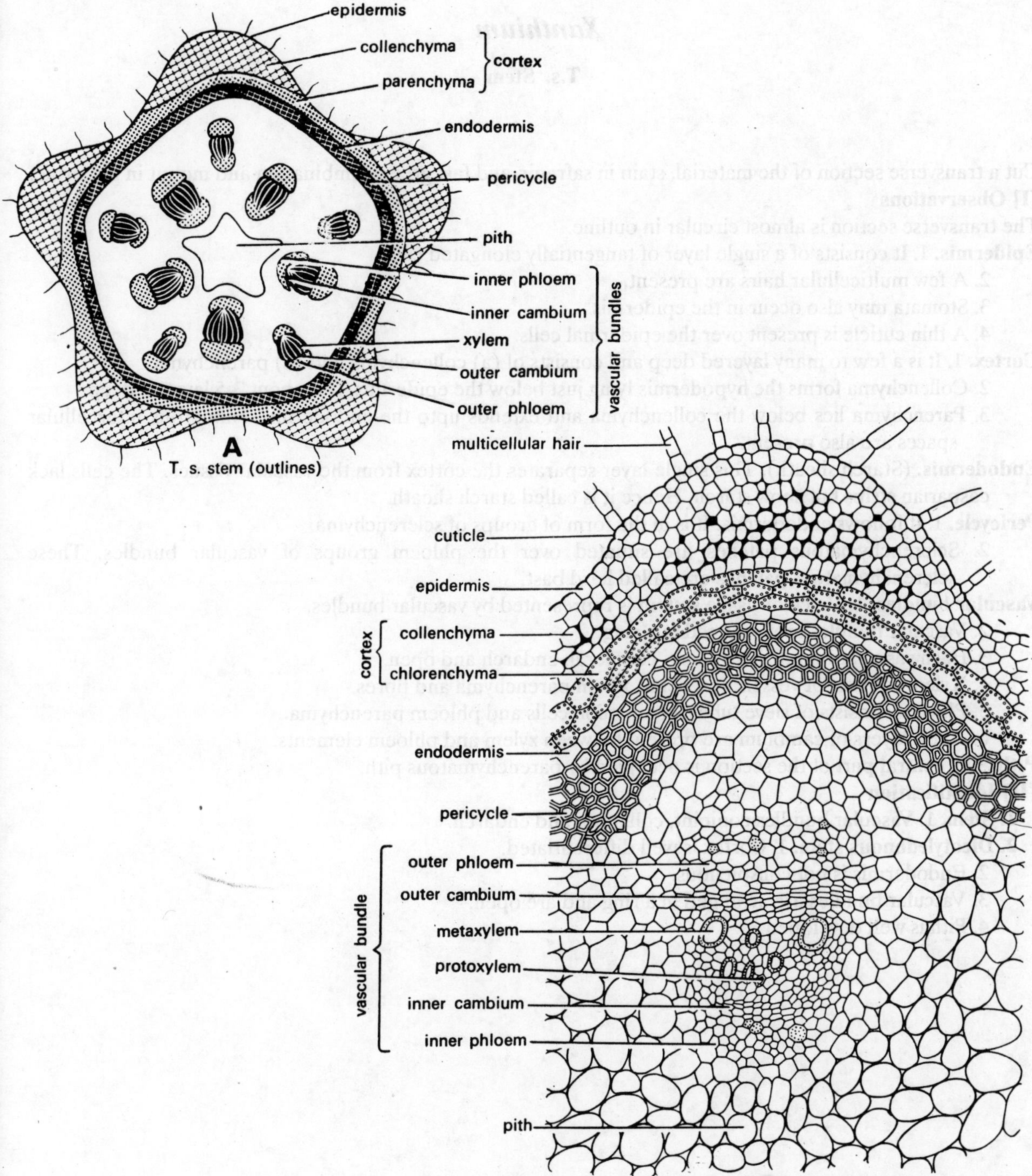

Fig. 17. ***Luffa***. T. s. stem.

Luffa **Family** – Cucurbitaceae
English name – Dish-Clothgourd.
Vernacular name – Ghia tori.

Xanthium

T.s. Stem

Cut a transverse section of the material, stain in safranin and fast green combination and mount in glycerine.

[I] Observations

The transverse section is almost circular in outline.

Epidermis. 1. It consists of a single layer of tangentially elongated cells.

2. A few multicellular hairs are present.
3. Stomata may also occur in the epidermis.
4. A thin cuticle is present over the epidermal cells.

Cortex. 1. It is a few to many layered deep and consists of (a) collenchyma and (b) parenchyma.

2. Collenchyma forms the hypodermis lying just below the epidermis. It is about 3-5 layered deep.
3. Parenchyma lies below the collenchyma and extends upto the endodermis. Numerous intercellular spaces are also present.

Endodermis. (Starch sheath). This single layer separates the cortex from the vascular tissues. The cells lack casparian strips but show starch. Hence it is called starch sheath.

Pericycle. 1. It follows endodermis. It is in the form of groups of sclerenchyma.

2. Sclerenchymatous patches are situated over the phloem groups of vascular bundles. These sclerenchymatous patches are called hard bast.

Vascular bundles. 1. Vascular tissue system is represented by vascular bundles.

2. Vascular bundles are arranged in a ring.
3. Each vascular bundle is conjoint, collateral, endarch and open.
4. Xylem consists of vessels, tracheids, xylem parenchyma and fibres.
5. Phloem consists of sieve tubes, companion cells and phloem parenchyma.
6. A few layers of cambium are present between xylem and phloem elements.

Pith. The central part of the section is occupied by parenchymatous pith.

[II] Identification

1. Stem. 1. Vascular bundles conjoint, collateral and endarch.

2. Dicotyledonous stem. 1. Cortex is well differentiated.

2. Endodermis is not conspicuous.
3. Vascular bundles are arranged in a ring and are open.
4. Pith is well developed.

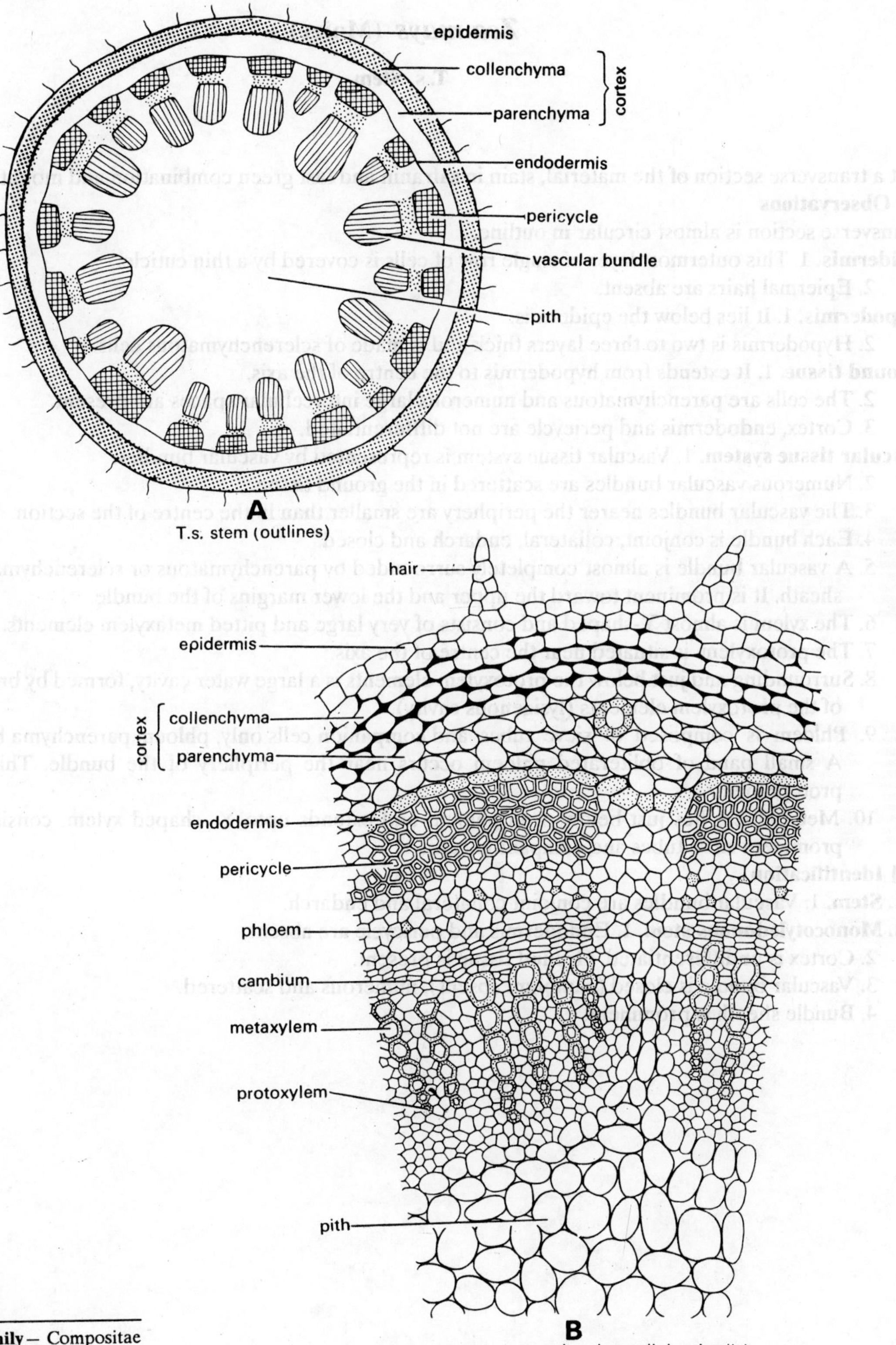

T.s. stem (A sector showing cellular details)

Fig. 18. ***Xanthium.*** T. s. stem.

Xanthium **Family** – Compositae
English name – Cocklebur
Vernacular names – Banokra, Adhasisí

Zea mays (Maize)

T. s. Stem

Cut a transverse section of the material, stain in safranin and fast green combination and mount in glycerine.

[I] Observations

Transverse section is almost circular in outline.

Epidermis. 1. This outermost layer of single row of cells is covered by a thin cuticle.

2. Epiermal hairs are absent.

Hypodermis. 1. It lies below the epidermis.

2. Hypodermis is two to three layers thick and is made of sclerenchymatous cells.

Ground tissue. 1. It extends from hypodermis to the centre of the axis.

2. The cells are parenchymatous and numerous large intercellular spaces are present.
3. Cortex, endodermis and pericycle are not diffferentiated.

Vascular tissue system. 1. Vascular tissue system is represented by vascular bundles.

2. Numerous vascular bundles are scattered in the ground tissue.
3. The vascular bundles nearer the periphery are smaller than in the centre of the section.
4. Each bundle is conjoint, collateral, endarch and closed.
5. A vascular bundle is almost completely surrounded by parenchymatous or sclerenchymatous bundle sheath. It is prominent toward the upper and the lower margins of the bundle.
6. The xylem is almost Y-shaped and consists of very large and pitted metaxylem elements.
7. The protoxylem is situated near the centre of the axis.
8. Surrounding and just below the protoxylem elements is a large water cavity, formed by breaking down of the protoxylem elements (lysigenous cavity).
9. Phloem is composed of sieve tubes and companion cells only, phloem parenchyma being absent. A small band of obliterated phloem occurs near the periphery of the bundle. This represents protophloem.
10. Metaphloem lies just below protophloem and extends upto Y- shaped xylem, consisting of very prominent sieve tubes and companion cells.

[II] Identification

1. Stem. 1. Vascular bundles are conjoint collateral and endarch.

2. Monocotyledonous stem. 1. Endodermis and pericycle are absent.

2. Cortex is undifferentiated. Ground tissue is present.
3. Vascular bundle is closed (cambium absent), numerous and scattered.
4. Bundle sheath is prominent.

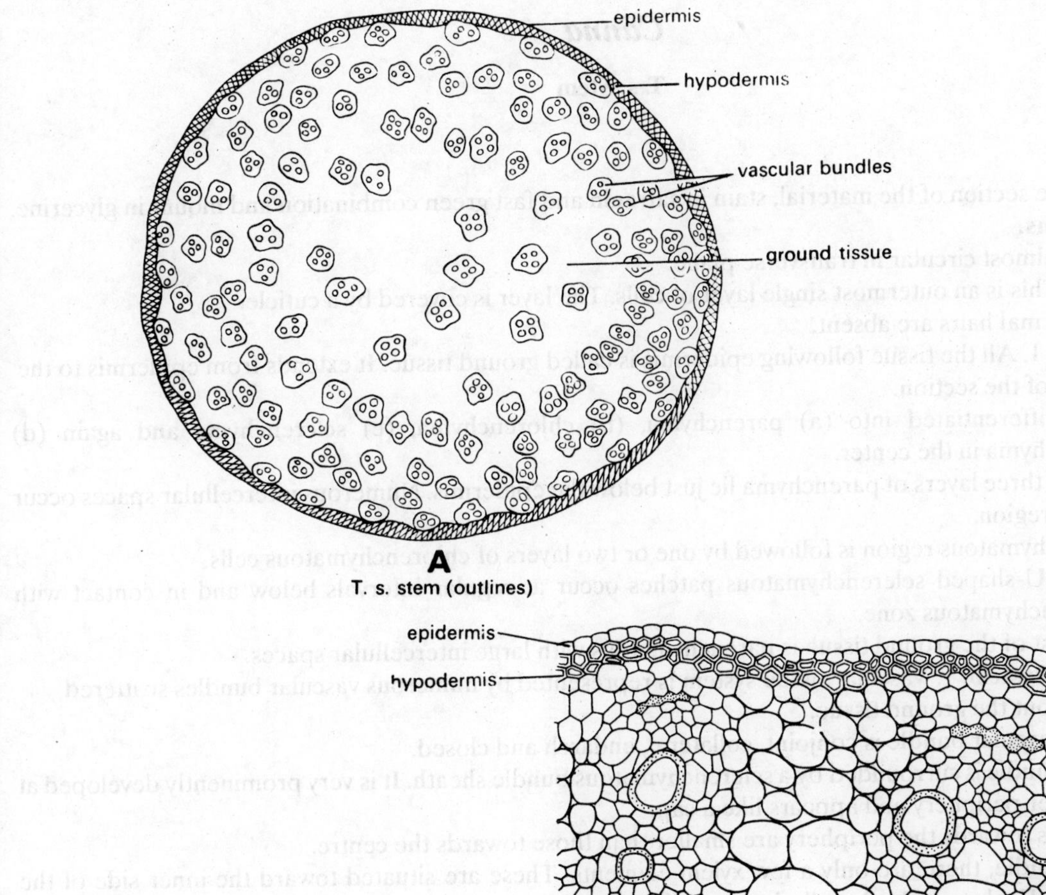

Fig. 19. ***Zea mays.*** T. s. stem.

Zey mays **Family** – Gramineae
English names – Maize, Corn
Vernacular names – Makka, Bhutta

Canna

T. s. Stem

Cut a transverse section of the material, stain in safranin and fast green combination and mount in glycerine.

[I] Observations.

The section is almost circular in transverse plane.

Epidermis. 1. This is an outermost single layer of cells. The layer is covered by a cuticle.

2. Epidermal hairs are absent.

Ground tissue. 1. All the tissue following epidermis is called ground tissue. It extends from epidermis to the centre of the section.

2. It is differentiated into (a) parenchyma, (b) chlorenchyma, (c) sclerenchyma and again (d) parenchyma in the center.
3. Two to three layers of parenchyma lie just below the epidermis. Numerous intercellular spaces occur in this region.
4. Parenchymatous region is followed by one or two layers of chlorenchymatous cells.
5. A few U-shaped sclerenchymatous patches occur at regular intervals below and in contact with chlorenchymatous zone.
6. The rest of the ground tissue is parenchymatous with large intercellular spaces.

Vascular tissue system. 1. Vascular tissue system is represented by numerous vascular bundles scattered throughout the ground tissue.

2. Each vascular bundle is conjoint, collateral, endarch and closed.
3. Each bundle is surrounded by a sclerenchymatous bundle sheath. It is very prominently developed at the outer periphery and appears like a cap.
4. Bundles towards the periphery are smaller than those towards the centre.
5. In a bundle, there are only a few xylem elements. These are situated toward the inner side of the bundle. Each vascular bundle is generally represented by single or two large vessels and a small tracheid.
6. The phloem occupies the outer part of the vascular bundle – a region just below the sclerenchyma of the bundle sheath. It consists of sieve tubes and companion cells.

[II] Identification

1. Stem. 1. Vascular bundles are conjoint, collateral and endarch.

2. Monocotyledonous stem. 1. Endodermis and pericycle are absent.

2. Ground tissue is present.
3. Vascular bundles are closed (cambium absent), many and scattered throughout ground tissue.
4. Bundle sheath is prominent.

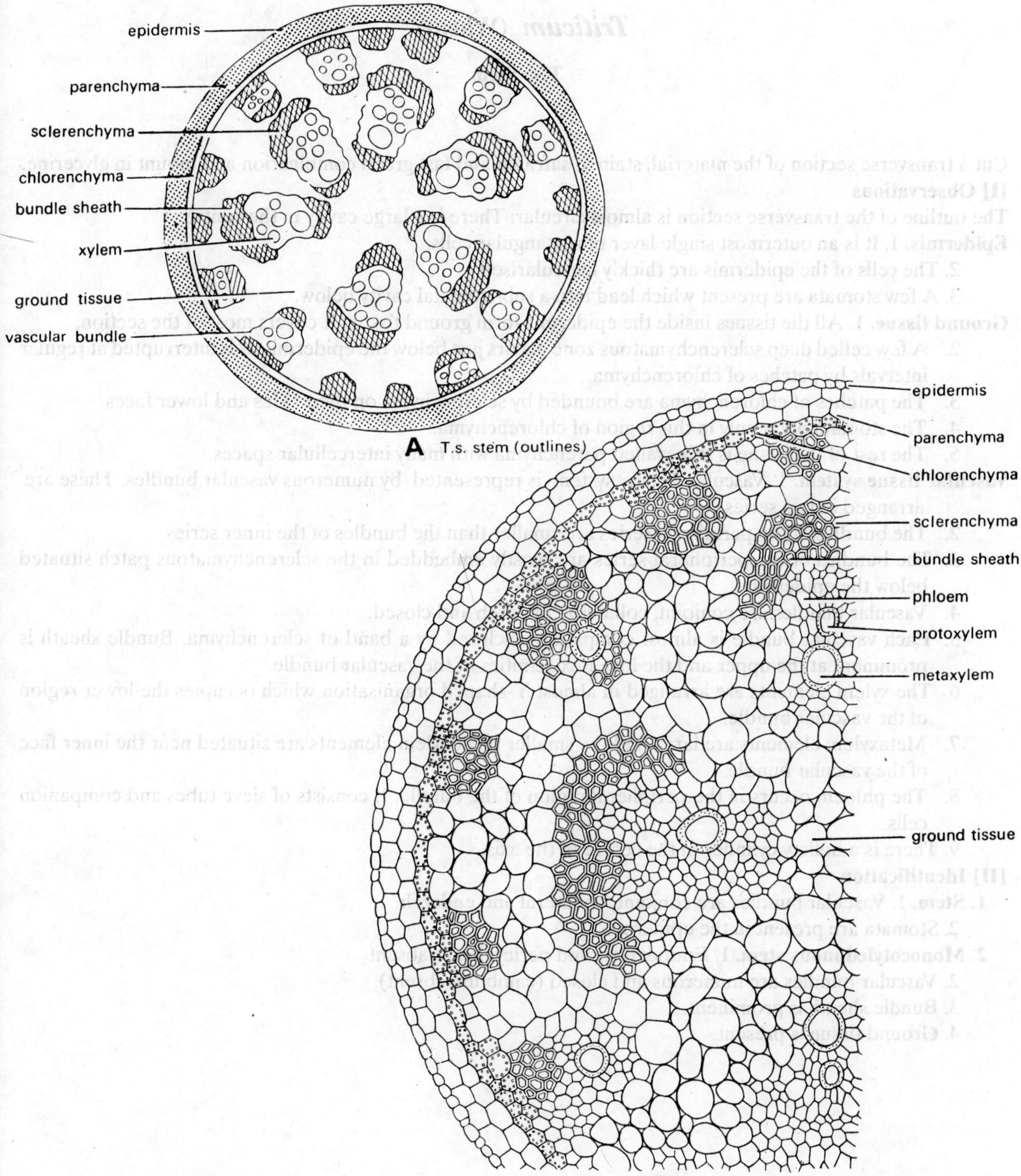

A T.s. stem (outlines)

B T.s. stem (A sector showing cellular details)

Fig. 20. *Canna*. T. s. stem

***Canna* Family – Cannaceae**
English name – Indian shot
Vernacular names – Sabbajaya, Keli

Triticum (Wheat)

T.s. Stem

Cut a transverse section of the material, stain in safranin and fast green combination and mount in glycerine.

[I] Observations

The outline of the transverse section is almost circular. There is a large cavity in the centre.

Epidermis. 1. It is an outermost single layer of rectangular cells.

2. The cells of the epidermis are thickly cuticularised.
3. A few stomata are present which lead into a sub-stomatal cavity below.

Ground tissue. 1. All the tissues inside the epidermis form ground tissue. It covers most of the section.

2. A few celled deep sclerenchymatous zone occurs just below the epidermis. It is interrupted at regular intervals by patches of chlorenchyma.
3. The patches of chlorenchyma are bounded by sclerenchyma on their sides and lower faces.
4. The stomata open only in this region of chlorenchyma.
5. The rest of the tissue is thin walled parenchyma with many intercellular spaces.

Vascular tissue system. 1. Vascular tissue system is represented by numerous vascular bundles. These are arranged in two series.

2. The bundles of the peripheral series are smaller than the bundles of the inner series.
3. The bundles of the peripheral series are mostly embedded in the sclerenchymatous patch situated below the epidermis.
4. Vascular bundles are conjoint, collateral, endarch and closed.
5. Each vascular bundle is almost completely enclosed by a band of sclerenchyma. Bundle sheath is prominent at the upper and the lower extremities of the vascular bundle.
6 The xylem elements are arranged in almost Y-shaped organisation which occupies the lower region of the vascular bundle.
7. Metaxylem elements are large and the smaller protoxylem elements are situated near the inner face of the vascular bundle.
8. The phloem occurs in the peripheral region of the bundle. It consists of sieve tubes and companion cells.
9. There is a hollow cylinder in the centre of the axis.

[II] Identification

1. Stem. 1. Vascular bundles are conjoint, collateral and endarch.

2. Stomata are present in the epidermis.

2. Monocotyledonous stem. 1. Endodermis and pericycle are absent.

2. Vascular bundles are numerous and closed (cambium absent).
3. Bundle sheath is prominent.
4. Ground tissue is present.

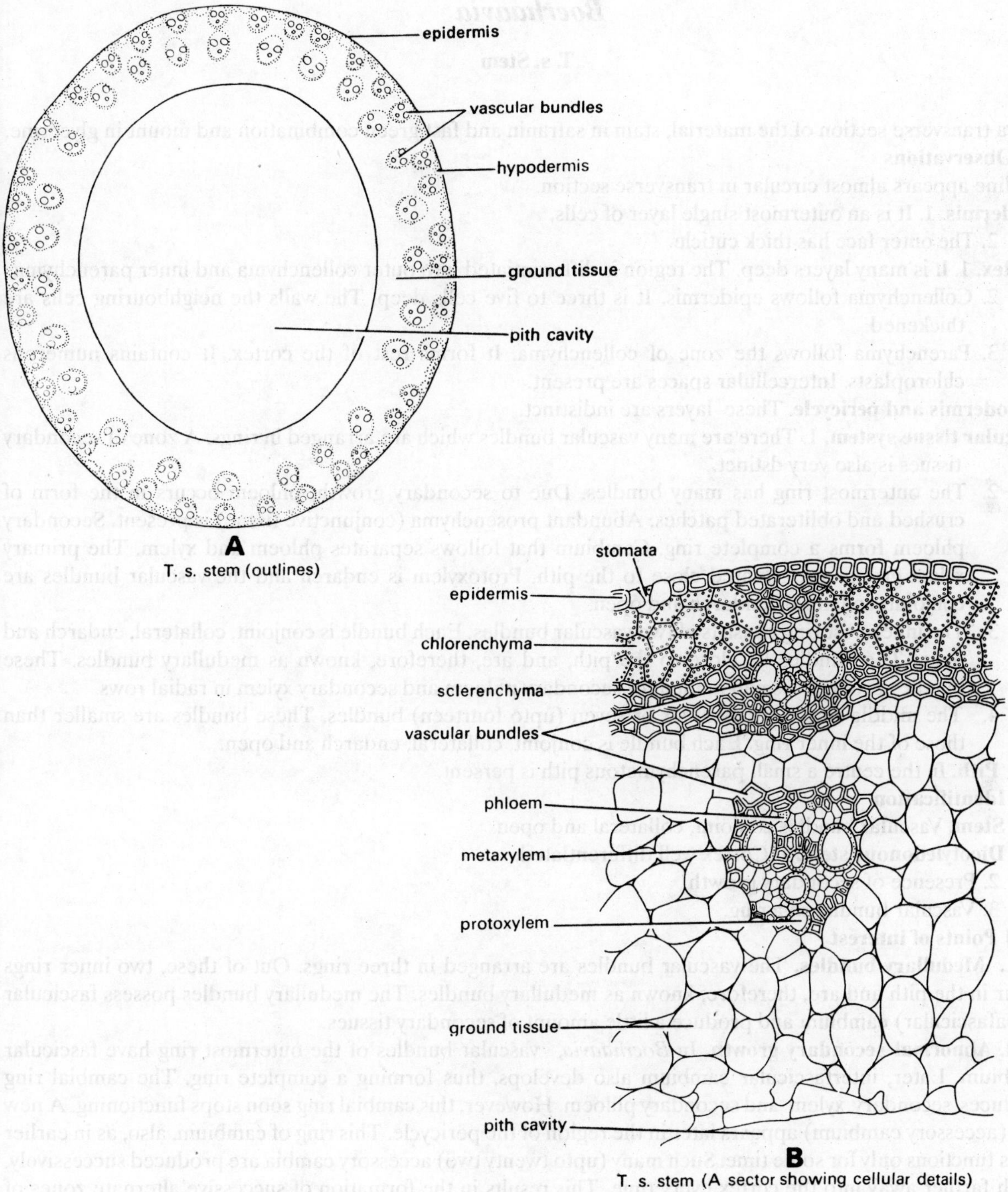

Fig. 21. ***Triticum.*** T.s. stem.

Triticum **Family** – **Gramineae**
English name – **Wheat**
Vernacular names – **Gehoon, Kanak**

Boerhaavia

T. s. Stem

Cut a transverse section of the material, stain in safranin and fast green combination and mount in glycerine.

[I] Observations

Outline appears almost circular in transverse section.

Epidermis. 1. It is an outermost single layer of cells.

2. The outer face has thick cuticle.

Cortex. 1. It is many layers deep. The region is differentiated into outer collenchyma and inner parenchyma.

2. Collenchyma follows epidermis. It is three to five cells deep. The walls the neighbouring cells are thickened.

3. Parenchyma follows the zone of collenchyma. It forms rest of the cortex. It contains numerous chloroplasts. Intercellular spaces are present.

Endodermis and pericycle. These layers are indistinct.

Vascular tissue system. 1. There are many vascular bundles which are arranged in rings. A zone of secondary tissues is also very dstinct.

2. The outermost ring has many bundles. Due to secondary growth, phloem occurs in the form of crushed and obliterated patches. Abundant prosenchyma (conjunctive tissue) is present. Secondary phloem forms a complete ring. Cambium that follows separates phloem and xylem. The primary xylem groups are situated close to the pith. Protoxylem is endarch and the vascular bundles are conjoint, collateral, endarch and open.

3. The innermost ring consists of two vascular bundles. Each bundle is conjoint, collateral, endarch and open. The bundles lie close to the pith, and are, therefore, known as medullary bundles. These bundles produce a small amount of secondary phloem and secondary xylem in radial rows.

4. The middle ring consists of six or seven (upto fourteen) bundles. These bundles are smaller than those of the inner ring. Each bundle is conjoint, collateral, endarch and open.

Pith. In the centre a small parenchymatous pith is persent.

[II] Identification

1. **Stem.** Vascular bundles conjoint, collateral and open.
2. **Dicotyledonous stem.** 1. Cortex well differentiated.

   2. Presence of secondary growth.

   3. Vascular bundles in a ring.

[III] Points of interest

1. **Medullary bundles.** The vascular bundles are arranged in three rings. Out of these, two inner rings occur in the pith and are, therefore, known as medullary bundles. The medullary bundles possess fascicular (intrafascicular) cambium and produce a little amount of secondary tissues.

2. **Abnormal secondary growth.** In *Boerhaavia,* vascular bundles of the outermost ring have fascicular cambium. Later, interfascicular cambium also develops, thus forming a complete ring. The cambial ring produces secondary xylem and secondary phloem. However, this cambial ring soon stops functioning. A new ring (accessory cambium) appears later in the region of the pericycle. This ring of cambium, also, as in earlier cases functions only for some time. Such many (upto twenty two) accessory cambia are produced successively, much farther away into the cortex every time. This results in the formation of successive alternate zones of secondary xylem and secondary phloem. These rings or zones (of secondary tissues) are sometimes eccentrically developed. Cambia produce a very large amount of prosenchyma into which xylem remains scattered and at times becomes indistinguishable from it.

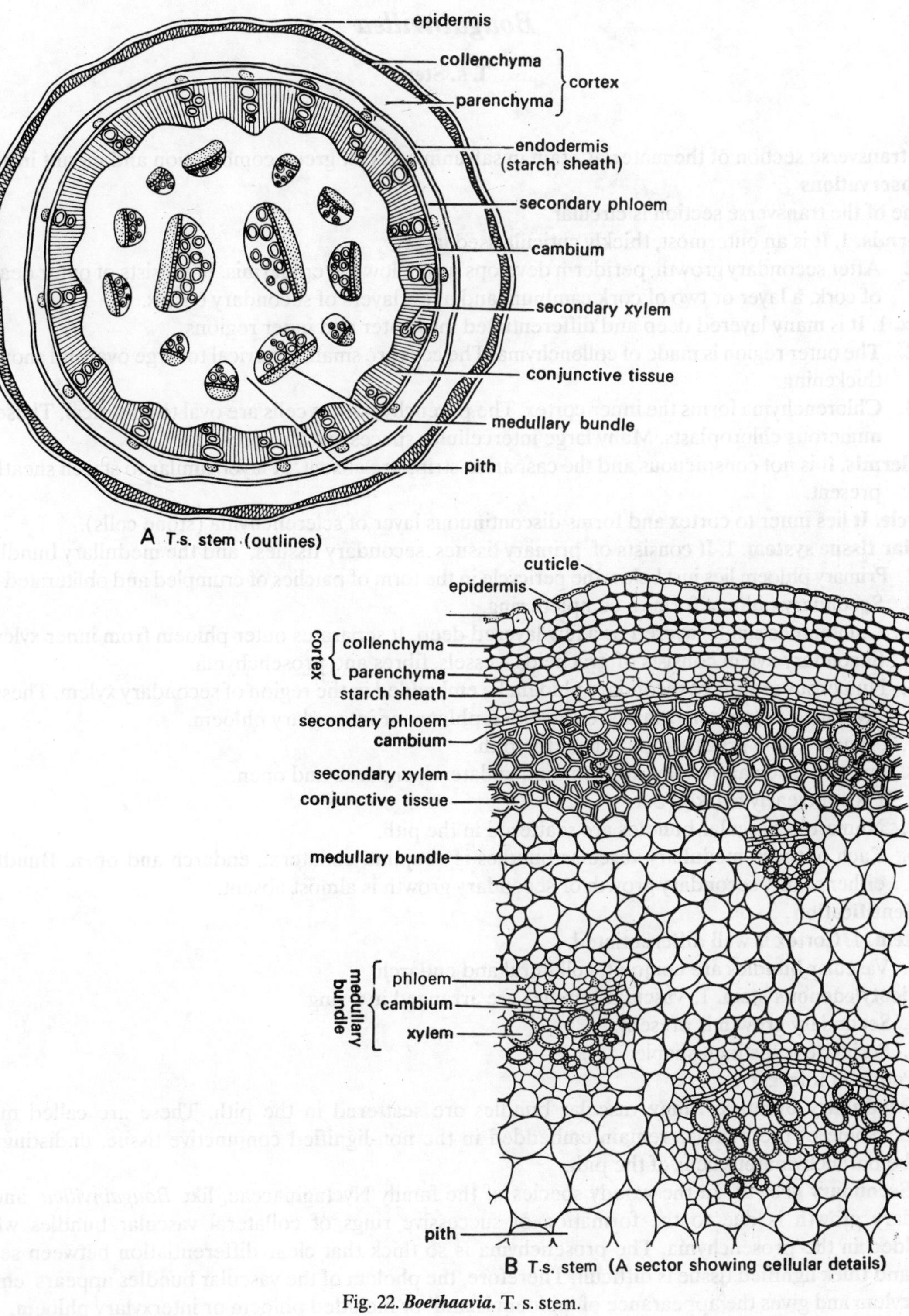

Fig. 22. ***Boerhaavia***. T. s. stem.

Boerhaavia **Family**—Nyctaginaceae
English names—Horse-purslane, hogweed.
Vernacular names—Punarnava, sant, santhi.

Bougainvillea

T. s. Stem

Cut a transverse section of the material, stain in safranin and fast green combination and mount in glycerine.

[I] Observations

Outline of the transverse section is circular.

Epidermis. 1. It is an outermost, thickly cuticularised layer.

2. After secondary growth, periderm develops just below the epidermis. It consists of outer dead tissues of cork, a layer or two of cork cambium and a few layers of secondary cortex.

Cortex. 1. It is many layered deep and differentiated into outer and inner regions.

2. The outer region is made of collenchyma. The cells are small, spherical to large oval and show angular thickening.
3. Chlorenchyma forms the inner cortex. The parenchymatous cells are oval to spherical. These contain numerous chloroplasts. Many large intercellular spaces are also present.

Endodermis. It is not conspicuous and the casparian strips are absent. A layer similar to starch sheath may be present.

Pericycle. It lies inner to cortex and forms discontinuous layer of sclerenchyma (stone cells).

Vascular tissue system. 1. It consists of primary tissues secondary tissues, and the medullary bundles.

2. Primary phloem lies just below the pericycle in the form of patches of crumpled and obliterated tissues.
3. Secondary phloem forms a complete ring.
4. Cambium is single layered or a few layered deep. It separates outer phloem from inner xylem.
5. Secondary xylem consists of tracheids, vessels, fibres and prosenchyma.
6. Numerous groups of secondary phloem lie embedded in the region of secondary xylem. These groups are called as 'phloem islands' or included phloem or interxylary phloem.
7. Primary xylem groups appear near the pith.
8. Primary vascular bundles are conjoint, collateral, endarch and open.

Pith. 1. It is not clearly marked out.

2. Numerous vascular bundles are scattered in the pith.
3. Each of these medullary vascular bundles is conjoint, collateral, endarch and open. Bundles show either scanty secondary growth or secondary growth is almost absent.

[II] Identification

1. Stem. 1. Cortex is well differentiated.

2. Vascular bundles are conjoint, collateral and endarch.

2. Dicotyledonous stem. 1. Vascular bundles are arranged in a ring.

2. Secondary growth is present.
3. Pericycle is distinguishable.

[III] Points of interest

1. Medullary bundles. Many vascular bundles are scattered in the pith. These are called medullary bundles. Some of the bundles remain embedded in the non-lignified conjunctive tissue, undistinguishable from the parenchymatous cells of the pith.

2. Secondary growth. In the woody species of the family Nyctaginaceae, like *Bougainvillea,* anomalous secondary growth is due to the formation of successive rings of collateral vascular bundles which get embedded in the prosenchyma. The prosenchyma is so thick that clear differentiation between secondary xylem and thick lignified tissue is difficult. Therefore, the pholem of the vascular bundles appears embedded in the xylem and gives the appearance of 'phloem island' or included phloem or interxylary phloem.

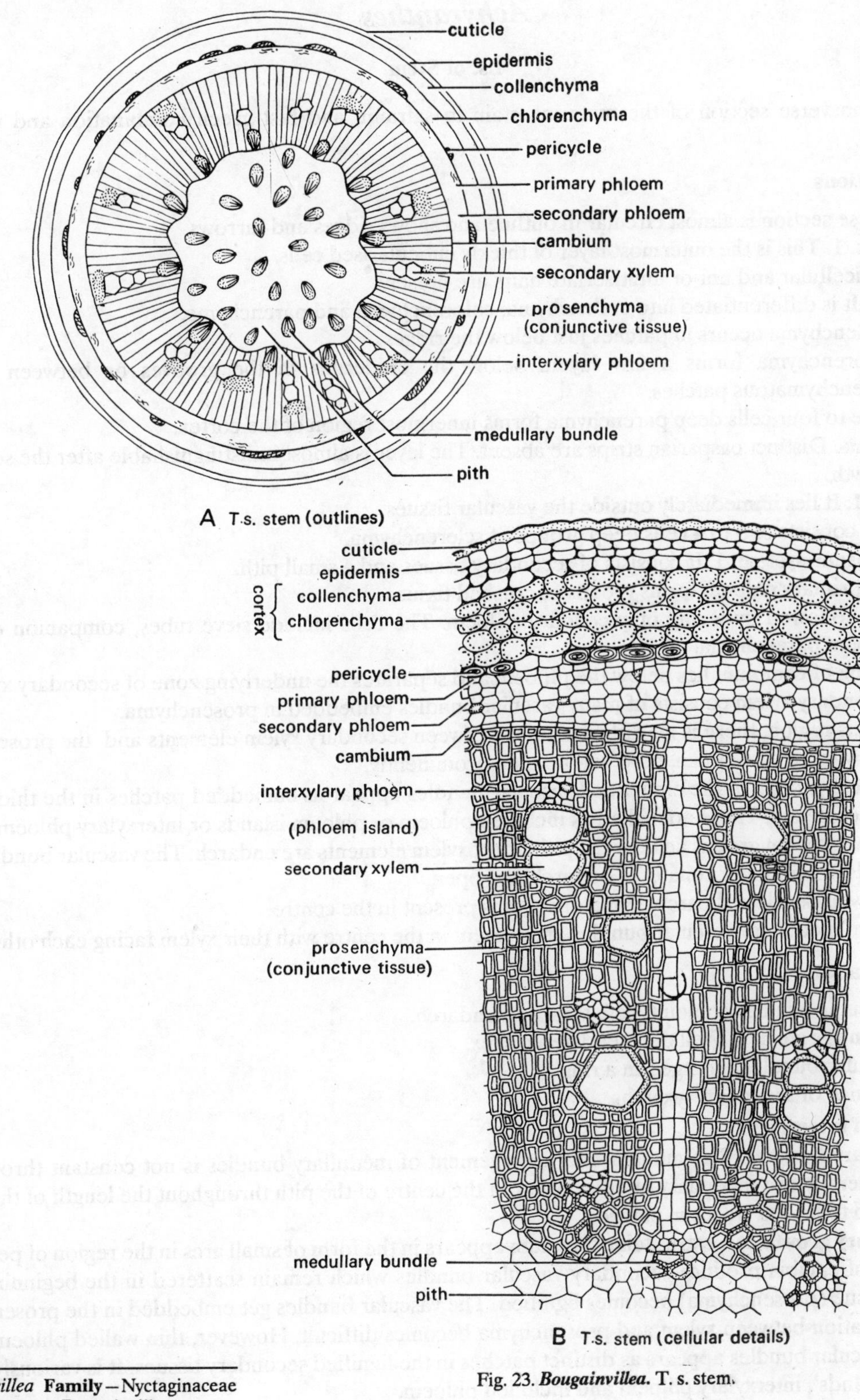

Fig. 23. ***Bougainvillea.*** T. s. stem.

Bougainvillea **Family** – Nyctaginaceae
English name – Bougainvillea
Vernacular name – Baganvilas

Achyranthes

T.s. of Stem

Cut a transverse section of the material, stain in safranin and fast green combination and mount in glycerine.

[I] Observations

The transverse section is almost circular in outline and shows ridges and furrows.

1. Epidermis. 1. This is the outermost layer of thickly cuticularised cells.
 2. Multicellular and uni-or multiseriate hairs are present.

2. Cortex. 1. It is differentiated into collenchyma, chlorenchyma and parenchyma.
 2. Collenchyma occurs in patches just below the ridges.
 3. Chlorenchyma forms a few layers below the epidermis in the grooves or between the two collenchymatous patches.
 4. Three to four cells deep parenchyma forms innermost region of the cortex.

3. Endodermis. Distinct casparian strips are absent. The layer is almost indistinguishable after the secondary growth.

4. Pericycle. 1. It lies immediately outside the vascular tissues.
 2. It consists of 3 to 4 cells deep groups of sclerenchyma.

5. Vascular tissue system. 1. It consists of secondary tissues and a small pith.
 2. The primary phloem forms groups of crushed tissues.
 3. It is followed by a ring of secondary phloem. The cells include sieve tubes, companion cells and phloem parenchyma.
 4. A ring of cambium lies below the phloem and separates the underlying zone of secondary xylem.
 5. Secondary xylem consists of many vascular bundles embedded in prosenchyma.
 6. In this region, there is no differentiation between secondary xylem elements and the prosenchyma. A few large vessels can, however, be seen prominently.
 7. Phloem groups of the embedded vascular bundles appear as embedded patches in the thick walled prosenchyma. These are called as included phloem or phloem islands or interxylary phloem.
 8. Primary xylem groups lie near the pith. Protoxylem elements are endarch. The vascular bundles, thus, would be conjoint, collateral, endarch and open.

6. Pith. 1. A well developed parenchymatous pith is present in the centre.
 2. Two medullary vascular bundles are present in the centre with their xylem facing each other.

[II] Identification

1. Stem. Vascular bundles conjoint, collateral and endarch.

2. Dicotyledonous stem. 1. Well differentiated cortex.
 2. Vascular bundles arranged in a ring.
 3. Presence of secondary growth.

[III] Points of interest

1. Medullary bundles. The number and arrangement of medullary bundles is not constant throughout. However, generally two medullary bundles occur in the centre of the pith throughout the length of the plant. These are said to be leaf traces in nature.

2. Secondary growth. An extra stelar cambium appears in the form of small arcs in the region of pericycle. These strips of cambia produce secondary vascular bundles which remain scattered in the beginning. The conjuntive tissue (prosenchyma) becomes lignified. The vascular bundles get embedded in the prosenchyma and differentiation between xylem and prosenchyma becomes difficult. However, thin walled phloem of the secondary vascular bundles appears as distinct patches in the lignified secondary tissues. It is variously called as 'phloem islands', interxylary phloem and included phloem.

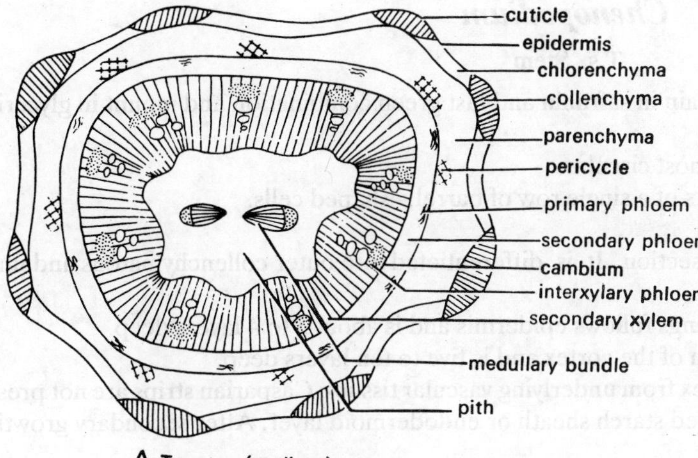

A. T.s. stem (outlines)

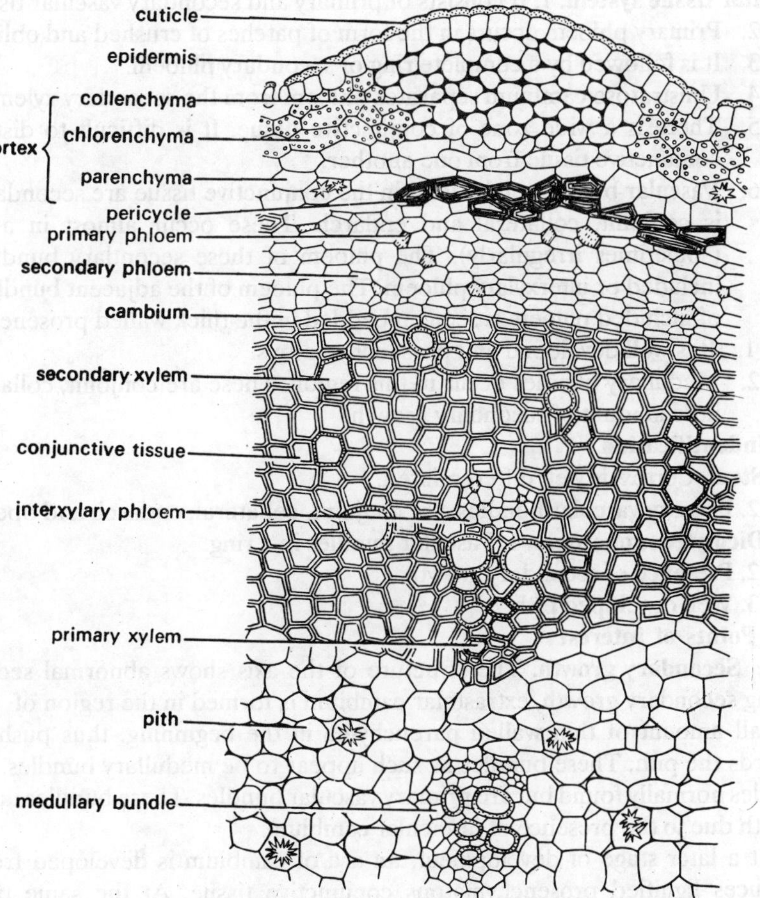

B T.s. stem (A sector showing cellular details)

Fig. 24. *Achyranthes*. T. s. stem.

Achyranthes **Family** – Amaranthaceae
English name – Chaff flower
Vernacular names – Puthkunda, Chirchitta.

Chenopodium

T.s. Stem

Cut a transverse section of the material, stain in safranin and fast green combination and mount in glycerine.

[I] Observations

The outline of the transverse section is almost circular.

Epidermis. 1. This outermost layer consists of a single row of barrel – shaped cells.

2. The cells are thickly cuticularised.

Cortex. 1. It forms a small part of the section. It is differentiated into outer collenchymatous and inner parenchymatous regions.

2. Collenchyma with angular thickenings follows epidermis and is about 3 to 4 layers deep.
3. Parenchyma forms the inner region of the cortex and is five to ten layers deep.

Endodermis. This layer separates the cortex from underlying vascular tissues. Casparian strips are not present and, therefore, the layer is called starch sheath or endodermoid layer. After secondary growth it becomes indistinguishable.

Pericycle. A distinct pericycle is absent.

Vascular tissue system. 1. It consists of primary and secondary vascular tissues in the following order.

2. Primary phloem occurs in the form of patches of crushed and obliterated tissues.
3. It is followed by a complete ring of secondary phloem.
4. Unistratose cambium separates phloem from the secondary xylem tissues located inner to it.
5. There is a wide zone of conjunctive tissue. It is difficult to distinguish secondary xylem and the conjunctive tissue from one another.
6. Vascular bundles embedded in the conjunctive tissue are secondary in origin. Each vascular bundle is conjoint, collateral and endarch. These occur almost in a ring being distributed regularly (sometimes irregularly). The phloem of these secondary bundles appears in patches similar to included or interxylary phloem. The phloem of the adjacent bundles coalesce and a continuous zone of included phloem is seen embedded in the thick walled prosenchymatous tissue.

Pith. 1. It is well developed and prosenchymatous.

2. Medullary bundles occur in this region. These are conjoint, collateral, endarch and open and show little amount of secondary growth.

[II] Indentification

1. Stem. Cortex is well differentiated.

2. Primary vascular bundles are conjoint, collateral, endarch and open.

2. Dicotyledonous stem. 1. Vascular bundles in a ring.

2. Presence of secondary growth.
3. Well developed pith.

[III] Points of interest

1. Secondary growth. The structure of the axis shows abnormal secondary growth. In *Chenopodium,* during secondary growth, extrastelar cambium is formed in the region of pericycle. This cambium produces a small amount of thin walled parenchyma in the beginning, thus pushing the primary vascular bundles towards the pith. These bundles as such appear to be medullary bundles. However, these are not leaf trace bundles normally found but are primary vascular bundles. These bundles undergo a little amount of secondary growth due to the presence of fascicular cambium.

At a later stage of development, an arc of cambium is developed from the tissues of the pericycle. It produces lignified prosenchymatous conjunctive tissue. At the same time the cambium forms vascular bundles. These get embedded in the prosenchymatous conjunctive tissue. The phloem is developed centripetally and gets buried in this conjunctive tissue, forming included or interxylary phloem or phloem islands. The secondary cambium (extra stelar) continues to function indefinitely and forms complex secondary tissues.

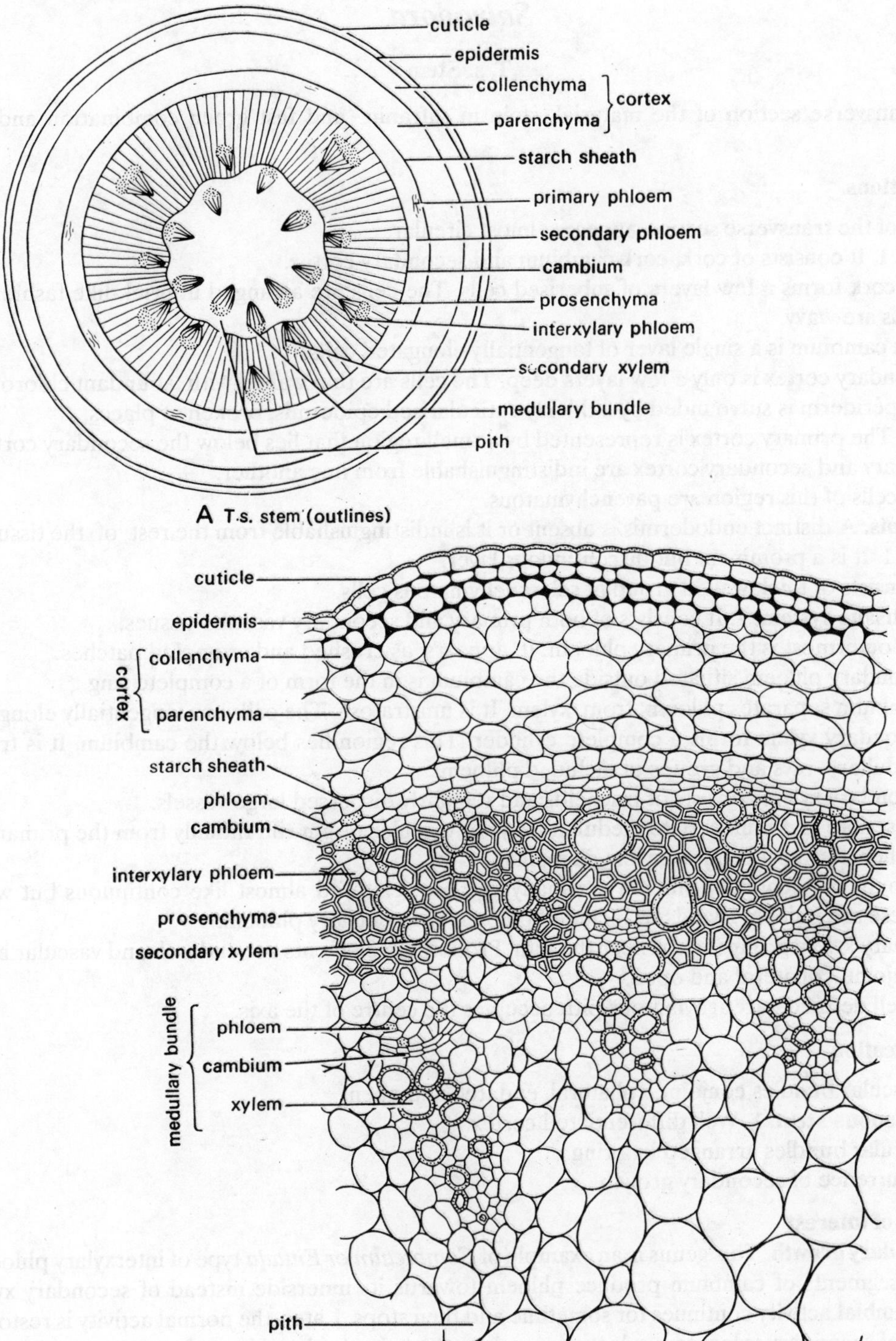

Fig. 25. ***Chenopodium.*** T. s. stem.

Chenopodium **Family –** Chenopodiaceae
English names – Pigweed, Lambs-quarters
Vernacular name – Bathua

Salvadora

T. s. Stem

Cut a transverse section of the material, stain in safranin and fast green combination and mount in glycerine.

[I] Observations

The outline of the transverse section appears almost circular.

1. Periderm. 1. It consists of cork, cork cambium and secondary cortex.

2. The cork forms a few layers of suberised cells. The cells are arranged in brick-like fashion. The cell walls are wavy.
3. Cork cambium is a single layer of tangentially elongated cells.
4. Secondary cortex is only a few layers deep. The cells are thin walled with abundant chloroplasts.
5. The periderm is surrounded by a thickly cuticularised epidermis, broken at places.

2. Cortex. 1. The primary cortex is represented by a small region that lies below the secondary cortex. Both primary and secondary cortex are indistinguishable from one another.

2. The cells of this region are parenchymatous.

3. Endodermis. A distinct endodermis is absent or it is indistinguishable from the rest of the tissues.

4. Pericycle. 1. It is a prominent but discontinuous layer.

2. It consists of thick walled group of sclerenchymatous cells.

5. Vascular tissue system. 1. It consists of both primary and secondary vascular tissues.

2. The outermost is the primary phloem. It appears as crushed and crumpled patches.
3. Secondary phloem situated outside the cambium is in the form of a complete ring.
4. Cambium separates phloem from xylem. It is unistratose. The cells are tangentially elongated.
5. Secondary xylem forms a complete cylinder. This region lies below the cambium. It is traversed by medullary rays and groups of included phloem.
6. Secondary xylem consists of tracheids and regularly dispersed large vessels.
7. Uniseriate and multiseriate medullary rays of vascular origin run radially from the primary phloem to the innermost primary xylem elements.
8. Groups of secondary phloem are many and are scattered almost like continuous but wavy zones. These are phloem islands or included phloem or interxylary phloem.
9. Primary xylem groups occur near the pith. Protoxylem elements are endarch and vascular bundles are conjoint, collateral and open.

6. Pith. A well defined parenchymatous pith occupies the centre of the axis.

[II] Identification

1. Stem. Vascular bundles conjoint, collateral, endarch and open.

2. Dicotyledonous stem. 1. Well differentiated cortex.

2. Vascular bundles arranged in a ring.
3. Occurrence of secondary growth.

[III] Points of interest

1. Secondary growth. This genus is an example of *Combretum or Entada* type of interxylary phloem. In this case, small segments of cambium produce phloem towards its innerside instead of secondary xylem. This abnormal cambial activity continues for sometime and then stops. Later, the normal activity is restored by the production of secondary xylem towards the innerside. As a result, the phloem formed toward the innerside for a short period gets embedded in the xylem elements. These groups of embedded phloem are called as 'phloem islands' or included phloem or interxylary phloem. The development is said to be centripetal.

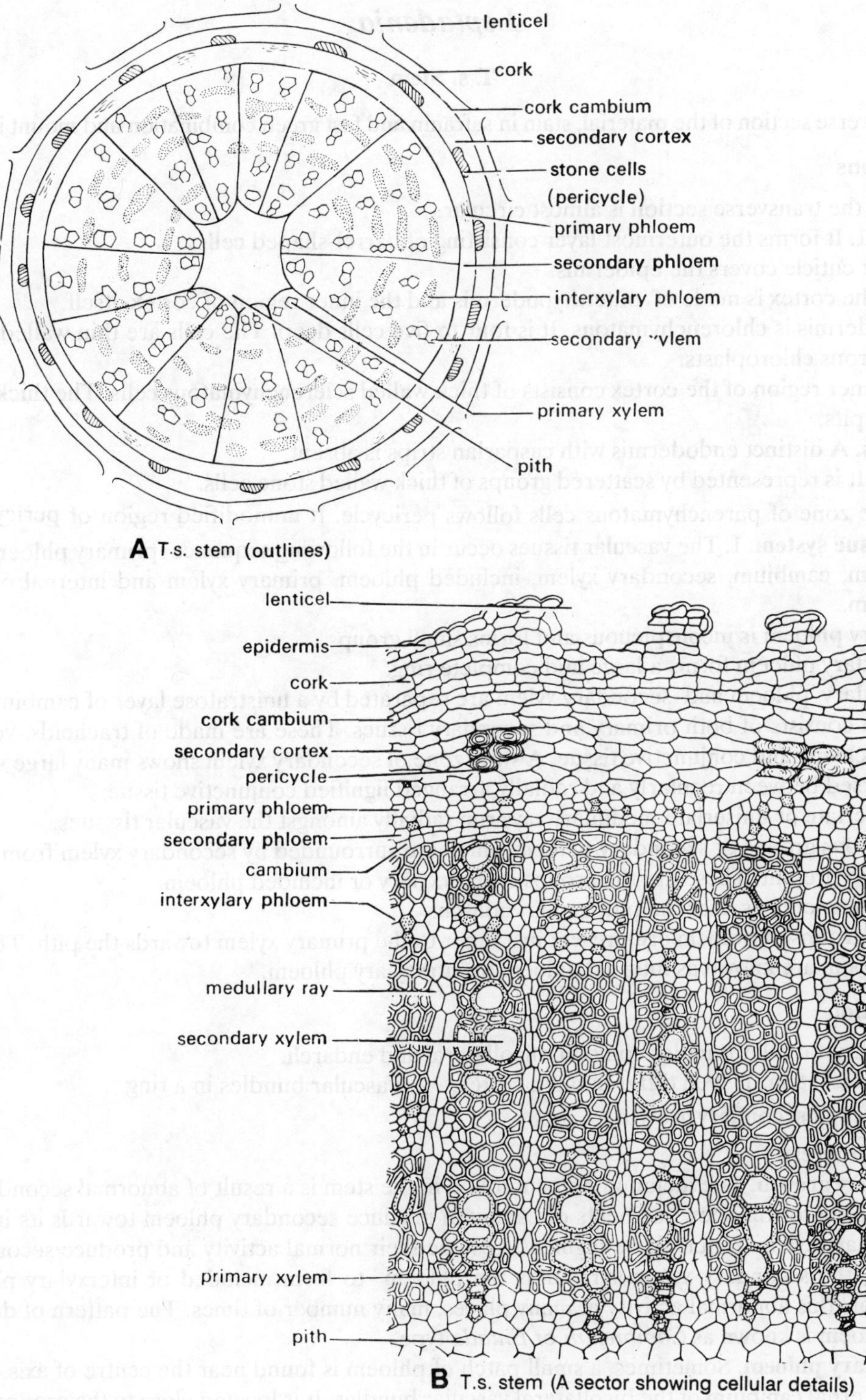

Fig. 26. ***Salvadora.*** T. s. stem.

Salvadora **Family** – Salvadoraceae
English name – Mustard tree
Vernacular names – Chhota pilu, Jhal, Kharjal.

Leptadenia

T. s. Stem

Cut a transverse section of the material, stain in safranin and fast green combination and mount in glycerine.

[I] Observations

The outline of the transverse section is almost circular.

1. Epidermis. 1. It forms the outermost layer consisting of barrel-shaped cells.
2. A thick cuticle covers the epidermis.

2. Cortex. 1. The cortex is made of outer hypodermis and the inner region of cortex itself.
2. Hypodermis is chlorenchymatous. It is four to five cells deep. The cells are thin walled and possess numerous chloroplasts.
3. The inner region of the cortex consists of thick walled sclerenchymatous cells. The thickenings show many pits.

3. Endodermis. A distinct endodermis with casparian strips is absent.

4. Pericycle. 1. It is represented by scattered groups of thick walled stone cells.
2. A wide zone of parenchymatous cells follows pericycle. It unmodified region of pericycle.

5. Vascular tissue system. 1. The vascular tissues occur in the following sequence–primary phloem, secondary phloem, cambium, secondary xylem, included phloem, primary xylem and internal or interxylary phloem.
2. Primary phloem is inconspicuous and forms small groups.
3. Secondary phloem forms a large and complete ring.
4. Secondary phloem and secondary xylem are separated by a unistratose layer of cambium.
5. Xylem consists of both primary and secondary tissues. These are made of tracheids, vessels, xylem parenchyma and conjunctive tissue. A wide zone of secondary xylem shows many large sized vessels, dispersed between regularly and radially arranged lignified conjunctive tissue.
6. Multiseriate or uniseriate medullary rays run radially amongst the vascular tisssues.
7. Numerous groups of secondary phloem which are surrounded by secondary xylem from all the sides are also present. These are the groups of interxylary or included phloem.
8. Primary xylem lies near the pith and is endarch.
9. A few groups of phloem are present just inner to the primary xylem towards the pith. These patches of phloem are known as internal phloem or intraxylary phloem.

[II] Identification

1. **Stem** . Primary vascular bundles conjoint, bicollateral and endarch.
2. **Dicotyledonous stem.** 1. Well differentiated cortex. 2. Vascular bundles in a ring.
3. Presence of secondary growth.

[III] Points of interest

1. Secondary growth. The included phloem found in the stem is a result of abnormal secondary growth. During secondary growth, a few segments of cambium produce secondary phloem towards its inner side in place of secondary xylem. Later, these segments resume their normal activity and produce secondary xylem as usual. Thus, the secondary xylem surrounds the phloem to form included or interxylary phloem. The cambium repeats this abnormal activity at many places, many number of times. The pattern of development of included phloem is known as *Combretum* or *Entada* type.

2. Intraxylary phloem. Sometimes, a small patch of phloem is found near the centre of axis. This is due to activity of internal cambium of the bicollateral vascular bundles. It is located close to the groups of primary xylem towards the pith. These groups represent the internal or inner phloem of the primary bicollateral vascular bundles.

3. Xerophytic characters. Presence of thick cuticle, chlorenchyma in the cortex and sclerenchymatous pericycle are xeromorphic characters shown by the stem.

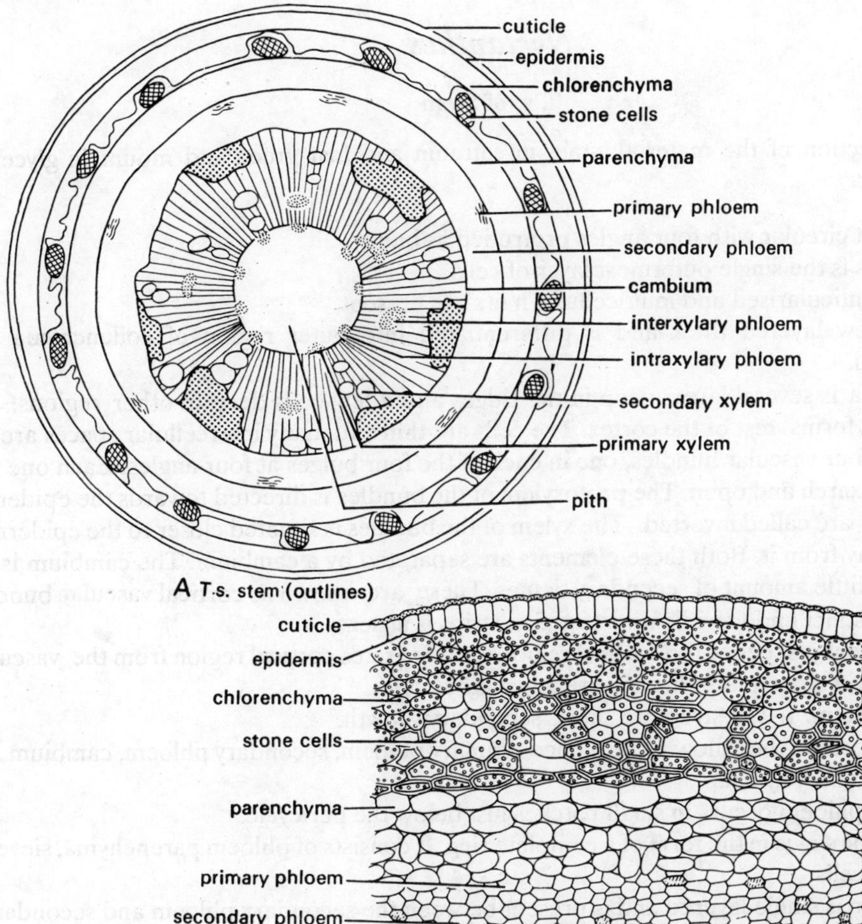

B T.s. stem (A sector showing cellular details)

Fig. 27. ***Leptadenia.*** T. s. stem.

Leptadenia **Family** – Asclepiadaceae
Vernacular name – Dori

Nyctanthes

T. s. of Stem

Cut a transverse section of the material, stain in safranin and fast green and mount in glycerine.

[I] Observations

The outline is almost circular with four angles protruded as bulges.

1. Epidermis. 1. This is the single outermost layer of cells.
2. It is thickly cuticularised and multicellular hairs are present.

2. Cortex. 1. It is few layered thick and is differentiated into outer region of collenchyma and inner parenchyma.
2. Collenchyma is several layers deep in the ridges and a few cells deep in other regions.
3. Parenchyma forms rest of the cortex. The cells are thin and many intercellular spaces are present.
4. Cortex has four vascular bundles, one in each of the four bulges at four angles. Each one is conjoint, collateral, exarch and open. The protoxylem of the bundles is directed towards the epidermis, hence the bundles are called inverted. The xylem of the bundles is situated closer to the epidermis and the phloem away from it. Both these elements are separated by a cambium. The cambium is active and produces a little amount of secondary tissues. These are known as cortical vascular bundles.

3. Endodermis. A distinct endodermis with caspaian strips is absent.

4. Pericycle. It is present just below the cortical region and separates cortical region from the vascular tissues. It forms almost a complete ring of parenchymatous cells.

5. Vascular tissue system. 1. The structure shows secondary growth.
2. The tissues occur in the following sequence–primary phloem, secondary phloem, cambium, secondary xylem and primary xylem.
3. The primary phloem occurs in small patches just below the pericycle.
4. Secondary phloem is in the form of a complete ring. It consists of phloem parenchyma, sieve tubes and companion cells.
5. The cambium is single layered and is present between the secondary phloem and secondary xylem.
6. Secondary xylem occupies most of the region towards the centre of the axis. It consists of tracheids, vessels and xylem parenchyma. A few vessels are very distinct. Annual rings are not very distinct.
7. Primary xylem lies close to the pith. The protoxylem is endarch. Primary vascular bundles are conjoint, collateral, endarch and open.

6. Pith. A large parenchymatous pith is present in the centre.

[II] Identification

1. Stem. Vascular bundles conjoint, collateral and endarch.

2. Dicotyledonous stem. 1, Cortex well differentiated.
2. Pericycle distinguishable.
3. Vascular bundles in a ring.
4. Secondary growth present.
5. Pith well developed.

[III] Point of interest

Cortical vascular bundles. The stem shows four vascular bundles in the cortex, one each in four corners of the angular stem. These bundles called as cortical bundles due to their location in the cortex, are in fact leaf trace bundles. Bundles arise at much lower a node. These pass through the cortex of the upper internode before supplying the leaf at the next upper node. During the course of their upward passage, the bundles become inversely oriented. Thus, the phloem of the bundles is directed away from the epidermis while the endarch protoxylem is closer to the epidermis.

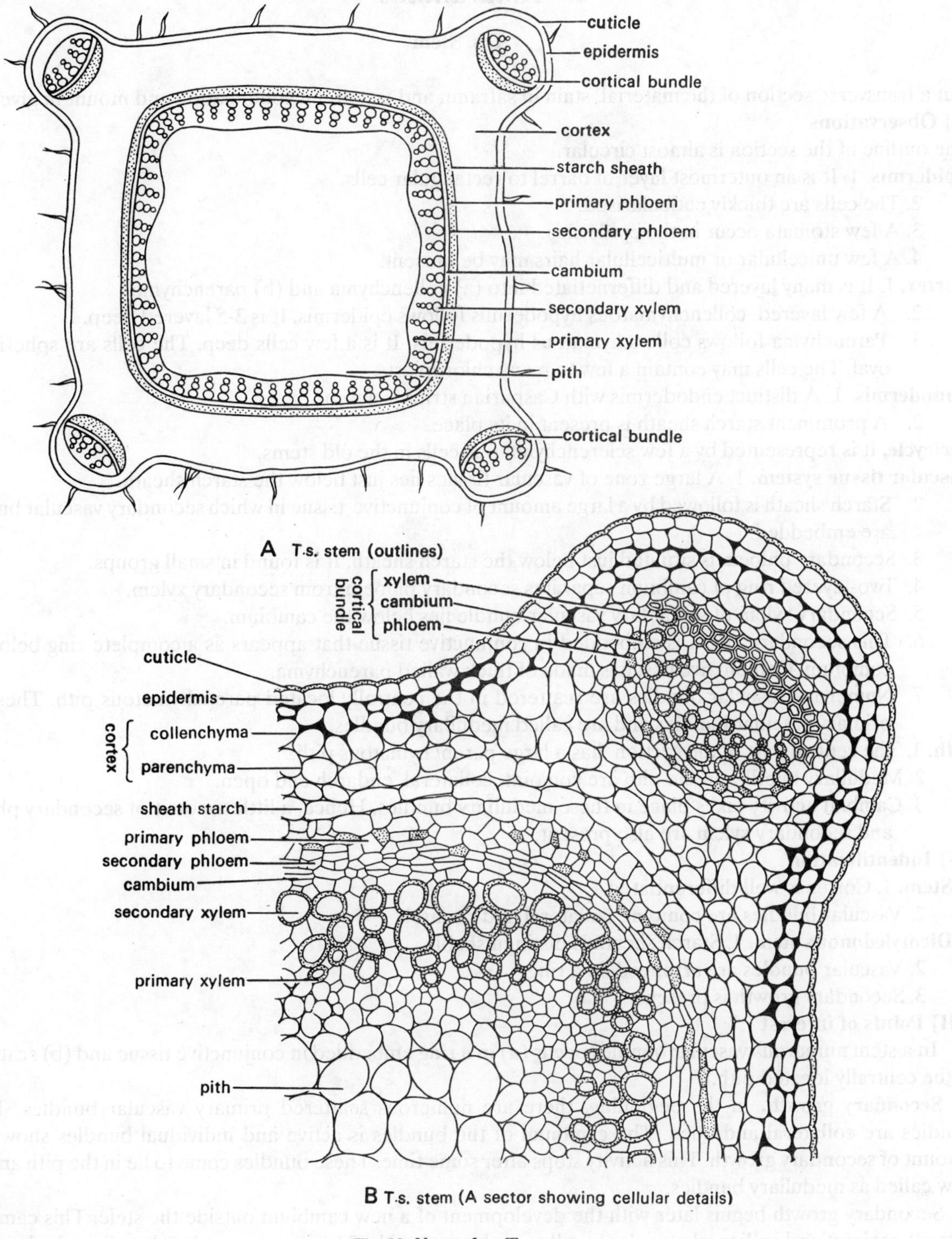

Fig. 28. *Nyctanthes.* T. s. stem.

Nyctanthes **Family** – Nyctanthaceae.
English name – Tree of sorrow
Vernacular names – Harsinghar, Sephalika.

Amaranthus

T. s. Stem

Cut a transverse section of the material, stain in safranin and fast green combination and mount in glycerine.

[I] Observations

The outline of the section is almost circular.

Epidermis. 1. It is an outermost layer of barrel to rectangular cells.
2. The cells are thickly cuticularised.
3. A few stomata occur in the epidermis.
4. A few unicellular or multicellular hairs may be present.

Cortex. 1. It is many layered and differnetiated into (a) collenchyma and (b) parenchyma.
2. A few layered collenchymatous hypodermis follows epidermis. It is 3-5 layered deep.
3. Parenchyma follows collenchymatous hypodermis. It is a few cells deep. The cells are spherical to oval. The cells may contain a few to many chloroplasts.

Endodermis. 1. A distinct endodermis with Casparian strips is absent.
2. A prominent starch sheath is present in its place.

Pericycle. It is represented by a few sclerenchymatous cells in the old stems.

Vascular tissue system. 1. A large zone of vascular tissues lies just below the starch sheath.
2. Starch sheath is followed by a large amount of conjunctive tissue in which secondary vascular bundles are embedded.
3. Secondary phloem is situated just below the starch sheath. It is found in small groups.
4. Two-layered ring of cambium separates secondary phloem from secondary xylem.
5. Secondary xylem of secondary vascular bundle lies below the cambium.
6. This secondary xylem is embedded in conjunctive tissue that appears as a complete ring below the cambium. Conjunctive tissue is made of thick walled parenchyma.
7. Numerous vascular bundles are scattered in the centrally located parenchymatous pith. These are primary vascular bundles and are called medullary bundles.

Pith. 1. The central part of the section has a large parenchymatous pith.
2. Medullary bundles in the pith are conjoint, collateral, endarch and open.
3. Cambial activity takes place in these medullary bundles. Hence, a little amount of secondary phloem and secondary xylem are also present.

[II] Indentification

1. Stem. 1. Cortex is well differentiated.
2. Vascular bundles are conjoint, collateral and endarch.

2. Dicotyledonous stem. 1. Starch sheath is distinguishable.
2. Vascular bundles are arranged in a ring.
3. Secondary growth is present.

[III] Points of interest

In a stem numerous vascular bundles occur (a) in a ring embedded in conjunctive tissue and (b) scattered in the centrally located pith.

Secondary growth. In the beginning, there are numerous scattered primary vascular bundles. These bundles are collateral and open. The cambium of the bundles is active and individual bundles show little amount of secondary growth. This activity stops after some time. These bundles come to lie in the pith and are now called as medullary bundles.

Secondary growth begins later with the development of a new cambium outside the stele. This cambium cuts off conjoint and collateral vascular bundles on the outer side. These are secondary bundles which remain embedded in the large amount of conjunctive tissue formed by the cambium.

Such many rings of vascular bundles are formed which remain embedded in the conjunctive tissue and their phloem consequently gives an appearnace of included phloem or phloem islands at number of places.

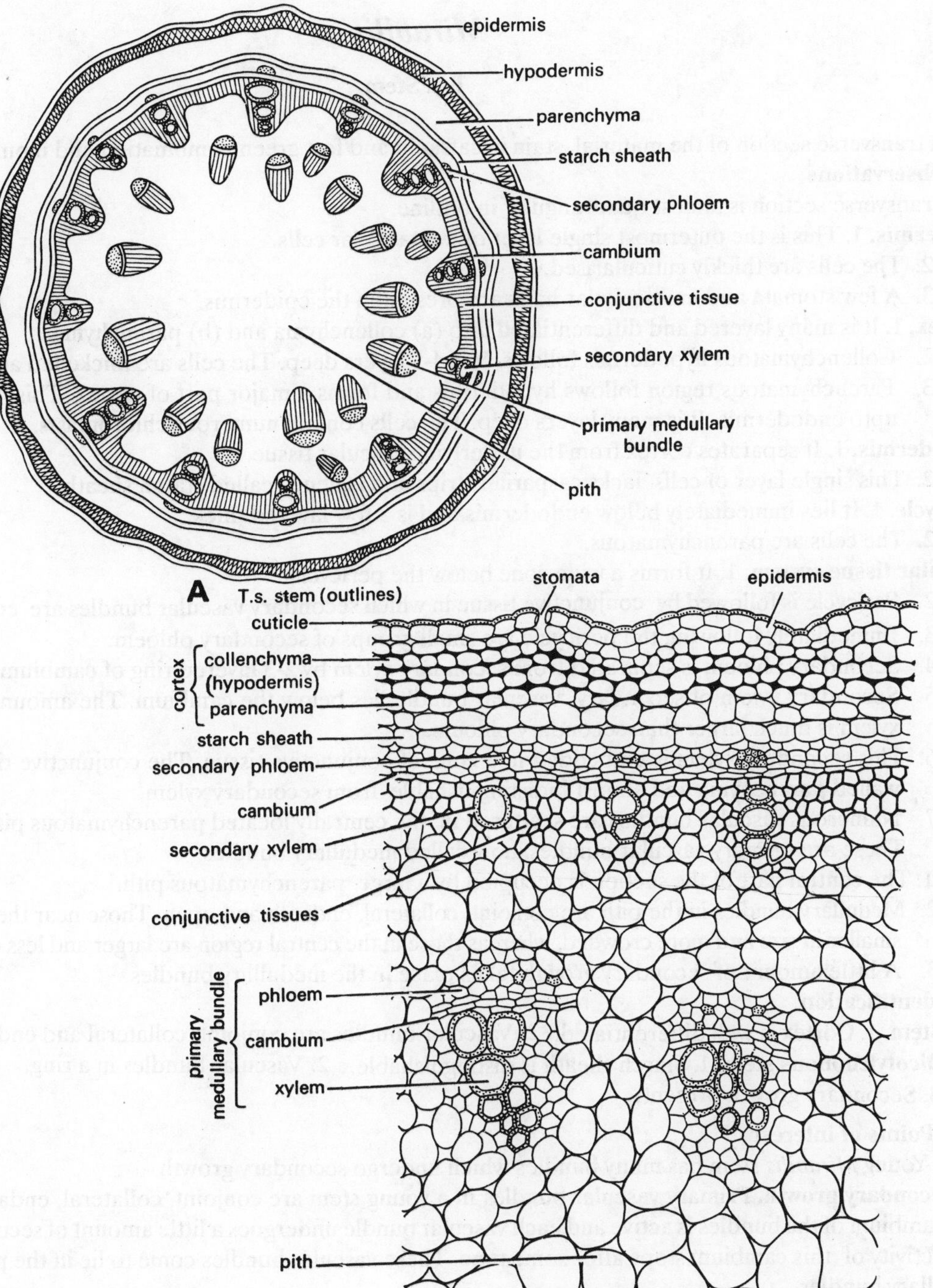

Fig. 29. ***Amaranthus.*** T. s. stem.

Amaranthus **Family** – Amaranthaceae
English names – Amaranth, African/Chinese spinach
Vernacular names – Chaulai, Lal sag, Ramdana

Mirabilis

T. s. Stem

Cut a transverse section of the material, stain in safranin and fast green combination and mount in glycerine

[I] Observations

The transverse section is almost quadrangular in outline.

Epidermis. 1. This is the outermost single layer of rectangular cells.
2. The cells are thickly cuticularised.
3. A few stomata and multicellular hairs are present in the epidermis.

Cortex. 1. It is many layered and differentiated into (a) collenchyma and (b) parenchyma.
2. Collenchymatous hypodermis follows. It is 4-5 layers deep. The cells are thickened at the corners.
3. Parenchymatous region follows hypodermis and forms a major part of cortex. This region extends upto endodermis. It is many layers deep. The cells contain numerous chloroplasts.

Endodermis. 1. It separates cortex from the underlying vascular tissue.
2. This single layer of cells lacks casparian strips and is hence called starch sheath.

Pericycle. 1. It lies immediately below endodermis and is a few layered thick.
2. The cells are parenchymatous.

Vascular tissue system. 1. It forms a wide zone below the pericycle.
2. Pericycle is followed by conjunctive tissue in which secondary vascular bundles are embedded.
3. Immediately following the pericycle are small groups of secondary phloem.
4. Secondary phloem is separated from secondary xylem by 2-3 layered ring of cambium.
5. Secondary xylem of secondary vascular bundle lies below the cambium. The amount of secondary xylem is much larger than secondary phloem.
6. This secondary xylem is embedded in a zone of conjunctive tissue. The conjunctive tissue is a thick walled parenchyma and almost indistinguishable from secondary xylem.
7. Numerous vascular bundles are scattered in the centrally located parenchymatous pith. These are primary vascular bundles, now called medullary bundles.

Pith. 1. The central part of the section is occupied by a large parenchymatous pith.
2. Medullary bundles in the pith are conjoint, collateral, endarch and open. Those near the periphery are smaller in size and more crowded, whereas those in the central region are larger and less crowded.
3. A little amount of secondary growth takes place in the medullary bundles.

[II] Identification.

1. Stem. 1. Cortex is well differentiated. 2. Vascular bundles are conjoint, collateral and endarch.

2. Dicotyledonous stem. 1. Starch sheath is distinguishable. 2. Vascular bundles in a ring.
3. Secondary growth present.

[III] Points of interest

Young *Mirabilis* stem has many bundles which undergo secondary growth.

Secondary growth. Primary vascular bundles in a young stem are conjoint, collateral, endarch and open. The cambium of the bundles is active and each vascular bundle undergoes a little amount of secondary growth. The activity of this cambium stops after some time. These vascular bundles come to lie in the pith and called medullary bundles.

Secondary growth starts with the formation of secondary cambium originating in the parenchyma closer to pericycle. This cambium cuts off secondary xylem on its inner side. It remains embedded in thick walled conjunctive tissues. A very small amount of secondary phloem elements are formed by the cambium on its outer side.

Due to successive cambial ring formation, rings of vascular tissues embedded in the conjunctive tissue are formed.

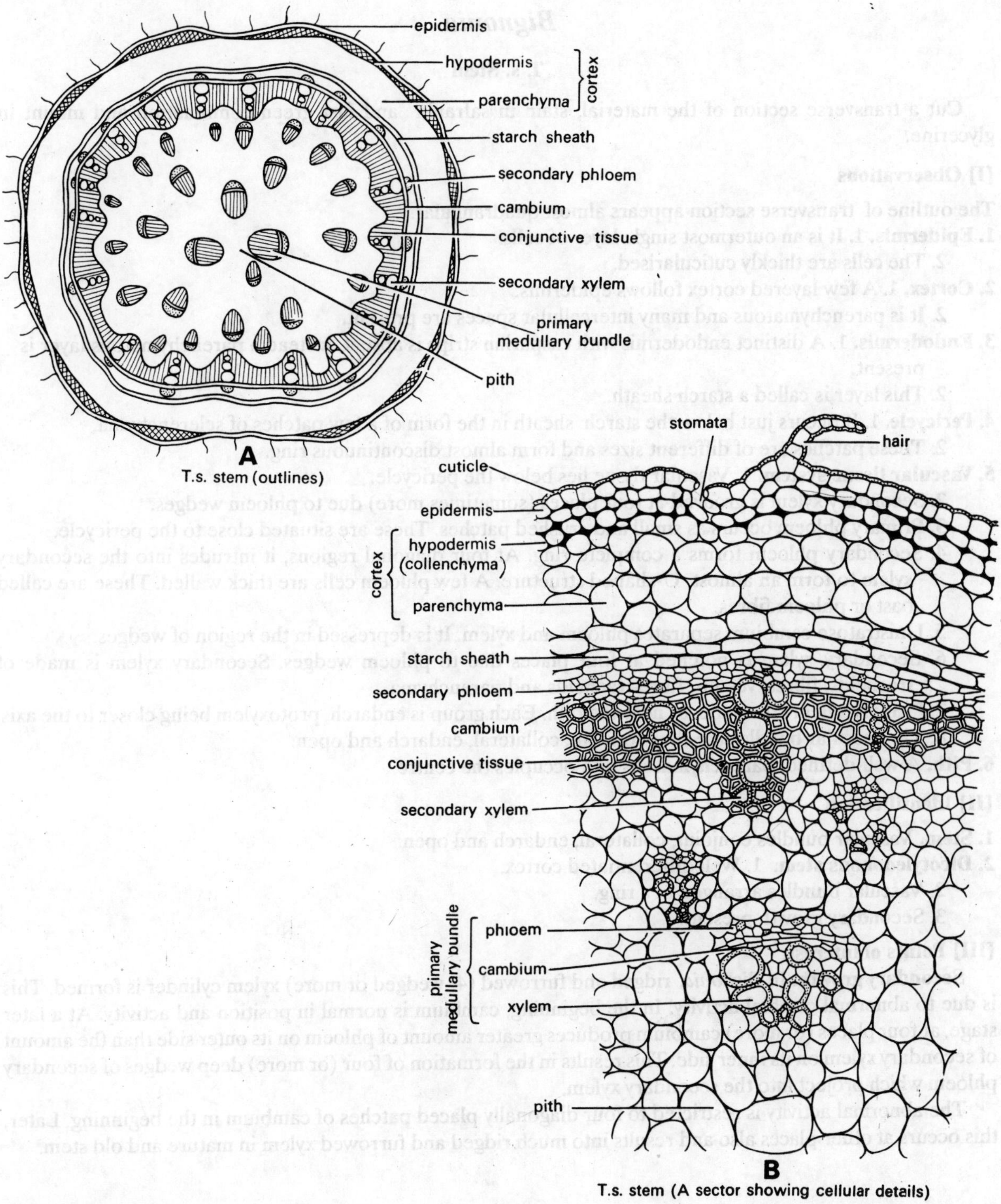

Fig. 30. ***Mirabilis.*** T. s. stem.

Mirabilis **Family** – Nyctaginaceae
English name – Four-o'-clock plant.
Vernacular name – Gulabas.

Bignonia

T. s. Stem

Cut a transverse section of the material, stain in safranin and fast green combination and mount in glycerine.

[I] Observations

The outline of transverse section appears almost quadrangular.

1. Epidermis. 1. It is an outermost single layer of cells.
   2. The cells are thickly cuticularised.

2. Cortex. 1. A few layered cortex follows epidermis.
   2. It is parenchymatous and many intercellular spaces are present.

3. Endodermis. 1. A distinct endodermis with casparian strips is absent, instead a parenchymatous layer is present.
   2. This layer is called a starch sheath.

4. Pericycle. 1. It occurs just below the starch sheath in the form of a few patches of sclerenchyma.
   2. These patches are of different sizes and form almost discontinuous ring.

5. Vascular tissue system. 1. Vascular tissue lies below the pericycle.
   2. Secondary xylem is grooved at four places (sometimes more) due to phloem wedges.
   3. Primary phloem occurs as small and crushed patches. These are situated close to the pericycle.
   4. Secondary phloem forms a complete ring. At four diagonal regions, it intrudes into the secondary xylem to form an almost U-shaped structure. A few phloem cells are thick walled. These are called bast or phloem fibres.
   5. Unistratose cambium separates phloem and xylem. It is depressed in the region of wedges.
   6. Secondary xylem is notched at four places due to phloem wedges. Secondary xylem is made of tracheids, fibres, vessels, fibre-tracheids and parenchyma.
   7. Primary xylem groups occur near the pith. Each group is endarch, protoxylem being closer to the axis.
   8. The vascular bundles are thus conjoint, collateral, endarch and open.

6. Pith. A well-defined, parenchymatous pith occupies the centre.

[II] Identification

1. Stem. Vascular bundles conjoint, collateral, endarch and open.

2. Dicotyledonous stem. 1. Well differentiated cortex.
   2. Vascular bundles arranged in a ring.
   3. Secondary growth present.

[III] Points of interest.

Secondary growth. In *Bignonia,* ridged and furrowed (4- wedged or more) xylem cylinder is formed. This is due to abnormal cambial activity. In the beginning, cambium is normal in position and activity. At a later stage, at four places (or more) cambium produces greater amount of phloem on its outer side than the amount of secondary xylem on its inner side. This results in the formation of four (or more) deep wedges of secondary phloem which project into the secondary xylem.

The abnormal activity is restricted to four diagonally placed patches of cambium in the beginning. Later, this occurs at other places also and results into much ridged and furrowed xylem in mature and old stem.

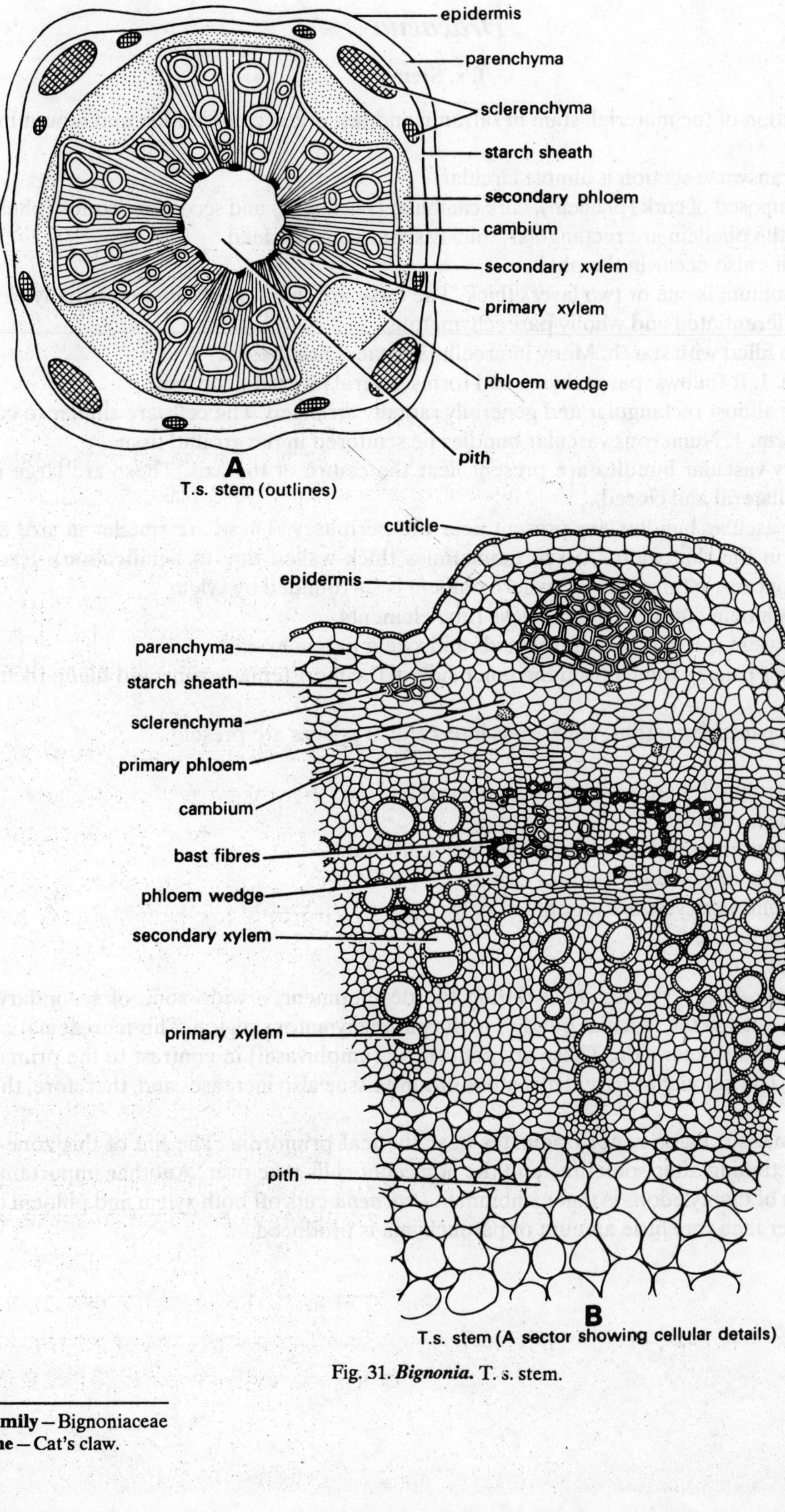

Fig. 31. ***Bignonia.*** T. s. stem.

Bignonia **Family** – Bignoniaceae
English name – Cat's claw.

Dracaena

T. s. Stem

Cut a transverse section of the material, stain in safranin and fast green combination and mount in glycerine.

[I] Observations

The outline of the transverse section is almost circular.

Periderm. 1. It is composed of cork (phellem), cork cambium (phellogen) and secondary cortex (phelloderm).

2. The cells of the phellem are rectangular, thickly suberised and dead.
3. A few lenticles also occur in the phellem.
4. The cork cambium is one or two layers thick. The cells are thin walled and tangentially elongated.

Cortex. 1. It is undifferentiated and wholly parenchymatous.

2. The cells are filled with starch. Many intercellular spaces are present.

Meristematic tissue. 1. It follows parenchyma and forms several layered deep zone.

2. The cells are almost rectangular and generally radially arranged. The cells are similar to cambium.

Vascular tissue system. 1. Numerous vascular bundles lie scattered in the ground tissue.

2. The primary vascular bundles are present near the centre of the axis. These are large in size and typically collateral and closed.
3. Secondary vascular bundles are present near the periphery. These are smaller in size and remain embedded in the thin walled tissue (sometimes thick walled due to lignification). Each vascular bundle is concentric (amphivasal) where phloem is surrounded by xylem.
4. Secondary phloem consists of short sieve tube elements.
5. Secondary xylem is composed of tracheids and xylem parenchyma.

Ground tissue. 1. This tissue extends from the inner side of the meristematic zone and fill up the major part of the axis.

2. The cells are parenchymatous. Numerous intercellular spaces are present.

[II] Identification

1. Stem. 1. Vascular bundles are conjoint and collateral.

2. Ground tissue is present.

2. Monocotyledonous stem. 1. Vascular bundles are scattered.

2. Cambium is absent (vascular bundles closed).
3. Endodermis and pericycle are absent.
4. Pith is not well defined.

[III] Point of interest

Secondary growth. At a very late stage during the development, a wide zone of secondary meristem (cambium) develops outside the vascular bundles in the parenchymatous region. This meristematic tissue cuts off vascular bundles on its inner side. These are concentric (amphivasal) in contrast to the primary bundles which are collateral. The amount of parenchymatous ground tissue also increases and, therefore, the diameter of the stem.

The cambium (meristermatic zone) originates near the leaf primordia. The life of this zone or layer is limited. It stops functioning after sometime and the adjaceent cells take over. Another important feature in contrast to cambium of dicotyledons is that cambium in *Dracaena* cuts off both xylem and phloem on its inner side while on its outer face very little amount of parenchyma is produced.

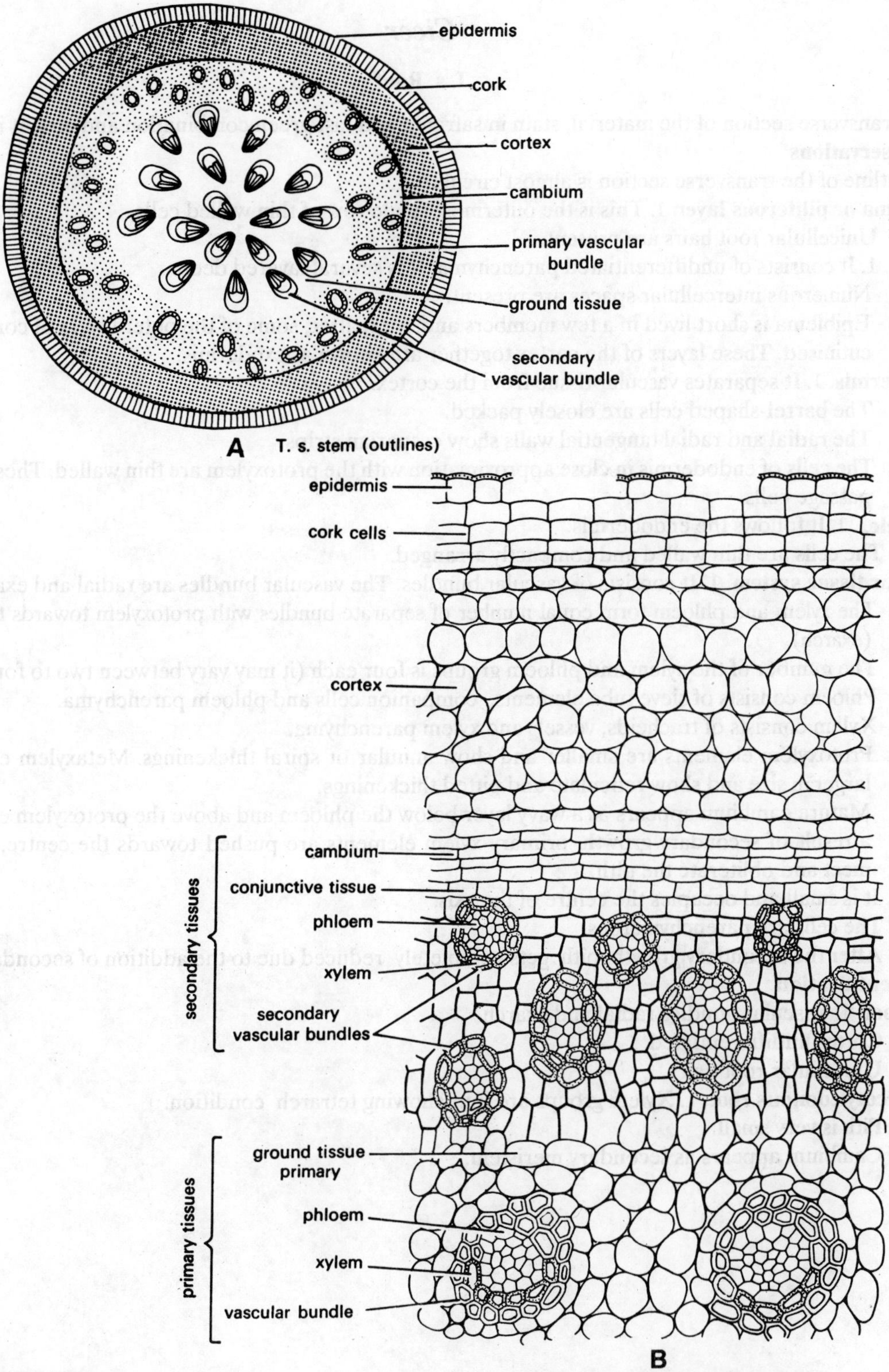

B
T. s. stem (A sector showing cellular details)

Fig. 32. ***Dracaena.*** T. s. stem.

Dracaena **Family** – Liliaceae
English name – Dragon plant

Cicer

T. s. Root

Cut a transverse section of the material, stain in safranin and fast green combination and mount in glycerine.

[I] Observations

The outline of the transverse section is almost circular.

Epiblema or piliferous layer. 1. This is the outermost single row of thin walled cells.

2. Unicellular root hairs are present.

Cortex. 1. It consists of undifferentiated parenchyma. It is several layered deep.

2. Numerous intercellular spaces are present.
3. Epiblema is short lived in a few members and, thereafter, some of the outer layers of cortex become cutinised. These layers of the cortex together are known as exodermis.

Endodermis. 1. It separates vascular tissue from the cortex.

2. The barrel-shaped cells are closely packed.
3. The radial and radial tangential walls show casparian strips
4. The cells of endodermis in close approximation with the protoxylem are thin walled. These are called passage cells.

Pericycle. 1. It follows the endodermis.

2. The cells are thin walled and compactly arranged.

Vascular tissue system. 1. It consists of vascular bundles. The vascular bundles are radial and exarch.

2. The xylem and phloem form equal number of separate bundles with protoxylem towards the pericycle (exarch).
3. The number of the xylem and phloem groups is four each (it may vary between two to four).
4. Phloem consists of sieve tube elements, companion cells and phloem parenchyma.
5. Xylem consists of tracheids, vessels and xylem parenchyma.
6. Protoxylem elements are smaller and show annular or spiral thickenings. Metaxylem elements are larger in size and show reticulate and pitted thickenings.
7. Mature cambium appears as a wavy layer below the phloem and above the protoxylem elements. As a result of secondary growth, primary xylem elements are pushed towards the centre, where they meet and obliterate the pith.

Pith. 1. It is small and occupies the centre of the axis.

2. The cells are parenchymatous.
3. After the secondary growth, pith gets completely reduced due to the addition of secondary tissues.

[II] Identification

1. Root. 1. Vascular bundles radial and exarch.

2. Cortex undifferentiated.
3. Unicellular root hairs.

2. Dicotyledonous root. 1. Xylem groups are four showing tetrarch condition.

2. Pith is very small.
3. Cambium appears as secondary meristem.

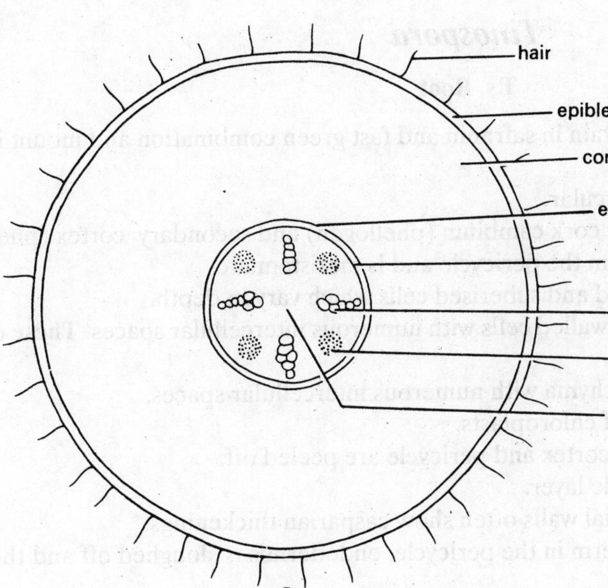

A
T. s. root (outlines)

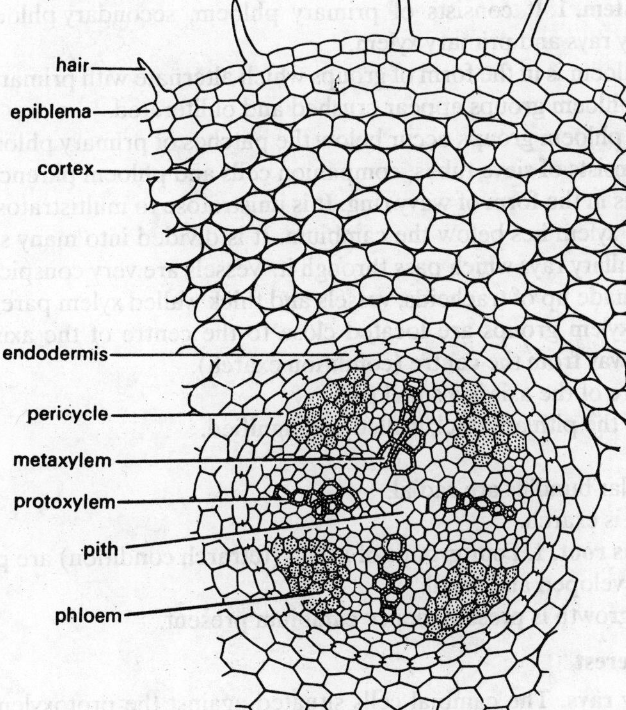

B
T. s. root (A sector showing cellular details)

Fig. 33. *Cicer*. T. s. root.

Cicer **Family –** Papilionaceae
English names – Gram, chick pea
Vernacular name – Chana.

Tinospora

T.s. Root

Cut a transverse section of the material, stain in safranin and fast green combination and mount in glycerine.

[I] Observations

The outline of the transverse section is circular.

Periderm. 1. It consists of cork (phellem), cork cambium (phellogen) and secondary cortex (phelloderm).
2. The cork cambium originates from the pericycle and is meristematic.
3. Cork is made of rectangular, dead and suberised cells which vary in depth.
4. Secondary cortex consists of thin walled cells with numerous intercellular spaces. These cells contain large number of chloroplasts.

Cortex. 1. It consists of thin walled parenchyma with numèrous intercellular spaces.
2. The cells possess large number of chloroplasts.
3. After the formation of periderm, cortex and pericycle are peeled off.

Endodermis. 1. It is well demarcated single layer.
2. The tangential and radial tangential walls often show casparian thickenings.
3. Due to the development of periderm in the pericycle, endodermis is sloughed off and therefore, it is not visible in the old structure.

Pericycle. 1. It follows endodermis and is in the form of a complete ring of barrel-shaped cells.
2. This is the place where cork cambium originates to form periderm.

Vascular tissue system. 1. It consists of primary phloem, secondary phloem, cambium, secondary xylem, medullary rays and primary xylem.
2. Primary phloem is in the form of groups which alternate with primary xylem groups near the centre of axis. The phloem groups appear crushed and obliterated.
3. Secondary phloem groups occur below the patches of primary phloem and are massive.
4. Phloem consists of sieve tubes, companion cells and phloem parenchyma.
5. Cambium is in the form of wavy ring. It is unistratose to multistratose.
6. Secondary xylem lies below the cambium. It is divided into many smaller and larger regions due to wide medullary rays which pass through it. Vessels are very conspicuous due to their large diameter. Xylem is made up of tracheids, vessels and thick walled xylem parencyhyma.
7. Primary xylem groups are located close to the centre of the axis. Protoxylem of these groups is directed away from the centre (condition exarch).

Pith. 1. In the centre of the axis is a small pith.
2. The cells of the pith are thick walled and lignified.

[II] Identification

1. **Root.** 1. Vascular bundles are radial.
2. Protoxylem is exarch.

2. **Dicotyledonous root.** 1. Four groups of xylem (tetrarch condition) are present.
2. Pith is ill developed and small.
3. Secondary growth is present, hence cambium present.

[III] Points of Interest

1. **Wide medullary rays.** The cambial cells situated against the protoxylem elements produce multiseriate, parenchymatous and broad vascular (medullary) rays. These run between and through xylem and phloem, dividing the secondary vascular tissues into smaller groups.
2. **Xerophytic characters.** Presence of chlorenchyma in the cortex exhibits the aerial nature of the root.

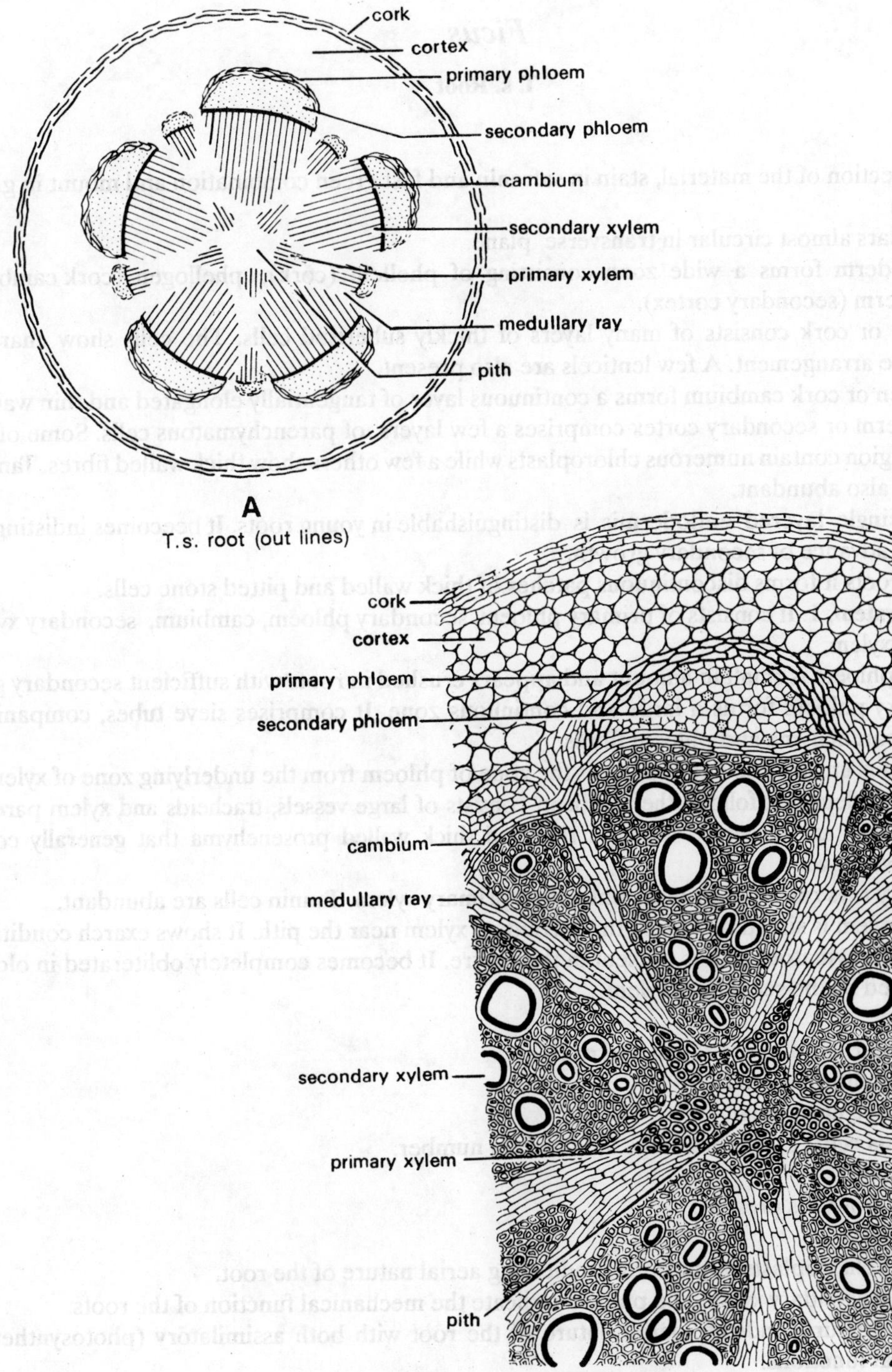

Fig. 34. ***Tinospora.*** T. s. root.

Tinospora **Family** – Menispermaceae
Vernacular names – Gulancha, Giloe.

Ficus

T. s. Root

Cut a transvere section of the material, stain in safranin and fast green combination and mount in glycerine.

[I] Observations

The section appears almost circular in transverse plane.

Periderm. 1. Periderm forms a wide zone consisting of phellem (cork), phellogen (cork cambium) and phelloderm (secondary cortex).

2. Phellem or cork consists of many layers of thickly suberised cells. The cells show characteristic brick-like arrangement. A few lenticels are also present.
3. Phellogen or cork cambium forms a continuous layer of tangentially elongated and thin walled cells.
4. Phelloderm or secondary cortex comprises a few layers of parenchymatous cells. Some of the cells of this region contain numerous chloroplasts while a few others show thick walled fibres. Tannin filled cells are also abundant.

Endodermis. A single layered endodermis is distinguishable in young roots. It beecomes indistinguishable with the advance of secondary growth.

Pericycle. In old roots it forms discontinuous patches of thick walled and pitted stone cells.

Vascular tissue system. 1. It consists of primary phloem, secondary phloem, cambium, secondary xylem and primary xylem.

2. Primary phloem is small in amount and appears crushed in roots with sufficient secondary growth.
3. Secondary phloem forms a large and continuous zone. It comprises sieve tubes, companion cells, phloem parenchyma and phloem fibres.
4. Cambium is unistratose and separates the zone of phloem from the underlying zone of xylem.
5. Secondary xylem that follows the cambium consists of large vessels, tracheids and xylem parenchyma. These tissues are dispersed amongst thin and thick walled prosenchyma that generally constitutes conjunctive tissue.
6. Medullary rays run from primary phloem to primary xylem. Tannin cells are abundant.
7. Primary xylem is situated close to the secondary xylem near the pith. It shows exarch condition.

Pith. A small parenchymatous pith is present in the centre. It becomes completely obliterated in older roots being occupied by the secondary xylem.

[II] Identification

1. Root. 1. Vascular bundles are radial and exarch.
2. Cortex is undifferentiated.
3. Root hairs are unicellular.

2. Dicotyledonous root. 1. Xylem groups are fewer in number.
2. Pith is small.
3. Secondary growth is present.

[III] Points of interest

1. Presence of chloroplasts in the cortex indicating aerial nature of the root.
2. Abundant seecondary xylem and phloem indicate the mechanical function of the roots.
3. The above features indicate aerial nature of the root with both assimilatory (photosynthetic) and mechanical functions.

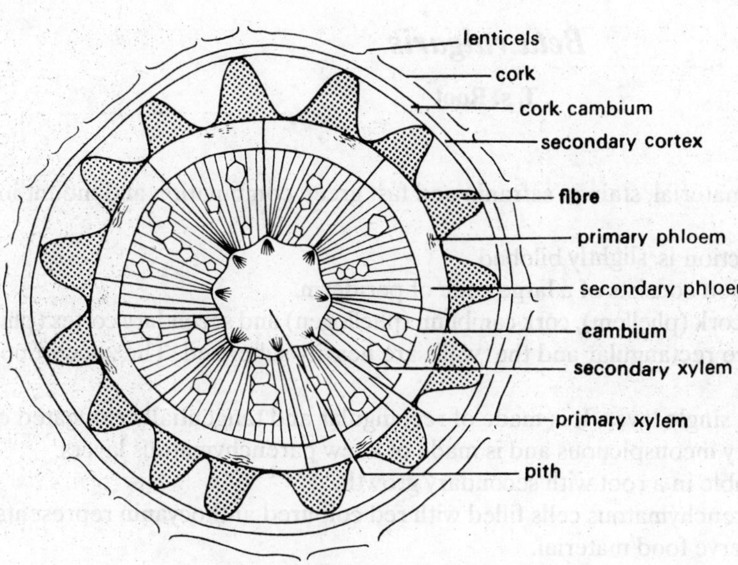

A T.s. root (outlines)

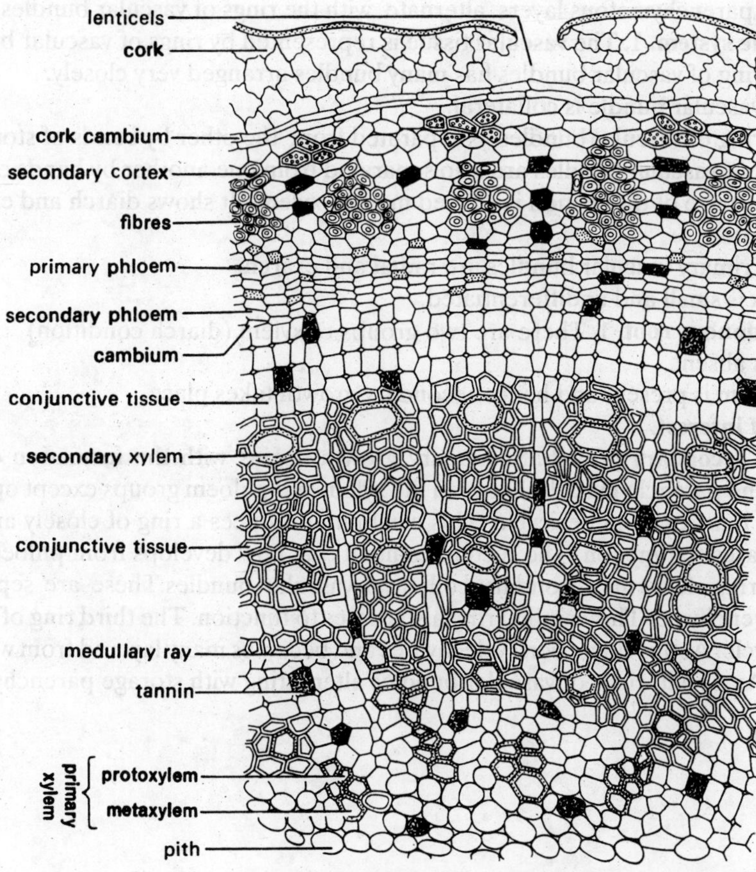

B T.s. root (A sector showing cellular details)

Fig. 35. *Ficus.* T. s. root.

Ficus. **Family** – Moraceae
English name – Banyan
Vernacular name – Barh, Bargad

Beta vulgaris

T. s. Root

Cut a transverse section of the material, stain in safranin and fast green combination and mount in glycerine.

[I] Observations

The outline of the transverse section is slightly bilobed.

Periderm. 1. The outermost region consists of a large zone of periderm.
2. Periderm is made up of cork (phellem), cork cambium (phellogen) and secondary cortex (phelloderm).
3. The cells of the cork are rectangular and the walls are heavily suberised. The zone of cork is about 8-10 layers deep.
4. Cork cambium forms a single layer. It is made of rectangular and tangentially elongated cells.
5. Secondary cortex is very inconspicuous and is made of a few parenchymatous layers.

Endodermis. It is indistinguishable in a root with secondary growth.

Pericycle. 1. A large zone of parenchymatous cells filled with red coloured anthocyanin represents pericycle. The cells are rich in reserve food material.
2. The pericycle becomes proliferated due to repeated divisions and forms many pericyclic layers.
3. These parenchymatous layers alternate with the rings of vascular bundles.

Vascular tissue system. 1. The vascular tissue is represented by rings of vascular bundles.
2. Each ring of vascular bundles has many bundles arranged very closely.
3. Each vascular bundle is collateral.
4. Each ring of vascular bundles is separated from the other by bands of storage parenchyma.
5. Adjacent vascular bundles are also separated from one another by bands of radial parenchyma.
6. In the centre of the section is a fused mass of xylem . It shows diarch and exarch condition.

[II] Identification

1. Root. 1. Primary vascular bundles are radial and exarch.
2. Cortex is small and undifferentiated.

2. Dicotyledonous root. 1. There are two groups of xylem (diarch condition)
2. Pith as absent.
3. Cambium is present and hence secondary growth takes place.

[III] Points of interest.

Abnormal secondary growth. Secondary growth begins with the formation of primary cambium. It is formed from the parenchyma cells between the xylem and phloem groups except opposite the two protoxylem groups where it arises from pericycle. This cambium produces a ring of closely arranged collateral vascular bundles. It ceases to function. The second cambial ring now develops from phloem parenchyma outside the first cambial ring. It forms secondary collateral vascular bundles.These are separated by radially formed secondary parenchyma. This cambial ring also ceases to function. The third ring of cambium is now produced from the pricycle. At this stage, pericycle divides and becomes many layered from which cambial rings develop successively. As a rsult, rings of vascular bundles alternating with storage parenchyma are formed.

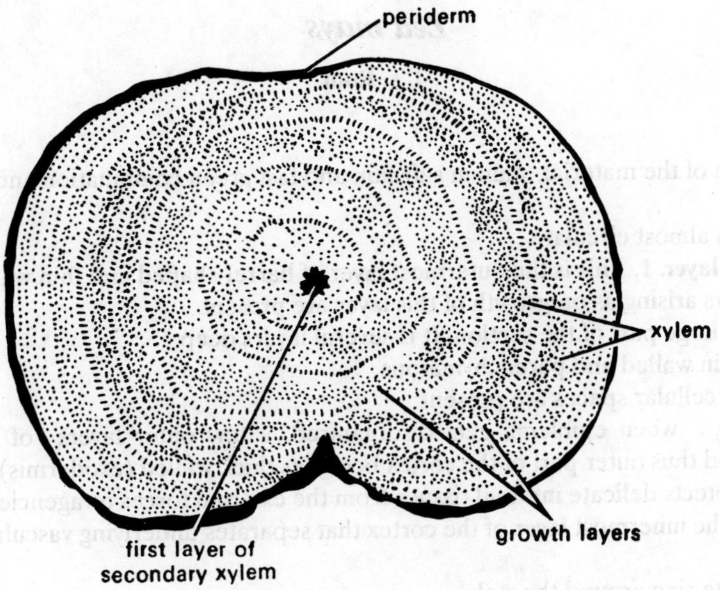

A T. s. root (outlines)

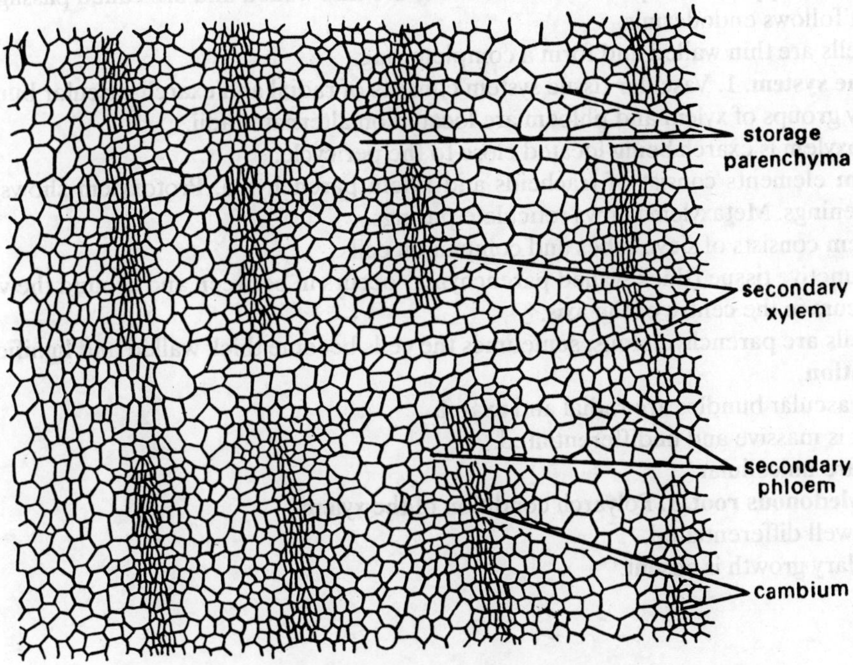

B T. s. root (A sector showing cellular details)

Fig. 36. ***Beta vulgaris.*** T. s. root.

Beta vulgaris **Family** – Chenopodiaceae
English names – Beet root, Garden beet.
Vernacular name – Chukander.

Zea mays

T. s. Root

Cut a transverse section of the material, stain in safranin and fast green combination and mount in glycerine.

[I] Observations

Outline of the section is almost circular.

Epiblema or piliferous layer. 1. This is the outermost layer of barrel-shaped and thin walled cells.

2. Unicellular hairs arising as outgrowth of this layer are present.

Cortex. 1. It occupies a large part of the section. It is several layers deep.

2. The cells are thin walled and parenchymatous.
3. Numerous intercellular spaces are present.
4. In an old root, when epiblema gets disorganised, a few outer layers of the cortex undergo suberisation and thus outer part of the cortex becomes thick walled (exodermis). This is a protective layer which protects delicate internal tissues from the external forces or agencies.

Endodermis. 1. This is the innermost layer of the cortex that separates underlying vascular tissue from the cortex.

2. It forms a definite ring around the stele.
3. The cells are barrel-shaped, compactly arranged and casparian strips are present.
4. A few cells opposite the protoxylem elements are thin walled and are called passage cells.

Pericycle. 1. It follows endodermis.

2. The cells are thin walled and form a complete ring.

Vascular tissue system. 1. Vascular tissue system consists of radial and exarch vascular bundles.

2. Many groups of xylem and phloem are located on alternate radii.
3. Protoxylem is exarch being located close to the pericycle.
4. Xylem elements consist of tracheids and xylem parenchyma. Protoxylem shows annular or spiral thickenings. Metaxylem shows reticulate pittings.
5. Phloem consists of sieve tubes and companion cells.
6. Conjunctive tissue (thick walled parenchyma) occurs in between and around the vascular tissues.

Pith. 1. It occcurs in the centre of the axis.

2. The cells are parenchymatous, sometimes the cells become thick walled and lignified.

[II] Identification

1. Root. 1. Vascular bundles are radial and exarch.

2. Cortex is massive and undifferentiated.
3. Hairs are unicellular.

2. Monocotyledonous root. 1. Polyarch condition of the xylem.

2. Pith is well differentiated.
3. Secondary growth is absent.

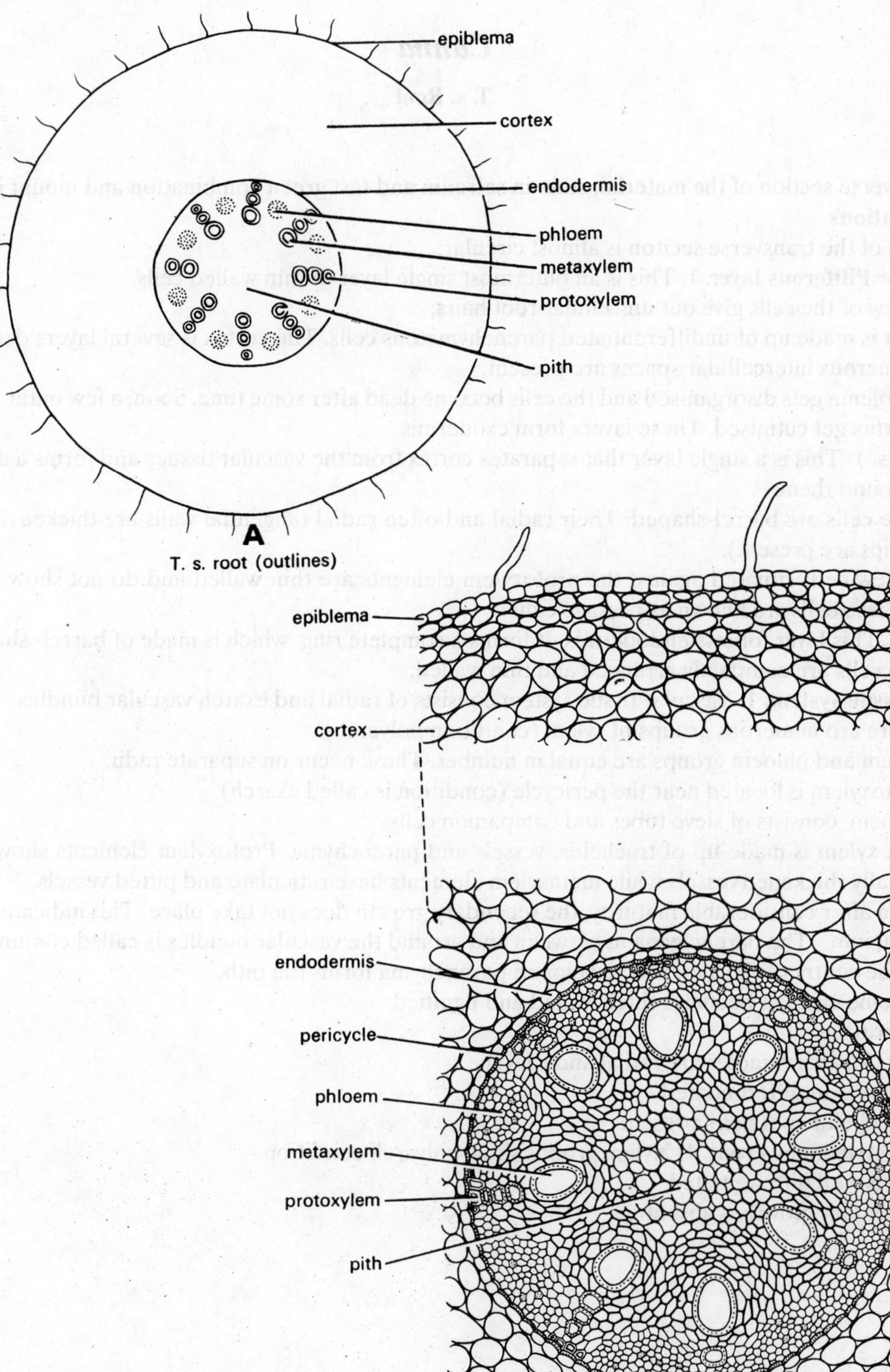

Fig. 37. *Zea mays.* T. s. root.

Zea mays **Family –** Gramineae
English names – Maize, Corn.
Vernacular names – Makka, Bhutta.

Canna

T. s. Root

Cut a transverse section of the material, stain in safranin and fast green combination and mount in glycerine.

[I] Observations

The outline of the transverse seciton is almost circular.

Epiblema or **Piliferous layer.** 1. This is an outermost single layer of thin walled cells.

2. A few of the cells give out unicellular root hairs.

Cortex. 1. It is made up of undifferentiated parenchymatous cells. The cortex is several layers deep.

2. Numerous intercellular spaces are present.

3. Epiblema gets disorganised and the cells become dead after some time. Soon, a few outer layers of the cortex get cutinised. These layers form exodermis.

Endodermis. 1. This is a single layer that separates cortex from the vascular tissues and forms a definite ring around them.

2. The cells are barrel-shaped. Their radial and often radial tangential walls are thickened (casparian strips are present).

3. A few cells situated against the protoxylem elements are thin walled and do not show thickenings. (These cells are known as passage cells).

Pericycle. 1. This layer follows endodermis. It forms a complete ring which is made of barrel- shaped cells.

2. The cells are compactly arranged and thin walled.

Vascular tissue system. 1. Vascular tissue system consists of radial and exarch vascular bundles.

2. There are numerous groups of xylem (condition polyarch).

3. Xylem and phloem groups are equal in number. These occur on separate radii.

4. Protoxylem is located near the pericycle (condition is called exarch).

5. Phloem consists of sieve tubes and companion cells.

6. The xylem is made up of tracheids, vessels and parenchyma. Protoxylem elements show annular or spirally thickened vessels while metaxylem elements have reticulate and pitted vessels.

7. Even after considerable maturity, the secondary growth does not take place. This indicates absence of cambium. The parenchyma in between and around the vascular bundles is called conjunctive tissue.

Pith. 1. In the centre of the axis, well developed parenchyma forms the pith.

2. In some cases, it becomes thick walled and lignified.

[II] Identification

1. Root. 1. Vasular bundles are radial and exarch.

2. Cortex is undifferentiated.

3. Unicellular root hairs present.

2. Monocotyledonous root. 1. Xylem groups show polyarch condition.

2. Pith is well differentiated.

3. Secondary growth is absent.

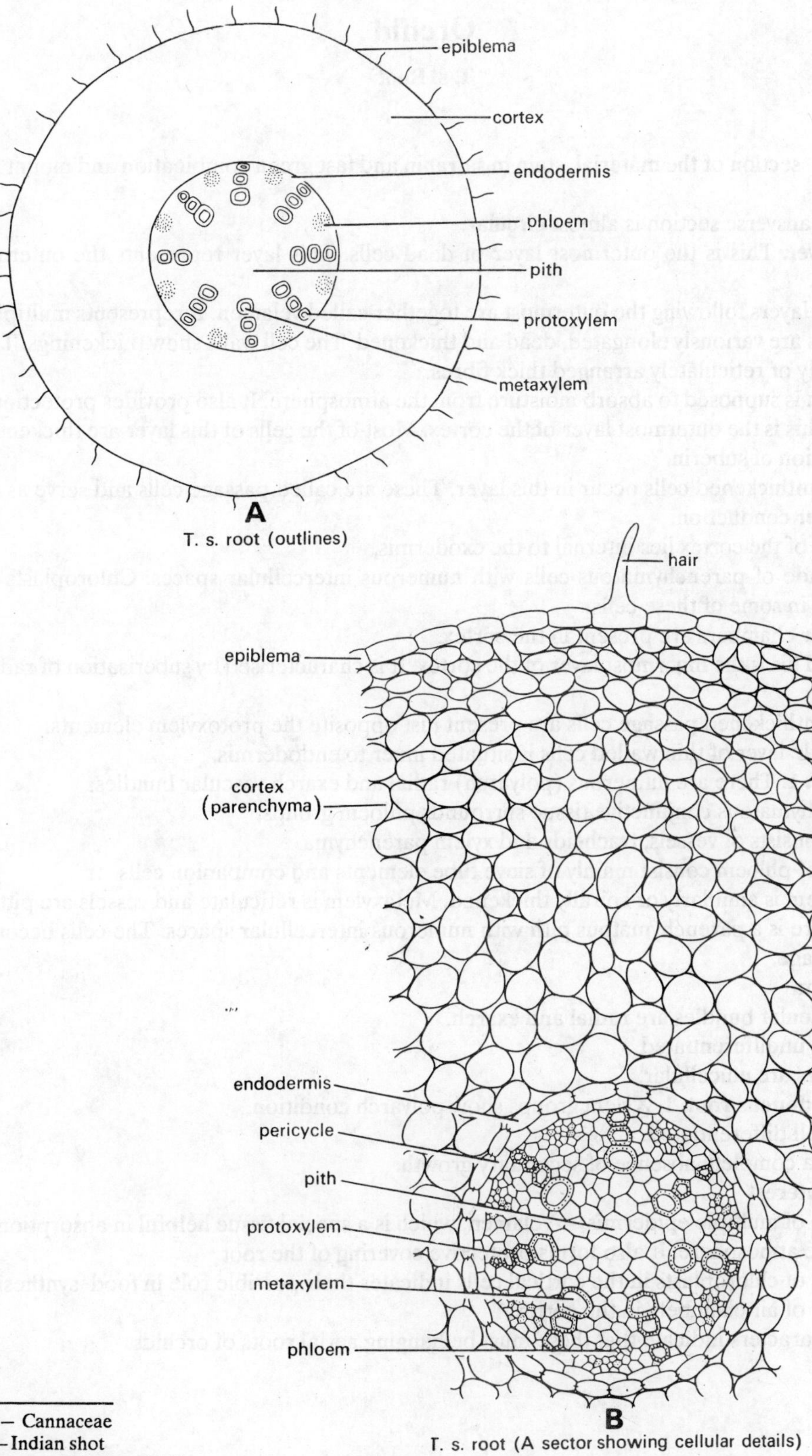

Canna **Family** – Cannaceae
English name – Indian shot
Vernacular names – Sabbajaya, Keli.

Fig. 38. ***Canna.*** T. s. root.

Orchid

T. s. Root

Cut a transverse section of the material, stain in safranin and fast green combination and mount in glycerine.

[I] Observations

Outline of the transverse section is almost circular.

The limiting layer. This is the outermost layer of dead cells. This layer represents the outermost layer of velamen.

Velamen. 1. The layers following the outermost are together called velamen. It represents multiple epidermis. The cells are variously elongated, dead and thickened. The cell walls show thickenings. These are due to spirally or reticulately arranged thick fibres.

2. Velamen is supposed to absorb moisture from the atmosphere. It also provides protection to the root.

Exodermis. 1. This is the outermost layer of the cortex. Most of the cells of this layer are thickened due to the deposition of suberin.

2. A few unthickened cells occur in this layer. These are called passage cells and serve as the channels for water conduction.

Cortex . 1. Most of the cortex lies internal to the exodermis.

2. It is made of parenchymatous cells with numerous intercellular spaces. Chloroplasts may also be present in some of these cells.

3. A few air chambers are present in the cortex.

Endodermis. 1. This is the innermost layer of the cortex. It is characterised by suberisation of radial and inner walls.

2. A few unthickened passage cells are present just opposite the protoxylem elements.

Pericycle. A single layer of thin walled cells is situated inner to endodermis.

Vascular tissues. 1. There are numerous (polyarch) radial and exarch vascular bundles.

2. Sclerenchymatous conjunctive tissue surrounds phloem groups.
3. Xylem consists of vessels, tracheids and xylem parenchyma.
4. Groups of phloem consist mainly of sieve tube elements and companion cells.
5. Protoxylem is annularly or spirally thickened. Metaxylem is reticulate and vessels are pitted.

Pith. In the centre is a parenchymatous pith with numerous intercellular spaces. The cells become sclerified at a later stage.

[II] Identification

1. Root. 1. Vascular bundles are radial and exarch.

2. Cortex is undifferentiated.
3. Root hairs are unicellular.

2. Monocotyledonous root. 1. Xylem groups show polyarch condition.

2. Pith is well differentiated.
3. There is a complete absence of secondary growth.

[III] Points of interest

1. Presence of multiple epidermis– Velamen, which is a special tissue helpful in absorption of moisture from the atmosphere. It also forms protective covering of the root.
2. Presence of chloroplasts in the cortical cells indicates their possible role in food synthesis.
3. Presence of air chambers in the cortex.
4. These characters indicate that these must be hanging aerial roots of orchids.

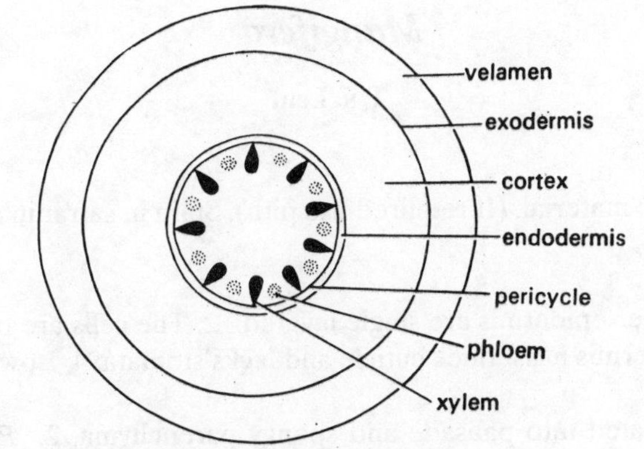

A T.s. root (outlines)

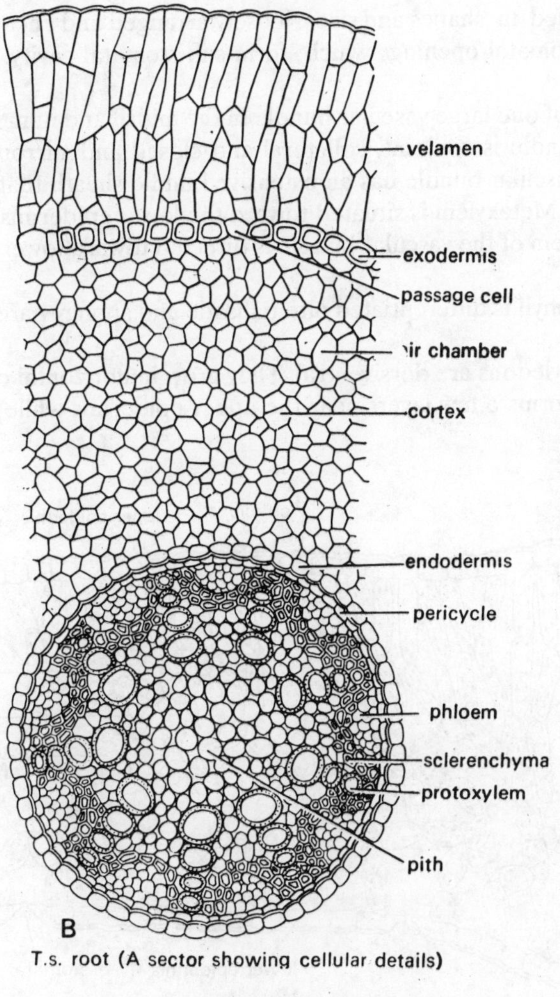

B
T.s. root (A sector showing cellular details)

Fis 39. **Orchid, T. s. root.**

Orchid **Family**— Orchidaceae

Mangifera

T. s. Leaf

Cut a transverse section of the material. (If required use pith). Stain in safranin and fast green combination and mount in glycerine.

[I] Observations

Epidermis. 1. Lower and upper epidermis are single layered. 2. The cells are barrel-shaped and compactly arranged. 3. Upper epidermis has a thick cuticle and lacks stomata. 4. Lower epidermis has thin cuticle and stomata are present.

Mesophyll. 1. It is differentiated into palisade and spongy parenchyma. 2. *Palisade* occurs below upper epidermis in two layers, with parenchyma near the larger vascular bundle. The cells are compactly arranged, long and tubular and chloroplasts are present. 3. *Spongy parenchyma* forms rest of the tissue. The cells are small, varied in shapes and sizes, loosely arranged and enclose small air spaces. 4. A few air spaces lead to the stomatal openings which form sub-stomatal cavity. Numerous chloroplasts are present near the walls.

Vascular tissue. 1. It consists of one large vascular bundle in the midril and numerous small vascular bundles in the wings. 2. Each bundle is conjoint, collateral and closed and surrounded by a parenchymatous bundle sheath. Larger vascular bundle has an extensive bundle sheath that extends both toward lower and upper epidermis. 3. Metaxylem is situated toward the lower epidermis and protoxylem toward the upper epidermis. 4. Phloem of the vascular bundle is directed toward lower epidermis.

[II] Identification

Dorsiventral leaf. Mesophyll is differentiated into palisade and spongy parenchyma.

[III] Points of interest

Most of the leaves of dicotyledons are dorsiventral. They grow in horizontal direction with distinct upper and lower surfaces. Palisade forms a few layers near the upper epidermis while spongy parenchyma occurs near the lower epidermis.

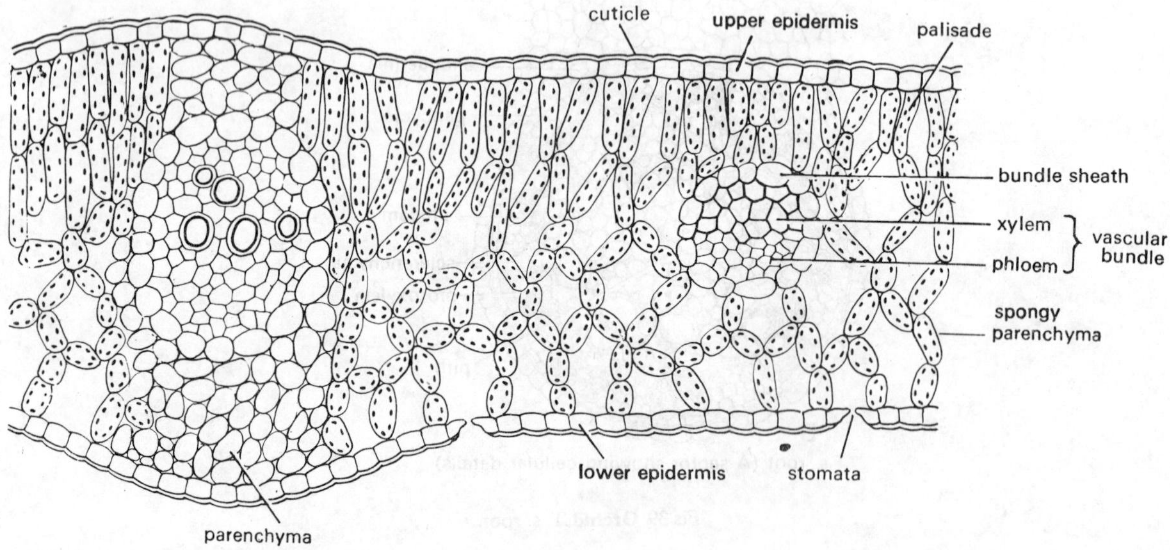

Fig. 40. ***Mangifera.*** T. s. leaf (A part cellular).

Zea mays

T. s. Leaf

Cut a transverse section of the leaf by keeping the piece of leaf in the pith. Stain in safranin and fast green combination and mount in glycerine.

[I] Observations

Epidermis. 1. Leaf is bounded by lower and upper epidermal layers. Both layers are thickly cuticularised. 2. Stomata are present in both epidermal layers. 3. A few large, empty and colourless bulliform (or motor) cells occur in upper epidermis.

Mesophyll. 1. It is not differentiated into palisade and spongy parenchyma. It occurs between upper and lower epidermis. 2. The cells are isodiametric and contain numerous chloroplasts. These are compactly arranged and leave only a few intercellular spaces.

Vascular tissue. 1. There are numerous vascular bundles of variable sizes arranged in a parallel series. Each bundle is collateral and closed. There is a distinct parenchymatous bundle sheath. The cells of the sheath possess plastids and starch grains (this layer, thus serves as a temporary storage tissue and also transports the products of photosynthesis to the phloem). 2. A patch of sclerenchyma each is present above and below the larger vascular bundles and extends up to the upper and lower epidermal layers respectively. 3. Larger bundles have distinct and more amount of xylem and phloem than the smaller ones. 4. Bundles possess xylem on their upper side (toward upper epidermis) and phloem on its lower side (toward lower epidermis).

[II] Identification

Isobilateral leaf. 1. Mesophyll is not differentiated into palisade and spongy parenchyma.
2. Stomata are present on both lower and upper epidermal layers.

[III] Points of interest

Most of the leaves of monocotyledons are isobilateral. The stomata are present on both lower and upper epidermal layers. Mesophyll, in these cases, is undifferentiated into palisade and spongy parenchyma.

Bulliform cells are present in the upper epidermis. This is characteristic of plants (monocotyledonous) growing under dry conditions. These motor cells help the leaf to roll due to the changes in their turgidity, thereby reducing the stomatal transpiration, under xeric conditions. Other xerophytic characters include: thick cuticle, sclerenchymatous patches and more stomata on lower surface.

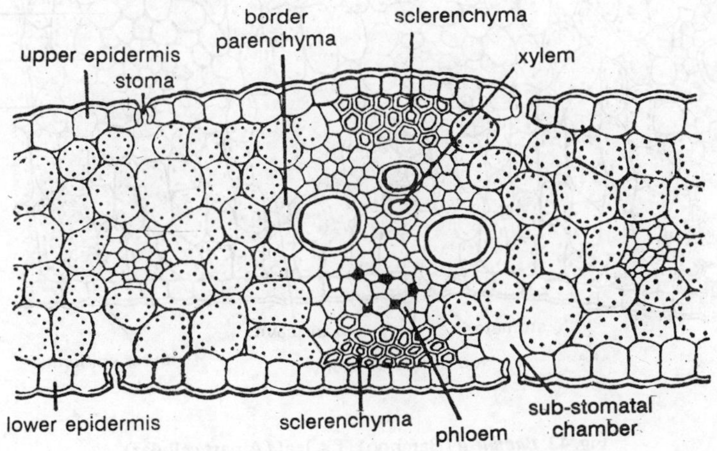

Fig. 41. ***Zea mays*** (Maize). T. s. leaf (A part cellular).

Bambusa (Bamboo)

Cut a transverse section of the leaf. Use pith if necessary. Stain in safranin and fast green combination and mount in glycerine.

[I] Observations

Epidermis. 1. Lower and upper epidermis are single-celled layers. The cells are arranged compactly. 2. Upper epidermis has thin cuticle, lacks stomata and a few enlarged cells – bulliform (or motor) cells are present. 3. Lower epidermis has a strong cuticle and numerous stomata. Outer surface has heavy deposition of silicon. A few stiff and sharply pointed hairs are present.

Mesophyll. 1. It is not differentiated into palisade and spongy parenchyma. The entire tissue between upper and lower epidermis is palisade-like. 2. Intercellular spaces are absent but few air cavities are present.

Vascular tissue. 1. It consists of numerous vascular bundles, arranged in parallel series. 2. Each bundle is collateral and closed, surrounded by a distinct bundle sheath. A patch of sclerenchyma is present above and below the bundle and extends up to upper and lower epidermis respectively. Larger bundles have distinct and more amount of xylem and phloem than the smaller one. 3. Phloem lies toward lower epidermis. 4. Metaxylem is located toward lower epidermis and protoxylem toward the upper epidermis.

[II] Identification

Isobilateral leaf. Mesophyll is not differentiated into palisade and spongy parenchyma.

[III] Points of interest

Most of the monocotyledonous plants show isobilateral leaves. They show stomata on both of their surfaces (amphistomatic). Mesophyll is undifferentiated.

However, in this case, characteristic bulliform cells (motor cells) are present in the upper epidermis. These are enlarged and colourless cells. The cells bring inrolling of the leaf by the changes in the turgor pressure. The inrolling is very effective in checking the stomatal transpiration. Other xerophytic characters are – thick cuticle, sclerenchymatous patches and stomata on the lower surface

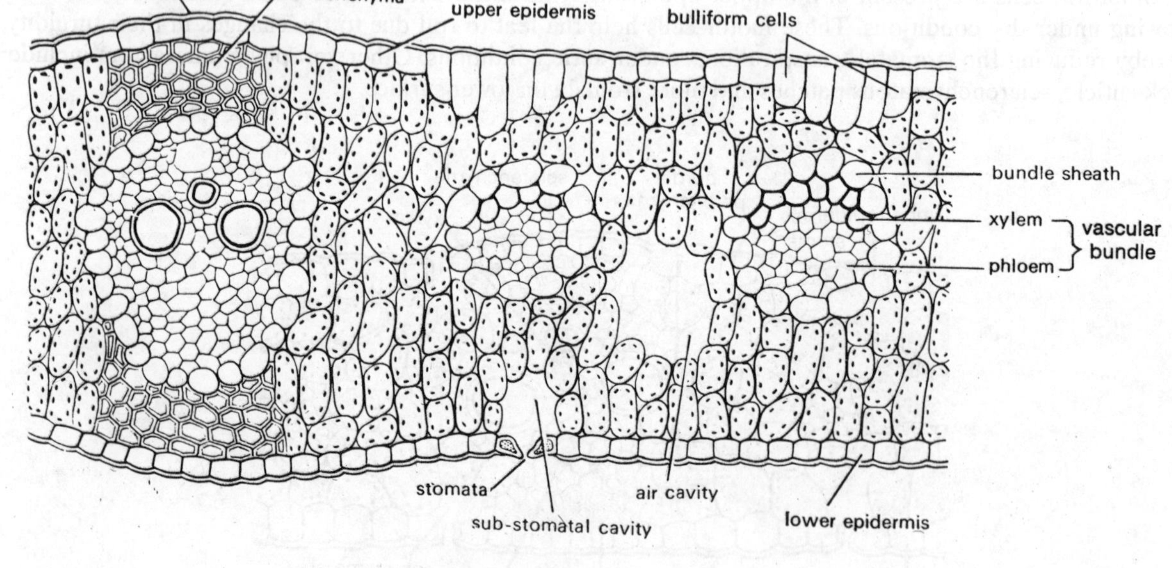

Fig. 42. ***Bambusa*** (Bamboo). T.s. leaf (A part cellular).

Acacia moniliformis

T.s. Phyllode

Cut a transverse section of the material, stain in safranin and fast green combination and mount in glycerine.

[I] Observations

The transverse section of the material shows the following anatomical characters.

The outline appears like a T.s. of leaf, with a distinct midrib – like portion and lateral wings.

Epidermis. 1. Both upper and lower epidermal layers are made of single row of cells. The cells are thickly cuticularised.

2. These are rectangular to radially elongated.
3. Both the epidermises are interrupted by numerous sunken stomata which open in the substomatal cavities.

Mesophyll. 1. The region between upper and lower epidermal layers is occupied by mesophyll.

2. It is made of palisade and parenchyma.

*(a) **Palisade.*** 1. The palisade is located inner to both upper and lower epidermal layers.

2. The cells are radially elongated and tubular. These possess numerous chloroplasts. Intercellular spaces are absent. This zone is about two cells deep.

*(b) **Parenchyma.*** 1. This tissue occupies the central region. The cells are thin walled and vary from oval to spherical. Numerous intercellular spaces are present.

Vascular tissue. 1. It is represented by many vascular bundles, situated just below the palisade on either side.

2. Vascular bundles in the centre and at the tips of the wings are bigger in size than those present in the wings.
3. Bigger vascular bundles are surrounded by a massive zone of sclerenchyma. Smaller bundle remains enveloped by a single layer of thin-walled cells. However, a few layers of sclerenchyma form a cap above smaller vascular bundles.
4. Each of the vascular bundles consists of xylem and phloem. Xylem is directed toward the centre and phloem towards the epidermis.
5. Xylem consists of tracheary elements, vessels and parenchyma.
6. Phloem is made of sieve tube elements, companion cells and parenchyma.

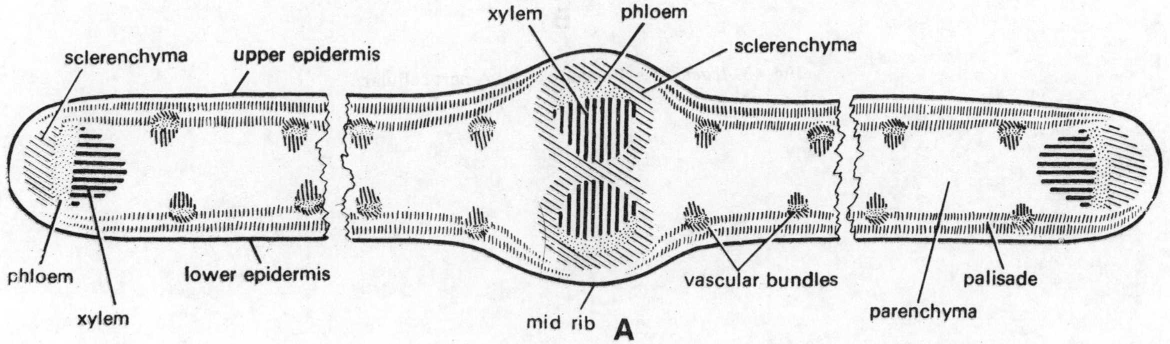

Fig. 43. **Acacia.** T.s. phyllode, A. Outlines

[II] Identification

Petiole. Vascular bundles are arranged in a complete ring which has formed two rows due to flattening.

[III] Points of interest

The structure shows a flattened petiole which has become leaf- like. This modified organ is known as phyllode. It is generally borne vertically by the plant, so that both the surfaces receive equal amount of illumination. It shows a few characters of the leaf e.g. presence of palisade tissue and a flattened leaf-like feature.

This modification is found in xerophytic plants. The phyllode shows xerophytic characters such as a thick cuticle, sunken stomates, radially elongated epidermal cells, presence of palisade, well-developed sclerenchyma, etc.

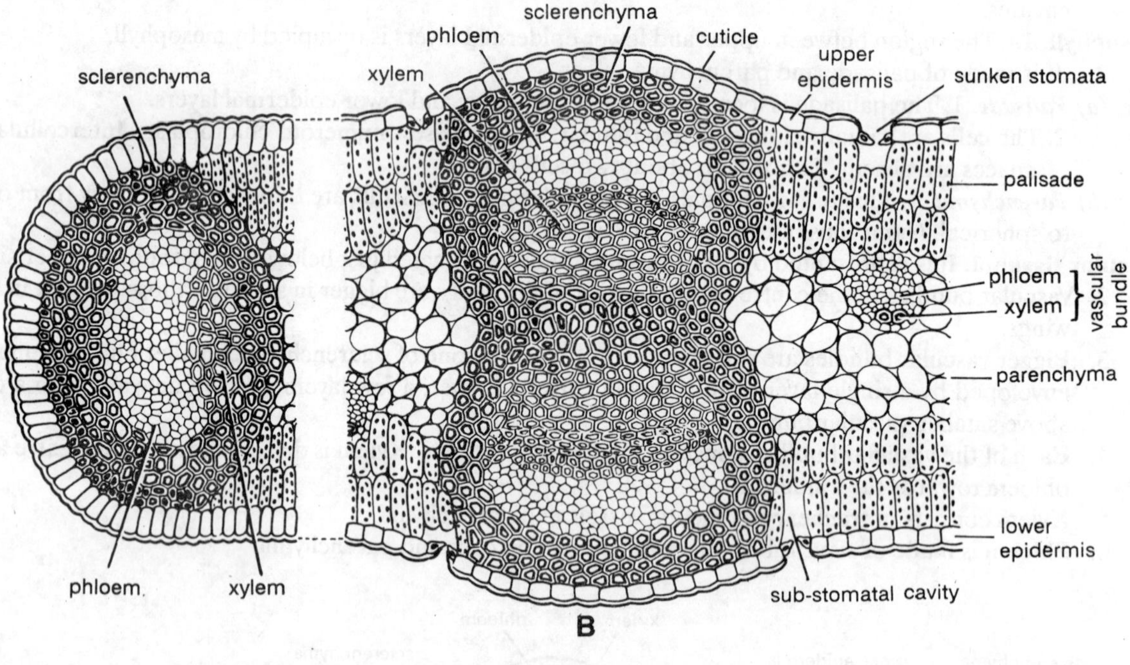

Fig. 43. *Acacia.* T.s. Phyllode B. A part cellular.

Ruscus aculeatus

T.s. Phylloclade

Cut a transverse section of the material stain in safranin and fast green combination and mount in glycerine.

[I] Observations

The transverse section of the material shows central bulged region and lateral wings.

Epidermis. 1. The section is bound by thickly cuticularised upper and lower epidermal layers.

2. Numerous stomata occur throughout both the epidermal layers.
3. The outline of the lower epidermis is angular.

Chlorenchyma. 1. Just below the epidermis are a few layers of chlorenchyma that are 2-4 cells deep.

2. The cells are rounded or oval and contain numerous chloroplasts.

Parenchyma. 1. It occupies larger part of the section. Parenchyma is made of thin walled cells which are variable in shape and size.

2. Numreous intercellular spaces are present. The cells are loosely arranged.

Vascular tissue. 1. There are many vascular bundles in almost parallel series. A few vascular bundles are aggregated in the bulged central region.

2. Each vascular bundle is surrounded by a thick bundle sheath. It is concentric and amphivasal.
3. In the central bulge a few vascular bundles together are surrounded by sclerenchymatous layer. In the centre of the bulge parenchymatous tissue is present.

[II] Identification

1. Stem. 1. Cortex is well differentiated.

2. Vascular bundles are concentric and amphivasal.

2. Monocotyledonous stem. Vascular bundles are scattered.

[III] Points of interest

In this case, stem has become flattened and green, like the leaves. Such modified stems are known as phylloclades or cladophylls and are often mistaken for leaves. Phylloclades of *Ruscus* look exactly like those of leaves with veins. However, their stem-like nature is revealed when flowers are brone on them at the 'nodal' positions.

It shows the following **leaf-like characters.**

1. A flattened and leaf-like external appearance,
2. presence of upper and lower epidermal layers,
3. the central bulge similar to a midrib region,
4. presence of chlorenchyma and
5. presence of stomata.

The following are the **characteristics of stem.**

1. Concentric-amphivasal vascular bundles,
2. vascular bundle in the bulge without any uniform arrangement and
3. phloem not located toward the lower epidermis as in leaves.

It also exhibits the following **xerophytic characters :** thick cuticle, presence of photosynthetic tissue and sclerenchyma. This modification checks the loss of water by cutting off the growth of leaves and develops photosynthetic tissue, thereby taking up the function of leaves.

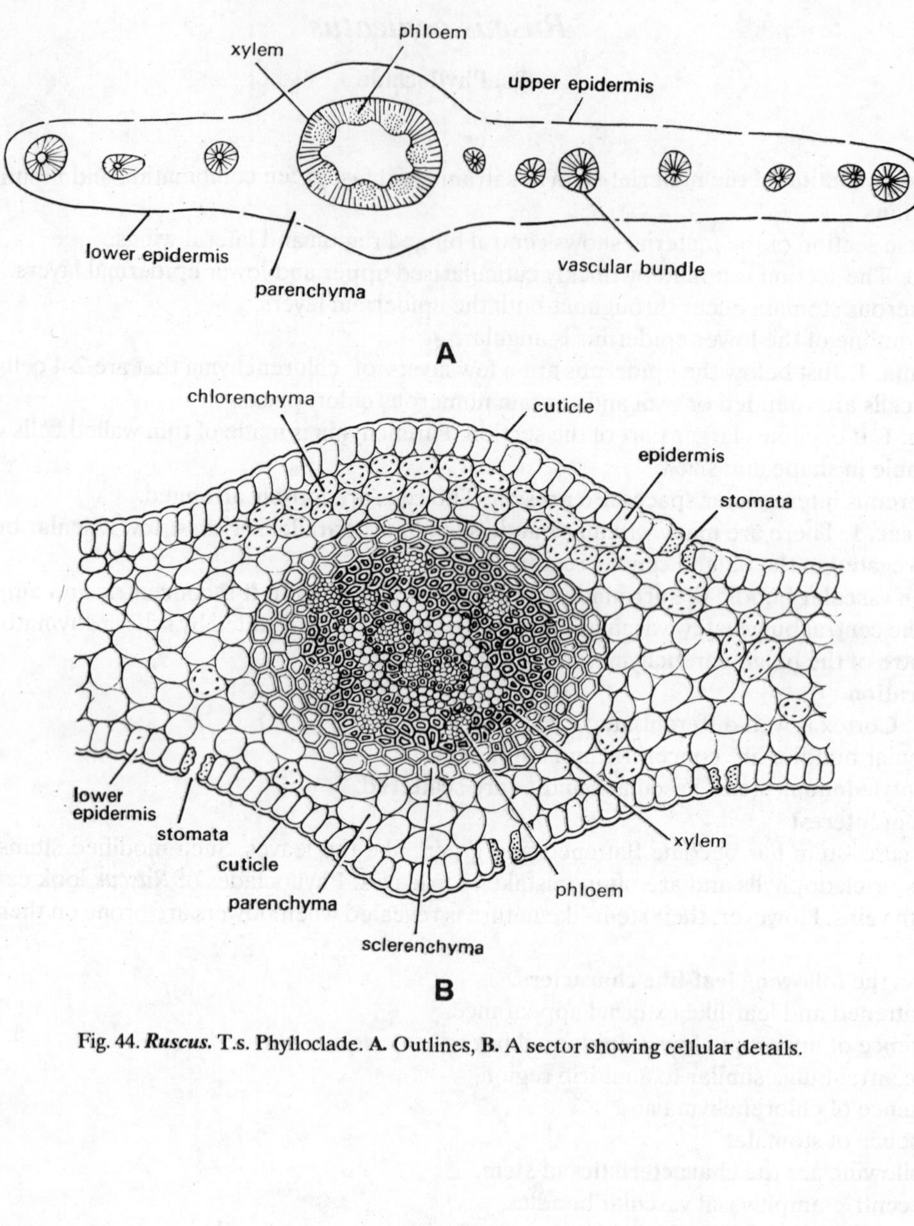

Fig. 44. ***Ruscus.*** T.s. Phylloclade. A. Outlines, B. A sector showing cellular details.

7

Illustrated Glossary of Anatomical Terms

TYPES OF CELLS

[I] Parenchyma

A tissue made of living and thin walled cells (Fig. 1). Parenchyma is of following four types.

1. Chlorenchyma. Parenchymatous tissue containing many chloroplasts.

2. Palisade parenchyma. Parenchymatous cells which are radially elongated and contain many chloroplasts situated closer to the cell wall (Fig. 2).

3. Spongy parenchyma. The cells of different shapes and sizes occurring in the mesophyll of the leaf. Cells contain chloroplasts and leave many intercellular spaces (Fig. 3).

4. Aerenchyma. Parenchymatous tissue with large intercellular spaces formed due to partitions (Fig. 4).

[II] Collenchyma

It is a supporting tissue composed of more or less living cells with unevenly thickened walls (Fig. 5). It is of following three types —

1. Angular. Collenchyma tissue in which cell walls are thick at angles where several cells join together.

2. Lamellar. Collenchyma tissue in which tangential walls of the cells are thickened.

3. Lacunar. Collenchyma tissue in which intercellular spaces become thick due to deposition.

[III] Sclerenchyma

A supporting tissue made of lignified and thick walled cells. The cells are devoid of protoplast and hence dead. The main types are —

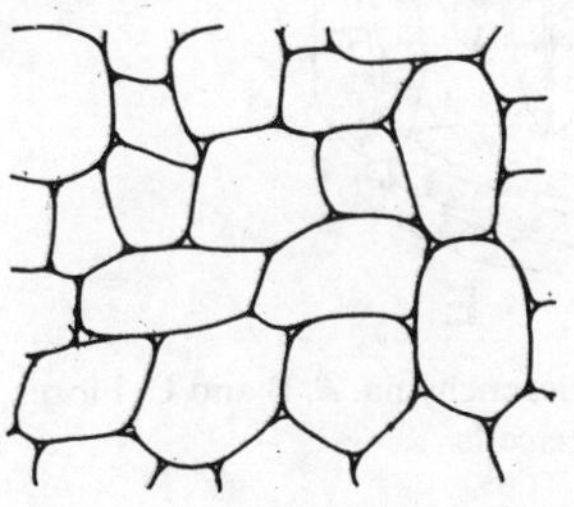

Fig. 1. Parenchyma.

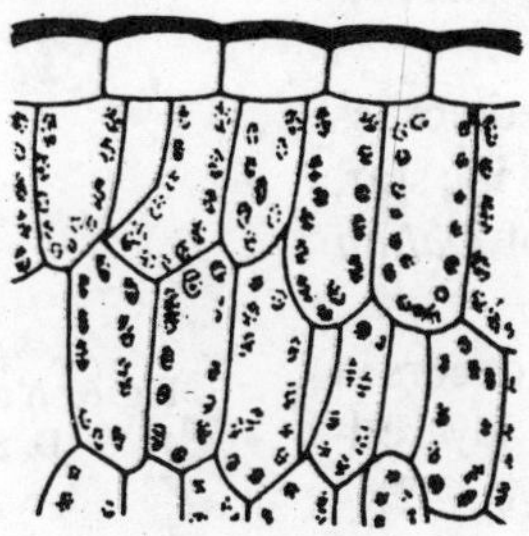

Fig. 2. Palisade parenchyma.

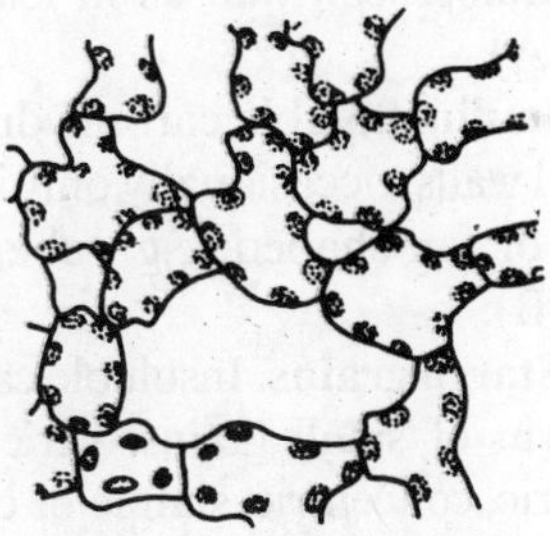

Fig. 3. Spongy parenchyma.

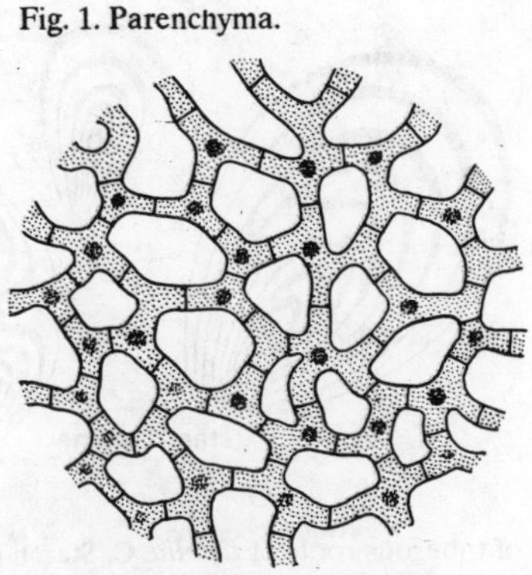

Fig. 4. Aerenchyma.

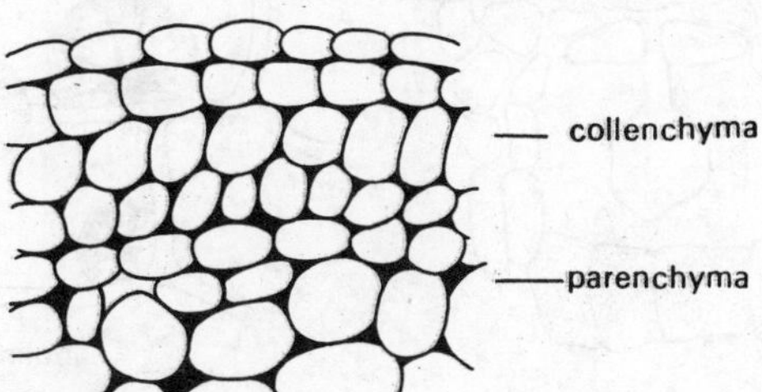

Fig. 5. Collenchyma.

1. Fibre. An elongated tapering sclerenchyma cell with more or less thick, lignified secondary walls, generally dead at maturity (Fig. 6 A,B,C).

2. Sclereid. A sclerenchyma cell; varied in shape and size but not elongated. The walls are thick and lignified with simple pits (Fig. 6.D).

3. Stone cell (Brachysclereid). A short, roughly isodiametric sclereid; similar to parenchymatous cells (Fig. 6 E).

[IV] Special types of cells

1. Bulliform cell. (Motor cell). An enlarged epidermal cell in the leaves of grasses. These are hygroscopic and help the leaves to roll upwards.

2. Idioblast. A special cell in the tissue which differs in form, size and contents from other cells in the same tissue. It may be filled with oils, tannins, gums, resins, etc.

CELL INCLUSIONS

These are the non-protoplasmic components of the cell; reserve or waste products.

1. Crystal sand. A mass of very fine free crystals.

2. Crystalloid. Protein crystal that is less angular than mineral crystal; swells in water.

3. Cystolith. Grape-like cluster formed by the deposition of calcium carbonate on an ingrowth of the cellulose cell wall as in leaves of *Ficus elastica* (Fig .7A).

4. Inulin. Soluble carbohydrate deposited across the cell walls; occasionally only in the cell cavity; star, wheel or fan-shaped; e.g. tuberous roots of *Dahlia* (Fig. 7B).

5. Starch grains. Insoluble carbohydrate, occurs in the form of small grains; varied in shape; layered-eccentric, concentric, simple or compound (Fig. 7C).

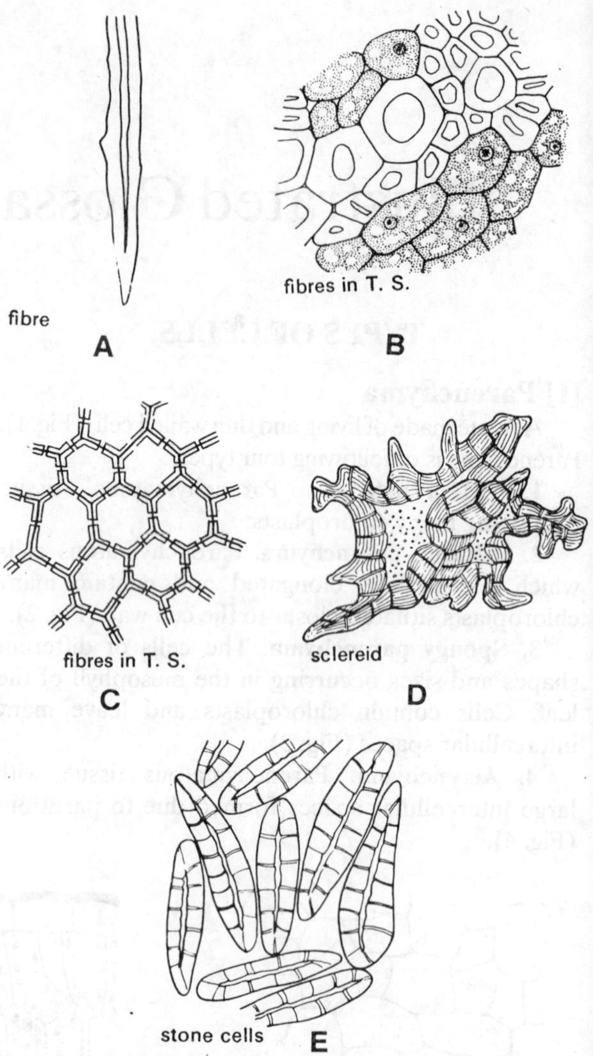

Fig. 6. **A** to **E.** Types of sclerenchyma. **A, B** and **C.** Fibres, **D.** Sclereid, **E.** Stone cells.

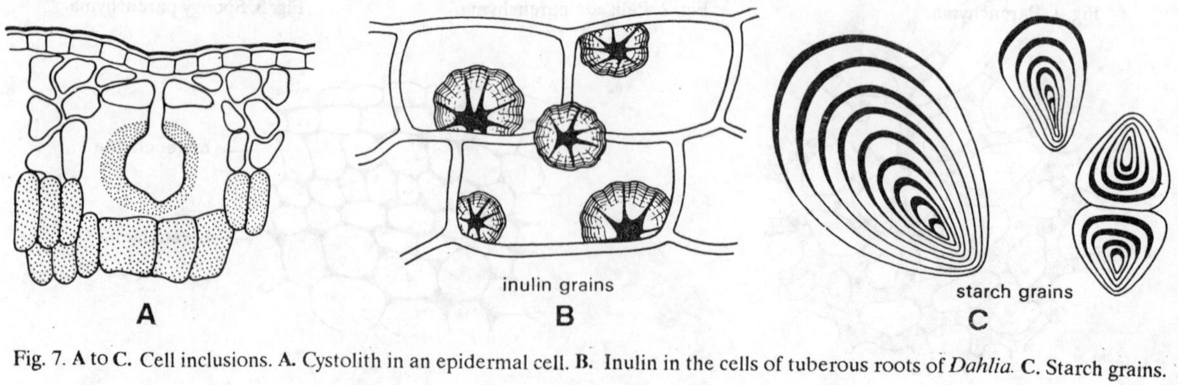

Fig. 7. **A** to **C.** Cell inclusions. **A.** Cystolith in an epidermal cell. **B.** Inulin in the cells of tuberous roots of *Dahlia.* **C.** Starch grains.

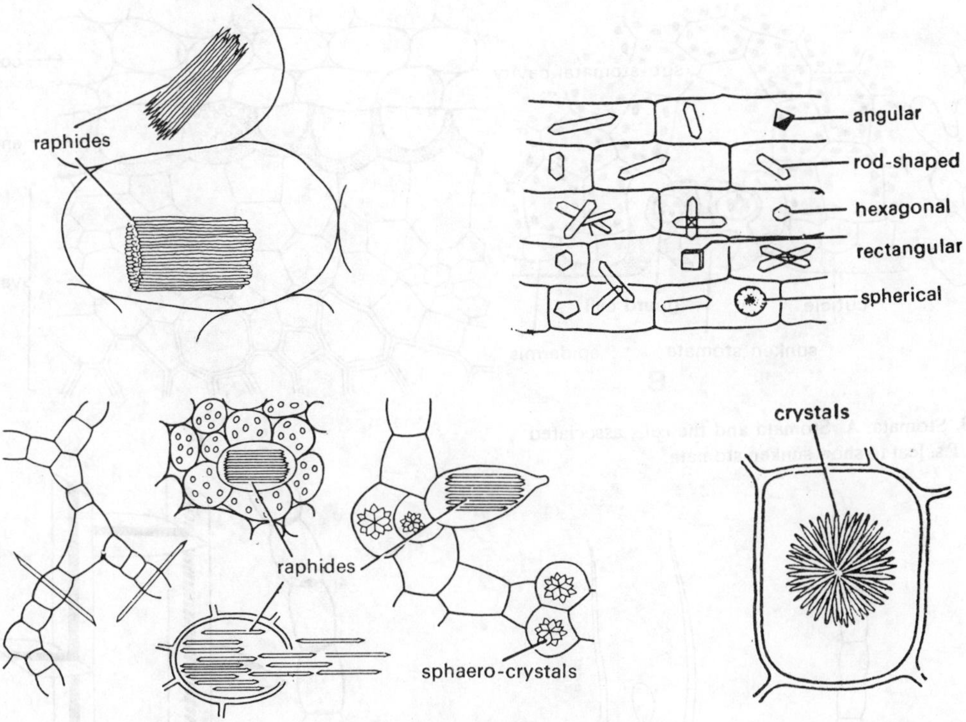

Fig. 8. Different types of raphides.

6. Raphide. Different types of crystals of calcium oxalate; though mostly needle-shaped may be angular, rod-shaped, hexagonal, rectangular, spherical, etc. These may occur single or in bundles (Fig. 8).

TISSUES AND TISSUE SYSTEMS

Tissues. Groups or masses of cells which are similar in origin, structure and function.

Tissue System. A tissue or tissues in a plant or plant organ structurally and functionally similar.

1. Dermal or tegumentary tissue system. Outer tissue which covers the plant i.e. epidermis or periderm.

2. Ground or fundamental tissue system. The entire complex of ground tissues i.e. tissues other than epidermis and periderm on one hand and vascular tissues on the other.

3. Primary vascular tissue system. Vascular tissues differentiated from procambium during primary growth, i.e. xylem and phloem.

[I] Epidermis

Outer layer of cells which is primary in origin (Fig. 9A).

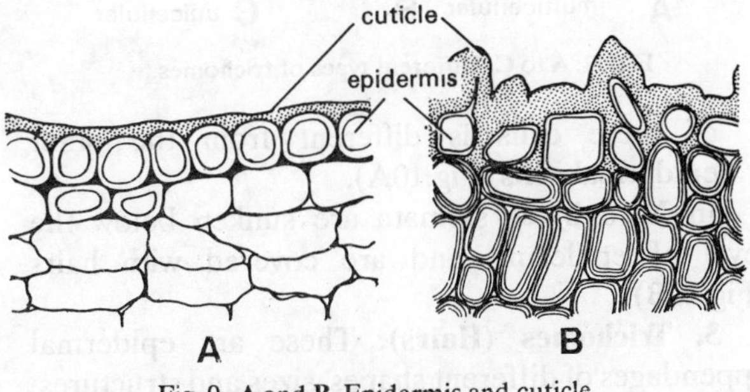

Fig. 9. A and B. Epidermis and cuticle.

1. Cuticle. A layer of waxy material more or less impervious to water; present on the outer wall of epidermis (Fig. 9B).

2. Stomata. An opening in the epidermis surrounded by two guard cells. The different types of cells associated with stomata are —

(a) ***Guard cells.*** Two guard cells surround a pore in the epidermis. These undergo turgor changes which cause opening and closing of stomata.The guard cells are generally kidney shaped. The walls facing the opening is thickened.

(b) ***Subsidiary cells*** (Accessory cells). An epidermal cell/cells associated with guard cells. The shape

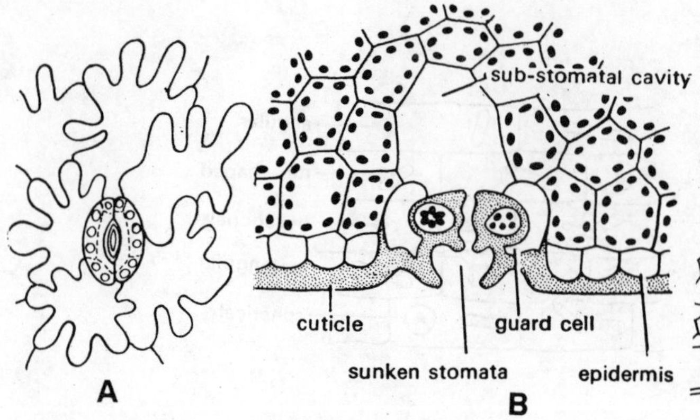

Fig. 10. **A** and **B.** Stomata. **A** Stomata and the cells associated with it. **B.** T.s. leaf to show sunken stomata.

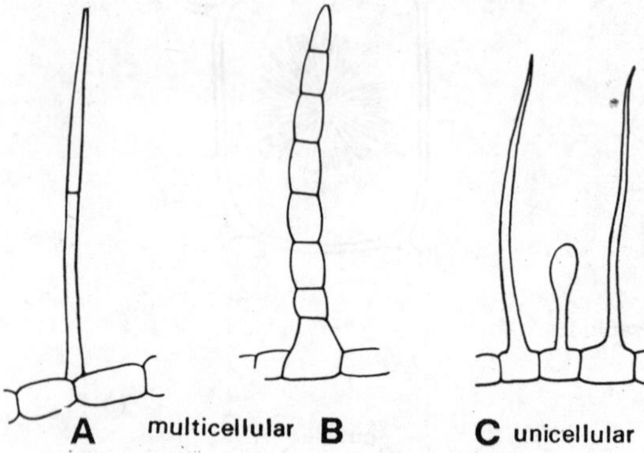

Fig. 11. **A** to **C.** Different types of trichomes.

of these cells is different from the other epidermal cells (Fig.10A).

In **Xerophytes** stomata are sunken below the level of epidermis and are covered with hairs (Fig.10B).

3. Trichomes (Hairs). These are epidermal appendages of different shapes, sizes and structures. Some of the common types include glandular, non-glandular, scales, papillae, etc. (Fig. 11A ,B , C).

[II] Cortex

The region of ground tissue situated between the vascular system and the epidermis.

1. Hypodermis. Layer or layers of the cells just beneath the epidermis. This term is used only if these layers are different from rest of the cortex.

2. Endodermis. A layer of ground tissue surrounding the vascular region.The cells are characterised by suberised casparian strips. It is the innermost layer of cortex in stems and roots of seed plants (Fig. 12A and B).

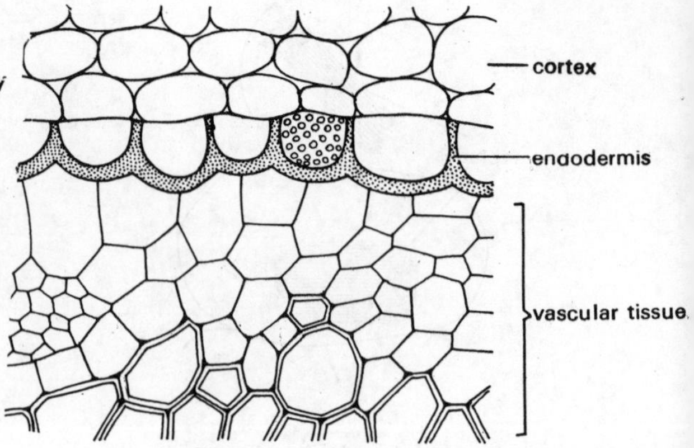

A

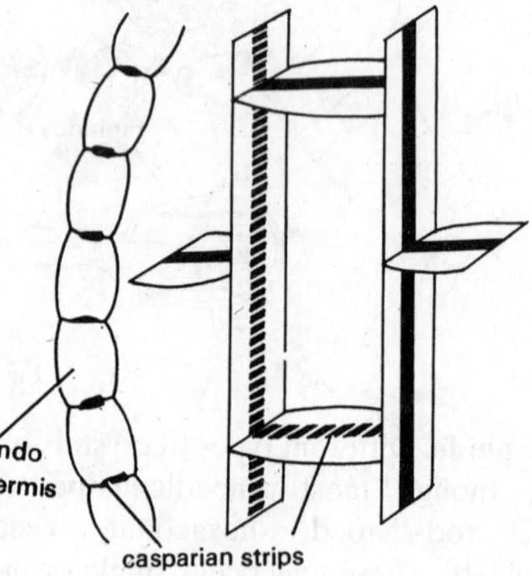

B

Fig. 12. **A** and **B.** Endodermis and pericycle. **A.** T.s. to show positions of endodermis and pericycle. **B.** Casparian strips in the endodermal cells.

3. Endodermoid. A layer made of cells which are similar to those of endodermis but without casparian strips. It is generally found in the stems of gymnosperms and angiosperms in place of endodermis.

4. Pericycle. A part of the ground tissue of the stele located between phloem (or vascular bundle) and endodermis (Fig.12A).

5. Pith. Ground tissue in the centre of the stem or root.

XYLEM

This tissue is mainly responsible for conduction of water. It also acts as supporting tissue. Xylem consists of tracheary elements viz. tracheids, vessels, fibres and xylem parenchyma.

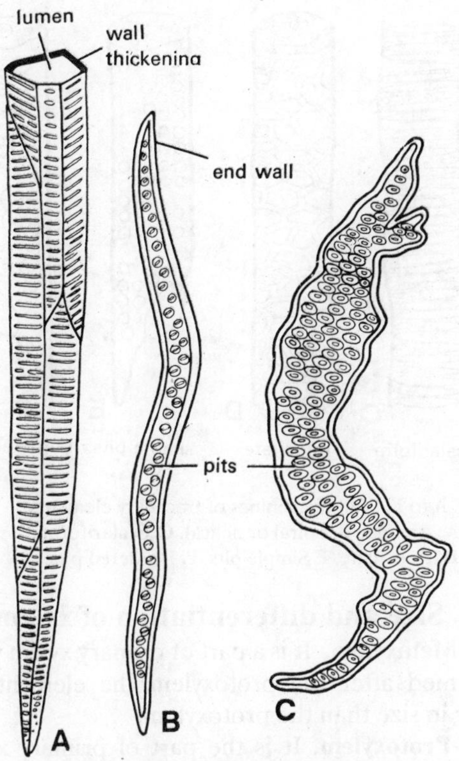

Fig. 13. A to C. Different types of tracheids.

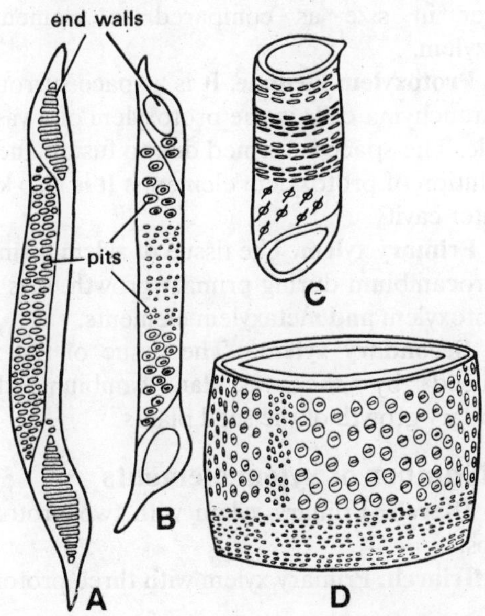

Fig. 14. A to D. Different types of vessels.

[I] Elements of xylem

1. Tracheid. A tracheary element of xylem which unlike vessel members does not possess perforated cross walls; may have any of the different types of secondary wall thickenings (Figs. 13A,B,C).

2. Vessel. A tube-like series of vessel members, the common walls of which are perforated. (Fig.14A,B,C,D).

3. Fibre tracheids. These fibre-like tracheids occur in the wood. They are thick walled with pointed ends and lenticular slit-like apertures. (Fig.15B).

4. Libriform Fibre. These thick walled fibres occur in the wood; show simple pits; perhaps the longest cells in the wood (Fig.15A).

5. Parenchyma cells. These are thin walled cells which store starch, oil and many other ergastic substances; the walls may be secondarily thickened or lignified (Figs.15C D).

(a) ***Tylosis.*** These occur in the wood. Tylosis is an outgrowth from xylem parenchyma cell through a pit cavity in a vessel wall, partially or completely blocking the lumen of the vessel (Fig.16).

[II] Wall thickenings of tracheary elements

1. Annular cell wall thickening. Secondary wall material is deposited on the primary wall in the form of rings (Fig.17A).

2. Spiral or helical cell wall thickening. Secondary wall material is deposited on the primary wall in the form of spirals or helix (Fig. 17B).

3. Scalariform cell wall thickening. Secondary cell wall material is deposited on the primary cell wall forming a ladder- like pattern (Fig. 17C).

4. Reticulate cell wall thickening. Secondary wall material is deposited on the primary wall giving an appearance of net (Fig.17D).

5. Pits. A thin region in the secondary wall where lignin is not deposited. Pits may be of two types.

(a) ***Simple pits.*** A pit in which the cavity becomes wider; remains almost constant in width or only gradually becomes narrower during the growth in thickness of secondary wall (Fig.17E).

(b) ***Bordered pits.*** A pit in which the pit membrane is overarched by the secondary wall, e.g. wood of *Pinus* (Fig.17F).

[III] Different positions of xylem

Following are some of the terms used in reference to the position of protoxylem in a vascular bundle.

1. Endarch. A xylem group or strand where protoxylem elements are closest to the centre of the axis or pith. It is typical of stems and leaves of seed plants.

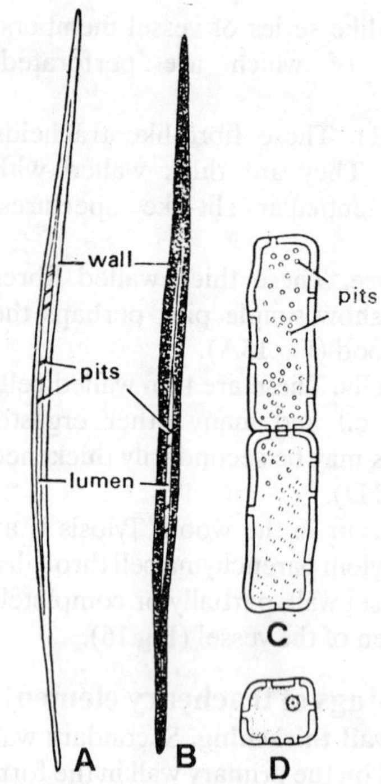

Fig. 15. **A** to **D.** Elements of xylem. **A.** Libriform fibre. **B.** Fibre tracheid, **C** and **D.** Parenchyma cells.

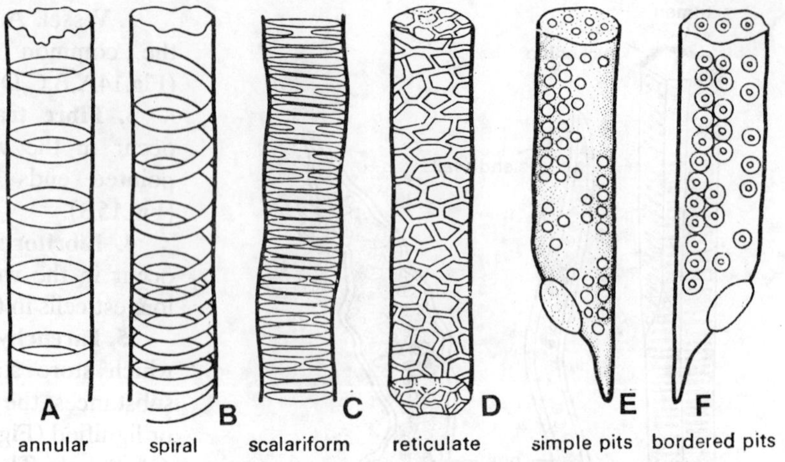

Fig. 17. **A** to **F.** Wall thickenings of tracheary elements. **A.** Annular **B.** Spiral or helical. **C.** Scalariform. **D.** Reticulate. **E** Simple pits. **F.** Bordered pits.

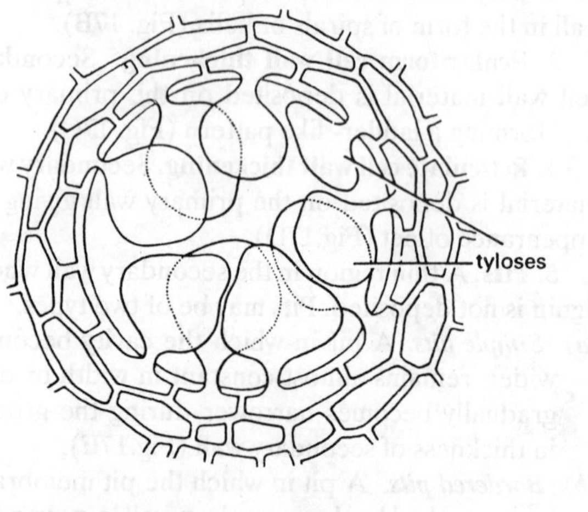

Fig. 16. Section showing tyloses in the vessel.

2. Exarch. A xylem group or strand where protoxylem elements are directed away from the centre of the axis or pith. It is typical of roots of seed plants.

3. Mesarch. A xylem group or strand where protoxylem occurs in the centre and is surrounded by metaxylem elements.

[IV] Size and differentiation of xylem

1. Metaxylem. It is a part of primary xylem which is formed after the protoxylem.The elements are larger in size than the protoxylem.

2. Protoxylem. It is the part of primary xylem. These are the first formed elements of xylem and are smaller in size as compared to elements of metaxylem.

3. Protoxylem lacunae. It is a space surrounded by parenchyma cells in the protoxylem of a vascular bundle. The space is formed due to fusion and then dissolution of protoxylem elements. It is also known as water cavity.

4. Primary xylem. The tissue of xylem formed by the procambium during primary growth. It is made of protoxylem and metaxylem elements.

5. Secondary xylem. The tissue of the xylem produced by the vascular cambium during secondary growth of the seed plants.

[V] Number of xylem elements

1. Diarch. Primary xylem with two protoxylem groups.

2. Triarch. Primary xylem with three protoxylem groups.

3. Tetrarch. Primary xylem with four protoxylem groups.

4. Polyarch. Primary xylem with more than four protoxylem groups.

PHLOEM

Phloem is the major food conducting tissue of the vascular plants. It is made of sieve elements, parenchyma cells, fibres and sclereids.

[I] Elements of Phloem

The following are major components of the phloem.

1. Sieve cells. These sieve elements lack sieve plates at their end walls. Sieve areas, however, are present all over the walls.

2. Sieve tube member. One of the elements or a cell of which sieve tube is made of. Cells with sieve plates at the cross walls. The cell has protoplasm but nucleus is absent.

3. Sieve tube. It is made of a series of sieve tube members arranged end to end and are connected through their sieve plates (Fig. 18).

4. Companion cell. A sieve element, occurring as a specialised parenchyma cell associated with sieve tube members. It is characteristic of phloem of angiosperms (Figs. 18, 19B).

5. Fibre sclereid or phloem fibre. Phloem fibres developing from parenchyma cells of non-functioning phloem (Fig . 19A).

6. Phloem parenchyma. Parenchyma cells distributed amongst the elements of phloem (Figs. 19C,D).

[II] Position of phloem

1. External phloem. Primary phloem situated outside the primary xylem of a bicollateral vascular bundle e.g. stem of *Cucurbita.*

2 Internal phloem. (Intraxylary phloem). Primary phloem situated inside the primary xylem of a bicollateral vascular bundle e.g. stem of *Cucurbita.*

3. Included phloem (Interxylary phloem). Secondary phloem, included or embedded in the secondary xylem of certain dicotyledons, e.g., *Salvadora, Leptadenia*, etc.

[III] Size and differentiation of phloem

1. Metaphloem. It is a part of primary phloem which develops after the formation of protophloem. The elements are larger in size as compared to protophloem elements.

2. Protophloem. It is a part of primary phloem. These elements develop earlier than the others in the phloem i.e., metaphloem. Protophloem elements are smaller as compared to metaphloem elements.

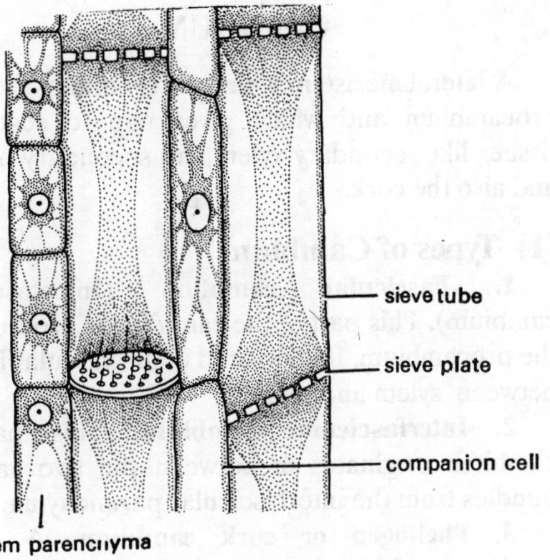

Fig. 18. Sieve tube and companion cell.

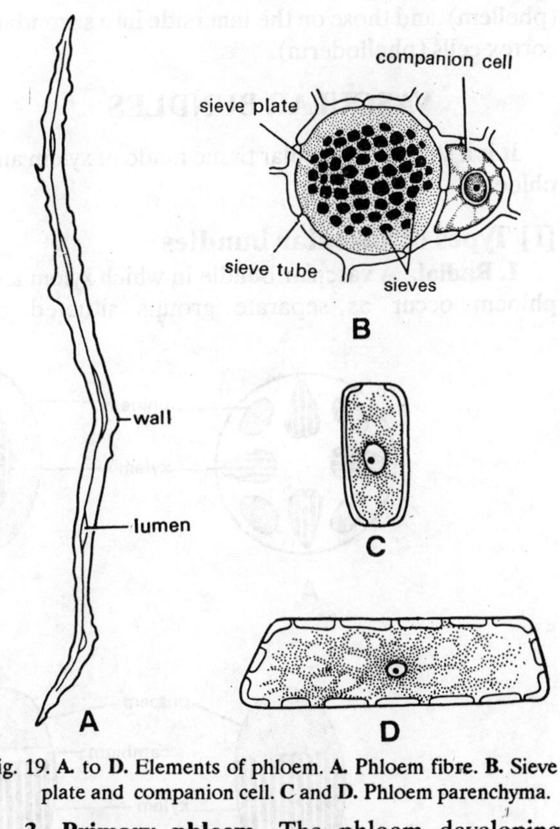

Fig. 19 A. to D. Elements of phloem. A. Phloem fibre. B. Sieve plate and companion cell. C and D. Phloem parenchyma.

3. Primary phloem. The phloem developing directly from procambium during primary growth. The first formed phloem elements are protophloem followed by the formation of metaphloem.

4. Secondary phloem. The phloem which develops from the vascular cambium during secondary growth of the plant.

CAMBIUM

A lateral meristem which differentiates from the procambium and which gives rise to secondary tissues like secondary xylem and secondary phloem and also the cork.

[I] Types of Cambium

1. Fascicular cambium (Intrafascicular cambium). This part of the cambium is produced by the procambium. It is situated in the vascular bundle between xylem and phloem.

2. Interfascicular cambium. This part of cambium originates in between the two vascular bundles from the interfascicular parenchyma.

3. Phellogen or cork cambium. A lateral meristem which is secondary in origin. The derivatives on its outerside mature into cork cells (phellem) and those on the innerside into secondary cortex cells (phelloderm).

VASCULAR BUNDLES

It is a strand of vascular tissue made of xylem and phloem.

[I] Types of vascular bundles

1. Radial. A vascular bundle in which xylem and phloem occur as separate groups situated on different radii alternating each other. It is typical of roots (Fig.20A).

2. Concentric. A vascular bundle in which one of the two vascular tissues (i.e. xylem or phloem) occupies the centre and is completely surrounded by another (i.e. phloem or xylem). These bundles are of two types.

(a) ***Amphicribal vascular bundle*** (Hadrocentric). It is a concentric vascular bundle where xylem occupies the centre and is surrounded by phloem (Fig. 20B).

(b) ***Amphivasal vascular bundle*** (Leptocentric). It is a concentric vascular bundle where phloem occupies the centre and is surrounded by xylem (Fig. 20C).

3. Conjoint. It is a vascular bundle in which both xylem and phloem lie on the same radius and form a single group. These are of following two types —

(a) ***Collateral vascular bundle.*** A conjoint vascular bundle where xylem forms the inner part and the phloem forms the outer part (Fig. 20D).

(b) ***Bicollateral vascular bundle.*** A conjoint vascular bundle where phloem is present on both inner and outer faces of xylem (Fig. 20F).

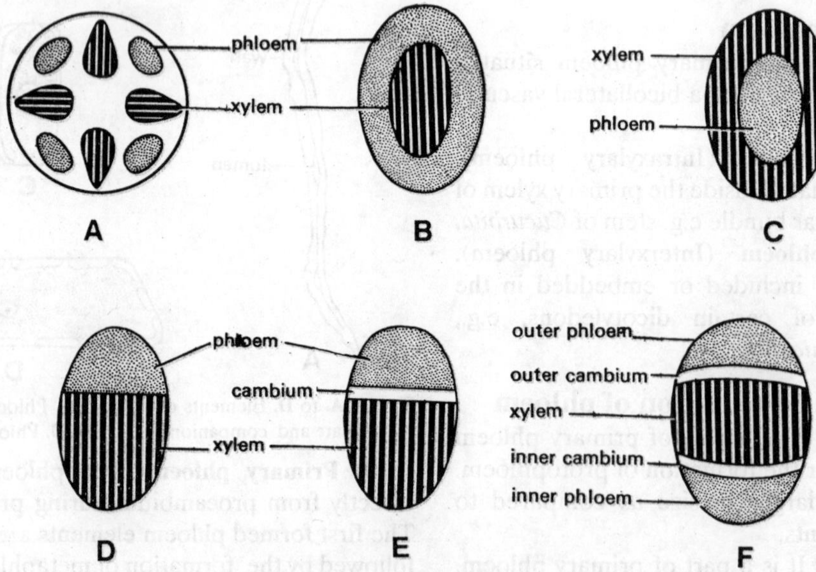

Fig. 20. A to F. Types of vascular bundles. A. Radial. B. Amphicribal. C. Amphivasal. D. Collateral and closed. E. Collateral and open. F. Bicollateral.

[II] SOME OTHER TYPES

1. Medullary vascular bundle. Type of vascular bundle occurs in the pith, more or less close to the centre of the stem, e.g. *Boerhaavia.*

2. Cortical vascular bundle. A vascular bundle that occurs in the region of cortex, e.g. *Nyctanthes.*

[III] Vascular bundle in relation to cambium

1. Open vascular bundle. When cambium is present in between the xylem and phloem of a conjoint (collateral or bicollateral) vascular bundle (Fig. 20E), e.g. vascular bundles in dicot stems.

2. Closed vascular bundle. A vascular bundle where cambium is absent (Fig. 20D) e.g. vascular bundles in monocot stems.

[IV] Associated structures

1. Bundle cap. It is thick walled parenchyma or sclerenchyma associated with a vascular bundle. In cross section it appears like a cap over phloem or xylem.

2. Bundle sheath. Layer or layers of parenchyma or sclerenchyma which surround a vascular bundle.

STELE

The central cylinder of the axis organised as a unit of the plant body and made of vascular system and the associated ground tissue (pericycle, interfascicular region and pith).

[I] Types of steles

1. Protostele. It is the simplest type of stele made of central solid core of xylem surrounded by phloem (Fig.21A).

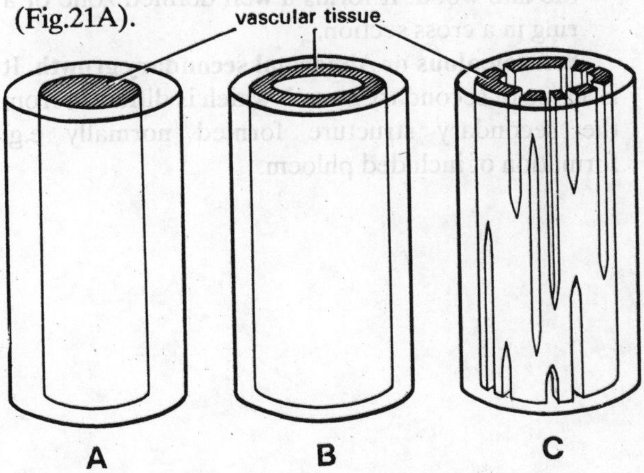

Fig. 21. A to C. Different types of steles. A. Protostele . B. Siphonostele, C. Solenostele.

2. Siphonostele. A type of stele where central part is occupied by pith and hence it is considered to be hollow cylinder of vascular tissue. Leaf gaps are absent (Fig. 21B). There are two major types.

(a) ***Amphiphloic siphonostele.*** A siphonostele in which there are two phloem rings one external and the other internal to xylem.

(b) ***Ectophloic siphonostele.*** A siphonostele with pith and only one phloem ring, external to the xylem.

3. Solenostele. A type of amphiphloic siphonostele in which successive leaf gaps are considerably distant from one another (Fig. 21C).

4. Dictyostele. A stele in which leaf gaps are large and partly overlap one another dividing it into small strands called meristeles in each of which phloem surrounds the xylem.

5. Eustele. It is the most advanced type of stele found in dicotyledons and gymnosperms. Vascular cylinder is hollow with parenchymatous pith in the centre and a ring of collateral or bicollateral vascular bundles.

6. Atactostele. In this type, vascular bundles are scattered throughout the ground tissue as in stems of monocotyledons.

SECONDARY GROWTH

1. Primary growth. This is the growth of roots, shoots and reproductive structures from the time of their origin, from the apical meristem until the complete formation of organs.

2. Secondary growth. This results in the increase in thickness of root and stem. It takes place due to activity of cambium and results in the formation of secondary tissues. Vascular cambium produces secondary xylem (wood) and secondary phloem. Cork cambium (phellogen) divides to produce cork and secondary cortex.

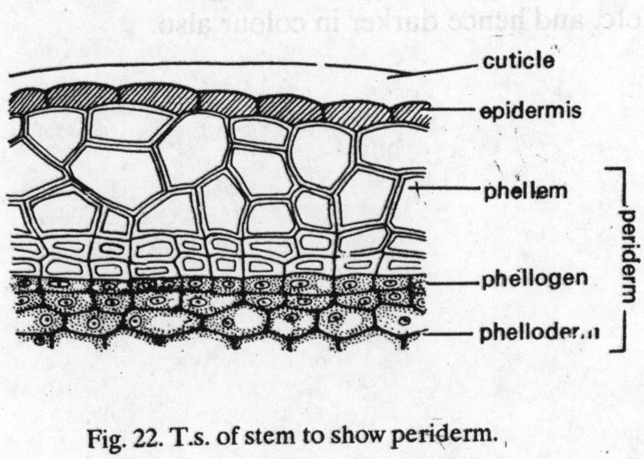

Fig. 22. T.s. of stem to show periderm.

[I] Secondary growth in cortex

1. Bark. It is a non- technical term which includes all the tissues outside the vascular cambium.

2. Periderm. It is a secondary protective tissue derived from the phellogen (cork cambium). It is made of cork (phellem), cork cambium (phellogen) and secondary cortex (phelloderm) Fig. 22.

3. Phellogen or cork cambium. A lateral meristem which is secondary in origin. The derivatives produced on the inner side mature into secondary cortex (phelloderm) and those on the outer side mature into cork (phellem).

4. Phellem or cork. It is a protective tissue made of non-living dead cells with heavily suberised walls (Fig. 23).

5. Phelloderm or secondary cortex. It is a tissue formed by phellogen on its inner side. The cells are parenchymatous and form a region similar to cortex.

6. Lenticels. These are special areas with openings in between suberised cork cells. The surrounding parenchymatous tissue has numerous intercellular spaces.

[II] Secondary growth in vascular region

1. Wood or secondary xylem. It is a region of secondary xylem produced by the vascular cambium.

2. Annual ring. It is a growth layer of xylem, one is formed each year. It consists of spring wood and autumn wood.

3. Spring wood or early wood. It is the secondary xylem formed during spring. The elements are large and thin forming a distinct concentric ring.

4. Autumn wood or late wood. It is the secondary xylem formed during autumn. The elements are small and thick forming a distinct concentric ring.

5. Heart wood. The term used to refer to inner layers of wood. It is the non-functional part of the wood the cells being filled with gums, tannins, resins, etc. and hence darker in colour also.

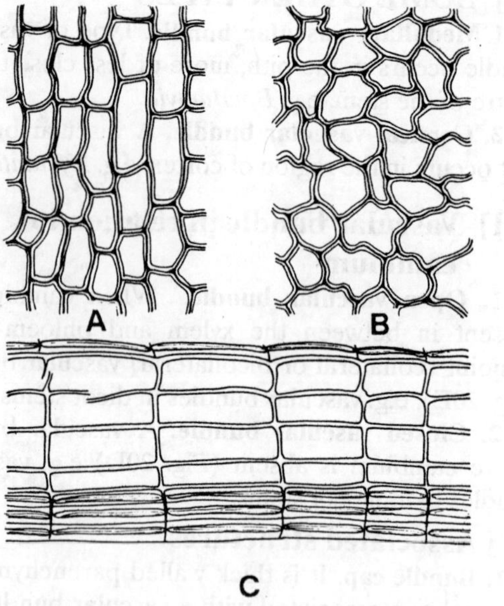

Fig. 23. A to C. Different types of cork cells.

6. Sap wood. The term used to refer to outer small region of wood. It is the functional part of the water conducting tissue. The region appears lighter in colour.

7. Porous wood. Secondary xylem (wood) with vessels. This is of following two types—

(a) Diffuse porous wood. Wood in which pores (vessels) are distributed fairly uniformly throughout the growth layer or change only gradually in size from early to late wood.

(b) Ring porous wood. Wood in which pores (vessels) of the early wood are distinctly larger than that of the late wood. It forms a well defined zone or a ring in a cross section.

8. Anomalous or Abnormal secondary growth. It is a type of secondary growth which is different from the secondary structure formed normally e.g. formation of included phloem.

8

Ecology

Ecology is defined as a branch of science which deals with reciprocal relationships between an organism and its environment. Ecologists consider ecology as the study of structure and function of ecosystem. This concept is one of the most prevalent and forms the present definition. Ecosystem consists of two major components-biotic and abiotic. The biotic components include all the living organisms of a particular habitat Abiotic components in fact form the environment.

I THE PLANTS

The best ecological classification of plants is based on water availability in the habitat. Accordingly following three major groups of plants are recognised–

(1) **Hydrophytes**–Plants growing in water or in habitat rich in water.

(2) **Xerophytes**–Plants growing in habitats where available water is practically negligible.

(3) **Mesophytes**–Plants growing in habitats where available water is moderately sufficient.

The Hydrophytes

[I] Classification of Hydrophytes

The following is one of the most practical classification of hydrophytes.

1. Free floating hydrophytes. These plants float freely on the water surface and are not rooted, e.g. *Eichhornia*, *Lemna*, *Limnanthemum*, *Pistia*, *Wolffia*, etc.

2. Floating but rooted hydrophytes. These plants float on the surface of water but remain attached to the bottom of water reservoir by their roots, e.g. *Aponogeton*, *Jussiaea*, *Nymphaea*, *Potamogeton*, *Trapa*, etc.

3. Submerged but not rooted. These plants occur below the water surface and remain free being not rooted, e.g. *Ceratophyllum*, *Najas*, etc.

4. Submerged but rooted. These plants remain below the water surface but are attached to the reservoir bottom by their roots, e.g. *Hydrilla*, *Utricularia*, *Vallisneria*, etc.

5. Amphibious and rooted. These plants grow near the water reservoirs in shallow and muddy places, e.g. *Polygonum*, *Marsilea*, etc.

6. Emergent but rooted. These plants are found in shallow water. They grow half below the water and the half above it, e.g. *Cyperus*, *Ranunculus*, *Typha*, etc.

[II] External features of hydrophytes

The following are some of the common morphological features shown by hydrophytes.

1. Root. A few major characters are listed below–

1. It is often very poorly developed. The roots may even be absent e. g. *Ceratophyllum*, *Wolffia*, etc.
2. In some hydrophytes root system is well developed mainly for the purpose of attachment, e.g. *Nymphaea*, *Cyperus*, *Typha*, etc.
3. In free floating plants, adventitious roots are developed not for anchorage but for buoyancy e.g. *Eichhornia*, *Pistia*, etc.
4. Sheath-like root pockets are developed in *Azolla*, *Lemna*, *Pistia*, etc. instead of root cap. It helps the plants to float.
5. Spongy roots which are negatively geotropic develop for floating in *Pistia*.

2. Shoot. The stems are spongy, delicate and flexible.

3. Petiole. The following are the hydrophytic characters.

1. Petiole is very long and delicate in plants with roots attached and leaves floating, e.g. *Nymphaea*, *Sagittaria*, etc.
2. Bulbous petiole of *Eichhornia* helps the plant to float on water surface.

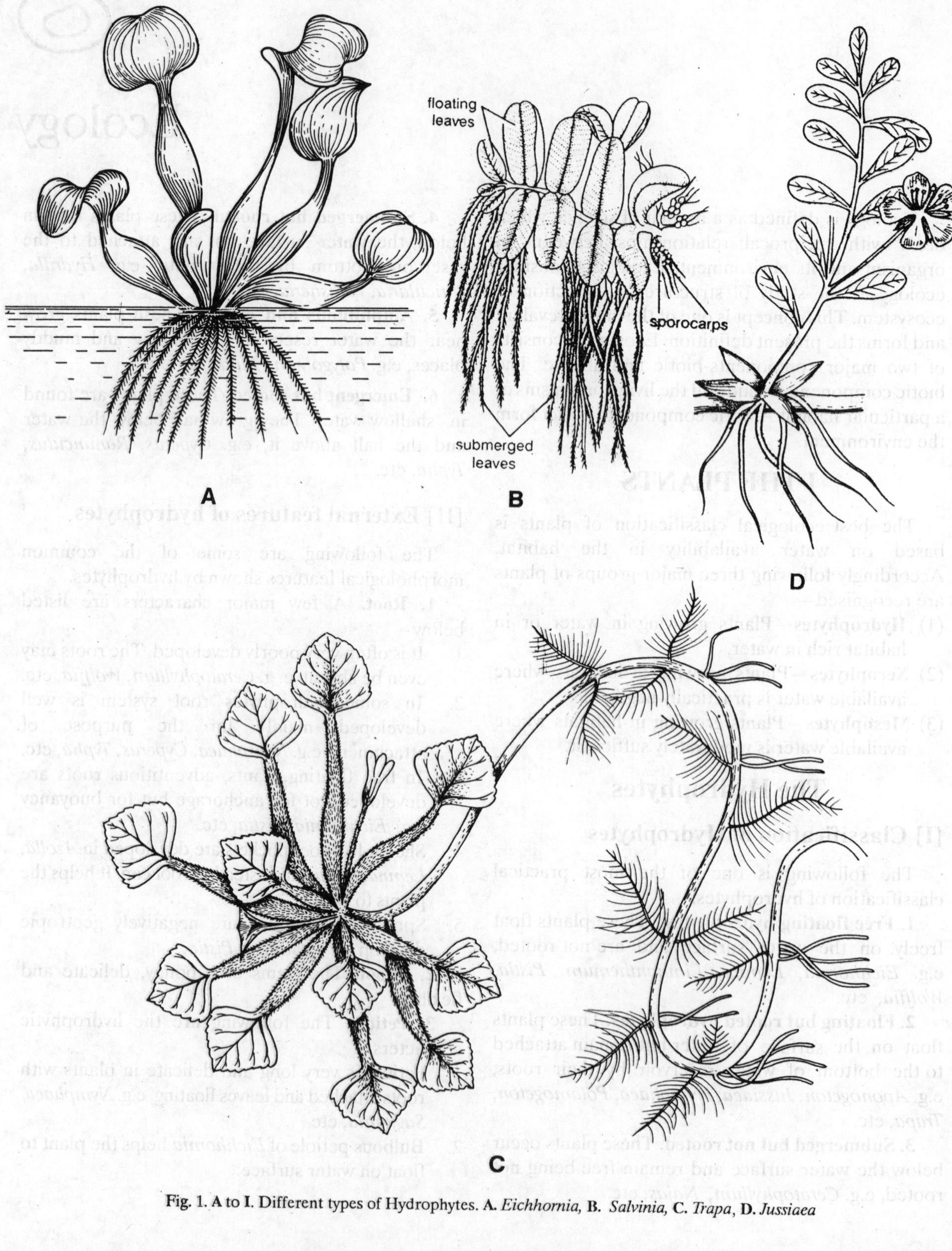

Fig. 1. A to I. Different types of Hydrophytes. A. *Eichhornia*, B. *Salvinia*, C. *Trapa*, D. *Jussiaea*

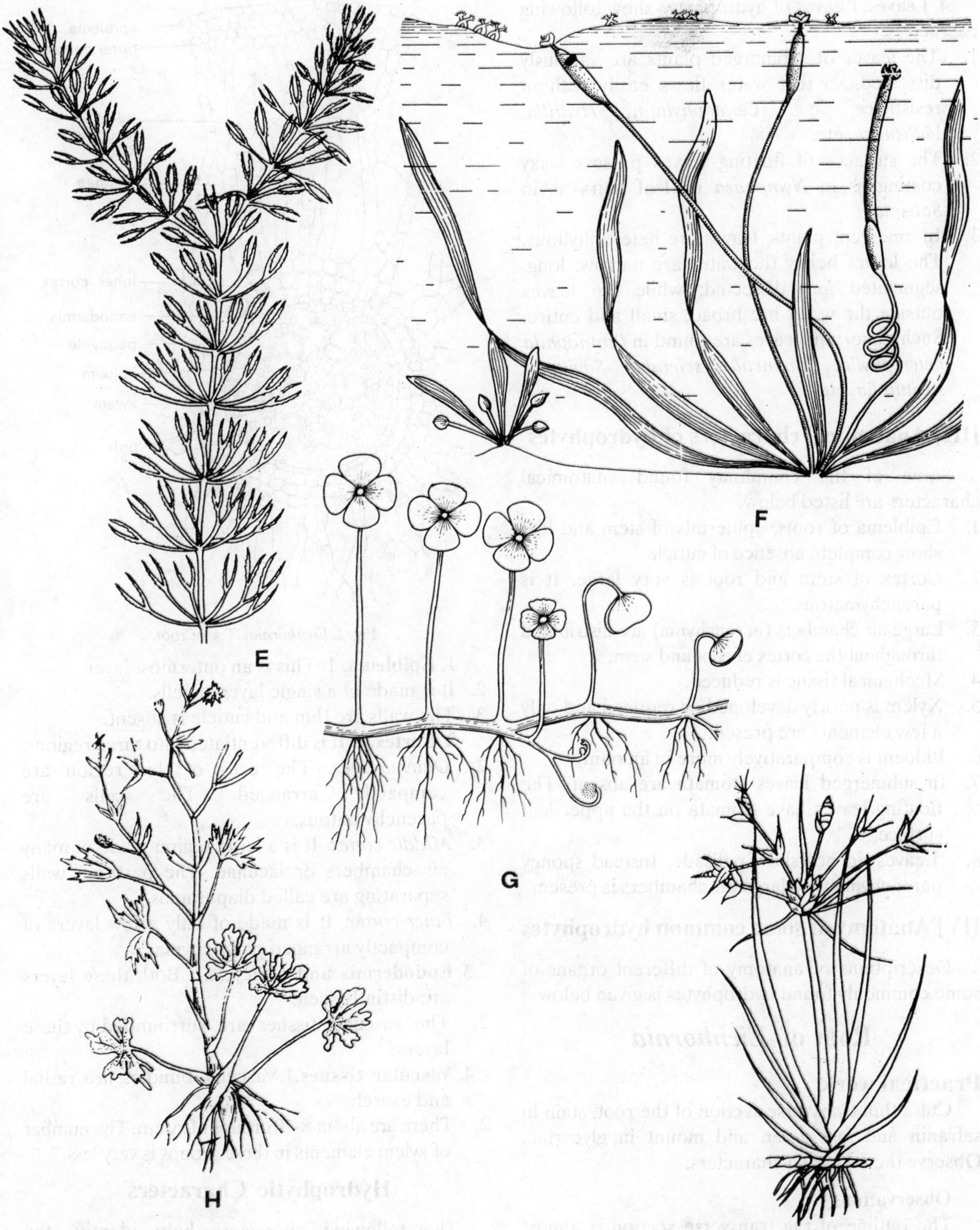

Fig. 1. (contd.) **E.** *Ceratophyllum*, **F.** *Vallisneria*, **G.** *Marsilea*, **H.** *Ranunculus*, **I.** *Cyperus*.

4. **Leaves.** Leaves of hydrophytes show following characters.

1. The leaves of submerged plants are variously dissected, so that water flows easily without resistance; e.g. *Ceratophyllum*, *Hydrilla*, *Vallisneria*, etc.
2. The surfaces of floating leaves possess waxy coating as in *Nymphaea* or leaf hairs as in *Salvinia*.
3. In emergent plants, leaves are heterophyllous. The leaves below the water are narrow, long, segmented and dissected; while the leaves outside the water are broad, small and entire. Such dimorphic leaves are found in *Limnophila heterophylla*, *Ranunculus scleratus*, *Sagittaria sagittifolia*, etc.

[III] Anatomical characters of hydrophytes

Some of the commonly found anatomical characters are listed below.

1. Epiblema of roots, epidermis of stem and leaf show complete absence of cuticle.
2. Cortex of stem and root is very large. It is parenchymatous.
3. Large air chambers (aerenchyma) are distributed throughout the cortex of root and stem.
4. Mechanical tissue is reduced.
5. Xylem is poorly developed or reduced and only a few elements are present.
6. Phloem is comparatively more in amount.
7. In submerged leaves stomata are absent. The floating leaves have stomata on the upper leaf surface.
8. Leaves do not show palisade. Instead spongy parenchyma with large air chambers is present.

[IV] Anatomy of some common hydrophytes

Descriptions of anatomy of different organs of some commonly found hydrophytes is given below.

Root of *Eichhornia*

Practical work

Cut a thin transverse section of the root, stain in safranin and fast green and mount in glycerine. Observe the following characters.

Observations

The outline of the transverse section is almost circular.

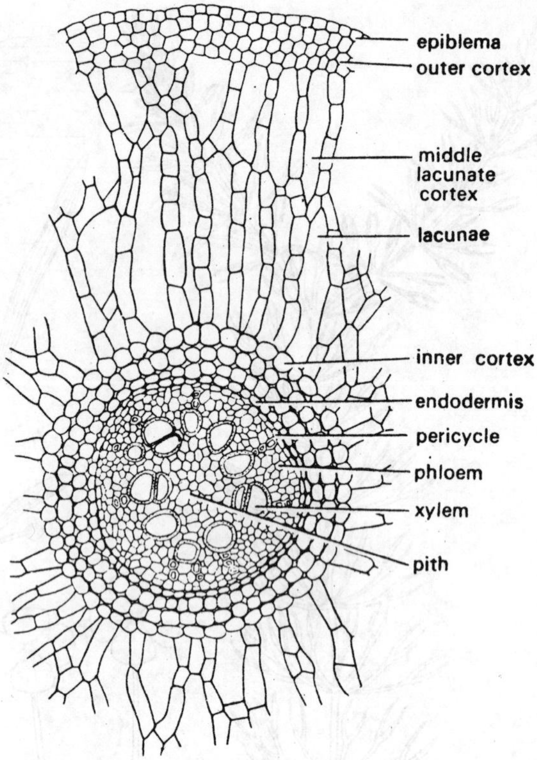

Fig. 2. ***Eichhornia.*** T.s. of root.

1. Epiblema. 1. This is an outermost layer.
2. It is made of a single layer of cells.
3. The walls are thin and cuticle is absent.

2. Cortex. 1. It is differentiated into three regions.
2. *Outer cortex.* The cells of this region are compactly arranged. The cells are parenchymatous.
3. *Middle cortex.* It is a large region made of many air chambers or lacunae. The partition walls separating are called diaphragms.
4. *Inner cortex.* It is made of only a few layers of compactly arranged parenchyma.

3. Endodermis and pericycle. 1 .Both these layers are distintly seen.
2. The vascular tissues are surrounded by these layers.

4. Vascular tissues. 1.Vascular bundles are radial and exarch.
2. There are about 8-10 groups of xylem. The number of xylem elements in these groups is very less.

Hydrophytic Characters

The following characters help identify the material as hydrophyte.

1. Undifferentiated parenchymatous tissue.
2. Abundance of aerenchyma.
3. Absence of mechanical tissue.
4. Vascular tissue poorly developed.
5. Xylem elements fewer in number.
6. The above characters indicate that the plant is a hydrophyte. Since it shows radial and exarch conditions of vascular bundles it is a root.

Stem of *Hydrilla*

Practical work

Cut a thin transverse section of the material; stain in safranin and fast green combination, mount in glycerine and study.

Observations

The outline of the section is almost circular. It shows following characters.

1. Epidermis. 1. This is the outermost single layer of cells.
2. Cutcle is absent.

2. Cortex. 1. It occupies most part of the section.
2. It is made of many, large air chambers.
3. Air chambers are separated from one another by partitions called diaphragms.
4. A few layers just below the epidermis (outer cortex) and a few layers close the endodermis (inner cortex) are compact and parenchymatous.

3. Endodermis and pericycle. 1. Distinct endodermis and pericycle are present.
2. These enclose the underlying vascular tissue.

4. Vascular tissues. 1. It is extremely reduced.
2. Most of the tissue is phloem.
3. Xylem is represented by a single large element situated in the centre.

Hydrophytic Characters

1. Epidermis is made of thin walled cells.
2. Cuticle is absent.
3. Absence of mechanical tissue.
4. Aerenchyma and air chambers present.
5. Extremely reduced xylem.
6. Comparatively well developed phloem.

Petiole of *Eichhornia*

Practical work

Cut a transverse section of petiole of *Eichhornia*, stain with safranin and fast green, mount in glycerine and study.

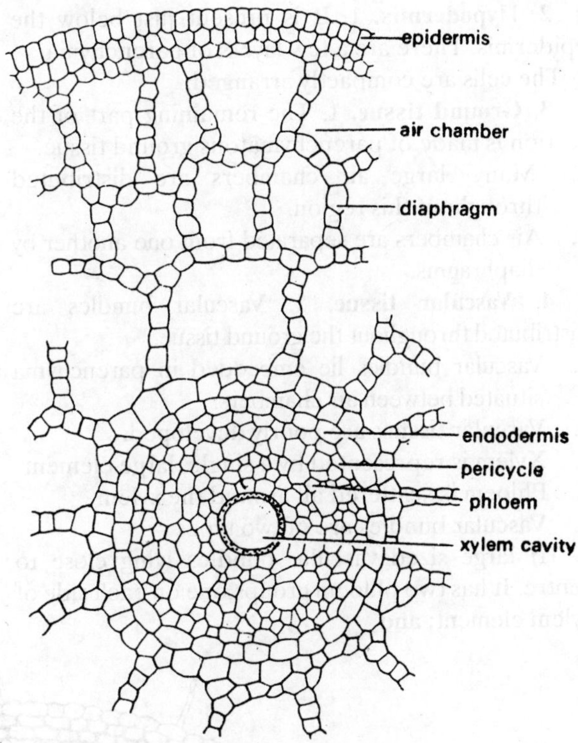

Fig. 3. ***Hydrilla.*** T.s. of stem.

Observations

The transverse section is almost circular in outline. It shows following characters.

1. Epidermis. 1. It is the outermost layer made of parenchymatous cells.
2. Cuticle is absent.

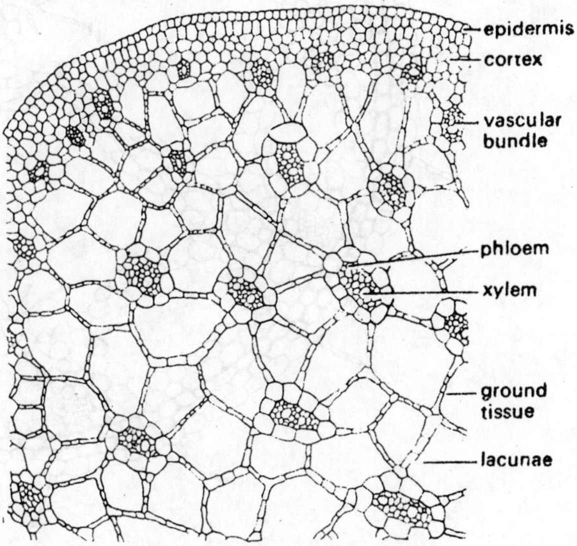

Fig. 4. ***Eichhornia.*** T.s. of petiole.

2. Hypodermis. 1. It is present just below the epidermis. There are a few layers of parenchyma.
2. The cells are compactly arranged.

3. Ground tissue. 1. The remaining part of the section is made of parenchymatous ground tissue.
2. Many large air chambers are distributed throughout this region.
3. Air chambers are separated from one another by diaphragms.

4. Vascular tissue. 1. Vascular bundles are distributed throughout the ground tissue.
2. Vascular bundles lie embedded in parenchyma situated between air chambers.
3. Vascular tissues are poorly developed.
4. Xylem is represented by a single, large element.
5. Phloem is scattered all around the xylem.
6. Vascular bundles are of two types –

(i) large sized vascular bundles lying close to centre. It has two phloem groups, one on each side of xylem element; and

(ii) small sized vascular bundles lying in the outer region of ground tissue. It has only one phloem group situated on its outer side.

Hydrophytic characters

The following hydrophytic characters are shown by the section –

1. The cells of the epidermis are thin walled.
2. Cuticle absent.
3. Absence of mechanical tissue.
4. Ground tissue parenchymatous.
5. Presence of aerenchyma.
6. Vascular tissues poorly developed.

Petiole of *Nymphaea*

Practical work

Cut a transverse section of petiole of *Nymphaea*, stain in safranin-fast green combination, mount in glycerine and study.

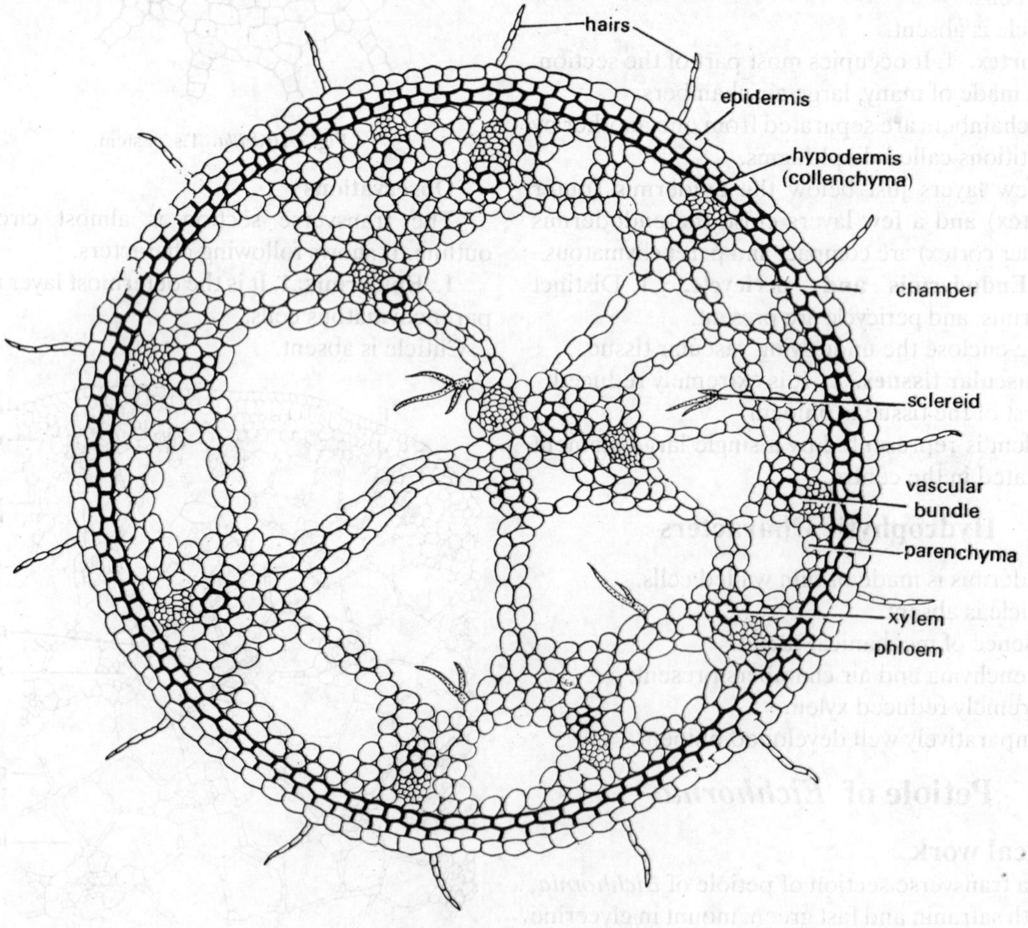

Fig. 5. *Nymphaea*. T.s. of petiole.

Observations

The transverse section is almost circular in outline. It shows following characters.

1. Epidermis.1. This is an outermost layer made of parenchymatous cells with chloroplasts.

2. Cuticle is generally absent, if present, it is very thin.
3. A few multicellular, unbranched hairs are present.

2. Hypodermis. 1. It lies below the epidermis and is about 2-3 layered deep.

2. The cells are collenchymatous and compactly arranged.

3. Ground tissue. 1. The remaining part of the section is mostly filled with ground tissue.

2. There are many air chambers scattered throughout this region.
3. A few trichosclereids or internal hairs occur in the air chambers.

4. Vascular tissue. 1. Vascular bundles are distributed throughout the ground tissue.

2. These are situated in the parenchyma between air chambers.
3. Vascular bundles show poorly developed xylem, represented by a single lacuna.
4. Phloem of bundle lies on the outer side and is normally developed.
5. There are two types of bundles –

(i) larger sized towards the centre with two groups of phloem, one on either side of xylem element and

(ii) smaller in size towards periphery with only one (outer) group of phloem.

Hydrophytic characters

1. Thin walled epidermis.
2. Presence of chloroplasts in the epidermis
3. Cuticle absent or very thin.
4. Mechanical tissue reduced.
5. Ground tissue undifferentiated.
6. Presence of large number of air chambers.
7. Vascular tissue reduced.
8. Presence of trichosclereids.

Leaf of *Nymphaea*

Practical work

Cut a transverse section of the leaf, stain in safranin-fast green combination, mount in glycerine and study.

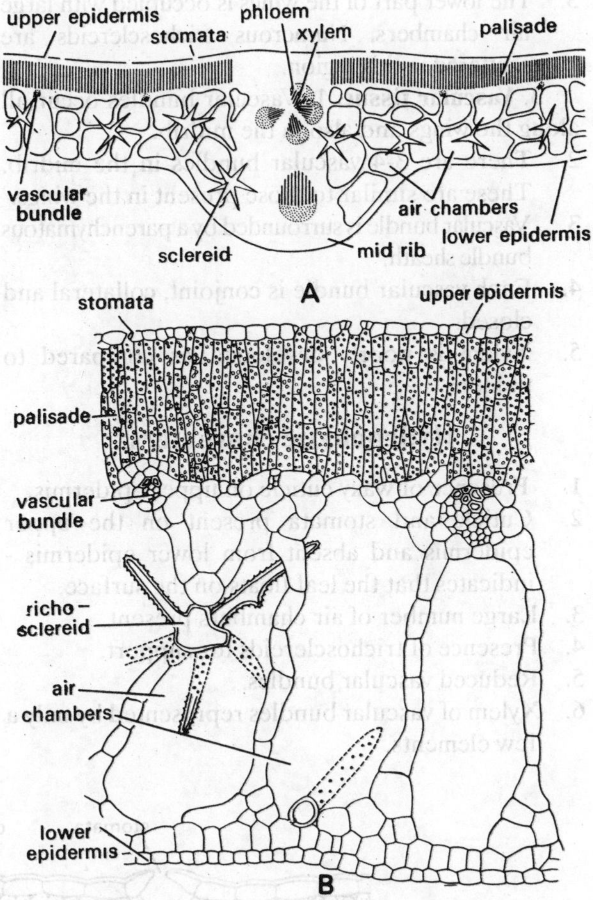

Fig. 6. ***Nymphaea***. T.s. of leaf. **A.** Outlines of the section, **B.** Details of a part of section.

Observations

The transverse section shows a bulged and distinct midrib and wings on its both sides. The following characters are seen.

1. Epidermis. 1. Both upper and lower epidermal layers are present.

2. Both are made of compactly arranged cells.
3. Upper epidermis has many stomata; which are lacking from lower epidermis.
4. Upper epidermis is covered with waxy cuticle. It is absent from lower epidermis.
5. A few slime glands occur on the lower epidermis.

2. Mesophyll. 1. It is differentiated into upper palisade and lower spongy parenchyma.

2. Upper palisade becomes discontinuous near epidermis to form sub-stomatal chambers.

3. The lower part of the wings is occupied with large air chambers. Numerous trichosclereids are scattered in this region.

3. Vascular tissue. 1. Vascular bundles occur all along the wings and also in the midrib.

2. There are 3-4 vascular bundles in the midrib. These are similar to those present in the wings.
3. Vascular bundle is surrounded by a parenchymatous bundle sheath.
4. Each vascular bundle is conjoint, collateral and closed.
5. Xylem is poorly developed as compared to phloem.

Hydrophytic characters

1. Presence of waxy cuticle on upper epidermis.
2. Cuticle and stomata present on the upper epidermis and absent from lower epidermis - indicates that the leaf floats on the surface.
3. Large number of air chambers present.
4. Presence of trichosclereids for support.
5. Reduced vascular bundles.
6. Xylem of vascular bundles represented by only a few elements.

Leaf of *Trapa*

Practical work

Cut a transverse section of the leaf, stain in safrain - fast green combination, mount in glycerine and study.

Observations

Transverse section shows a distinct midrib in the centre and the wings on either of its sides. The following are the major anatomical details.

1. Epidermis. 1. Both upper and lower epidermal cells are present.

2. A thin cuticle is present on the upper epidermis only.
3. Stomata occur on the upper epidermis only.
4. The cells of the lower epidermis are thin walled. Cuticle and stomata are absent.
5. A few multicellular hairs occur on the lower epidermis.

2. Mesophyll. 1. Mesophyll is present between upper and lower epidermis.

2. It is differentiated into upper layers of palisade and lower region occupied by spongy parenchyma.

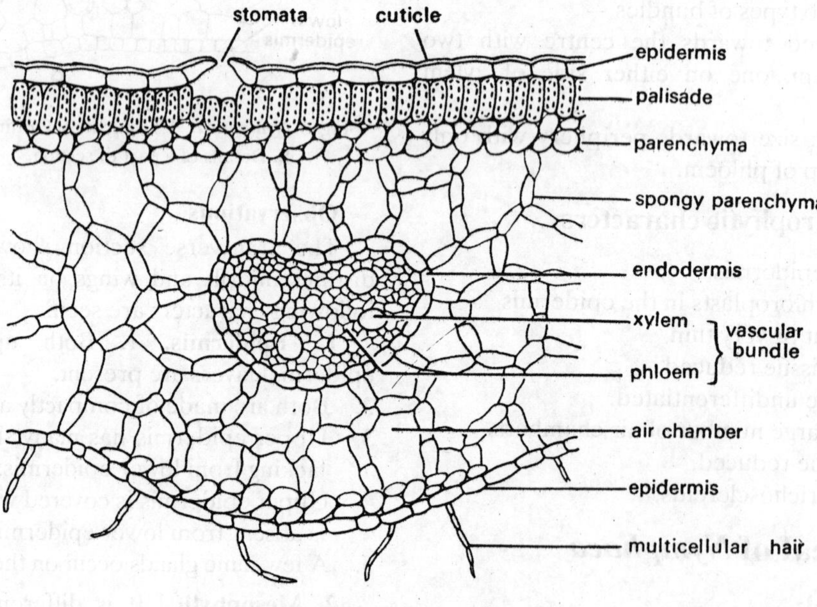

Fig. 7. ***Trapa***. T.s. of leaf.

3. The palisade cells are present just below the upper epidermis. The cells are radially elongated, contain numerous chloroplasts and are compactly arranged.
4. Sub-stomatal cavities occur in this region.
5. A few layers (about 2-3) of parenchyma lie just below the palisade.
6. The rest of the tissue near the lower epidermis is made of spongy parenchyma. It is loosely arranged to form numerous air chambers.

3. Vascular tissue. 1. There is a single vascular bundle in the midrib.

2. It is surrounded by a parenchymatous bundle sheath.
3. Vascular tissue is reduced.
4. Xylem is reduced to only a few lacunae.
5. Phloem is comparatively well developed.

Hydrophytic characters

1. Presence of thin cuticle on the upper epidermis; its absence from lower epidermis.
2. Presence of stomata only on the upper epidermis and their absence from lower epidermis.
3. Presence of air chambers.
4. Absence of mechanical tissue.
5. Vascular tissue reduced and ill developed.

The presence of cuticle and stomata in the upper epidermis indicates that these leaves float on water surface.

The Xerophytes

[I] Classification of Xerophytes

The following is one of the useful classifications of xerophytes.

1. Microphyllous. The leaves are small, scaly, reduced, modified or absent, e.g., *Acacia* (Australian), *Asparagus, Capparis aphylla, Casuarina, Euphorbia, Pinus,* etc.

2. Sclerophyllous. The leaves of these plants are thick, coarse and leathery due to excessive lignified and sclerified tissues, e.g., *Ficus, Nerium, Spartina, Banksia, Dasilirion,* etc.

3. Trichophyllous. These xerophytes have leaves covered with a thick felt of hairs, e.g., *Calotropis.*

4. Malacophyllous. The leaves of these plants are fleshy and thick e.g., *Agave, Aloe, Bryophyllum, Begonia, Salicornia,* etc.

Schimper (1903) classified xerophytes on the basis of external morphology of the leaf –

(1) **Sclerophylly :** leaves leathery.
(2) **Chylophylly :** (leaf succulence) : leaves fleshy.
(3) **Aphylly :** leaves rudimentary and caducous.
(4) **Sclerocauly :** axes slender, dry and hard.
(5) **Chylocauly :** (stem succulence) axes short, thick and filled with mucilaginous sap.

[II] External features of xerophytes

The following are some of the common morphological characters shown by xerophytes.

1. Root. A few major marphological characters of root are listed below.

1. The root system is very well developed and profusely branched.
2. These have a long tap root system that grows deep into the soil and reaches the water table.
3. In some desert plants, roots grow near the soil surface to absorb soil water whenever available.
4. The roots of many xerophytes are perennating.

2. Shoot. The following are morphological characteristics of the shoot.

1. The stem is generally hard and woody that remains covered with wax, silica, hairs, etc.
2. A few xerophytes possess fleshy and stunted stem. The cells may contain, large quantities of mucilage, thus allowing the stem to store water.
3. In extreme cases stem becomes modified into leaf-like structure to reduce the transpiring surfaces. In *Ruscus,* the stem becomes leaf-like and is known as phylloclade (also in *Opuntia, Muehlenbeckia,* etc). The internodes of *Asparagus* get modified into leaf-like cladodes, while the leaves are small and scaly.
4. In some xerophytes, the shoot becomes either fleshy, reduced cushion-like or stunted.

3. Leaves. A few typical morphological characters are given below.

1. In many xerophytes, leaves fall down as soon as they are formed (caducous leaves) e.g., in species of *Euphorbia. Capparis aphylla* shows complete absence of leaves.
2. In *Opuntia* and many cacti leaves get reduced to spine- like structures.
3. Rosette arrangement of the leaves is seen in *Bromelia* which cuts down the light and reduces transpiration.
4. The desert grasses show rolling of the leaves so that stomates located on the upper epidermis stop transpiring *e.g., Ammophila, Festuca, Stipa,* etc.

4. Reproduction. Xerophytes are characterised by following cycles of reproduction. Accordingly three categories can be recognised —

(a) Drought escaping (ephemerals). These plants complete their life cycle during the period of available moisture and before the onset of dry season e.g., *Artemesia, Astragalus,* etc.

(b) Drought enduring plants. These xerophytes continue to live during dry period without any injury or damage, though they are at their lowest activities *e.g.,* succulent plants.

(c) Drought resistant. These are structurally adapted to resist extreme drought conditions. Besides, most of the xerophytes perennate by roots. These flower only during the season when moisture is available.

[III] Anatomical characters of xerophytes

Some of the anatomical characteristics of xerophytes are given below.

1. Epidermal cells of the leaves and stems are thick and heavily cuticularised.
2. Presence of wax on the epidermal cells to reflect light.
3. The number of stomata per unit area is very less.
4. Stomata are mostly sunken.

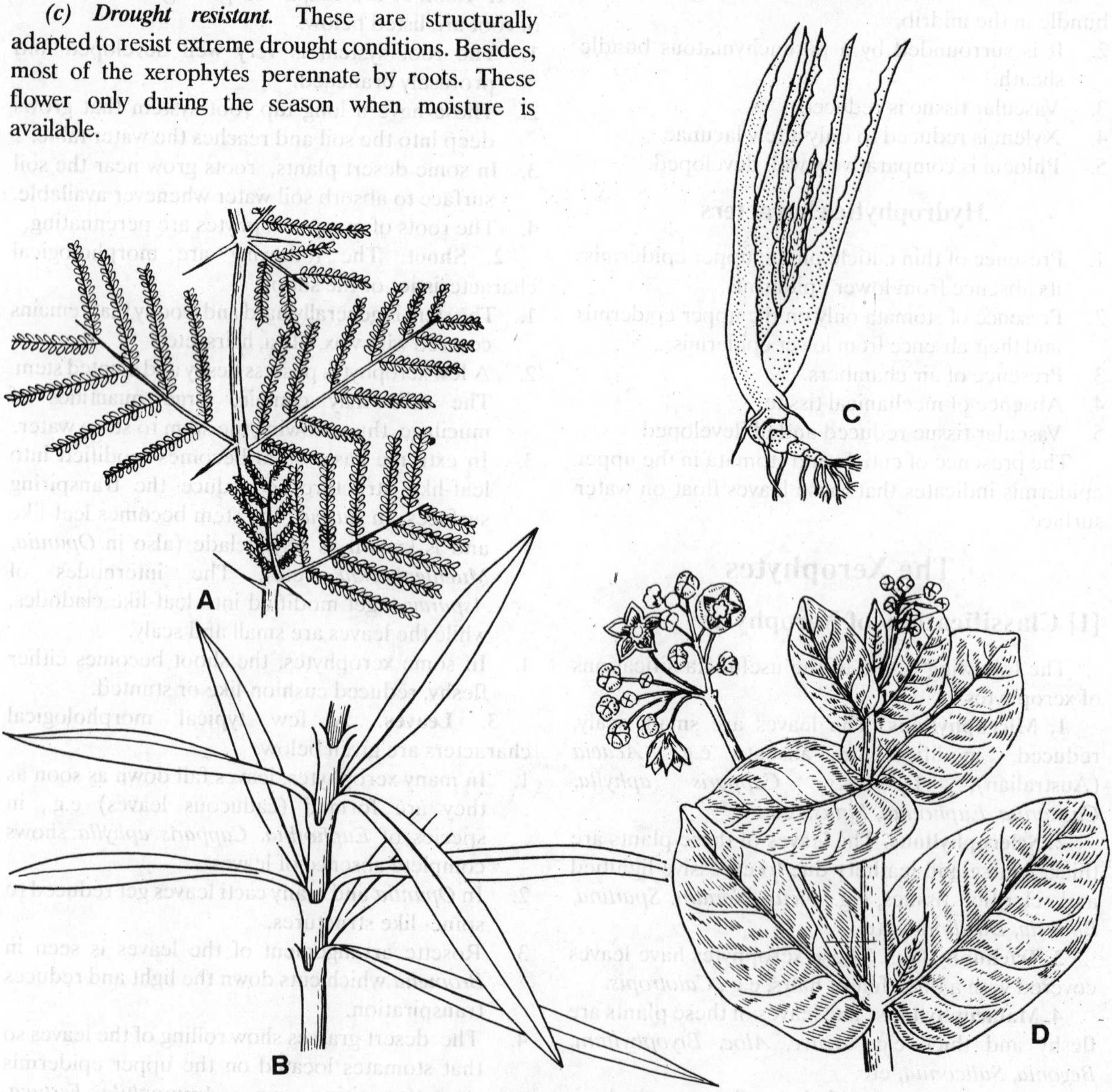

Fig. 8. A. to D. Different types of xerophytes. A. *Acacia* B. *Nerium*, C. *Aloe*, D. *Calotropis*.

5. A thick felt or dense covering of hairs is generally present over the epidermis and near the stomatal openings. Hairs are generally air-containing and form an insulating layer against the rise in temperature.
6. The epidermal cells are generally radially elongated to receive only required amount of light.
7. In case the leaves are small, reduced or absent, the cortex of the stem possesses palisade or chlorenchyma. Palisade cells are very much elongated.
8. Intercellular spaces which contain air, are small in size and their number is reduced to minimum. The transpiring surface is thus reduced.
9. The amount of mechanical tissue i.e., collenchyma and sclerenchyma is higher. It provides mechanical support to the plants which become hard.
10. Presence of water storing tissue e.g., double or multiple epidermis, aqueous tissue, mucilage cells, etc. Water storing cells are either dead tracheids, living parenchyma tissue, chlorenchyma, intercellular spaces of solitary living cells, etc. These are not uniformly distributed but confined to a few organs whose chief function is the storage of water e.g., succulent leaves and stems. Water cells reserve water as soon as it is available to them and allow other cells to utilise it when needed.
11. Increased amount of vessels allows easier conduction of water.
12. In some desert grasses, leaves roll down during excessive dry conditions. This is due to the modified, enlarged and colourless epidermal cells – bulliform or motor cells occurring in the upper epidermis. These cells are sensitive to turgor changes and collapse during dry and warm conditions. This results in the upward rolling of the leaf to close down the stomata located on the upper epidermis.

[IV] Anatomy of some common xerophytes

Descriptions of anatomy of different organs of some commonly found xerophytes is given below.

Stem of *Cynodon*

Practical work

Cynodon is a common lawn grass. A sharp razor or a new safety blade is necessary for cutting the section. Stain a thin section in safranin and fast green combination, mount in glycerine and study.

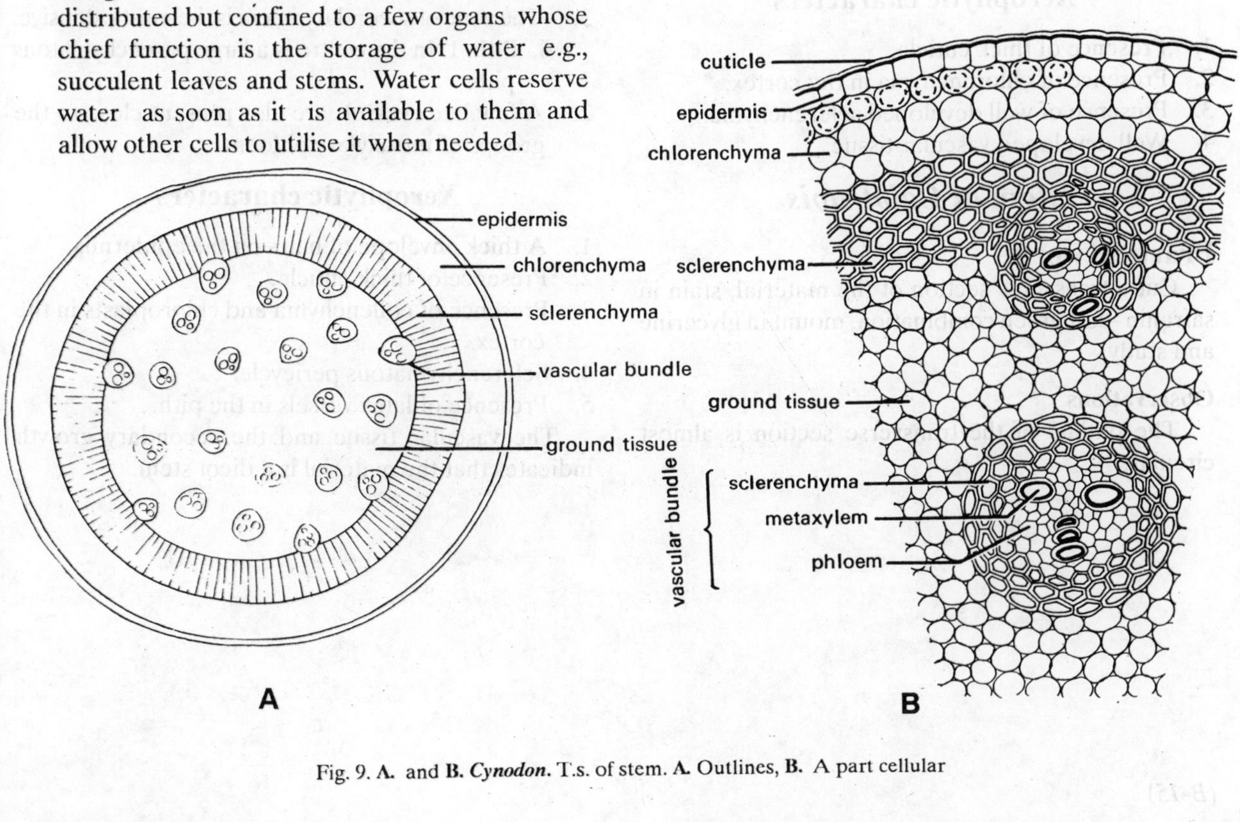

Fig. 9. A. and B. *Cynodon*. T.s. of stem. A. Outlines, B. A part cellular

Observations

The outline of the transverse section is almost circular. It shows following characters.

1. Epidermis. 1. This is an outermost single layer of cells.

2. The cells are thickly cuticularised.

2. Ground tissue. 1. Below the epidermis, 3-4 layers of chlorenchyma are present.

2. It is followed by a several celled deep band of sclerenchyma.
3. The rest of the ground tissue is parenchymatous with numerous intercellular spaces.

3. Vascular tissue. 1. Many vascular bundles are scattered in the ground tissue.

2. Each vascular bundle is collateral and closed. It is enveloped by a sclerenchymatous bundle sheath.
3. Xylem forms a V - shaped structure.
4. Phloem is situated between the arms of V.
5. The outer ring of bundles is partially embedded in the ring of sclerenchyma while the vascular bundles of the inner ring lie in the parenchy matous ground tissue.

Xerophytic characters

1. Presence of thick cuticle.
2. Presence of chlorenchyma in the cortex.
3. Presence of well developed sclerenchyma.
4. Well developed vascular tissue.

Stem of *Calotropis*

Practical work

Cut a transverse section of the material, stain in safranin - fast green combination, mount in glycerine and study.

Observations

The outline of the transverse section is almost circular.

1. Epidermis. 1. This is the outermost single layer of cells.

2. It is thickly cuticularised.
3. Numerous hairs produced by the epidermis form a thick cover.

2. Cortex. 1. It is many layers deep.

2. There are two distinct regions.
3. The outer region of the cortex is made of a few layers of collenchyma.
4. The inner region which forms larger part of the cortex is parenchymatous.

3. Endodermis. 1. This single layer forms a wavy layer around the vascular tissues.

2. The cells lack characteristic casparian strips. The cells are, however, filled with abundant starch.

4. Pericycle. 1. It occurs in the form of small patches of sclerenchymatous fibres.

2. In between sclerenchymatous patches, parenchyma is also present.

5. Vascular tissue. 1. It shows secondary growth.

2. As a result, groups of primary phloem, secondary phloem, cambium, secondary xylem, primary xylem and intraxylary (internal) phloem could be seen.
3. The zone of secondary xylem is the most extensive.

6. Pith. 1. In the centre is a large parenchymatous pith.

2. A few latex vessels are also present close to the groups of intraxylary phloem.

Xerophytic characters

1. A thick envelope of hairs on the epidermis.
2. Presence of thick cuticle.
3. Presence of collenchyma and chloroplasts in the cortex.
4. Sclerenchymatous pericycle.
5. Presence of latex vessels in the pith.

The vascular tissue and the secondary growth indicates that the material is a dicot stem.

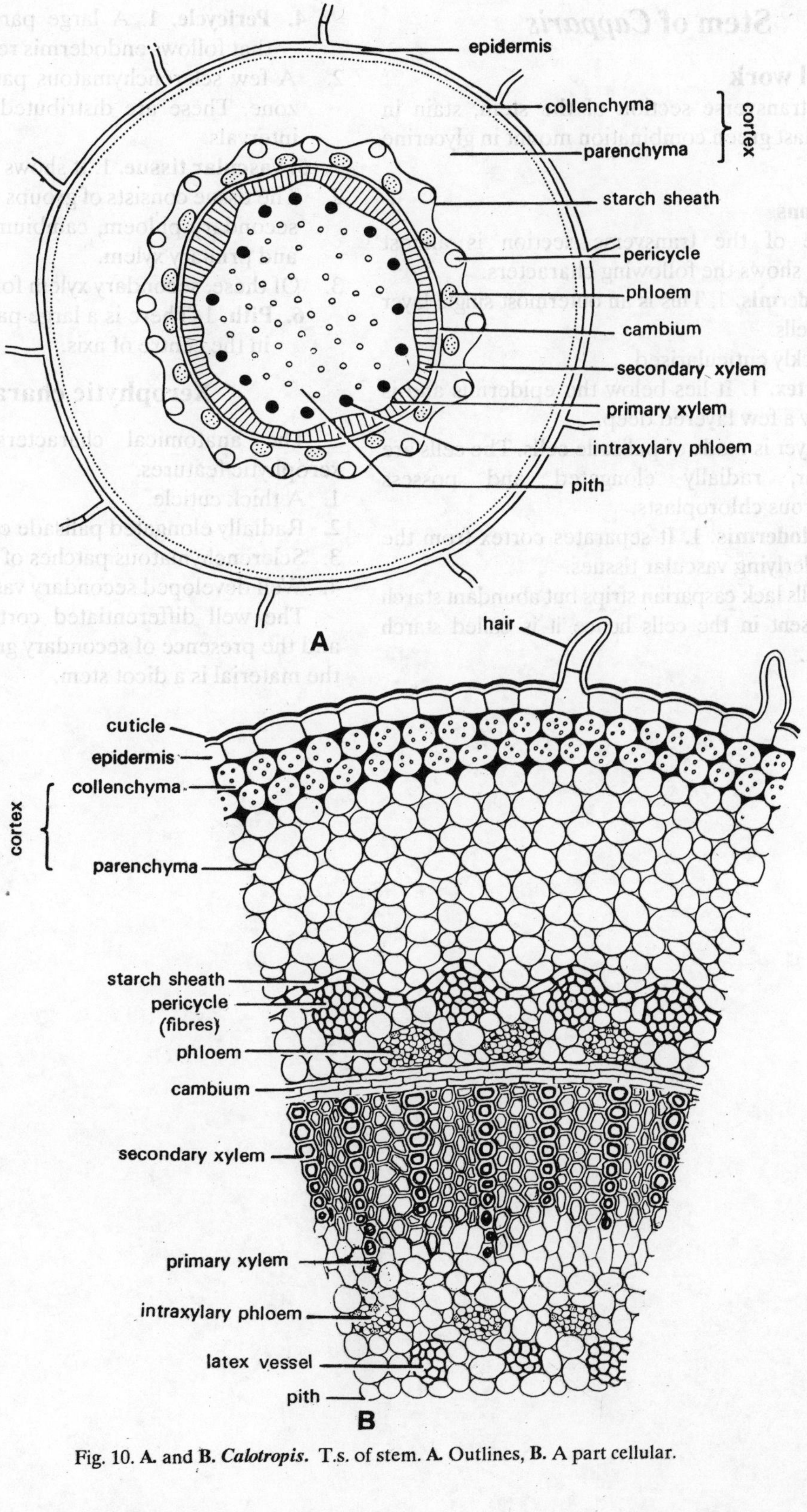

Fig. 10. A. and B. *Calotropis*. T.s. of stem. A. Outlines, B. A part cellular.

Stem of *Capparis*

Practical work

Cut a transverse section of the stem, stain in safranin - fast green combination mount in glycerine and study.

Observations

Outline of the transverse section is almost circular. It shows the following characters.

1. **Epidermis.** 1. This is an outermost single layer of cells.
2. It is thickly cuticularised.

2. **Cortex.** 1. It lies below the epidermis and is only a few layered deep.
2. This layer is made of palisade cells. The cells are tubular, radially elongated and possess numerous chloroplasts.

3. **Endodermis.** 1. It separates cortex from the underlying vascular tissues.
2. The cells lack casparian strips but abundant starch is present in the cells hence it is called starch sheath.

4. **Pericycle.** 1. A large parenchymatous zone that follows endodermis represents pericycle.
2. A few sclerenchymatous patches occur in this zone. These are distributed almost at regular intervals.

5. **Vascular tissue.** 1. It shows secondary growth.
2. The tissue consists of groups of primary phloem, secondary phloem, cambium, secondary xylem and primary xylem.
3. Of these, secondary xylem forms massive zone.

6. **Pith.** 1. There is a large parenchymatous pith in the centre of axis.

Xerophytic characters

The anatomical characters show following xerophytic features.

1. A thick cuticle.
2. Radially elongated palisade cells in the cortex.
3. Sclerenchymatous patches of the pericycle.
4. Well developed secondary vascular tissue.

The well differentiated cortex, vascular tissue and the presence of secondary growth indicates that the material is a dicot stem.

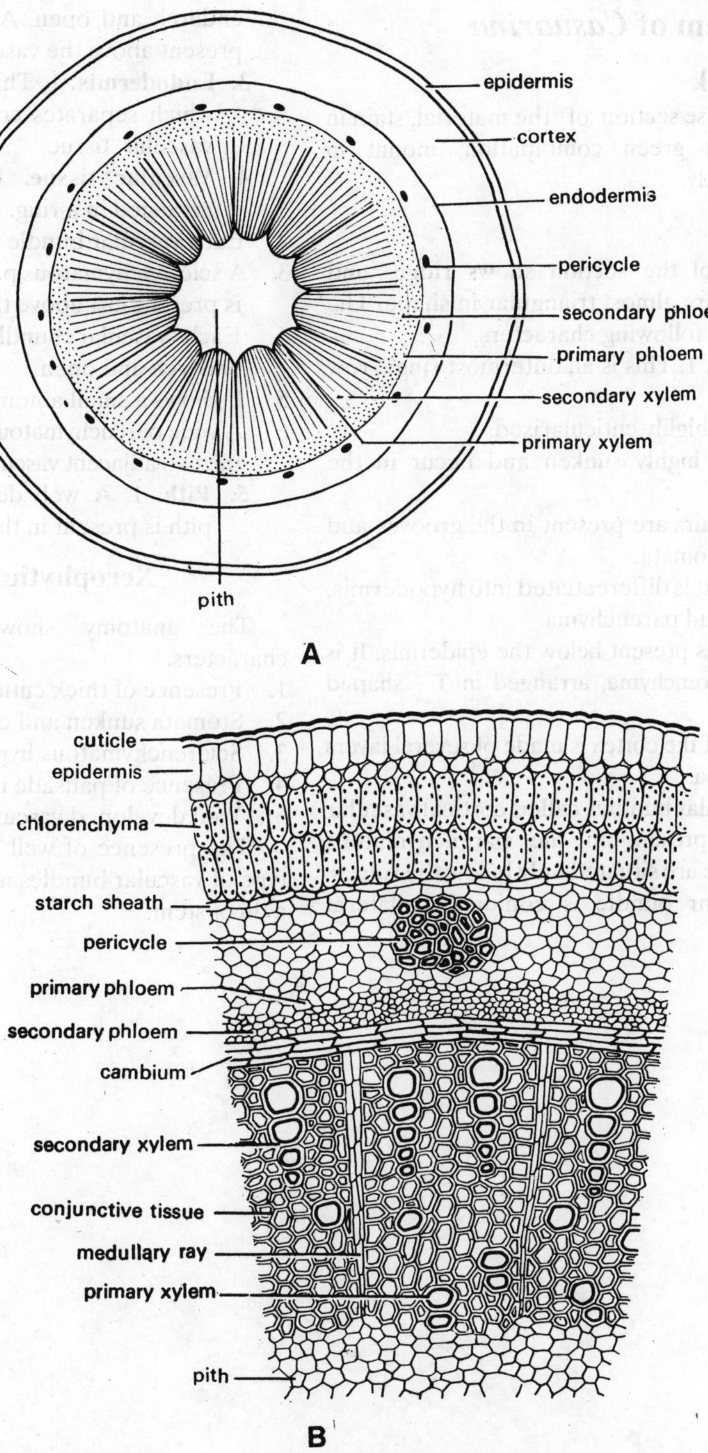

Fig. 11. A and B. *Capparis*. T.s. of stem. A. Outlines, B. A part cellular.

Stem of *Casuarina*

Practical work

Cut a transverse section of the material, stain in safranin – fast green combination, mount in glycerine and study.

Observations

The outline of the section shows ridges and grooves. Ridges are almost triangular in shape. The section shows the following characters.

1. **Epidermis.** 1. This is an outermost single row of cells.
2. The cells are highly cuticularised.
3. Stomata are highly sunken and occur in the grooves.
4. Numerous hairs are present in the grooves and around the stomata.

2. **Cortex.** 1. It is differentiated into hypodermis, palisade and parenchyma.
2. Hypodermis is present below the epidermis. It is made of sclerenchyma, arranged in T - shaped patches.
3. Larger part of the cortex is made of several layers of parenchyma.
4. Ring of vascular bundles called cortical vascular bundles is present in the parenchymatous region. These are situated only below the ridges. Each vascular bundle is conjoint, collateral endarch and open. A sclerenchymatous cap is present above the vascular bundle.

3. **Endodermis.** 1. This is a single layer of cells which separates cortex from the underlying vascular tissue.

4. **Vascular tissue.** 1. Vascular bundles are arranged in a ring.
2. Each vascular bundle occurs below the groove.
3. A sclerenchymatous patch, known as bundle cap is present just above the bundle.
4. Each vascular bundle is conjoint, collateral, endarch and open.
5. It shows a small amount of secondary growth.
6. A wide parenchymatous region is present between the two adjacent vascular bundles.

5. **Pith.** 1. A well developed parenchymatous pith is present in the centre.

Xerophytic characters

The anatomy shows following xerophytic characters.

1. Presence of thick cuticle.
2. Stomata sunken and covered with hairs.
3. Sclerenchymatous hypodermis and bundle cap.
4. Presence of palisade in the cortex.
5. Well developed vascular tissue.

The presence of well developed cortex and the type of vascular bundles indicate that the material is a dicot stem.

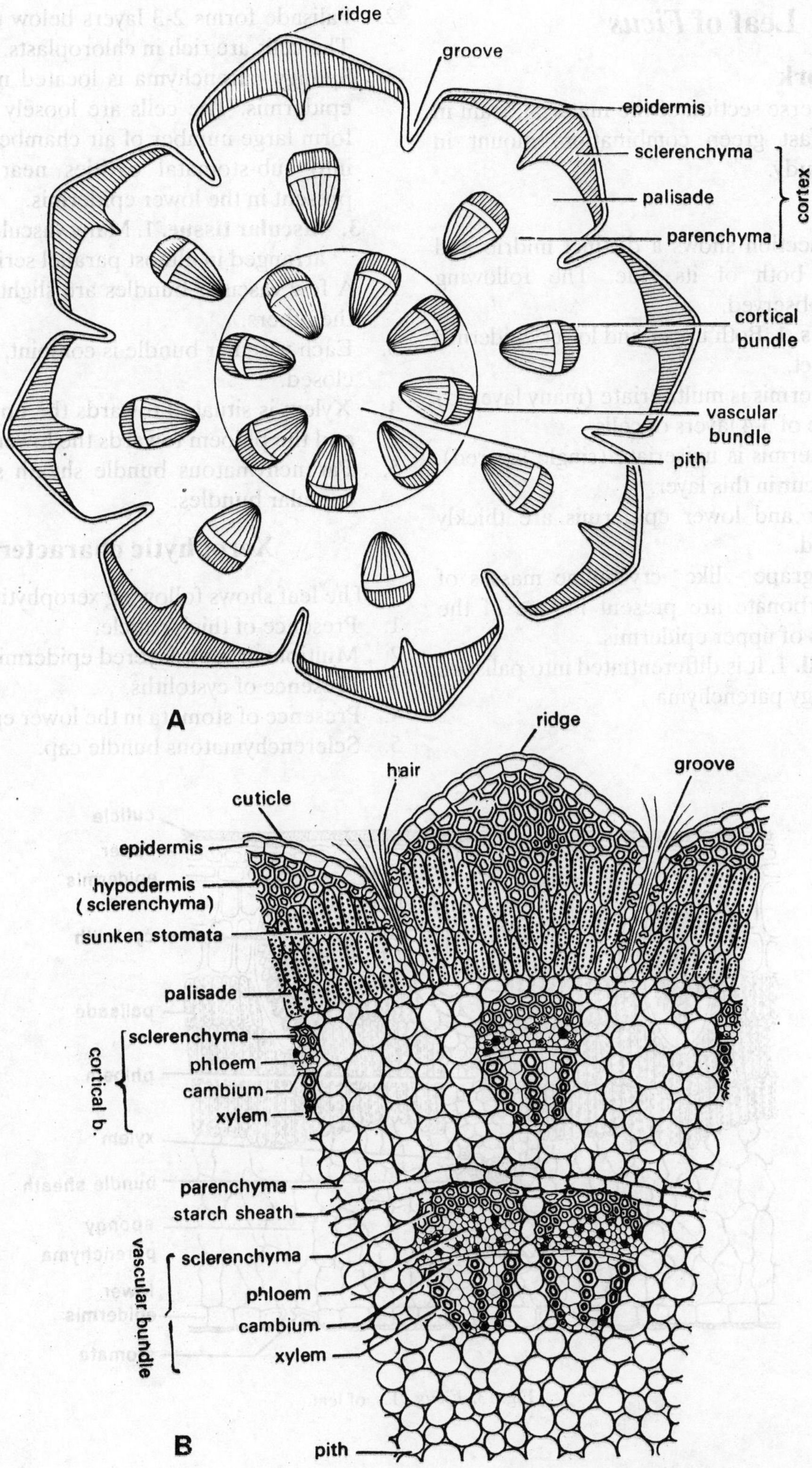

Fig. 12. A. and B. *Casuarina*. T.s. of stem. A. Outlines, B. A part cellular.

Leaf of *Ficus*

Practical work

Cut a transverse section of the material, stain in safranin and fast green combination, mount in glycerine and study.

Observations

Transverse section shows a distinct midrib and the wings on both of its side. The following characters are observed.

1. **Epidermis.** 1. Both upper and lower epidermis are distinct.
2. Upper epidermis is multiseriate (many layered) and is made of 3-4 layers of cells.
3. Lower epidermis is uniseriate (single layered). Stomata occur in this layer.
4. Both upper and lower epidermis are thickly cuticularised.
5. Cystolith, grape - like crystalline masses of calcium carbonate are present in one of the lower layers of upper epidermis.

2. **Mesophyll.** 1. It is differentiated into palisade and spongy parenchyma.
2. Palisade forms 2-3 layers below the epidermis. The cells are rich in chloroplasts.
3. Spongy parenchyma is located near the lower epidermis. The cells are loosely arranged and form large number of air chambers which open into sub-stomatal cavities near the stomata present in the lower epidermis.

3. **Vascular tissue.** 1. Many vascular bundles are arranged in almost parallel series.
2. A few vascular bundles are slightly bigger than the others.
3. Each vascular bundle is conjoint, collateral and closed.
4. Xylem is situated towards the upper epidermis and the phloem towards the lower epidermis.
5. Parenchymatous bundle sheath surrounds the vascular bundles.

Xerophytic characters

The leaf shows following xerophytic characters.

1. Presence of thick cuticle.
2. Multiple or multilayered epidermis.
3. Presence of cystoliths.
4. Presence of stomata in the lower epidermis only.
5. Sclerenchymatous bundle cap.

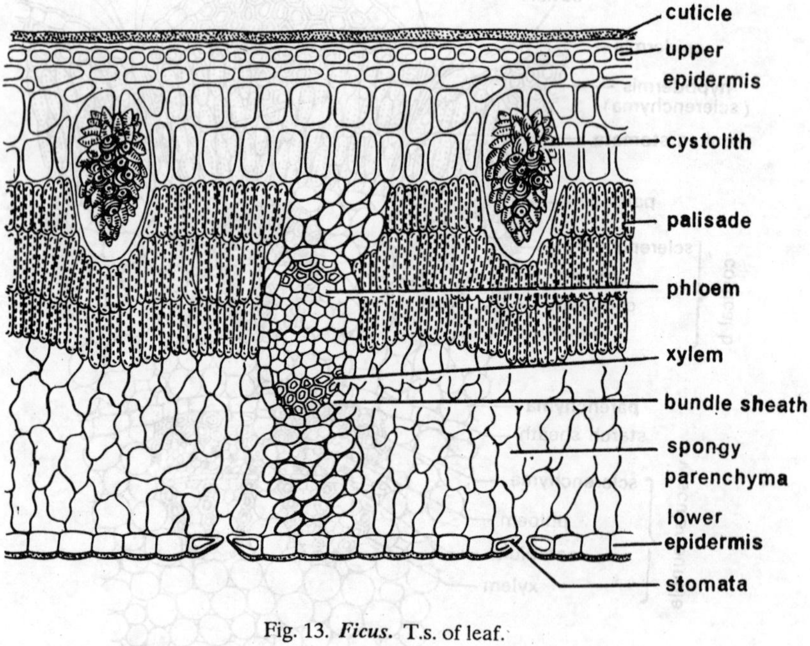

Fig. 13. ***Ficus.*** T.s. of leaf.

Leaf of *Nerium*

Practical work

Cut a transverse section of the material, stain in safranin-fast green combination, mount in glycerine and study.

Observations

The transverse section shows a distinct midrib and wings on either of its sides. Following characters are observed.

1. **Epidermis.** 1. Both, upper and lower epidermis are distinct.
2. Upper as well as lower epidermis are multiseriate (many layered). Each epidermis is made of about 3-4 layers. The cells are parenchymatous.
3. Both epidermal layers are thickly cuticularised.
4. Stomata occur only in the lower epidermis. These are highly sunken and are present in the infolded parts of lower epidermis.
5. The stomata are covered with hairs.

2. **Mesophyll.** 1. It consists of palisade tissue and spongy parenchyma.
2. Palisade lies just below the upper epidermis and is 4-5 cells deep. A few layers of compactly arranged palisade tissue are also present just above the lower epidermis.
3. Spongy parenchyma is present between the palisade of lower and upper epidermis. The cells are loosely arranged and form large air chambers.

3. **Vascular tissue.** 1. Many vascular bundles occur in the leaf.
2. Vascular bundle in the midrib is larger than the others.
3. Each vascular bundle is conjoint and collateral. The protoxylem is located towards the upper epidermis and the metaxylem towards the lower epidermis.

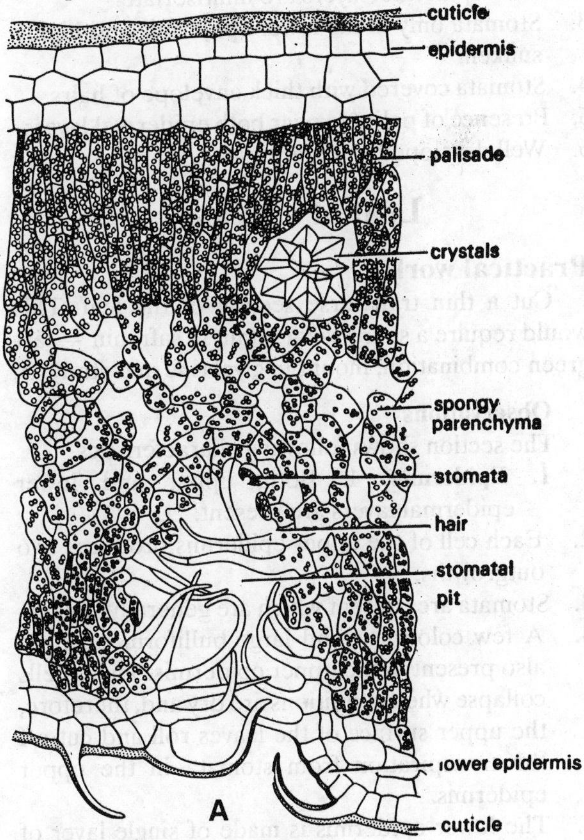

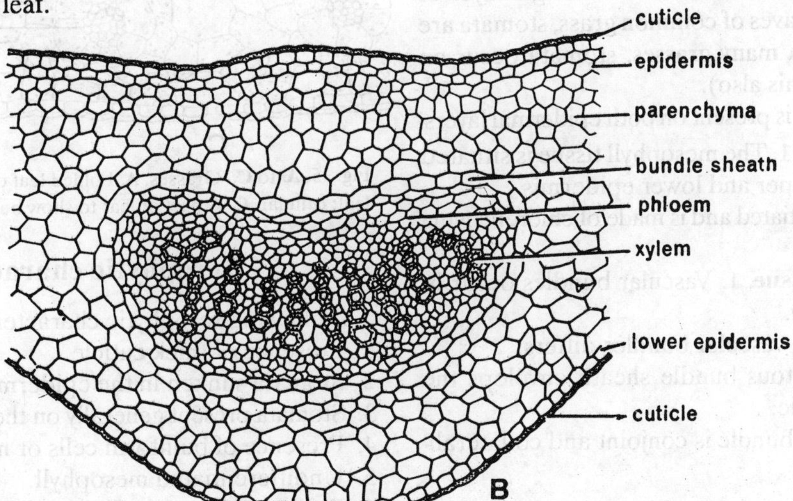

Fig. 14. A. and B. *Nerium*. T.s. of leaf. A. part of the wings: cellular. B. Part of the midrib: cellular.

4. Vascular bundle is surrounded by a parenchymatous bundle sheath.

4. Xerophytic characters. The leaf shows following xerophytic characters.

1. Presence of thick cuticle.
2. Both epidermal layers are multiseriate.
3. Stomata only in the lower epidermis and highly sunken.
4. Stomata covered with thick envelope of hairs.
5. Presence of palisade near both epidermal layers.
6. Well developed vascular tissues.

Leaf of a Grass

Practical work

Cut a thin transverse section of the leaf. This would require a sharp razor. Stain in safranin — fast green combination, mount in glycerine and study.

Observations

The section shows following characteristics.

1. Epidermis. 1. Both, upper and lower epidermal layers are present.

2. Each cell of the upper epidermis produces two outgrowths.
3. Stomata are present which are generally sunken.
4. A few colourless and large bulliform cells are also present in the upper epidermis. These cells collapse when conditions are dry and, therefore, the upper surface of the leaves roll and cut off the transpiration from stomata in the upper epidermis.
5. The lower epidermis is made of single layer of cells. In the leaves of common grass, stomata are absent (but in many grasses, stomata occur on lower epidermis also).
6. A thick cuticle is present on both epidermal layers.

2. Mesophyll. 1. The mesophyll tissue is situated between upper and lower epidermis.

2. It is undifferentiated and is made of chlorenchyma only.

3. Vascular tissue. 1. Vascular bundles occur in a single row.

2. The size of the vascular bundles differs.
3. Sclerenchymatous bundle sheath envelops the vascular bundle.
4. Each vascular bundle is conjoint and collateral.

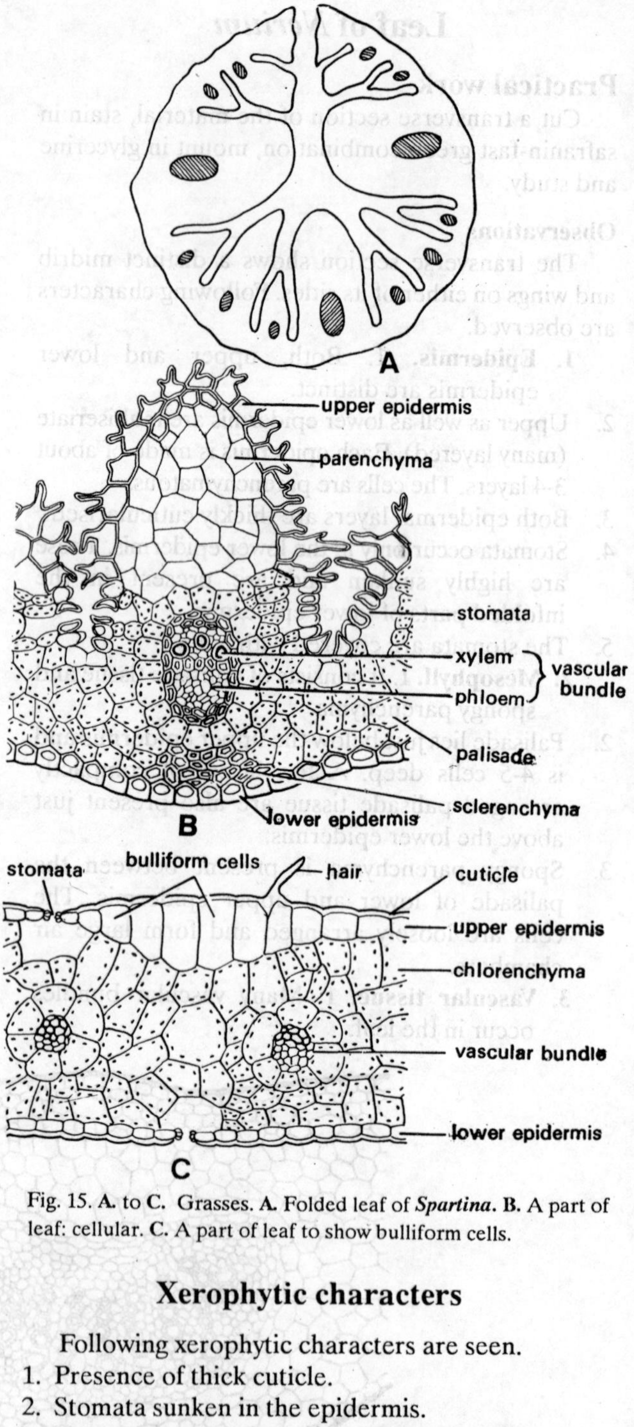

Fig. 15. A. to C. Grasses. A. Folded leaf of *Spartina*. B. A part of leaf: cellular. C. A part of leaf to show bulliform cells.

Xerophytic characters

Following xerophytic characters are seen.

1. Presence of thick cuticle.
2. Stomata sunken in the epidermis.
3. Stomata present generally on the upper epidermis.
4. Presence of bulliform cells or motor cells.
5. Undifferentiated mesophyll.
6. Rolling of leaves in dry conditions.

II. STUDY OF THE COMMUNITY

Exercise 1

Purpose : To determine the minimum size of the quadrat by Species- area curve.

Materials

Meter scale, string or cord, nails, paper, pencil, etc.

Procedure

1. Prepare a L-shaped structure in the field of 1 meter × 1 metre by using 3 nails and tying string with them.
2. Now measure 10 cm on one side of the arm of L and then the other.
3. Using another piece of string and nails prepare 10×10 sq cm area.
4. Count the number of species occurring in this area.
5. Increase this area to 20 × 20 sq cm and similarly record additional species occurring in this area.
6. Repeat the same procedure till 1×1 sq meter area is covered.
7. Note down the observations as follows.

***Table 1.*Total number of species and the area.**

Area	Total no. of species
10 × 10 sq.cm 20 × 20 sq.cm 30 × 30 sq.cm upto 100 × 100 sq.cm	

8. Using the above recorded data, prepare a graph. Number of species are plotted on Y axis and size of the quadrats on X axis.

Results

At one point of the graph, curve starts flattening or shows only a gradual increase.

Conclusion

The point of the graph, at which steep increase of the curve becomes gradual or curve flattens, denotes minimum area of the quadrat suitable for the study of an area under consideration.

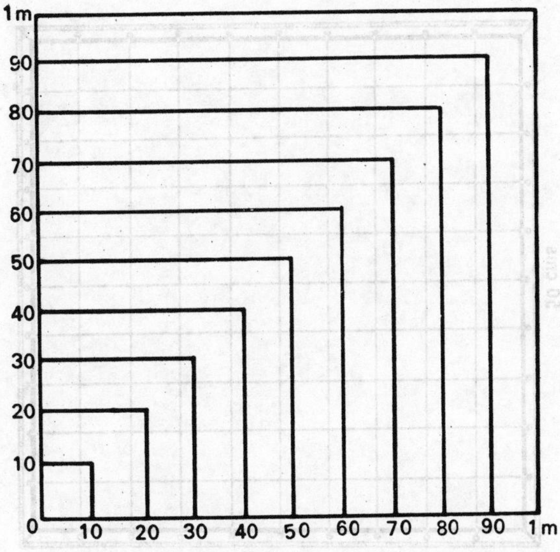

Fig. 16. Procedure to find out minimum required size of the quadrat.

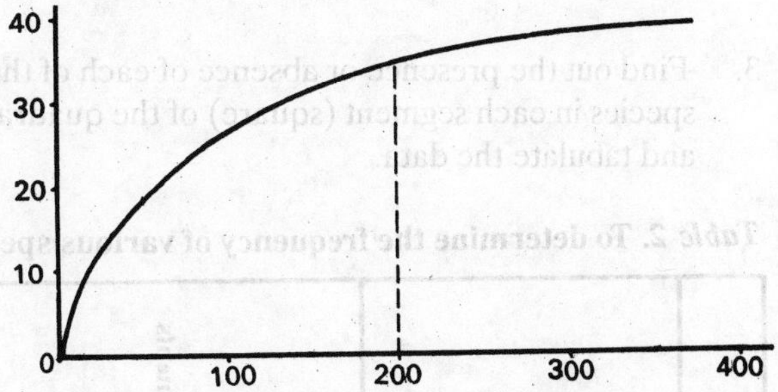

Fig. 17. Species-area curve to determine the size of the quadrat.

Exercise 2

Purpose : To determine the frequency of various species occurring in a given area.

Materials

Quadrats of required size, measuring tape, paper, pencil, etc.

Procedure

The following are some of the common methods.

[I] Quadrat

1. Take a quadrat of suitable size, lay it randomly at number of places.
2. Identify the species or distinguish them as **A, B, C**, etc.

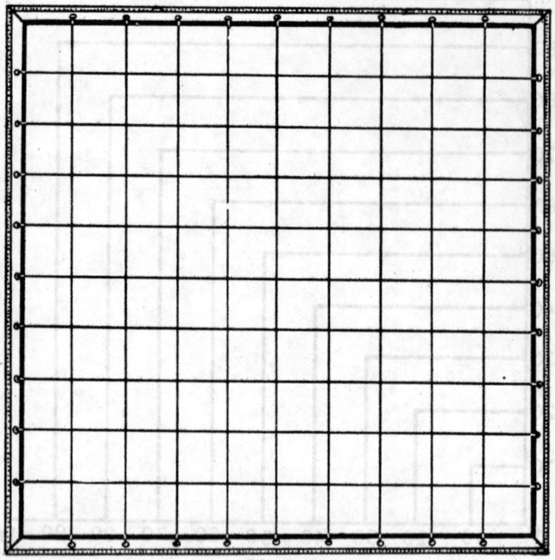

Fig. 18. A quadrat.

3. Find out the presence or absence of each of the species in each segment (square) of the quadrat and tabulate the data.

4. If the species are not identified taxonomically in the field, collect them, glue or fix with cellotape to herbarium sheets, use the same identification marks, e.g., **A, B, C,** etc. as used in the table and properly preserve the sheets.

[II] Line transect

1. In a grassland, line transect can also be used for determining frequency.
2. A measuring tape or a cord marked into one meter segments is used.
3. Take a tape or cord across the grassland in North-South direction.
4. Note the presence or absence of plant species in each one meter segment. Only those plant species are considered which touch the cord or tape.

[III] Belt transect

Similar method is used in belt transects. The plant species occurring in alternate segments or uniform area are recorded.

Results

The record of the observations is kept in the following way (refer to table 2)

***Table 2.* To determine the frequency of various species.**

Serial no.	Name of the plant species	No.of quadrats/segments					Total no. of a species	Total no. of quadrats in which species occurred	Total no. of quadrats studied	Frequency %	Frenquency class	Density	Abundance
		1	2	3	4	5							
1.	*Alysicarpus monilifer*	5	5		-		10	2	5	40	B	2	5
2.	*Convolvulus pluricaulis*	10	-	-	-	-	10	1	5	20	A	2	10
3.	*Cynodon dactylon*	15	10	12	13	15	65	5	5	100	E	13	13
4.	*Cyperus rotundus*	-	6	-	-	-	6	1	5	20	A	1.2	6
5.	*Desmodium triflorum*	-	12	-	-	-	12	1	5	20	A	2.4	12
6.	*Dichanthium annulatum*	12	-	12	10	11	45	4	5	80	D	9	11.25
7.	*Eclipta alba*	5	6	-	-	4	15	3	5	60	C	3	5
8.	*Euphorbia hirta*		-	-	6	-	4 10	2	5	40	B	2	5
9.	*Evolvulus nummularius*	-	-	3	-	-	3	1	5	20	A	0.3	6
10.	*Gomphrena globosa*	2	4	3	1	2	12	5	5	100	E	2.4	2.4
11.	*Indigofera linifolia*	-	-	-	6	-	6	1	5	20	A	1.2	6
12.	*Launea nudicaulis*	-	-	-	-	3	3	1	5	20	A	0.6	3
13.	*Phyllanthus niruri*	-	-	-	-	2	2	1	5	20	A	0.4	2
14.	*Rhynchosia minima*	-	-	-	4	3	7	2	5	40	B	1.4	3.5
15.	*Sida cordifolia*		-	-	6	4	2 12	3	5	60	C	2.4	4
16.	*Vernonia cinerea*	-	-	11	-	-	11	1	5	20	A	2.2	11

Number of plants in each frequency class. A = 8, B = 3, C = 2, D = 1, E = 2

Table 5. To determine vegetational cover.

Serial no.	Name of plant species	Length of Individuals					Total %
		1	2	3	4	5	
1	A						
2	B						
3	C						
4	D						
5	E						
Total no. of plant sps.		Total no. of individuals studied.					Total length of all the individuals

Calculate (a) total length of transect covered by all the species and (b) percentage of total length of transect covered by different species. This gives percentage cover.

Relative cover percentage =

$$\frac{\text{length of one type}}{\text{total length of all the individuals}} \times 100$$

II. Tabulate in the following form –

Table 6. To calculate vegetational cover.

Serial no.	Name of plant species	Diameter of Individuals					Total	Average
		1	2	3	4	5		
1	A							
2	B							
3	C							
4	D							
5	E							

Total basal area of all species -

Calculate by using Average basal area $= \pi r^2$

Where $r = \text{radius} = \frac{\text{diameter (Average)}}{2}$

If multiplied by the value of density (D) –

D × average basal area = ...sq cm/sq meter.

Exercise 5

Purpose : Estimation of biomass.*

Material

Scissors, polythene bags, oven, balance, etc.

Procedure

The following three methods are commonly used.

1. A small sampling unit (e.g. 25 × 25 cm) is chosen and plants are cut close to the ground surface.
2. Seclec andomly a few plants (e.g.,about five) from a sampling unit, the density for which has already been calculated.
3. In a pond, lower a container (known as dredge) of known volume which opens by special mechanism only after lowering it under water surface at desired depth and then close down.

In all the cases, each sample is packed in sulitable plastic bags, dried in the laboratory (blotting papers are used for aquatic plants), weighed and cut into in smaller and suitable pieces.

Take 1000 g of each sample and dry it in an oven at 70°C for 12- 24 hours. Note down the dry weight.

Calculate the biomass(dry weight) per meter square area.

(a) Take into consideration the fresh weight and the dry weight of 1000 g from the sample.

(b) Calculate the dry weight for this fresh weight of a sample.

(c) Now determine the area from which the sample is collected and calculate the value for one square meter.

Calculations. 1. Fresh weight ..... Xg

2. Weight after heating (at 74°C for 24 hrs) ..... Y g

∴ Dry weight ..... Y g

Find out the biomass per unit area e.g. the size of the quadrat used was 25 cm × 25 cm = 625 cm^2 and Y g was the dry weight

∴ biomass for 1m × 1m (100 cm × 100 cm) would be

$$\frac{Yg \times 100 \times 100}{625} = Zg/m^2$$

As such biomass would be Zg/m^2

Exercise 6

Purpose : Determination of local vegetation: frequency and relative frequency, density and relative density and importance value index.

Materials

Quadrats, measuring tape, paper pencil, etc.

*Biomass and standing crop, both are synonyms. Biomass can be expressed in terms of number and measured as fresh weight (living weight), dry weight, ash-free dry weight, energy or any conventional unit which is found useful for the purpose of comparison. Thus, the simplest way is to determine fresh weight of the samples and calculate it for a square meter area.

Table 7. **To determine frequency, relative frequency, density relative density and importance value index.**

1	2	3	4	5	6
Serial no.	**Name of plant species**	**Retative Domin-ance**	**Relative Density**	**Relative Frequ-ency**	**IVI (3+4+5)**
1	A				
2	B				
3	C				
4	D				
5	E				

Arrange the species in decreasing values of IVI.

Procedure

1. Lay the quadrats, identify the species, count their number in each quadrat and record the observations in a tabular form as done earlier (table 1).
2. Use line transect or belt transect as done earlier (exercise no.2) and record the observations as per table 1.

Calculations

Importance value index (IVI) is a measure of dominance and ecological success of a species. It takes into consideration relative dominance, relative density and relative frequency. These are calculated as follows –

1. Relative dominance =

$$\frac{\text{Total basal area of the species}}{\text{Total basal area all the species}} \times 100$$

2. Relative density =

$$\frac{\text{Number of individuals of the species}}{\text{Number of individuals of all the species}} \times 100$$

3. Relative frequency =

$$\frac{\text{Number of occurrences of the species}}{\text{Number of occurrences of all the species}} \times 100$$

Record the values obtanied in the following table

Exercise 7

Purpose : To study the species composition of an area for analysing biological spectrum and comparison with Raunkiaer's normal biological spectrum.

Materials

Record book, pen, pencil, etc.

Procedure

1. Visit the area under study.
2. Study the different life forms and their general appearance, spread, etc.
3. Place each one of the plant under different life forms as per the classification proposed by Raunkiaer (1934); as given below

Observations

1. Record the observations in the following table.

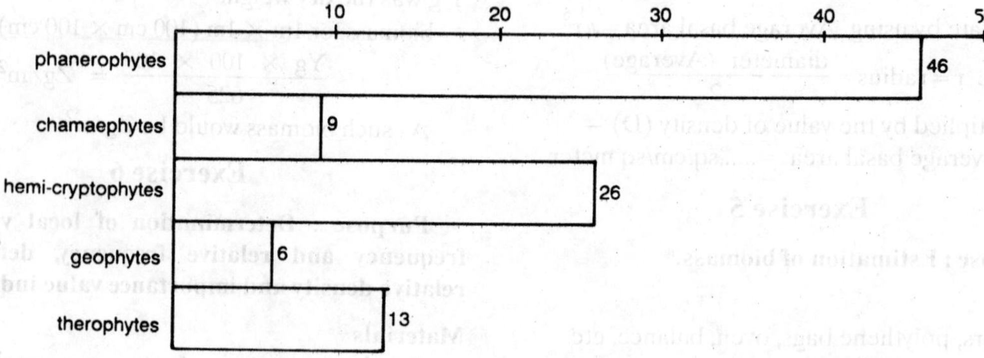

Fig. 21. Raunkiaer's normal biological spectrum for the world's phanerogamic flora.

Table 8. Raunkiaer's classification of life forms

Symbol	Life form	Characteristics
P	**I. Phanerophyte**	Perennating bud well above the ground
	These are the further sub-divided into following -	
MM	1. Megaphanerophyte	Perennating bud above 30m high.
	2. Mesophanerophyte	..... between 8 m and 30 m
M	3. Microphanerophyte	.... between 2 m and 8 m
N	4. Nanophanerophyte	.... under 2 m
Ch	**II. Chamaephyte**	Herbaceous or low woody plants whose perennating buds borne just above ground level up to 0.3 m.
H	**III. Hemicryptophyte**	Perennating buds close to the ground (rather half hidden in the soil).
	IV. Cryptophyte	Perennating organs below surface or water.
	These are further sub-divided into following-	
G	1. Geophyte	Perennating buds underground.
HH	2. Helophyte	Marsh plants with perennating buds in watterlogged mud.
	3. Hydrophyte	Perennating buds beneath the water.
Th	**V. Therophyte**	Survival in unfavourable season through seeds or spores; annuals.

Table 9. To determine biological spectrum.

Life form class	No. of individuals	Total no. in each class		%
MM	卌 卌 卌 |||	18		
M	卌 卌 卌 卌 卌 卌 卌 卌 卌 |||	48	128	47.4%
N	卌 卌 卌 卌 卌 卌 卌 卌 卌 卌 卌 卌 ||	62		
Ch	卌 卌 卌 卌 卌 |||	28		10.3%
H	卌 卌 卌 卌 卌 卌 卌 卌 卌 卌 卌 |||	58		21.4%
G	卌 卌 卌 |	16	20	7.4%
HH				
Th	卌 卌 卌 卌 卌 卌 卌 |	36		13.3%
	Total no. of individuals observed	270		

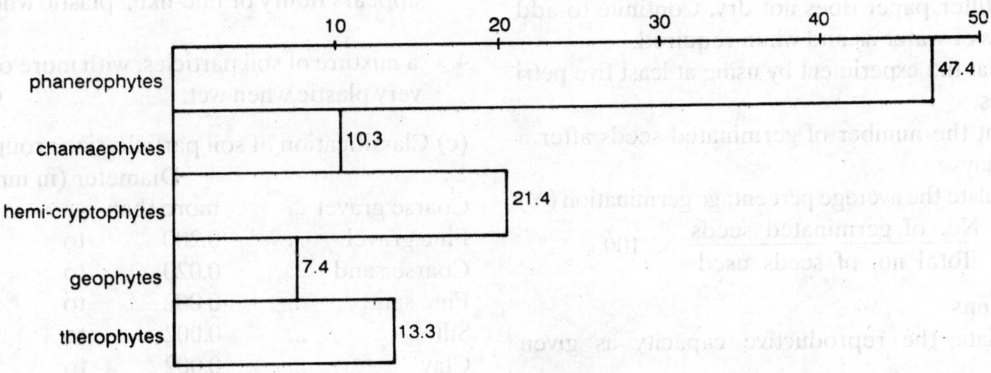

Fig. 22. Biological spectrum for the area studied.

2. Draw the percentage distribution of different life forms in a graph on Y-axis and different classes on X-axis.
3. Compare this biological spectrum with Raunkiaer's normal biological spectrum for the world's phanerogamic flora which shows
(1) phanerophytes 46%
(2) chamaephytes 9%
(3) hemi- cryptophytes 26%
(4) geophytes / or + helophytes and hydrophytes 6%
(5) therophytes 13%

Exercise 8

Purpose : To find out reproductive capacity of a species.

Materials

A plant, forceps, petri dishes, filter papers, seeds, polythene bags, etc.

Procedure

The experiment is to be carried out in two stages.

[I] Collection of seeds

1. Collect as many seeds as possible from a mature individual of a species.
2. Count the total number of seeds.
3. Repeat the procedure for at least five individuals of the same species.
4. Calculate the average number of seeds per plant (*x*).

[II] Germination of seeds

1. Place a filter paper in a petri dish.
2. Moisten the filter paper with water.
3. Place a few seeds on the filter paper. Take care that filter paper does not dry. Continue to add drops of water as and when required.
4. Repeat the experiment by using at least five petri dishes.
5. Count the number of germinated seeds after a few days.
6. Calculate the average percentage germination (Y)

$$\frac{\text{No. of germinated seeds}}{\text{Total no. of seeds used}} \times 100$$

Calculations

Calculate the reproductive capacity as given below.

Reproductive capacity

$$\frac{\text{Average no. of seeds (x)} \times \text{Average \% germination (y)}}{100}$$

III. THE ENVIRONMENT

Exercise 1

Purpose : To study the soil texture.

Materials

A pick, polythene bags, hand lens, meshes of different pore sizes, forceps, etc.

Procedure

A soil sample is collected, packed in the polythene bags and dried in the laboratory. Examine dry sample by a hand lens and feel it between fingers. Similarly examine a moist sample.

The soil can also he placed on meshes of different pore sizes and the amount of particles which pass through them are recorded.

Observations

(a) Soil can be indentified on the basis of particles –

1. soil particles very large: ... Gravel
2. particles small, apparent to the naked eye, gritty and non-plastic when wet; ... Sand
3. particles very small, very plastic when wet and hard when dry. ... Clay

(b) Some soils show mixture of various particles –

1. soil with an almost equal amount of sand and clay; Loam
2. a mixture of soil particles, with more of sand; ... Sandy loam
3. a mixture of soil particles, with more of silt; soil appears floury or talc-like, plastic when wet; Silt loam
4. a mixture of soil particles, with more of clay, soil very plastic when wet. ... Clay loam

(c) Classification of soil particle-size groups –

		Diameter (in mm)		
Coarse gravel	...	more than		5.000
Fine gravel	...	0.200	to	5.000
Coarse sand	...	0.020	to	2.000
Fine sand	...	0.002	to	0.200
Silt	...	0.002	to	0.020
Clay	...	0.002	to	less

Soil texture refers to the relative prcportions of the various size groups of the indvidual particles.

Exercise 2

Purpose : To measure the soil temperature.

Materials

Ordinary or soil thermometer.

Procedure

The soil temperature at various depths is measured by any one of the two following methods.

[I] Ordinary thermometer

A hole is dug in the soil up to a desired depth by means of a pointed iron or steel rod. Thermometer is then placed in this hole for about 15 minutes and temperature is recorded.

[II] Soil thermometer

These thermometers have a steel end near the mercury bulb. Thermometer is directly pushed into the soil by steel end to a desired depth and the temperature is recorded.

Exercise 3

Purpose : To determine the soil pH.

Materials

Soil sample, distilled water, pH paper/barium sulphate/comparometer/ tintometer, pH indicator etc.

Procedure

The following methods are commonly used.

[I] pH Paper

1. Add a pinch of soil to 5 ml distilled water.
2. Take a broad range pH paper indicator (a small piece) and dip it in the soil-water suspension. The colour of the paper changes.
3. Match the colour with the colour scale given on a booklet. This gives an approximate pH value.
4. For more correct value, narrow range pH paper indicator of the value indicated by broad range paper is now taken (i.e., if the pervious value comes to 8, now use indicator of the scale varying between 7.5 to 8.5).
5. The colour change is compared with the scale given on booklet and approximate pH value is determined.

(pH papers are those papers on which indicators of various pH ranges are absorbed).

[II] Barium sulphate test

1. A spoonful of soil is added to an equal amount of Barium sulphate.
2. About 10-20 ml of distilled water is added to the test tube containing soil suspension.
3. Now sufficient quantity of soil indicator is added to the test tube and contents are thoroughly shaken.
4. Allow the contents to stand.
5. Match the colour developed with the colour chart and note the pH value.

(For this purpose B.D.H. Barium sulphate soil testing outfit would be very useful).

[III] Comparometers/Tintometers.

1. These are boxes with two windows. In one of the windows of the box, test tube containing soil-water suspension is kept, while in another, a tube with standard solution is kept (or in tintometers a rotating colour disc is adjusted) and the comparisons are made.
2. To prepare a soil- water suspension, take a tube supplied with the apparatus.
3. Add a little Barium sulphate and almost twice the amount of soil.
4. Fill the tube up to the mark with distilled water and shake thoroughly. Allow the tube to stand till the clear liquid appears.
5. Place the tube in slot of the box and compare the colours to find out the pH value.

Exercise 4

Purpose : To determine water holding capacity.

Materials

Filter papers, brass or tin boxes, balance, soil sample, petri dishes, water, oven, etc.

Procedure

1. Take a soil sample, allow it to dry and crush it.
2. Take a brass or tin box with perforated bottom and weigh the box (1).
3. Take a filter paper and weigh it (2).
4. Now place a filter paper at the bottom of the box. Fill the box gradually with soil by tapping to ensure uniform filling.
5. Place such a soil filled box in a petri dish containing water and allow it to remain overnight. Weigh the container once again (3).

6. Now place this container in an oven at 105°C for about 24 hours, till constant weight is attained. Record the weight (4).
7. Take a few filter papers (similar to one used in container). Dip one in water and find out the average amount of water absorbed by the filter paper.

Results.

Results are computed in the following way.

[I] Observations

Record the observations as follows.

1. Weight of the box — 40.75 g
2. Weight of dry filter paper — 0.112 g
3. Weight of wet soil + box + wet filter paper — 111.50 g
4. Weight of dry soil + box + dry filter paper — 91.50 g
5. Weight of wet filter paper — 0.634 g

[II] Calculations

Calculate water holding capacity as follows

6. Weight of wet soil = (weight of wet soil + box + wet filter paper) – (weight of box + weight of wet filter paper).
= (3) – (1+5)
= 111.50 g – (40.75 g + 0.634 g)
= 70.12 g

7. Weight of oven dry soil = (weight of dry soil + box + dry filter paper) – (weight of box + weight of dry filter paper).
= (4) – (1+2)
= 91.50 g – (40.75 g + 0.112 g)
= 50.64 g

8. Water in soil = weight of wet soil – weight of oven dry soil
= (6) – (7)
= 70.12 g – 50.64 g
= 19.48 g

Water holding capacity

$$= \frac{\text{amount of water in the soil (8)}}{\text{weight of oven dry soil(7)}} \times 100$$

$$= \frac{19.48}{50.64} \times 100$$

$$= 38.46\ \%$$

Exercise 5

Purpose : To determine moisture percentage of soil.

Materials

Test tubes, box containers, soil sample, balance, oven, water, etc.

Procedure

The following procedure is used.

1. Collect the soil at desired depth and keep in closed test tubes or box.
2. Take an empty box or suitable container and weigh it (1).
3. Now fill the box with soil and weigh it (2).
4. Place this container in an oven at 105°C for about 24 hours till constant weight is attained. Note the weight after drying (3).

Results

Results can be obtained in the following way –

[I] Observations

Record the observations as follows –

1. Weight of the box — 25.0 g
2. Weight of the box + soil — 125.0 g
3. Weight of the box + oven dry soil — 105.0 g

[II] Calculations

Calculate the following values –

4. Weight of the soil = (weight of box + soil) – weight of box
= (2)-(1) = 125g – 25g
= 100g

5. Weight of dry soil = (weight of box + oven dry soil – weight of box
= (3)-(1) = 105g – 25g
= 80 g

5. Amount of moisture in the soil = weight of the soil − weight of dry soil
= (4)-(5) = 100g − 80g
= 20g

Moisture %

$$= \frac{\text{amount of moisture in the soil}}{\text{weight of dry soil}} \times 100$$

$$= \frac{20}{80} \times 100 = 25\%$$

Exercise 6

Purpose : To find out bulk density of a given soil sample.

Materials

Soil samples, petri dishes, oven, measuring cylinders, balance etc.

Procedure

1. Collect soil samples from different places at a depth of 15 cm.
2. Dry the soil in an oven at 105°C till constant weight is attained.
3. Transfer a part of this soil to the measuring cylinder and determine the volume (1).
4. Also determine the weight of soil by first weighing measuring cylinder and the soil (2) and then the weight of measuring cylinder alone (3).

Observations and Calculations

Record the observations as follows.

5. Volume of the soil (1)
6. Weight of measuring cylinder + soil (2)
7. Weight of measuring cylinder (3)

Calculate by using following formula

$$\textbf{Bulk density } (gm/cm^3) = \frac{\text{Weight of soil (gm)}}{\text{volume of soil}} = \frac{(2)-(3)}{(1)}$$

8. Place the soil in one of the three following classes

Soil classes	**Bulk density** (gm/cm^3)
(a) Medium to fine textured	1.1 − 1.5
(b) Coarse textured	1.2 − 1.65
(c) Alkaline saline	1.70 − 1.85

The bulk density is defined as dry weight of unit volume of soil (in gm/cm^3). It is inversely proportional to pore space of the soil.

Exercise 7

Purpose : To find out the porosity (per cent pore space) of a given soil sample.

Materials

Soil samples, petri dishes, beaker, measuring cylinders, beakers, balance, etc.

Procedure

1. Scrape the soil surface to flat.
2. Dig straight walled pit (10×10×10 cm).
3. Collect the removed soil in a beaker.
4. Dry the soil in an oven at 105°C till constant weight is attained.
5. Transfer a part of this soil to measuring cylinder and determine the volume (1).
6. Also determine the weight of soil (2) and then the weight of measuring cylinder alone (3).

Observations and calculations

Record the observations as follows.

7. Volume of the soil (1).
8. Weight of measuring cylinder + soil (2).
9. Weight of measuring cylinder (3).
10. Calculate the bulk density by using following formula

$$\textbf{Bulk density } (gm/cm^3) = \frac{\text{weight of the soil (2) − (3)}}{\text{volume of the soil (1)}}$$

11. Now calculate percentage pore space by the formula given below.

$$\textbf{Per cent pore space} = \frac{2.6 - \text{Bulk density}}{2.6} \times 100$$

Where 2.6 is the approximate specific gravity of soil.

Exercise 8

Purpose : Demonstration of different horizons of local soil profile.

Materials

Pick, trowel, etc.

Procedure

1. Dig a long trench of 75 cm wide and 1.5 m deep in an undisturbed area. (e.g. college campus)

(A narrow pit, dug in the study area of the college will also serve the purpose of demonstration).

***Table 10.* Characters of different horizons.**

Horizon	Sub-horizon	Depth (cm)	Profile characters
A	A oo	0-2	Uppermost layer, with freshly fallen organic matter such as dead leaves, branches, flowers, fruits, etc.
	Ao	2-15	Organic matter in different stages of decomposition mostly partially decomposed and called duff.
	A1	15 - 25	Dark, rich in organic matter, often mixed with mineral particles.
	A2	25-45	Lighter in colour with mineral particles of large size and little amount of organic matter.
B	B1	45-60	Zone of maximum leaching, humified organic matter present, particles coarse and colour dark.
	B2	60-62	Rich in clay - sesquioxides or silicate, clays mineral particles bonded by iron.
	B3	62-90	Contains sand, stones and gravel, light yellow in colour,
C	-	below 90	Consists of incompletely weathered, large masses of rocks.

Observations

1. The trench or a pit shows three horizons - A,B and C starting with upper surface downwards.
2. The horizons show following characters (table 8).

Exercise 9

Purpose : Test for the presence of carbonate, nitrate and deficiency of replaceable bases.

Materials

Hydrochloric acid, diphenylamine, sulphuric acid, ammonium thiocyanate, hydrogen peroxide, water, white glazed tiles, test tubes, soil samples, etc.

Procedure

Following are the methods for determination of contents of carbonate, nitrate and replaceable bases.

[I] Carbonate contents

It can be determined in the field by adding conc. HCl to the soil sample. This produces effervescence which indicates the presence of carbonate in the soil. If two samples are analysed, degree of effervescence is compared. More is the effervescence, more would be the carbonate contents.

[II] Nitrate contents

Prepare 1: 5 soil : water suspension. Shake it thoroughly. Add diphenylamine [prepared in conc. H_2SO_4 (0.2%)] to the clear solution. Take a few drops of soil suspension on a white tile and add a few drops of diphenylamine. Blue colour developed indicates the presence of nitrate. If two samples are to be compared, the comparison of depth of blue colour indicates the degree of nitrate contents. Darker the blue colour is, more would be the nitrate contents.

(For good results, use soil rich in organic contents, since these are generally rich in nitrate contents as well).

[III] Deficiency of replaceable bases (Ca, K, Mg, Na, etc.)

Take a pinch of soil and add it to a saturated alcoholic solution of ammonium thiocyanate. Shake the contents thoroughly. Allow the solids to settle down and a clear liquid is available. Now add a drop or two of H_2O_2 and note the red colour which develops. The degree of colour depth indicates the deficiency of replaceable bases.

Exercise 10

Purpose : Test for the presence of inorganic salts in the soil.

Materials

Test tubes, beaker, soil, conical flask, distilled water, barium chloride solution, hydrochloric acid sulphuric acid, nitric acid, ammonium nitrate ammonium molybdate, silver nitrate, etc.

Procedure

Take about 200 g of soil sample in a conical flask. Add 500 ml distilled water to the conical flask and shake vigorously. Keep the flask overnight so that soluble salts dissolve in water. Pour the water slowly and collect the filtrate (henceforth called water extract).

[I] Chloride

Take 20 ml of water extract of the soil in a beaker. Add 10 ml N/10, H_2SO_4 and thus neutralise carbonate and bicarbonate present in the extract. Now add silver nitrate to the solution.

A white precipitate develops to indicate the presence of chloride.

[II] Sulphate

Take 20 ml of water extract of the soil in a beaker. Add 2-5 ml of conc. HCl and boil. Add $BaCl_2$ solution to the beaker.

A white precipitate develops to indicate the presence of sulphate.

[III] Phosphate

Take 10 ml of water extract of the soil. Add a few drops of ammonium molybdate solution, conc. HNO_3 and NH_4NO_3.

A yellow colour develops to indicate the presence of phosphates.

Exercise 11

Purpose : Demonstration of CO_2, O_2, chlorine and ammonia in water.

Materials

Lime water, nitric oxide, alkaline pyragallate solution, ammoniacal cuprous chloride, iodide paper (paper soaked in potassium iodide solution and starch solution), Hydrochloric acid, glass rod, Nessler's solution, test tubes, water, pH indicator papers, etc.

Procedure and results

[I] Carbon dioxide

Take water sample and add to it freshly prepared lime water. Lime water turns milky. The degree of milky white colour indicates the amount of carbon dioxide. Clear lime water turns milky due to the formation of insoluble calcium.

[II] Chlorine

The presence of chlorine can be dectected in water sample by dipping starch-iodide paper which turns blue.

[III] Ammonia

The presence of ammonia in water can be demonstrated by any one of the following tests.

1. A glass rod dipped in concentrated hydrochloric acid is inserted in the test tube containing water sample. Dense white fumes of ammonium chloride are produced.
2. The sample turns brown on addition of Nessler's solution (Nessler' solution is prepared by pouring potassium iodide in mercuric chloride solution until the precipitate of mercuric iodide formed dissolves in excess of potassium iodide. The solution is then made alkaline with caustic potash.)

Exercise 12

Purpose : Determination of maximum and minimum temperature.

Materials

Maximum and minimum thermometer, etc.

Procedure

The thermometer consists of U-shaped tube, with bulb at each end. The bulbs are filled with alcohol and the glass tube with mercury. Inside each limb of the glass tube, there is an iron indicator (index).

As the temperature rises, the alcohol in the right hand limb of the glass tube expands and pushes the mercury down the right hand limb and up the left hand limb. The movement continues till the highest temperature is reached. The lower end of the indicator in the lift hand limb of the glass tube gives the maximum temperature.

When the temperature decreases, the alcohol in the glass tube contracts and the mercury moves up in the right hand limb of the glass tube. This causes the indicator of the right hand limb to move up. The position of the lower end of the indicator in the right hand limb indicates the minimum temperature during the day.

After noting the minimum and maximum temperature during the day, the iron indicators are

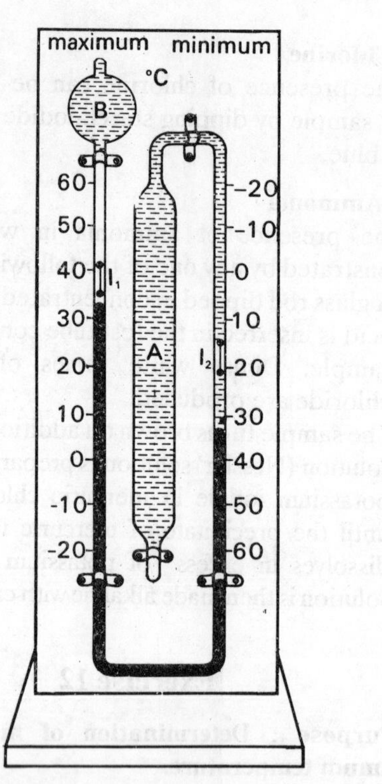

Fig. 23. Maximum and minimum thermometer.

brought down in contact with mercury by means of magnet. This is known as the setting of thermometers.

Exercise 13

Purpose : Determination of relative humidity.

Materials

Wet and dry bulb thermometers (hygrometer).

Procedure

These are two identical thermometers, mounted together. The bulb of one thermometer is exposed to the air while that of another is covered with a piece of muslin cloth kept constantly moist by a wick dipping into a small container filled with water.

The dry bulb thermometer indicates the actual air temperature. The temperature of wet bulb thermometer is low because of evaporation of water. When the air is saturated, there is no evaporation and both the thermometers show the same temperature. When the air is dry, there would be rapid evaporation and the temperature in the wet bulb thermometer would be lowered. The difference in the temperature indicated by these two thermometers is used to determine relative humidity of the air. The following table is used.

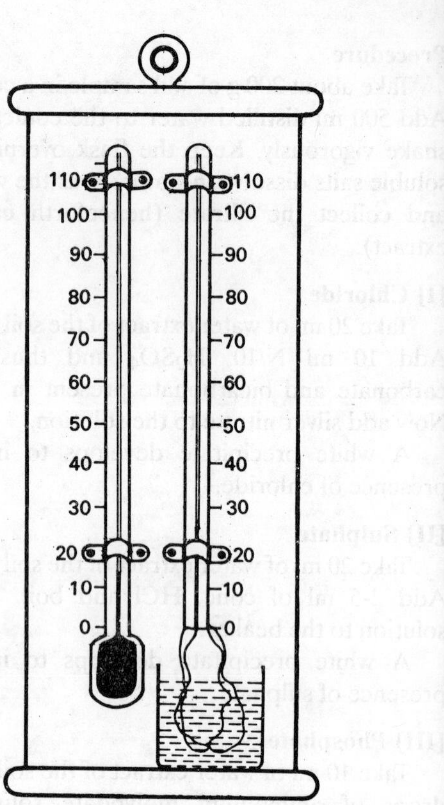

Fig. 24. Dry and wet bulb thermometer (hygrometer).

Table 11. **Showing Relative Humidity (in %) in the atmosphere.**

Temperature reading of dry bulb thermometer	Difference in temperature of two thermometers (in °C)									
	1	2	3	4	5	6	7	8	9	1
40	93	87	82	76	71	66	61	52	52	4
35	93	87	81	75	69	64	58	53	49	4
30	92	86	79	73	67	61	55	50	44	3
25	92	84	77	70	63	57	50	44	38	
20	91	83	74	66	59	51	44	37		
15	90	80	71	61	52	44	35			
10	88	76	65	54	44	34				
8	87	75	63	51	40					
6	86	73	60	47	35					
4	85	70	56	42						
2	84	68	52	37						
0	82	65	48							
2	80	61	42							

Suppose that the temperature readings of dry and we thermometers are 35°C and 30°C respectively. The differenc between the two is 5°C. Now find out the value of relativ humidity given in column showing 5°C difference, placed agains 35°C temperature of dry bulb thermometer. This comes out tc be 69 percent.

Exercise 14

Purpose : Soil testing for phosphorus.

Materials

Polythene bottles, beakers, glass vials, measuring cylinders, conical flasks, spot plates, etc. Glacial acetic acid, ammonia, ammonium molybdate, concentrated hydrochloric acid, stannous chloride, stannous oxalate, distilled water, etc.

Procedure

[I] Preparation of soil extract

1. Prepare 2.5% acetic acid extractant by diluting 25 ml glacial acetic acid to 11 with distilled water.
2. Prepare ammonium acetate extractant by adding 57.5 ml glacial acetic acid and 74.0 ml ammonia solution (sp. gr. 0.880) to 30 ml of distilled water in 11 volumetric flask Mix well. Dilute to the mark.
3. Place 1g of air-dry sieved mineral soil in a 50 ml conical flask. Add 25 ml ammonium acetate extractant prepared earlier and shake for 30 minutes.
4. Filter into polythene bottles, rejecting the first 5 ml of filtrate.
5. Adjust pH to 3.3 with drops of acetic acid or ammonia.

[II] Preparation of reagents

6. Dissolve 8 g of ammonium molybdate in 200 ml distilled water.
7. Prepare a mixture of 126 ml concentrated HCl and 74 ml distilled water.
8. Add this mixture to ammonium molybdate solution. Just before use, dilute 1 part of this reagent with 4 parts distilled water.

[III] The method

9. Mark 10 ml level in a glass vial. Fill the vial with reagent.
10. Add 1 level teaspoon of soil extract.
11. Shake the vial vigorously.
12. Filter the solution.
13. To 5 ml of filtrate add 0.1 ml of reagent.
14. Mix by rotation to make sure that sufficient amount of reagent is added.
15. Add stannous chloride or stannous oxalate powder till colour becomes intense.

Results

Light yellow to dark blue colour develops.

Conclusions

On the basis of intensity of colour following inferences can be drawn.

1. Very pale yellow - very low phosphorus.
2. Green or bluish green - medium phosphorus.
3. Light blue - medium phosphorus.
4. Medium blue - adequate phosphorus.
5. Dark blue - abundant phosphorus.

Exercise 15

Purpose : Soil testing for Potassium.

Materials

Polythene bottles, beakers, glass vials, conical flasks, measuring cylinders, conical flasks, spot plates, etc.

Ammonia (sp. gr. 0.880), glacial acetic acid, sodium cobalt nitrite, sodium nitrite, anhydrous isopropyl alcohol, distilled water,

Procedure

[I] Preparation of soil extract

1. Prepare ammonium acetate extractant by adding 60 ml glacial acetic acid and 74.0 ml ammonia solution (sp. gr. 0.880) to 20-30 ml of distilled water in 11 volumetric flask. Mix well. Dilute to the mark.
2. Place 1 g of air-dry dieved mineral soil in a 50 ml conical flask.
3. Add 25 ml of ammonium acetate extractant and shake for 30 minutes.
4. Filter into polythene bottles, rejecting the first 5 ml of filtrate
5. Adjust pH to 7.00 with drops of acetic acid or ammonia.

[II] Preparation of reagents

6. Dissolve 5 g of sodium cobalt nitrite ($Na_3CO(NO_2)_6$ and 30 g of sodium nitrite ($NaNO_2$) in 80 ml distilled water.
7. Add 50 ml glacial acetic acid and make up the volume to 100 ml. Allow to stand for several days.
8. Just before use, add 5 ml of the reagent to a solution of 15 g $NaNO_2$ in 100 ml distilled water. Adjust pH to 5.0 with acetic acid.

[III] The method

9. Mark 10 ml level in a glass vial. Fill upto mark with reagent.
10. Add 1 level teaspoon of air-dried soil. Shake vigorously for 1 minute.
11. Filter to 5 ml of filtrate add 2.5 ml of reagent.
12. Add anhydrous isopropyl alcohol. Mix thoroughly and let it stand for 3 minutes.

Results

Turbidity is developed.

Conclusions

On the basis of degree of turbidity following conclusions can be drawn.

1. Trace of turbidity - deficient potassium supply.
2. Medium turbidity - doubtful potassium supply
3. Very high turbidity - adequate potassium supply.

Exercise 16

Purpose : Soil testing for Nitrate.

Materials

Soil sample, polythene bottles, pipette,burette, beakers, measuring cylinder, centrifuge, filter papers (Whatman no. 1), white spot plate, test tube, balance, etc., Sodium chloride, diphenylamine, sulphuric acid,water, etc.

Procedure

1. Dig out a small amount of soil. Place about 25 g of this sample in polythene bottle.
2. Add 200 ml of 6% NaCl (propared by dissolving 6 g of NaCl in 100 ml of water)
3. Close the bottle tightly and shake it for 30 minutes. Allow this bottle to stand for about 30 minutes.
4. Pipette out about 100 ml of the suspension and distil to get clear extract. This can also be done by filtering soil suspension through Whatman no. 1 filter paper.
5. Prepare diphenylamine by dissolving 0.05 g in 25 ml of concentrated H_2SO_4.
6. Place one drop of soil extract on a spot plate. Add four drops of diphenylamine. Let it stand for 2 minutes.
7. Blue colour develops.

Result

1. Blue colour that develops indicates presence of nitrate.
2. If colour is deep blue - nitrate content is high.
3. If colour is pale blue - nitrate content is low.

Exercise 17

Purpose : Comparison of dissolved oxygen content of polluted and non-polluted water by iodometric titration method.

Materials

Manganous chloride (40% solution); a mixture of sodium hydroxide (33g) and potassium iodide (10g) dissolved in 100 ml of distilled water; standard sodium thiosulphate solution (N/40; i.e. 0.62 g of sodium thiosulphate dissolved in 100 ml of distilled water); concentrated sulphuric acid; starch solution; distilled water.

Burette, pipette, beakers, sampling bottles, measuring cylinders, etc.

Procedure

1. Take a narrow mouthed reagent bottle of about 250 ml capacity with a tight fitting ground glass stopper. Fill the water to be sampled in such a way that there is no bubbling. Allow plenty of water to overflow in the sample bottle.
2. Remove carefully the stopper of the sample bottle. Add 0.5 ml of manganous chloride and 0.1 ml of mixture of NaOH and KI for every 70 ml of sample. Use proportionately larger volumes of the two solutions for more quantity of samples.
3. Close the bottles firmly. Care should be taken to see that no air bubbles are included. Shake well and leave to stand for five minutes. A brown precipitate of manganic hydroxide appears and the oxygen in the sample is now fixed. This procedure can be easily carried out in the field and the remaining stages are completed in the laboratory.
4. Add 2 ml of concentrated sulphuric acid to the sample as above. Mix the contents thoroughly by rotation. The precipitate disappears. The liquid becomes clear golden brown in colour due to liberation of iodine.
5. Take about 25 ml of treated sample in a pipette, transfer it to conical flask and immediately titrate against standard sodium thiosulphate solution, using 2 ml of starch solution as indicator.
6. Starch is added until the yellow of iodine has nearly disappeared.

. The procedure should be repeated at least twice for each sample.

:alculations.

. ml of the standard sodium thiosulphate is equivalent to 0.1 mg of oxygen.

.et V_1 be the volume of thiosulphate used

V_2 be the volume of sample

$$\frac{V_1 \times 0.1 \times 1000}{V_2} = \text{mg oxygen per litre}$$

Now 1 ml of sodium thiosulphate

= 0.0001 g of oxygen

Therefore, 1 ml of sodium thiosulphate

$$= \frac{0.0001 \times 22.400}{32} \text{ mg of } O_2$$

Hence

$$\frac{V_1 \times 0.0001 \times 22.400 \times 1000}{32 \times V_2} = \frac{V_1 \times 70}{V_2}$$

= mg of oxygen per litre

9

Biostatistics (Biometry

Exercise 1

Purpose : Calculation of central tendencies-median and mode.

Method

Central tendency is a number or a quantity which is typical or representative of a set of data. Measures of this type are known as averages.

[I] The Median

Median or (middle item) is the middle value (or the mean of the two middle values) of a set of numbers arranged in order of magnitude.

e.g. in the set of numbers : 1, 2, 4, 6, 8, 9, 10.

the median is 6

Similarly, in the set of numbers : 1, 2, 3, 4, 5, 6.

the median is $\frac{3+4}{2} = 3.5$

The median number is calculated by

$\left(\frac{N+1}{2}\right)$, where N is the total number of observations.

Example 1

Calculation of median when the number of items is odd.

Find the median of the following observations.

5, 6, 7, 9, 6, 9, 11, 12, 13, 11, 13, 14, 13.

Step 1.

$$\text{Median number} = \frac{13+1}{2} = 7$$

Step 2.

Now arrange the figures in ascending order. 5, 6, 6, 9, 9, 11, 11, 13, 13, 13, 14.

Step 3.

Here 7th figure is 11, Therefore, median is 11.

Example 2

Calculation of median when the number of items is even.

Find the median of following observations.

5, 6, 6, 7, 9, 9, 11, 13, 8, 12.

Step 1

$$\text{Median number} = \frac{10+1}{2} = 5.5$$

In this case, two middle terms-5th and 6th ar considered and the mean of these is taken.

Step 2.

Now arrange the figures in ascending order, 5, 6, 6, 7, 8, 9, 9, 11, 12, 13.

Step 3.

Here, 5 th term = 8

6 th term = 9

$$\text{Therefore, median} = \frac{8+9}{2} = \frac{17}{2} = 8.5$$

Example 3

Calculation of median from frequenc distribution from discrete series.

Find out the median of the following discrete series.

Variate values – 2, 4, 6, 8, 10, 12.

Frequencies – 1, 3, 4, 6, 5, 1.

Step 1.

Calculate the cumulative frequencies

Variate values	Frequencies	Cumulative frequencies
2	1	1
4	3	4
6	4	8
8	6	14
10	5	19
12	1	20
	20	

Step 2.

Calculate median number $\left(\frac{N+1}{2}\right)$

$$= \frac{20+1}{2} = 10.5$$

Step 3.

Median number 10.5 is included in the cumulative frequency 14. It is placed against variate value 8.

i.e. 10th item = 8

11th item = 8

Therefore, median is 8.

Example 4

Calculation of median from frequency distribution from continuous series.

Find out the median from the data given below.

Class intervals	Frequencies	Cumulative frequencies
9–25	42	42
25–41	48	90
41–57	47	137
57–73	40	177
73–89	41	218
89–105	21	239
105–121	5	244
121–137	2	246
137–153	2	248
153–169	2	250
	250	

Step 1.

Calculate the median number.

$$\frac{N+1}{2} = \frac{250+1}{2} = 125.5$$

Step 2

Since this median number is lesser than cumulative frequency 137, therefore, median number lies between the range of 41–57.

Step 3.

Calculate the median by following formula.

$$\text{(1) Median} = l_1 + \frac{\frac{N}{2}-c}{f} \times i$$

or $$\text{(2) Median} = l_1 + \frac{m-c}{f} \times i$$

where l_1 lower limit of the class in which median is located.

m is $\frac{N+1}{2}$; median number

c is cumulative frequency of the class just lower than the median class.

f is the frequency of the median class.

i is the width of the median class.

Step 4.

Substitute the values.

l_1 = 41.00

m = 125.50

c = 90.00

f = 47.00

i = 16.00

N/2 = 125.5

Step 5.

Calculate median by using both the formulae.

Formula 1

$$41 + \left(\frac{125-90}{47} \times 16\right) = 41 + \left(\frac{35}{47} \times 16\right)$$
$$= 41 + (0.7446 \times 16)$$
$$= 41 + 11.914$$
$$= 52.914$$

Formula 2

$$41 + \left(\frac{125\cdot5-90}{47} \times 16\right)$$
$$= 41 + \left(\frac{35.5}{47} \times 16\right),$$
$$= 41 + (0.755 \times 16)$$
$$= 41 + 12.085, = 53.085$$

Formula no. 1 gives more accurate results.

[II] The Mode

The mode is the most commonly occurring value or the value of that variable which has the maximum frequency.

e.g. if the set of numbers is 2, 2, 5, 7, 9, 9, 9, 10, 11, 12, then the mode is 9.

Example 1

Computation from discrete series.

Mode can be easily found out by locating the value or item whose frequency is maximum. However, mode is determined by grouping when there are several items whose frequencies are maximum and equal or nearly equal, differing by a very small figure.

Find out the mode of the following discrete series.

Variate values – 5, 7, 9, 11, 13, 15, 17, 19, 21, 23, 25

Frequencies– 3, 5, 7, 8, 11, 11, 10, 9, 8, 6, 2.

Step 1.

Arrange the values in the table as shown.

Step 2.

Group two frequencies in one, starting from item no. 1, till all the items are consumed. Add them.

Step 3.

Repeat the same, but nów start from item no. 3.

Step 4.

Now group three frequencies together, starting from item no. 1, till all the items are consumed. Add them.

Repeat the same procedure but start with item no. 2.

Repeat the procedure once again but now start with item no. 3.

Step 5.

Find out the largest group in each series (given in bold letters).

(Variate values) Size of items	Individual frequencies	Frequencies				
		Grouping by twos		Grouping by threes		
	1	2	3	4	5	6
5	3					
7	5	8				
9	7		12	15		
11	**8**	15			20	
13	**11**		19			**26**
15	**11**	**22**		**30**		
17	10		**21**		**32**	
19	9	19				**30**
21	8		17	27		
23	6	14			23	
25	2		8			16

Step 6.

Prepare another table with only those items which fall in the largest group in each series.

Step 7.

Indicate occurrence of each of these items by cross (×) in the largest group.

Step 8.

The item which occurs for the maximum number is the mode.

Table of analysis

Column no.	items or groups with maximum frequency				
	11	13	15	17	19
1		×	×		
2		×	×		
3			×	×	
4	×	×	×		
5		×	×	×	
6			×	×	×
Total	1	4	6	3	1

Therefore, 15 is the mode though 13 and 15 both have the maximum frequencies.

Example 2

Computation of mode from continuous series with all items having different frequencies.

Find out the mode from the following data.

Number of stomata per sq. mm	Frequency
51–52	10
52–53	19
53–54	17
54–55	16
55–56	22
56–57	18
57–58	19
58–59	12
59–60	14
60–61	13
61–62	15

Here the modal class would be 55–56 with maximum frequency.

Now use the following formulae. Formula no. 1 gives more accurate results.

Formula 1.

$$\text{Mode} = l_1 + \frac{\Delta_1}{\Delta_1 + \Delta_2} \times i$$

Where l_1 = lower limit of modal class

Δ_1 = difference between the frequencies of the modal class and the next lower class

Δ_2 = difference between the frequencies of the modal class and next higher class

i = width of the modal class

Now calculate the values and substitutue

$l_1 = 55$, $\Delta_1 = 22 - 16 = 6$, $\Delta_2 = 22 - 18 = 4$, $i = 1$

$$\text{Mode} = 55 + \frac{6}{6+4} \times 1, = \frac{55+6}{10} \times 1$$

$$\text{Mode} = 55 + 0.6 \times 1, = 55.6$$

Formula 2.

$$\text{Mode} = l_1 + \frac{f_2}{f_1 + f_2} \times i$$

where l_1 = lower limit of modal class

f_1 = frequency of the next lower class

f_2 = frequency of the next higher class

i = width of the modal class

Now calculate the values and substitute

$l_1 = 55,\ f_1 = 16,\ f_2 = 18,\ i = 1$

$$\text{Mode} = 55 + \frac{18}{16+18} \times 1, \quad = 55 + \frac{18}{34} \times 1.$$

$$\text{Mode} = 55 + 0.529, = 55.529$$

Example 3

Computation of mode from continuous series, with more than one item having the same frequency.

Find out the mode the following data.

Number of seeds per pod	Frequency
5 – 6	5
6 – 7	8
7 – 8	14
8 9	13
9 – 10	15
10 – 11	15
11 – 12	12
12 – 13	10
13 – 14	9
14 – 15	6

Find out the median class by grouping method as described earlier.

Number of seeds per pod	Frequencies: Individual	Grouping by two's		Grouping by threes	
	1	2	3	4	5
5 – 6	5	13	22	27	35
6 – 8	8				
7 – 8	14	27			
8 –9	13		28	43	
9 – 10	15	30			42
10 – 11	15		27		
11 – 12	12	22		31	
12 – 13	10		19		25
13 – 14	9	15			
14 – 15	6				

Table of analysis

Column no.	Groups with maximum frequency: 8 — 9	9 — 10	10 — 11	11 — 12
1		x	x	
2		x	x	
3	x	x		
4	x	x	x	
5		x	x	x
Total	2	5	4	1

Here the modal class would be 9 – 10.

Now use the formulae

$$(1)\ \text{Mode} = l_1 + \frac{\Delta_1}{\Delta_1+\Delta_2} \times i$$

$$\text{or } (2)\ \text{Mode} = l_1 + \frac{f_2}{f_1+f_2} \times i$$

Formula 1

Calulate and substitute the values.

$l_1 = 9,\ \Delta_1 = 15-13 = 2,\ \Delta_2 = 15-15 = 0,\ i = 1.$

$$\text{Mode} = 9 + \frac{2}{2+0} \times 1, \quad = 9+0$$

$$\text{Mode} = 9$$

Formula 2.

Calculate and substitute the values

$l_1 = 9,\ f_2 = 13,\ f_1 = 15, i = 1$

$$\text{Mode} = 9 + \frac{15}{13+15} \times 1, \quad = 9 + \frac{15}{28} \times 1.$$

$$\text{Mode} = 9 + 0.535 \times 1, \quad = 9.535$$

Exercise 2

Purpose : Calculation of Inter Quartile Range.

Method

Interquartile range is a good measure of dispersion. It gives the range of variability which is sufficient for 50% of the population. The following are some of the terms –

Lower quartile (Q_1). "25th percentile is called lower quartile. The position of the lower quartile is given by N/4 if variable is continuous by and N+1/4 if it is discrete.

Upper quartile (Q_3). "75th percentile is called upper quartile. The position of the upper quartile is 3/4 N or 3/4 (N+1) respectively for continuous and discrete variables.

Interquratile range (Q_3-Q_1). The difference between the upper and the lower quartile is called interquartile range (i.e. Q_3-Q_1).

Example

Estimate the upper quartile (Q_3) and lower quartile Q_3 and Q_1, and interquartile range for the frequency table given on the next page.

Step 1.

Denote height (in cm.) on the x axis and cumulative frequency on y axis.

Step 2.

Plot the points (15,2), (20,7), (25,14), (30,25), (35,70), (40,94), (45,98) and (50,100).

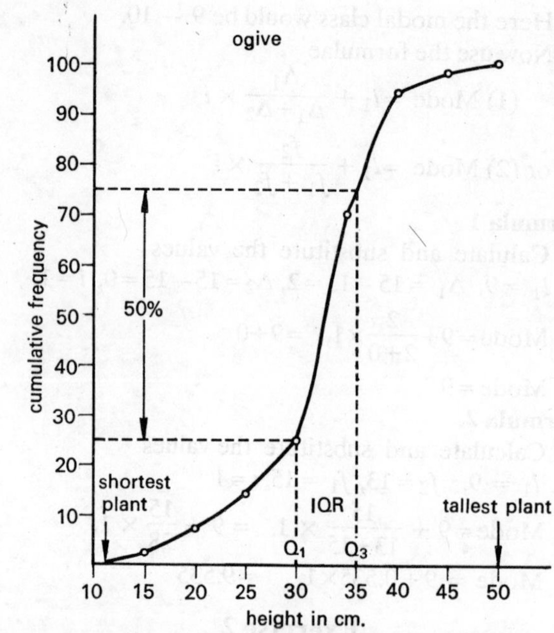

Height of plants (in cm.)	Frequency	Cumulative frequency
11 – 15	2	2
16 – 20	5	7
21 – 25	7	14
26 – 30	11	25
31 – 35	45	70
36 – 40	24	94
41 – 45	4	98
46 – 50	2	100

Step 3.

Find the lower quartile : N/4, i.e. 100/4 = 25. Intersect the ogive at 25. This gives the value of 30. Therefore, 30 is the lower quartile mark of $Q_1 = 30$

Step 4.

Similarly find the upper quartile : 3N/4 = 3/4×100 = 75. Intersect the ogive at 75. This gives the value of 35.5 Therefore, 35.5 is the upper quartile mark or $Q_3 = 35.5$.

Step 5.

Interquartile range would be Q3 – Q1 (35.5 – 30) i.e.5.5

Exercise 3

Purpose : Calculation of Standard Deviation.

Method

It is the most important measure of dispersion that gives the measure of the amount of deviation of individuals from the mean. It is calcualted by one of the following formulae.

Formula 1. $S = \sqrt{\dfrac{\Sigma(\bar{x}-x)^2}{n}}$

Formula 2. $S = \sqrt{\dfrac{\Sigma x^2}{n} - (\bar{x})^2}$

Where S or is the standard deviation

Σ = sign of summation

$\bar{x}$ = arithmetic mean

x = various values

n = number of values (items)

Example 1

Find the standard diviation of the set of values 50, 60. 70, 88, 32.

Formula 1

Step 1.

Calculate the artihmetic mean ($\bar{x}$) of the set of values.

$x/n = \bar{x}$; $x = 50+60+70+88+32 = 300$; $n = 5$, $300/5 = 60$, $\bar{x} = 60$

Step 2.

Calculate the difference of the items from this average (sign may be ignored).

$\bar{x}$–x, 10, 0, 10, 28, 28.

Step 3.

Calculate the squares of these differences.

$(\bar{x}-x)^2$ 10× 10 = 100, 0×0 = 0, 10×10 = 100, 28×28 = 784, 28×28 = 784

Step 4.

Calculate the sum of squares of differences to get the quantity known as the sample sum of squares.

$(\bar{x}-x)^2$, 100 + 0 + 100 + 784 + 784 = 1768

Step 5.

Divide the sample of sum squares by the number of items ($n = 5$). This the quantity known as 'sample variance'.

$$\sqrt{\frac{(\bar{x}-x)^2}{n}} = \sqrt{\frac{1768}{5}} = \sqrt{353.6}$$

Step 6.

Take square root of variance to obtain the standard deviation.

$$S = \sqrt{353} = 18.80$$

Formula 2.

Step 1.

Calculate the squares of different values and add them.

1. 50 = 2500
2. 60 = 3600
3. 70 = 4900
4. 88 = 7744
5. 32 = 1024

$\Sigma = 19768$

ep 2.

Divide this value by number of values.

19768/5 = 3953.6

ep 3.

Calculate arithmetic mean of the values.

$\bar{x} = x/n$

$= 50+60+70+88+32/5$

$= 300/5 = 60$

tep 4.

Square of 60 would be 3600. Subtract this value om that obtained in Step 2

$\sqrt{3953.6-3600}$

$= \sqrt{353.6}$

tep 5.

Take square root of 353.6

$\therefore$ S = 18.80

Exercise 4

Purpose : Calculation of Standard Error.

lethod

This method can be used when ratio between two lasses is to be tested –

$$\text{S.E.r} = \sqrt{\left(\frac{P.q}{n}\right)}$$

Where $P =$ one of the obtained percentages denoted by decimals)

q = another of the obtained percentages $(1-P)$

n = total number $(P+q)$

Deviation = the difference between expected nd obtained values.

If the ratio $\dfrac{\text{Deviation}}{S.E.r}$ is less than 1.96, the btained results are said to be a good fit.

xample

In F_2 generation Mendel obtained as follows –

Round seeds	Wrinkled seeds	Total
5,474 % = 0.74	1,850 % = 0.26	7,324

Expected ratio : 3:1 *i.e.* 0.75 : 0.25

$p = 0.74$ $q = 0.26$ $n = 7{,}324$

Deviation = 0.75 − 0.74 = 0.1

Substituting the values

$$\text{S.E.}r = \sqrt{\left(\frac{P\times q}{n}\right)}$$

$$= \sqrt{\frac{(0.74\times 0.26)}{7{,}324}}$$

$$= \sqrt{\frac{0.1924}{7324}}$$

$$\therefore \frac{Deviation}{S.E.r} = \frac{.01}{.005118} = 1.95$$

i.e. less than 1.96 and hence good fit.

Thus, the results obtained are close to the expected ratio and the hypothesis is acceptable.

Exercise 5

Purpose : The 't test' for significance.

Method

This is a method used to find out whether the differences between the two different samples are significant or mere fluctuations or errors.

$$t = \frac{\text{mean difference}}{\text{standard error of differences}}$$

$$\text{mean difference} = \frac{\text{sum of difference}}{\text{number of trials } (n)}$$

standard error of difference

$$\sqrt{\frac{(\text{sum of square of difference}) - \dfrac{(\text{sum of differences})^2}{n}}{(n-1).n}}$$

Example

The table below shows some hypothetical data on amino acid content of soyabean grown in ten different localities.

Locality or trials	Amino acid content data of Soyabean (in %) Amount of amino acid in % Variety A	Variety B	Difference	Square of difference
1.	3	8	5	25
2.	6	4	2	4
3.	9	6	3	9
4.	15	11	4	16
5.	10	13	3	9
6.	12	17	5	25
7.	7	9	2	4
8.	13	12	1	1
9.	8	6	2	4
10.	12	8	4	16
Sum			31	113

Step 1.
Calculate the mean difference.

$$\text{Mean difference} = \frac{\text{sum of difference}}{\text{number of trials } (n)} = \frac{31}{10} = 3.1$$

Step 2.
Calculate the standard error of differences.

$$\sqrt{\frac{(\text{sum of square of difference}) - \frac{(\text{sum of diferences})^2}{n}}{(n-1)\times n}}$$

Sum of square of difference $= 113$
(sum of differences)$^2 = (31)^2 = 961$
$n = 10$,
(sum of differences)$^2/n$ = 961/10 96.1

$$\sqrt{\frac{113-96.1}{(n-1).n}} = \sqrt{\frac{16.9}{(10-1).10}}$$

$$= \sqrt{\frac{16.9}{90}} = \sqrt{0.187}$$

$\sqrt{0.187} = 0.433$ (standard error of differences)

Step 3. Substitute the value.

$$t = \frac{\text{mean difference}}{\text{standard error of differences}} = \frac{3.1}{0.433} = 7.15^{**}$$

Step 4. Find out the value of p for 9 degrees of freedom (*d.f.* is one less than the number of trials or comparisons)

Degree of freedom (*d.f.*)	Probability of larger value of t (P)	
	0.05	0.01
1.	12.71	63.66
2.	4.30	9.92
3.	3.18	5.84
4.	2.78	4.60
5.	2.57	4.03
6.	2.45	3.71
7.	2.36	3.50
8.	2.31	3.36
9.	2.26	3.25
10.	2.23	3.17
11.	2.20	3.11
12.	2.18	3.06
13.	2.16	3.01
14.	2.14	2.98
15.	2.13	2.95
16.	2.12	2.92
17.	2.11	2.90
18.	2.10	2.88
19.	2.09	2.86
20.	2.09	2.84

For 9 *d.f.* t = 2.26 for *P* of 0.05 and 3.25 for *P* of 0.0 Hence *P* is much < 0.01. This means that chanc are much less than 0.01 (or 1% or 1.99). Th difference is a sample chance or error. As such t amino acid content difference observed is high significant. It is denoted by two asterisks (**). In tests $P < 0.05$ only is considered significant.

Exercise 6

Purpose : Calculation of x^2 (chi-square).

Method

This is one of the most versatile methods in th statistical theory. It permits the test—whethe observed frequencies in a distribution diffe significantly from the frequencies which can b expected according to some hypothesis.

x^2 is calculated by the following formula—

$$x^2 = \Sigma\left[\frac{(X_o - X_e)^2}{X_e}\right] \quad \text{......(1)}$$

Where Σ = sign of summation;
x_o = Observed numbers;
x_e = expected numbers.

Since $x_o - x_e = d$ *i.e.* deviation

$$x^2 = \frac{d^2}{X_e} \quad (2)$$

Example 1

In F_2 generation, Mendel obtained 787 ta plants and 277 dwarf, out of the total of 1,064. A might be expected for 3:1 ratio, plants should hav been 798 tall and 266 dwarf.

		Tall	Dwarf
1.	Observed no (X_o)	787	277
2.	Expected no. (X_e)	798	266
	$(X_o - X_e)$	11	11
	$(X_o - X_e)^2$	121	121
	$\frac{(X_o - X_e)^2}{X_e}$	$\frac{121}{798}$ +	$\frac{121}{266}$

$$x^2 = \frac{121}{798} + \frac{121}{266} = 0.15 + 0.45 = 0.60$$

*Pronounced as 'keye' square, *x* is a Greek letter.
** Values of *P* be determined using accurate tables given in the books on biometry.

Now value of x^{2}* is to be tested **

Degree of freedom (d.f.)	Probability of larger value of Chi-square (P)		
	0.99	0.50	0.05
1	0.00016	0.455	3.841
2	0.0201	1.386	5.991
3	0.115	2.366	7.815
4	0.297	3.337	9.488
5	0.254	4.351	11.070

d.f. = degree of freedom
= number of actual classes – 1

in this case *d. f.* = 2 – 1 = 1

Find out 0.60 value against the *d.f.* 1.

It falls between P 0.05 and 0.50. The probability, therefore, is 0.05 or 5% or 5 times in hundred that a higher value may be obtained. Being within the limits of higher values mentioned in the table the values are considered to be very good fit.

Example 2

Mendel found the following number for the colour of the unripe pods in F_2 generation.

		Green	Yellow	Total
1.	Observed number (X_o)	428	152	580
2.	Expected number (X_e)	435	145	580

$(X_o - X_e)$	7	7
$(X_o - X_e)^2$	49	49
$\frac{(X_o - X_e)^2}{X_e}$	$\frac{49}{435}$	$\frac{49}{145}$

$$x^2 = \frac{49}{435} + \frac{49}{145} = 0.11 + 0.33 = 0.44$$

Find out the P (probability of a larger value of x^2) with 1 degree of freedom.

(It shows that P = 5% or 5 chances in 100. the ratio is good to fit).

Example 3

Mendel observed the following during his dihybrid cross, involving shape of the seed and colour of the pods.

	Round Yellow	Round Green	Wrinkled Yellow	Wrinkled Green
1. Observed number (X_o)	315	108	101	32
2. Expected number (X_e)	312.75	104.25	104.25	34.75

$$(X_o - X_e) = (315 - 312.75), (108 - 104.25), (101 - 104.25), (32 - 34.75)$$

$$(X_o - X_e)^2 = (2.25)^2 \; (3.75)^2 \; (3.75)^2 \; (2.25)^2$$

$$\frac{(X_o - X_e)^2}{X_e} = \frac{5.0625}{312.75} + \frac{14.0625}{104.25} + \frac{10.5625}{104.25} + \frac{7.5625}{34.75}$$

$$x^2 = 0.01 + 0.12 + 0.12 + 0.21 = 0.48.$$

Find out the P (probability of a larger value of x^2) with degrees of freedom [number of actual classes (4 – 1)] = 3.

(It is less than the maximum. So the observations are good to fit.)

10

Cytology & Genetics

I. PLANT CELL

1. To study generalised plant cell

Take out a leaf of *Hydrilla* or peel off epidermis of leaf of any ongiospermic plant. Stain with safranin and mount in glycerine.

Comments

1. The outermost is the cell wall made of cellulose.
2. Cell wall is followed by cell membrane.
3. Inside the cell membrane is the cytoplasm and the nucleus.

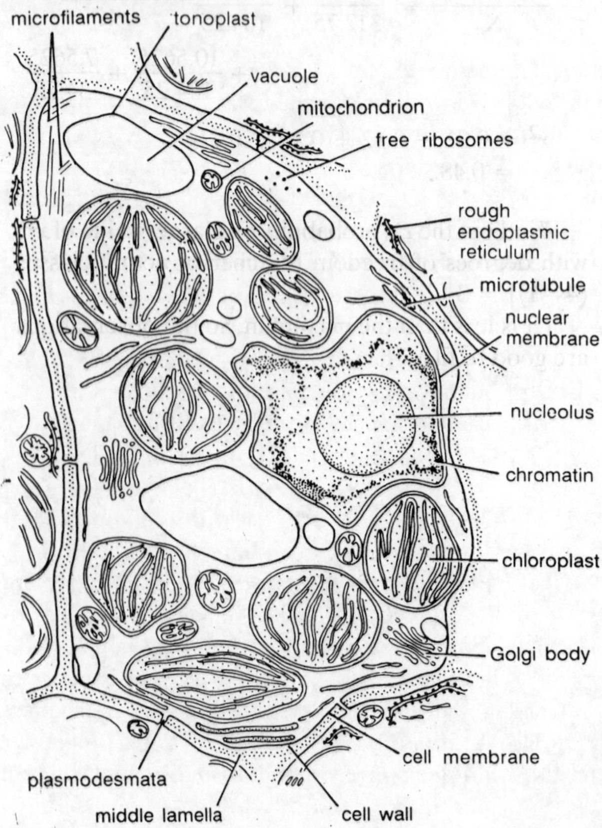

Fig. 1. Generalised plant cell.

4. Cytoplasm contains chloroplasts, mitochondria, golgi bodies, endoplasmic reticulum and ribosomes.
5. The characteristic green colour of the cell is due to the presence of many chloroplasts distributed throughout the cytoplasm.
6. Nucleus is situated in the cytoplasm. It shows nuclear membrane, nucleolus and chromatin network present in nucleoplasm.

Identification

Since the cell shows cell wall and chloroplasts, it is a plant cell.

2. To study the mitochondria

Study the microphotograph of mitochondria.

Comments

1. The mitochondria being small, ultrastructure can be observed only with the help of electron microscope.
2. Mitochondria appear almost rod-shaped.
3. It is made up of outer and inner membranes and matrix.
4. The outer membrane is smooth.
5. The inner membrane is folded inwards. The folds are called cristae.
6. The region between two membranes is known as perimitochondrial space.
7. Cristae possess many globose-stalked bodies called F_1 particles or elementary particles. These are concerned with synthesis of ATP or phosphorylation.
8. The inner region is filled with matrix. Reactions of the Kreb's Cycle of respiration occur in this region.
9. Matrix also shows the presence of small ring shaped DNA and 70 S ribosomes.

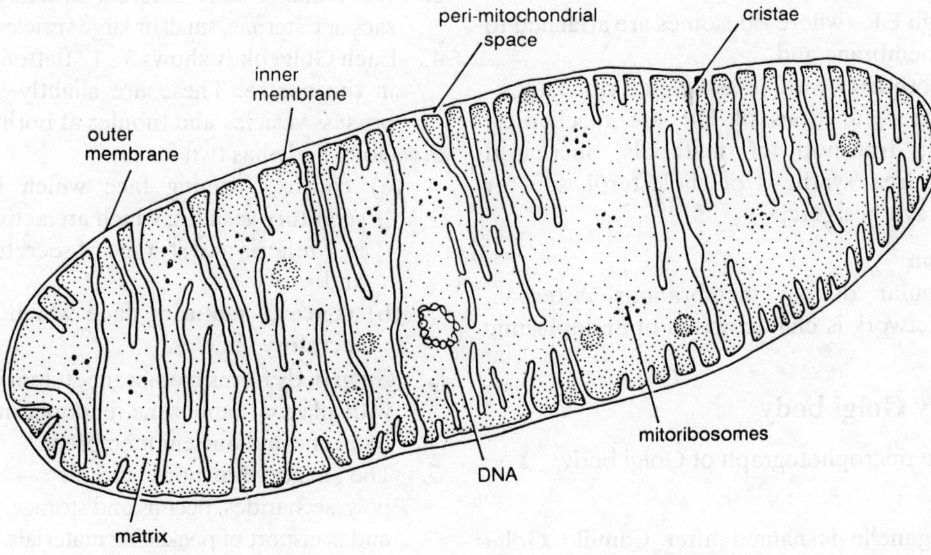

Fig. 2. Microphotograph of mitochondria showing structure

Identification

The characteristic double membrane and cristae being present, the structure is mitochondrion.

3. To study endoplasmic reticulum

Study the microphotograph of endoplasmic reticulum.

Comments

1. The endoplasmic reticulum was discovered by Porter (1945).
2. It forms the major part of the membrane system of the cell.
3. ER is made of cisternae, vesicles and tubules.

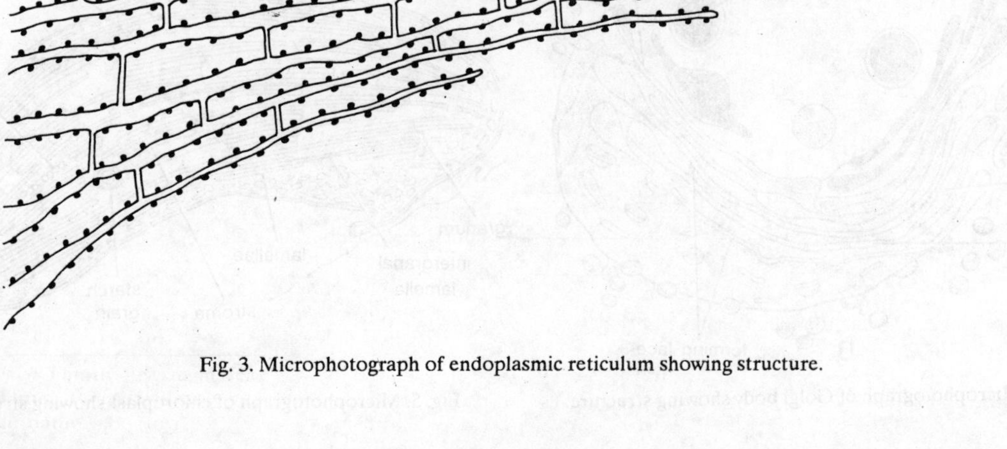

Fig. 3. Microphotograph of endoplasmic reticulum showing structure.

4. There are two types of ER –
   (a) Rough ER - where ribosomes are attached to the membrane and
   (b) Smooth ER - without associated ribosomes.
5. The major functions of ER are mechanical support, transport of materials, increased surface area, synthesis of cholesterol, site for protein synthesis, etc.

Identification

The tubular double membranous cisternae, forming a network is characteristic of endoplasmic reticulum.

4. To study Golgi body

Study the microphotograph of Golgi body.

Comments

1. The organelle is named after Camillo Golgi (1822) who discovered this structure.
2. Golgi body has an outer double membrane.
3. It is made of three different structures - flattened sacs or cisternae, small or large vesicles and tubules.
4. Each Golgi bkdy shows 3 - 12 flattened cisternae in the centre. These are slightly curved and possess vesicles and tubules at both the ends.
5. Golgi body has two faces –
   (a) convex, forming face which forms small secretory vesicles; which are actively engaged in synthesis and storage of secretory porducts and
   (b) concave, maturing face which forms large secretory vesicles.
6. Golgi body forms membrane system in association with plasma membrane, endoplasmic reticulum, lysosome and nuclear membrane.
7. The major functions include – synthesis of polysaccharides, pectins and storage, condensation and transport of packaging materials.

Identification

The presence of curved cisternae into a group generally ending into vesicles indicates that the organelle is Golgi body.

5. To study chloroplast

Study the microphotograph of chloroplast.

Comments

1. It is discoid in shape.
2. Many chloroplasts are present in a cell.
3. Each chloroplast is surrounded by 2 membranes. The space between the two membranes is called periplastidial space.

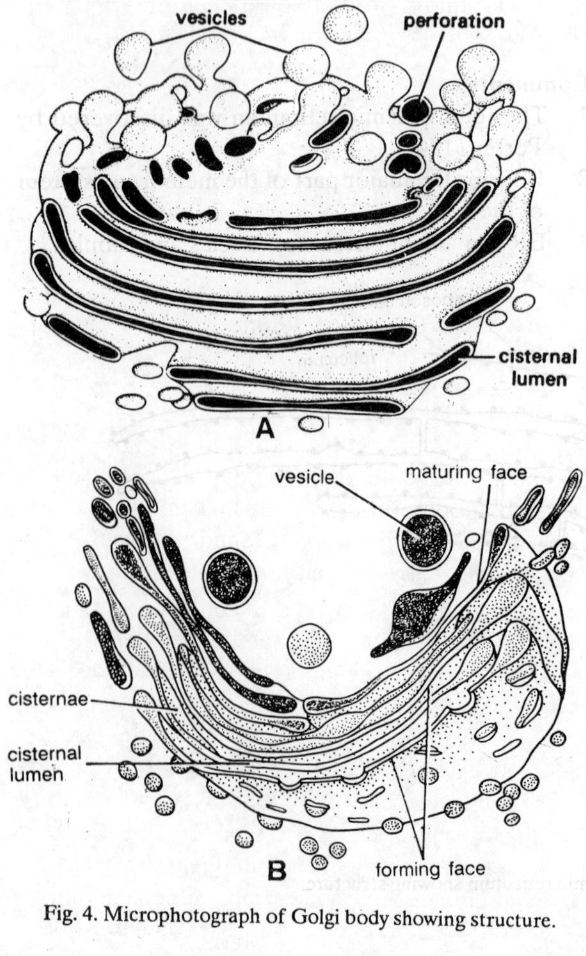

Fig. 4. Microphotograph of Golgi body showing structure.

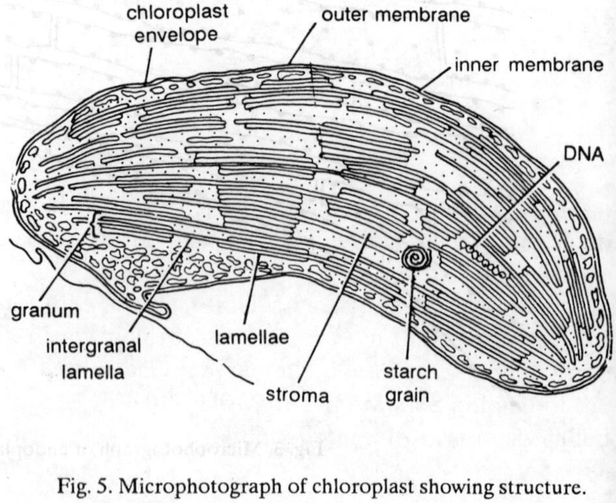

Fig. 5. Microphotograph of chloroplast showing structure.

4. The membranes enclose grana and stroma.
5. Granum is a stack or group of lamellae arranged one over the other. There may be 30 to 40 grana in each chloroplast. Grana are joined with one another by stroma lamellae or frets.
6. Grana lamellae are made of lipo-pigments. Major groups of pigments present are chlorophylls and carotenoids.
7. Grana are concerned with light reaction of photosynthesis.
8. Stroma is the ground substance of chloroplast. Dark reaction of photosynthesis takes place in the stroma.
9. Stroma also shows the presence of small piece of DNA and 70 S ribosomes. Chloroplasts are, therefore, genetically autonomous structures.

Identification

The chloroplasts are identified on the basis of grana and stroma surrounded by two membranes.

6. To study nucleus

Study the microphotograph of nucleus.

Comments

1. Each cell has one nucleus.
2. It is generally spherical to oval in shape.
3. Nucleus consists of nuclear membrane, chromatin network, mucleolus and nucleoplasm.
4. The boundary of nucleus is made of two unit membranes; called nuclear membrane.
5. The membrane has numerous pores called nuclear pores. These maintain continuity between nucleoplasm and cytoplasm.
6. Chromatin network is spread throughout the nucleus. This is made of densely coiled chromosomes – the hereditary material of the cell.
7. A large, densely stained, spherical body is also present in the chromatin network. This is nucleolus. It is essentially made of RNA and is the place where biosynthesis of ribosomes takes place.
8. Nucleoplasm is the ground substance of the nucleus.
9. Nucleus is the controlling centre of the cell. It is mainly concerned with hereditary characters.

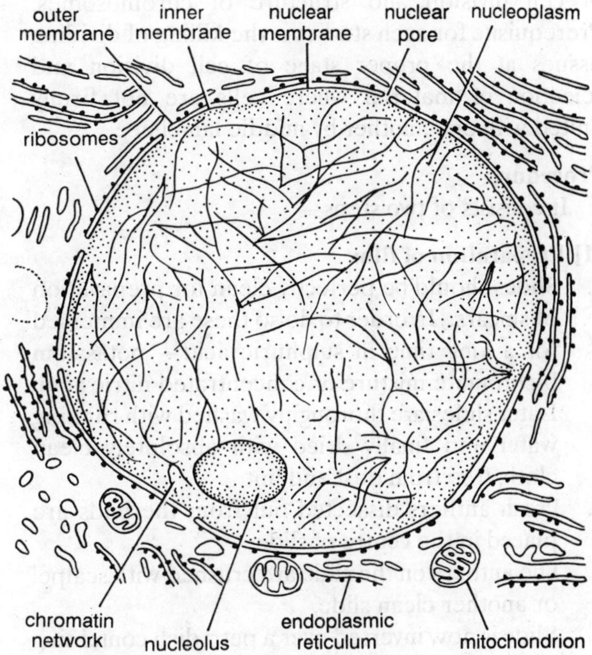

Fig. 6. Microphotograph of nucleus showing structure.

Identification

The two membrane boundary with pores, network of threads and rounded nucleolus indicates that the organelle is a nucleus.

II. CHROMOSOME

Exercise 1

Purpose : Preparation of smear.

Materials

Microsporocytes of *Asphodelus, Trillium, Lilium* and *Oenothera* as well as anthers of *Tradescantia, Triticum* and *Nicotiana* and root tips of onion, *Ficus*, etc. fixed at appropriate time are widely used for smear preparations.

Principle

The principle underlying this method consists of spreading the cells in a single layer. Almost all the cells remain adhered to the slide. The cells are smeared at a stage when they are in the process of cell division. This permits the study of various stages of cell division and structure of chromosomes. Prerequisite for such studies is the killing of dividing tissues at the proper stage of cell division and selection of material where cells are not firmly united with one another by middle lamellae.

Procedure

It consists of two steps –

[I] Preparation of film

1. Slides should be perfectly clean for preparation of smears. In order to do so these are immersed for a long time in sulphuric acid – potassium bichromate mixture or concentrated nitric acid. Later slides are thoroughly washed with running water and finally dried with absolutely clean cloth, free from dust and lint.
2. Fresh anthers dissected out from the buds are placed in the centre of slide.
3. The anthers on the slide are crushed with scalpel or another clean slide.
4. Slide is now inverted over a petri dish containing killing fluid (most suitable being Randolph modified Navashin fluid), in a way that smeared surface comes in contact with the fluid. It should be allowed in this position for about 10-15 minutes.
5. Slide is now inverted with smeared side upward.
6. Slide is ready for staining. It may also be immediately stained without immersing in killing fluid.

[II] Staining procedure

Many different methods have been used by different workers e.g., Johansen's methyl violet method, Newton's gentian violet iodine method, Backman's method, etc. Most common and popular method is that prescribed by Bellings (1926), known as Bellings iron – acetocarmine method. (The recipe of acetocarmine has already been described under the heading Stains). This method is as follows.

1. A few drops of acetocarmine are placed on the smeared material on slide.
2. After a few minutes, stain is replaced with a fresh drop of stain. At this stage, large pieces and debris of material are removed.
3. Slide is heated gently over the flame and uniform pressure is applied over the blotting paper placed on a cover glass.
4. A cover glas$ placed over the drop of stain is immediately sealed with melted wax.

Another simple method is followed –

1. Anthers are smeared on the cover glass.
2. It is then inverted on the slide in drop of acetocarmine.
3. Cover glass is sealed with melted wax.

Exercise 2

Purpose : Preparation of squash.

Materials

Onion root tips, acetic acid, aceto-carmine, slides, cover slips, etc.

Allow the onion bulbs to grow in bottles filled with water. If the lower root portion of the bulb dips in water, it quickly sends forth large number of roots. Cut the root tips between 9 a.m. to 12 noon and fix them in Carnoy's fluid.

Procedure

The following procedure is used.

1. Place the fixed root tip in a drop of 45% acetic acid.
2. Place a cover glass over the tip and diffuse aceto-carmine.
3. Tap and apply uniform pressure over the cover glass.
4. The squash preparation is ready.

Exercise 3

Purpose : Demonstration of salivary gland chromosomes from *Chironomous* larva by Aceto-orcein technique.

Materials

Salivary glands of *Chironomous* or *Chironomous* larvae (it is common blood-worm of ponds), needles, slides, coverslips, saline soluion, Mayer's albumen, petri dishes, Aceto-orcein, etc.

Procedure

The following procedure is used.

[I] Preparation of Aceto-orcein

1. Dissolve 2.2 g of Orcein in 100 ml of glacial Acetic acid by gentle boiling.
2. Cool, dilute (if necessary) and filter. (The best stain is 2% Orcein in 50% acetic acid).

[II] Dissection of larva

1. Take a full grown larva having established its sex if necessary and place it on a slide in a isotonic saline solution or a drop of fixative.

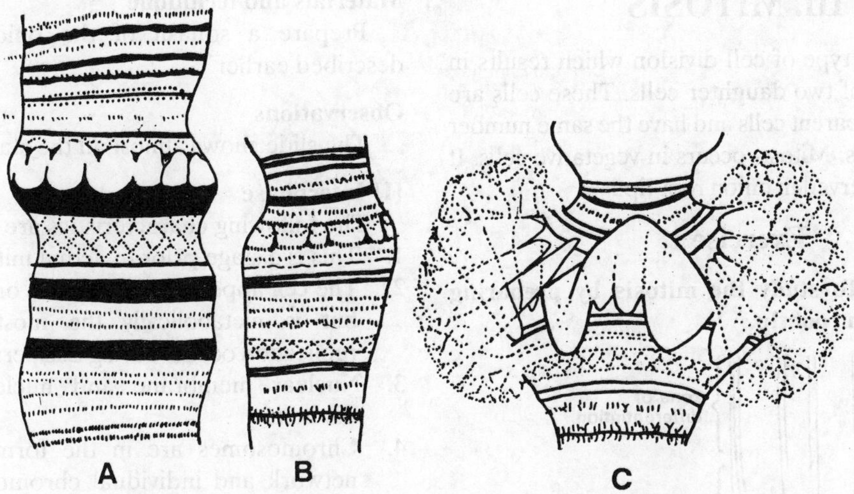

Fig. 7. Salivary gland chromosomes of *Chironomous larva*.A. Salivary gland chromosome with bands, B. unpuffed state, C. puffed state.

2. Cut off its head with a needle in right hand while pressing the body with a needle in the left. When the pressure is released, the salivary glands will float out and then can be put on another slide.
3. Fix the glands in Carnoy's fluid.

(Well-fed larvae ready for pupation have largest chromosomes. Each salivary gland of *Chironomous* contains 28 - 44 cells).

[III] Staining

1. Smear a slide with Mayer's albumen and place the salivary glands.
2. Place a drop or two of Aceto-orcein on the material.
3. Allow the stain to remain as such for 3-5 minutes.
4. Drain off the stain and replace it with fresh drops of stain.

[IV] Preparation of slide

1. Pass the slide quickly over the spirit flame, 5-6 times.
2. The solution of Aceto-orcein should not boil. Judge the heat by passing the slide over palm of the hand.
3. Cover glass is sealed with melted wax.

Another method consists of smearing the cover slip with egg albumen which is then inverted on the slide with material placed in Aceto-orcein. The cover slip is then sealed with melted wax.

If the **permanent preparation** is to be made pass the slide or cover slip through—

1. Aceto-orcein (2 minutes),
2. 1:3 acetic-alcohol (2 minutes),
3. Absolute alcohol, 2 changes (2 minutes each), and mount in Euparol or DPX (if cloudy, place on a hot plate for short time).

Observations

1. These chromosomes are very large in size than the normal somatic chromosomes.
2. These polytene chromosomes attain this size by duplication of chromonema. The duplication may be repeated 9-10 times and the duplicated chromosomes do not separate.
3. The process involved is called endomitosis during which abnormal somatic synapsis occurs.
4. Polytene chromosomes are permanent prophase chromosomes.
5. These show alternating dark and light transverse bands.
6. Dark bands are mainly composed of euchromatin and the light bands of heterochromatin.
7. The centromeres of all the chromosomes are attached to a common point, called chromocentre.
8. Chromosomal swellings known as chromosome puffs or bulbs are also present.
9. The chromonema of polytene chromosomes give out a series of lateral loops. These large sized chromosomal loops or puffs are called Balbiani rings.
10. Such chromosomes were first reported by Balbiani in 1881.

III. MITOSIS

Mitosis is a type of cell division which results in the formation of two daughter cells. These cells are identical to the parent cells and have the same number of chromosomes. Mitosis occurs in vegetative cells. It can be best observed in onion root tip.

Exercise 1

Purpose : To study the mitosis by preparing squash of onion root tip.

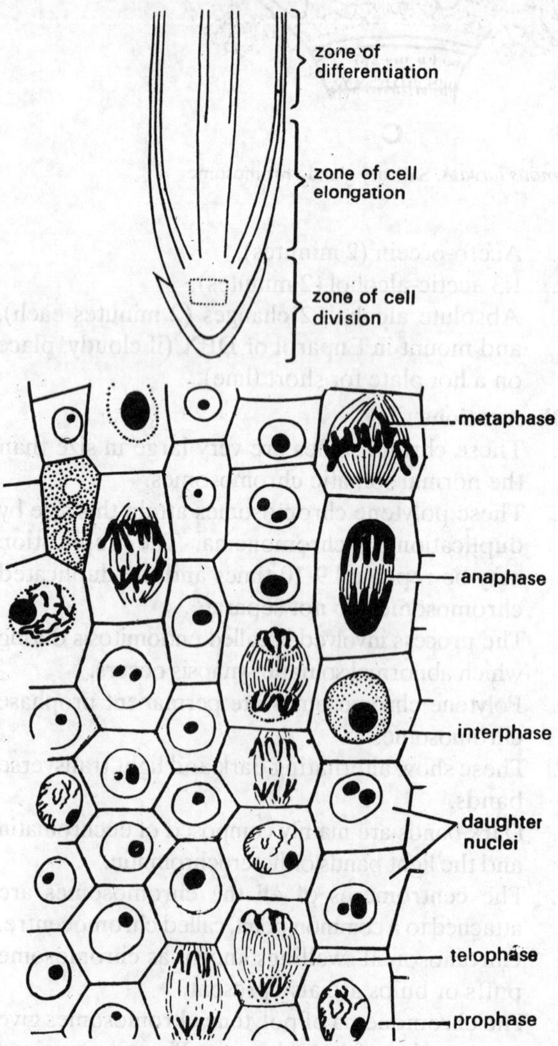

Fig. 8. L. s. onion root tip showing different stages of mitosis.

Materials and technique

Prepare a squash of the onion root tip as described earlier.

Observations

The slide shows almost all the stages of mitosis.

[I] Interphase

The following characteristics are seen,—

1. This is a stage prior to actual mitotic cycle.
2. The cell appears to be inactive or in resting stage but is metabolically the most active. DNA replication occurs during this period.
3. Nuclear membrane and nucleolus are very distinct.
4. Chromosomes are in the form of chromatin network and individual chromosomes can not be seen separately.
5. The chromosome appears double stranded i.e. made of two chromatids.

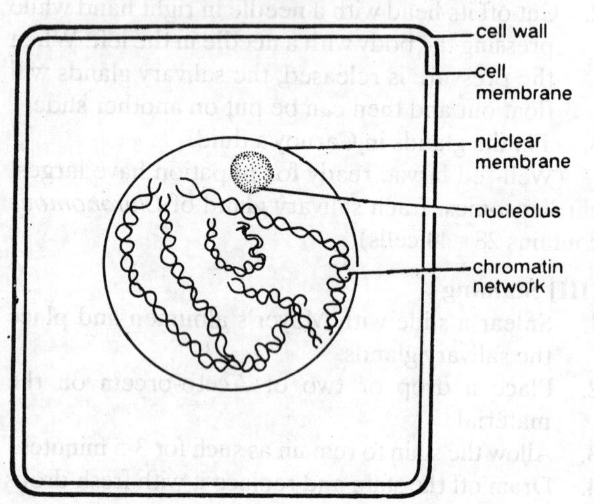

Fig. 9. **Mitosis**. Cell showing interphase.

[II] Early prophase

The following characteristics are seen—

1. This is the first stage of mitosis which is observed under the microscope.
2. Nuclear membrane appears distinct.
3. Nucleolus is also seen clearly.
4. Chromosomes become coiled and shortened and more distinct.

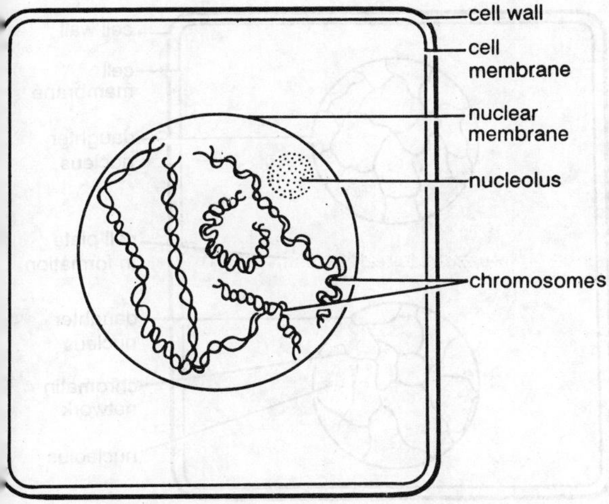

Fig. 10. **Mitosis.** Cell showing early prophase.

III] Late prophase

The following characteristics are seen—

The nuclear membrane and nucleolus have partially or completely disappeared.

Each chromosome now begins to show chromatids, primary constriction, secondary constriction and centromeres.

The equatorial region appears clearly in the centre of the cell.

Chromosomes begin to move and gather near the equatorial plate.

Chromosomes are condensed and thus short and thick.

Spindle fibres also begin to appear.

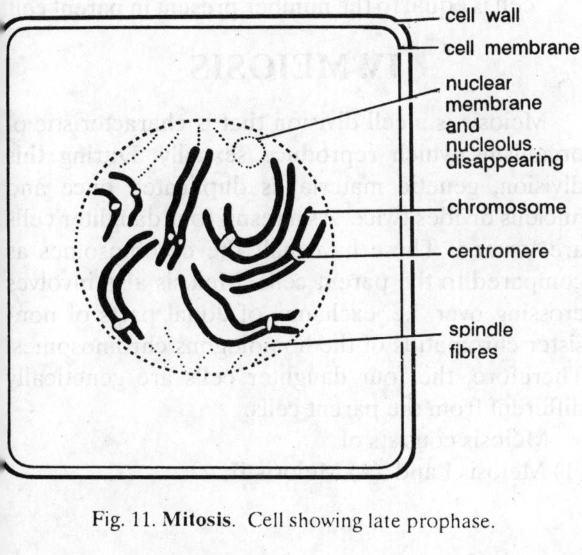

Fig. 11. **Mitosis.** Cell showing late prophase.

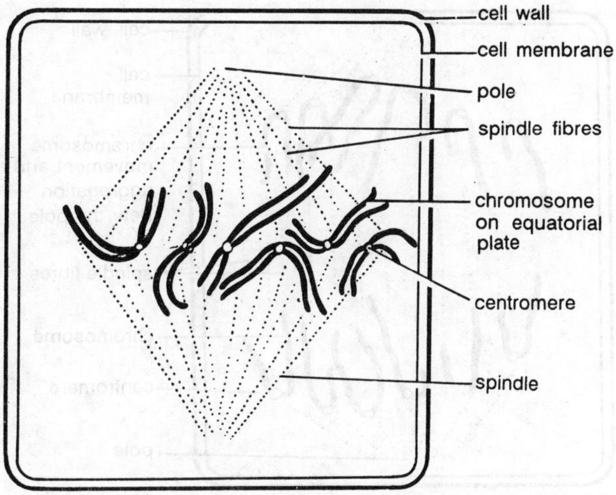

Fig. 12. **Mitosis.** Cell showing metaphase.

[IV] Metaphase

The following characteristics are seen.

1. Nuclear membrane and nucleolus are absent having disappeared.
2. Centromeres of the chromosomes are arranged on the equatorial plate and each is attached to the spindle fibres.
3. Centrioles are absent and hence aster is not formed in plant cells. This type of mitosis is known as anastral mitosis.
4. The spindle is made of fibres only. The absence of centrioles indicates that it is a plant cell.
5. The chromosomes at metaphase are very distinct. Thus, number and morphology of chromosome is studied at this stage. Each chromosome shows two chromatids, centromere, primary constriction, euchromatic and heterochromatic regions, chromomeres, etc.

[V] Anaphase

The following characteristics are seen—

1. This stage is completed in a very small period of time.
2. The centromere of each chromosome gets split into two.
3. The chromosome also gets divided into two chromatids. Each chromatid now bears one centromere each.
4. The chromosome becomes shorter and thicker.
5. The separated chromatids are now pulled towards the opposite poles due to contraction of spindle fibres.

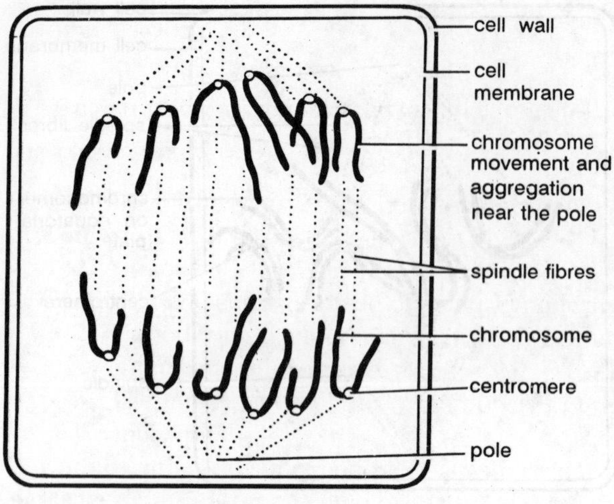

Fig. 13. **Mitosis.** Cell showing anaphase.

6. During movement, each chromosome shows characteristic shape which is dependent on the position of centromere.

[VI] Telophase

The following characteristics are seen—

1. The chromosomes are present at both the poles of a parent cell.
2. The chromosomes increase in length and become thread-like. All the chromosomes together form chromatin network and their individuality is now lost.
3. The groups of chromatin network at each are surrounded by nuclear membrane Nucleolus is also present.

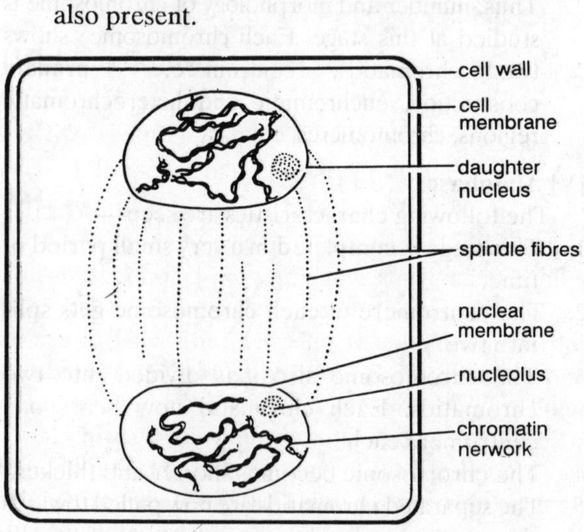

Fig. 14. **Mitosis.** Cell showing telophase.

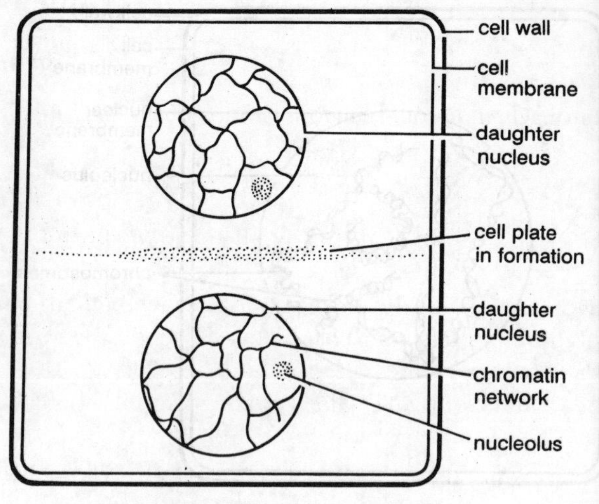

Fig. 15. **Mitosis.** Cell showing cytokinesis.

4. Thus two fully formed nuclei, one at each pole are present in the parent cell.
5. Spindle fibres are absent.

[VII] Cytokinesis

The following characteristics are seen—

1. In this stage, cytoplasm divides into two. It results in the formation of two daughter cells.
2. Division of the cytoplasm is due to formation of a cell plate in the equatorial region.
3. Cell plate formation begins in the centre of the cell and gradually progresses towards the periphery.
4. This results in the formation of two daughter cells. Organelles are also present.
5. The number of chromosomes in each daughter cell is equal to the number present in parent cell.

IV. MEIOSIS

Meiosis is a cell division that is characteristic of organisms which reproduce sexually. During this division, genetic material is duplicated once and nucleus divides twice. As a result four daughter cells are formed. These have half the chromosomes as compared to the parent cells. Meiosis also involves crossing over, i.e. exchange of equal parts of non-sister chromatids of the homologous chromosomes. Therefore, the four daughter cells are genetically different from the parent cells.

Meiosis consists of
(1) Meiosis I and (2) Meiosis II.

Meiosis I involves some very characteristic and important stages such as—

(1) Synapsis or pairing of homologous chromosomes,
(2) Recombinations due to crossing over and
(3) Segregation of homologous chromosomes.

The stages included in Meiosis I are Prophase I, Metaphase I, Anaphase I and Telophase I. At the end of meiosis I, two daughter cells are formed. Each cell has half the number of chromosomes compared to parent cell.

Meiosis II is similar to mitosis. It results in the formation of four daughter cells, each having the same chromosome number as was present at the end of Meiosis I. Meiosis II is also sub-divided into Prophase II, Metaphase II, Anaphase II and Telophase II.

Exercise 1

Purpose : To study meiosis by smear preparation.

Materials and Technique

Prepare a smear of young anthers of *Asphodelus* or *Tradescantia* as described earlier.

Observations

Following stages can be seen in different slides of meiosis—

[I] Leptotene (Leptonema) of Prophase I

The following characteristics are seen—

1. Nuclear membrane and nucleolus are intact.
2. Chromosomes are long thread-like structures. All the chromosomes are intertwined to form chromatin network.
3. Chromosomes appear beaded due to chromomeres which are distinct at this stage.
4. All the chromosomes finally move towards one part of the nucleus. This stage is known as synizesis or boquet formation.
5. Centrioles are not present. This indicates that it is a dividing plant cell.

[II] Zygotene (Zygonena) of Prophase I

The following characteristics are seen—

1. Nuclear membrane and nucleolus are still very clear.
2. The major character of this stage is synapsis – pairing of homologous chromosomes.
3. Synaptonemal complex is formed as a result of synapsis. This complex is made of two lateral elements and a central region which is bisected by a narrow central component.
4. Synapsis can occur at more than one points along the length of the chromosome.
5. At each place a pair showing two chromatids is present.

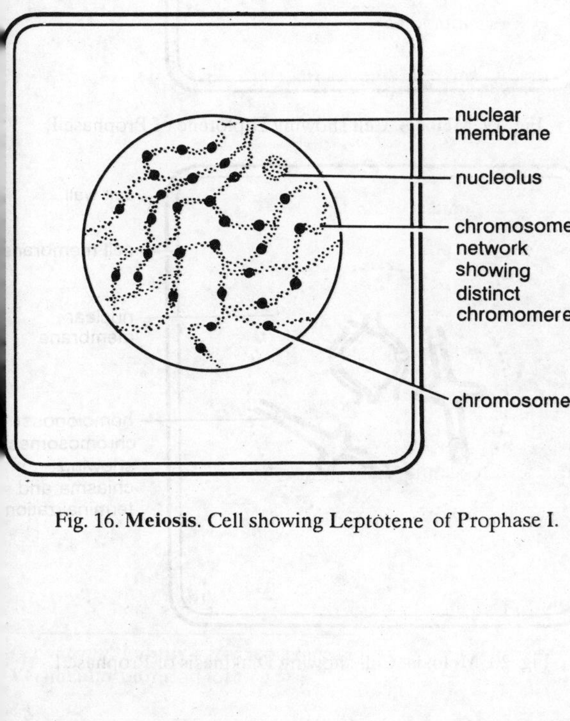

Fig. 16. **Meiosis**. Cell showing Leptotene of Prophase I.

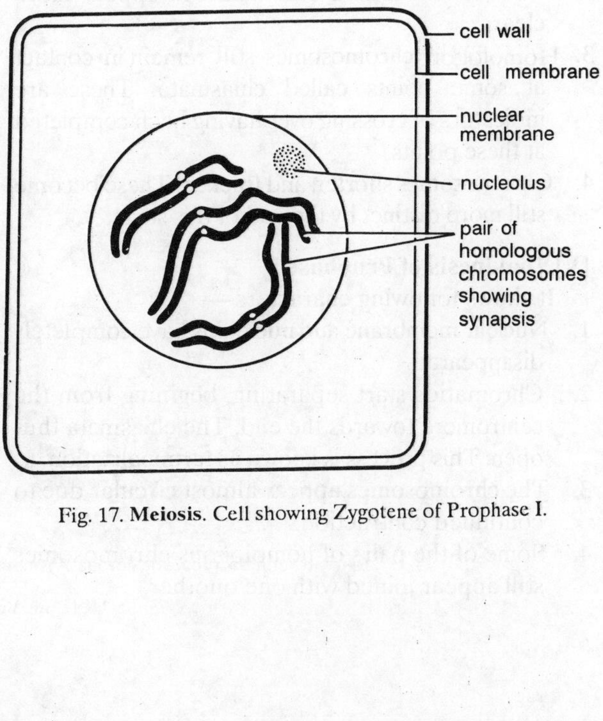

Fig. 17. **Meiosis**. Cell showing Zygotene of Prophase I.

[III] Pachytene (Pachynema) of Prophase I

The following characteristics are seen—

1. Nucleolus and nuclear membrane are distinct.
2. Chromosomes are thickened, coiled and thread-like.
3. Chromosomes are very closely coiled. Each chromosome shows its two chromatids. A pair of homologous chromosomes which is intimately coiled upon one other shows four chromatids together.
4. Pair of homologous chromosomes is called bivalent. It is made of four chromatids and hence known as tetrad.
5. The stage is characterised by crossing over. It is the exchange of equal parts of chromatids of two different but homologous chromosomes.
6. Nucleolus is distinctly attached to nucleolar organising chromosome.
7. The length of the chromosome being more than that found at metaphase, the chromosome at this stage is also used for the study of morphology.

[IV] Diplotene (Diplonema) of Prophase I

The following characteristics are seen—

1. The nucleolus is disappearing while nuclear membrane is still intact.
2. The close and tight coiling of chromosomes becomes loose and chromosomes appear more clear.
3. Homologous chromosomes still remain in contact at some points called chiasmata. These are indicators of crossing over having been completed at these points.
4. Chromosomes shorten and thicken. These become still more distinct by the end of this stage.

[V] Diakinesis of Prophase I

It shows following characters—

1. Nuclear membrane and nucleolus have completely disappeared.
2. Chromatids start separating, begining from the centromere towards the end. The chiasmata thus open. This process is known as terminalization.
3. The chromosomes appear almost circular due to continued contraction.
4. Some of the pairs of homologous chromosomes still appear joined with one onother.

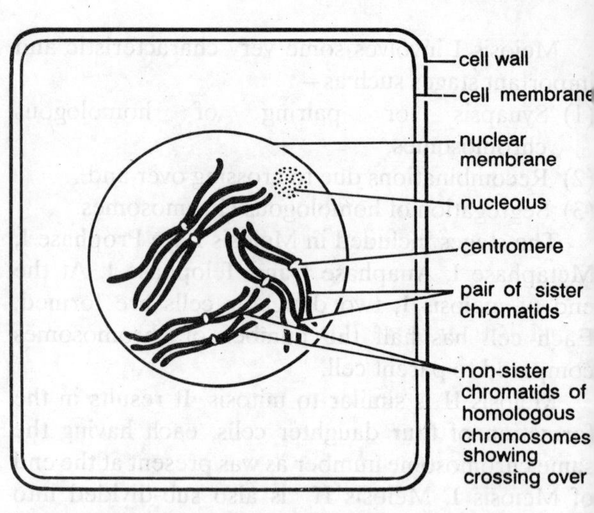

Fig. 18. **Meiosis.** Cell showing Pachytene of Prophase I.

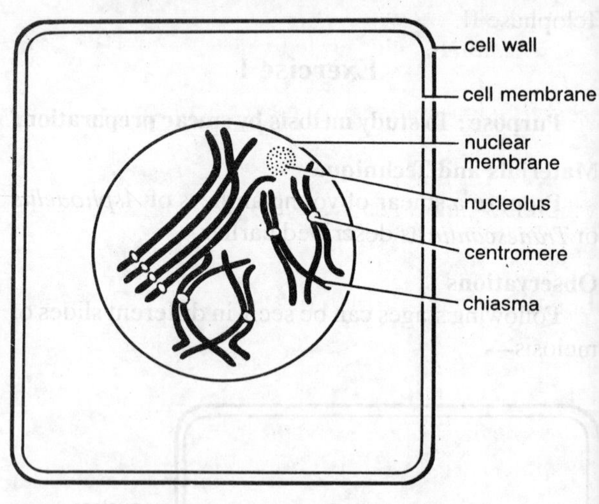

Fig. 19. **Meiosis.** Cell showing Diplotene of Prophase I.

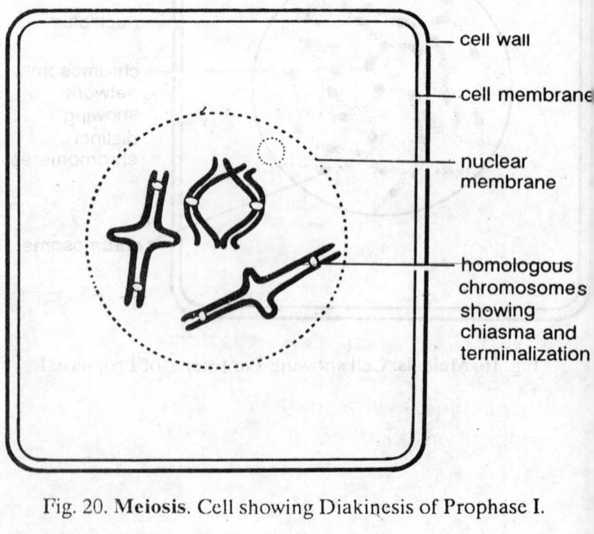

Fig. 20. **Meiosis.** Cell showing Diakinesis of Prophase I.

[VI] Metaphase I

The characters observed during Metaphase I are –

1. Nuclear membrane and nucleolus have completely disappeared.
2. Spindle formed by fibres is distinct.
3. Bivalents are arranged on the equatorial plate.
4. Each chromosome of a bivalent is attached to the spindle fibres by its centromere.
5. Centromeres are arranged on both the sides of the equatorial region, almost at equal distance.

[VII] Anaphase I

The following are characteristics of this stage —

1. Nuclear membrane and nucleolus are completely absent.
2. The chromosomes separate out of the pair of homologous chromosomes.
3. Spindle fibres contract and pull the centromere alongwith the chromosome to opposite poles.
4. This results in two haploid sets of chromosomes, one at each pole of the cell.
5. Each chromosome shows characteristic shape during movement.

[VIII] Telophase I

The stage shows following characteristics —

1. Nuclear membrane and nucleolus have reappeared and are clearly seen.
2. There are two nuclei one each at the poles of the cell.
3. Each daughter cell has half the number of chromosomes compared to the parent cell. Chromosomes are thin and long. They are intermingled with one another to form a network.
4. Spindle fibres are totally absent.

[IX] Prophase II

The following characteristics are seen –

1. Nuclear membrane and nucleolus are distinct in the early stages. In late prophase, both these structures disappear gradually.
2. Chromosomes are short and thick.
3. Each chromosome is made of two chromatids bound together by a centromere.
4. The spindle fibres also begin to appear.
5. Chromosomes move towards the equatorial plate which is generally formed at right angles to the plate formed during meiosis I.

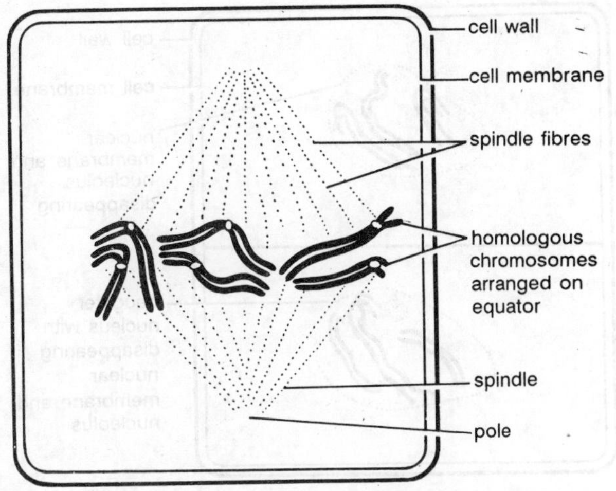

Fig. 21. **Meiosis**. Cell showing Metaphase I.

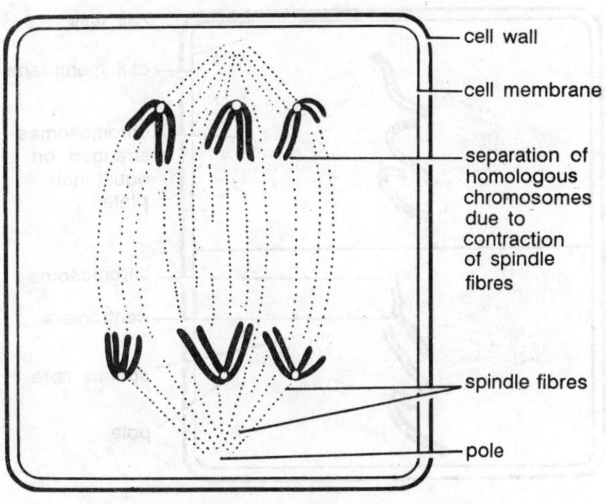

Fig. 22. **Meiosis**. Cell showing Anaphase I.

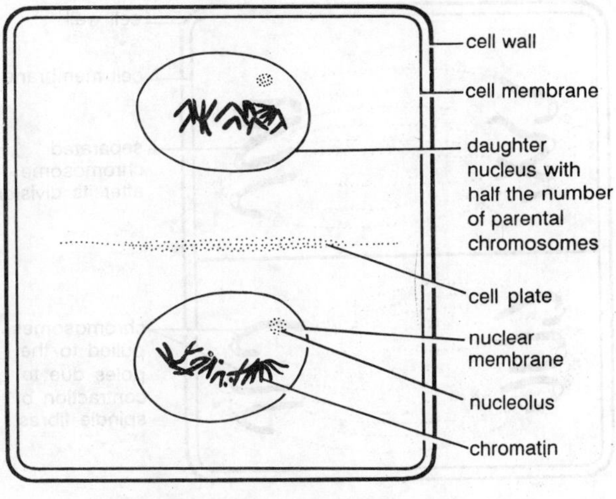

Fig. 23. **Meiosis**. Cell showing Telophase I.

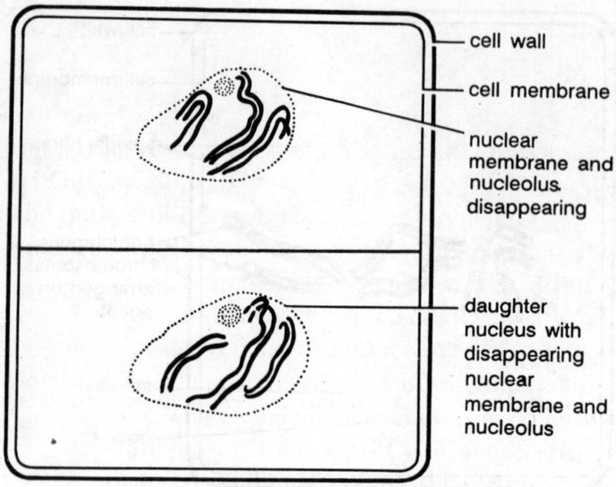

Fig. 24. **Meiosis**. Cell showing Prophase II.

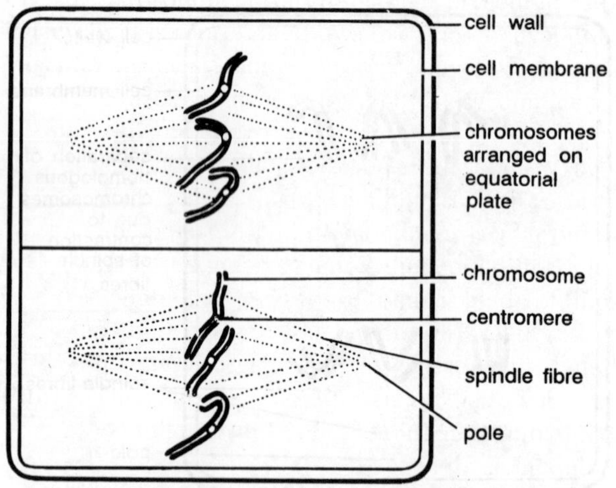

Fig. 25. **Meiosis**. Cell showing Metaphase II.

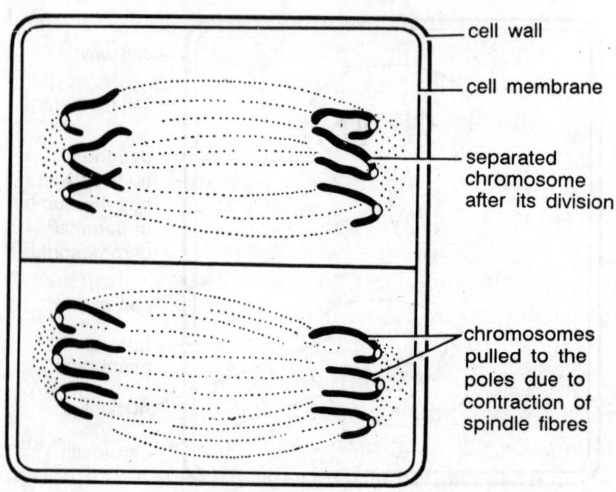

Fig. 26. **Meiosis**. Cell showing Anaphase II.

[X] Metaphase II

It shows following characteristics—

1. Nuclear membrane and nucleolus both are absent, having disappeared.
2. Spindle fibres are formed. These are organised into a spindle.
3. Spindle fibres are joined with centromeres of the chromosomes.
4. All the chromosomes are aranged on the equatorial plate.
5. Each chromosome is made of two chromatids held together by a centromere.

[XI] Anaphase II

This stage is characterised by the following—

1. Nuclear membrane and nucleolus are absent.
2. Centromere that holds two chromatids splits. Each chromatid now has an individual centromere.
3. Spindle fibres contract and each chromosome is now pulled to the opposite poles.
4. Chromatids (now called chromosomes) show characteristic shape during their movement.

[XII] Telophase II

The following are characteristic features of this stage—

1. Chromosomes are in the form of groups at each end of the parent cell.
2. Nuclear membrane reappears and surrounds the group of chromosomes. This results in the formation of daughter nuclei at the opposite poles of the cells.
3. Spindle fibres disappear completely.

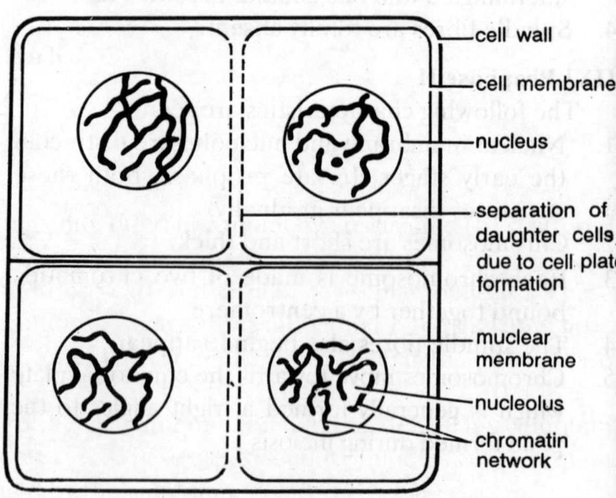

Fig. 27. **Meiosis**. Cell showing Telophase II.

V. MENDELIAN GENETICS

Gregor Johann Mendel is known as 'Father of Genetics'. He is famous for his work on garden pea which led to the formulation of fundamental work in genetics. He used seven contrasting pairs of characters in pea.

Table 1. **Seven pairs of contrasting characters studied by Mendel.**

Trait	Dominant	Recessive
1. Shape of seed	Round	Wrinkled
2. Colour of seed	Yellow	Green
3. Colour of seed coat	Grey	White
4. Shape of fruit (pod)	Inflated	Constricted
5. Colour of fruit (pod)	Green	Yellow
6. Position of flowers	Axial	Terminal
7. Length of stem	Long (Tall)	Short (Dwarf)

Mendel's observations include certain generalisations and two rules or law. These are
(1) Dominance,
(2) Law of Segregation and
(3) Law of Independent Assortment.

[I] Dominance

P or *Parental generation* with one parent homozygous for dominant character (AA) and the other individual homozygous for recessive character (aa) are taken. The cross between the two is made. The resulting $\mathbf{F_1}$ generation (*First filial generation*) or hybrid will show heterozygous genotype (Aa). The phenotype shall be a dominant trait which shall be due to dominant gene. Dominant phenotype is expressed in both homozygous and heterozygous conditions. In Mendel's words "characters which are transmitted entire or almost unchanged in the hybridization, and therefore in themselves constitute the characters of the hybrid, are termed the *dominant* and those which become latent in the process are *recessive.*"

phenotypes Round seeded plant × Wrinked seeded plant — **P** (Parental generation)
genotypes (RR) (rr)
↓
Round seeded (Rr) — $\mathbf{F_1}$ (First filial generation)

In this case, round shape of the seeds is a dominant character. This allele affects the phenotype when present in a homozygous (e.g. RR) or heterozygous (e.g. Rr) condition while recessive gene affects the phenotype only in case it is present in a homozygous (e.g. rr) condition.

[II] Law of Segregation (Monohybrid cross)

In the first generation in Mendel's experiments the characters (phenotypes) produced were uniform i.e. all the plants were heterozygous and showed dominant character only. Now plants of the F_1 generation were selfed to produce F_2 generation. In contrast to F_1 generation (where all the plants expressed phenotypically only dominant traits), in F_2 generation two different phenotypes appeared
(1) Round seeded, like one parent and
(2) Wrinkled seeded, like the other one. This shows that traits have separated from F_1 hybrid.

Round seeded plant (RR) × Wrinkled seeded plant (rr) — **P**
Round seeded plant (Rr) — $\mathbf{F_1}$
↓
Phenotypes: 3 Round seeded plants : 1 Wrinkled seeded plant — $\mathbf{F_2}$
Genotypes: 1RR : 2Rr : 1rr

[III] Law of Independent Assortment (Dihybrid cross)

Dihybrid cross involves two pairs of independent characters (two pairs of alleles). If these pairs of alleles occur on two different (two non-homologus) chromosomes, they shall separate (segregate) or assort independently of one another during meiosis. The separation of one pair of allele regulating one phenotypic expression has no effect on another pair of allele.

Round seeded Yellow (RR Y Y) × Wrinkled seeded Green (rr yy) — **P**
Round seeded Yellow (Rr Yy) — $\mathbf{F_1}$
↓

Phenotypes	Round Yellow	Round Green	Wrinkled Yellow	Wrinkled Green
Genotypes	RRYY 1	RRyy 1	rrYY 1	yyrr 1
	RYy 2	Rryy 2	rrYy 2	
	RrYY 2			
	RrYy 4			
	9 :	3 :	3 :	1

Phenotypic ratio 9 : 3 : 3 : 1
Genotypic ratio 1 : 2 : 2 : 4 : 1 : 2 : 1 : 2 : 1

Of the four phenotypic classes, Round Yellow and Wrinkled Green are parental combinations while the other two i.e. Round Green and Wrinkled Yellow are newly formed and are called recombinations. This is a result of independent assortment of characters.

[IV] Test Cross

Test cross is defined as a cross between F_1 hybrid with its recessive parent. Two test crosses are given below.

MONOHYBRID CROSS

P_1 Red flower (RR) × White flower (rr) P_2

Red (Rr) F_1

MONOHYBRID TEST CROSS

Red (from F_1) (Rr) × White (from P_2) (rr)

Ratio: Red (Rr) 1 : White (rr) 1

DIHYBRID CROSS

P_1 Round Yellow (RRYY) × Wrinkled & Green (rryy) P_2

Round Yellow (RrYy) F_1

DIHYBRID TEST CROSS

(from F_1) Round & Yellow (RrYy) × Wrinkled & Green (rryy) (from P_2)

	Round & Yellow (RrYy)	Round & Green (Rryy)	Wrinkled & Yellow (rrYy)	Wrinkled & Green (rryy)
Ratio	1 :	1 :	1 :	1

The progeny of test cross shows following in the above example

1. **Monohybrid cross :** Heterozygous Red (Rr) 1 homozygous White (rr)
2. **Dihybrid cross:** 1 heterozygous Round Yellow (RrYy): 1 heterozygous Round Green (Rryy) 1 heterozygous Wrinkled Yellow (rrYy) 1 homozygous Wrinkled Green (rryy).

[V] Exceptions to Mendelism

The following are some of the exceptions to Mendel's work.

1. Incomplete dominance as in *Mirabilis jalapa* (4 O'clock plant).
2. Interaction of genes.
3. Multiple alleles.
4. Linkage.

Exercise 1

Purpose : Determination of probability by tossing coins.

Materials

Fifty, one rupee coins or fifty paise coins.

Procedure

Toss each coin and note the head or tails it falls. Find out the ratio of heads to tails.

Explanation

Probability means 'likely hood' or chance. If a coin is tossed in the air, the chance of its falling head is one half. Hence $p = 1/2$. However, there are two ways the spin may turn up: head or tail. Both are equally likely, but it is absolutely certain that the coin will finish up head *or* tail; Hence, $p = 1$ which is shared between the two possible results equally, *i.e.* $p = 1/2$ for a head and $p = 1/2$ for a tail. The expected ratio of heads to tails is 1:1. If a coin is tossed four times, there should be two heads and two tails. This, however, may not be possible until a large number of coins, say 400 are tossed. Only then ratio close to 1:1 is obtained.

This is possible because each toss is independent of the influence of the other. The law of probability is that, the chance of any number of independent things happening together is equal to the product of the chances that each will happen separately, e.g. chance of obtaining two heads on any one toss is one-half; the chance of obtaining two heads on two separate tosses each would be $1/2 \times 1/2 = 1/4$.

Example 1

Homozygote *AA* is crossed with heterozygote *Aa*. What kind of offspring do we expect ?

Gametes of parent AA $\quad 1/1A$ (or $1/2A + 1/2A$)
Gametes of parent Aa $\quad 1/2A + 1/2a$
multiply the above two $\quad 1/2AA + 1/2Aa$

The probabilities among the zygotes would be

$$1/2AA + 1/2Aa$$

Example 2

If two heterozygous parents with genotype *Aa* and *Aa* respectively are crossed, what kinds of offsprings would be produced ?

Games of parent Aa $\quad = 1/2A + 1/2a$
Gametes of another parent Aa $= 1/2A + 1/2a$
multiply the above two $\quad 1/4AA + 1/4Aa$
$\quad 1/4Aa + 1/4aa$

The probabilities among the zygotes would be $= 1/4AA + 1/2Aa + 1/4\ aa$

Exercise 2

Purpose : Demonstration of phenomenon of segregation.

Materials

Two bóxes, 100 yellow coloured balls, 100 green coloured balls, paper, pencil, etc.

Procedure

Count 50 yellow balls and 50 green balls. Put them in box *A* and mix them thoroughly. Repeat the same procedure for box *B*. You now have 100 balls in each box, of both colours, equal in number.

Now, without looking withdraw one ball from each box and record the colour of pairs. Continue until the boxes are empty and you have hundred pairs.

Add up the number of three combinations viz. yellow and yellow, yellow and green and green and green.

Find out it they approach 1 : 2 : 1 ratio, assuming that yellow ball represents yellow colour (Y) of the seed (dominant) and the green ball represents green colour (y) of the seed (recessive).

Your chances of getting more acurate ratio would also increase if you increase the number of balls in the boxes.

Explanation

The boxes represent the plant and balls the gametes carrying different alleles or factors. The random selection of pairs correspond to random fusion of male and female gametes. The pairs of balls thus represent zygotic combinations.

Since each box contains equal number of yellow and green balls, there is an equal chance at each random selection that the combination will be any one of the following.

(1) Yellow from box *A* with yellow from box *B*.
(2) Yellow from box *A* with green from box *B*.
(3) Green from box *A* with yellow from box *B*.
(4) Green from box *A* with green from box *B*.

Round seeded plant (RR) × Wrinkled seeded plant (rr) ..... (P_1 generation)

Round seed (Rr) .. (F_1 generation)

male gametes \ female gametes	R	r
R	RR (Round)	Rr (Round)
r	Rr (Round)	rr (Wrinkled)

The phenotypic ratio of Round : Wrinkled is 3:1 in case of monohybrid cross. Genotypically the ratio shows homozygous dominant (1): heterozygous dominant (2): homozygous recessive (1).

Exercise 3

Purpose : Demonstration of phenomenon of Independent Assortment.

Materials

Two boxes, four types of coloured balls viz. red, blue, yellow and green in multiples of 16 (say 80 each), paper, pencil, etc.

Procedure

Count 40 balls of each colour. Put them in box *A* and mix thoroughly. Repeat the same procedure for box *B*. You have now 160 balls in each box, of four colours, in equal numbers.

Now, without looking, withdraw one ball each from each of the boxes and record the colour of pairs, Continue until the boxes are empty and you have 160 pairs.

Calculate the ratio assuming that both boxes represent the two plants and the balls, the gametes carrying different alleles or factors.

Explanation

Each box contains equal numbers of four types of balls representing gametes. If the two plants crossed were phenotypically round seeded and seeds yellow coloured (round seed is dominant over wrinkled seed and yellow colour of the seed is dominant over green colour), with genotype RrYy, then the four types of gametes would be RY, Ry, rY and ry. Let them be represented as follows–

RY is represented by red ball,
Ry is represented by blue ball,
rY is represented by yellow ball and
ry is represented by green ball.

Find out the phenotypes by using these indicators and whether the ratio approaches 9 : 3 : 3 : 1. There would be any one of the following combinations because there are equal number of balls in each of the boxes and there is an equal chance at each random selection for such a combination.

(1) Red from box *A* with red from box *B*.
(2) Red from box *A* with blue from box *B*.
(3) Red from box *A* with yellow form box *B*.
(4) Red from box *A* with green from box *B*.
(5) Blue from box *A* with red from box *B*.
(6) Blue from box *A* with blue from box *B*.
(7) Blue from box *A* with yellow from box *B*.
(8) Blue from box *A* with green from box *B*.
(9) Yellow from box *A* with red from box *B*.
(10) Yellow from box *A* with blue from box *B*.
(11) Yellow from box *A* with yellow from box *B*.
(12) Yellow from box *A* with green from box *B*.
(13) Green from box *A* with red from box *B*.
(14) Green from box *A* with blue from box *B*.
(15) Green from box *A* with yellow from box *B*.
(16) Green from box *A* with green from box *B*.

Round & Yellow (RR YY) × Wrinkled & Green .... (rr yy) **P**

↓

Round & Yellow (Rr Yy) **F_1**

Phenotype	**9 Round &Yellow**	**3 Round & Green**	**3 Wrinkled & Yellow**	**1 Wrinkled & Green**
Genotype	RRYY 1 RRYy 2 RrYY 2 RrYy 4	RRyy 1 Rryy 2	rrYY 1 rrYy 2	yyrr 1
	9 :	3 :	3 :	1

Phenotypic ratio 9 : 3 : 3 : 1
Genotypic ratio 1 : 2 : 2 : 4 : 1 : 2 : 1 : 2 : 1

[VII] Some of the Exampies

Example 1

Yellow (Y) is dominant over the green (y) colour of the pea seeds. In the following crosses find out the genotype of parents.

Parents	**Progeny**	
	Yellow	**Green**
(a) Yellow × Green	72	80
(b) Yellow × Yellow	125	42
(c) Yellow × Green	74	0
(d) Green × Green	0	50

Explanation

(a) The ratio is close to 1: 1, therefore, this is a test cross

Yy × yy
(From F_1) (From P)

(b) The ratio is close to 3: 1, therefore, this is interbreeding between two F_1 plants, genotypes would be Yy × Yy.

(c) There is no segregation and only dominant phenotype is expressed, genotype would be YY × yy.

(d) There is no segregation and only reccessive therefore, genotypes would be yy×yy.

Example 2

A tall (TT) pea plant with smooth seeds (SS) was crossed with plants with dwarf (rr) and wrinkled (ss) seeds. Find out the following–

(a) Genotype and phenotype in F_1.

(b) Genotypes and phenotypes in a cross between F_1 plant and tall (TT) and smooth seeded (SS) plant.

(c) Genotypes and phenotypes in a cross between F_1 plant and dwarf (tt) and wrinkled seeded (ss) plant.

(d) Genotype and phenotype in F_2.

Explanation

(a) F_1 of TT SS × tt ss

Genotype	Phenotype
Tt Ss	Tall and smoth seeded plant

gametes of one parent ↓ ; gametes of another parent ←

	TS	TS	TS	TS
ts	Tt Ss	Tt Ss	Tt Ss	Tt Ss
ts	Tt Ss	Tt Ss	Tt Ss	Tt Ss
ts	Tt Ss	Tt Ss	Tt Ss	Tt Ss
ts	Tt Ss	Tt ss	Tt Ss	Tt Ss

All plants of F_1 show same phenotype and genotype.
Phenotype : Tall and smooth
Genotype : Tt Ss

(b) Cross between TtSs (F_1) × TT SS

Genotypes	Phenotypes
TT SS TT Ss Tt SS Tt Ss	Ali tall and smooth seeded plant

(c) Cross botween Tt Ss (F_1)× tt ss

Genotypes	Phenotypes
1 : Tt Ss 1 : Tt ss 1 : tt Ss 1 : tt ss	1 : Tall and smooth seeded 1 : Tall and wrinkled seeded 1 : Dwarf and smooth seeded 1 : Dwarf and wrinkled seeded

(d) Genotype and phenotype of F_2 (i. e. cross between Tt Ss× Tt Ss)

Genotypes		Phenotypes
TT SS Tt SS TT Ss Tt Ss	1 2 2 4	9 : Tall and smooth seeded plants
TT ss Tt ss	1 2	3 : Tall and wrinkled seeded plants
tt Ss tt Ss	1 2	3 : Dwarf and Smooth seeded plants
tt ss	1	1 : Dwarf and wrinkled seeded plant

F_1 plants selfed to produce F_2 generation

male gametes ↓ ; **female gametes** ←

	TS	Ts	tS	ts
TS	TT SS	TT Ss	Tt SS	Tt Ss
Ts	TT Ss	TT ss	Tt Ss	Tt ss
tS	Tt Ss	Tt Ss	tt SS	tt Ss
ts	Tt Ss	Tt ss	tt Ss	tt ss

Phenotypes :	Tall smooth	Tall wrinkled	Dwarf smooth	Dwarf wrinkled
Genotypes :	TTSS 1 TtSS 2 TTSs 2 TtSs 4	TTss 1 Ttss 2	ttSS 1 ttSs 2	ttss 1
Phenotype : ratio	9	3	3	1

Example 3

In snap-dragon, homozygous flowers may be red or white. The heterozygous flowers are pink. What would be the genotypes and phenotypes of F_2 generation.

Explanation

Homozygous red (RR) × Homozygous white (rr) **P**

↓

Heterozygous pink (Rr) **F_1**

F_2 generation is obtained by selfing

Rr× Rr

Genotypes		Phenotypes
RR	1	1 : Red flower
Rr	2	2 : Pink flowers
rr	1	1 : White flower

This is an example of **incomplete dominance.**

Example 4

In sweet pea *Lathyrus odoratus*, purple flowers are dominant over white flowers. A cross between two white flowered plants (cc pp × cc PP), purple flower was obtained in F_1. Find out the genotypes and phenotypes of F_2

Explanation

White (CC pp) × White (cc PP) **P**

↓

Purple (Cc Pp) **F_1**

F_2 generation is obtained by selfing Cc Pp.

Since purple colour is developed only when both C and P are present following genotypes and phenotypes would be obtained.

Genotypes		Phenotypes
CC PP	1	9 : Purple flowered
CCPp	2	
CcPP	2	
Cc Pp	4	
CC pp	1	7 : White flowered
Cc pp	2	
cc PP	1	
cc Pp	2	
cc pp	1	

This is an example of **duplicate recessive epistasis.**

Example 5

In poultry there are three comb types- rose (R), pea (P) and walnut (RP). Recessive genes produce fourth type – the single (rr or pp). Rose (RR pp) and pea (rr PP) were crossed. F_1 offspring was walnut (Rr Pp). Find out genotypes and phenotypes of a cross between two walnut (Rr Pp) combed chicken.

Explanation

Rr Pp × Rr Pp would produce following genotypes and phenotypes

Genotypes		Phenotypes
RR PP	1	9 : Walnut
Rr PP	2	
RR Pp	2	
Rr Pp	4	
RR pp	1	3 : Rose
Rr pp	2	
rr PP	1	3 : Pea
rr Pp	2	
rr pp	1	1 : Single

This is an example showing **modified dihybrid ratio.**

11

Experiments in Plant Physiology

The Procedure

In a physiology laboratory student either watches a demonstration or performs the experiment himself. He is expected to follow certain instructions so that laboratory work becomes useful.

The following are some of the useful hints.

1. A student should first read the procedure of the experiment from the book and then attend the laboratory.
2. The details and the instructions given by the teacher in the laboratory should be patiently heard and carefully understood.
3. The theoretical aspects involving the experiment may also please be already read and kept in mind while conducting or observing the experiment.
4. It is important to remember the equipment required and how to assemble it.
5. After procuring the necessary equipment assemble it and then experiment should be started.
6. The expected observations may be carefully noted.
7. Once the experiment is over, write the various details under following heads –
   (a) Object
   (b) Materials required
   (c) Procedure or method
   (d) Observations or results
   (e) Conclusions
8. See that conclusions drawn are compatible with the theoretical background.

I. Cell : Protoplasm and Membranes

Preamble

The plant is made of many basic structural and functional units – the cell. It is a unit of protoplasm surrounded by a membrane. A cell is dynamic and highly organised system of interdependent and interacting components. The protoplasm which is a viscous fluid, comprises 5 to 90 or more percent of water. Large number of protoplasmic inclusions (organelles) remain embedded in this protoplasm. Some of the significant organelles are – **mitochondria** – concerned with respiration; **Golgi apparatus** or dictyosomes – supposed to have role in secretion; **plastids** (particularly chloroplasts) – concerned with trapping of light energy and synthesis of carbohydrates (photosynthesis); ribosomes – site of protein synthesis, **nucleus** – controlling the cell metabolism, etc.

The protoplasm, with much of particulate phase colloidal in nature, consists of hydrophilic and hydrophobic colloidal complexes. Hydrophilic sol is formed mainly of amino acids, sugars and inorganic ions while hydrophobic system consists of fats and oils which appear suspended as droplets. The substances of hydrophilic system are attracted into the bulk phase, where they absorb water molecules, thus maintaining continuous aqueous phase of the protoplasmic colloid. The fats and oils due to their property to repel water molecules tend to collect in interfacial films of the cytoplasm.

The protoplasm of the living cell shows constant movement known as cyclosis – a characteristic of plant cells. The cessation of this movement is one of the first signs of cell death.

Nearly all plant cells possess a cell wall around the cell membrane or plasma membrane. The cell wall is primarily a rigid structure which provides skeletal support and protects against osmotic pressure. Cell membrane regulates continuous movements of substances into and out of the cell. It is a selectively permeable membrane which allows certain substances to pass through it more easily than others.

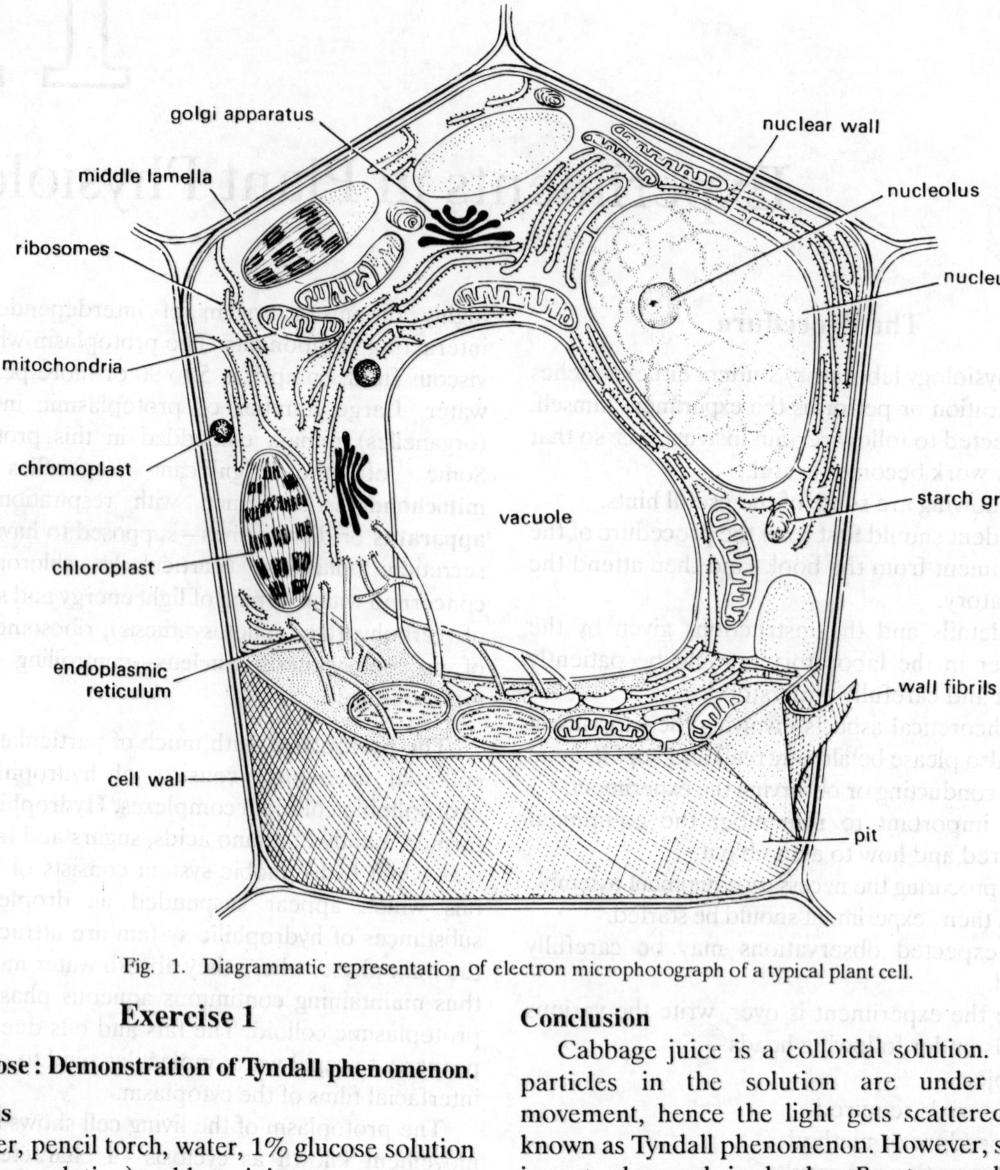

Fig. 1. Diagrammatic representation of electron microphotograph of a typical plant cell.

Exercise 1

Purpose : Demonstration of Tyndall phenomenon.

Materials

Beaker, pencil torch, water, 1% glucose solution (or any true solution), cabbage juice, etc.

Procedure

1. Pour cabbage solution in beaker *A* and 1% glucose solution in beaker *B* (or any true solution).
2. Pass a beam of light by pencil torch through both the beakers placed in the dark.
3. Observe the beam of light at right angles.

Results

1. When passed through beaker *A*, the light gets scattered in the direction of the observer.
2. This phenomenon is not observed when light is passed through beaker *B*.

Conclusion

Cabbage juice is a colloidal solution. Colloidal particles in the solution are under constant movement, hence the light gets scattered. This is known as Tyndall phenomenon. However, scattering is not observed in beaker *B* a true solution, (a particle-free homogenate), Tyndall phenomenon is a method to distinguish a true solution from a colloidal solution.

Exercise 2

Purpose : Preparation of a suspension.

Materials

Barium chloride solution, dilute sulphuric acid, test tube, test tube holder, test tube stand, etc.

Procedure

1. Pour a little of barium chloride solution in a test tube.

2. Add little amount of sulphuric acid to the test tube.
3. Shake well. Keep the tube undisturbed.

Results

A precipitate of barium sulphate settles down.

Conclusion

Precipitate is a suspension where particles do not separate and remain dispersed as such throughout the liquid. The suspensions form unstable system and the particles gradually settle down in the container.

Exercise 3

Purpose : Preparation of an emulsion.

Materials

Olive oil or mustard oil (or any non- volatile oil), water, test tube, etc.

Procedure

1. Pour a few drops of oil in a test tube filled with water.
2. Shake well and keep undisturbed for some time.

Results and conclusions

The droplets of oil remain dispersed even after vigorously shaking the test tube. The oil and water appear as separate layers, after sometime.

In an emulsion dispersed phase (oil) remains dispersed in the dispersion phase (water). The droplets of oil coalesce to form larger droplets until two distinct layers are formed.

Two immiscible liquids form an emulsion. The particles of dispersed phase are generally larger than the colloidal particle size.

Exercise 4

Purpose : To prepare a suspensoid.

Materials

Water, ferric chloride, test tube, spirit lamp, etc.

Procedure

1. Heat water in test tube over spirit lamp.
2. Add ferric chloride till a concentrated solution is prepared.

Results and conclusion

Ferric hydroxide molecules are formed as a result of chemical reaction. These form the dispersed phase of the colloidal solution known as suspensoid (= lyophobic solution = hydrophobic solution = irreversible colloid). In this case, there is a complete lack of strong affinity between a dispersed phase and the liquid in which it is dispersed.

(Similarly colloidal suspension of arsenic sulphide can be prepared by bubbling H_2S gas into a solution of arsenic oxide).

Exercise 5

Purpose : To Prepare an emulsoid.

Materials

Starch (agar-agar or gelatin etc.), hot water, test tube, a glass rod, spirit lamp, etc.

Procedure

1. Take a test tube. Pour little amount of water. Heat over spirit lamp and bring water to boil.
2. Add starch (agar-agar or gelatin, etc.) to the test tube. Keep stirring with a glass rod till the solid gets evenly dispersed.

Results and conclusions

The colloidal solution or emulsoid is formed in this way. It is lyophilic with a strong affinity between a dispersed phase and the liquid in which it is dispersed. If the dispersion medium used is water, the colloidal solution is known as hydrophilic.

Exercise 6

Purpose : Demonstration of Brownian movement.

Materials

Slide, cover-slip, microscope, latex from *Calotropis* (or India ink or plant or fruit juice, etc.)

Procedure

1. Place a drop of latex (or India ink or cabbage juice) on a slide and cover with a glass cover-slip.
2. Examine the slide under the high power of the microscope. (If possible, use a strong beam of light, allowing only diffused light to reach the object).

Results and conclusions

The particles in the material appear as bright illuminated points moving randomly and irregularly.

In a colloidal solution, uneven bombardment of the minute colloidal particles is caused by the molecules of the dispersion medium (solvent). This results in movement of the colloidal particles in the direction of least resistance (which continues to change constantly). This phenomenon of irregular movement of colloidal particles is known as Brownian movement.

Exercise 7

Purpose : To observe streaming movement (cyclosis) of the protoplasm.

Materials

Leaves of *Hydrilla, Vallisneria, Elodea* (or staminal hair of *Tradescantia*) or Moss (fresh), slide, cover-slip, water, microscope, etc.

Procedure

1. Pluck a young and living leaf. Tear off the epidermis or mount entire leaf (Moss) in a drop of water.
2. Observe under the microscope, especially the chloroplasts.

Results

Chloroplasts appear to move. This is due to the streaming movement of the protoplasm. This is known as rotation. (In *Tradescantia* small parts of protoplasm move independently and in different directions. This phenomenon of cyclosis is called circulation).

(*Use young leaves near the tip*).

Exercise 8

Purpose : To demonstrate the importance of living membrane.

Materials

Beet root (roots of *Beta vulgaris),* cork borer, water, ice, spirit lamp, beaker, test tubes, test tube stand, wire gauze, tripod stand, thermometer, alcohol, etc.

Procedure

1. Cut eight slices of beet root with cork borer.
2. Fill in eight test tubes with water. Place a piece of beet root in each test tube after it has been repeatedly washed with water.
3. Warm water in beaker. Dip one test tube each, in the beaker when temperature of the water reaches 30°C, 40°C, 50°C, 80°C, and 100°C.
4. Also add ice cold water and alcohol to the remaining test tubes.

Results

The intensity of the red colour increases with increase in temperature. The water becomes red when ice cold water or alcohol is added.

Conclusions

The appearance of the red colour in the test tube is due to diffusion of anthocyanin pigment from inside the cell to external medium. In a living cell the selectively permeable membrane does not allow anthocyanin to diffuse out. However, with the increase in temperature, the cell is killed and the selective permeability of the cell membrane is lost. Hence, the anthocyanin diffuses out freely. Living membrane, therefore, controls the passage of cell contents as long as it is living.

Ice cold water and chemicals like alcohol also have similar effects.

II. Osmosis, Imbibition and Plasmolysis

Preamble

The cytoplasm and organelles of a cell are surrounded by a cell membrane. It is a selectively permeable membrane which controls the movement of solutes and solvents in and out of the cell. The movement of water through a semi-permeable or selectively permeable membrane is called osmosis. Water moves into the cell, when placed in pure water. The entry of water produces an outward pressure called turgor pressure. The elastic cell membrane exerts an equal and opposite pressure called wall pressure. The cell with maximum amount of water pressing against the wall is called turgid. A cell without a turgor pressure is known as flaccid.

With the entry of water into the cell, turgor pressure increases while the osmotic concentration decreases. The difference between osmotic pressure (osmotic concentration) and the turgor pressure allows the passage of water, in and out of the cell. This difference is known as Diffusion Pressure Deficit (DPD). Gradually osmotic pressure becomes equal to the turgor pressure. At this stage, the DPD is zero and the cell is called turgid.

The following conditions would show how the changes occur when the concentrations of solutions are altered –

Cell Sap	External Medium	The Result
1. Concentration more i.e. (a) cell sap concentrated or (b) less solvent mols. Cell sap **Hypertonic**	1. Concentration less i.e. solution dilute or more solvent mols. Solution **Hypotonic.**	(i) external solution hypotonic, (ii) water moves into the cell, (iii) cell volume increases, (iv) process is **endosmosis.**
2. Concentration less i.e. (a) cell sap dilute or (b) more solvent mols Cell sap **Hypotonic**	2. Concentration more i.e. solution concentrated or less solvent mols. 3. Solution **Hypertonic**	(i) external solution hypertonic, (ii) water moves out of the cell, (iii) cell volume decreases, (iv) process is **exosmosis.**
3. Concentration same in both. same number of solvent mols.	Solution **Isotonic**	(i) both solutions **isotonic** (ii) no movement of water, (iii) no change in volume.

If a dry material (e.g., seeds) is placed in water, it wells up considerably. This is due to imbibition. It s a special type of diffusion between solvent and dry naterial called imbibant. As a result of swelling, great amount of imbibition pressure is developed.

Exercise 1

Purpose : To demonstrate the phenomenon of osmosis by using goat bladder/parchment paper.

Materials

Sugar solution, water, thistle funnel, parchment paper or membrane from goat's bladder, thread, beaker, stands, razor or safety blade, etc.

Procedure

1. Tie a piece of parchment paper or membrane from goat's bladder to the broad mouth of the thistle funnel.
2. Fill the thistle funnel with concentrated sugar solution. Mark the level of sugar solution in the funnel.
3. Dip the funnel into the beaker containing water. Allow the experiment to stand for some time.

Results

The level of sugar solution in the thistle funnel rises.

Conclusions

The rise is due to entry of water into the thistle funnel (the region of low concentration of water molecules) from the beaker (the region of high concentration of its molecules) through the cell membrane. The movement of water molecules from its region of higher concentration to its region of lower concentration through a semi-permeable membrane (cell membrane) is known as osmosis.

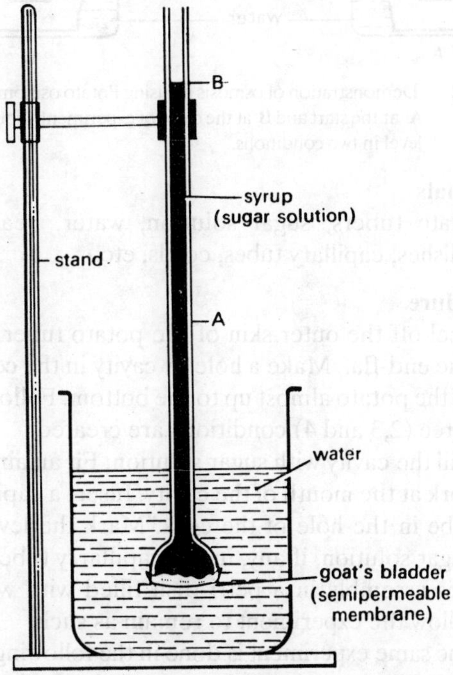

Fig. 1. Demonstration of osmosis by using goat bladder.

After allowing the experiment to remain as such watch the rise in the level after some time. It does not change at all, indicating that the concentration of water molecules in the beaker and inside the thistle funnel has become equal.

Exercise 2

Purpose : To domonstrate the osmosis by using potato osmometer.

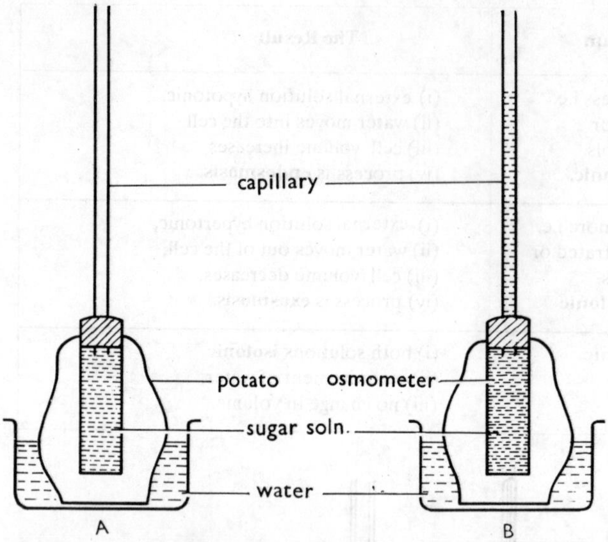

Fig. 2. Demonstration of osmosis by using Potato osmometer. **A** at the start and **B** at the close of experiment. Note the level in two conditions.

Materials

Potato tubers, sugar solution, water, beakers, petri dishes, capillary tubes, cords, etc.

Procedure

1. Peel off the outer skin of the potato tuber. Cut one end-flat. Make a hole or cavity in the centre of the potato almost up to the bottom. Following three (2,3 and 4) conditions are created.
2. Fill the cavity with sugar solution. Fit an airtight cork at the mouth of the cavity. Insert a capillary tube in the hole of the cork. Mark the level of sugar solution, if any, in the capillary tube. Put this assembly in a petri dish filled with water. Allow the experiment to remain as such.
3. The same experiment is done in the following way also. Fill the cavity of the potato tuber with sugar solution. Mark the level in the cavity by piercing a pin. Place this tuber in a petri dish containing pure water.
4. The cavity of the other tuber is filled with water and the level is marked by piercing a pin. This tuber is placed in a petri dish containing concentrated sugar solution.

Results and conclusions

In case **2**, the level in the capillary begins to rise and becomes stable after sometime. This is due to osmosis where water moves from the petri dish into the cavity of the tuber through semi- permeabl tuber cells.

In case **3**, the initial level 'A' rises to level 'B' afte some time. The increase is due to the movement o water from the outside (*i.e.* petri dish) throug semi-permeable membranes of the potato tuber Since the osmosis shows the movement of wate from outside into the tuber, the process i endosmosis. There is an increase in the volum whenever endosmosis takes place.

In case **4**, the initial level 'A' falls to 'B', afte sometime. The decrease or fall in the level is due t the movement of water from inside the tuber to th outside. The outer solution in this case is hypertoni and hence the water moves out of the cavity of tuber This phenomenon of osmosis is called exosmosis.

Demonstration of exosmosis and endosmosis ca also be repeated by placing fresh grapes, potat slices, garden beet, etc. in sugar solution and water respectively.

Exercise 3

Purpose : To prepare a semi-permeabl membrane – collodion bag.

Materials

Wide mouthed tube, collodion (cellulose nitrat dissolved in alcohol and ether), water, toluol, etc.

Procedure

1. Take a wide mouthed tube. Clean and dry i thoroughly.
2. Pour a small amount of collodian solution int the tube. Gradually pour back collodion whil revolving the tube gently so that the liquid get evenly spread over the inner wall.
3. Invert the tube and allow the contents to dry fo about 10-15 minutes.
4. Another layer of collodion is formed inside the tub in the same fashion. The tube with collodion layer i now allowed to dry for about 5-7 hours.
5. After the collodion is dry, loosen the membran gently and cautiously. Pour water into the tub between the glass wall and the membrane.
6. Lift the sac of collodion membrane out of the tub very carefully.

This collodion bag can be used as a semi-permeabl membrane. It is preserved in distilled water to which a few drops of toluol are added.

Exercise 4

Purpose : To demonstrate the phenomenon of lialysis.

/laterials

Collodion bag, starch, common salt, water, •eaker, silver nitrate, iodine, a rod, thread, etc.

'rocedure

.. Prepare a mixture of starch and common salt solution.
:. Fill the collodion bag with this mixture. Close the mouth of bag with thread and suspend it into a beaker containing water.
;. Allow the experiment to remain as such for some time.
l. Test the solution in the beaker for common salt with silver nitrate and for starch with iodine.

Results

The silver nitrate test is positive. This indicates he presence of common salt. The iodine test is legative, showing that the starch is absent.

Conclusions

The experiment shows that the starch has failed :o move out of the collodion bag into water, while common salt (sodium chloride) moved out into the beaker. The starch is a crystalloid and can not diffuse hrough the membrane in the form of molecules. The common salt is a not a colloid and its particles can pass through the membrane. This is due to the size of he colloidal particles and their rate of diffusion. This phenomenon or property of colloids is used in separating them from a true solution by the process called dialysis.

Exercise 5

Purpose : Measurement of the Diffusion Pressure-Deficit (Suction pressure) of plant cells.

Materials

Sugar, water, cork borer (hollow cylinder with piston), petri dishes, pipette, scale, watch glass, balance with weighing box, etc.

Procedure

1. Take a potato tuber and remove the skin. Then bore a hollow cylinder into the tuber and with the piston take out a cylinder of tissue. Cut the cylinder into about 20 equal- sized slices.
2. Also prepare 0.10M, 0.20M, 0.25M and 0.30M solutions of sugar. Pour approximately equal quantity of each solution into four different petri dishes and mark them as A, B, C and D respectively.
3. Weigh the cylinders or slices of tuber. Place the slices into the petri dishes containing different molar concentrations of sugar solutions. Cover the petri dishes.
4. After some time (preferably 24 hours), remove the cylinders, blot away the excess solution and reweigh. Record the gain or loss of weight.

Results

A tentative scheme is privided herewith.

Sr. No.	Conc. of the soln. M	Initial wt. of the potato slices (in g)	Final wt. of the potato slices (in g)	Loss/gain
A	0.10	0.423	0.517	Gain
B	0.20	0.435	0.495	Gain
C	0.25	0.558	0.556	Almost negligible.
D	0.30	0.497	0.463	Loss

There is no change in the weight of potato slices placed in the 0.25 molar concentration of sugar solution.

Conclusions

1. In petri dishes A and B weight increases because the volume of the cell increases when placed in a hypotonic solution. This is due to endosmosis.
2. In case of D the weight decreases because the volume of the cell decreases when water moves from inside to the outside. Thus the solution outside is hypertonic.

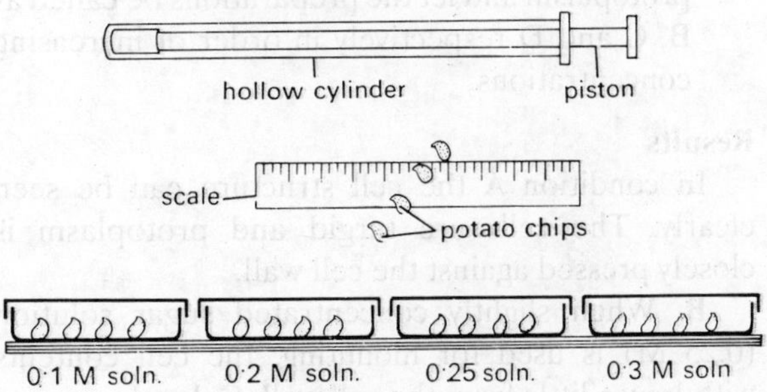

Fig. 4. Measurement of DPD. A. cylinder and potato slices. B Potato slices in different solutions.

3. In petri dish C, there is no change in the weight (the loss shown in observations being taken as negligible). This happens only if there is no movement of water molecules from inside the cell or into the cell. Thus, the sugar solution (0.25 M) should be isotonic with the cell sap. This indicates that the osmotic concentration of the cell sap is equal to 0.25 molar.

The osmotic presure of the solution, in which no gain or loss of weight occurs, is considered to be equal to the diffusion- pressure deficit of the cells of the potato tuber (DPD-OP). Therefore, the DPD is 0.25 M.

Exercise 6

Purpose : To study the phenomenon of plasmolysis.

Materials

Tradescantia/Rhoeo discolor leaf, safety blade, sugar solutions of different concentrations, cover-slips, slides, water, microscope, etc.

Procedure

1. Peel off a small segment from the lower leaf surface. This can be done by tearing the leaf obliquely with a single jerk or scraping it with safety blade.
2. Mount the peel in a drop of water on a slide and then place a cover-slip. Observe under the microscope. Draw the protoplasm and let the preparation be called as A.
3. Take another peel and similarly mount pieces in a drop of sugar solutions of different concentrations (0.25 M, 0.5 M and 0.75 M). Observe each preparation under the microscope. Draw the boundaries of protoplasm and let the preparations be called as B, C and D respectively in order of increasing concentrations.

Results

In condition **A** the cell structure can be seen clearly. The cells are turgid and protoplasm is closely pressed against the cell wall.

B. When slightly concentrated sugar solution (0.25 M) is used for mounting, the cell contents withdraw a little from the cell wall. Colourless space between cell wall and the coloured cell sap, is distinct.

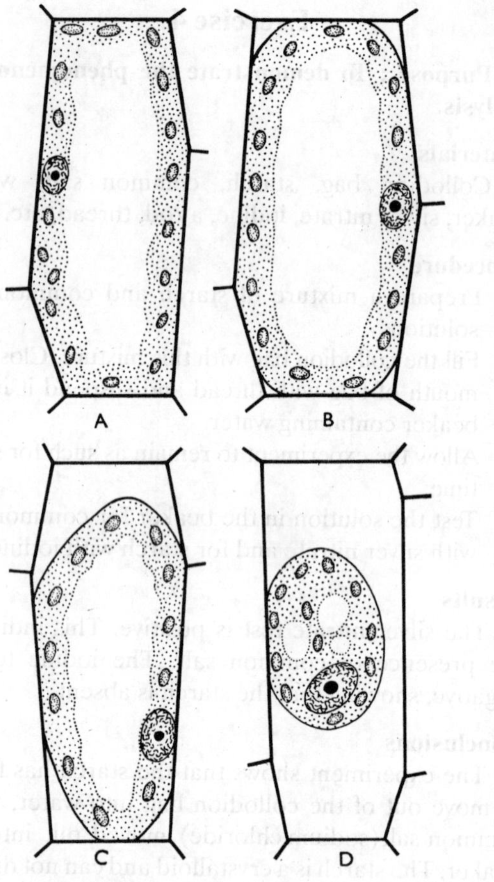

Fig. 5. Cells showing phenomenon of plasmolysis. A. Normal cell, **B.** Cell showing contraction of cytoplasm beginning at the corners in contact with cell wall (incipient plasmolysis), **C.** Contraction of cytoplasm proceeds further and **D.** plasmolysed cell.

C. When a little more concentrated sugar solution (0.5 M) is used, the cell contents move appreciably away from the cell wall, leaving a considerable space between the wall and the sap.

D. When the peel is mounted in a drop of concentrated sugar solution (0.75 M) the cell contents withdraw from the cell wall and shrink into a small, round and ball-like form.

Conclusions

Preparation **A** shows normal condition where cell sap presses the protoplasm against the cell wall which is slightly inflated. The cell is called turgid.

B. The withdrawal of the cell contents is due to the loss of water from the cell (exosmosis). The small space between the cell wall and the contents indicates the beginning of plasmolysis, and is known as incipient plasmolysis.

C and **D.** With the increase in the concentration of sugar solution outside, the space between the cell wall and the contents increases. Finally, due to continued exosomosis the cell contents shrink and collect on one side.Such a cell is called plasmolysed.

In a plasmolysed cell, the space between the cell wall and the contents is filled with the hypertonic solution placed outside the cell. The incipient plasmolysis can be stopped if such a cell is placed either in pure water or hypotonic solution. The cell then attains its normal structure (turgidity) due to endosmosis. The process is known as deplasmolysis. But if the plasmolysis continues, the cells show desiccation and plant becomes permanently wilted.

(This experiment can also be done by using petals of *Thunbergia* and *Luffa,* leaves of *Zebrina* and *Hydrilla,* staminal hairs of *Tradescantia,* and vegetative and large filaments of *Spirogyra*).

Exercise 7

Purpose : To demonstrate the phenomenon of imbibition.

Materials

Gram seeds, water, watch-glasses, etc.

Procedure

1. Take a few gram seeds. Put them in water in a watch- glass.
2. Keep the seeds for 10-15 minutes as such.

Results

After some time seeds appear considerably swollen.

Conclusions

The increase in the volume of seeds is due to a special type of diffusion called imbibition. Seeds which are particulary high in colloidal material are very good imbibants. The proteins and carbohydrates are hydrophilic colloids and major imbibants. The diffusion pressure of water present in

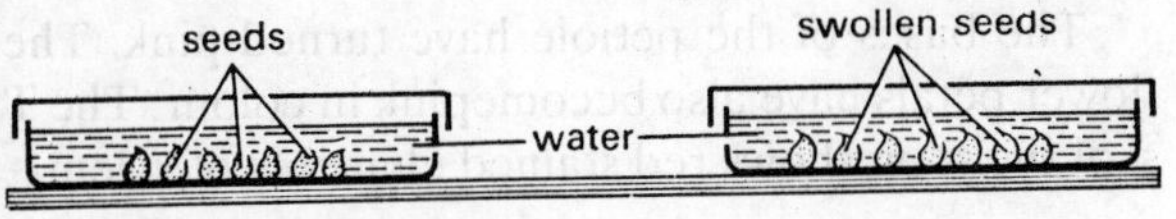

Fig. 6 Demonstration of imbibition. **A.** Seeds at the beginning of experiment and **B.** Seeds swollen due to imbibition.

these dry colloids is practically zero. Hence, when the material is immersed in water a sharp diffusion pressure gradient is established. Thus, the water moves rapidly into the imbibant till the diffusion pressure of the imbibant and water becomes equal.

Exercise 8

Purpose : To demonstrate that pressure is developed during imbibition.

Materials

A bottle with airtight cork, an airtight disc fitting into the bottle to which a pointer is attached outside the cork of bottle, a scale attached to the stand, water and a few gram seeds, etc.

Procedure

1. Pour water into bottle and put a few seeds upto the water surface.
2. Adjust the disc just over the seeds and the pointer over zero mark on the scale.
3. Allow the experiment to remain as such overnight.

Results

The pointer moves down. The disc has moved a little upwards. The seeds are swollen considerably.

Conclusions

The hydrophilic colloids of the gram seeds imbibe water and, therefore, swell up. The increase in size is accompanied with pressure that pushes the disc. Subsequently, the pointer also moves down. Though the term "imbibition pressure" is the maximum potential pressure that an imbibant will develop if submerged in pure water, the actual pressure that develops, such as the one in this experiment is a result of osmotic phenomenon and

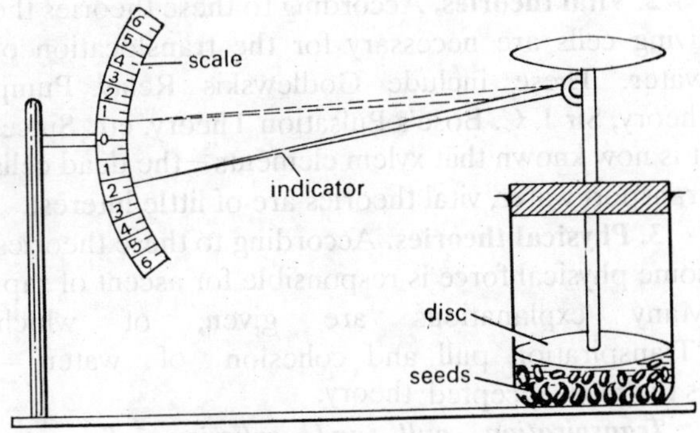

Fig. 7. Apparatus to demonstrate imbibiton pressure.

is, therefore logically a turgor pressure. This pressure, however, will not develop in an unconfined imbibant (i.e., till the seeds are enclosed and prevented from swelling.)

III. Ascent of Sap

Preamble

Water is mostly absorbed from the soil by the roots. It is lost (transpired) by the aerial organs of the plant especially the leaves. The distances between absorbing and transpiring organs vary from a few inches to about 400 feet. This requires an effective water transport mechanism. The process by which water is transported from the roots to the tops of the plant is called Ascent of Sap.

The water is absorbed from the soil by root hairs. It moves through the cortex, endodermis and pericycle before reaching the xylem elements of the root. The xylem elements of the root are in contact with the xylem ducts of the stem. Thus, the water is transported to the xylem of the stem. Ultimately the xylem of stem being in contact with xylem of the leaf, water reaches the leaves. consequently, water from the leaf veins moves into mesophyll cells and is lost through the stomates to the environment. The above cells and tissues form the path of water movement.

Many theories are given to explain the movements of water and forces responsible for it.

1. Root pressure. The exudation of water from the cut end of the stem is due to root pressure. It is defined as "a pressure developing in the tracheary elements of xylem as a result of metabolic activities of the roots". The pressure developed is very less and insufficient to transport the water to great heights.

2. Vital theories. According to these theories the living cells are necessary for the translocation of water. These include Godlewskis Relay Pump theory, Sir J. C. Bose's Pulsation Theory, etc. Since, it is now known that xylem elements – the dead cells transport water, vital theories are of little interest.

3. Physical theories. According to these theories some physical force is responsible for ascent of sap. Many explanations are given, of which "Transpiration pull and cohesion of water" – is the most accepted theory.

Transpiration pull and cohesion of water. According to this theory, a continuous water column is formed through the path described earlier. The water in the cells adjacent the sub- stomatal cavity is lost (transpired) through the stomates of the leaf. The sap of these cells now becomes more concentrated than the neighbouring cell. Hence, there is a movement of water (along diffusion gradient) to the cell which has lost water. This makes up the water deficit of the cell. The neighbouring cell having lost its water would similarly require water from another neighbouring cell (with more concentration of water molecules). This chain continues through the same path but in the direction of stomates to root hair. This force of gradual movement of water from one cell to another is known as transpiration pull.

The water column throughout the network of tracheary elements remains unbroken because of the cohesive force among water molecules. The water molecules remain attracted to the wall of the tracheary elements because of their adhesive force for the wall. Therefore, the water column shall not break until cohesive and adhesive forces are overcome.

Exercise 1

Purpose : To demonstrate that water moves through the xylem.

Materials

Eosin solution, a small potted plant (*e.g. Impatiens*), stand, test tube, cotton plug, razor slide, cover- slip, glycerine, microscope, etc.

Procedure

1. Fill the test tube with eosin solution. Insert the roots of small plant into the tube. Plug the mouth of the tube with cotton. Keep the tube fixed to a stand.
2. After a few hours watch the colour of the base of the petioles and the flower petals.
3. Cut a T. s. of the stem and observe under the microscope.

Results

The bases of the petiole have turned pink. The flower petals have also becomepink in colour. The T s. of the stem shows red stained elements of xylem.

Conclusions

The bases of the petioles and the flower petals become pink indicating that the eosin has reached

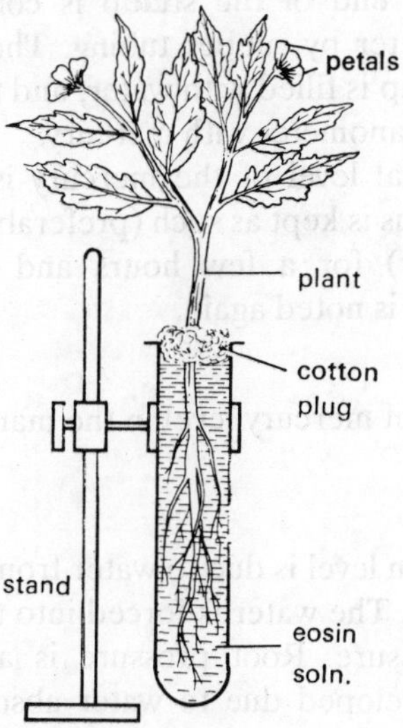

Fig. 1. Demonstration that water moves through xylem.

these organs. The movement of water, therefore, takes place from the roots to the leaves and flowers through the stem. This experiment demonstrates that (a) water is absorbed by the roots and (b) is transported upwards up to leaves.

The xylem takes up the stain of eosin. It shows that the eosin solution (and similarly water) moves through the xylem elements. The path of water, therefore, is through the xylem of the root, stem and leaves.

Exercise 2

Purpose : To demonstrate that ascent of sap takes place through the xylem by ringing method.

Materials

A twig or part of the plant, beaker, water, razor and wax, etc.

Procedure

1. Take a plant and remove a ring of a bark (all the tissues from epidermis upto phloem) about one inch in length without causing injury to the cambium below.
2. Take another twig and remove xylem elements without injuring the cortex and the phloem. (This can be done by using wax or vaseline. The xylem or phloem and cortex can be blocked by applying wax or grease to these elements.)

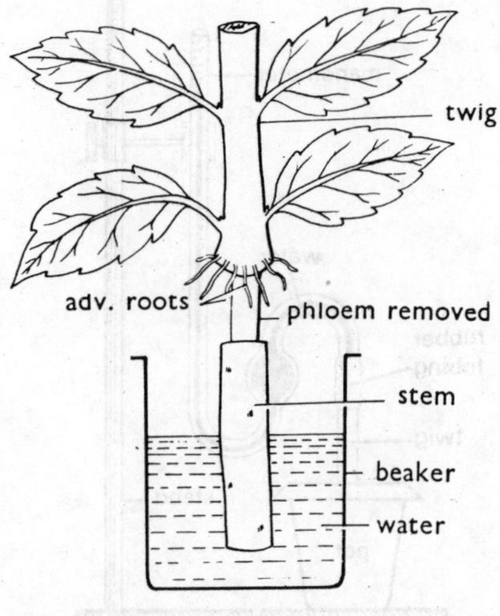

Fig. 2. Ringing experiment to demonstrate that ascent of sap takes place through xylem.

3. The ringing (removal of tissues) should always be done while the twigs are under water. Immerse the twigs in separate beakers containing water. Allow them to stand for a few hours.

Results

In condition 1 the plant remains unchanged and the leaves are turgid even after ringing. In condition 2 the leaves wilt and loose their normal condition if xylem is blocked.

Conclusions

1. The leaves remain turgid because of continued transport of water. The removal of phloem and cortex (bark) has not disturbed the water movement. This indicates that cortex and phloem do not play any role in this process. The undisturbed xylem must have transported water upwards.
2. The wilting occurs when water does not reach the leaves to keep them turgid. The xylem being removed, the path of water transport is disturbed. It shows that even though the cortex and phloem are present, ascent of sap does not take place if xylem is blocked. The xylem, therefore, is the tissue which conducts the water.

Exercise 3

Purpose : To demonstrate the root pressure.

Materials

A well-watered potted plant, a razor, rubber tubing, manometer, mercury, water, stand, etc.

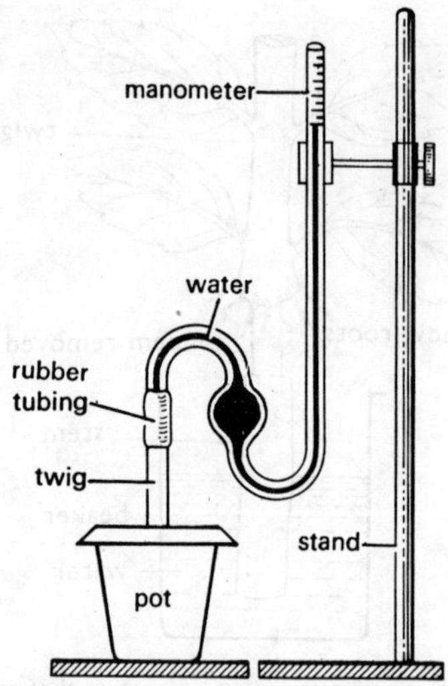

Fig. 3. Demonstration of root pressure.

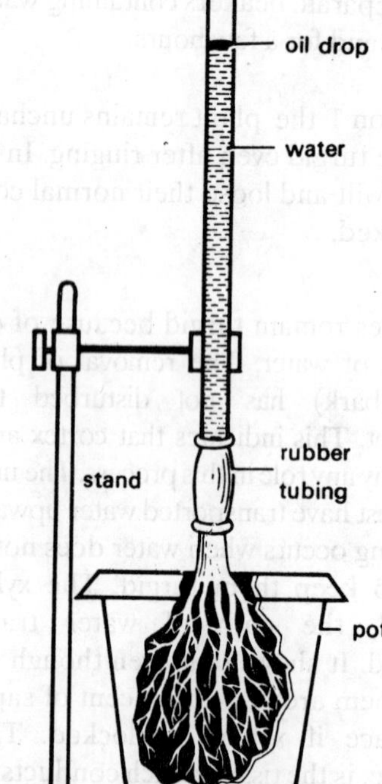

Fig. 4. Apparatus used for the demonstration of root pressure.

Procedure

1. The plant is watered heavily. The shoot of the potted plant is cut off a few inches above soil level just below the first leaf.
2. The cut end of the stump is connected to a manometer by rubber tubing. The tube above the stump is filled with water, and the bent tube of the manometer with mercury.
3. The initial level of the mercury is noted. The apparatus is kept as such (preferably in a humid chamber) for a few hours and the level of mercury is noted again.

Results

The rise of mercury level in the manometer tube is observed.

Conclusions

The rise in level is due to water from the cut end of the stamp. The water is forced into the stem due to root pressure. Root pressure is a hydrostatic pressure developed due to water absorbed by the roots.

If plant is not heavily watered, the water level falls down, because water is used by the cut end of the 'stump'. This is called negative root pressure. It occurs if absorption of water is less than the rate of transpiration. The conditions which do not allow proper absorption of water such as poor aeration, cold or dry soil, high concentration of solutes in the soil or presence of toxic substances, as well as those conditions which allow high rate of transpiration, either reduce or prevent root pressure. Hence the water from the water reservoir (or plant) shall be absorbed by the twig. The positive root pressure is seen early in the morning because all the favourable conditions are available to the plant during night.

The root pressure is said to be responsible for the ascent of sap. However, a very little pressure is developed which transports water only to a few feet

Exercise 4

Purpose : To demonstrate water lifting power of transpiration.

Materials

Stand, beaker, a glass tube or capillary tube with a wide mouth, cork, oil cloth, plant or twig, water, mercury, beaker, etc.

Procedure

1. Fill beaker (or petri dish) with mercury. Invert a capillary over the mercury and fill it with water.
2. Insert the twig through hole into the cork in a way that the cut end of the plant is dipped in the

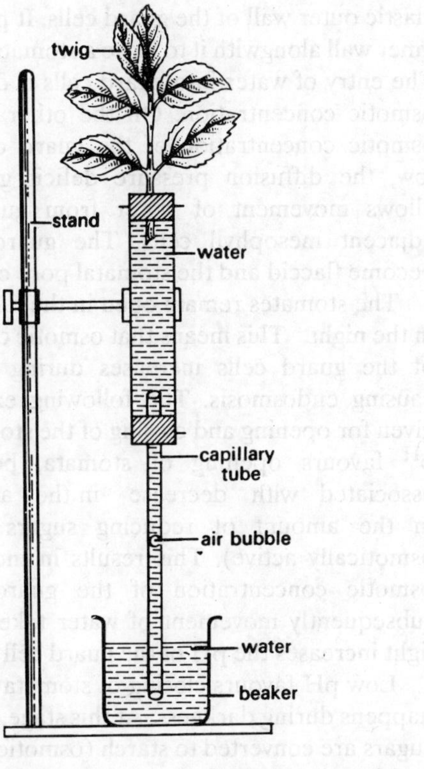

Fig. 5. Demonstratation of water lifting power of transpiration.

water. Make the cork and hole airtight by applying vaseline or tie oilcloth securely around it.

3. Note the initial level of mercury in the capillary.
4. Allow the experiment to stand in open and sunny place. Note the level of mercury at the end of the experiment.

Results

The level of mercury rises.

Conclusions

The plant transpires and absorbs water to make up the deficit thus created. This results in pull or suction, called as transpiration pull.

The transpiration pull exerts a tension on the water present in the conducting tracheary elements. This tension is passed down to the roots. Thus, the whole column of water is lifted. The mercury column is similarly pulled upward exhibiting transpiration pull.

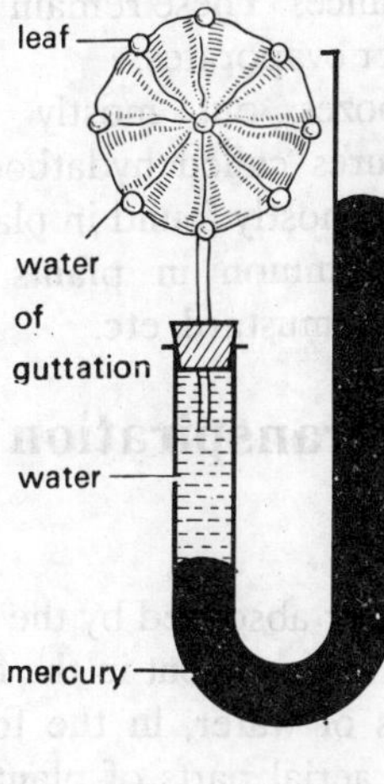

Fig. 6. Demonstration of guttation.

Exercise 5

Purpose : To demonstrate the phenomenon of guttation.

Materials

U-tube, mercury, water, a cork with a single hole, a leaf of garden nasturtium, etc.

Procedure

1. Fill the water in the U tube through one end.
2. Fit a leaf through one-holed cork in a smaller arm of the tube. Make it airtight.
3. Pour a little amount of mercury in the other limb. (The mercury is placed in order to force the water into the petiole.)
4. Allow the experiment to stand for some time.

Results

The drops of water appear at the margins of the leaf near vein endings.

Conclusions

The process of water exudation from the margins of the leaf at vein endings is known as guttation. It occurs under conditions favourable for rapid water absorption, but unfavourable for rapid loss (transpiration). This is commonly evident in the morning, because water is absorbed throughout the night while transpiration is practically negligible. At this time root pressure is high and causes guttation.

The water of guttation also contains a few solutes e.g., carbohydrates, mineral salts, organic acids and nitrogenous substances. These remain as crystals on the leaf when water evaporates.

The water oozes out mostly through the specialised structures called hydathodes or water stomata which are mostly found in plants of humid tropics. This is common in plants like garden Nasturtium, grasses, mustard, etc.

IV. Transpiration

Preamble

Of the total water absorbed by the plants, about 99% is lost to the environment in the form of water vapours. The loss of water, in the form of water vapours from the aerial parts of plant is known as transpiration.

Three types of transpiration are known— (a) stomatal, (b) cuticular and (c) lenticular. The amount of water lost by cuticular and lenticular transpirations is insignificant. Major amount of water is lost through stomata.

Stomatal transpiration occurs through stomata on the leaves. Stoma is surrounded by two kidney or bean-shaped guard cells. The wall of the guard cell towards the stomatal pore is thick and inelastic while the wall away from the pore is thin and elastic. Stomata may be present on both the leaf surfaces, but are more common on lower leaf surface. The stomatal pore opens into a substomatal cavity lined by cells which are interconnected with intercellular spaces. Thus, the internal atmosphere of the leaf is in direct contact with the external environment.

The stomatal pore opens when the guard cells are turgid. At this stage, the turgor pressure pushes the elastic outer wall of the guard cells. It pulls inelastic inner wall alongwith it to leave a stomatal pore open. The entry of water into guard cells is due to higher osmotic concentration. On the other hand, if the osmotic concentration of the guard cell becomes low, the diffusion pressure deficit gradient now allows movement of water from guard cells to adjacent mesophyll cells. The guard cells then become flaccid and the stomatal pore closes.

The stomates remain open in the day and closed in the night. This means that osmotic concentration of the guard cells increases during light period causing endosmosis. The following explanation is given for opening and closing of the stomata: A high p^H favours opening of stomata, because it is associated with decrease in the and increase in the amount of reducing sugars (which are osmotically active). This results in increase in the osmotic concentration of the guard cells and subsequently movement of water takes place. The light increases the pH of the guard cell (pH 7).

Low pH favours closing of stomata (pH 5). This happens during darkness. At this stage, the reducing sugars are converted to starch (osmotically inactive) and lowers the osmotic concentration of the guard cells. Hence, subsequently water diffuses out from them to mesophyll cells. Guard cells become flaccid and the stomatal pore closes.

$$\text{Starch} \underset{\substack{\text{phosphorylase} \\ \text{pH 5}}}{\overset{\substack{\text{phosphorylase} \\ \text{pH 7}}}{\rightleftharpoons}} \text{sugar}$$

The stomatal movement is responsible for transpiration. Besides light, it depends upon

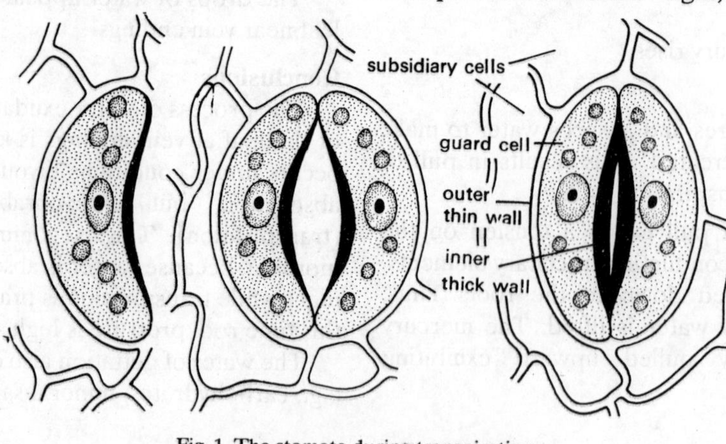

Fig. 1. The stomata during transpiration.

humidity of air, wind, temperature, leaf area and leaf structure.

The transpiration is known as "necessary evil". The loss of water is continuous even when plant needs it which is so due to structure and anatomy of leaf. However, transpiration is said to be useful in lowering the temperature, growth and development, mineral and water absorption and ascent of sap.

For study of the stomatal structure peel off tender leaves of plants such as snapdragon, Iris, daffodils, etc.

Exercise 1

Purpose : To demonstrate the phenomenon of transpiration.

Materials

A potted plant, glass plate, bell jar, oil cloth, grease, etc.

Procedure

1. Keep a potted plant on glass plate. Cover the pot and the soil with oil cloth. Invert a bell jar over the potted plant. Observe after some time.
2. Set up another experiment in exactly the same way but omit the plant. However, use the pot containing soil covered with oil cloth.

Results

1. In the first set up the drops of water appear on the inner surface of the bell jar.
2. In the second set up there is no visible change.

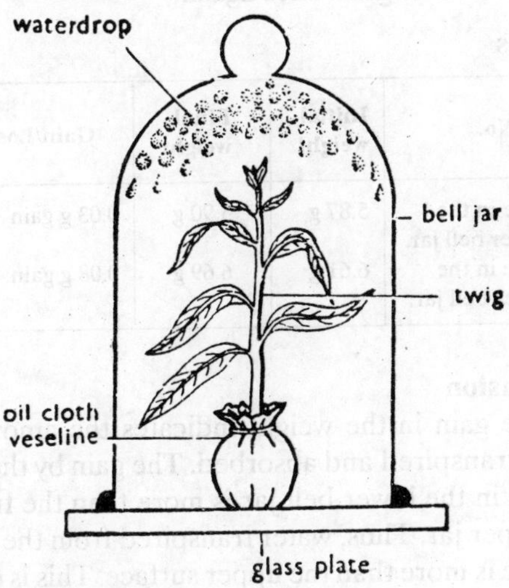

Fig. 2. Demonstration of transpiration.

Conclusion

Considering both the experiments, the moisture in the first set up is considerable while in the second set up it is practically negligible. Thus, the excess moisture must have come from the plant. This is evident because in the second set up where plant is omitted (other things being the same) there is no moisture. This moisture comes from transpiration.

Exercise 2

Purpose : To study the relative rates of water-vapour loss (transpiration) from the leaf surfaces of different plants.

Materials

A potted plant, stop-watch, filter papers, cobalt chloride solution (3%), glass slides, clips, desiccator, punching machine, etc.

Procedure

1. Dip filter papers in 3% cobalt chloride solution. Squeeze out excess solution. Dry the filter papers and cut discs of suitable sizes of punch the holes with punching machine. Store these discs in a desiccator.
2. Take a potted and well watered plant. Place the dried discs of cobalt chloride filter paper, one each on the upper and lower leaf surfaces. Press them closer to surfaces by glass slides. Clip the slides together.
3. Note the time taken by the filter paper to change its blue colour to pink.
4. Repeat the experiment under different conditions and with different types of plants

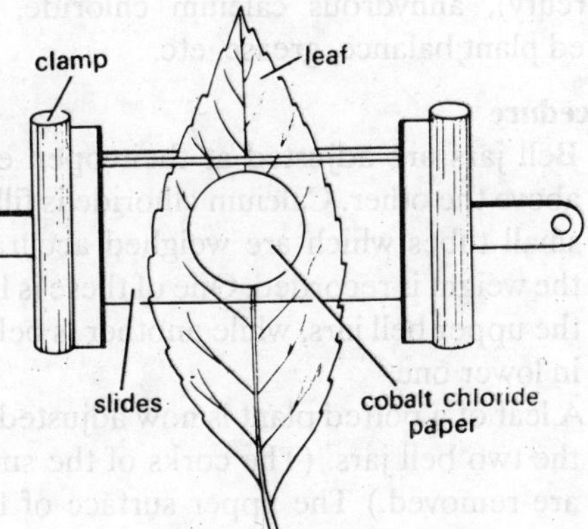

Fig. 3. Cobalt Chloride method to compare the rate of transpiration from leaf surfaces.

Results

Plants : (Different plants can be used.)

Condition : Exccessive light/shade/wind/etc.

Sr. No.	Time taken by cobalt chloride paper to turn pink.	
	Lower Surface	Upper Surface
1.	25 seconds	30 seconds
2.	22 seconds	30 seconds
3.	20 seconds	28 seconds
4.	24 seconds	30 seconds
5.	18 seconds	26 seconds

The time taken for change in colour from blue to pink on the lower leaf surface is less as compared to the upper surface.

Conclusion

The quick change in the colour of cobalt chloride paper on the lower surface indicated higher rate of loss of water vapours from this surface than the upper one.

This is due to more stomata per unit area (frequency) on the lower surface than the upper one. In hypostomatic leaves (stomata only on the lower surface) the change in the cobalt chloride paper is faster on the lower surface than the upper where only cuticular transpiration takes place.

Exercise 3

Purpose : To compare the rates of transpiration from the lower and upper surfaces of the leaf by bell jar method.

Materials

Bell jars, small tubes, manometer, glycerine (mercury), anhydrous calcium chloride, stand, a potted plant,balance, grease, etc.

Procedure

1. Bell jars are adjusted at their open ends, one above the other. Calcium clhoride is filled in the small tubes which are weighed accurately and the weight is recorded. One of these is hanged in the upper bell jars, while another is bell jar kept in lower one.
2. A leaf of a potted plant is now adjusted between the two bell jars. (The corks of the small tubes are removed.) The upper surface of leaf faces the upper bell jar while the lower faces the lower bell jar.

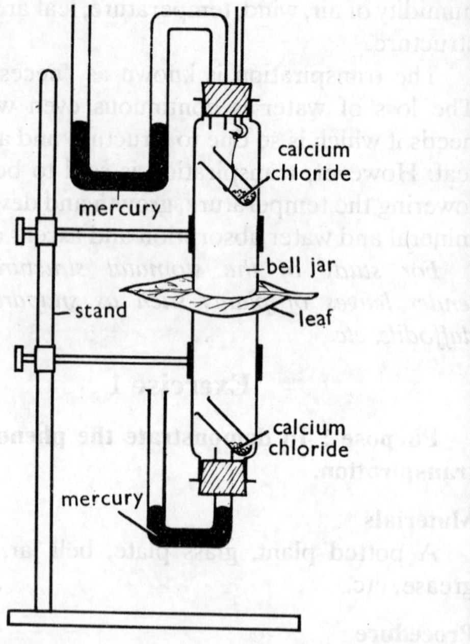

Fig. 4. Bell jar method for the comparison of rates of transpiration.

3. The manometers at the ends of bell jars are filled with glycerine (or mercury or non-volatile oil). The region between the leaf and bell jars is made airtight by applying suitable and required quantity of grease.
4. The apparatus is allowed to stay in this state for a few hours.
5. Later small tubes with calcium chloride are taken out and weighed once again.

Results

Sr. No.	Initial weight	Final weight	Gain/Loss
1. Tube in the upper bell jar.	5.87 g	5.90 g	0.03 g gain
2. Tube in the lower bell jar.	6.61 g	6.69 g	0.08 g gain

Conclusion

The gain in the weight indicates the amount of water transpired and absorbed. The gain by the tube placed in the lower bell jar is more than the tube in the upper jar. Thus, water transpired from the lower surface is more than the upper surface. This is due to more frequency of stomata on the lower surface of the leaf, as compared to that on the upper surface of the leaf.

(For example, in most horizontal leaves the number of stomata is greater on the lower side. Occasionally as in apple, liliac leaves, etc. there are no stomata on the upper surface and the leaves of aquatic plants possess no stomata on either of its surfaces.)

Exercise 4

Purpose : To demonstrate the loss in the total weight of the plant (leaf) during transpiration.

Materials

Stands, spring balances, two leaves of almost equal size and ages, grease, water, test tubes with corks, etc.

Procedure

1. Fill both the test tubes with water. Insert a fresh leaf through the cork hole into each tube.
2. Apply grease to both the surfaces of leaf B, leaving leaf A as such.
3. Hang the tubes on the spring balances.
4. Note the initial weight of the tubes.
5. Make sure at the begining of the experiment that both the corks are made airtight and the petiole of the leaf is dipped in water.
6. Keep the apparatus in open air and then note the weight once again after a few hours.

Results

Leaves	Initial weight	Final weight	Loss/ gain
A	26.3 g	25.9 g	0.4 g loss.
B	30.4 g	10.4 g	No change.

Conclusion

Leaf B being greased, its stomata are closed, therefore, it does not show any transpiration. Hence, there is no change in weight. The leaf A is non-greased and its stomata are open. Thus water is lost by transpiration and hence decrease in the weight of tube A. The loss of weight of tube A indicates the amount of water lost by the leaves. The experiment, therefore, shows that there is a loss in the total weight during transpiraion.

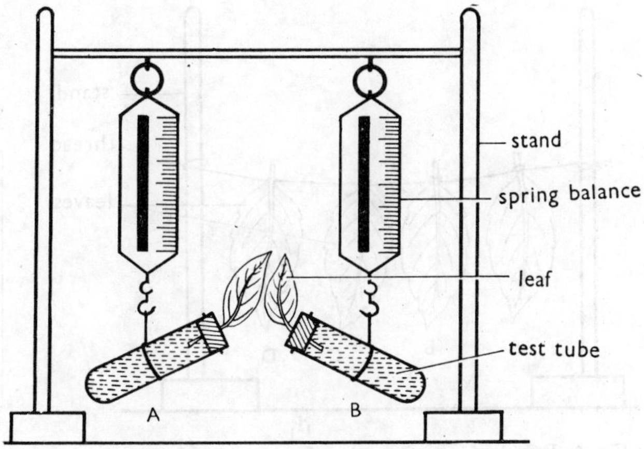

Fig. 5. Experiment to demonstrate the loss of weight during transpiration.

Exercise 5

Purpose : Demonstration of the stomatal transpiration by four leaves method.

Materials

Four fresh dorsiventral leaves, thread, stands, grease, etc.

Procedure

1. Take four similarly grown leaves of a plant. Smear grease at the cut end of the petiole.
2. Apply grease on both the surfaces of leaf A, lower surface of leaf B, and on upper surface of leaf C. Leave leaf D without grease.
3. Note the changes in the leaves after some time.

Results

Leaves	Surface with grease	Results
D	No grease	first to dry
C	upper	second to dry
B	lower	third to dry
A	both	little change

Conclusion

The dorsiventral leaves possess stomata on both the surfaces. The frequency of stomata on the lower surface is more than the upper surface. Hence following conclusions are drawn.

Leaf A. The grease applied on both the surfaces checks any loss of water and, therefore, the leaf does not wilt.

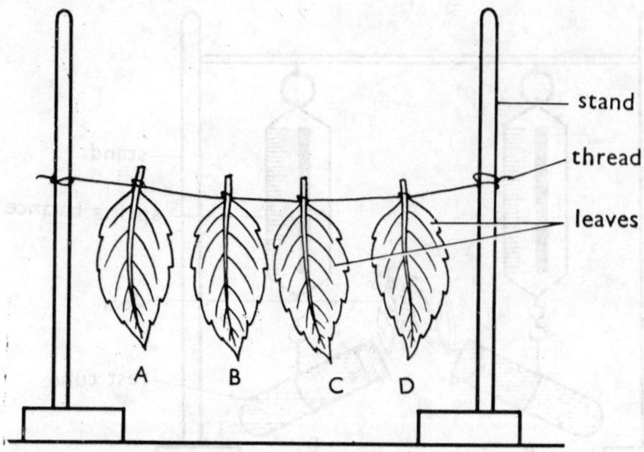

Fig. 6. Four-leaf experiment to demonstrate the stomatal transpiration.

Leaf B. The grease applied on the lower surface blocks most of the stomata. Thus, there is no transpiration from the lower surface. The transpiration from the upper leaf surface continues at a low rate, number of stomata being very less.

Leaf C. The grease on the upper surface blocks only a few stomata. The lower surface with large number of stomata continues to loose water. Thus, this leaf dries faster than leaf A (with no transpiration) and leaf B (with transpiration from upper only).

Leaf D. The first leaf to dry is, however, D. This is because the leaf transpires water from both upper and lower surfaces.

Exercise 6

Purpose : To demonstrate the relation between absorption of water and transpiration.

Materials

A bottle with cork at one end (or Vosuque's potometer), water, twig (or entire small plant), balance, graduated U-tube, oil, etc.

Procedure

1. Potometer is completely filled with water up to the neck. It is fitted with one-holed cork, through which a twig is inserted so as to dip its cut end in water.
2. A few drops of oil are added to the side tube. The apparatus is made airtight.
3. The bottle is covered with black cloth so that light does not reach the roots.
4. The whole apparatus is weighed and the level in the graduated tube is marked.
5. Allow the experiment to stay undisturbed for some time. Then weigh the apparatus and note the level of water in the graduated tube.

Results

Condition	After experiment	Result
1. Weight of apparatus 926.8 g	924.7 g	loss of 2.1 g
2. Level of the graduated tube 0.4 cc	2.6 cc	fall of 2.2 cc

Calculations

Consider 1 g of water = 1 cc of water

Loss of water (transpired)
= Loss of weight = X

Loss of water (absorbed)
= Loss of water from graduated tube = Y

$$\frac{X}{Y} = \frac{\text{water transpired}}{\text{water absorbed}}$$

Conclusions

The loss in weight of apparatus is the amount of water transpired. Also, the difference in the level of the graduated tube shows the amount of water absorbed by the plant.

Under normal conditions the amount of water absorbed is almost equal to that transpired. The present experiment reveals that this is generally true However, more of water is absorbed than transpired.

Exercise 7

Purpose : To demonstrate the rate of transpiration by using potometer(s).

Materials

Choose any of the following potometers— Simple potometer/Farmer's potometer/ Ganong's potometer/Improved type large capacity potometer/ Bose's potometer; water, plants, grease, beaker, stop-watch, etc.

Procedure

Since there are many types of potometers, the construction of each one of them is described separately.

1. Simple potometer. It consists of a glass tube (U-shaped) with a side arm. The upper end of tube is fitted with one-holed cork while the side arm is

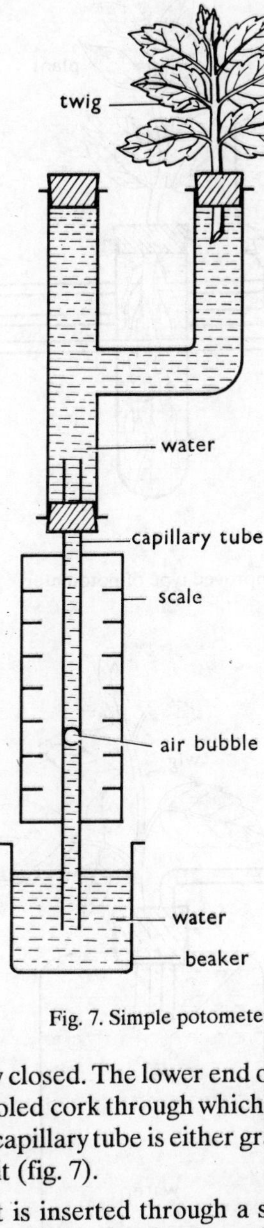

Fig. 7. Simple potometer.

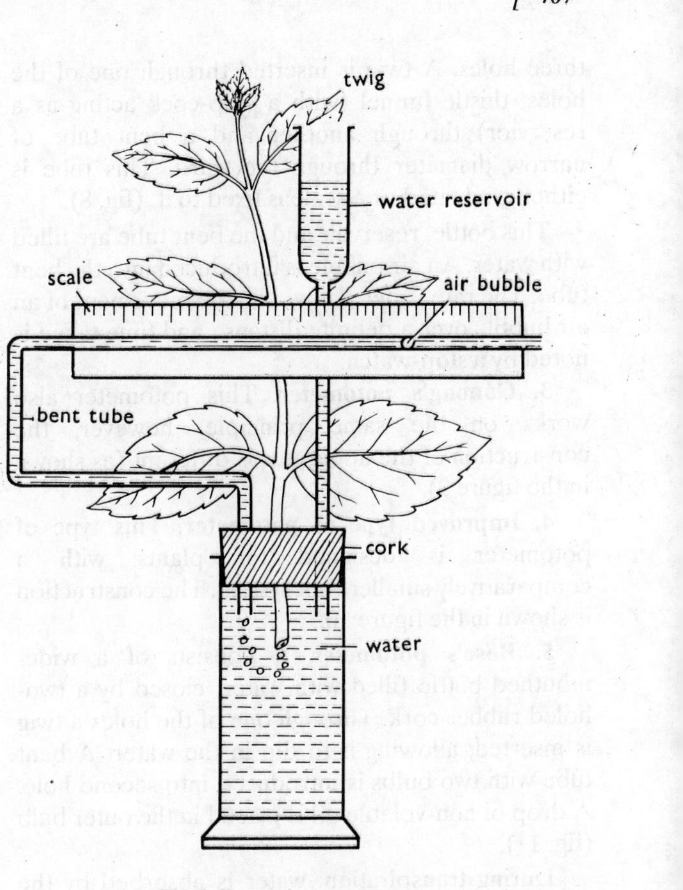

Fig. 8. Farmer's potometer.

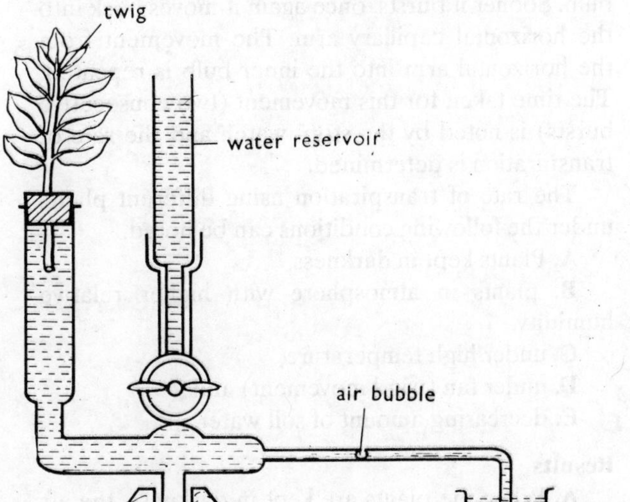

Fig. 9. Ganong's potometer.

completely closed. The lower end of the tube is fitted with one holed cork through which passes a capillary tube. The capillary tube is either graduated or a scale is fixed to it (fig. 7).

A plant is inserted through a single-holed cork, into the side tube, allowing it to dip into the water. The transpiration begins and the water in the capillary tube rises. At this time, the lower end of capillary is dipped into a beaker containing water, thereby introducing an air bubble. The rate of movement of bubble is measured by allowing it to move a definite distance and the time taken by it is noted by a stop-watch.

2. Farmer's potometer. It is made up of a wide mouthed bottle which is closed by a rubber cork with three holes. A twig is inserted through one of the holes, thistle funnel (with a stop-cock acting as a reservior) through another and a bent tube of narrow diameter through the third. This tube is either graduated or a scale is fixed to it. (fig. 8).

This bottle, reservoir and the bent tube are filled with water. An air bubble is introduced into the bent tube. The rate is determined by the movement of an air bubble over a definite distanse and time taken is noted by a stop-watch.

3. Ganong's potometer. This potometer also works on the same principle, however, the construction of the apparatus is different (as shown in the figure 9).

4. Improved type of potometer. This type of potometer is designed for plants with a comparatively smaller root system. The construction is shown in the figure 10.

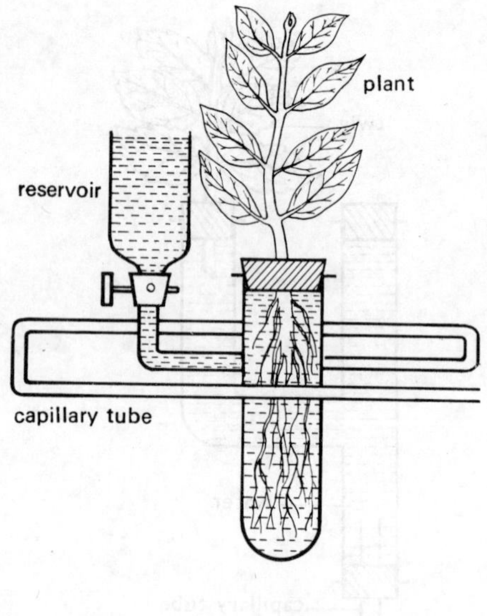

Fig. 10. Improved type of potometer.

5. Bose's potometer. It consists of a wide-mouthed bottle filled with water, closed by a two-holed rubber cork. Through one of the holes a twig is inserted, allowing it to dip in the water. A bent tube with two bulbs is introduced into second hole. A drop of non-volatile oil is placed in the outer bulb (fig. 11).

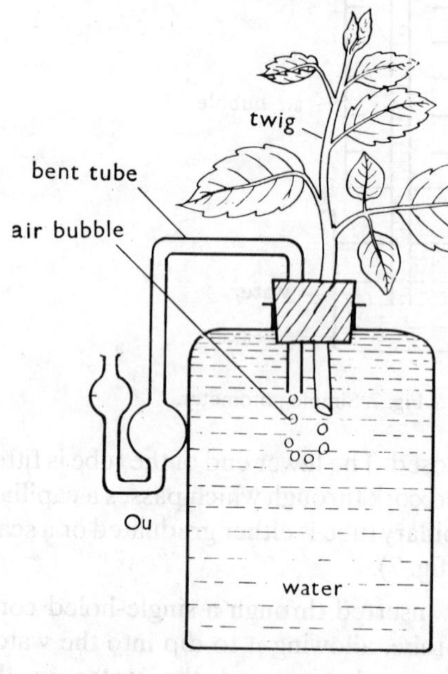

Fig. 11. Bose's potometer.

During transpiration, water is absorbed by the plant pulling the oil drop towards the inner oil bulb through the arm. It bursts after reaching the inner bulb. Sooner it bursts, once again it moves back into the horizontal capillary arm. The movement from the horizontal arm into the inner bulb is repeated. The time taken for this movement (two consecutive bursts) is noted by the stop- watch and the rate of transpiration is determined.

The rate of transpiration using different plants under the following conditions can be noted.

A. Plants kept in darkness,

B. plants in atmosphere with higher relative humidity,

C. under high temperature,

D. under fan (wind movement) and

E. decreasing amount of soil water.

Results

A. When the plants are kept in darkness, the air bubble does not move.

B. When the plants are kept in atmosphere with higher relative humidity, the air bubble moves slowly.

C. When the plants are kept in place with high temperature, the air bubble moves faster.

D. When the plants are kept under fan, the air bubble moves faster.

E. When the plant is not properly watered, the air bubble moves slowly.

onclusions

A. When the plants are kept in darkness.

The air bubble does not move, indicating that anspiration does not take place in the dark.

The stomates remain close in the dark. Absence f photosynthesis in the dark results in accumulation f CO_2 from respiration. The cytoplasm becomes cidic and pH is lowered to 5. Under this condition ıgar (osmotically active) in the guard cells is onverted to starch (osmotically inactive). The smotic concentration of the guard cells is lowered, xosmosis takes place, turgor pressure is reduced nd walls of the guard cells return to normal osition, closing the stomatal pore.

$$\text{Sugar} \xrightarrow[\text{phosphorylase}]{\text{pH 5}} \text{Starch}$$

B. Plants are kept in atmosphere with high elative humidity.

The air bubble then moves slowly, indicating low ate of transpiration.

Normally, the internal atmosphere of the leaf is aturated with water vapours, while the external tmosphere is generally less humid. Therefore, a apour pressure gradient exists between the internal nd the external atmosphere. The vapours diffuse om inside the leaf to external atmosphere. The esser is the relative humidity of the external tmosphere, more rapid will be the diffusion from ıside the leaf. However, in the present case external tmosphere being more humid (i.e. more amount of vater vapours) the difference between the internal leaf tmosphere and the external atmosphere is lesser. At ıis stage, diffusion of vapours from saturated internal tmosphere to almost saturated external atmosphere is ery less. The rate of transpiration is very low. It shall how a higher rate if the external atmosphere is less umid i.e. when air is dry.

C. The plants are kept in a region of high emperature.

With increase in temperature of the external tmosphere, air bubble moves faster, thus indicating ıcrease in the rate of transpiration. This is due to

(i) stomatal movement,

(ii) change in the vapour pressure gradients. and

(iii) increased evaporation.

(i) Higher temperatures increase the stomatal pening. Temperatures approaching 0°C result in tomatal closure while there is gradual increase in stomatal opening up to about 30°C. Thus higher is the temperature, stomatal opening is wider. The rate of transpiration increases.

(ii) The vapour pressure changes with the temperature. Higher is the temperature, the external atmosphere becomes less denser and thus contains lesser water vapours. The internal leaf atmosphere being saturated, vapours diffuse outward to the external atmosphere (containing less vapour). Thus, higher temperature steepens the vapour pressure gradient.

(iii) The higher is the temperature, more would be the heat, hence more would be the evaporation of water. Hence, rate of transpiration is higher.

D. If plants are kept under fan (air movement).

The rate of transpiration increases under fan (or high velocity of wind). Saturated air surrounding the leaf is removed by wind.

The air surrounding the plants is generally saturated with water vapours due to transpiration. The vapour pressure gradient becomes less steeper. The rate of transpiration is lowered. However, the wind carries away water vapours accumulated around the leaf. The concentration of vapours becomes lower. The vapour pressure gradient becomes sharper. The transpiration increases.

E. When amount of available soil water is less.

Transpiration depends upon the absorption of soil water. As long as an equilibrium between the water absorbed from the soil and the water lost by transpiration is maintained, the rate of transpiration does not fall. The higher rate of transpiration reduces amount of soil water. The water absorption is reduced and so also the rate of transpiration. Continued transpiration would finally result into wilting.

Exercise 8

Purpose : To demonstrate the stomatal opening by Darwin's porometer.

Materials

Darwin's porometer, beaker, potted plant, water (or mercury), clips, stopwatch, adhesive (durofix, etc.), etc.

Procedure

1. Darwin's porometer consists of a T-tube. One of the arms is attached to a small cup with rubber tubing while the other to a rubber tubing which can be closed by a clip.

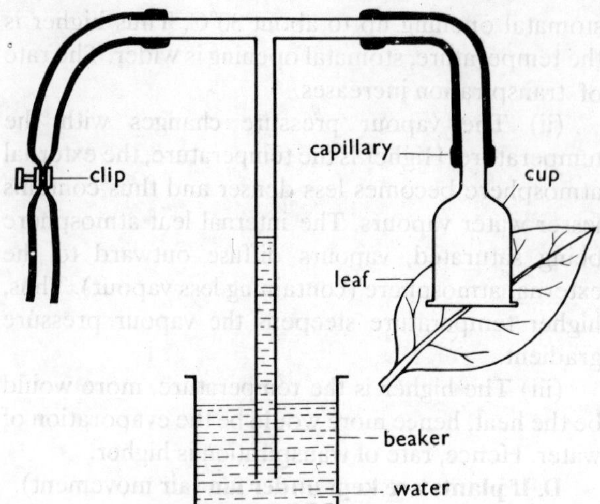

Fig. 12. Darwin's porometer.

2. The cup is cemented by adhesive (durofix, chewing gum, etc.) to the lower surface of the leaf of a potted plant.
3. The vertical arm is dipped in a beaker containing water (or mercury).
4. The clip is opened and water sucked through it. It is seen that the water rises in the vertical arm. The level is then marked.
5. The leaf is cut from the plant and level is again marked.

Results

1. The level falls down gradually when the leaf is attached.
2. The level remains stationary, if leaf is cut and removed.

Conclusion

The air inside the porometer remains under reduced pressure when air is sucked through the rubber tubing.

In a potted plant the stomates remain open. The transpiration continues. The water vapours, thus enter the chamber of the cup. This results in the fall of the water column. This fall in the level indicates that the stomates are open.

The cutting of leaf from the plant results in the closure of the stomates. The vapours due to transpiration do not enter the chamber of the cup. Therefore, the water level remains stationary.

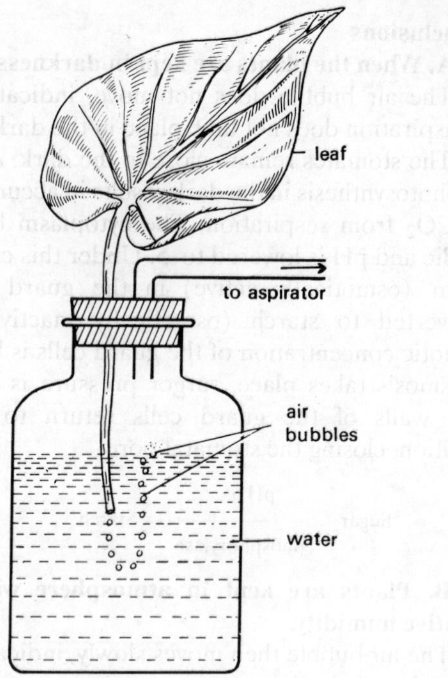

Fig. 13. Apparatus used to demonstrate continuity of air spaces.

The porometer is used to measure the stomata opening. The time taken for the fall of definite leve (e.g. 1 cc/1 cm) is noted under various conditions. I the time is more, the stomates are partially closec When stomata are fully open, more vapours ente the chamber of the cup and the fall of the level sha be rapid. In the latter case, lesser amount of vapour due to the partially open stomates, shall take mor time to bring fall in the level. Thus the rate at whic the water column falls indicates the degree c stomatal opening.

Exercise 9

Purpose : To demonstrate the continuity of th air spaces.

Materials

A bottle, a large petioled leaf, two-holed rubbe cork, bent tube, aspirator, grease, etc.

Procedure

1. Fill bottle with water. Close with two-holed cork Insert a bent glass tube through one hole, but d not allow it to dip in the water.

2. Pass a petiole (cut under water) through the second hole in a way, so that the cut end is under water.
3. The bent glass tube is connected to an aspirator which is allowed to run.

Results

A continuous stream of bubbles is formed from the cut end of the petiole.

Conclusion

The experiment shows that the intercellular spaces of the leaf are directly in contact with the atmosphere through the stomata. As soon as the aspirator is set to work, it sucks the air from the bottle. This creates vacuum. To overcome it, the outside air enters through the stomata into the air spaces (intercellular spaces) of the leaf and finally into the water through the continuous channel of the intercellular spaces. The air appears in the form of bubbles. The bubbles can only be seen if air is sucked through the leaf. The leaf must, therefore, possess a continuous column which can hold water. Since the petiole is cut, the intercellular spaces are open and directly in contact with water.

V. Photosynthesis

Preamble

[I] The Process

The green plants are autotrophic i.e. they synthesis their own food material. Food material is mostly synthesised in the form of carbohydrates especially the starch. Synthesis of starch takes place in chlorophyll containing leaves. It also requires light and CO_2 from atmosphere and water from the soil. The complex reactions involved in the process finally reduce CO_2 to starch. These reactions together are called photosynthesis. During this process gaseous oxygen is released as a by-product. Photosynthesis is summarised as follows.

$$6CO_2 + 12H_2O^* \xrightarrow[\text{Chlorophyll}]{\text{Light}} C_6H_{12}O_6 + H_2O + 6O_2^*$$

[II] The Pigments

The important chemical compounds which absorb light energy are the pigments. These are present in the chloroplasts or chromoplasts of the plant cell. Photosynthetically active pigments are chlorophylls – *a,b,c,d* and *e*, bacteriochlorophyll *a* and *b* and bacteriovirdin. Of these, chlorophyll *a* and *b* occur most widely. Chlorophyll *a* consists of a tetrapyrrolic (porphyrin) ring with magnesium atom in its center and a long chain phytol attached to one of the pyrrol rings. The minor difference in the structure of chlorophyll *a* and *b*, results in absorption of different wavelengths of light e.g. chlorophyll *a* and *b* show maximum absorption in the blue-violet region at the peaks of 429 mμ and 453 mμ respectively; with minor peaks at 410 mμ and 430 mμ. Another secondary absorption maximum for chlorophyll *a* and *b* is in the red region of 660 mμ and 642 mμ respectively. Thus, blue and red wavelengths are most effective in photosynthesis which are absorbed heavily by the chloroplast. Other pigments taking part in the photosynthesis are carotenoids and phycobilins. These pigments, absorb light energy but cannot convert it into chemical energy, hence are called accessory pigments.

[III] The Mechanism

Photosynthesis consists of two steps –
(1) light reaction and
(2) dark reaction.

1. Light reaction is complex and involves two photochemical acts – (i) photochemical reaction brought about by pigment system I (PS I) where ATP is formed and (ii) another photochemical reaction brought about by pigment system II (PS II) where photolysis of water takes place and as a result ATP and $NADPH_2$ are formed while oxygen is released as a by-product.

Thus at the end of light reaction ATP and $NADPH_2$ are formed which are used in the dark reaction.

2. Dark reaction does not require light energy but requires the products formed in the light reaction. The process begins when CO_2 is accepted by Ribulose-bi-phosphate. At the end of the process starch accumulates as the reserve food. The entire process is called Calvin Cycle or C_3 cycle.

[IV] The Factors

The process of photosynthesis is affected by many factors, viz. light (instensity, quality and duration), carbon dioxide, temperature, oxgyen and water. Blackman (1905) postulated the law of limiting factor. It states that when a process is conditioned as to its rapidity by a number of separate factors, the rate of the process is limited by the pace of the 'slowest factor'. Thus, if all the other factors are kept constant, the factor affecting the rate is at minimum (e.g. CO_2). The rate gradually increases with the increase in the amount of this factor till the rate becomes constant. The rate now does not increase even though the amount of this factor is increased (e.g. CO_2) because another factor (e.g. light) has now become factor in the minimum. The rate of photosynthesis is, therefore, dependent on the factor available in relatively smaller amounts when many factors are involved.

1. Light. Average intensity of sunlight is sufficient for normal photosynthesis. The plants can photosynthesise even at a low light intensity but at a very low rate. The rate, however, continues to increase with increase in the light intensity till some other factor becomes limiting. Higher intensity as inhibitory effect. It also brings about closure of the stomata, thus restricting the diffusion of CO_2. Photosynthesis takes place only in the visible part of the spectrum. Most effective wavelengths are red and blue-violet.

2. Carbon dioxide. Atmosphere has 0.03% carbon dioxide wherefrom it is absorbed by the plants. Photosynthesis tolerate considerable fluctuation in the concentration of CO_2, however, with the increase or decrease in CO_2 concentration, corresponding increase or decrease in the photosynthesis takes place. Higher concentration reduces the rate.

3. Temperature. The photosynthesis takes place over a wide range of temperature which differs with habitat and plant. The average suitable temperature is about 24°C to 30°C. The higher is the temperature (beyond maximum), there is a decrease in the rate.

4. Water. The water is needed for photosynthesis in very small quantity (about 1% of the water absorbed by the plant). This amount is always available and the rate is not affected appreciably by the water.

5. Other factors. Besides the above factors, chlorophyll content, protoplasmic factors, accumulation of end products of photosynthesis, etc. also affect the rate of photosynthesis.

Exercise 1

Purpose : To demonstrate that oxygen is evolved during photosynthesis by inverted funnel method.

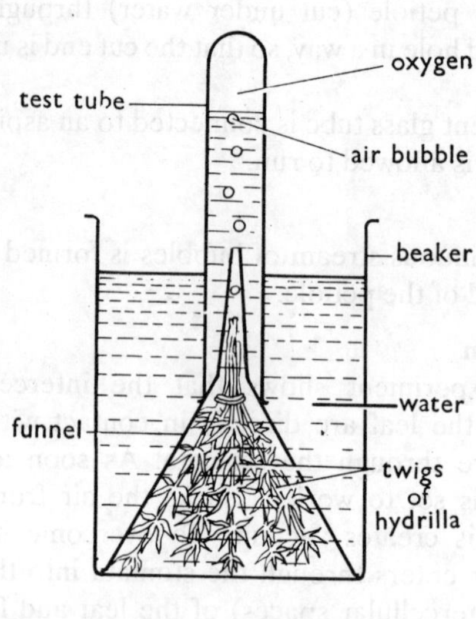

Fig. 1. Experiment to demonstrate evolution of oxygen during photosynthesis.

Materials

A beaker, funnel, test tube, twigs of *Hydrilla* (an aquatic plant), water, thread, etc.

Procedure

1. Beaker is filled with water. The twigs of *Hydrilla* are inserted in the funnel in a way, that the cut ends are firmly introduced in the tube of funnel but spreading in its wide mouth. The funnel is then fully immersed in the water.
2. A test tube filled with water is inverted over the stem of the funnel. It is seen that water does not flow out of the test tube and it remains fully filled with water.
3. The experiment is placed in sunlight.

Results

Air bubbles come out from the cut ends of the plant, escape upwards through the stem of the funnel and collect in the tube. The gas is tested by pyrogallic acid or a burnt match stick is inserted in the tube.

Conclusion

The pyrogallic acid or a burnt match stick indicates the presence of oxygen in the test tube. It comes from the photosynthesizing plant placed under water. The evolution Of O_2 takes place due to photolysis of water.

$$H_2O \rightarrow (H) + (OH)$$
$$2(OH) \rightarrow 2H + O_2 \uparrow$$

The oxygen is liberated into the air spaces or intercellular spaces and escapes outside because of the continuity of air spaces.

This experiment can also be used to show effects of various factors.

A. If boiled water is used instead of pond water in which *Hydrilla* grows –

The air bubbles would not be produced, since the photosynthesis is not taknig place.

This is due to the absence of CO_2 in the water which gets removed when water is boiled.

B. If sodium bicarbonate is added to the water –

The rate of photosynthesis increases. This is due to the availability of more CO_2, as a result of addition of $NaHCO_3$

$$2NaHCO_3 + H_2O \rightarrow Na_2CO_3 + H_2CO_3$$

$$H_2CO_3 \rightarrow H_2O + CO_2$$

This released CO_2 is utilised during photosynthesis and the rate increases. The CO_2 is generally a limiting factor and, therefore, more of this gas causes increase in rate till some other factor becomes limiting.

C. If some toxic, anaesthetic or harmful substance is added to water.

The photosynthetic rate decreases. This is due to the harmful effects of the substances on the enzymes and finally the protoplasm of the cell gets killed. The photosynthesis stops.

D. In case a terrestrial plant (e.g. mango) or a mesophyte is used.

It can not absorb CO_2 from the water. Moreover, the stomates which are the main organs of gaseous exchange get clogged and closed due to water.

Exercise 2

Purpose : To compare the rate of photosynthesis under different conditions.

Materials

Wilmott's bubbler, water, twigs of *Hydrilla*, stopwatch, etc.

Procedure

Wilmott's bubbler can be prepared in the laboratory as given below.

1. A wide-mouthed bottle is taken. It is completely filled with pond water. A cork is then fitted, through which a glass tube (glass reservoir)wide at its open end is passed in a way, that its lower end dips in the water.

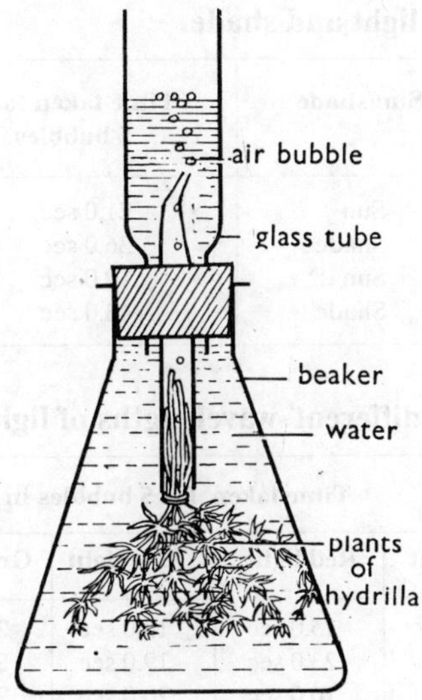

Fig. 2. Wilmott's bubbler to compare the rate of photosynthesis under different conditions.

2. Another narrow glass tube open at both the ends is made into a bent jet and introduced into the glass reservoir. The twigs of *Hydrilla* are tied at the lower end of this narrow glass tube inside the bottle.

For studying the rate of photosynthesis following different conditions are given.

A. Different amounts of sodium bicarbonate are added to the pond water.

B. The bubbler is kept in sunlight and shade alternately.

C. The bubbler is covered with red, green and blue cellophane papers.

D. The temperature of the water in the bottle is raised by keeping it near a strong source of electric light.

In each case the number of bubbles and time taken are noted –

Results

A. Effect of CO_2

Sr. No.	Conc. of $NaHCO_3$	Time taken for 5 bubbles
1.	Tap water	No bubbles
2.	5.5 g	10.1 sec
3.	1.0 g	4.9 sec
4.	2.0 g	3.0 sec
5.	3.9 g gm	No bubbles

B. Effect of light and shade

Sr. No.	Sun/shade	Time taken for 5 bubbles
1.	Sun	21.0 sec
2.	Shade	36.0 sec
3.	Sun	19.0 sec
4.	Shade	43.0 sec

C. Effect of different wavelengths of light

Sr. No.	Time taken for 5 bubbles in			
	Sun light	Red light	Blue light	Green light
1.	20.1 sec	15.0 sec	18.0 sec	21.0 sec
2.	28.0 sec	23.0 sec	19.0 sec	23.0 sec
3.	25.0 sec	16.0 sec	20.0 sec	24.0 sec
4.	39.0 sec	32.0 sec	36.3 sec	42.0 sec
5.	33.0 sec	28.0 sec	32.0 sec	38.0 sec
Average	29.2 sec	22.8 sec	25.4 sec	32.8 sec

D. Effect of temperature

Sr. No.	Temperature	Time taken for 5 bubbles
1.	10°C	25.5 sec
2.	20°C	20.0 sec
3.	25°C	18.3 sec
4.	30°C	15.8 sec
5.	35°C	12.5 sec

Conclusion

The rate of evolution of oxygen bubbles is a measure of photosynthetic rate.

A. Effect of CO_2. When tap water is used in the bubbler, bubbles are not evolved. This shows that photosynthesis is not taking place. This is because tap water does not contain sufficient CO_2. The rate of photosynthesis increases with the addition of sodium-bi-carbonate because it increases the supply of CO_2. The increase in the rate continues till some other factor becomes limiting.

B. Effect of light and shade . In shade the rate of photosynthesis slows down as compared to in sunlight.

Normally, light is never a limiting factor. About 1-2% of the total light falling upon the leaves is used. Thus, maximum rate of photosynthesis is attained at intensities much below those of the full sunlight.

However, low light intensity may become a limiting factor and photosynthesis is lesser in plants exposed to weak light than in plants exposed to strong light. Thus, the rate of photosynthesis is lesser in shade than in sun light.

If alternate light and dark periods (intermittent) are given, the efficiency of photosynthesis is higher. One of the reasons being, the accumulation of CO_2 in the leaves and translocation or conversion of photosynthate into soluble form. This helps to increase the rate of photosynthesis during light periods.

C. Effect of different wavelengths of light. Under the sunlight, plants continue to show a definite rate of photosynthesis because the pigments active in photosynthesis absorb the respective wavelengths. These wavelengths being most effective, the rate of photosynthesis is almost maximum if other factors are also favourable.

If the red wavelengths (647-660 mμ) are available, the rate of photosynthesis is the maximum. The wavelength (near 670 mμ) is known to be maximally effective.

Similarly, net higher peak of absorption in the blue wavelengths is 422-492 mμ. It is absorbed in larger quantities than other wavelengths. These wavelengths (near 440 mμ) are second most effective. The rate of photosynthesis, in this case, would be lesser as compared to red wavelengths.

The rate of photosynthesis is practically zero in the region of green wavelengths. This is because the chlorophylls reflect green wavelengths.

D. Effect of temperature. The rate of photosynthesis increases with increase in temperature from 10°C to 35°C.

Photosynthesis occurs in a temperature range, similar to that tolerated by protein compounds i.e. between 0°C-60°C. The temperatures do not affect the photochemical process but the biochemical part i.e. formation of starch is affected. This is because the enzymes are involved in this reaction. The range of temperature at which photosynthesis occurs at a relatively rapid rate is 10°C-35°C, provided other factors are not limiting. If the temperature is raised within this limit, there shall be an increase in the rate of photosynthesis.

Exercise 3

Purpose : To demonstrate the effect of different avlengths of light during photosynthesis.

laterials

A large box where leaf can be inserted (similar to anong's light screen), glass top covered by red, reen and blue colours, a twig, ethyl alcohol 90%, pirit lamp, beaker, iodine, etc.

rocedure

. The leaf is destarched by keeping the plant in dark for about 24 hours.

. This leaf is inserted below the glass top of the apparatus.

. The apparatus is kept in sunlight.

. The leaf is detached in the evening (or after a few hours).

. The chlorophyll is removed by boiling it in alcohol.

. The leaf is now tested for starch by staining with iodine.

. Compare the intensity of staining of different parts of the leaf under red, blue and green light.

esults

. The part of leaf receiving red light is darkly stained.

. The part under the blue light is slightly lighter than in red.

. The part under green light shows almost negative staining.

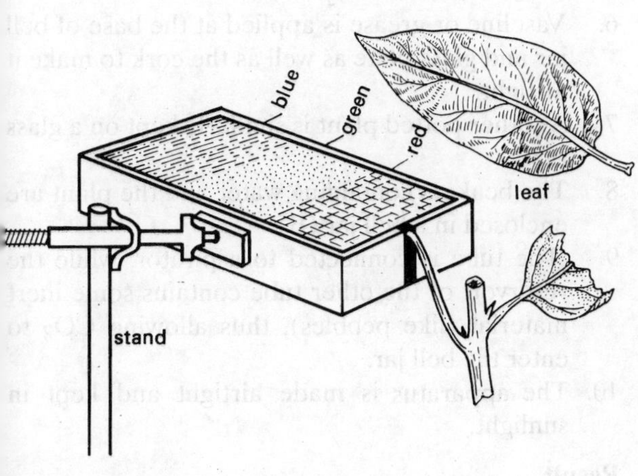

Fig. 3. Apparatus used for determining the effect of different wavelengths of light during photosynthesis.

Conclusion

1. The maximum photosynthesis occured in red region. Thus there is more amount of starch which is the end product of photosynthesis.
2. The next effective are the blue wavelenghts. This also shows lesser amount of starch manufactured during the same time. Photosynthesis in this wavelength of light is at a lower rate than that in the red region.
3. Staining indicates that no photosynthesis has taken place in green wavelength and hence it is not effective in this process.

Exercise 4

Purpose : To demonstrate the presence of starch in chloroplast.

Materials

Leaves of moss or filaments of *Spirogyra*, chloral hydrate, iodine, slides, coverslips, microscope, etc.

Procedure

1. Pluck the moss leaves or place a few filaments of *Spirogyra* on a slide.
2. Place a few drops of chloral hydrate and a drop of iodine.
3. Allow the plant material to remain so in the reagents. Observe under the microscope.

Result and Conclusion

The starch is accumulated in the chloroplasts after photosynthesis is completed. These starch grains take blue stain of the iodine.

Exercise 5

Purpose : To demonstrate that light is necessary for photosynthesis.

Materials

Ganong's screen, a twig, ventilated box, iodine, etc.

Procedure

1. Destarch leaf of a potted plant by diping it in dark for about 24 hours.
2. Place it between Ganong's screen.
3. Cut a pattern (A in this case) in black paper, so that light passes only through this design. Place it over the leaf and below the screen.
4. The twig is allowed to stand in sunlight. Take out the leaf and test for starch.

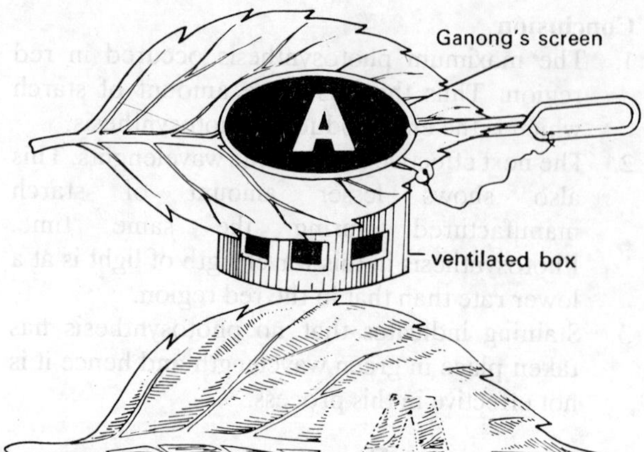

Fig. 4. To demonstrate that light is necessary for photosynthesis using Ganong's screen. A. Leaf with Ganong's screen. B. Leaf after iodine test.

Result

The positive iodine test shows presence of starch, only in the region where letter A was cut in the black paper.

Conclusion

The final product of the photosynthesis is starch. It is formed in the leaf only when all the essential factors for photosynthesis are available to the plant. The iodine test shows that starch is manufactured in the region exposed to light while the region of the leaf which was covered with black paper does not show any starch.

Therefore, starch formation needs the presence of light while in its absence starch cannot be produced. This indicates the necessity of light for photosynthesis.

Exercise 6

Purpose : To demonstrate that CO_2 is necessary for photosynthesis.

Materials

Two bell jars, beakers, glass plates, aspirators, soda lime, caustic potash, water, two twigs (potted plants), etc.

Procedure

1. The potted plants are kept in darkness for about two days to destarch the leaves.

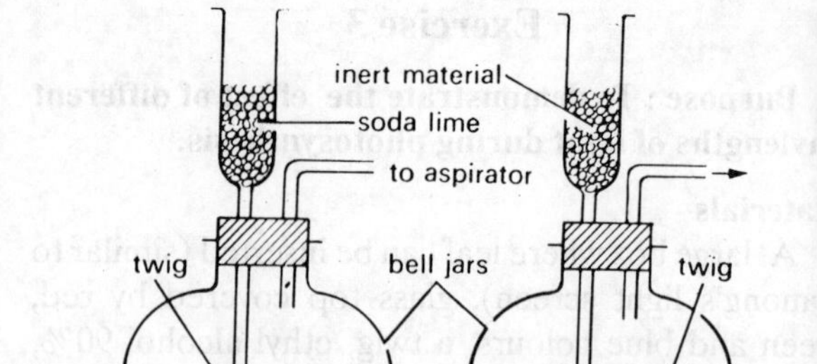

Fig. 5. To demonstrate that CO2 is necessary for photosynthesis.

2. A plant is kept under a bell jar (A) along with two beakers filled with caustic potash (to absorb any CO_2 present).
3. The bell jar is connected to an aspirator through a tube inserted in its cork.
4. Another tube with reservoir containing soda lime is also inserted through the cork.
5. This arrangement is made so that when an aspirator is run, air rushes into the bell jar through the tube with soda lime. Thus, air free of CO_2 enters the bell jar.
6. Vaseline or grease is applied at the base of bell jar and glass plate as well as the cork to make it airtight.
7. Another potted plant is similarly kept on a glass plate.
8. The beakers containing water and the plant are enclosed in a bell jar (B).
9. The tube is connected to aspirator, while the reservoir of the other tube contains some inert material (like pebbles), thus allowing CO_2 to enter the bell jar.
10. The apparatus is made airtight and kept in sunlight.

Result

After a few hours, leaves are tested for starch with iodine. The leaves of the plant in bell jar A show negative test while those in bell jar B give positive test.

Conclusion

The negative test shows that starch is not formed in the plant kept in CO_2 free atmosphere.

The other plant kept in atmosphere of CO_2 shows positive iodine test. This indicates that photosynthesis takes place in presence of CO_2.

The comparison shows that besides water, light, chlorophyll and temperature, CO_2 is also necessary for the photosynthesis.

Exercise 7

Purpose : To demonstrate that carbon dioxide water, light and chlorophyll are essential for photosynthesis by 'Moll's half leaf' experiment.

Materials

A potted plant, wide-mouthed bottle, split cork, caustic potash, water, stand, iodine, etc.

Procedure

1. A potted plant is kept in the dark for about two days to destarch its leaves.
2. One of the leaves of this plant is half inserted in a bottle through a split cork. The bottle is partly filled with a strong solution of caustic potash.
3. The bottle is then kept in the light for the whole day. The leaf is then tested for starch.

Result

1. The portion of the leaf inside the bottle shows negative test.
2. The portion of the leaf between the two halves of the split cork also shows negative results.
3. The portion of the leaf outside the cork and bottle gives the positive test.

Conclusion

Photosynthesis requires CO_2, light, water and chlorophyll without any of which the process cannot continue.

1. The portion of the leaf inside the bottle does not receive CO_2 which is absorbed by caustic potash. This part of the leaf receives light, water and possesses chlorophyll but does not receive CO_2. Hence photosynthesis does not take place and starch is not formed.
2. The portion of the leaf between the two halves of the split cork does not receive CO_2 and light as well. Therefore, the photosynthesis does not take place and consequently there is no starch formation.

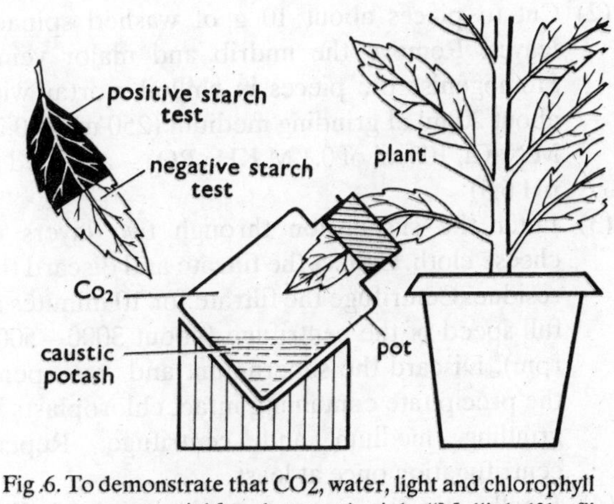

Fig .6. To demonstrate that CO2, water, light and chlorophyll are essential for photosynthesis by "Moll's half leaf" experiment.

3. The portion of the leaf outside the cork and the bottle receives CO_2 and light from the atmosphere, water from the pot and possesses chlorophyll. Thus all the essential factors are available to this part of leaf. Consequently, starch is formed giving positive iodine test.

[If a variegated leaf e.g., Croton leaf (where chlorophyll is present only at a few regions which are green and lacking at others where it is white) is used, starch is formed only in the regions where chlorophyll is present. This shows that, besides all other requirements, pigment chlorophyll is also essential].

Comparing the results from all the three portions of a leaf used in Moll's experiment, reveal that chlorophyll, CO_2, water and light are essential for photosynthesis.

Exercise 8

Purpose : Dye reduction by isolated chloroplasts or to demonstrate Hill activity.

Materials

Spinach leaves, sodium chloride, (also prepare 0.25 M NaCl), 0.1 M KH_2PO_4, 2-6-dichlorophenol-indophenol (0.1%), 2 ice baths, water bath, mortar and pestle, cheese cloth, test tubes, etc.

Procedure

It consists of following two major steps.

1. Isolation of chloroplasts.

(1) Prepare two baths of chipped ice and NaCl in large beakers. Use these baths to cool all reagents, glassware and chloroplast suspension.

(2) Cut to pieces about 10 g of washed spinach leaves. Remove the midrib and major veins. Homogenise the pieces in chilled mortar with about 20 ml of grinding medium (250 ml of 0.24 M NaCl, 100 ml of 0.1 M KH_2PO_4 – adjusted at pH 6.5)

(3) Filter the suspension through two layers of cheese cloth. Collect the filtrate and discard the residue. Centrifuge the filtrate for 10 minutes at full speed of the centrifuge (about 3000 – 5000 rpm). Discard the supernatant and resuspend the precipitate containing intact chloroplasts in grinding medium and centrifuge. Repeat centrifugation once at least.

(4) Finally stir the suspension kept in grinding medium with glass rod and immerse the container in an ice bath.

2. Dye reduction.

(1) Add 5.0 ml of buffer (grinding medium), 6.0 ml of distilled water and 2.0 ml of chloroplast suspension each to two test tubes.

(2) Cover one of the tubes with aluminium foil or black paper so completely that light does not reach the tube.

(3) Now add a few drops of dye 2-6 dichlorophenol indophenol (DCPIP) to both the tubes.

(4) Place both the tubes in a strongly illuminated (200 watt bulb) water bath at room temperature.

Result

The tube with aluminium foil cover does not show any change in blue colour. The tube exposed to light turns blue dye to colourless.

Conclusion

During photosynthesis water is split to release oxygen and yields hydrogen that combines with NADP. The process is known as photolysis of water. This photochemical part of the photosynthesis, if carried out with isolated chloroplasts, is known as Hill reaction. Hydrogen acceptor is needed during this process. The role of hydrogen acceptor is played by 2-6 dichlorophenol – indophenol.

$$\underset{\text{(oxidized, blue)}}{\text{2, 6 dichlorophenol indophenol}} + 2H_2O \xrightarrow[\text{chlorophyll}]{\text{Light}} \underset{\text{(reduced, colourless)}}{\text{2 indophenol} -2H + O_2}$$

The Hill reaction shows that photosynthesis is an oxidation – reduction reaction.

VI. Respiration & Respiratory Enzymes

Preamble

[I] The Process

Respiration is a catabolic process during which many complex organic substances (like carbohydrates, fats and proteins) are oxidised to simpler products (like carbon dioxide and water). The reaction also results in the formation of energy rich compound – ATP, which is used for other vital processes of the cell.

There are two types of respiration. These are ,

(1) **Aerobic respiration** – where oxygen is necessary for the oxidation of organic compounds and

(2) **Anaerobic respiration** – where organic compounds are broken down in the absence of oxygen.

[II] Aerobic respiration

It consists of two major steps.

(1) **Glycolysis.** In this reaction mediated by many enzymes, sugars are broken down, into two molecules of pyruvic acid accompanied with formation of 2 ATP (net gain) and 2 mols of $NADH_2$. This process takes place in the cytoplasm.

(2) **Kreb's cycle** or Tricarboxylic acid cycle or Citric acid cycle. During this cycle involving complex reactions and requiring oxygen, pyruvic acid molecule is further oxidised. Carbon dioxide and water are released while energy released is stored in the form of ATP.

At the end of these two steps of aerobic respiration 38 molecules of ATP are formed. The Kreb's cycle takes place in mitochondria, the 'Power House of the Cell'.

[III] Anaerobic respiration

Here also there are two steps.

(1) **Glycolysis.** This reaction, as in aerobic respiration results in the formation of two molecules of pyruvic acid from a molecule of sugar 2 mols of ATP and 2 mols of $NADH_2$.

(2) **Further oxidation of pyruvic acid.** This process takes place in the absence of oxygen and, therefore, does not require mitochondria but occurs in the cytoplasm like glycolysis. The end products are alcohol and carbon dioxide.

[IV] Fermentation

The terms fermentation and anaerobic respiration are sometimes used as synonyms. However, the term fermentation is used for a type of anaerobic respiration which is carried on by some fungi and bacteria. Moreover, the substrate is outside the cell and the process can be called as extracellular. Fermentation is brought about by an enzyme or a group of enzymes, zymase.

[V] Respiratory activity

The cells rich in protoplasm, generally the young and meristematic cells, show higher rate of respiration. The rate of the process varies with tissues and organs, age of the plant and also the environmental factors.

[VI] The Respiratory Quotients

The substances oxidised during respiration are called respiratory substrates. These include carbohydrates, fats and proteins. Respiratory quotients for these substrates vary. The RQ is the ratio between the volume of carbon dioxide given out and the volume of oxygen absorbed, by a given weight of tissue in a given period of time.

$$RQ = \frac{CO_2 \text{ evolved}}{O_2 \text{ absorbed}}$$

Three values of RQ are generally known. These are

1. RQ equal to unity. (Substrates : Carbohydrates found in most of the tissues and organs).

$$C_6H_{12}O_6 + 6O_2 = 6CO_2 + 6H_2O + 673 \text{ k cal}$$

$$RQ = \frac{CO_2 \text{ evolved}}{O_2 \text{ absorbed}} = \frac{6}{6} = 1$$

2. RQ less than unity. (Substrates : Fats – fatty seeds, fats transformed to carbohydrates – germinating fatty seeds, carbohydrates – incomplete oxidation to organic acids in succulent plants during night).

(i) Respiration of fats and proteins:

$$2C_{51}H_{98}O_6 + 145\, O_2 = 102\, CO_2 + 98\, H_2O$$

$$RQ = \frac{CO_2}{O_2} = \frac{102}{145} = 0.7$$

$$C_{57}H_{104}O_6 + 80\, O_2 = 57\, CO_2 + 52\, H_2O$$

$$RQ = \frac{CO_2}{O_2} = \frac{57}{80} = 0.7$$

(ii) Incomplete oxidation of carbohydrates:

$$2C_6H_{12}O_6 + 3\, O_2 = 3\, \underset{\text{(Malic acid)}}{C_4H_6O_5} + 3\, H_2O$$

$$RQ = \frac{CO_2}{O_2} = \frac{0}{3} = 0$$

In some cases, carbohydrates are incompletely oxidised to certain organic acids. This is not accompanied with any evolution of CO_2 and water. Such a process takes place in succulent plants (e.g.*Opuntia*) and the plants with red coloured leaves due to the presence of anthocyanin pigment. In all these cases the value of RQ is always less than one.

Incomplete oxidation normally takes place in the night and results in the accumulation of organic acids. During the day these organic acids are completely oxidised and release carbon dioxide. (The value of RQ in the day, therefore, is more than one).

3. RQ more than one. (Substrates : Carbohydrates undergoing anaerobic respiration, carbohydrates synthesised from fats as in maturing fatty seeds, organic acids – in succulents during day time)

(i) $\underset{\text{(Malic acid)}}{C_4H_6O_5} + 3\, O_2 = 4\, CO_2 + 3\, H_2O$

$$RQ = \frac{CO_2}{O_2} = \frac{4}{3} = 1.3$$

(ii) Respiration in absence of oxygen (anaerobic respiration)

$$C_6H_{12}O_6 \xrightarrow{\text{zymase}} 2\, C_2H_5OH + 2CO_2 + 21 \text{ k cal}$$

$$RQ = \frac{CO_2}{O_2} = \frac{2}{0} = 2$$

(iii) Respiration of maturing fatty seeds:

The oxygen is used in other metabolic processes e.g. formation of anthocyanin, conversion of fats into carbohydrates, etc. Thus, there is no evolution of carbon dioxide. In such cases RQ is less than one. However, during transformation of carbohydrates to fats (in maturing fatty seeds) oxygen is released internally and used up immediately without corresponding release of carbon dioxide. The value of RQ, therefore, is greater than one.

[VII] The Factors affecting

Many factors affect the rate of respiration. These include – temperature, oxygen, carbon dioxide, light, moisture, substrates, protoplasmic factor, etc.

1. Temperature. The rate of respiration increases with the increase in temperature. It follows Vant Hoff's Law which states that the rate of respiration increases two to three folds but within certain limits, for every rise of 10°C. However, the rate of respiration decreases below 0°C and above 55°C.

2. Oxygen. The rate of respiration decreases with the decrease in the supply of oxygen.

3. Carbon dioxide. Though CO_2 concentration in the atmosphere remains fairly constant, high concentration of CO_2 reduces the rate of respiration.

4. Light. The rate of respiration increases with the availability of light. The effect of light on respiration is indirect in enhancing the rate of photosynthesis and thus increasing the supply of respirable material.

5. Water. If water is in short supply, the conversion of starch to sugars is slowed down and the rate of respiration decreases.

6. Respiratory substrates. The rate of respiration increases with the increase in the supply of respirable material.

7. Protoplasmic contents. Young and meristematic tissues with higher protoplasmic contents show higher rate of respiration than the cells or tissues poor in protoplasm and the cells with thick walls.

Exercise 1

Purpose : To demonstrate anaerobic respiration.

Materials

A test tube, petri dish, stand, KOH crystals, mercury, germinating seeds, forceps, etc.

Procedure

1. A petri dish is filled half with mercury.
2. A test tube is completely filled with mercury and inverted over this petri dish.
3. Germinating seeds (soaked gram seeds) are introduced into the tube by forceps through its open end. The seeds rise to the top of the tube.
4. The apparatus is allowed to remain as such for a few hours.

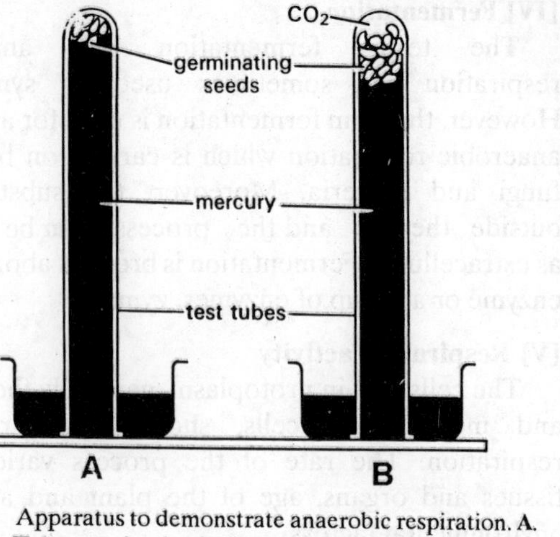

Fig. 7. Apparatus to demonstrate anaerobic respiration. **A.** Tube at the beginning of experiment. **B.** Tube showing accumulation of CO2 after anaerobic respiration.

Result

The level of mercury falls down. Now KOH crystal is inserted into the tube. The mercury again begins to rise.

Conclusion

At the beginning of the experiment, test tube has no air. Germinating seeds respire at the tip of the tube in the absence of air. It results in formation of alcohol and CO_2.

$$C_6H_{12}O_6 \rightarrow 2CO_2 + 2\,C_2H_5OH$$

The CO_2 produced pushes down the mercury column. On the introduction of KOH crystal this CO_2 is absorbed. Thus mercury rises once again.

Exercise 2

Purpose : To demonstrate the process of fermentation.

Materials

Kuhne's fermentation vessel, beaker, glucose, water, baker's yeast, etc.

Procedure

1. Prepare 10% solution of glucose in a beaker.
2. Add a small quantity of baker's yeast to the beaker.
3. Pour the mixture into Kuhne's fermentation vessel. The complete upright tube and half of the bent bulb is filled.

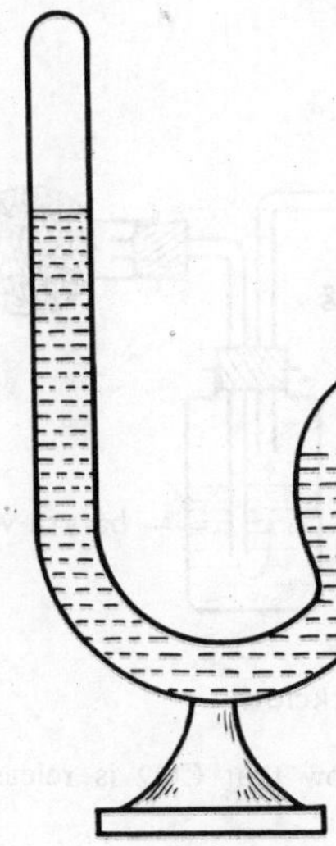

Fig. 2. Kuhne's fermentation vessel.

4. The open end of the bent bulb is plugged with cotton or cork.
5. The apparatus is allowed to stand for some hours.

Result

The gas begins to collect in the upright arm of the vessel with a consequent fall in the level of solution.

Conclusion

Gas collecting in the tube is CO_2 which can be tested by introducing caustic potash in the vessel. The smell of alcohol can also be detected from the remaining solution.

The process that occurs in the tube is fermentation. In this case sugar is fermented by the addition of zymase (from baker's yeast) resulting in the production of carbon dioxide and alcohol. Pure zymase is not known to bring about fermentation. It requires presence of phosphate which acts as a coenzyme. Thus, the fermentation reactions can be summarised as follows –

(i) $2C_6H_{12}O_6 + 2R_2HPO_4 = 2CO_2 + 2C_2H_5OH + 2H_2O + C_6H_{10}O_4(R_2PO_4)_2$ (Hexose diphosphate)

(ii) $C_6H_{10}O_4(R_2PO_4)_2 + 2H_2O = 2R_2HPO_4 + C_6H_{12}O_6$ (Hexose diphosphate)

Final equation, therefore,

$C_6H_{12}O_6 = 2CO_2 + 2C_2H_5OH$

The fermentation of sugar stops when the concentration of ethyl alcohol reaches 10-15% and al' the yeast cells are killed at this stage.

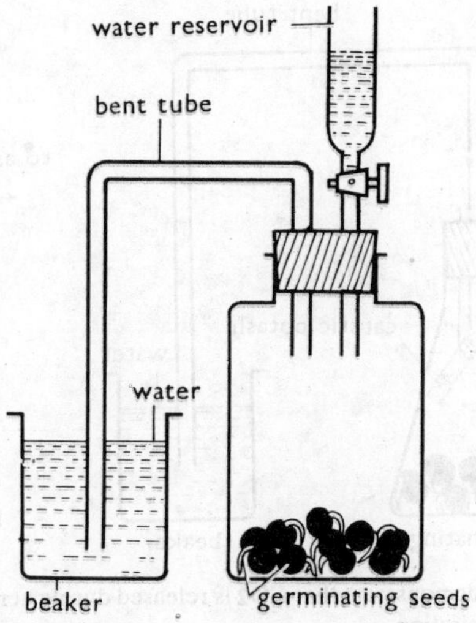

Fig. 3. To demonstrate the release of CO2 during aerobic respiration.

Exercise 3

Purpose : To demonstrate liberation of carbon dioxide during aerobic respiration.

Materials

A bottle, two holed cork, bent tube, reservoir with tube and stop cock, beakers, stand, water, lime water, germinating seeds, etc.

Procedure

1. Germinating seeds are placed in a bottle.
2. It is closed by a cork through which a glass tube is inserted, bent twice at right angles. The free lower end is allowed to dip in water.
3. Through another hole is inserted a tube holding a water reservoir with a stop cock.
4. The water seal (water in beaker) and stop cock of the reservoir are closed. The seeds are allowed to respire for some time.
5. Water seal is then replaced by beaker containing lime water. Stop cock of the reservoir is opened and air inside the bottle is driven out.

Result

The air bubbles come out through the bent tube into the beaker containing lime water which turns milky.

Conclusion

The turning milky of lime water indicates the presence of carbon dioxide. This gas is apparently released during germination of soaked seeds.

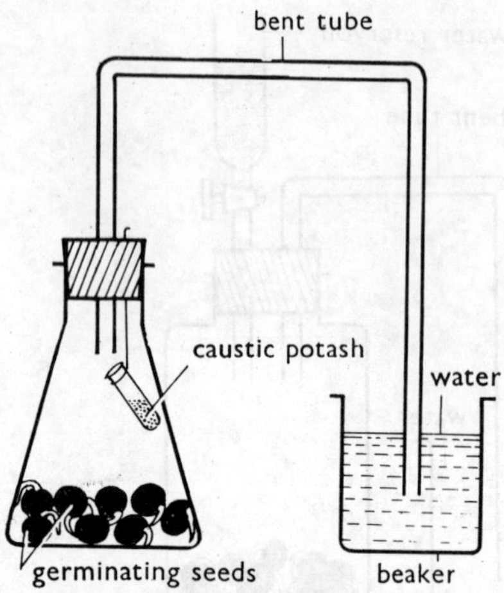

Fig. 4. To demonstrate that CO2 is released during aerobic respiration.

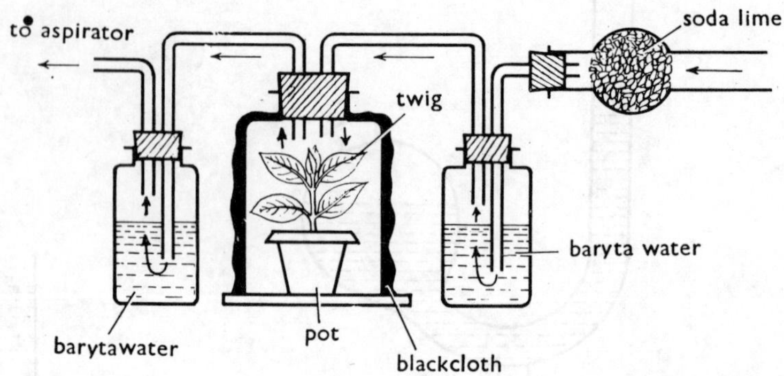

Fig. 5. Apparatus to show that CO2 is released during respiration.

During the process of respiration respiratory substrate is broken down with the apparent release of carbon dioxide.

(This process can also be demonstrated by other apparatus as shown in (a) fig. 4 and (b) fig. 5 .

Materials (for apparatus shown in fig. 4)

A conical flask, cork, bent glass tube, a small test tube, thread, water, KOH, germinating seeds, etc.

Procedure

(1) Germinating seeds are placed in a flask.
(2) A bent tube is introduced thorugh the cork.
(3) The free end of the tube is allowed to dip into a beaker containing water.
(4) A small test tube containing KOH crystals is hung inside the flask.
(5) The apparatus is made airtight and respiration is allowed to continue (fig. 4).

Results

Water in beaker rises in glass tube.

Conclusions

Seeds take oxygen and liberate an equal amount of carbon dioxide. Thus, there should not be any change in the volume of air. However, KOH crystals in the test tube absorb carbon dioxide creating a vacuum in the flask. This results in the rise of water in the glass tube.

Materials (for apparatus shown in fig. 5)

A bell jar, two bottles, bent tubes, a bulb, soda lime, water, aspirator, connecting rubber tubes, corks, grease, cloth, a potted plant, etc. (Fig. 5).

Procedure

(1) A potted plant is covered by a bell jar. (If germinating seeds are to be used bell jar is replaced by a tube).
(2) The bell jar is connected by connecting tubes to the bottles on both the sides. The bottles contain lime water or baryta water.
(3) Bottle at one end is connected with a bulb containing soda lime which is in contact with air.
(4) The bottle at other end is connected with an aspirator. The apparatus is made airtight.
(5) The bell jar is covered with black cloth to prevent photosynthesis.
(6) To begin the experiment aspirator is allowed to run. (fig. 5).

Results

The lime water in a bottle close to aspirator turns milky while that placed in a bottle at another end does not.

Conclusions

The air enters the glass bulb filled with KOH. This removes carbon dioxide from the air. The air now enters the bottle containing lime water where carbon dioxide if any is also absorbed. The air completely free from carbon dioxide now reaches the bell jar.

The plant inside the bell jar cannot undergo photosynthesis because light is not available. However, plant can respire since carbon dioxide free air still supplies oxygen needed for this process. The respiration releases carbon dioxide which enters the bottle with lime water turning it milky.

This experiment shows that, if a plant is given air free of carbon dioxide, even then it turns the lime water milky. This demonstrates that carbon dioxide is released during respiration of the plant in a bell jar.

Exercise 4

Purpose : To demonstrate that carbon dioxide is produced during aerobic respiration by using retorts.

Materials

Three beakers, three stands, three retorts, dry seeds, soaked seeds, caustic potash, salt solution, water, etc.

Procedure

1. Introduce a few dried seeds in the retort. Now dip the drawn tube of retort in the caustic potash solution in the beaker (marked A).
2. Introduce soaked seeds in the retort. Dip the drawn tube of the retort in the salt solution in the beaker (marked B).
3. Introduce a few soaked seeds in the retort. Dip the drawn tube in caustic potash solution (marked C).
4. Allow the experiment to stand as such for some time.

Results

There is no change in 1 and 2 conditions. In 3, the KOH solution rises in the tube.

Conclusions

1. When dry seeds are placed (in case A).

Water is required as a medium for enzyme activity. Hence dry seeds do not respire.

2. When soaked seed are placed (in case B)

Soaked seeds germinate because water is available as ınedium for respiratory enzymes. During seed germination respiration takes place. It uses oxygen and an equal amount of carbon dioxide is released. Thus volume of the air in the retort remains the same except that it is now rich in CO_2. Carbon dioxide is insoluble in salt solution placed outside in the beaker. Therefore, water rises in the retort.

3. When soaked seeds are placed (in case C)

Soaked seeds in this case respire and release carbon dioxide equal to the amount of oxygen absorbed. Since the free end of the retort is dipped

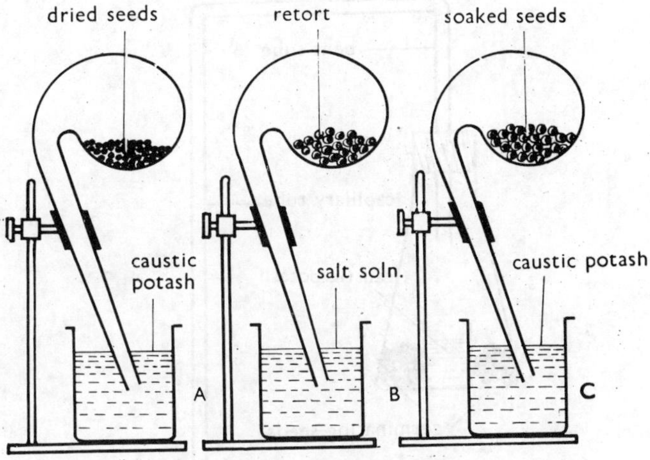

Fig. 6. To demonstrate that CO2 is released during aerobic respiration by using retorts.

into the KOH solution, carbon dioxide produced shall be absorbed and solution shall rush into the tube. This indicate the production of carbon dioxide during respiration.

The comparison of the there conditions show that

(1) dried seeds do not respire,
(2) the volume of air remains unchanged during the process because the carbon dioxide produced is equal in volume to oxygen absorbed and
(3) when germinating seeds respire, carbon dioxide is released.

Exercise 5

Purpose : To demonstrate that oxygen is used during respiration.

Materials

A conical flask, small beaker, bent capillary tube, trough, mercury, germinating seeds, caustic potash, stands, etc.

Procedure

1. Take a conical wide-mouthed flask, introduce a few germinating seeds and a small beaker containing caustic potash.
2. The mouth of the flask is closed by a single-holed cork through which is inserted a capillary tube bent twice.
3. The free end of the tube is dipped in a trough containing mercury.
4. The experiment is allowed to stand.

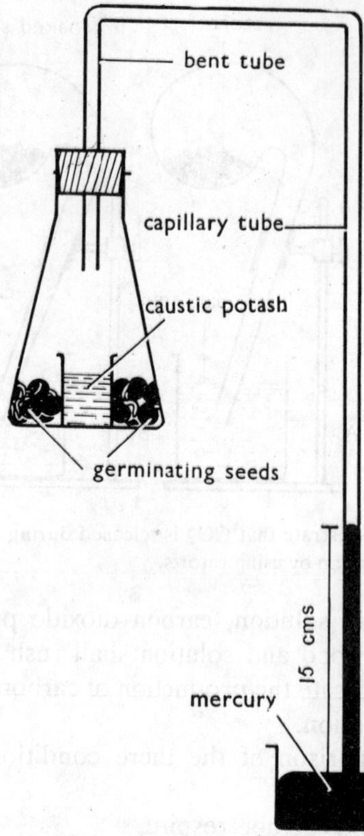

Fig. 7. To demonstrate that oxygen is used during respiration.

Results

The mercury rises up in the capillary tube up to about 15 cm.

Conclusions

The germinating seeds respire releasing carbon dioxide. It is immediately absorbed by the KOH. As a result mercury begins to rise in the capillary tube.

After reaching the 15 cm mark of the capillary tube, mercury stops to rise. This indicates that there is no further production of carbon dioxide and the respiration has stopped.

The rise of mercury to 15 cm indicates that this is about one- fifth of the normal atmospheric pressure. Thus, the seeds must have used about one-fifth of the volume of the air. Oxygen makes up about one-fifth of the volume of air. Therefore, it is concluded that the seeds have absorbed oxygen which accounts for this one-fifth of air.

Actually the rise of mercury is equal to the carbon dioxide absorbed by the caustic potash. This indicates that about one fifth of the atmospheric volume of carbon dioxide is produced during respiration. The amount of carbon dioxide being equal to the oxygen absorbed, this rise in the mercury level further indicates that one-fifth of the volume of air i.e. the total oxygen content of the air has been used up. There being no further oxygen left in the conical flask, respiration ceases and consequently, the level of mercury stops to rise.

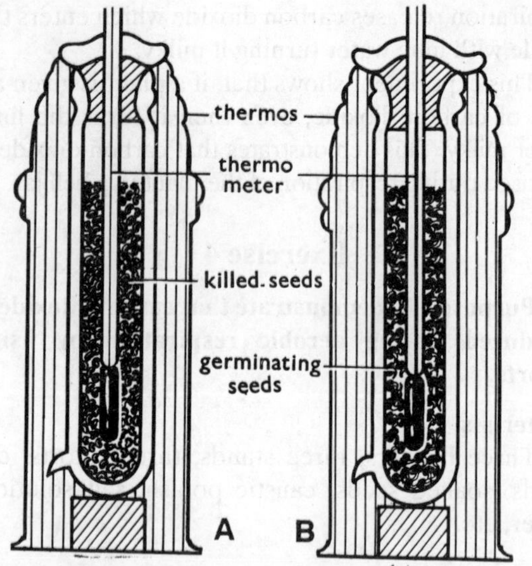

Fig. 8. To demonstrate that energy is released in the form of heat during respiration.

Exercise 6

Purpose : To demonstrate that energy is released in the form of heat during respiration.

Materials

Two thermos flasks, germinating seeds, mercuric chloride, two thermometers, rubber corks, etc.

Procedure

1. Take two thermos flasks.
2. Introduce seeds which are boiled or dried and treated with mercuric chloride in A. (The mercuric chloride treatment also eliminates fungi or bacteria from the seeds and consequently their respiration is prevented.)
3. In flask B germinating seeds are placed.
4. Both the flasks are closed by rubber stopper. Thermometers are inserted through each of these. The thermometers should be buried in the seeds.

5. The temperatures at the beginning of the experiment are noted.
6. The apparatus is allowed to stand for some time and then the temperatures are recorded once again.

Results

The temperature of the flask A with killed seeds remains unchanged while there is a rise in temperature of the flask B where germinating seeds were placed.

Conclusions

Respiration breaks down respiratory substrate and release about 673 Kcal of energy. Of this, most of the energy is converted and stored (as ATP) before being actually used in other metabolic activities of the cells.

However, some amount of energy escapes as free energy (heat) resulting in the increase in temperature.

In flask A the seeds being killed do not respire, therefore, the temperature remains unchanged. However, the seeds in flask B undergo respiration. The energy escaping as heat during this process; consequently causes rise in temperature.

Exercise 7

Purpose : To determine the value of RQ of different respiratory substrates.

Materials

Ganong's respirometer, respiratory substrates, caustic potash, saline water, filter paper, stand, etc.

Procedure

1. Open the bulb of the respirometer and pour a few drops of water.
2. Place a filter paper at its base.
3. Place a few germinating seeds in the bulb.
4. Saline water is filled through the other end of tube (called levelling arm). Saline water is used because carbon dioxide is insoluble in this solution.
5. Now place the stopper of the bulb. It is first adjusted in a way that a hole in the bulb and those in the stopper come to lie opposite each other. Air enters through them into the bulb.
6. The solution in the arm is brought to the same level by raising or lowering the levelling arm.
7. The stopper is then rotated, so that the contact between the two holes is cut off.

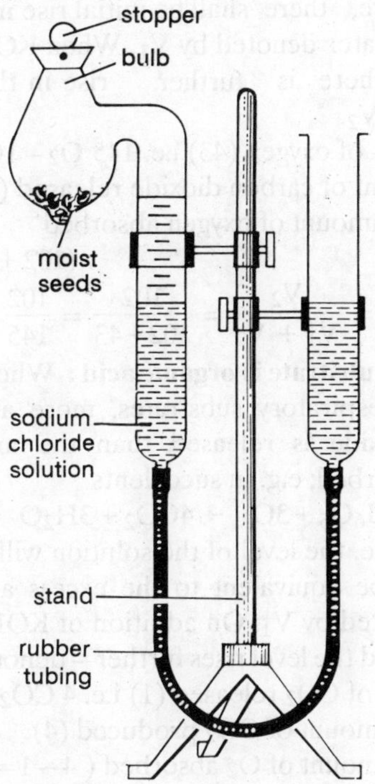

Fig. 9. To determine RQ by using Ganong's respirometer.

8. The initial level of the solution is noted again.
9. The experiment is allowed to proceed for a few hours. The level is noted once again.
10. A KOH crystal is introduced in the tube and change in the level is noted

Results and conclusions

1. If the respiratory substrate is corbohydrate : Germinating grains of cereals e.g. wheat, rice, maize, etc. are rich in carbohydrates. During their respiration, the amount of carbon dioxide released shall be equal to the amount of oxygen absorbed. Thus, there shall neither be rise nor fall in the level. The RQ is, therefore, equal to unity. Similarly, RQ for the leaves of many species of plants and flowers usually have a respiratory quotient of approximately one.

$$C_6H_{12}O_6 + 6O_2 = 6CO_2 + 6H_2O$$

$$\therefore \quad RQ = \frac{6}{6} = 1$$

2. If the respiratory substrate is fat : In case of fats (e.g. castor seeds, mustard seeds, ground nut etc.), the amount of carbon dioxide released is less than the amount of oxygen absorbed, e.g.

$$2C_{51}H_{98}O_6 + 145\ O_2 \rightarrow 102\ CO_2 + 98\ H_2O$$

Therefore, there shall be initial rise in the level of saline water denoted by V_1. When KOH crystal is added, there is further rise in the level– denoted by V_2.

V_1 = excess of oxygen (43) i.e. 145 O_2 – 102 CO_2

V_2 = amount of carbon dioxide released (102)

$V_1 + V_2$ = amount of oxygen absorbed (102 + 43 = 145)

$$RQ = \frac{CO_2}{O_2} = \frac{V_2}{V_1 + V_2} = \frac{102}{102+43} = \frac{102}{145} = 0.7$$

3. If the substrate is organic acid : When organic acids are respiratory substrates, more amount of carbon dioxide is released than the amount of oxygen absorbed; e.g. in succulents.

$$C_4H_6O_5 + 3O_2 \rightarrow 4CO_2 + 3H_2O$$

Therefore, the level of the solution will fall. This fall would be equivalent to the excess amount of CO_2 – denoted by V_1. On addition of KOH, CO_2 is absorbed and the level rises further – denoted by V_2.

V_1 = excess of CO_2 released (1) i.e. 4 CO_2 – 3 O_2.

V_2 = total amount of CO_2 produced (4)

$V_2 - V_1$ = amount of O_2 absorbed (4 – 1 = 3)

$$RQ = \frac{CO_2}{O_2} = \frac{V_2}{V_2 - V_1} = \frac{4}{(4-1=3)} = \frac{4}{3} = 1.3$$

This type of respiration occurs in succulents during daytime. (Succulents show incomplete oxidation of carbohydrates during night producing organic acids. These are later oxidised during daytime. Thus, if the bulb is covered with black cloth, succulents would show incomplete oxidation of carbohydrates and the value of RQ would be zero or less than one).

Exercise 8

Purpose : To compare and calculate the resspiratory quotients by means of a pair of respiroscopes.

Materials

Double respiroscopes, wooden stand, beakers, caustic potash, starchy seeds (wheat, maize, oat, etc.), oily seeds (castor, mustard, etc.), cotton plug, a small test tube, thread, etc.

Procedure

1. A pair of respiroscopes is placced on a wooden stand
2. Almost equal quantities of seeds are taken and inserted in the bulged part of the tube.
3. The lower free ends of the tubes are dipped in water placed in the beakers below.

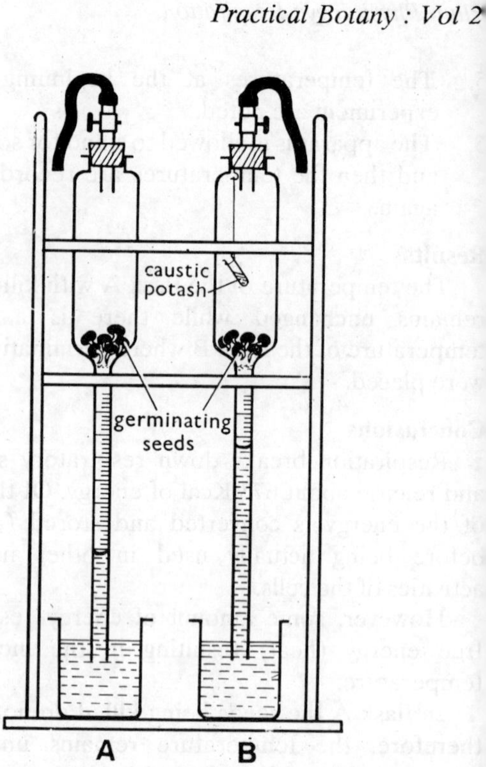

Fig. 10. Double respiroscopes to compare and measure RQ of different substances. Note the levels in respiroscpes A and B.

4. A tube containing caustic potash is hung by the thread in the respiroscope B.
5. The stop cocks of both the respiroscopes are kept open. Air is sucked through the rubber tubing and water is allowed to rise in the graduated tubes up to a prefixed mark. The stop cocks and clips of the rubber tubings are closed.
6. The apparatus is allowed to remain as such for an hour or so. The experiment is repeated with different respiratory substrates.

Results and conclusions

1. If starchy seeds are used (i.e. if the respiratory substrate is carbohydrate), there is no change in the level of tube A. The water rises in tube B. The maintenance of level in tube A indicates that absorption of oxygen is equal to release of carbon dioxide. The rise in the level of B denotes the amount of carbon dioxide released.
2. If the fatty seeds are placed (i.e. if the respiratory substrate is fat or oil), the water level in the tube A rises. This shows that more amount of oxygen is used as compared to amount of carbon dioxide released. The rise in the level of tube B, indicates the amount of carbon dioxide released.

RQ can also be calculated.
Rise in the level in tube A is denoted by V_1.
V_1 = excess of oxygen used
Rise in the level in tube B is denoted by V_2.
V_2 = total amount of carbon dioxide released.
$V_1 + V_2$ = total amount of oxygen used

$$RQ = \frac{CO_2}{O_2} = \frac{V_2}{V_1 + V_2}$$

If the succulent plants are placed (i.e. if the respiratory substrate is organic acid, the water level in the tube A falls. This shows that more amount of carbondioxide is produced than the amount of oxygen absorbed. The rise in level of tube B, indicates the amount of carbondioxide released.

RQ can be calculated as follows—
Fall in level of tube A is denoted by V_1
V_1 = excess of carbondioxide released
Rise in level of tube B is denoted by V_2
V_2 = total amount of carbondioxide released
$V_2 - V_1$ = total amount of oxygen used

$$RQ = \frac{CO_2}{O_2} = \frac{V_2}{V_2 - V_1}$$

Exercise 9

Purpose : To measure the rate of respiration by olumetric method using Pettinkoffer's tubes.

laterials

Pettinkoffer's apparatus, respiratory substrate, ressure regulator, soda lime, barium hydroxide, xalic/hydrochloric acid, phenolphthalein, caustic otash, burette, measuring cylinder, beakers, jars, alance, weight box, vaseline or grease, etc.

Procedure

1. The jars or bottles are filled with soda lime.
2. The respiratory material (about 100 g) is placed in U-tube chamber.
3. Long and narrow Pettinkoffer's tubes are filled with barium hydroxide solution of known concentration (*N/10*). The tubes are placed on a wooden stand in such a way that they are obliquely oriented.
4. The tubes are connected to a pressure regulator (suction pump).
5. Apparatus is made airtight.
6. The pressure regulator is allowed to work. A slow current of air rushes into soda lime towers. This removes carbon dioxide from the air current. The air now reaches the plant material placed in a respiratory chamber.
7. The air from the chamber is bubbled through the barium hydroxide solution filled in the Pettinkoffer's tubes.
8. A pressure regulator is put to work to regulate a slow movement of air and bubbles are regulated. The bubbles are moved slowly in such a way that they do not coalesce with one another. Air is first passed through one of the Pettinkoffer's tubes and then the flow of air is diverted to the second tube.
9. The first tube is removed and its contents are titrated.
10. The contents show turbidity due to the presence of preciptated $BaCO_3$.
11. About 25 cc of $BaCO_3$ (or contents of Pettinkoffer's tube) are measured.
12. It is now titrated against *N/10* solution of oxalic acid or hydrochloric acid.

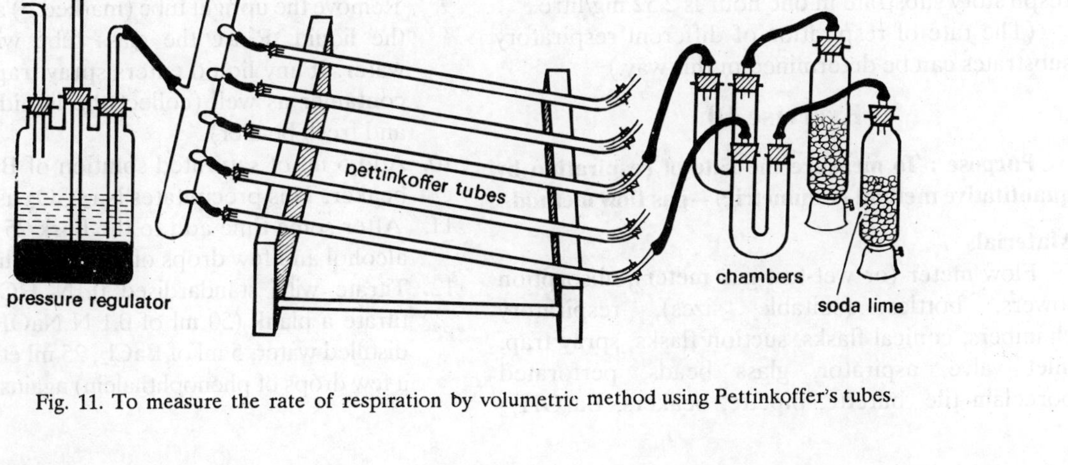

Fig. 11. To measure the rate of respiration by volumetric method using Pettinkoffer's tubes.

13. A drop of phenolphthalein is used as indicator which is added to the beaker containing $BaCO_3$.
14. The end point is then noted.

Results and conclusions

S. No.	Volume of $BaCO_3$	Volume of Oxalic acid		
		Initial reading	Final reading	Volume used
1	25 cc	0 cc	10.0 cc	10 cc
2	25 cc	11.0 cc	20.0 cc	9 cc
3	25 cc	21.0 cc	32.0 cc	11 cc
4	25 cc	33.0 cc	42.0 cc	9 cc
5	25 cc	43.0 cc	54.0 cc	11 cc
				Average : 10 cc

$N_1 V_1 = N_2 V_2$

N_1 = Known normality of oxalic acid.

N_1 is calculated as follows –

Molecular weight of oxalic acid = 126

$$\text{Equivalent weight} = \frac{126}{2} = 63$$

$$\therefore N = 63$$

$\therefore \frac{N}{10}$ = 6.3 g of oxalic acid dissolved in 1000cc water

$\therefore \quad N_1 = 6.3$

V_1 = Known volume of oxalic acid used = 10 cc

N_2 = Normality of barium hydroxide soln. (To be determined).

V_2 = Volume of $BaCO_3$ = 25 cc

Substituting the values in $N_1 V_1 = N_2 V_2$

$6.3 \times 10 = N_2 \times 25$

$$\therefore \quad N_2 = \frac{6.3 \times 10}{25} = 2.52$$

The amount of CO_2 produced by 100 g of respiratory substrate in one hour is 2.52 mg/litre.

(The rate of respiration of different respiratory substrates can be determined in this way.)

Exercise 10

Purpose : To measure the rate of respiration by quantitative method (volumetric) – gas flow method.

Materials

Flow meter (or wet-test gas meter), absorption towers, bottles (suitable sizes), respiratory chambers, conical flasks, suction flasks, spray trap, inlet valve, aspirator, glass beads, perforated porcelain tile, burette, pipette, beakers, $Ba(OH)_2$ solution (20%), soda lime, 0.1N NaOH, $BaCl_2$ (saturated), ethyl alcohol (95%), phenolphthalein 0.1N HCl, potatoes, (or germinating seeds or any respiratory substrate under study), etc.

Procedure

1. Set up the apparatus in the following sequence:
(A) a calibrated flow meter or wet-test gas meter,
(B) a CO_2 absorption tower (filled with soda lime),
(C) a bottle containing 20% $Ba(OH)_2$ solution,
(D) respiratory chamber,
(E) a flask with absorption tower (filled with soda lime),
(F) spray trap,
(G) suction flask with
(H) one way valve,
(I) inlet for flow rate adjustment and
(J) water aspirator.
2. Absorption tower (B) is a 2 cm wide tube. At its bottom is a perforated procelain plate on which glass beads and soda lime are packed.
3. The size of the respiratory chamber (D) is chosen according to the need.
4. The rate of air flow should be adjusted in a way that its rate is sufficient to prevent any appreciable accumulation of CO_2 in respiratory chamber.
5. To proceed, place the respiratory substrate in a respiratory chamber (D).
6. Now pour 50 ml of 0.1N NaOH in absorption flask (marked C).
7. Make the connections airtight and run aspirator. Take care to see that level of the liquid in absorption flask (E) does not rise more than halfway to the top during the experiment.
8. Allow the experiment to run for about an hour.
9. Remove the upright tube (marked F) and pour off the liquid. Rinse the glass tube with distilled water. If any liquid enters spray trap, rinse this container as well (collect the liquid in a clean and fresh beaker).
10. Add 5 ml of saturated solution of $BaCl_2$ to the beaker. This precipitates Na_2CO_3 as $BaCO_3$.
11. After some time add to the flask 25 ml of ethyl alcohol and few drops of phenolphthalein.
12. Titrate with standardised 0.1N HCl. Similarly titrate a blank (50 ml of 0.1 N NaOH, 200ml of distilled water, 5 ml of $BaCl_2$, 25 ml ethyl alcohol, a few drops of phenophthalein) against 0.1N HCl.

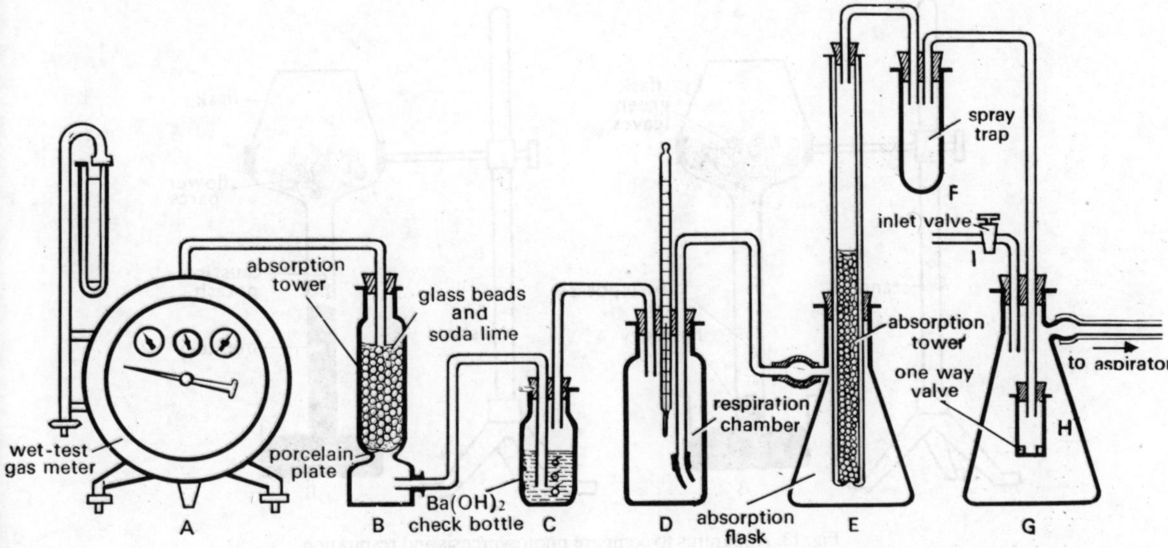

Fig.12. Assembly of apparatus for measuring the rate of respiration by gas flow method.

Results

1. Weight of CO_2 liberated during respiration is computed as follows—
   CO_2 in milligrams = $V \times N \times 22.0$
   V = Difference between blank and experimental titrations (in millilitres)
   N = normality of HCl used.
2. Calculate the milligrams of CO_2 evolved per hour per gram of the substrate as follows—
   $N_1V_1 = N_2V_2$ where
   N_1 = normality of HCl;
   V_1 = Known volume of HCl used;
   N_2 = ? and V_2 = volume of $BaCO_3$
   $\therefore$ N_2 = amount of CO_2 in mg/litre/hour/gram of respiratory substrate.

Exercise 11

Purpose : To compare the processes of photosynthesis and respiration.

Materials

Two long necked flasks, two petri dishes, stands, mercury, caustic potash, green leaves, flowers, etc.

Procedure

1. Introduce moistened green leaves in flask A.
2. A few moistened flowers are placed in flask B.
3. Invert the flasks so that their necks dip in mercury in petri dishes.
4. The experiment s kept in diffused light.
5. In the evening introduce a crystal of caustic potash into the neck of each flask.

Results

1. The mercury shall rise very little or there shall be no rise at all in the neck of the flask A, where green leaves are placed.
2. There shall be an appreciable rise in the level of mercury in the neck of flask B where flowers are placed.

Conclusion

Green leaves respire and also photosynthesize. In respiration, oxygen is absorbed and carbon dioxide is released. However, in photosynthesis carbon dioxide is used and oxygen is released.

During the experiment both the processes continue. In diffused light, the rate of photosynthesis would be slower and hence oxygen released shall also be less. This oxygen shall be completely used up in respiration and carbon dioxide is released. This carbon dioxide can not be fully absorbed by photosynthesis because it is slow due to diffused light. Hence, some quantity of carbon dioxide accumulates. Thus, mercury rushes in the tube as soon as caustic potash is introduced which absorbs carbon dioxide present in the flask.

2. In flask B there is almost no photosynthesis due to absence of chlorophyll in the flower parts. Only respiration takes place resulting in the production of carbon dioxide alone. The mercury rises higher in the flask B after the insertion of caustic potash which absorbs carbon dioxide present in the flask.

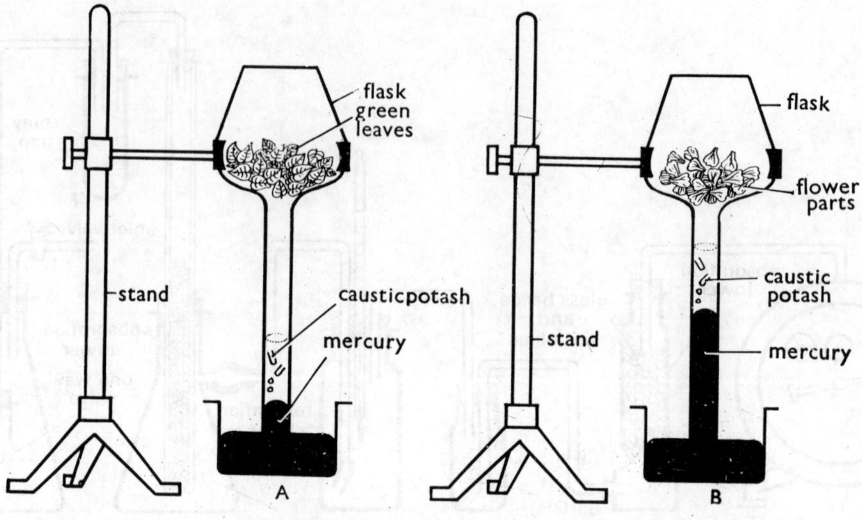

Fig. 13. Apparatus to compare photosynthesis and respiration.

Exercise 12

Purpose : Demonstration of respiratory enzymes in plant tissues.

Materials

Potato, razors, petri dishes, spirit lamp, test tubes, water, alcohol, gum guaiacum (Benzidine), hydrogen peroxide, 2,3,5 triphenyl tetrazolium chloride, etc.

Procedure

(1) **Oxidase.** A thin transverse section of the potato tuber is cut and placed in a petri dish. Section is immersed completely in 2% alcoholic solution of gum guaiacum (Benzidine). Ten to fifteen minutes are allowed for results to appear. The process is repeated with a boiled section of another potato slice.

(2) **Peroxidase.** Repeat the same procedure as above using another potato slice. Remove all the gum guaiacum (Benzidine) solution after 10-15 minutes. Add dilute solution of hydrogen peroxide (3% commercial hydrogen peroxide in 30 parts of water). Repeat the procedure with a boiled section of another potato slice.

(3) **Dehydrogenase.** Cut a thin section of potato tuber. Add 2,3,5 triphenyl tetrazolium chloride (0.5%) to the section in petri dish. Repeat with a boiled section of a potato tuber.

(4) **Catalase.** To a cut and thin potato slice, add hydrogen peroxide solution (30 parts of water to 1 part of H_2O_2). Note the changes. Repeat with a potato slice boiled in water.

Results

(1) **Oxidase.** Blue colour is developed due to oxidization of gum guaiacum.

(2) **Peroxidase**. The rapidity with which the intensity of the blue colour develops, changes as compared to 1 (oxidase).

(3) **Dehydrogenase**. Red colour is developed.

(4) **Catalase.** Oxygen bubbles are evolved.

Explanations

(1) **Oxidase**. During oxidative phase of the Kreb's cycle, hydrogen electrons are transfered from the substrate to atmospheric oxygen through a chain of hydrogen acceptors. In cells, hydrogen acceptors transfer the hydrogens from one substance to another until they reach a compound called cytochrome. The enzymes oxidases, peroxidases and dehydrogenases catalyse the transfer from one kind of molecule to another. The type reaction may be –

$$A.H_2 + B \xrightarrow[\text{enzymes}]{\text{oxidising}} A + B.H_2$$

A = hydrogen donor, B = hydrogen acceptor,

In a reaction catalysed by the enzyme cytochrome oxidase, the hydrogens are finally transferred to molecular oxygen to form water.

(2) **Peroxidase**. These are of wide occurrence in the plant tissues and oxidise various substrates (viz. phenols, amines) in the presence of H_2O_2 as electron acceptors. Hydrogen peroxide with an addition of hydrogen atoms and electrons form water.

$$A.H_2 + H_2O_2 \xrightarrow{\text{Peroxidase}} A + 2H_2O$$

(3) **Dehydrogenase**. These also remove hydrogen atoms like oxidases and peroxidases to oxidise the substrate. The acceptors receive hydrogen atoms and get reduced (e.g., hydrogen acceptors – NAD or NADP). In plant cells, oxidase results in the formation of H_2O_2. The evidence, however, fails to show accumulation of hydrogen peroxide due to respiration. Further, H_2O_2 is known inhibitor of many enzymes and needs destruction.

(4) **Catalase**. It is an enzyme which brings about decomposition of H_2O_2 into water and oxygen.

$$2H_2O_2 \xrightarrow{\text{Catalase}} 2H_2O + O_2$$

Exercise 13

Purpose : To study the effect of amylase (diastase) on starch.

Materials

Starch solution (or extract or slurry of potato pulp), taka diastase or extract from germinating barley seeds, (both are used for amylase), iodine solution, Benedict's solution, test tubes, spirit lamp, etc.

Procedure

1. Take two test tubes.
2. Add a tablet of taka diastase (to 100 ml of water in each test tube).
3. Heat and bring to boil a solution in one test tube (A) while keep another (B) as such.
4. Add soluble starch solution to both.
5. Test the solutions in tubes A and B with iodine on porecelain tile or with Benedict' solution.

Results

1. The intensity of the colour in tube A remains unchanged while the colour is intense in tube B which decreases with time.
2. In tube B first test for the presence of starch should be done soon after the mixture is ready. Then tests are made for starch after 2, 5, 15 and 20 minutes. Two drops of solution and a drop of iodine on a porcelain tile gives the test. (Also use Benedict's solution.) If blue colour does not appear, dilute stock soln. of amylase with equal volume of $CaCl_2$ soln. and restart.

The intense colour in the tube A indicates presence of starch. This intense colour also appears in tube B, thereby indicating presence of starch. Later, intensity decreases (in tube B) showing disappearance of the starch.

Conclusions

Amylase (Taka diastase) is an enzyme. It is widely distributed in plant tissues particularly germinating seeds. It is specific for starch and breaks it to simple monosaccharides (glucose). It functions to meet the glucose need especially during seed germination.

The tube A when heated does not show reactions because the enzyme is denatured at high temperature. Enzymes are proteins and are most effective in concentrated solutions. Effective temperature and pH range is very narrow and beyond this enzyme is inactivated irreversibly.

Second experiment shows the effect of enzyme concentration on the rate of reaction. The amount of starch (indicated by the comparative intensity of the blue colour) will be highest in a sample where enzyme concentration was lowest. The tube with minimum starch shall have maximum enzyme.

If the amount of starch (substrate) is sufficient and does not limit the reaction rate, then the rate of reaction is usually directly proportional to enzyme concentration.

VII. Growth and Growth Hormones

Preamble

[I] The Definition

The growth is defined as irreversible increase in volume associated with increase in dry weight. In plants growth is localised to meristems only e.g. (1) apical meristems – root and shoot apices, (2) lateral meristems – vascular cambium and cork cambium and (3) intercalary meristem.

[II] Growth curve

The meristematic cells pass through three phases viz. cell division, cell enlargement and cell maturation. The growth rate exhibits S-shaped curve. The maximum growth rate occurs durring cell enlargement phase and gradually declines towards the phase of cell maturation.

[III] Growth substances

The growth of a plant is mostly due to certain chemical substances which plant synthesizes in very small quantities. These are produced at places other than the growth points and are then transported to places where they produce specific effects. These are variously known as plant hormones, phytohormones, growth substances, growth regulators, etc. Three categories of hormones are recognised chemically— (1) auxins, (2) gibberellins and (3) cytokinins.

1. Auxins. Auxins form an important group. Indole-acetic-acid (IAA) is the most common and naturally occurring auxin in the plants. Synthetic substances found to act as auxins are indole-butyric-acid (IBA), α and β naphthalene -acetic acid, phenyl-acetic acid and 2-4, dichlorophenoxy-acetic acid (2-4 D), etc.

The studies about the distribution of auxin were made on *Avena* coleoptile during its phototropic movement. It is now known that stimulus (illumination) induces auxin at the apex and that it was water soluble. The auxin is generally inhibited and photochemically inactivated on the illuminated side. This substance is inhibited in its down ward movement on the illuminated side. It was furthermore demonstrated that auxins move away from the illuminated side and are concentrated on the side towards dark. This substance causes cell to divide on the side where it is most concentrated i.e. on the dark side, thus resulting in a curvature towards the source of light.

Auxins affect the overall process of growth. It is responsible for cell division, cell elongation, shortening of internodes, initiation of roots, prevention of abscission layer, apical dominance, parthenocarpy, flower initiation, etc.

2. Gibberellins. Gibberellins which form a distinct group of growth substances were first isolated from a fungus *Gibberella fujikuroi*. This growth substance causes surprising elongation of the stem, breaks genetic dwarfism, produces parthenocarpic fruits, breaks dormancy and promotes flowering in long day plants.

3. Cytokinins. Cytokinins are substances causing cells to divide and coconut milk, zeatin are examples of cytokinins. These are also known to delay senescence.

Exercise 1

Purpose : Measurement of growth using auxanometer.

Materials

1. Lever auxanometer, potted plant, weights, string, etc. 2. Pfeffer's auxanometer, potted plant, weight, smoked paper, etc.

Procedure

Two types of auxanometers are commonly used— 1. Lever auxanometer or arc indicator and 2. pulley auxanometer or Pfeffer's auxanometer.

1. Lever auxanometer or **arc indicator.** In this type an indicator is fixed to a wheel around which passes a cord. One end of the cord is tied, gummed or taped to the apex of the stem. The cord is now passed over a small wheel to which an indicator is fixed. The other end of the cord carries a weight.

2. Pfeffer's auxanometer or **pulley auxanometer.** It gives a permanent record of growth within a specified time. A thread is tied to the tip of the stem. It is then passed over a small wheel attached to a large wheel and accurately centered around the same axis. At the other end of this thread a small weight is tied. Round the bigger wheel (to which a smaller wheel carrying a thread from plant passes) passes another cord, both ends of which carry one small weight each. A smaller pointer is attached to the cord passing over the bigger wheel. It is in contact with the drum which is placed close to the pointer. The drum is wrapped with a smoked paper and is rotated by a clockwork mechanism.

Result

1. The arc indicator moves along the arc.
2. The smoked paper shows marks of the pointer movement.

Conclusion

1. Lever auxanometer. As the growth takes place, stem increases in length. The wheel slowly rotates due to the pressure of weight. This results in the movement of indicator along the arc scale. The growth of the plant is thus recorded.

From the records, actual growth can be obtained. The magnification of growth given by the indicator is first made known. For example, if the size of pulley is

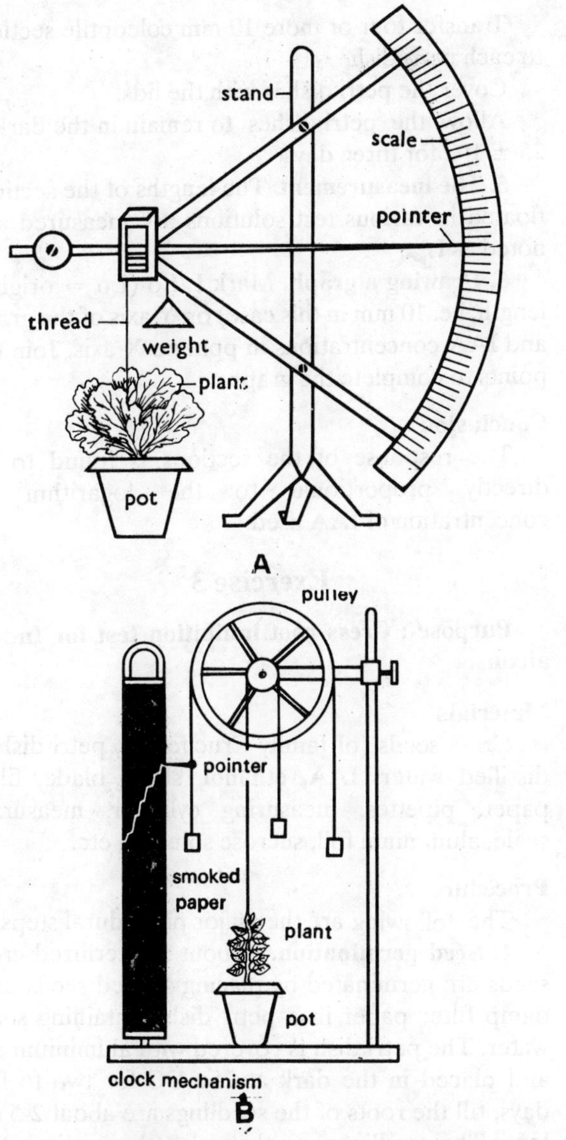

Fig. 1. Auxanometers. A Arc indicator. B. Pfeffer's auxanometer.

4 inches and needle 20 inches from the centre of the disc, the magnification of growth shown is 10 times.

Now, in the auxanometer indicator has traversed a distance of 5 cm, in 20 hours and the magnification is 10 times, the actual growth during this period shall be

$$\frac{5}{10} \text{ cm} = 0.25 \text{ or } 2.5 \text{ mm in 20 hours.}$$

$$\therefore \text{ in an hour } \frac{2.5 \text{ mm}}{20} = 0.1 \text{ mm/hour.}$$

2. Pfeffer's auxanometer. In this case as the stem tip grows, pointer leaves a mark on the smoked paper of the rotating drum on a magnified scale. If there is no growth, a straight horizontal line is obtained. On the other hand, during growth the line moves downward and traces a downward spiral on the smoked paper.

For a permanent record, smoked paper is dipped in varnish, to fix the smoke. A staircase curve is then traced on to a paper. The horizontal portion of the curve indicates no growth. A diagonal curve is obtained if the growth is continuous. The time period and magnification of growth given by drum curve being known, actual rate of growth during a specified period can be calculated.

During elongation or growth of stem the following processes take place—

1. Active cell division of the apical region of the shoot,
2. The newly added cells (derivatives) undergo elongation or expansion and
3. There is consequent increase in the length of the stem.

Exercise 2

Purpose : Demonstration of *Avena* straight growth test.

Materials

Avena (oat) fruits (caryopsis), filter paper, aluminium foil, petri dishes, test tubes, pipettes, measuring cylinder, coleoptile cutter (or sharp blade), hair brush, pencil, graph paper, distilled water, ethanol, IAA, 2% sucrose solution, etc.

Procedure

The following are the major steps—

1. Seed germination. About 50 or more *Avena* seeds are germinated by placing soaked seeds in water and then placed on a damp filter paper in petri dish containing a small amount of water. Petri dish is covered with aluminium foil and placed in the dark at 25 ± 1°C for 2 to 5 days.

2. Preparation of sections. After germination when coleoptiles are aobut 2-3 cm long, the apical tip, about 4 mm, of each coleoptile is removed. This is done in order to prevent natural auxins produced by the coleoptile from affecting the growth.

Cut sections of 10 mm length of the remaining part of the coleoptile with the help of coleoptile cutter or a very sharp blade.

3. Preparation of IAA concentrations. Dissolve 100 mg of IAA in 2 ml of ethanol (IAA is not soluble in water, hence it is first dissolved in ethanol). Dilute

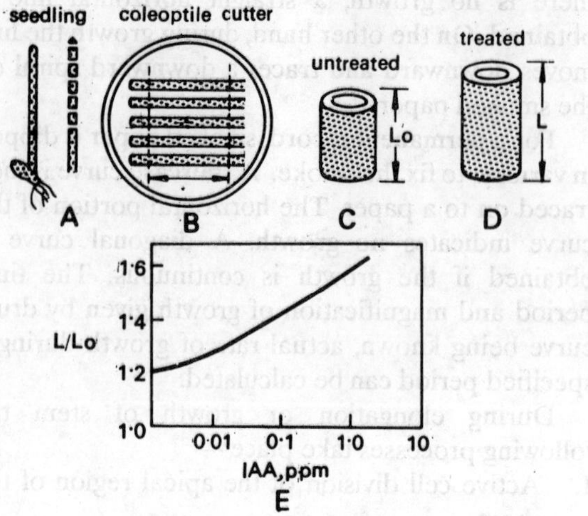

Fig. 2. Diagrammatic representation of *Avena* straight growth test, **A.** *Avena* seedling, **B.** Cutting of sections, C. Lo = length of freshly cut segment, D. L = length of treated segments, E. graph showing relationship between dose and response.

to 900 ml with distilled water. Warm the solution to 80°C and keep at this temperature for 5 minutes. Make up to one litre with distilled water. This stock solution gives 100 ppm concentration of IAA.

Take six test tubes marked A to F. Add 10 ml of 2% sucrose solution to each test tube. Now do as follows to obtain desired concentrations.

Tube A. Add 2 ml of IAA stock solution to 18 ml sucrose solution already present. Mix the contents thoroughly. This gives 10 ppm IAA solution.

Tube B. Add 2 ml solution from tube A to 18 ml sucrose solution already present. This gives 1 ppm IAA solution.

Tube C. Add 2 ml solution from tube B to 18 ml of sucrose solution already present. This gives 0.1 ppm IAA solution.

Tube D. Add 2 ml solution from tube C to 18 of sucrose solution already present. This gives 0.01 ppm IAA solution.

Tube E. Add 2 ml sucrose solution to 18 ml sucrose solution in the test tube. There is no IAA in the tube.

Tube F. Add 2 ml of distilled water to 18 ml of sucrose solution already present.

The tubes E and F act as control.

4. The treatment. Transfer solution from tubes A to F to similarly marked petri dishes.

Transfer four or more 10 mm coleoptile sections to each petri dish.

Cover the petri dishes with the lids.

Allow the petri dishes to remain in the dark at 25 ± 1°C for three days.

5. The measurement. The lengths of the sections floated in various test solutions are measured and noted as L.

6. Drawing a graph. Mark L/Lo (Lo = original length, i.e. 10 mm in this case) on Y axis of the graph and IAA concentrations in ppm on X axis. Join the points to complete the graph.

Conclusion

The response of the sections is found to be directly proportional to the logarithm of concentration of IAA used.

Exercise 3

Purpose : Cress root inhibition test for Indole auxins.

Materials

Cress seeds (of family Cruciferae), petri dishes, distilled water, IAA, ethanol, sharp blade, filter paper, pipettes, measuring cylinder, measuring scale, aluminium foil, sucrose solution, etc.

Procedure

The following are the major procedural steps—

1. Seed germination. About 50 sterilized cress seeds are germinated by placing soaked seeds on a damp filter paper in a petri dish containing some water. The petri dish is covered with aluminium foil and placed in the dark at 25±1°C for two to five days, till the roots of the seedlings are about 2-5 cm long. The seedlings are then placed in various test solutions.

2. Preparation of IAA solutions. Dissolve 10 mg of IAA in 2 ml of ethanol (IAA is not soluble in water, hence it is first dissolved in ethanol). Dilute 900 ml with distilled water. Warm the solution to 80°C and keep at this temperature for 5 minutes. Make up to one litre with distilled water. This stock solution gives 10 ppm concentration of IAA.

Take five test tubes, marked A to E. Add 18 ml of sucrose solution (2%) to each of the five test tubes. Now proceed as follows to prepare different IAA concentrations.

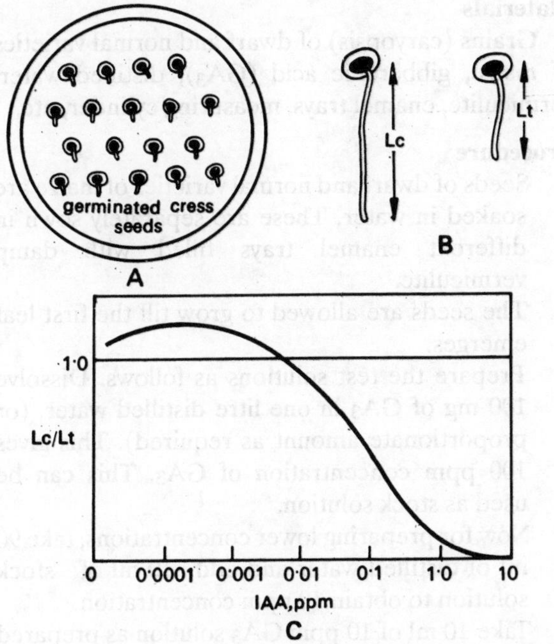

Fig. 3. Diagrammatic representation of cress inhibition test, for Indole auxins. A. Germinating cress seeds, B. treated and controlled seedlings (Lc = length of controlled seedling root; Lt = length of treated seedling root), C. graph showing relationship between dose and response.

Tube A. Add 2 ml of IAA stock solution to obtain 1 ppm IAA concentration.

Tube B. Add 2 ml of solution from tube A and obtain 0.1 ppm IAA concentration.

Tube C. Add 2 ml of solution from tube B and obtain 0.01 ppm IAA concentration.

Tube D. Add 2 ml of solution from tube C and obtain 0.001 ppm IAA concentration.

Tube E. Add 2 ml of solution from tube D and obtain 0.0001 ppm IAA concentration.

3. The treatment. Transfer the solutions from test tubes A to E to similarly marked petri dishes.

Transfer a few germinated seeds to each petri dish after measuring their root length (Lt).

Cover the petri dishes with lids.

Allow the petri dishes to remain in the dark at 25±1°C for 48 hours.

4. Measurement. Measure lengths of roots of seedlings placed in various test solutions, after the test period.

5. Drawing a graph. Mark Lt/Lc (Lt = length of treated seedling root at the end of test period; Lc = length of control seedling root at the end of test period) on Y axis of the graph and IAA concentration on X axis.

Conclusion

The roots are much more sensitive to auxin than the stem and are, in fact, inhibited by concentration of auxins that normally stimulate stem growth. However, at very low concentration of auxin, root growth may be stimulated. The value of root test, therefore, is that the effect of extremely low concentration of auxin, such as found in plant extracts, may be measured. It is capable of detecting concentrations of IAA as low as 1/100,000 mg. The response is roughly proportional to the logarithm of auxin concentration.

Exercise 4

Purpose : To study the effect of gibberellic acid on plant growth.

Materials

Pea (*Pisum sativum*), bean (*Phaseolus vulgaris*) plants, gibberellic acid, ethanol, distilled water, a tray with sand, plastic covering for plants, etc.

Procedure

1. Sow pea seeds (preferably dwarf variety) or bean seeds in a tray containing sand. Maintain the seeds in moist condition by occasionally watering the tray.
2. Cover some of the two-week old pea plants by plastic covers. Spray the rest with gibberellic acid solution (100 mg/litre; dissolve GA in 1 to 2 ml of 95% ethanol and dilute to 1 litre with water). Remove the cover and spray the uncovered plants with amount of ethanol used for GA preparation. (This serves as control.) Allow the plants to grow and measure the following periodically :
(a) height of plants (from soil level),
(b) length of internodes,
(c) length of leaves and
(d) blade width.

Measure the above values for both—treated and control plants.

3. Select 2 week old bean plants of approximately the same height. Apply following solutions of GA to the growing tip of two plants each :
(a) Distilled water (control),
(b) GA 10^{-1}M,

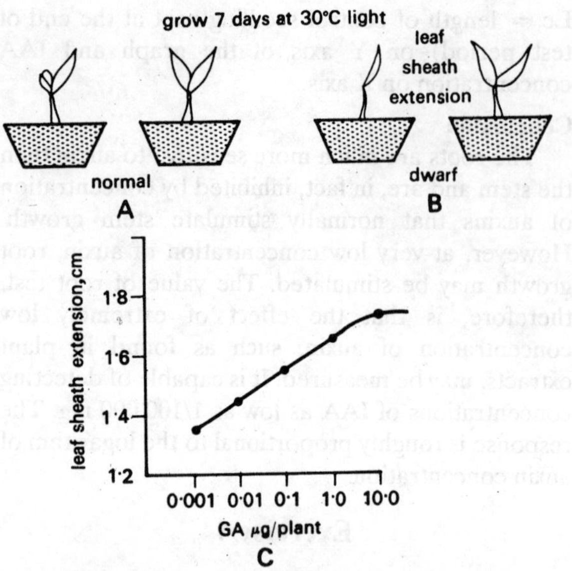

Fig. 4. Diagrammatic representation of dwarf maize test for gibberellins. A. Response of normal plants to treatments, B. response of dwarf plants to treatments, C. graph showing relationship.

(c) GA 10^{-2}M,
(d) GA 10^{-3}M and
(e) GA 10^{-4}M.

Allow the plants to grow for 2-3 weeks and measure the characters given above.

Tabulate the observations.

Result and conclusion

Growth of Pea plants shows response to gibberellic acid treatment. The bean plants would exhibit effect of GA on stem tip.

1. Genetic dwarfism. The GA eliminates genetic dwarfism in certain plants. The pea plants (dwarf) elongate and acquire the height of the normal plant. The normal plants, however, show no effect of GA on height.

2. Effect on stem tip. GA treatment growing tip of bean seedling shortens the time to flowering and hastens maturity.

Besides stem elongation and promoting flowering in long-day plants, gibberellins can break dormancy and also produce parthenocarpic fruits.

Exercise 5

Purpose : Demonstration of gibberellin activity by bioassay.

Materials

Grains (caryopsis) of dwarf and normal varieties of maize, gibberellic acid (GA_3), distilled water, vermiculite, enamel trays, measuring cylinder, etc.

Procedure

1. Seeds of dwarf and normal varieties of maize are soaked in water. These are separately sown in different enamel trays filled with damp vermiculite.
2. The seeds are allowed to grow till the first leaf emerges.
3. Prepare the test solutions as follows. Dissolve 100 mg of GA_3 in one litre distilled water. (or proportionate amount as required). This gives 100 ppm concentration of GA_3. This can be used as stock solution.
4. Now for preparing lower concentrations, take 90 ml of distilled water and add 10 ml of stock solution to obtain 10 ppm concentration.
5. Take 10 ml of 10 ppm GA_3 solution as prepared above and to it add 90 ml of distilled water in another beaker. This gives 1 ppm concentration. Repeat the procedure to obtain 0.1, 0.01 ppm concentrations of GA_3.
6. Add test material as prepared above to the cup formed by the emerging first leaf. Allow the plants to grow for 7 days 30°C in light to observe the response.

Observations

Note the observations as given below.

GA concentration (in ppm)	Leaf sheath extension (in cm)
0.001	1.36
0.01	1.45
0.1	1.52
1.0	1.66
10.0	1.73

Draw a graph showing leaf sheath extension on Y axis and GA concentrations used on X axis.

Conclusion

The dwarf habit in many plants is due to single recessive gene. In gibberellin assays only single-gene dwarfs are used. It is specific for gibberellins and the growth reponse is linear in the range of 0.001-10 ppm (or μg) of GA_3 per plant.

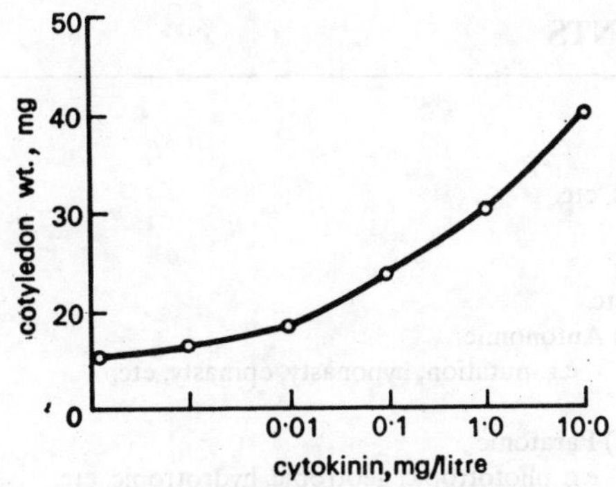

Fig. 5. Diagrammatic representation of radish cotyledon test for cytokinins. Graph to show relationship between dose and response.

Exercise 6

Purpose : Demonstration of cytokinin activity by bioassay.

Materials

Seeds of radish, cytokinin, distilled water, petri dishes, measuring cylinder, beakers, etc.

Procedure

1. Radish seeds are soaked in water. These are allowed to germinate for 30 hours in complete darkness on moistened filter paper, at 26± 1°C.
2. Prepare the test solutions as follows. Dissolve 100 mg of cytokinin in one litre of water (or proportionate amount as desired). This gives 100 ppm concentration of cytokinin and serves as a stock solution.
3. Now for preparing lower concentrations, take 45 ml of distilled water in a test tube and add 5 ml of stock solution. This gives 10 ppm concentration of cytokinin.
4. To prepare 1 ppm concentratioin, take 45 ml of distilled water in a test tube and add 5 ml of 10 ppm cytokinin solution prepared as given above.
5. To prepare 0.1 ppm concentration, take 45 ml distilled water in a test tube and 5 ml of 1 ppm cytokinin solution prepared as given above.
6. To prepare 0.01 ppm concentration, take 45 ml of distilled water in a test tube and add 5 ml of 0.1 ppm cytokinin solution prepared as above.
7. To prepare 0.001 ppm concentration, take 45 ml of distilled water in a test tube and add 5 ml of 0.01 ppm cytokinin solution as prepared above.
8. Thus solutions with 10, 1, 0.1, 0.01 and 0.001 ppm concentration of cytokinin are prepared. Filter paper discs of appropriate sizes are cut and placed in different petri dishes. Cytokinin solutions of different concentrations are poured in separate petri dishes to moisten filter paper discs placed in them.
9. Smaller of the cotyledons from each radish seedling is removed and weighed. These are placed on filter discs containing test solutions.
10. Petri dishes are covered and placed under continuous fluroscent illumination for 3 days at 25±1°C. The cotyledons are reweighed.

Observations

Cytokinin concentration (in ppm)	Weight (in mg)		
	Before treatment	After treatment	Increase
0.001	30.2	45.3	15.1
0.01	22.6	40.6	18.0
0.1	26.3	48.7	22.4
1.0	25.4	55.6	30.2
10.0	28.5	67.3	30.8

Draw a graph showing increase in the weight of cotyledons on Y axis and concentration on X axis.

Conclusion

The increase in weight is related to the concentrations of the applied cytokinin. Concentrations of cytokinins between 0.001 and 10 mg per litre (or ppm) can be assayed by this procedure.

VIII. Movements

Preamble

Plant movements are of universal occurrence. These movements are not visible because plants generally do not move bodily. The plants are sensitive to changes in the environment e.g. light, heat, touch, contact, etc. The change which induces a movement in the plant is called stimulus, while reaction (movement) of the plant is known as response. This is due to the irritability or sensitiveness of protoplasm. The stimulus may be given or received by any plant organ, while response may be shown by some other organ.

PLANT MOVEMENTS

A. VITAL MOVEMENTS

- **1. Movements of locomotion**
  - (a) Autonomic (spontaneous) *e.g.* ciliary, amoeboid, cyclosis, etc. locomotion
  - (b) Paratonic (induced) or tactic *e.g.* chemotactic, phototactic, etc.
- **2. Movements of curvature**
  - (a) Movements of growth
    - (i) Autonomic *e.g.* nutation, hyponasty, epinasty, etc.
    - (ii) Paratonic *e.g.* phototropic, geotropic, hydrotropic, etc.
  - (b) Movements of variation
    - (i) Autonomic *e.g.* in *Desmodium gyrens*
    - (ii) Paratonic *e.g.* nyctinasty, seismonasty, thigmonasty, etc.

B. MECHANICAL MOVEMENTS. *e.g.* hygroscopic movements as in opening of fern sporangia, opening of peristome in moss, coiling and uncoiling elaters of *Equisetum* spores, etc.

Exercise 1

Purpose : To demonstrate geotropism by clinostat.

Materials

Clinostat, potted plant, etc.

Procedure

Clinostat consists of a disc (or drum) which rotates by clock-work mechanism. A rod is fitted to this disc which also rotates. A pot is fixed at the end of the rod.

1. A potted plant is fitted horizontally on the clinostat. It is slowly rotated by hand or electric mechanism. This gives an equal stimulation of gravity all over the plant.
2. The plant is allowed to stop at a particular position for a few minutes at regular intervals.

Result

1. The shoot as well as roots do not show any curvature.
2. The shoots bend away from the force of gravity while roots grow towards the gravity.

Conclusion

1. In the first case, the plant fails to show any movement in response to stimulus of gravity. This is because all sides of the plant are equally stimulated by gravity.
2. The shoots show negative geotropism (i.e. grow away from the force of gravity) while roots grow toward the stimulus of gravity, thus showing positive geotropism. This is because a particular region of the plant receives more gravitational stimulus than the others.

The stimulus should be received by the plant for some minimum period before curvature is produced. This period is called the presentation time. If time is less than minimum, there shall be no response to the stimulus. The visible response appears after sometime (after the stimulus is given for minimum period many times) – this period between the presentation and the apparent movement is known as reaction time.

The movement depends upon concentration of auxin. In roots and shoots concentration of auxins towards the side of stimulus is more. In case of roots, more amount of auxins inhibit cell elongation while in stems they promote the growth. Therefore, in roots the lower side with more auxins shows lesser growth than the upper side with less auxins. As such, curvature toward gravitational force results. In shoots, on the contrary, lower side toward the gravitational stimulus has more auxin concentration This results in cell elongation on the lower side producing curvature towards the upper side which would be away from the gravitational stimulus (negative geotropism).

(Geotropism can be demonstrated by growing oat seedlings on a wire guaze and placing the roots in horizontal position. Wire guaze is placed in a beaker

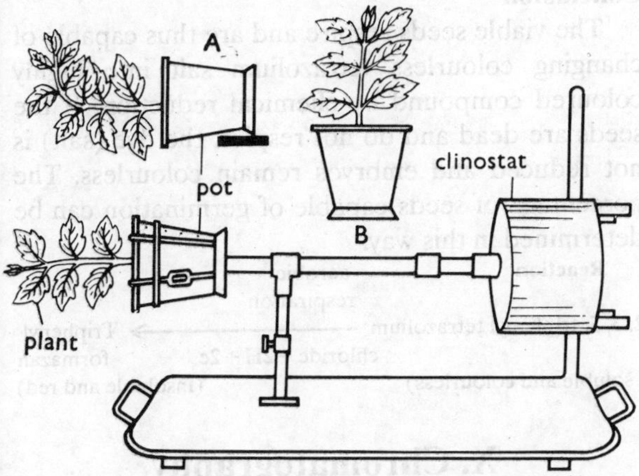

Fig. 1. To demonstrate geotropism by clinostat. A. Potted plant showing negative geotropism of the shoot. B. Potted plant when rotated continuously shows no response to gravitational stimulus.

in a way so that water reaches the seedlings. The seedling shows that roots grow downwards in response to gravitational stimulus.)

Exercise 2

Purpose : To demonstrate phototropism.

Materials

A chamber (painted black from inside) with a hole on one side, a potted plant.

Procedure

1. Keep a potted plant in a dark chamber and allow it to remain so for 2-3 days.

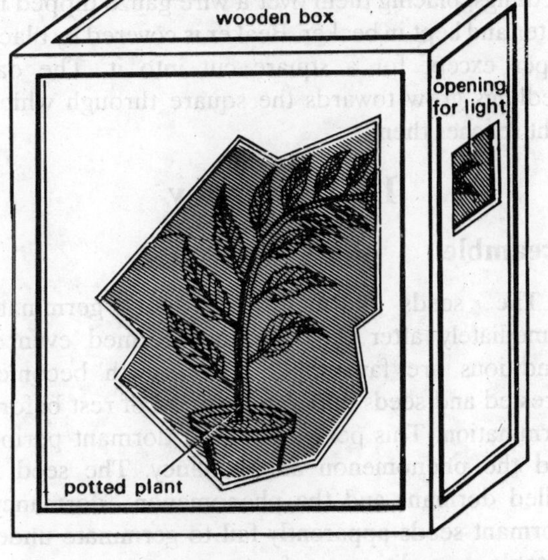

Fig. 2. Experiment to demonstrate phototropism.

2. The hole should be directed towards the source of light.

Result and conclusion

The stem curves and grows towards the source of light through the hole on one side.

A movement induced by unilateral source of light is known as phototropism. The response is due to unequal growth rates on the two sides of the stem. The side away from the source of light shows more growth than the illuminated side. This is due to higher auxin concentration on the side away from the source of light.

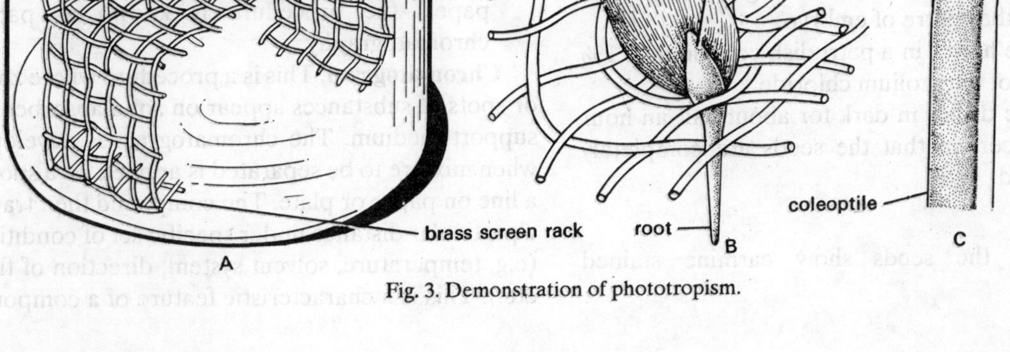

Fig. 3. Demonstration of phototropism.

(The experiment can be repeated by growing oat seedlings, placing them over a wire gauze dipped in water and kept in beaker. Beaker is covered by black paper except for a square cut into it. The oat seedlings grow towards the square through which light reaches them.)

IX. Dormancy

Preamble

The seeds normally do not germinate immediately after they are fully formed even if conditions are favourable. The growth becomes arrested and seeds undergo a period of rest before germination. This period is called dormant period and the phenomenon as dormancy. The seed is called dormant and the phenomenon – dormancy. Dormant seeds apparently fail to germinate under suitable conditions of temperature, oxygen, moisture, etc. because seed coat may be impermeable to water, impermeable to oxygen, mechanically resistant or immature embryo, germination inhibitors, etc. There are many methods, used to break the dormancy of seeds. These consist of scarification (weakening or rupturing the seed coat), low temperature treatments, alternate temperature treatments, light, pressure, etc.

Exercise 1

Purpose : To test the germinability of seeds with tetrazolium.

Materials

Barley seeds, distilled water, petri dish, filter papers, safety razor blade, tetrazolium salt (tetrazolium chloride), etc.

Procedure

1. Soak the barley seeds in water for about 2 hours. Cut carefully each seed in longitudinal halves through the centre of embryo.
2. Place the halves in a petri dish containing 0.1% solution of tetrazolium chloride.
3. Keep the dishes in dark for about half an hour making certain that the seeds are completely immersed.

Results

Some of the seeds show carmine stained embryos.

Conclusion

The viable seeds respire and are thus capable of changing colourless tetrazolium salt into highly coloured compound by chemical reduction. If the seeds are dead and do not respire, the dye (salt) is not reduced and embryos remain colourless. The percentage of seeds capable of germination can be determined in this way.

Reaction

$$\text{2, 3, 5, triphenyl tetrazolium chloride} + 2H + 2e \xrightarrow{\text{aerobic respiration}} \text{Triphenyl formazan}$$

(soluble and colourless) → (insoluble and red)

X. Chromatography

Preamble

In recent years chromatography has come to occupy a very significant place in the studies of biology and chemistry. It consists of separation of constituents of a mixture. Separation of these components is a function of their different affinities for a stationary phase such as a solid or liquid and their differential solubility in a moving phase such as liquid or gas. Most commonly stationary phase is solid and moving phase is liquid. In this case, the separation of compounds is controlled by their character to distribute themselves between solution in the liquid and absorption on the solid surface; e.g., paper, silica gel, etc.

There are three major methods.

(1) **Column chromatography:** If bulk solids are used by packing them into column, the procedure is referred to as column chromatography.

(2) **Thin-layer chromatography:** If bulk solids are employed as a thin layer on supporting glass or plastic plate, the procedure is known as thin-layer chromatography (TLC).

(3) **Paper-chromatography:** If the solid used is paper, the procedure is known as paper-chromatography.

Chromatogram. This is a procedure where zones or spots of substances appear on solid absorbent or support medium. The chromatogram is developed when mixture to be separated is applied as a spot or a line on paper or plate. The compound then travels a particular distance under specific set of conditions (e.g. temperature, solvent system, direction of flow, etc.). This is a characteristic feature of a compound d is used for its identification. Rf value is cordingly calculated. It is a ratio between distance avelled by a compound to that of distance travelled solvent.

$$Rf = \frac{\text{distance from origin travelled by compound}}{\text{distance of solvent front from origin}}$$

Rf values are constant and thus used for an entification of a particular compound. The known is chromatographed along with series of own compounds and Rf values are then compared determine and identify the compound.

Exercise 1

Purpose : Separation of chloroplast pigments by romatographic technique (Paper and thin-layer romatography).

aterials

Spinach leaves, chromatography paper Whatman o. 1, microscope slides, mortar, pestle, separatory nnel, beakers, capillary tube, split corks, tubes, hromotographic chambers, pencil, drier, split orks, tubes, sand, silica gel, cellulose, distilled ater, benzene, acetone, calcium carbonate, ethyl her, methyl alcohl, KOH, n-butanol, acetic acid, arbon tetrachloride, anhydrous sodium sulphate, etroleum ether, etc.

rocedure

The following are major steps—

. **Preparation of paper.** (1) Cut chromatography paper Whatman No. 1 into square sheets to a size which would fit in easily in the chromatography jar (or a specimen tube).

2) Draw a pencil line 1/2 inch above the bottom of each sheet.

. **Preparation of plates.** (1) Prepare a slurry of silica gel by blending cellulose with silica gel in distilled water (10 g cellulose : 4 g silica gel : 80 ml distilled water).

2) Another method to prepare slurry is to suspend 2 g of kieselgel in 10ml of distilled water.

3) The homogeneous slurry is spread uniformly over the clean mcroscope slides. Allow the gel to set and to oven dry them overnight at 40°C.

. **Preparation of extract.** Cut fine strips of spinach leaves, place in a clean mortar and reduce it to pulp with pestle. There are two possible methods. The first *(a)* is simple for the use of under graduate classes.

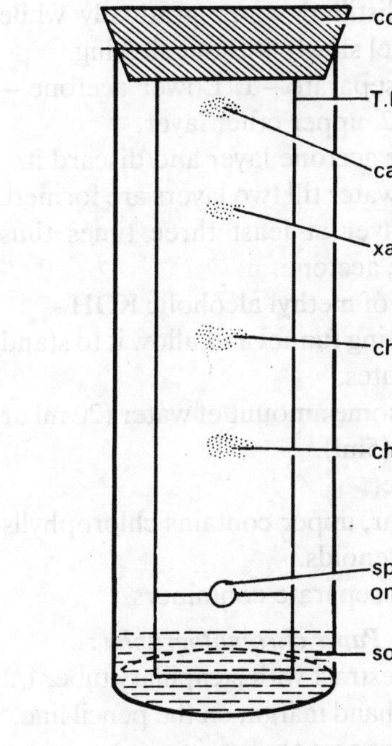

Fig. 1. Thin layer chromatography.

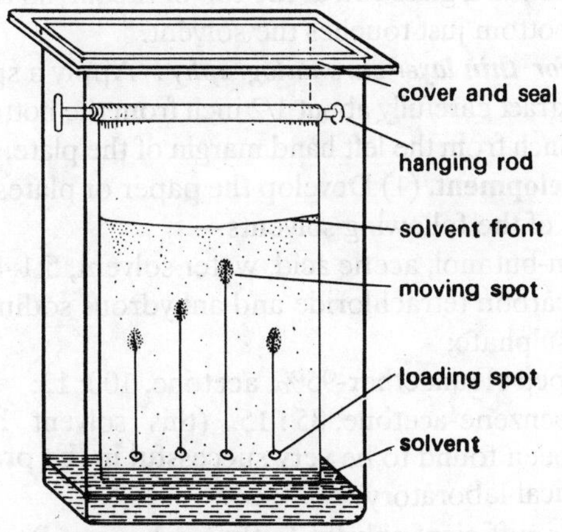

Fig. 2. Chromatography chamber.

(a) Extraction of leaf pigment: Add 50 ml of procooled acetone to leaf pulp, stir well and filter through fine linen cloth.

(b) Separation of chlorophylls and carotenoid extracts: (1) Add 50 ml of procooded 80% acetone to leaf pulp to which small quantities of acid-washed sand and a small amount of $CaCO_3$ is added.

(2) Transfer the clear supernatant green coloured liquid to 10 ml of ethyl ether in a separatory funnel.

(3) Add 60 ml of distilled water gradually while rotating the funnel slowly without shaking.
(4) Two layers now separate – 1. Lower acetone – water layer, and 2. upper ether layer.
(5) Run off the lower acetone layer and discard it.
(6) Continue to add water till two layers are formed.
(7) Run off lower layer at least three times thus discarding all the acetone.
(8) Add about 30 ml of methyl alcoholic KOH.
(9) Shake the separating funnel and allow it to stand for about 15 minutes.
(10) Add once again some amount of water (20 ml or more) and ether (5ml).
(11) Rotate and shake.
(12) Two layers appear, upper contains chlorophylls while lower carotenoids.
(13) Preserve them in separate containers.

4. Application. ***(a) Paper chromatography :***
(1) Put a spot of the extract with a capillary tube, 1/2 inch form the left hand margin on the pencil line.
(2) Allow the pigment spot to dry.
(3) Fix the strip with clips to the cork of tube or roll it around a glass rod at the top of the jar, so that its bottom just touches the solvent.

(b) For thin layer chromatography : Apply a spot of the extract carefully about 1/2 inch from the bottom and 1/2 inch from the left hand margin of the plate.

5. Development. (1) Develop the paper or plates in one of the following solvents –
(a) n-butanol, acetic acid, water solvent, 5:1:4;
(b) carbon tetrachloride and anhydrous sodium sulphate;
(c) petroleum ether-95%, acetone, 100: 12;
(d) benzene-acetone, 85 : 15. (this solvent has been found to be very successful in the practical laboratory).

(2) Pour sufficient solvent (either a, b, c or d) into chromatography jar (or tube) filling aobut inch from the bottom.
(3) Place the spotted slide or paper vertically, so that spot is just above the solvent level.
(4) Cover the jar and close the lid tightly.
(5) Allow 1-2 hours for development.
(6) The solvents shall move up the paper or plate (slide).
(7) Remove the chromatogram when the solvent reaches the top and allow it to dry.
(8) Since the colours of the pigments fade, examine the paper or plate when fresh.

Results

The sequence of pigments from top to bottom shall be –

Carotenes : orange yellow;
Xanthophylls : one or more yellow bands;
Chlorophyll *a*: blue green;
Chlorophyll *b*: yellow green.

Determine the Rf values by following formula –

$$Rf = \frac{\text{distance from origin travelled by compound}}{\text{distance of solvent front from origin}}$$

Identify the components by comparing result with standardised values.

Exercise 2

Purpose : Technique of two dimensional paper-chromatography of amino acids.

Materials

Water imbibed seeds (or germinated seeds) ethyl alcohol, phenol, butanol, glacial acetic acid water, ninhydrin spray agent, chromatography jars, capillary tubes, staples and stapler, atomizer (or spraying apparatus), etc.

Procedure

The following are major steps.

1. **Amino acid extract.** (1) Grind about 10 g of imbibed germinating seeds in about 50 ml of 80% ethyl alcohol.
(2) Filter and evaporate the filtrate to near dryness.
(3) Redissolve the solid in distilled water to make up the volume of extract to about 2 ml.

(Instead, a mixture of known amino acids can also be used e.g. Glycine + aspartic acid; phenylalanine + tryptohan, etc.)

2. **Chromatography chambers.** (1) Use suitable containers (depending upon the size of the paper to be used). Use proper lids so that containers would be airtight.
(2) Of the two chambers, fill phenol in one while in the remaining n-butanol, acetic acid water (3 : 1:1) solvent is poured. Level of the solvent should be inch from the bottom.

3. **Application and development.** (1) Cut chromatography paper Whatman No. 1 into quarters of suitable sizes (depending upon the size of containers).
(2) Mark a dot by pencil about 1 inch from the bottom and 2 inches from left hand edge.

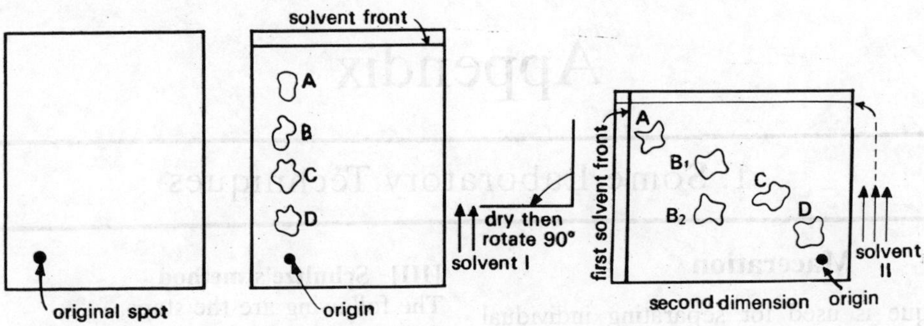

Fig. 3. Two dimensional chromatography.

3) Deposit a small amount of extract gradually on the pencil dot.

4) Hang the paper along the glass rod with dot at the base after spot of the extract is dry.

5) Allow the paper edge to dip in the solvent (phenol) but keep the pencil mark well above the solvent level.

6) Close the chamber airtight and permit 16-18 hours to develop the chromatogram.

(7) Remove the paper and allow it to dry.

(8) Mark the position of the solvent.

(9) Now turn the paper 90° (i.e. the original spot should now be in the right hand lower corner instead of left).

(10) Place paper in the direction in another chamber with n-butanol-acetic acid-water solvent.

(11) Allow to develop for 10-12 hours.

(12) Remove paper before solvent reaches its tip.

(13) Dry the paper and spray uniformly with ninhydrin (triketohydrindene hydrate or ninhydrin 0.1 g dissolved in 100 ml of water saturated n-butanol).

(14) Heat the paper at 90°C for 5 minutes.

(15) Outline the spots with pencil.

Results

Most amino acids react with spray agent to give various colours; generally amino acids give purple colours;

Phenylalanine, tyrosine, and aspartic acid – blue colours; Tryptophan-olive brown;

Asparagine, cystine and cyeine – brown;

Proline – yellow.

Determine the Rf value by following formula –

Indentify the components by comparing results with standardised values.

$$Rf = \frac{\text{distance from origin travelled by compound}}{\text{distance of solvent front from origin}}$$

Chromatography of anthocyanins. Anthocyanins from *Impatients balsamina* flowers can also be separated. Exract is prepared by grinding the material with 1% HCl in 95% ethyl alcohol. The solvent used for thin layer chromatography is n-butanol- acetic acid – water (5 : 1 : 4). For two dimensional paper chromatography of anthocyanins use solvent I *t*-butanol- acetic acid-water (3: 1: 1) and solvent II; 10% acetic acid.

The chromatogram is run as described above.

Circular chromatography. (1) A disc of Whatman no. 1 paper is cut and radial sectors are marked.

(2) A hole is made in the centre and a wick is passed through it.

(3). A spot is placed near the inner edge of the sector.

(4) A 3/4 petri dish is filled with butanol-acetic acid-water (4: 1: 5) solvent.

(5) A wick is placed in the solvent and disc of paper with a spot extract is kept horizontally over this petri dish.

(6) The petri dish is covered by a suitable chamber or kept in a desiccator.

Appendix

1. Some Laboratory Techniques

Maceration

This technique is used for separating individual cells from a group or tissue by dissolution of pectic middle lamella. There are three common methods.

[I] Jeffery's method

Proceed as follows.

1. Cut the fresh or dried material into small slices thinner than a tooth-pick.
2. Boil material in test tube filled with water till it settles down at the bottom.
3. Replace water with the following solution
   10% Nitric acid
   (90 cc water + 10 cc nitric acid)
   10% Chromic acid
   (90 cc water + 10 cc chromic acid)
   Mix both these acids in equal parts.
4. Heat the test tube filled with macerating fluid.
5. Stop heating when material becomes soft.
6. Transfer the test tube fluid to a watch glass.
7. Drain out all the macerating fluid. Wash with water to remove traces of acid.
8. The material is now stained with safranin and destained with water.
9. The material is crushed with glass rod, teased by a needle and spread over the slide.
10. The material is mounted in glycerine or glycerine jelly.

[II] Harlow's method

The following are the steps.

1. Sliced and boiled material is treated with chlorine water for two hours.
2. It is then washed with tap water.
3. Boil the material in sodium sulphate for about 15 minutes.
4. The liquid is now transferred to a watch glass.
5. The material is repeatedly washed in water.
6. It is teased with needle or crushed with glass rod on a slide.
7. The teased material is evenly spread on the slide, stained in safranin and then mounted in glycerine or glycerine jelly.

[III] Schultze's method

The following are the steps.

1. Material is sliced and boiled in a test tube filled with water.
2. Concentrated nitric acid is added to the tube. A few crystals of potassium chlorate are added later.
3. The mixture is heated slowly and gradually till the material is bleached white.
4. The liquid is then transferred to watch glass and drained out leaving only the material.
5. The material is now washed with water.
6. Later it is teased or crushed, till individual cells appear isolated.

Peelings

Peeling is the removal of leaf epidermis, to study the number, arrangement, distribution and structure of stomata. The method consists of breaking the leaf irregularly with a force. Thus separating a little part of the lower epidermis. It is later pulled out. If lower epidermis does not separate easily, a needle or forceps is inserted and a small part is first slowly broken. This can now be held in hand and considerably large strip is pulled apart.

The stripped lower epidermis is stained in safranin and washed. It can be mounted in glycerine or glycerine jelly. Permanent preparation is also made if necessary.

Smearing

Smearing is used to study the chromosome structure and stages of cell division. The method consists of spreading the cells in a single layer. The cells are smeared when they are dividing. It requires killing of dividing tissues at a proper stage of cell division and selection of material where cells are not firmly united by middle lamellae. Microsporocytes of *Trillium* spp., *Lilium* spp. and *Oenothera* spp., as well as anthers of *Tradescantia* spp., *Triticum* spp., and *Nicotiana* spp., root tips of nion, *Ficus*, etc. fixed at appropriate time are idely used for smear preparations.

1. Technique. The following are the steps.

) Slides should be perfectly clean for preparation of smears. Cleaning is done by immersing the slides in sulphuric acid-potassium bichromate mixture or concentrated nitric acid for a long time.

2) Slides are thoroughly washed with running water and finally dried with absolutely clean cloth, free from dust and lint.

3) Fresh anthers are placed on slide and crushed with scalpel or another clean slide.

4) Slide is now inverted over a petri dish containing Randolph modified Navashin fluid in a way that smeared surface comes in contact with the fluid. It should be allowed to remain in this position for about 10-15 minutes.

5) Slide is now inverted with smeared side upward. It is now ready for staining.

2. Staining procedure. The method described elow is called Belling's iron acetocarmine method. The slides are stained in the following way.

1) A few drops of acetocarmine are placed on the smeared material or unsmeared anthers are kept on slide in a drop of acetocarmine. After a few minutes, stain is replaced with a fresh drop of stain.

2) At this stage, unsmeared anthers are crushed and large pieces and debris is removed.

3) Slide is gently heated over a flame, cover glass is placed on the material and uniform pressure is applied after placing a piece of blotting paper on glass.

4) Slide is immediately sealed with melted wax.

Squash

This technique is also useful in the study of cell ivision especially mitosis and the chromosome tructure. For this purpose onion bulbs are grown n bottle filled with water. If the lower root portion f the bulb touches the water, it quickly sends orth large number of roots. Cut the root tips and ix them.

. Place root tips in a drop of 45% acetic acid.

. Place a cover glass over the tip and diffuse acetocarmine.

. Tap and apply uniform pressure over the cover glass.

. The squash preparation is ready.

Micrometry

This is the procedure used to measure the size of microscopic objects like cell, spore, pollen grain, etc. The method consists of using a calibrated ocular micrometer (a glass disc with engraved scale). The calibration is done by comparing ocular with stage micrometer (a slide bearing an engraved scale of known values). Each of the 100 parts of stage micrometer scale represents 0.01 mm or 10μ (1 mm = 1000 microns or μ).

1. Calibration of ocular micrometer. The calibration is done as follows.

(1) Place the ocular micrometer inside the eye piece by unscrewing the upper lens.

(2) Place the stage micrometer slide on microscope stage and focus the scale.

(3) The stage micrometer scale is moved in such a way that it lies by the side of the scale of ocular micrometer when focussed.

(4) Now compare and count the divisions on both micrometers to find out the number of divisions where both scales are equally opposite or coincide.

(5) For example when 45x objective and 10x eye piece are used, 50 divisions of ocular micrometer are found equal coinciding with 72 divisions of stage micrometer.

(6) Calibrate the ocular micrometer as given below.

100 dns of stage micrometer = 1 mm (= 1000 μ or microns)

1dn of stage micrometer = 0.01 mm (= 10 μ or microns)

if, 50 dns (ocular micrometer) = 72 dns (stage micrometer)

then, 50 dns (ocular micrometer) = 0.72 mm (= 720 μ or microns)

therefore, 1 dn (ocular micrometer) = 0.14 mm (14.4 μ or microns)

One millimeter = 1,000 μ

(μ : Greek letter for micron.)

2. Measurement of objects. Determine the size of an object as per the example given below.

(1) With objective 45x and eye piece 10x in use, each division of ocular (micrometer) would measure 14.4 μ or microns.

(2) Now remove the stage micrometer and place a slide with object to be measured.

(3) Use oculometer (micrometer) to measure the width of a bacillus or diameter of a pollen

grain or a fungal spore. For example a fungal spore measures 2 divisions of ocular.

(4) The diameter of a fungal spore would b $(2 \times 14.4\ \mu) \cdot 28.8\ \mu$.
The length, breadth, diameter, etc. of differer structures can be measured in this way.

2. Fixing Agents, Stains and Mounting Media

Fixing Agents and Preservatives

1. Carnoy's fluid

100% ethyl alcohol	—	30 cc
Glacial acetic acid	—	5 cc
Chloroform	—	15 cc

It is used for root tips, anthers, etc. and is preferred for its great penetrating power.

2. Formalin-Aceto-Alcohol

50% or 70% ethyl alcohol	—	90 cc
Glacial acetic acid	—	5 cc
Formalin		5 cc

It is popularly known as FAA and is a standard universal fixative. It is the most extensively used fixing and killing agent.

3. Formalin-Propiono-Alcohol

In the preparation of FAA use propionic acid instead of acetic acid.

4. Randolph's modified Navashin fluid

Solution A.	Chromic acid	—	5 gm
	Glacial acetic acid	—	50 cc
	Distilled water		320 cc
Solution B.	Natural formalin	—	200 cc
	Saponin	—	3 gm
	Distilled water	—	175 cc

At the time of use, mix solutions A and B in equal amounts. Recommended for buds, roots tips and similar objects.

5. Bouin's fluid

Picric acid (1.5% aq. solution)	—	75 cc
Formalin	—	25 cc
Glacial acetic acid	—	5 cc

This fixative is more useful than those with chromic acid.

Stains

1. Acetocarmine

Dissolve 1 gm of stain in 100 cc of boiling 45% acetic acid (or propionic acid). Cool and decant. Add a few drops of saturated aqueou solution of ferric acetate. Cool by keeping i ice for at least twelve hours. Filter and store the stock in refrigerator. For storage use dropping bottle that is dark or covered with a black paper.

2. Aniline blue

(cotton blue, china blue, water blue)

Aniline blue	—	1 gm
Alcohol 90% or water	—	100 cc

For better results stain or alcohol should be slightly acidified with hydrochloric acid.

3. Crystal violet (Gentain violet)

Crystal violet	—	1 gm
Distilled water		100 c

4. Erythrosine

The following are two recipes :

(a) Erythrosine	—	1 gm
Alcohol 90%	—	100 c
(b) Erythrosine	—	1 gm
Absolute Alcohol	—	5 cc
Clove oil	—	95 cc

5. Fast green

The following are two recipes :

(a) Fast green	—	0.5 gm
Alcohol 90%	—	100 c
(b) Fast green	—	0.5 gm
Absolute alcohol	—	25 cc
Clove oil	—	75 cc

6. Gram's iodine

Iodine	—	2 gm
Potassium iodide (KI)	—	3 cc
Distilled water	—	300 c

7. Hematoxylin

It is a chromogen derived from logwood *Haematoxylon campechianum* of Leguminosae. Two types of hematoxylins are commonl employed (a) Heidenhain's and (b) Delafied's hematoxylin.

(a) Heidenhain's hematoxylin.
Half per cent solution of the stain is prepared in warm and distilled water. It is then stored in dark in a closed bottle to ripen for at least four days before use.

(b) Delafield's hematoxylin.
(i) A saturated aqueous solution (100 cc) of ferric ammonium sulphate is prepared.
(ii) One gram of stain is dissolved in 6 cc of absolute alcohol.
(iii) Mixture of solutions 1 and 2 is prepared. Add to this solution 25 cc of glycerine and 25 cc of absolute alcohol are added to this mixture.
(iv) The solution thus prepared is allowed to remain for sufficient time till the colour becomes dark red.

8. Safranin

(a) Safranin	—	1gm
Alcohol 90%	—	50 cc
Distilled water	—	50 cc
(b) Safranin	—	1 gm
Distilled water	—	100 cc

Mounting Media

1. Glycerine jelly
Soak some gelatin for 2 to 3 hours in cold water, pour off the excess water and heat until melted. To 1 part of this, add 1 $\frac{1}{2}$ parts of glycerine and filter while still hot. Add 2 or 3 percent phenol. Still keeping the mixture hot and fluid, add drop by drop a saturated solution of methyl green in 50 percent alcohol, until the glycerine becomes fully as dark as green ink.

2. Lactophenol
Mix equal parts of phenol crystals, lactic acid glycerine and distilled water. Cotton blue may be mixed to stain fungi.

3. Laboratory Reagents

For Physiology Experiments and Microchemical Tests

Acetone. (a) 80% Acetone AR 800 ml; distilled water to make 1000 ml

(b) 80% Acetone 800 ml; distilled water to make 1000 ml.

Acids.

	Mol. wt.	Gm/ litre	Molarity	ml required for 1000 ml. N soln.
HCl	36.47	445	12.2	82.0
HNO_3	63.02	989	15.7	63.8
H_2SO_4	98.08	1742	17.8	28.2
CH_3COOH	60.03	1046	17.4	57.4
$CH_3(CHOH)COOH$	90.08	1032	11.5	87.3

Agar-Agar. Bring 1000 ml distilled water to boil, add 30 gm of agar with constant stirring. Pour uniformly in petri dishes after agar has dissolved completely. If desire to store for more than twelve hours, autoclave the containers with agar-agar.

Ammonium hydroxide. Mol. wt. 17.03%, by weight 21.0 gm/litre 252, molarity 14.8, ml required for 1000 ml N solution 67.6.

Barium chloride. 20 gm of Barium chloride dissolved in 100 ml water.

Barium hydroxide. N/10.

$Ba(OH)_2$ 12.15 gm.

Boiled and distilled water 500 ml.

Benedict's solution. (a) Dissolve 173 gm of sodium citrate and 100 gm of sodium carbonate (Na_2CO_3) in about 600 ml of distilled water. Warm the solution. Filter if necessary.

(b) Dissolve 17.3 gms of cupric sulphate in about 150 ml of distilled water. Add the latter solution to the former slowly and with constant stirring. Dilute to one litre.

Benzidine solution. Dissolve 4 gm of benzidine (p - diaminodiphenyl) in 100 ml of glacial acetic acid.

Calcium chloride.

1.48 gm	$CaCl_2$	added to 1000 ml water makes 0.01 M
14.8 gm	$CaCl_2$	added to 1000 ml water makes 0.1 M
74.0 gm	$CaCl_2$	added to 1000 ml water makes 0.5 M
148.0 gm	$CaCl_2$	added to 1000 ml water makes 1.0 M

Caustic potash.

10% : 10 gm in 1000 ml of water
1 N : 56.11 gm in 1000 ml of water

Chloral hydrate-iodine. Add about 1 cc iodine to about 10-15 cc of chloral hydrate and shake the mixture.

Cobalt chloride. For 3% : 3 gm of cobalt chloride dissolved in 100 ml of water.

Collodion. A solution of pyroxylin (cellulose nitrates) in ether or acetone, available commercially as reagent.

Copper sulphate. For 1% : 1 gm of $CuSO_4.5H_2O$, per 100 ml water. For 10% : 10 gm of $CuSO_4.5H_2O$ per 100 ml of water.

Dichlorophenol indophenol (DCPIP). For 0.1% : 0.1 gm of DCPIP dissolved in 100 ml of water; For 2.5×10^{3} M : dissolve 1 gm of DCPIP in 100 ml of water.

Eosin. For 1% : 1 gm of eosin dissolved in 100 ml of water.

Fehlings solution. Fehlings A : Dissolve 34.65 gm of $CuSO_4.5H_2O$ in water and make the volume upto 500 ml.

Fehlings B : Dissolve 173 gm of potassium sodium tartarate and 125 gm of potassium hydroxide in 500 ml of water.

Mix both solutions A and B in equal amount just before use.

Ferric chloride.

13.516 gm $FeCl_3$ dissolved in 1000 ml water makes 0.05 M
135.16 gm $FeCl_3$ dissolved in 1000 ml water makes 0.5 M

Gibberellic acid.

Concentration	GA%	Water
(μ gm/L)		(Dilute to)
10	0.01	1000 ml
50	0.05	1000 ml
100 mgm/5 ml	0.1	1000 ml
0.01	0.2	100 ml
0.1	2.0	100 ml
1.0	20.0	100 ml

Glucose.

Desired Molarity %	Amount (gm)	Adjust to (water) ml
2.0	360.32	1000
1.0	180.16	1000
0.5	90.80	1000
0.1	18.016	1000
0.01	1.801	1000
1%	10.0	1000

Grinding medium.

(a) NaCl (0.25M)	(b) KH_2PO_4 (0.1M)
add 1000 ml 1.6125 gm or alternatively 250 ml to 3.6531 gm	add 1000 ml water to 13.62 gm or alternatively 100 ml to 1.362 g

To prepare add (a) 250 ml of NaCl (0.25M) (b) 100 ml of KH_2PO_4 (0.1M)

Gum guiacum. For 2% : 2 gm of gum guiacum dissolved in 100 ml of 95% ethyl alcohol.

Hydrogen peroxide. Dilute 10 ml of 30% H_2O to 100 ml of water.

Iodine. Iodine (I_2) 5 gms, Potassium iodide (KI) 10 gm, distilled water to 100 ml. For less intense solution : iodine 1 gm, potassium iodide 2 gm, distilled water 300 ml.

Millon's reagent. (a) Digest one part by weight of mercury with two parts by weight of concentrated nitric acid. Dilute the resulting solution into twice its volume of water or

(b) 10% $HgSO_4$ in 10% sulphuric acid.

Ninhydrin (Triketohydrindine hydrate) (a) 0.1 gm of ninhydrin dissolved in n-butanol and volume is made upto 100 ml. The reagent is stored in dark bottle and not for more than a week.

(b) To 50 ml of absolute ethyl alcohol add 0.0 gm of ninhydrin, 2 ml of collodine and 0.5 ml of glacial acetic acid.

Osmic acid. For 1% : 1 gm of osmic acid dissolved in 100 ml of water.

Phenolphthalein solution. Dissolve 1 gm of phenolphthalein in 50 ml of 95% ethyl alcohol and then add 50 ml of water.

Phloroglucinol. Dissolve 1 gm of phenolphthalein in 50 ml of 95% ethyl alcohol and then add 50 ml of water.

Potassium hydroxide. 30 gm of potassium hydroxide per 100 ml of methyl alcohol.

Potassium permanganate. Dissolve 1 gm of potassium permanganate in 100 ml of water.

Potassium phosphate (monobasic) (KH_2PO_4)

Molarity	Amount mg/gm	Adjust volume with distilled water (ml)
0.001 M	0.013	100
0.01 M	0.136	100
0.1 M	1.362	100
0.2 M	2.724	100

Silver nitrate. For 10% : 10 gm of $AgNO_3$ dissolved in 100 ml of water.

Sodium carbonate. For 1 M solution $Na_2CO_3.H_2O$ 124.2 gm, distilled water to 1000 ml

Sodium chloride.

Molarity	Amount (gm)	Adjust Vol. with water (ml)
5.0 M	292.25	1000
2.5 M	146.125	1000
2.0 M	116.90	1000
1.0 M	58.45	1000

Sodium hydroxide.
For 0.1N : 4.0 gm dissolved in 1000 ml;
For 20% : 20.0 gm dissolved in 1000 ml.

Sodium hypochlorite. For 1% : 1 gm of sodium hypochlorite dissolved in 100 ml of water.

Solvents (chromatography)

for chlorophylls		
(a)	n-butanol	500 ml
	glacial acetic acid	100 ml
	water	400 ml
	(5 : 1 : 4)	
(b)	petroleum ether	200 ml
	acetone	24 ml
	(100 : 12)	
(c)	benzene	85 ml
	acetone	15 ml
	(85 : 15)	
for amino acids		
	n-butanol	300 ml
	glacial acetic acid	100 ml
	water	100 ml
	(3 : 1 : 1)	

Sucrose.

Molarity	Amount (gm)	Distilled water (ml)
1%	10.0 gm	1000
2%	20.0 gm	1000
1M	342.30 gm	1000
2M	684.60 gm	1000

Two dimensional chromatography

I solvent	
t-butanol	300 ml
glacial acetic acid	100 ml
water	100 ml
(3 : 1 : 1)	
II solvent	
10% acetic acid	10 ml of acetic acid in 1000 ml of water.

Starch.

2 % 20 gm of starch, 1000 ml (water)
1% 10 gm of starch, 1000 ml
Boil for 30 minutes and then adjust volume.

Sudan III. Add sudan III slowly in 70% alcohol. Warm to dissolve.

Sudan IV. Add sudan IV slowly in 70% alcohol. Warm to dissolve.

Tetrazolium chloride. 0.1 gm of 2, 3, 5 triphenyl tetrazolium chloride per 100 ml of water, keep in brown bottle.

Thin layer plates.

(a) 10 gm cellulose
4 gm silicalgel
80 gm distilled water.

Prepare a homogeneous slurry, spread uniformly, use 1 ml per 19 sq cm or dip slides in slurry for photosynthetic pigments experiment.

(b) Suspend 2 gm of Kiesel gel G or H (E. Merck) in 10 ml of water, spread the suspension over 3 to 5 slides. Allow the slides to set for about 30 minutes at 120°C.

Index

Alphabetical Lists
Of Important Families And Botanical Names Of Plants Appearing In The Book.

I. *FAMILIES OF FLOWERING PLANTS*

(*For Chapter 3 : Description of Plants*)

II. *BOTANICAL NAMES*

(*For Chapter 3 : Description of Plants*)

BOTANICAL NAMES

(For Chapter 4 : Plants & Human Welfare)

(For Chapter 6 : Anatomy)

(For Chapter 8 : Plant Ecology)